Utilization-Focused Evaluation

TO JEANNE

For teaching me daily that:

What's useful is knowledge,
What's important is love.

Utilization-Focused Evaluation

The New Century Text

Edition 3

Michael Quinn Patton

SAGE Publications
International Educational and Professional Publisher
Thousand Oaks London New Delhi

For information address:

SAGE Publications, Inc.
2455 Teller Road
Thousand Oaks, California 91320
E-mail: order@sagepub.com

SAGE Publications Ltd.
6 Bonhill Street
London EC2A 4PU
United Kingdom

SAGE Publications India Pvt. Ltd.
M-32 Market
Greater Kailash I
New Delhi 110 048 India

Printed in the United States of America

Library of Congress Cataloging-in-Publication Data

Patton, Michael Quinn.
Utilization-focused evaluation: the new century text / author, Michael Quinn Patton. — 3rd ed.
p. cm.
Includes bibliographical references and index.
ISBN 0-8039-5265-1 (pbk.: acid-free paper). — ISBN 0-8039-5264-3 (cloth: acid-free paper)
1. Evaluation research (Social action programs)—United States.
I. Title.
H62.5.U5P37 1996
361.6′1′072—dc20 96-25310

98 99 00 01 02 03 10 9 8 7 6 5 4

Acquiring Editor: C. Deborah Laughton
Editorial Assistant: Dale Grenfell
Production Editor: Diana E. Axelsen
Production Assistant: Sherrise Purdum
Typesetter/Designer: Janelle LeMaster
Cover Designer: Ravi Balasuriya
Print Buyer: Anna Chin

Contents

Detailed Table of Contents

Preface

Sufi stories are tales used to pass on ancient wisdom. One such story tells of a revered teacher, Mulla Nasrudin, who was asked to return to his home village to share his wisdom with the people there.

Mulla Nasrudin mounted a platform in the village square and asked rhetorically, "O my people, do you know what I am about to tell you?"

Some local rowdies, deciding to amuse themselves, shouted rhythmically, "NO. . . ! NO. . . ! NO. . . ! NO. . . !"

"In that case," said Mulla Nasrudin with dignity, "I shall abstain from trying to instruct such an ignorant community," and he stepped down from the platform.

The following week, having obtained an assurance from the hooligans that they would not repeat their harassment, the elders of the village again prevailed upon Nasrudin to address them. "O my people," he began again, "do you know what I am about to say to you?"

Some of the people, uncertain as to how to react, for he was gazing at them fiercely, muttered, "Yes."

"In that case," retorted Nasrudin, "there is no need for me to say more." He then left the village square.

On the third occasion, after a deputation of elders had again visited him and implored him to make one further effort, he stood before the people: "O my people! Do you know what I am about to say?"

Since he seemed to demand a reply, the villagers shouted, "Some of us do, and some of us do not."

"In that case," said Nasrudin as he withdrew, "Let those who know teach those who do not."

—Adapted from Shah, 1964:80-81

This book records the things that I have learned about doing program evaluation from those who know. The pages that follow represent an accumulation of wisdom from many sources: from interviews with 40 federal decision makers and evaluators who participated in a study of the use of federal health evaluations; from conversations with program staff and funders about their evaluation experiences; from evaluation colleagues; from participants in my evaluation workshops and university classes, who are struggling to conduct useful evaluations; and from 25 years of evaluation practice.

The evaluation profession has developed dramatically since the last edition of this book 10 years ago. Updating this edition with recent evaluation research and thinking proved a formidable task, and it substantially increased the length of the book because so much has happened on so many fronts. New chapters have been added on new forms of uses, alternative roles for evaluators, and new concerns about ethics. Yet, the central challenge to professional practice remains—*doing evaluations that are useful and actually used!*

The tone and substance of this new edition have been influenced by the fact that *utilization-focused evaluation* is now more than 20 years old. The first edition, published in 1978 and based on research done in 1975, had the tone of a toddler throwing a temper tantrum because no one seemed to be paying attention. The second edition, published in 1986, was alternatively brash and shy, assertive and uncertain, like an adolescent coming of age. By that time, the first edition had attracted both praise and skepticism, support and opposition, and the premises undergirding the approach had been sufficiently disseminated to be distorted, misquoted, and miscategorized. I wanted the second edition to set the record straight and clarify points of confusion. By my own criteria, I only partially succeeded, and reading that edition now, after having received useful feedback from students and teachers of evaluation, I find it less clear on some points than I would have wished. I have attempted to correct those deficiencies.

Now that utilization-focused evaluation has survived to voting age (or even drinking age), I feel liberated to be more celebratory and less argumentative in tone. While my colleagues Joe Wholey, Harry Hatry, and Kathryn Newcomer (1994) may have overstated the case when they observed that "in recent years the watchword of the evaluation profession has been utilization- focused evaluation" (p. 5), I can say without hubris that the widespread acceptance of the premises of utilization-focused evaluation has influenced my voice. In this edition, I have strived to achieve the more mature tone of the elder, which I find I'm becoming. My professional development parallels the maturation of our profession. As a field of professional practice, we have reached a level where we know what we're doing and have a track record of important contributions to show. That knowledge and those contributions are the bedrock of this new edition.

While I have learned from and am indebted to many more people than I can acknowledge, the personal and professional contributions of a few special colleagues have been especially important to me in recent years, particularly in the writing of this edition. Marv Alkin, Jean King, and Hallie Preskill read portions of the revision and offered instructive feedback. Other colleagues whose writings and wisdom have informed this edition include Eleanor Chelimsky, Huey Chen, Bob

Covert, David Fetterman, Mike Hendricks, Ernie House, Ricardo Millett, Sharon Rallis, Jim Sanders, Michael Scriven, Will Shadish, Midge Smith, Yoland Wadsworth, Carol Weiss, and Joe Wholey. Minnesota provides a thriving evaluation community in which to work and an active local chapter of the American Evaluation Association where friends and colleagues share experiences; among local evaluators who have been especially helpful to me in recent years are John Brandl, Tom Dewar, Jean King, Dick Krueger, Steve Mayer, Paul Mattessich, Marsha Mueller, Ruth Anne Olson, Greg Owen, and Stacey Stockdill. I also want to thank several colleagues and clients currently or formerly in government who have contributed ideas and experiences that have influenced this edition: Valerie Caracelli, Kay Knapp, Gene Lyle, Meg Hargreaves, Laurie Hestness, Dennis Johnson, Mike Linder, Richard Sonnichsen, and Jennifer Thurman. I thank the Union Institute Graduate School, especially Dean Larry Ryan, for sabbatical support to complete this revision. Ongoing encouragement from Union Institute faculty and learners supports both my teaching and writing.

That this new edition was written at all owes much to the patient nurturing and unwavering support of Sage editor C. Deborah Laughton. Sage has a commitment to keep major texts current, but what began as an update became, for me, a major rewrite as I worked to capture all the new developments in evaluation over the last decade. When I was tempted to go on to other projects, C. Deborah helped rekindle my commitment to this book. Her knowledge about both good writing and evaluation made the difference. Expert and thorough copy editing by Jacqueline A. Tasch also contributed by enhancing the quality of the final production.

Jeanne Campbell has been editor, critic, colleague, and collaborator. Most of all, she has been a source of power through her caring, belief, and support. She has helped me keep my priorities straight in the struggle to balance family, writing, teaching, and consulting, and somehow integrating them all in a rich and loving life together with our children. My daily experience of her provides ongoing evidence that getting older does mean getting better. I dedicate this book to her.

One final note of thanks to evaluation sage Halcolm (pronounced and interpreted, *How come?* as in "Why?"). Since the first edition, rumors have persisted that Halcolm doesn't really exist despite stories and quotations from him in my writings. Such ignominious scuttlebutt notwithstanding, I can assure the reader that Halcolm exists vitally in my mind.

* * *

This book is both practical and theoretical. It tells readers how to conduct program evaluations and why to conduct them in the manner prescribed. Each chapter contains both a review of the relevant literature and actual case examples to illustrate major points. Over 50 menus and exhibits have been added to this edition, with *exhibits* offering summaries and illustrations, and *menus* designed to present options as evaluators work with users to make selections from the vast smorgasbord of evaluation approaches. Finally, the book offers a definite point of view developed from the observation that much of what has passed for program evaluation has not been very useful; *that evaluation ought to be useful;* and, therefore, that something different must be done if evaluation *is* to be useful. Based on research and professional experience, and integrating theory and practice, this book provides both an overall framework and concrete advice for how to conduct useful evaluations.

PART 1

Toward More Useful Evaluations

In the beginning, God created the heaven and the earth.

And God saw everything that he made. "Behold," God said, "it is very good." And the evening and the morning were the sixth day.

And on the seventh day God rested from all His work. His archangel came then unto Him asking, "God, how do you know that what you have created is 'very good'? What are your criteria? On what data do you base your judgment? Just exactly what results were you expecting to attain? And aren't you a little close to the situation to make a fair and unbiased evaluation?"

God thought about these questions all that day and His rest was greatly disturbed. On the eighth day God said, "Lucifer, go to hell."

Thus was evaluation born in a blaze of glory. . . .

—From Halcolm's *The Real Story of Paradise Lost*

1

Evaluation Use: Both Challenge and Mandate

The human condition: insidious prejudice, stultifying fear of the unknown, contagious avoidance, beguiling distortion of reality, awesomely selective perception, stupefying self-deception, profane rationalization, massive avoidance of truth—all marvels of evolution's selection of the fittest. Evaluation is our collective effort to outwit these human propensities—if we choose to use it.

—Halcolm

On a cold November morning in Minnesota, some 15 people in various states of wakefulness have gathered to discuss evaluation of a county human services program. Citizen evaluation advisory board representatives are present; the county board and state representatives have arrived; and members of the internal evaluation staff are busy with handouts and overheads. We are assembled at this early hour to review the past year's evaluation efforts.

They review the problems with getting started (fuzzy program goals, uncertain funding); the data collection problems (lack of staff, little program cooperation, inconsistent state and county data processing systems); the management problems (unclear decision-making hierarchies, political undercurrents, trying to do too much); and the findings despite it all ("tentative to be sure," acknowledges the internal evaluator, "but more than we knew a year ago").

Advisory board members are clearly disappointed: "The data just aren't solid enough." A county commissioner explains why board decisions have been contrary to evaluation recommendations: "We didn't really get the information we needed when we wanted it, and it wasn't what we wanted when we got it." The room is filled with disappointment, frustration, defensiveness, cynicism, and more than a little anger. There are charges, countercharges, budget threats, moments of planning, and longer moments of explaining away problems. The chairperson ends the meeting in exasperation, lamenting: "What do we have to do to get results we can actually use?"

This book is an outgrowth of, and answer to, that question.

Evaluation Use as a Critical Societal Issue

If the scene I have described were unique, it would merely represent a frustrating professional problem for the people involved. But if that scene is repeated over and over on many mornings, with many advisory boards, then the question of evaluation use would become what sociologist C. Wright Mills (1959) called a critical public issue:

> *Issues* have to do with matters that transcend these local environments of the individual and the range of his inner life. They have to do with the organization of many such milieux into the institutions of an historical society as a whole. . . . An issue, in fact, often involves a crisis in institutional arrangements. (pp. 8-9)

In my judgment, the challenge of using evaluation in appropriate and meaningful ways represents just such a crisis in institutional arrangements. How evaluations are used affects the spending of billions of dollars to fight problems of poverty, disease, ignorance, joblessness, mental anguish, crime, hunger, and inequality. How are programs that combat these societal ills to be judged? How does one distinguish effective from ineffective programs? And how can evaluations be conducted in ways that lead to use? How do we avoid producing reports that gather dust on bookshelves, unread and unused? Those are the questions this book addresses, not just in general, but within a particular framework: utilization-focused evaluation.

The issue of use has emerged at the interface between science and action, between knowing and doing. It raises fundamental questions about human rationality, decision making, and knowledge applied to creation of a better world. And the issue is as fresh as the morning news. To wit, a recent newspaper headline: "Agency Evaluation Reports Disregarded by Legislators Who Had Requested Them" (Dawson 1995; see Exhibit 1.1). Let's look, then, at how the crisis in utilization has emerged. Following that, we'll outline how utilization-focused evaluation addresses this crisis.

A Larger Perspective: Using Information in the Information Age

The challenge of evaluation use epitomizes the more general challenge of knowl-

EXHIBIT 1.1
Newspaper Column on Evaluation Use

Agency Evaluation Reports Disregarded by Legislators Who Had Requested Them

Minnesota lawmakers who mandated that state agencies spend a lot of employee hours and money developing performance evaluation reports pretty much ignored them. . . . The official word from the state legislative auditor's evaluation of the performance evaluation process: Legislators who asked for the reports did not pay much attention to them. They were often full of boring and insignificant details. . . .

Thousands of employee hours and one million taxpayer dollars went into writing the 21 major state agency performance evaluation reports. The auditor reports the sad results:

- Only three of 21 state commissioners thought that the performance reports helped the governor make budget choices regarding their agencies.
- Only seven of 21 agencies were satisfied with the attention given the reports in the House committees reviewing their programs and budgets. And only one agency was satisfied with the attention it received in the Senate.

Agency heads also complained to legislative committees this year that the 1993 law mandating the reports was particularly painful because departments had to prepare new two-year budget requests and program justifications at the same time. That "dual" responsibility resulted in bureaucratic paperwork factories running overtime.

"Our experience is that few, if any, legislators have actually read the valuable information contained in our report . . . ," one agency head told auditors.

"The benefits of performance reporting will not materialize if one of the principal audiences is uninterested," said another.

"If the Legislature is not serious about making the report 'the key document' in the budget decision process, it serves little value outside the agency," said a third department head.

Mandating the reports and ignoring them looks like another misguided venture by the 201-member Minnesota Legislature. It is the fifth-largest Legislature in the nation and during much of the early part of this year's five-month session had little to do. With time on their hands, lawmakers could have devoted more time to evaluation reports. But if the reports were dull and of little value in evaluating successes of programs, can they be blamed for not reading them?

Gary Dawson, "State Journal" column
Saint Paul Pioneer Press, August 7, 1995, p. 4B

SOURCE: Reprinted with permission of *Saint Paul Pioneer Press.*

edge use in our times. Our age—the Age of Information and Communications—has developed the capacity to generate, store, retrieve, transmit, and instantaneously communicate information. Our problem is keeping up with, sorting out, absorbing, and *using* information. Our technological capacity for gathering and computerizing information now far exceeds our human ability to process and make sense out of it all. We're constantly faced with deciding what's worth knowing versus what to ignore.

Getting people to use what is known has become a critical concern across the different knowledge sectors of society. A major specialty in medicine (compliance research) is dedicated to understanding why so many people don't follow their doctor's orders. Common problems of information use underlie trying to get people to use seat belts, quit smoking, begin exercising, eat properly, and pay attention to evaluation findings. In the fields of nutrition, energy conservation, education, criminal justice, financial investment, human services, corporate management, international development—the list could go on and on—a central problem, often *the* central problem, is getting people to apply what is already known.

In agriculture, a major activity of extension services is trying to get farmers to adopt new scientific methods. Experienced agricultural extension agents like to tell the story of a young agent telling a farmer about the latest food production techniques. As he begins to offer advice, the farmer interrupts him and says, "No sense in telling me all those new ideas, young man. I'm not doing half of what I know I should be doing now."

I remember coming across a follow-up study of participants in time-management training. Few were applying the time-management techniques they had learned. When graduates of time-management training were compared with a sample of nonparticipants, the differences were not in how people in each group managed their time. The time-management graduates had quickly fallen back into old habits. The difference was: the graduates felt much more guilty about how they wasted time.

Research on adolescent pregnancy illustrates another dimension of the knowledge use problem. Adolescent health specialist Michael Resnik (1984) interviewed teenagers who became pregnant. He found very few cases in which the problem was a lack of information about contraception, about pregnancy, or about how to avoid pregnancies. **The problem was not applying—just not using—what they knew.** Resnick found "an incredible gap between the knowledge and the application of that knowledge. In so many instances, it's heartbreaking—they have the knowledge, the awareness, and the understanding, but somehow it doesn't apply to them" (p. 15).

These examples of the challenges of putting knowledge to use are meant to set a general context for the specific concern of this book: **narrowing the gap between generating evaluation findings and actually using those findings for program decision making and improvement.** Although the problem of information use remains central to our age, we are not without knowledge about what to do. We've learned a few things about overcoming our human resistance to new knowledge and change, and over the last two decades of professional evaluation practice, we've learned a great deal about how to increase evaluation use. Before presenting what we've learned, let's look more closely at the scope of the challenge of using evaluation processes and findings.

High Hopes for Evaluation

Evaluation and Rationality

Edward Suchman (1967) began his seminal text on evaluation research with

Hans Zetterberg's observation that "one of the most appealing ideas of our century is the notion that science can be put to work to provide solutions to social problems" (p. 1). Social and behavioral science embodied the hope of finally applying human rationality to the improvement of society. In 1961, Harvard-educated President John F. Kennedy welcomed scientists to the White House as never before. Scientific perspectives were taken into account in the writing of new social legislation. Economists, historians, psychologists, political scientists, and sociologists were all welcomed into the public arena to share in the reshaping of modern postindustrial society. They dreamed of and worked for a new order of rationality in government—a rationality undergirded by social scientists who, if not philosopher-kings themselves, were at least ministers to philosopher-kings. Carol Weiss (1977) has captured the optimism of that period.

> There was much hoopla about the rationality that social science would bring to the untidy world of government. It would provide hard data for planning . . . and give cause-and-effect theories for policy making, so that statesmen would know which variables to alter in order to effect the desired outcomes. It would bring to the assessment of alternative policies a knowledge of relative costs and benefits so that decision makers could select the options with the highest payoff. And once policies were in operation, it would provide objective evaluation of their effectiveness so that necessary modifications could be made to improve performance. (p. 4)

One manifestation of the scope, pervasiveness, and penetration of these hopes is the number of evaluation studies actually conducted. While it is impossible to identify all such studies, as early as 1976, the *Congressional Sourcebook on Federal Program Evaluations* contained 1,700 citations of program evaluation reports issued by 18 U.S. Executive Branch agencies and the General Accounting Office (GAO) during fiscal years 1973 through 1975 (Office of Program Analysis, GAO 1976:1). The numbers have grown substantially since then. In 1977, federal agencies spent $64 million on program evaluation and more than $1.1 billion on social research and development (Abramson 1978). The third edition of the *Compendium of Health and Human Services Evaluation Studies* (U.S. Department of Health and Human Services 1983) contained 1,435 entries. The fourth volume of the U.S. Comptroller General's directory of *Federal Evaluations* (GAO 1981) identified 1,429 evaluative studies from various U.S. federal agencies completed between September 1, 1979, and September 30, 1980. While the large number of and substantial funding for evaluations suggested great prosperity and acceptance, under the surface and behind the scenes, a crisis was building—*a utilization crisis.*

Reality Check: Evaluations Largely Unused

By the end of the 1960s, it was becoming clear that evaluations of Great Society social programs were largely ignored or politicized. The utopian hopes for a scientific and rational society had somehow failed to be realized. The landing of the first human on the moon came and went, but poverty persisted despite the 1960s "War" on it—and research was still not being used as the basis for government decision making.

While all types of applied social science suffered from underuse (Weiss 1977), nonuse seemed to be particularly characteristic of evaluation studies. Ernest House (1972) put it this way: "Producing data is one thing! Getting it used is quite another" (p. 412). Williams and Evans (1969) wrote that "in the final analysis, the test of the effectiveness of outcome data is its impact on implemented policy. By this standard, there is a dearth of successful evaluation studies" (p. 453). Wholey et al. (1970) concluded that "the recent literature is unanimous in announcing the general failure of evaluation to affect decision making in a significant way" (p. 46). They went on to note that their own study "found the same absence of successful evaluations noted by other authors" (p. 48). Cohen and Garet (1975) found "little evidence to indicate that government planning offices have succeeded in linking social research and decision making" (p. 19). Seymour Deitchman (1976), in his *The Best-Laid Schemes: A Tale of Social Research and Bureaucracy,* concluded that "the impact of the research on the most important affairs of state was, with few exceptions, nil" (p. 390). Weidman et al. (1973) concluded that "on those rare occasions when evaluations studies have been used . . . the little use that has occurred [has been] fortuitous rather than planned" (p. 15). In 1972, Carol Weiss viewed underutilization as one of the foremost problems in evaluation research: "A review of evaluation experience suggests that evaluation results have not exerted significant influence on program decisions" (pp. 10-11). This conclusion was echoed by four prominent commissions and study committees: the U.S. House Committee on Government Operations, Research and Technical Programs Subcommittee (1967); the Young Committee report published by the National Academy of Sciences (1968); the Report of the Special Commission on the Social Sciences (1968) for the National Science Foundation; and the Social Science Research Council's (1969) prospective on the Behavioral and Social Sciences.

British economist L. J. Sharpe (1977) reviewed the European literature and commission reports on use of social scientific knowledge and reached a decidedly gloomy conclusion:

> We are brought face to face with the fact that it has proved very difficult to uncover many instances where social science research has had a clear and direct effect on policy even when it has been specifically commissioned by government. (p. 45)

Ronald Havelock (1980) of the Knowledge Transfer Institute generalized that "there is a gap between the world of research and the world of routine organizational practice, regardless of the field" (p. 13). Rippey (1973) commented,

> At the moment there seems to be no indication that evaluation, although the law of the land, contributes anything to educational practice, other than headaches for the researcher, threats for the innovators, and depressing articles for journals devoted to evaluation. (p. 9)

It can hardly come as a surprise, then, that support for evaluation began to decline. During the Reagan Administration, the GAO (1987) found that federal evaluation received fewer resources and that "findings from both large and small studies have become less easily available for use by the Congress and the public" (p. 4). In both 1988 and 1992, the GAO prepared status reports on program evaluation to inform changing executive branch administrations at the federal level.

> We found a 22-percent decline in the number of professional staff in agency program evaluation units between 1980 and 1984. A follow-up study of 15 units that had been active in 1980 showed an additional 12% decline in the number of professional staff between 1984 and 1988. Funds for program evaluation also dropped substantially between 1980 and 1984 (down by 37% in constant 1980 dollars).... Discussions with the Office of Management and Budget offer no indication that the executive branch investment in program evaluation showed any meaningful overall increase from 1988 to 1992. (GAO 1992a:7)

The GAO (1992a) went on to conclude that its 1988 recommendations to enhance the federal government's evaluation function had gone unheeded: "The effort to rebuild the government's evaluation capacity that we called for in our 1988 transition series report has not been carried out" (p. 7). **Here, ironically, we have an evaluation report on evaluation going unused.**

In 1995, the GAO provided another report to the U.S. Senate on *Program Evaluation,* subtitled *Improving the Flow of Information to the Congress.* GAO analysts conducted follow-up case studies of three major federal program evaluations: the Comprehensive Child Development Program, the Community Health Centers program, and the Chapter 1 Elementary and Secondary Education Act aimed at providing compensatory education services to low-income students. The analysts concluded that

> lack of information does not appear to be the main problem. Rather, the problem seems to be that available information is not organized and communicated effectively. Much of the available information did not reach the [appropriate Senate] Committee, or reached it in a form that was too highly aggregated to be useful or that was difficult to digest. (GAO 1995:39)

Many factors affect evaluation use in Congress (Boyer and Langbein 1991), but politics is the overriding factor (Chelimsky 1995a, 1992, 1987a, 1987b). Evaluation use throughout the U.S. federal government appears to have continued its spiral of decline through the 1990s (Wargo 1995; Popham 1995; Chelimsky 1992). In many federal agencies, the emphasis shifted from program evaluation to inspection, auditing, and investigations (N. L. Smith 1992; Hendricks et al. 1990). However, anecdotal reports from state and local governments, philanthropic foundations, and the independent sector suggest a surge of interest in evaluation. I believe that whether this initial interest and early embrace turn into long-term support and a sustainable relationship will depend on the extent to which evaluations prove useful.

Nor is the challenge only one of increasing use. "An emerging issue is that of misuse of findings. The use-nonuse continuum is a measure of degree or magnitude; misuse is a measure of the manner of use" (Alkin and House 1992:466). Marv Alkin (1991, 1990; Alkin and Coyle 1988), an early theorist of user-oriented evaluation, has long emphasized that evaluators must attend to *appropriate* use, not just amount of use. Ernest House (1990a), one of the most astute observers of how the evaluation profession has developed, observed in this regard: "Results from poorly conceived studies have frequently been given wide publicity, and findings from good studies have been improperly used" (p. 26). The field faces a dual challenge then: supporting and enhancing appropriate uses while also working to eliminate improper uses.

We are called back, then, to the early morning scene that opened this chapter: decision makers lamenting the disappointing results of an evaluation, complaining that the findings did not tell them what they needed to know. For their part, evaluators complain about many things, as well, "but their most common complaint is that their findings are ignored" (Weiss 1972d:319). The question from those who believe in the importance and potential utility of evaluation remains: What has to be done to get results that are appropriately and meaningfully used? This question has taken center stage as program evaluation has emerged as a distinct field of professional practice.

Historical Context

The Emergence of Program Evaluation as a Field of Professional Practice

Like many poor people, evaluation in the United States has grown up in the "projects"—federal projects spawned by the Great Society legislation of the 1960s. When the federal government of the United States began to take a major role in alleviating poverty, hunger, and joblessness during the Depression of the 1930s, the closest thing to evaluation was the employment of a few jobless academics to write program histories. It was not until the massive federal expenditures on an awesome assortment of programs during the 1960s and 1970s that accountability began to mean more than assessing staff sincerity or political head counts of opponents and proponents. A number of events converged to create a demand for systematic empirical evaluation of the effectiveness of government programs (Walters 1996; Wye and Sonnichsen 1992), although that was often threatening to programs since many had come to associate evaluation with an attack and to think of evaluators as a program termination squad.

Education has long been a primary target for evaluation. Beginning with Joseph Rue's comparative study of spelling performance by 33,000 students in 1897, the field of educational evaluation has been dominated by achievement testing. During the Cold War, after the Soviet Union launched *Sputnik* in 1957, calls for better educational assessments accompanied a critique born of fear that the education gap was even larger than the "missile gap." Demand for better evaluations also accompanied the growing realization that, years after the 1954 Supreme Court *Brown* decision requiring racial integration of schools, "separate and unequal" was still the norm rather than the exception. Passage of the U.S. Elementary and Secondary Education Act in 1965 contributed greatly to more comprehensive approaches to evaluation. The massive influx of federal money aimed at desegregation, innovation, compensatory education, greater equality of opportunity, teacher training, and higher student achievement was accompanied by calls for evaluation data to assess the effects on the nation's children. To what extent did these changes really make an educational difference?

But education was only one arena in the War on Poverty of the 1960s. Great Society programs from the Office of Economic Opportunity were aimed at nothing less than the elimination of poverty. The creation of large-scale federal health programs, including community mental health

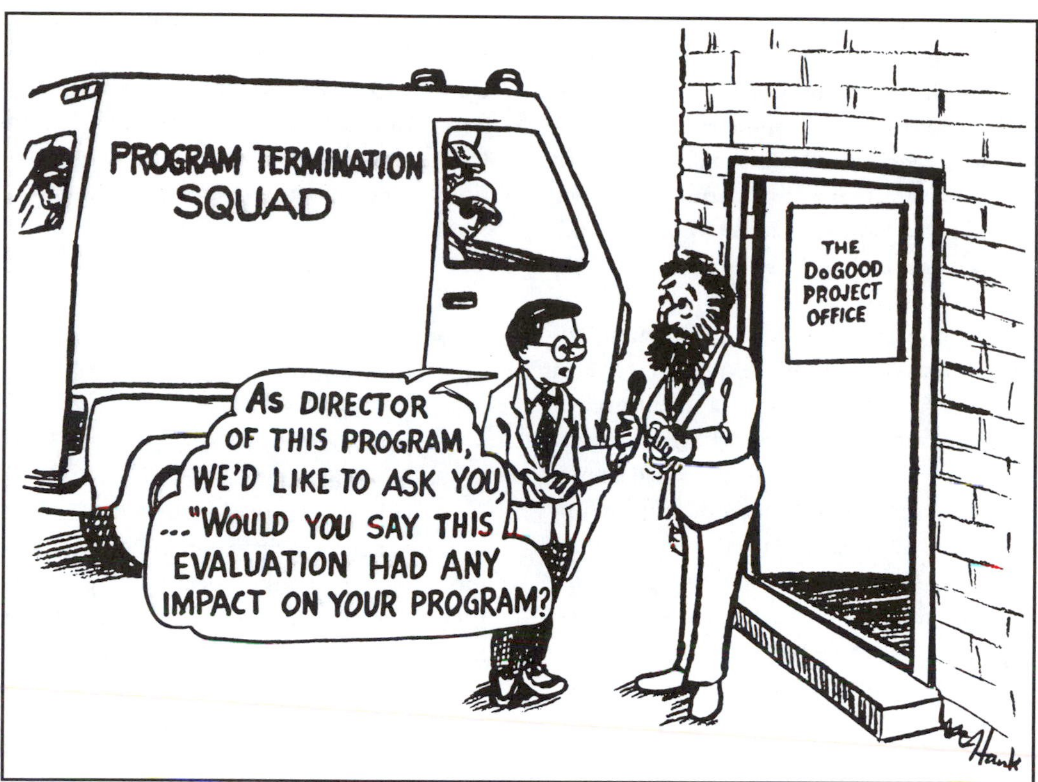

centers, was coupled with a mandate for evaluation, often at a level of 1% to 3% of program budgets. Other major programs were created in housing, employment, services integration, community planning, urban renewal, welfare, family programs (Weiss and Jacobs 1988), and so on—the whole of which came to be referred to as "butter" (in opposition to the "guns") expenditures. In the 1970s, these Great Society programs collided head on with the Vietnam War, rising inflation, increasing taxes, and the fall from glory of Keynesian economics. All in all, it was what sociologists and social historians, with a penchant for understatement, would characterize as "as a period of rapid social and economic change."

Program evaluation as a distinct field of professional practice was born of two lessons from this period of large-scale social experimentation and government intervention: First, there is not enough money to do all the things that need doing; and, second, even if there were enough money, it takes more than money to solve complex human and social problems. **As not everything can be done, there must be a basis for deciding which things are worth doing.** Enter evaluation.[1]

While pragmatists turned to evaluation as a commonsensical way to figure out what works and is worth funding, visionaries were conceptualizing evaluation as the centerpiece of a new kind of society: *the experimenting society.* Donald T. Campbell ([1971] 1991) gave voice to this vision in his 1971 address to the American Psychological Association.

> The experimenting society will be one which will vigorously try out proposed solutions to recurrent problems, which will make hard-headed and multidimensional evaluations of the outcomes, and which will move on to other alternatives when evaluation shows one reform to have been ineffective or harmful. We do not have such a society today. (p. 223)

Early visions for evaluation, then, focused on evaluation's expected role in guiding funding decisions and differentiating the wheat from the chaff in federal programs. But as evaluations were implemented, a new role emerged: helping improve programs as they were implemented. The Great Society programs foundered on a host of problems: management weaknesses, cultural issues, and failure to take into account the enormously complex systems that contributed to poverty. Wanting to help is not the same as knowing how to help; likewise, having the money to help is not the same as knowing how to spend money in a helpful way. Many War on Poverty programs turned out to be patronizing, controlling, dependency generating, insulting, inadequate, misguided, overpromised, wasteful, and mismanaged. Evaluators were called on not only to offer final judgments about the overall effectiveness of programs, but to gather process data and provide feedback to help solve programming problems along the way (Sonnichen 1989; Wholey and Newcomer 1989).

By the mid-1970s, interest in evaluation had grown to the point where two professional organizations were established: the academically oriented Evaluation Research Society and the practitioner-oriented Evaluation Network. In 1984, they merged to form the American Evaluation Association. By that time, interest in evaluation had become international, with establishment of the Canadian Evaluation Society and the Australasian Evaluation Society. In 1995, the first International Evaluation Conference included participation from new professional evaluation associations representing Central America, Europe, and the United Kingdom.

New Directions in Accountability

A predominant theme of the 1995 International Evaluation Conference was worldwide interest in reducing government programs and making remaining programs more effective and accountable. This theme first took center stage in the United States with the election of Ronald Reagan as President in 1980. He led a backlash against government programming, especially welfare expenditures. Decline in support for government programs was fueled by the widespread belief that such efforts were ineffective and wasteful. While the Great Society and War on Poverty programs of the 1960s had been founded on good intentions and high expectations, they came to be perceived as failures. The "needs assessments" that had provided the rationales for those original programs had found that the poor, the sick, the homeless, the uneducated—the needy of all kinds—needed services. So services and programs were created. Thirty years down the road from those original efforts, and billions of dollars later, most social indicators revealed little improvement. Poverty statistics—including the number of multigenerational welfare recipients and rates of homelessness, hard-core unemployment, and underemployment—as well as urban degradation and increasing crime combined to raise questions about the effectiveness of services. Reports on effective programs (e.g., Guttmann and Sussman 1995; Kennedy School of Government 1995; Schorr 1988) received relatively little media attention compared to the relentless press about waste and ineffectiveness (Wortman 1995). In the 1990s, growing concerns about federal budget deficits and runaway entitlement costs intensified the debate about the effectiveness of government programs. Both conservatives and liberals were faced with public demands to know what had been achieved by all the programs created and all the money spent. The call for greater accountability became a watershed at every level—national, state, and local; public sector, nonprofit agencies, and the private sector (Bonsignore 1996; HFRP 1996a, 1996b; Horsch 1996; Brizius and Campbell 1991).

Clear answers were not forthcoming. Few programs could provide data on results achieved and outcomes attained. Internal accountability had come to center on how funds were spent (inputs monitoring), eligibility requirements (who gets services, i.e., client characteristics), how many people get services, what activities they participate in, and how many complete the program. These indicators of inputs, client characteristics, activities, and outputs (program completion) measured whether providers were following government rules and regulations rather than whether desired results were being achieved. Control had come to be exercised through audits, licensing, and service contracts rather than through measured outcomes. The consequence was to make providers and practitioners compliance-oriented rather than results-focused. Programs were rewarded for doing the paperwork well rather than for making a difference in clients' lives.

Public skepticism turned to deep-seated cynicism. Polling data showed a widespread perception that "nothing works." As an aside, and in all fairness, this perception is not unique to the late twentieth century. In the nineteenth century, Spencer traced 32 acts of the British Parliament and discovered that 29 produced effects contrary to those intended (Edison 1983:I, 5). Given today's public cynicism, 3 effective programs out of 32 might be considered a pretty good record.

More damning still, the perception has grown in modern times that no relationship exists between the amount of money spent on a problem and the results accomplished, an observation made with a sense of despair by economist John Brandl in his keynote address to the American Evaluation Association in New Orleans in 1988. Brandl, a professor in the Hubert H. Humphrey Institute of Public Affairs at the University of Minnesota (formerly its Director), was present at the creation of many human services programs during his days at the old Department of Health, Education, and Welfare (HEW). He created the interdisciplinary Evaluation Methodology training program at the University of Minnesota. Brandl later moved from being a policy analyst to being a policy formulator as a Minnesota state legislator. His opinions carry the weight of both study and experience. In his 1988 keynote address to professional evaluators, he opined that **no demonstrable relationship exists between program funding levels and impact, that is, between inputs and outputs; more money spent does *not* mean higher quality or greater results.**

In a 1994 article, Brandl updated his analysis. While his immediate focus was on Minnesota state government, his comments characterize general concerns about the effectiveness of government programs in the 1990s:

> The great government bureaucracies of Minnesota and the rest of America today are

EXHIBIT 1.2
Premises of Reinventing Government

- What gets measured gets done.
- If you don't measure results, you can't tell success from failure.
- If you can't see success, you can't reward it.
- If you can't reward success, you're probably rewarding failure.
- If you can't see success, you can't learn from it.
- If you can't recognize failure, you can't correct it.
- If you can demonstrate results, you can win public support.

SOURCE: From Osborne and Gaebler (1992: chapter 5, "Results-Oriented Government").

> failing for the same reason that the formerly Communist governments in Europe fell a few years ago and Cuba is teetering today. There is no systematic accountability. People are not regularly inspired to do good work, rewarded for outstanding performance, or penalized for not accomplishing their tasks.
>
> In bureaus, people are expected to do well because the rules tell them to do so. Indeed, often in bureaus here and abroad, able, idealistic workers become disillusioned and burned out by a system that is not oriented to produce excellent results. No infusion of management was ever going to make operations of the Lenin shipyard in Gdansk effective.
>
> Maybe—I would say *surely*—until systematic accountability is built into government, no management improvements will do the job. (p. 13A).

Similar indictments of government effectiveness are the foundation for efforts at Total Quality Management, Re-engineering Government, or Reinventing Government. These and other management innovations make new forms of accountability —and greater use of evaluation processes and results—the centerpiece of reform. This is illustrated in Exhibit 1.2 by the premises for results-oriented government promulgated by Osborne and Gaebler (1992) in their influential and best-selling book, *Reinventing Government: How the Entrepreneurial Spirit is Transforming the Public Sector.*

The future of evaluation is tied to the future effectiveness of programs. New calls for results-oriented, accountable programming challenge evaluators to increase the use and effectiveness of evaluations. Indictments of program effectiveness are, underneath, also indictments of evaluation. The original promise of evaluation was that it would point the way to effective programming. Later, that promise broadened to include providing ongoing feedback for improvements during implementation. Evaluation cannot be considered to have fulfilled its promise if, as is increasingly the case, the general perception is that few programs have attained desired outcomes, that "nothing works."

Such conclusions about programs raise fundamental questions about the role of evaluation. Can evaluation contribute to increased program effectiveness? Can evaluation be used to improve programs? Do evaluators bear any responsibility for use and program improvement? This book will answer these questions in the affirmative and offer utilization-focused evaluation as an approach for realizing evaluation's original vision of contributing to long-term program effectiveness and improved decision making.

Worldwide Demand for Evaluation

The challenge to evaluation extends well beyond government-supported programming. Because of the enormous size and importance of government efforts, program evaluation is inevitably affected by trends in the public sector, but evaluation has also been growing in importance in the private and independent sectors (Independent Sector 1993). Corporations, philanthropic foundations, and nonprofit agencies are increasingly turning to evaluators for help in enhancing their organizational effectiveness.

Nor is interest in empirically assessing policies and programs limited to the United States. The federal government of Canada, especially the Auditor General's Office, has demonstrated a major commitment to conducting program evaluations at both national and provincial levels (Comptroller General of Canada 1989; Rutman and Mayne 1985), and *action-oriented evaluation* has emerged as an importance practice in many Canadian organizations (Hudson, Mayne, and Thomlison 1992). The Canadian Evaluation Society is active in promoting the appropriate practice and use of program evaluations throughout Canada, as is the Australasian Evaluation Society in Australia and New Zealand (AES 1995; Sharp 1994; Caulley 1993; Funnell 1993; Owen 1993; Sharp and Lindsay 1992). European governments are routinely using evaluation and policy analysis too, although the nature, location, and results of evaluation efforts vary from country to country (see, for example, Hoogerwerf 1985; Patton 1985). International agencies have also begun using evaluation to assess the full range of development efforts under way in Third World countries. The World Bank, UNICEF, the Australian Development Assistance Bureau (1982), and the U.S. Agency for International Development are examples of international development organizations with significant and active evaluation offices. Global interest in evaluation culminated in the first-ever International Evaluation Conference in Vancouver, Canada, in November 1995. With over 1,500 participants from 61 countries, this conference made it clear that evaluation had become a global challenge. In his keynote address to the conference, Masafumi Nagao (1995) from Japan's Sasakawa Peace Foundation challenged evaluators to think globally even as they evaluate locally, that is, to consider how international forces and trends affect project outcomes, even in small and remote communities. This book will include attention to how utilization-focused evaluation offers a process for adapting evaluation processes to address multicultural and international issues and constituencies.

Standards of Excellence for Evaluation

One major contribution of the professionalization of evaluation has been articulation of standards for evaluation. The standards make it clear that *evaluations ought to be useful.*

In the past many researchers took the position that their responsibility was merely to design studies, collect data, and publish findings; what decision makers did with those findings was not their problem. This stance removed from the evaluator any responsibility for fostering use and placed all the blame for nonuse or underutilization on decision makers.

Academic aloofness from the messy world in which research findings are translated into action has long been a characteristic of basic scientific research. Before the field of evaluation identified and adopted its own standards, criteria for judging evaluations could scarcely be differentiated from criteria for judging research in the traditional social and behavioral sciences, namely, technical quality and methodological rigor. Use was ignored. Methods decisions dominated the evaluation design process. Methodological rigor meant experimental designs, quantitative data, and sophisticated statistical analysis. Whether decision makers understood such analyses was not the researcher's problem. Validity, reliability, measurability, and generalizability were the dimensions that received the greatest attention in judging evaluation research proposals and reports (e.g., Bernstein and Freeman 1975). Indeed, evaluators concerned about increasing a study's usefulness often called for ever more methodologically rigorous evaluations to increase the validity of findings, thereby supposedly compelling decision makers to take findings seriously.

By the late 1970s, however, it was becoming clear that greater methodological rigor was not solving the use problem. Program staff and funders were becoming openly skeptical about spending scarce funds on evaluations they couldn't understand and/or found irrelevant. Evaluators were being asked to be "accountable," just as program staff were supposed to be accountable. The questions emerged with uncomfortable directness: Who will evaluate the evaluators? How will evaluation be evaluated? It was in this context that professional evaluators began discussing standards.

The most comprehensive effort at developing standards was hammered out over five years by a 17-member committee appointed by 12 professional organizations, with input from hundreds of practicing evaluation professionals. The standards published by the Joint Committee on Standards in 1981 dramatically reflected the ways in which the practice of evaluation had matured. Just prior to publication, Dan Stufflebeam (1980), chair of the committee, summarized the committee's work as follows:

> The standards that will be published essentially call for evaluations that have four features. These are *utility, feasibility, propriety,* and *accuracy.* And I think it is interesting that the Joint Committee decided on that particular order. Their rationale is that an evaluation should not be done at all if there is no prospect for its being useful to some audience. Second, it should not be done if it is not feasible to conduct it in political terms, or practicality terms, or cost-effectiveness terms. Third, they do not think it should be done if we cannot demonstrate that it will be conducted fairly and ethically. Finally, if we can demonstrate that an evaluation will have utility, will be feasible, and will be proper in its conduct, then they said we could turn to the difficult matters of the technical ade-

EXHIBIT 1.3
Standards for Evaluation

Utility

The Utility Standards are intended to ensure that an evaluation will serve the practical information needs of intended users.

Feasibility

The Feasibility Standards are intended to ensure that an evaluation will be realistic, prudent, diplomatic, and frugal.

Propriety

The Propriety Standards are intended to ensure that an evaluation will be conducted legally, ethically, and with due regard for the welfare of those involved in the evaluation, as well as those affected by its results.

Accuracy

The Accuracy Standards are intended to ensure that an evaluation will reveal and convey technically adequate information about the features that determine worth or merit of the program being evaluated.

SOURCE: Joint Committee 1994.

quacy of the evaluation. (p. 90; emphasis in the original).

In 1994, revised standards were published following an extensive review spanning several years (Joint Committee 1994; Patton 1994a). While some changes were made in the 30 individual standards, the overarching framework of four primary criteria remained unchanged: utility, feasibility, propriety, and accuracy (see Exhibit 1.3). Taking the standards seriously has meant looking at the world quite differently. Unlike the traditionally aloof stance of basic researchers, evaluators are challenged to take responsibility for use. No more can we play the game of blame the resistant decision maker. **Implementation of a utility-focused, feasibility-conscious, propriety-oriented, and accuracy-based evaluation requires situational responsiveness, methodological flexibility, multiple evaluator roles, political sophistication, and substantial doses of creativity, all elements of utilization-focused evaluation.**

From Problem to Solution: Toward Use in Practice

This chapter has reviewed the emergence of program evaluation as a professional field of practice with standards of excellence and a mandate to be useful. The early utilization crisis called into question whether the original hopes for evaluation would be, or even could be, realized. Utilization-focused evaluation developed in response to that crisis and as a way of fulfilling, in practice, the mandate of the utility standard. With this background as context, we turn in the next chapter to an overview of utilization-focused evaluation.

Note

1. For a full discussion of evaluation's emergence as both a discipline and a field of professional practice, see House (1993).

2

What Is Utilization-Focused Evaluation?

How Do You Get Started?

When I was a child, I spake as a child, I understood as a child. I thought as a child: but when I became an adult, I put away childish things. I decided to become an evaluator. My only problem was, I didn't have the foggiest idea what I was getting into or how to begin.

—Halcolm

A modern version of an ancient Asian story (adapted from Shah 1964:64) casts light on the challenge of searching for evaluation use.

A man found his neighbor down on his knees under a street lamp looking for something. "What have you lost, friend?"

"My key," replied the man on his knees.

After a few minutes of helping him search, the neighbor asked, "Where did you drop it?"

"In that dark pasture," answered his friend.

"Then why, for heaven's sake, are you looking here?"

"Because there is more light here."

The obvious place to look for use is in what happens *after* an evaluation is completed and there's something to use. What we shall find, however, is that the search for use takes us into the "dark pasture" of decisions made before any data are ever collected. The reader will find relatively little in this book about what to do when a study is over. At that point, the potential for use has been largely determined. Utilization-focused evaluation emphasizes that what happens from the very beginning of a study will determine its eventual impact *long before a final report is produced.*

A Comprehensive Approach

The question of how to enhance the use of program evaluation is sufficiently complex that a piecemeal approach based on isolated prescriptions for practice is likely to have only piecemeal impact. Overviews of research on evaluation use (e.g., Huberman 1995; Lester and Wilds 1990; Connor 1988; Greene 1988b; McLaughlin et al. 1988; M. F. Smith 1988; Cousins and Leithwood 1986; Leviton and Hughes 1981) suggest that the problems of underuse will not be solved by compiling and following some long list of evaluation axioms. It's like trying to live your life according to *Poor Richard's Almanac.* At the moment of decision, you reach into your socialization and remember, "He who hesitates is lost." But then again, "Fools rush in where angels fear to tread." Advice to young evaluators is no less confusing: "Work closely with decision makers to establish trust and rapport," but "maintain distance to guarantee objectivity and neutrality."

Real-world circumstances are too complex and unique to be routinely approached through the application of isolated pearls of evaluation wisdom. What is needed is a comprehensive framework within which to develop and implement an evaluation ***with attention to use built in.*** In program evaluation, as in life, it is one's overall philosophy integrated into pragmatic principles that provides a guide to action. Utilization-focused evaluation offers both a philosophy of evaluation and a practical framework for designing and conducting evaluations.

Since its original publication in 1978, *Utilization-Focused Evaluation* has been tested and applied in thousands of evaluations in the United States and throughout the world. This reservoir of experience provides strong confirmation that evaluations will be used if the foundation for use is properly prepared. Evidence to that effect will be presented throughout this book. First, let me outline the utilization-focused approach to evaluation and indicate how it responds to the challenge of getting evaluations used.

Utilization-Focused Evaluation

Utilization-Focused Evaluation begins with the premise that evaluations should be judged by their utility and actual use; therefore, evaluators should facilitate the evaluation process and design any evaluation with careful consideration of how everything that is done, *from beginning to end,* will affect use. Nor is use an abstraction. Use concerns how real people in the real world apply evaluation findings and experience the evaluation process. Therefore, the *focus* in utilization-focused evaluation is on *intended use by intended users.*

In any evaluation, there are many potential stakeholders and an array of possible uses. Utilization-focused evaluation requires moving from the general and abstract, that is, possible audiences and po-

EXHIBIT 2.1
Guiding Principles for Evaluators

Systematic Inquiry
Evaluators conduct systematic, data-based inquiries about what is being evaluated.

Competence
Evaluators provide competent performance to stakeholders.

Integrity/Honesty
Evaluators ensure the honesty and integrity of the entire evaluation process.

Respect for People
Evaluators respect the security, dignity, and self-worth of the respondents, program participants, clients, and other stakeholders with whom they interact.

Responsibilities for General and Public Welfare
Evaluators articulate and take into account the diversity of interests and values that may be related to the general and public welfare.

SOURCE: American Evaluation Association Guiding Principles for Evaluators, Shadish et al. 1995.

tential uses, to the real and specific: actual primary intended users and their explicit commitments to concrete, specific uses. The evaluator facilitates judgment and decision making by intended users rather than acting as a distant, independent judge. Since no evaluation can be value-free, utilization-focused evaluation answers the question of whose values will frame the evaluation by working with clearly identified, primary intended users who have responsibility to apply evaluation findings and implement recommendations. In essence, I shall argue, evaluation use is too important to be left to evaluators.

Utilization-focused evaluation is highly personal and situational. The evaluation facilitator develops a working relationship with intended users to help them determine what kind of evaluation they need. This requires negotiation: The evaluator offers a menu of possibilities within the framework of established evaluation standards and principles. While concern about utility drives a utilization-focused evaluation, the evaluator must also attend to the evaluation's accuracy, feasibility, and propriety (Joint Committee on Standards 1994). Moreover, as a professional, the evaluator has a responsibility to act in accordance with the profession's adopted principles of conducting systematic, data-based inquiries; performing competently; ensuring the honesty and integrity of the entire evaluation process; respecting the people involved in and affected by the evaluation; and being sensitive to the diversity of interests and values that may be related to the general and public welfare (AEA Task Force 1995:20; see Exhibit 2.1).

Utilization-focused evaluation does not advocate any particular evaluation content, model, method, theory, or even use. Rather, it is a process for helping primary intended users select the most appropriate content, model, methods, theory, and uses for their particular situation. Situational responsiveness guides the interactive process between evaluator and primary intended users. This book will present and discuss the many options now available in the feast that has become the field of evaluation. As we consider the rich and varied menu of evaluation, it will become clear that utilization-focused evaluation can include any evaluative purpose (formative, summative, developmental), any kind of data (quantitative, qualitative, mixed), any kind of design (e.g., naturalistic, experimental), and any kind of focus (processes, outcomes, impacts, costs, and cost-benefit, among many possibilities). Utilization-focused evaluation is a process for making decisions about these issues in collaboration with an identified group of primary users focusing on their intended uses of evaluation.

A psychology of use undergirds and informs utilization-focused evaluation. In essence, research and my own experience indicate that intended users are more likely to use evaluations if they understand and feel ownership of the evaluation process and findings; they are more likely to understand and feel ownership if they've been actively involved; and by actively involving primary intended users, the evaluator is training users in use, preparing the groundwork for use, and reinforcing the intended utility of the evaluation every step along the way. The rest of this chapter will offer some ways of working with primary intended users to begin the process of utilization-focused evaluation. Beyond the heuristic value of these examples, they are meant to illustrate how the philosophy of utilization-focused evaluation is translated into practice.

The First Challenge: Engendering Commitment

Utilization-focused evaluators begin their interactions with primary intended users by working to engender commitments to both evaluation *and* use. Even program funders and decision makers who request or mandate an evaluation often don't know what evaluation involves, at least not in any specific way. And they typically haven't thought much about how they will use either the process or the findings.

In working with program staff and administrators to lay the groundwork for an evaluation, I often write the word *evaluate* on a flip chart and ask those present to free-associate with the word. They typically begin with synonyms or closely related terms: *assess, measure, judge, rate, compare*. Soon they move to connotations and feelings: *waste, crap, cut our funding, downsize, attack, demean, put down, pain, hurt, fear*.

Clearly, evaluation can evoke strong emotions, negative associations, and genuine fear. To ignore the perceptions, past experiences, and feelings stakeholders bring to an evaluation is like ignoring a smoldering dynamite fuse in hope it will burn itself out. More likely, unless someone intervenes and extinguishes the fuse, it will burn faster and eventually explode. Many an evaluation has blown up in the face of well-intentioned evaluators because they rushed into technical details and methods decisions without establishing a solid foundation for the evaluation in clear purposes and shared understandings. To begin, both evaluators and those with whom we work need to develop a shared definition of evaluation and mutual understanding about what the process will involve.

What Is Program Evaluation?

I offer the clients with whom I work the following definition:

> Program evaluation is the systematic collection of information about the activities, characteristics, and outcomes of programs to make judgments about the program, improve program effectiveness, and/or inform decisions about future programming. Utilization-focused program evaluation (as opposed to program evaluation in general) is evaluation done for and with specific, intended primary users for specific, intended uses.

The general definition above has three interrelated components: (1) the systematic collection of information about (2) a potentially broad range of topics (3) for a variety of possible judgments and uses. The definition of utilization-focused evaluation adds the requirement to specify intended use by intended users.

This matter of defining evaluation is of considerable import because different evaluation approaches rest on different definitions. The use-oriented definition offered above contrasts in significant ways with other approaches. One traditional approach has been to define program evaluation as determining the extent to which a program attains its goals. However, as we shall see, program evaluation can and does involve examining much more than goal attainment, for example, implementation, program processes, unanticipated consequences, and long-term impacts. Goal attainment, then, takes too narrow a focus to encompass the variety of ways program evaluation can be useful.

Another common definition states that evaluation determines the worth, merit, or value of something (Joint Committee on Standards 1994; House 1993:1; Scriven 1991a:139). This admittedly commonsensical definition omits specifying the basis for determining merit or worth (that is, systematically collected data) or the purposes for making such a determination (program improvement, decision making, or knowledge generation). In advocating for this narrow and simple definition of evaluation, Stufflebeam (1994) warned against "obscuring the essence of evaluation —to assess value—by overemphasizing its constructive uses" (p. 323). However, for me, use is the essence, so I choose to include it in my definition as a matter of emphasis to reinforce the point that concern about use is a distinguishing characteristic of program evaluation, even at the point of defining what program evaluation is. I'm not interested in determining merit or worth as an end in itself. I want to keep before us the questions: Why is merit or worth to be judged? What will be done with whatever judgments are made?

A different approach is represented by the widely used Rossi and Freeman (1993) textbook, *Evaluation: A Systematic Approach*. They define *evaluation research* as the systematic application of social research procedures in assessing social intervention programs. But notice, they are defining evaluation *research*, and their text emphasizes applying social science methods, so naturally they include that in their definition of evaluation.

The definition of evaluation I've offered here emphasizes systematic data collection rather than applying social science methods. This is an important distinction in

emphasis, one in keeping with the Principle of Systematic Inquiry adopted by the American Evaluation Association (AEA Task Force on Guiding Principles 1995:22). From my perspective, program evaluators may use research methods to gather information, but they may also use management information system data, program monitoring statistics, or other forms of systematic information that are not research-oriented. Program evaluation differs fundamentally from research in the purpose of data collection and standards for judging quality. Basic scientific research is undertaken to discover new knowledge, test theories, establish truth, and generalize across time and space. Program evaluation is undertaken to inform decisions, clarify options, identify improvements, and provide information about programs and policies within contextual boundaries of time, place, values, and politics. The difference between research and evaluation has been called by Cronbach and Suppes (1969) the difference between conclusion-oriented and decision-oriented inquiry. Research aims to produce knowledge and truth. Useful evaluation supports action. The evaluation research of Rossi and Freeman is a hybrid that tends, in my reading of it, to be more knowledge-oriented than action-oriented.

Stake (1981) and Cronbach (1982) have emphasized that evaluation differs from research in the relative importance attached to making generalizations. In any data collection effort, the extent to which there is concern about utility, generalizability, scientific rigor, and relevance of the findings to specific users will vary. Each of these dimensions is a continuum. Because this book emphasizes meeting the information needs of specific intended users, the focus will most often be on program evaluation rather than evaluation research. This focus derives from my work with small, community-based programs where the idea of conducting "research" may be intimidating or where practitioners consider research "academic and irrelevant." On the other hand, national programs or those staffed or funded by people with advanced degrees may attach positive associations to conducting research, in which case they may prefer to call the process evaluation research. The language, like everything else in utilization-focused evaluation, depends on the program context and the explicit needs and values of primary intended users. In short, how to define evaluation and what to call a particular evaluation are matters for discussion, clarification, and negotiation.

What is not negotiable is that the evaluation be data-based. Both program evaluation and evaluation research bring an empirical perspective to bear on questions of policy and program effectiveness. This *data-based* approach to evaluation stands in contrast to two alternative and often competing ways of assessing programs: the charity orientation and pure pork barrel politics. I sometimes introduce these distinctions in working with clients to help them more fully appreciate the sine qua non nature of evaluation's commitment to systematic data collection.

Charitable Assessment

nd now abideth faith, hope, charity, these three; but the greatest of these is charity.

—Paul's First Letter to the Corinthians

Modern social service and education programs are rooted in charitable and philanthropic motives: helping people. From a charity perspective, the main criterion for evaluation is the sincerity of funders and program staff; the primary measure of program worth is that the program organizers care enough to try their very best to help the less fortunate. As an agency director told me after a measurement training session, "All I want to know is whether or not my staff are trying their best. When you've got a valid and reliable and all-that-other-stuff instrument for love and sincerity, come back and see me."

Sometimes religious motives can also be found in this mix. As a United Way agency director once told me, "God has mandated our helping the less fortunate, so God alone will judge the outcomes and effectiveness of our efforts." The implication was that God needed no assistance from the likes of social scientists, with their impersonal statistics and objective analyses of human suffering.

Data-oriented evaluators have little to offer those who are fully ensconced in charitable assessment. Others, however (and their numbers are increasing), have come to believe that, even for the sincere, indeed *especially* for the sincere and caring, empirically based program evaluations can be valuable. After all, sincerity and caring mean that one wants to do a good job, wants to be effective, and wants to make a difference. The purpose of program evaluation is precisely that—to increase effectiveness and provide information on whether hopes are actually being realized. People who really care about their work are precisely the people who can benefit greatly from utilization-focused program evaluation.

Pork Barrel Assessment

A second historically important approach to evaluating programs has been pork barrel politics, which takes as its main criterion the political power of a program's constituency: If powerful constituents want the program, or if more is to be gained politically by support for, rather than opposition to, the program, then the program is judged worthwhile; no other evidence of program effectiveness is needed, although data may be sought to support this predetermined political judgment. Pork barrel evaluations are one reason it is so difficult to terminate government-funded programs and agencies. Programs rapidly develop constituencies whose vested interests lie in program continuation. The driving force of the pork barrel approach is to give out money where it counts politically, not where it will be used most effectively.

The pork barrel criterion is not unique to elected politicians and governmental bodies. The funding boards of philanthropic foundations, corporate boards, and service agencies have their own constituencies to please. Political debts must be paid, so programs are judged effective as long as they serve powerful interests. Empirical evaluation findings are of interest only insofar as they can be manipulated for political and public relations purposes. (Chapter 14 will address in more depth the relationship, often healthy when properly approached, between politics and evaluation.)

Learning to Value Evaluation

So, we're working on engendering commitment to data-based evaluation and use. We want to get beyond charitable assessments and pork barrel assessments. Research on "readiness for evaluation" (D. S. Smith 1992; Studer 1978; Mayer 1976, 1975) has found that "valuing evaluation" is a necessary condition for evaluation use (see Exhibit 2.2). Valuing evaluation cannot be taken for granted. Nor does it happen naturally. Users' commitment to evaluation is typically fragile, often whimsical, and must be cultivated like a hybrid plant that has the potential for enormous yields, but only if properly cared for, nourished, and appropriately managed.

Reality Testing

I find the idea of "reality testing" helpful in working with intended users to increase the value they attach to evaluation and, correspondingly, their willingness to be actively engaged in the work necessary to make the evaluation useful. I include in the notion of testing reality gathering varying perceptions of reality in line with the axiom that "what is perceived as real is real in its consequences."[1] The phrase "reality testing" implies that being "in touch with reality" can't simply be assumed. When individuals lose touch with reality, they become dysfunctional, and, if the distortions of re-

EXHIBIT 2.2

Items on Belief in Program Evaluation, From Readiness for Evaluation Questionnaire

Rank Order by Factor	*Item*	*Factor Loading*
1	Program evaluation would pave the way for better programs for our clientele	.777
2	This would be a good time to begin (or renew or intensify) work on program evaluation	.732
3	Installing a procedure for program evaluation would enhance the stature of our organization	.723
4	We don't need to have our program evaluated	–.689
5	The amount of resistance in the organization to program evaluation should not be a deterrent to pursuing a policy of program evaluation	.688
6	I have yet to be convinced of the alleged benefits of program evaluation	–.669
7	Program evaluation would only increase the workload	–.668
8	"Program evaluation" and "accountability" are just fads that hopefully will die down soon	–.650
9	Program evaluation would tell me nothing more than I already know	–.645
10	I would be willing to commit at least 5% of the program budget for evaluation	.624
11	A formal program evaluation would make it easier to convince administrators of needed changes	.617
12	We could probably get additional or renewed funding if we carry out a plan for program evaluation	.587
13	Program evaluation might lead to greater recognition and rewards to those who deserve it	.548
14	It would be difficult to implement a procedure for program evaluation without seriously disrupting other activities	–.518
15	No additional time and money can be made available for program evaluation	–.450
16	Most of the objections one hears about program evaluation are really pretty irrational	.442
17	Some money could probably be made available to provide training to staff in program evaluation skills	.385

SOURCE: Smith 1992:53-54).
NOTE: Factor analysis is a statistical technique for identifying questionnaire or test items that are highly intercorrelated and therefore may measure the same factor, in this case, belief in evaluation. The positive or negative signs on the factor loadings reflect whether questions were worded positively or negatively; the higher a factor loading, the better the item defines the factor.

EXHIBIT 2.3

Reality Testing: Example of a Good Idea That Didn't Work Out

The Robert Wood Johnson Foundation funded an eight-year effort to establish and evaluate new ways of helping doctors and patients deal with death in hospitals. Called SUPPORT (Study to Understand Prognoses and Preferences for Outcomes and Risks of Treatment), the project placed nurses in five teaching hospitals to facilitate communications between physicians and families facing the death of a family member. The idea was that by increasing doctors' understanding of what patients and their families wanted and didn't want, pain could be diminished, the appropriateness of care would increase, and fewer "heroic measures" would be used to prolong life for short periods.

The evaluation found that the culture of denial about death could not be overcome through better communication. Major gaps remained between what patients privately said they wanted and what doctors, dedicated to saving lives, did. Living wills didn't help. Half the patients still died in pain. Many died attached to machines, and died alone.

Dr. Joanne Lynn, a co-director of the project, expressed dramatically the importance of testing good ideas in practice to see if they really work: "We did what everyone thought would work and it didn't work at all, not even a quiver."

While the idea didn't work, important lessons were learned, she concluded. "This wasn't a group of doctors dedicated to finding the last possible date on the tombstone. What we learned was that the conspiracy of silence about death was stronger than we expected, and the force of habit was also stronger than we expected. We are all involved in the dance of silence."

NOTE: Quotations attributed to Dr. Lynn are taken from Goodman 1995:17A.

ality are severe, they may be referred for psychotherapy. Programs and organizations can also "lose touch with reality" in the sense that the people in those programs and organizations are operating on myths and behaving in ways that are dysfunctional to goal attainment and ineffective for accomplishing desired outcomes. Program evaluation can be a mechanism for finding out whether what's supposed to be or hoped to be going on is, in fact, going on—a form of reality testing.

Some people would just as soon not be bothered dealing with programmatic or organizational reality. They've constructed their own comfortable worlds built on untested assumptions and unexamined beliefs. Evaluation is a threat to such people. Evaluators who ignore the threatening nature of reality testing and plow ahead with their data collection in the hope that knowledge will prevail are engaged in their own form of reality distortion. Utilization-focused evaluators, in contrast, work with intended evaluation users to help them understand the value of reality testing and buy into the process, thereby reducing the threat of evaluation and resistance (conscious or unconscious) to evaluation use. One way to do this is to look for and use examples from the news of good ideas that haven't worked out. Exhibit 2.3 presents an example I've used with several groups.

As I work with intended users to agree on what we mean by evaluation and engender a commitment to use, I invite them to assess incentives for and barriers to reality testing and information use in their own program culture. Barriers typically include fear of being judged, cynicism about whether anything can really change, skepticism about the worth of evaluation, concern about the time and money costs of evaluation, and frustration from previous bad evaluation experiences, especially lack of use. As we work through these and related issues to "get ready for evaluation," the foundation for use is being built in conjunction with a commitment to serious and genuine reality testing. Because evaluators have typically internalized the value of data-based reality testing, it is easy to assume that others share this perspective. But a commitment to examine beliefs and test actual goal attainment is neither natural nor widespread. People involved in program management and service delivery can become quite complacent about what they're doing and quite content with the way things are. Reality testing will only upset things. "Why bother?" they ask.

Nor is it enough that an evaluation is required by some funder or oversight authority. Indeed, under such conditions, evaluation often becomes an end in itself, something to be done because it is mandated, not because it will be useful or because important things can be learned. Doing an evaluation because it is required is entirely different from doing it because one is committed to grounding decisions and action in a careful assessment of reality. Ironically, mandated evaluations can actually undercut utility by making the reason for the evaluation compliance with a funding requirement rather than genuine interest in being more effective.

Because evaluation use is so dependent on the commitment to reality testing, evaluators need ways to cultivate that commitment and enlarge the capacity of intended users to undertake the process. This means engaging program staff, managers, funders, and other intended users in examining how their beliefs about program effectiveness may be based on selective perception, predisposition, prejudice, rose-colored glasses, unconfirmed assertions, or simple misinformation. The irony of living in the information age is that we are surrounded by so much misinformation and act on so many untested assumptions. By putting intended users in touch with how little they really know, and how flimsy is the basis for much of what they think they know, we are laying the groundwork for use. We are, in fact, identifying that there are useful things to be found out and creating the expectation that testing reality will be a valuable activity, not just an academic or mandated exercise. In short, we are establishing the program's readiness for evaluation.

Generating Real Questions

One way of facilitating a program's readiness for evaluation is to take primary intended users through a process of generating meaningful evaluation questions. I find that when I enter a new program setting as an external evaluator, the people with whom I'm working typically expect me to tell them what the focus of the evaluation will be. They're passively waiting to be told by the evaluation expert—me—what questions the evaluation will answer. But I don't come with specific evaluation questions. I come with a process for generating *their* questions. Taking them through that process is aimed at engendering their commitment to data-based evaluation and use. Let me share an example.

The Frontier School Division in Manitoba, Canada, encompasses much of northern Manitoba—a geographically immense school district. The Deputy Minister of Education in Manitoba thought evaluation might be a way to shake things up in a district he considered stagnant, so he asked me to facilitate an evaluation process with district officials. The actual form and content of the evaluation were to be determined internally, by them. So I went up to Winnipeg and met with the division administrators, a representative from the parents' group, a representative from the principals' group, and a representative from the teachers' union. I had asked that all constituencies be represented in order to establish credibility with all the people who might be involved in using the evaluation.

Inasmuch as I had been brought in from outside by a superordinate official, it was not surprising that I encountered reactions ranging from defensiveness to outright hostility. They had not asked for the evaluation, and the whole idea sounded unsavory and threatening.

I began by asking them to tell me what kinds of things they were interested in evaluating. The superintendent frowned and responded, "We'd like to see the evaluation instruments you've used in assessing other school districts."

I replied that I would be happy to share such instruments if they should prove relevant, but it would be helpful to first determine the evaluation issues and priorities of Frontier School Division. They looked skeptical, and after a lingering silence, the superintendent tried again: "You don't need to show us all the instruments you intend to use. Just show us one so we have an idea of what's going to happen."

I again replied that it was too early to talk about instruments. First, we had to identify their evaluation questions and concerns. Then we would talk about instruments. However, their folded arms and scowling faces told me that what they interpreted as my evasiveness was only intensifying their initial suspicions and fears. I was deepening their resistance by what they perceived as my secretiveness about the content of *my* evaluation scheme. The superintendent tried again: "How about just showing us one part of the evaluation, say the part that asks teachers about administrative effectiveness."

At that point I was about to throw in the towel, give them some old instruments, and let them use what they wanted from other evaluations. But first, I made one more attempt to get at *their* issues. I said, "Look, maybe your questions will be the same as questions I've used on surveys elsewhere. But I'm not even sure at this point that any kind of survey is appropriate. Maybe you don't need an evaluation. I certainly don't have any questions I need answered about your operations and effectiveness. Maybe you don't either. In which case, I'll tell the Deputy Minister that evaluation isn't the way to go. But before we decide to quit, let me ask you to participate in a simple little exercise. It's an old complete-the-blank exercise from grade school." I then turned to the chalkboard and wrote a sentence in capital letters.

> I WOULD REALLY LIKE TO KNOW ____________ ABOUT FRONTIER SCHOOL DIVISION.

I turned back to them and continued, "I want to ask each of you, individually, to complete the blank 10 times. What are 10 things about Frontier School Division that you'd like to know, things you aren't certain about, that would make a difference in what you do if you had more information? Take a shot at it, without regard to methods, measurement, design, resources, precision—just 10 basic questions, real questions about this division."

After about 10 minutes I divided the participants into three groups of four people each and asked them to combine their lists into a single list of 10 things that each group wanted to know—in effect, to establish each group's priority questions. Then we pulled back together and generated a single list of 10 basic evaluation questions—answers to which, they agreed, could make a real difference to the operations of Frontier School Division.

The questions they generated were the kind an experienced evaluator could anticipate being asked in a districtwide educational evaluation because there are only so many things one can ask about a school division. But the questions were phrased in *their* terms, incorporating important local nuances of meaning and circumstance. Most important, they had discovered that they had questions they cared about—not my questions but their questions, because *during the course of the exercise it had become their evaluation*. The whole atmosphere had changed. This became most evident as I read aloud the final list of 10 items they had generated that morning. One item read, "How do teachers view the effectiveness of administrators and how often do they think administrators ought to come into classrooms?" One of the administrators who had been most hostile at the outset said, "That would be dynamite information. We have no idea at all what teachers think about us and what we do. I have no idea if they want me in their classrooms or not, or how often they think I ought to visit. That could turn my job around. That would be great to know."

Another question concerned the relationship between the classroom and the community. Both the teacher and parent representatives said that nobody had ever thought about that in any real way: "We don't have any policy about that. We don't know what goes on in the different schools. That would be important for us to know."

We spent the rest of the day refining questions, prioritizing, formalizing evaluation procedures, and establishing an agenda for the evaluation process. The hostility had vanished. By the end of the day they were anxious to have me make a commitment to return. They had become excited about doing their evaluation. The evaluation had credibility because the questions were their questions. A month later, they found out that budget shifts in the Ministry meant that the central government would not pay for the evaluation. The Deputy Minister told them that they could scrap the evaluation if they wanted to, but they decided to pay for it out of local division funds.

The evaluation was completed in close cooperation with the task force at every step along the way. The results were disseminated to all principals and teachers. The conclusions and recommendations formed the basis for staff development conferences and division policy sessions. The evaluation process itself had an impact on the Division. Over the last several years, Frontier School Division has gone through many changes. It is a very different place in terms of direction, morale, and activity than it was on my first visit. Not all those changes were touched on in the evaluation, nor are they simply a consequence of the evaluation. But generating a list of real and meaningful evaluation questions played a critical part in getting things started. Exhibit 2.4 offers criteria for good utilization-focused questions.

EXHIBIT 2.4
Criteria for Utilization-Focused Evaluation Questions

1. Data can be brought to bear on the question; that is, it is truly an *empirical* question.
2. There is more than one possible answer to the question; that is, the answer is not predetermined by the phrasing of the question.
3. The primary intended users want information to help answer the question. They care about the answer to the question.
4. The primary users want to answer the question for themselves, not just for someone else.
5. The intended users can indicate how they would use the answer to the question; that is, they can specify the relevance of an answer to the question for future action.

Communicating Professional Commitment to Use From the Beginning

The criterion I offered the primary intended users in Winnipeg for generating meaningful questions was "Things you'd like to know that would make a difference to what you do." This criterion emphasizes knowledge for action—finding out things that can be used. But generating a list of potentially useful questions is only one way to start interacting with primary users. How one begins depends on what backgrounds, experiences, preconceptions, and relationships the primary users bring to the table. In Winnipeg, I needed to get the group engaged quickly in reframing how they were thinking about my role because their resistance was so palpable and because we didn't have much time.

With a seemingly more neutral group, one that is neither overtly hostile nor enthusiastic (Yes, some groups are actually enthusiastic at the beginning!), I may begin, as I noted earlier in this chapter, by asking participants to share words and feelings they associate with evaluation. Then, we explore how this "baggage" they've brought with them may affect their expectations about the evaluation's likely utility. As we work toward a shared definition of evaluation and a clear commitment to use, I look for opportunities to review the development of program evaluation as a field of professional practice and present the standards for and principles of evaluation (see the index). This material, presented earlier in this chapter and in Chapter 1, communicates to primary intended users that you, as the evaluator, are a professional—part of an established profession—and that, as such, you have an obligation to facilitate and conduct evaluations in accordance with professional standards and principles, including priority attention to utility.

Few non-evaluators are aware of the field's professional associations, conferences, journals, standards, and principles. By associating your effort with the larger profession, you can elevate the status, seriousness, and meaningfulness of the process you are facilitating and help the primary intended users understand the sources of wisdom you are drawing on and applying

EXHIBIT 2.5

Themes of Annual American Evaluation Association National Conferences

1986	What Have We Learned?
1987	The Utilization of Evaluation
1988	Evaluation and Politics
1989	International and Cross-Cultural Perspectives
1990	Evaluation and Formulation of Public Policy
1991	New Evaluation Horizons
1992	Synthesizing Evaluation: Perspectives, Practices, and Evidence
1993	Empowerment Evaluation
1994	Evaluation and Social Justice
1995	Evaluation for a New Century: A Global Perspective
1996	A Decade of Progress: Looking Back and Looking Forward
1997	Evaluation Theory Informing Practice, Practice Informing Theory

as you urge them to attend carefully to utilization issues from the start. Thus, the history of the profession presented in the first chapter can be shared with intended users to communicate the larger context within which any particular evaluation takes place and to show sophistication about the issues the profession has focused on over time (see Exhibit 2.5). I consider this so important that I have students practice 10-minute minilectures on the development of evaluation as a field of professional practice, one guided by standards and principles (see Exhibits 1.3 and 2.1), so they can hold forth at a moment's notice, whether the opportunity be a workshop or a cocktail party.

Creative Beginnings

Authors of all races, be they Greeks, Romans, Teutons, or Celts, can't seem just to say that anything is the thing it is; they have to go out of their way to say that it is like something else.

—Ogden Nash

With easy-going, relaxed groups that seem open to having some fun, I'll often begin with a metaphor exercise. Metaphors, similes, and analogies help us make connections between seemingly unconnected things, thereby opening up new possibilities by unveiling what had been undetected. Bill Gephart (1981), in his 1980 presidential address to evaluators, drew an analogy between his work as a watercolor artist and his work as an evaluator. Gephart compared the artist's efforts to "compel the eye" to the evaluator's efforts to "compel the mind." Both artist and evaluator attempt to focus the attention of an audience by highlighting some things and keeping other things in the background. He also examined the ways in which the values of an audience (of art critics or program decision makers) affect what they see in a finished piece of work.

Nick Smith (1981) directed a Research on Evaluation Program in which he and others thought about evaluators as poets, architects, photographers, philosophers, operations analysts, and artists. They consciously and creatively used metaphors and analogies to understand and elaborate the many functions of program evaluation. Use of these forms of figurative speech can help evaluators communicate the nature and practice of evaluation. Many of the problems encountered by evaluators, much of the resistance to evaluation, and many failures of use occur because of misunderstandings and communications problems. What we often have, between evaluators and non-evaluators, is a classic "failure to communicate."

One reason for such failures is that the language of research and evaluation—the jargon—is alien to many laypersons, decision makers, and stakeholders. From my point of view, the burden for clear communications rests on the evaluator. It is the evaluator who must find ways of bridging the communications gap.

To help intended users and stakeholders understand the nature of evaluation, I like to ask them to construct metaphors and similes about evaluation. This exercise helps participants in the process discover their own values concerning evaluation while also giving them a mechanism to communicate those values to others. The exercise can be used with a program staff, an evaluation task force, evaluation trainees, workshop participants, or any group for whom it might be helpful to clarify and share perceptions about evaluation. The exercise goes like this.

> One of the things that we'll need to do during the process of working together is come to some basic understandings about what evaluation is and can do. In my experience, evaluation can be a very creative and energizing experience. In particular, interpreting and using evaluation findings for program improvement requires creativity and openness to a variety of possibilities. To help us get started on this creative endeavor, I'm going to ask you to participate with me in a little exercise.
>
> In this box I have a bunch of toys, household articles, office supplies, tools, and other miscellaneous gadgets and thingamajigs that I've gathered from around my house. I'm going to dump these in the middle of the table and ask each of you to take one of them and use that item to make a statement about evaluation. Evaluation is like ___________ because . . .

To illustrate what I want people to do, I offer to go first. I ask someone to pick out any object in the room that I might use for my metaphor. What follows are some examples from actual workshops:

> Someone points to a coffee cup: "This cup can be used to hold a variety of things. The actual contents of the cup will vary depending on who is using it and for what purpose

they are using it. Utilization-focused evaluation is a process like this cup; it provides a form but is empty until the group of people working on the evaluation fill it with focus and content and substance. The potential of the cup cannot be realized until it holds some liquid. The potential of utilization-focused evaluation cannot be realized until it is given the substance of a concrete evaluation problem and situation. One of the things that I'll be doing as we work together is providing an evaluation framework like this cup. You will provide the substance."

Someone points to a chalkboard: "Evaluation is like a chalkboard because both are tools that can be used to express a variety of different things. The chalkboard itself is just an empty piece of slate until someone writes on it and provides information and meaning by filling in that space. The chalkboard can be filled up with meaningless figures, random marks, obscene words, mathematical formulas, or political graffiti—or the board can be filled with meaningful information, insights, helpful suggestions, and basic facts. The people who write on the chalkboard carry the responsibility for what it says. The people who fill in the blanks in the evaluation and determine its content and substance carry the responsibility for what the evaluation says. The evaluation process is just a tool to be used—and how it is used will depend on the people who control the process—in this case, you."

I'll typically take a break at this point and give people about 10 minutes to select an item and think about what to say. If there are more than 10 people in the group, I will break the larger group into small groups of 5 or 6 for sharing analogies and metaphors so that each person is given an opportunity to make an evaluation statement. Below are some examples from actual workshops.

This empty grocery bag is symbolic of my feelings about evaluation. When I think about our program being evaluated, I want to find someplace to hide, and I can put this empty bag over my head so that nobody can see me and I can't see anything else, and it gives me at least the feeling that I'm able to hide. (She puts the bag over her head.)

Evaluation can be like this toothbrush. When used properly it gets out the particles between the teeth so they don't decay. If not used properly, if it just lightly goes over the teeth or doesn't cover all the teeth, then some of the gunk will stay on and cause the teeth to decay. Evaluation should help get rid of any things that are causing a program to decay so it stays healthy.

Evaluation for me is like this rubber ball. You throw it down and it comes right back at you. Every time I say to my staff we ought to evaluate the program, they throw it right back at me and they say, "you do the evaluation."

Evaluation is like this camera. It lets you take a picture of what's going on, but it can only capture what you point it at, and only at a particular point in time. My concern about this evaluation is that it won't give the whole picture, that an awful lot may get left out.

Evaluation for me is like this empty envelope. You can use it to send a message to someone. I want to use evaluation to send a message to our funders about what we're doing in the program. They don't have any idea about what we actually do. I just hope they'll read the letter when they get it.

> Evaluation for me is like this adjustable wrench. You can use this wrench to tighten nuts and bolts to help hold things together. If used properly and applied with the right amount of pressure, it holds things together very well. If you tighten the bolt too hard, however, you can break the bolt, and the whole thing will fall apart. I'm in favor of evaluation if it's done right. My concern is that you can overdo it and the program can't handle it.

The process of sharing is usually accompanied by laughter and spontaneous elaborations of favorite metaphors. It's a fun process that offers hope the evaluation process itself may not be quite as painful as people thought it would be. In addition, participants are often surprised to find that they have something to say. They are typically quite pleased with themselves. Most important, the exercise serves to express important thoughts and feelings that can be dealt with once they are made explicit.

Participants are typically not even aware that they have these feelings. By providing a vehicle for discovering and expressing their concerns, it is possible to surface major issues that may later affect evaluation use. Shared metaphors can help establish a common framework for the evaluation, capturing its purpose, its possibilities, and the safeguards that need to be built into the process. Robert Frost once observed, "All thought is a feat of association: Having what's in front of you bring up something in your mind that you almost didn't know you knew." This exercise helps participants bring to mind things about evaluation they almost didn't know they knew.

By the way, I've used this exercise with many different groups and in many different situations, including cross-cultural settings, and I've never yet encountered someone who couldn't find an object to use in saying something about evaluation. One way of guaranteeing this is to include in your box of items some things that have a pretty clear and simple message. For example, I'll always include a lock and key so that a very simple and fairly obvious analogy can be made: "Evaluation is like a lock and key, if you have the right key you can open up the lock and make it work. If you have the right information you can make the thing work." Or I'll include a lightbulb so that someone can say "evaluation is like this lightbulb, it's purpose is to shed light on the situation."

The Cutting Edge of Metaphors

Metaphors can open up new understandings and enhance communications. They can also distort and offend. At the 1979 meeting of the Midwest Sociological Society, well-known sociologist Morris Janowitz was asked to participate in a panel on the question "What is the cutting edge of sociology?" Janowitz (1979), having written extensively on the sociology of the military, took offense at the "cutting edge" metaphor. He explained, " 'Cutting edge' is a military term. I am put off by the very term, cutting edge, like the parallel term breakthrough: slogans which intellectuals have inherited from the managers of violence" (p. 601).

Strategic planning is a label with military origins and connotations, as is *rapid reconnaissance*, a phrase sometimes used to describe certain quick, exploratory evaluation efforts. Some stakeholder groups will object to such associations; others will relate positively. Evaluators, therefore, must be sensitive in their selection of metaphors to avoid offensive comparisons and match analogies to stakeholders' interests. Of particular importance, in this regard, is avoiding the use of metaphors with possible racist and sexist connotations, for example, "It's black and white" or "We want to get inside the Black Box of evaluation."

As Minnich (1990) has observed in her important book, *Transforming Knowledge*, our language and thinking can perpetuate "the old exclusions and devaluations of the majority of humankind that have pervaded our informal as well as formal schooling" (p. 1). She observed further that

> even when we are all speaking the same languages, there are many "languages" at play behind and within what the speakers mean and what we in turn understand . . . , levels and levels of different meanings in even the most apparently simple and accessible utterance. (p. 9)

Minnich's point was nicely illustrated at a conference on educational evaluation where a Women's Caucus formed to express concerns about the analogies used in evaluation and to suggest some alternatives.

> To deal with diversity is to look for new metaphors. We need no new *weapons* of assessment—the violence has already been done! How about *brooms* to sweep away the attic-y cobwebs of our male/female stereotypes? The tests and assessment techniques we frequently use are full of them. How about *knives, forks*, and *spoons* to sample the feast of human diversity in all its richness and color? Where are the techniques that assess the deliciousness of response variety, independence of thought, originality, uniqueness? (And lest you think those are female metaphors, let me do away with that myth—at our house everybody sweeps and everybody eats!) Our group talked about another metaphor—the cafeteria line versus the smorgasbord banquet styles of teaching/learning/assessing. Many new metaphors are needed as we seek clarity in our search for better ways of evaluating. To deal with diversity is to look for new metaphors. (Hurty 1976)

As we look for new metaphors in evaluation, we would do well to do so in the spirit of Thoreau, who observed, "All perception of truth is the detection of an analogy." The added point for utilization-focused evaluators is the admonition to be sensitive in selecting metaphors that are meaningful to specific intended users. The importance of such sensitivity stems from the centrality of "the personal factor" in evaluation use, the subject of the next chapter. First, however, a closing metaphor.

Navigating Evaluation's Rough Seas

A common error made by novice evaluators is believing that because someone has requested an evaluation or some group has been assembled to design an evaluation, the commitment to reality testing and use is already there. Quite the contrary, these commitments must be engendered (or revitalized if once they were present) and then reinforced throughout the evaluation process. Utilization-focused evaluation makes this a priority.

It's all too easy for those of us trained in research methods to forget that "evaluation is an unnatural act." (Buttons and bumper stickers with this slogan evoke interesting responses from intended users.) Evaluation is not natural to managers, funders, policymakers, program staff, or program participants. That's why they need professional assistance, support, training, and facilitation.

Utilization-focused evaluation offers a philosophical harbor to sail toward when the often rough and stormy seas of evaluation threaten to blow the evaluator off course. With each new evaluation, the evaluator sets out, like an ancient explorer, on a quest for useful knowledge, not sure whether seas will be gentle, tempestuous, or becalmed. Along the way the evaluator will often encounter any number of challenges: political intrigues wrapped in mantles of virtue; devious and flattering antagonists trying to co-opt the evaluation in service of their own narrow interests and agendas; unrealistic deadlines and absurdly limited resources; gross misconceptions about what can actually be measured with precision and definitiveness; deep-seated fears about the evils-incarnate of evaluation, and therefore, evaluators; incredible exaggerations of evaluators' power; and insinuations about defects in the evaluator's genetic heritage. The observant evaluator is also likely to encounter tremendously dedicated staff working under difficult conditions for pitiable wages; program participants who have suffered grievous misfortunes and whose lives seem to hang by the most fragile of threads; administrators working feverishly to balance incredible needs against meager resources; funders and policymakers struggling to make sensible and rational decisions in a world that often seems void of sense and reason. The seas of evaluation offer encounters with discouraging corruption and inspiring virtue, great suffering and hopeful achievements, unmitigated programmatic disasters and solidly documentable successes, and an abundance of ambiguity between these poles of the human experience. The voyage is worth taking, despite the dangers and difficulties, because the potential rewards include making a meaningful difference in the effectiveness of important programs and thereby improving the quality of people's lives. That only happens, however, if the evaluation process and findings are used.

Note

1. I want to emphasize that I am using the term *reality testing* in its commonsense connotation of finding out what is happening. While philosophers of science will rightly point out that the whole notion of reality is an epistemological quagmire, I find that the people I work with in the "real world"—their phrase—resonate to the notion of reality testing. It is their own sense of reality I want to help them test, not some absolute, positivist construct of reality. The notion that reality is socially constructed doesn't mean it can't be tested and understood. At the 1995 International Evaluation Conference in Vancouver, Ernie House, Will Shadish, Michael Scriven, and I (evaluation theorists with quite different perspectives) participated in a session on theory in which we agreed on the following two propositions, among others: (1) Most theorists postulate a real physical world, although they differ greatly as to its knowability and complexity; and (2) logical positivism is an inadequate epistemology that few theorists advocate any more, either in evaluation or philosophy.

3

Fostering Intended Use by Intended Users

The Personal Factor

There are five key variables that are absolutely critical in evaluation use. They are, in order of importance: people, people, people, people, and people.

—Halcolm

On a damp summer morning at Snow Mountain Ranch near Rocky Mountain National Park, some 40 human service and education professionals have gathered from all over the country in a small, dome-shaped chapel to participate in an evaluation workshop. The session begins like this:

Instead of beginning by my haranguing you about what you should do in program evaluation, we're going to begin with an evaluation exercise to immerse us immediately in the process. I'm going to ask you to play the dual roles of participants and evaluators since that's the situation most of you find yourselves in anyway in your own agencies and programs, where you have both program and evaluation responsibilities. We're going to share an experience to loosen things up a bit . . . perhaps warm you up, wake you up, and allow you to get more comfortable. The exercise will also allow us to test your participant observer skills and provide us with a common experience as evaluators. We'll also generate some personal data about the process of evaluation that we can use for discussion later.

So what I want you to do for the next five minutes is move around this space in any way you want to. Explore this environment. Touch and move things. Experience different parts of this lovely setting. And while you're observing the physical environment, watch what others do. Then, find a place where you feel comfortable to write down what you observed, and also to evaluate the exercise. Experience, explore, observe, and evaluate. That's the exercise.

At the end of the writing time, participants shared, on a voluntary basis, what they had written.

First Observer: People slowly got up. Everybody looked kind of nervous 'cause they weren't sure what to do. People moved out toward the walls, which are made of rough wood. The lighting is kind of dim. People sort of moved counterclockwise. Every so often there would be a nervous smile exchanged between people. The chairs are fastened down in rows so it's hard for people to move in the center of the room. A few people went to the stage area, but most stayed toward the back and outer part. The chairs aren't too comfortable, but it's a quiet, mellow room. The exercise showed that people are nervous when they don't know what to do.

Second Observer: The room is hexagon-shaped with a dome-shaped ceiling. Fastened-down chairs are arranged in a semicircle with a stage in front that is about a foot high. A podium is at the left of the small stage. Green drapes hang at the side. Windows are small and triangular. The floor is wood. There's a coffee table in back. Most people went to get coffee. A couple people broke the talking rule for a minute. Everyone returned to about the same place they had been before after walking around. It's not a great room for a workshop, but it's OK.

Third Observer: People were really nervous about what to do because the goals of the exercise weren't clear. You can't evaluate without clear goals so people just wandered around. The exercise shows you can't evaluate without clear goals.

Fourth Observer: I said to myself at the start, this is a human relations thing to get us started. I was kind of mad about doing this because we've been here a half hour already, and we haven't done anything that has to do with evaluation. I came to learn about evaluation, not to do touchy-feely group stuff. So I just went to get coffee. I didn't like wasting so much time on this.

Fifth Observer: I felt uneasy, but I told myself that it's natural to feel uneasy when you aren't sure what to do. But I liked walking around, looking at the chapel, and feeling the space. I think some people got into it, but we were stiff and uneasy. People avoided looking at each other. Sometimes there was a nervous smile when people passed each other, but by kind of moving in a circle, most people went the same direction and avoided looking at each other. I think I learned something about myself and how I react to a strange, nervous situation.

These observations were followed by a discussion of the different perspectives reported on the same experience and speculation on what it would take to produce a more focused set of observations and evaluations. Suggestions included establishing clear goals; specifying evaluation criteria; figuring out what was supposed to be observed in advance so everyone could observe it; giving clearer directions of what to do; stating the purpose of evaluation; and training the evaluation observers so that they all recorded the same thing.

Further discussion revealed that before any of these evaluation tasks could be completed, a prior step would be necessary: **determining who the primary intended users of the evaluation are.** This task constitutes the first step in utilization-focused evaluation. Taking this first step is the focus of this chapter.

The First Step in Utilization-Focused Evaluation

Many decisions must be made in any evaluation. The purpose of the evaluation must be determined. Concrete evaluative criteria for judging program success will usually have to be established. Methods will have to be selected and time lines agreed on. All of these are important issues in any evaluation. The question is: Who will decide these issues? The utilization-focused answer is: primary intended users of the evaluation.

Clearly and explicitly identifying people who can benefit from an evaluation is so important that evaluators have adopted a special term for potential evaluation users: *stakeholders*. This term has been borrowed from management consulting, where it was coined in 1963 at the Stanford Research Institute as a way of describing people who were not directly stockholders in a company but "without whose support the firm would cease to exist" (Mendelow 1987:177).

> Stakeholder management is aimed at proactive action—action aimed, on the one hand, at forestalling stakeholder activities that could adversely affect the organization and on the other hand, at enabling the organization to take advantage of stakeholder opportunities. . . This can be achieved only through a conscious decision to adopt the stakeholder perspective as part of a strategy formulation process. (Mendelow 1987:177-78)

Evaluation stakeholders are people who have a stake—a vested interest—in evaluation findings. For any evaluation, there are multiple possible stakeholders: program funders, staff, administrators, and clients or program participants. Others with a direct, or even indirect, interest in program effectiveness may be consid-

ered stakeholders, including journalists and members of the general public, or more specifically, taxpayers, in the case of public programs. Stakeholders include anyone who makes decisions or desires information about a program. However, stakeholders typically have diverse and often competing interests. No evaluation can answer all potential questions equally well. This means that some process is necessary for narrowing the range of possible questions to focus the evaluation. In utilization-focused evaluation, this process begins by narrowing the list of potential stakeholders to a much shorter, more specific group of primary intended users. Their information needs, that is, their *intended uses*, focus the evaluation.

The workshop exercise that opened this chapter illustrates the importance of clearly identifying primary intended users. The participants in that exercise observed different things in part because they were interested in different things. They "evaluated" the exercise in different ways, and many had trouble "evaluating" the exercise at all, in part because they didn't know for whom they were writing. There were several potential users of an evaluation of the "explore the environment" exercise:

1. As a workshop leader, I might want to evaluate the extent to which the exercise accomplished my objectives.
2. Each individual participant might conduct a personal evaluation according to his or her own criteria.
3. The group could establish consensus goals for the exercise, which would then serve as focus for the evaluation.
4. The bosses, agency directors, and/or funding boards who paid for participants to attend might want an assessment of the return on the resources they have invested for training.

5. The Snow Mountain Ranch director might want an evaluation of the appropriateness of the chapel for such a workshop.
6. The building architects might want an evaluation of how participants responded to the space they designed.
7. Professional workshop facilitators might want to evaluate the exercise's effectiveness for opening a workshop.
8. Psychologists or human relation trainers might want to assess the effects of the exercise on participants.
9. Experiential learning educators might want an assessment of the exercise as an experiential learning tool.
10. The janitors of the chapel might want an evaluation of the work engendered for them by an exercise that permits moving things around (which sometimes occurs to destructive proportions when I've used the exercise in settings with moveable furniture).

This list of people potentially interested in the evaluation (stakeholders) could be expanded. The evaluation question in each case would likely be different. I would have different evaluation information needs as workshop leader than would the camp director; the architects' information needs would differ from the janitors' "evaluation" questions; the evaluation criteria of individual participants would differ from those reached by the total group through a consensus-formation process.

Beyond Audience

The preceding discourse is not aimed at simply making the point that different people see things differently and have varying interests and needs. I take that to be on the order of a truism. The point is that this truism is regularly and consistently ignored in the design of evaluation studies. To target an evaluation at the information needs of a specific person or a group of identifiable and interacting persons is quite different from what has been traditionally recommended as "identifying the audience" for an evaluation. Audiences are amorphous, anonymous entities. Nor is it sufficient to identify an agency or organization as a recipient of the evaluation report. Organizations are an impersonal collection of hierarchical positions. **People, not organizations, use evaluation information.** I shall elaborate these points later in this chapter. First, I want to present data from a study of how federal health evaluations were used. Those findings provide a research foundation for this first step in utilization-focused evaluation. In the course of presenting these data, it will also become clearer how one identifies primary intended users and why they are the key to specifying and achieving intended uses.

Studying Use: Identification of the Personal Factor

In the mid-1970s, as evaluation was emerging as a distinct field of professional practice, I undertook a study with colleagues and students of 20 federal health evaluations to assess how their findings had been used and to identify the factors that affected varying degrees of use. We interviewed the evaluators and those for whom the evaluations were conducted.[1] That study marked the beginning of the formulation of utilization-focused evaluation presented in this book.

We asked respondents to comment on how, if at all, each of 11 factors extracted from the literature on utilization had affected use of their study. These factors were methodological quality, methodological appropriateness, timeliness, lateness of report, positive or negative findings, surprise of findings, central or peripheral program objectives evaluated, presence or absence of related studies, political factors, decision maker/evaluator interactions, and resources available for the study. Finally, we asked respondents to "pick out the single factor you feel had the greatest effect on how this study was used."

From this long list of questions, only two factors emerged as consistently important in explaining utilization: (a) political considerations, to be discussed in Chapter 14, and (b) a factor we called *the personal factor*. This latter factor was unexpected, and its clear importance to our respondents had, we believed, substantial implications for the use of program evaluation. None of the other specific literature factors about which we asked questions emerged as important with any consistency. Moreover, when these specific factors were important in explaining the use or nonuse of a particular study, it was virtually always in the context of a larger set of circumstances and conditions related to either political considerations or the personal factor.

The personal factor is the presence of an identifiable individual or group of people who personally care about the evaluation and the findings it generates. Where such a person or group was present, evaluations were used; where the personal factor was absent, there was a correspondingly marked absence of evaluation impact.

The personal factor represents the leadership, interest, enthusiasm, determination, commitment, assertiveness, and caring of specific, individual people. These are people who actively seek information to make judgments and reduce decision uncertainties. They want to increase their ability to predict the outcomes of programmatic activity and thereby enhance their own discretion as decision makers, policymakers, consumers, program participants, and funders, or whatever role they play. These are the primary users of evaluation.

Data on the Importance of the Personal Factor

The personal factor emerged most dramatically in our interviews when, having asked respondents to comment on the importance of each of our 11 utilization factors, we asked them to identify the single factor that was most important in explaining the impact or lack of impact of that particular study. Time after time, the factor they identified was not on our list. Rather, they responded in terms of the importance of individual people:

> *Item:* I would rank as the most important factor this division director's interest, [his] interest in evaluation. Not all managers are that motivated toward evaluation. [DM353:17].[2]

> *Item:* [The single most important factor that had the greatest effect on how the study got used was] the principal investigator. . . . If I have to pick a single factor, I'll pick people any time. [DM328:20]

> *Item:* That it came from the Office of the Director—that's the most important factor. . . . The proposal came from the Office of the Director. It had his attention and he was interested in it, and he implemented many of the things. [DM312:21]

> *Item:* [The single most important factor was that] the people at the same level of decision making in [the new office] were not interested in making decisions of the kind that the people [in the old office] were, I think that

probably had the greatest impact. The fact that there was no one at [the new office] after the transfer who was making programmatic decisions. [EV361:27]

Item: Well, I think the answer there is in the qualities of the people for whom it was made. That's sort of a trite answer, but it's true. That's the single most important factor in any study now that's utilized. [EV232:22]

Item: Probably the single factor that had the greatest effect on how it was used was the insistence of the person responsible for iitiating the study that the Director of _______ become familiar with its findings and arrive at judgment on it. [DM369:25]

Item: [The most important factor was] the real involvement of the top decision makers in the conceptualization and design of the study, and their commitment to the study. [DM268:9]

While these comments concern the importance of interested and committed individuals in studies that were actually used, studies that were not used stand out in that there was often a clear absence of the personal factor. One evaluator, who was not sure how his study was used, but suspected it had not been, remarked,

I think that since the client wasn't terribly interested . . . and the whole issue had shifted to other topics, and since we weren't interested in doing it from a research point of view . . . nobody was interested. [EV264:14]

Another highly experienced evaluator was particularly adamant and articulate on the theory that the major factor affecting use is the personal energy, interests, abilities, and contacts of specific individuals. When asked to identify the one factor that is most important in whether a study gets used, he summarized his viewpoint as follows:

The most important factor is desire on the part of the managers, both the central federal managers and the site managers. I don't think there's [any doubt], you know, that evaluation should be responsive to their needs, and if they have a real desire to get on with whatever it is they're supposed to do, they'll apply it. And if the evaluations don't meet their needs, they won't. About as simple as you can get. **I think the whole process is far more dependent on the skills of the people who use it than it is on the sort of peripheral issues of politics, resources. . . .** Institutions are tough as hell to change. You can't change an institution by coming and doing an evaluation with a halo. Institutions are changed by people, in time, with a constant plugging away at the purpose you want to accomplish. And if you don't watch out, it slides back. [EV346:15-16]

His view had emerged early in the interview when he described how evaluations were used in the U.S. Office of Economic Opportunity (OEO):

In OEO, it depended on *who* the program officer was, on the program review officials, on program monitors for each of these grant programs. . . . Where there were aggressive program people, they used these evaluations whether they understood them or not. They used them to effect improvements, direct allocations of funds within the program, explain why the records were kept this way, why the reports weren't complete or whatever. Where the program officials were unaggressive, passive—*nothing!*

Same thing's true at the project level. Where you had a director who was aggres-

> sive and understood what the hell the structure was internally, he used evaluation as leverage to change what went on within his program. Those who weren't—*nothing*! [EV346:5]

At another point he observed, "The basic thing is how the administrators of the program view themselves and their responsibilities. That's the controlling factor" [EV346:8].

The same theme emerged in his comments about each possible factor. Asked about the effects on use of methodological quality, positive or negative findings, and the degree to which the findings were expected, he always returned eventually to the importance of managerial interest, competence, and confidence. **The person makes the difference.**

Our sample included another rather adamant articulation of this premise. An evaluation of a pilot program involving four major projects was undertaken at the instigation of the program administrator. He made a special effort to make sure that his question (i.e., Were the pilot projects capable of being extended and generalized?) was answered. He guaranteed this by personally taking an active interest in all parts of the study. The administrator had been favorable to the program in principle, was uncertain what the results would be, but was hoping that the program would prove effective. The evaluation findings were, in fact, negative. The program was subsequently ended, with the evaluation carrying "considerable weight" in that decision [DM367:8]. Why was this study used in such a dramatic way? His answer was emphatic:

> Look, we designed the project with an evaluation component in it, so we were committed to use it and we did. . . . It's not just the fact that [evaluation] was built in, but the fact that we built it in on purpose. That is, **the agency head and myself had broad responsibilities for this, wanted the evaluation study results, and we expected to use them. Therefore, they were used. That's my point.** If someone else had built it in because they thought it was needed, and we didn't care, I'm sure the use of the study results would have been different. [DM367:12]

The evaluator (an external agent selected through an open request-for-proposal process) independently corroborated the decision maker's explanation:

> The principal reason [for use] was that the decision maker was the guy who requested the evaluation and used its results. That is, the organizational distance between the policymaker and the evaluator was almost zero in this instance. That's the most important reason it had an impact. . . . It was the fact that the guy who was asking the question was the guy who was going to make use of the answer. [EV367:12].

Here, then, is a case in which a decision maker commissioned an evaluation knowing what information he needed; the evaluator was committed to answering the decision maker's questions; and the decision maker was committed to using the findings. The result was a high level of use in making a decision contrary to the director's initial personal hopes. In the words of the evaluator, the major factor explaining use was that "the guy who was going to be making the decision was aware of and interested in the findings of the study and had some hand in framing the questions to be answered; that's very important" [EV367:20].

The program director's overall conclusion gets to the heart of the personal factor:

> Factors that made a positive contribution to use? One would be that the decision makers themselves want the evaluation study results. I've said that several times. If that's not present, it's not surprising that the results aren't used. [DM367:17]

This point was made often in the interviews. One highly placed and widely experienced administrator offered the following advice at the end of a four-hour interview:

> Win over the program people. Make sure you're hooked into the people who're going to make the decision in six months from the time you're doing the study, and make sure that *they* feel it's *their* study, that these are *their* ideas, and that it's focused on *their* values. [DM283:40]

Presence of the personal factor increases the likelihood of long-term follow-through, that is, persistence in getting evaluation findings used. One study in particular stood out in this regard. It was initiated by a new office director with no support internally and considerable opposition from other affected agencies. The director found an interested and committed evaluator. The two worked closely together. The findings were initially ignored because it wasn't a hot political issue at the time, but over the ensuing four years, the director and evaluator personally worked to get the attention of key members of Congress. The evaluation eventually contributed to passing significant legislation in a new area of federal programming. From beginning to end, the story was one of personal human commitment to getting evaluation results used.

Although the specifics vary from case to case, the pattern is markedly clear: Where the personal factor emerges, where some individuals take direct, personal responsibility for getting findings to the right people, evaluations have an impact. Where the personal factor is absent, there is a marked absence of impact. Use is not simply determined by some configuration of abstract factors; it is determined in large part by real, live, caring human beings.

Supporting Research on the Personal Factor

James Burry (1984) of the UCLA Center for the Study of Evaluation conducted a thorough review of the voluminous literature on evaluation utilization. That review was the basis for a synthesis of factors that affect evaluation use (Alkin et al. 1985). The synthesis grew out of empirical research on evaluation utilization (Alkin, Daillak, and White 1979) and organizes the various factors in three major categories: human factors, context factors, and evaluation factors.

> Human factors reflect evaluator and user characteristics with a strong influence on use. Included here are such factors as people's attitudes toward and interest in the program and its evaluation, their backgrounds and organizational positions, and their professional experience levels.
>
> Context factors consist of the requirements and fiscal constraints facing the evaluation, and relationships between the program being evaluated and other segments of its broader organization and the surrounding community.
>
> Evaluation factors refer to the actual conduct of the evaluation, the procedures used in the conduct of the evaluation, and the quality of the information it provides. (Burry 1984:1)

The primary weakness of this framework is that the factors are undifferentiated in terms of importance. Burry ended up with a checklist of factors that may influence evaluation, but no overall hierarchy was presented in his synthesis; that is, a hierarchy that places more importance on certain factors as necessary and/or sufficient conditions for evaluation use. At a 1985 conference on evaluation use sponsored by the UCLA Center for the Study of Evaluation, I asked Jim Burry if his extensive review of the literature suggested any factors as particularly important in explaining use. He answered without hesitation:

> There's no question about it. The personal factor is far and away the most important. You're absolutely right in saying that the personal factor is the most important explanatory variable in evaluation use. The research of the last five years confirms the primacy of the personal factor. (personal conversation 1985)

Lester and Wilds (1990) conducted a comprehensive review of the literature on use of public policy analysis. Based on that review, they developed a conceptual framework to predict use. Among the hypotheses they found supported were these:

- The greater the interest in the subject by the decision maker, the greater the likelihood of utilization.
- The greater the decision maker's participation in the subject and scope of the policy analysis, the greater the likelihood of utilization. (p. 317)

These hypotheses were further confirmed in the evaluation literature in special issues of *New Directions for Program Evaluation* devoted to "Stakeholder-Based Evaluation" (Bryk 1983), "The Client Perspective in Evaluation" (Nowakowski 1987), and "Evaluation Utilization" (McLaughlin et al. 1988). Marvin Alkin (1985), founder and former director of the Center for the Study of Evaluation at the University of California, Los Angeles, made the personal factor the basis for his *Guide for Evaluation Decision-Makers*. Jean King concluded from her research review (1988) and case studies (1995) that *involving the right people* is critical to evaluation use. In a major analysis of "the Feasibility and Likely Usefulness of Evaluation," Joseph Wholey (1994) has shown that involving intended users early is critical so that "the intended users of the evaluation results have agreed on how they will use the information" (p. 16) before the evaluation is conducted. Cousins, Donohue, and Bloom (1995) reviewed a great volume of research on evaluation and found that "a growing body of data provide support" for the proposition that "increased participation in research by stakeholders will heighten the probability that research data will have the intended impact" (p. 5). Johnson (1995) used conjoint measurement and analysis to estimate evaluation use and found that evaluators attribute increased use to increased participation in the evaluation process by practitioners. And Carol Weiss (1990), one of the leading scholars of knowledge use, concluded in her keynote address to the American Evaluation Association:

> First of all, it seems that there are certain participants in policy making who tend to be 'users' of evaluation. The personal factor—a person's interest, commitment, enthusiasm—plays a part in determining how much

> influence a piece of research will have. (p. 177)

The need for interactive dialogue at a personal level applies to large-scale national evaluations as well as smaller-scale, local evaluations (Dickey 1981). Wargo (1995) analyzed three unusually successful federal evaluations in a search for "characteristics of successful program evaluations"; he found that active involvement of key stakeholders was critical at every stage: during planning, while conducting the evaluation, and in dissemination of findings (p. 77). In 1995, the U.S. General Accounting Office (GAO) studied the flow of evaluative information to Congress by following up three major federal programs: the Comprehensive Child Development Program, the Community Health Centers program, and the Chapter 1 Elementary and Secondary Education Act, aimed at providing compensatory education services to low-income students. Analysts concluded that underutilization of evaluative information was a direct function of poor communications between intended users (members of the Senate Committee on Labor and Human Resources) and responsible staff in the three programs:

> Finally, we observed that communication between the Committee and agency staff knowledgeable about program information was limited and comprised a series of one-way communications (from the Committee to the agency or the reverse) rather than joint discussion. This pattern of communication, which was reinforced by departmental arrangements for congressional liaison, affords little opportunity to build a shared understanding about the Committee's needs and how to meet them. (GAO 1995:40)

The GAO (1995) report recommended that Senate Committee members have "increased communication with agency program and evaluation staff to help ensure that information needs are understood and that requests and reports are suitably framed and are adapted as needs evolve" (p. 41). This recommendation affirms the importance of personal interactions as a basis for mutual understanding to increase the relevance and, thereby, the utility of evaluation reports.

Another framework that supports the importance of the personal factor is the "Decision-Oriented Educational Research" approach of Cooley and Bickel (1985). Although the label for this approach implies a focus on decisions rather than people, in fact the approach is built on a strong "client orientation." This client orientation means that the primary intended users of decision-oriented educational research are clearly identified and then involved in all stages of the work through ongoing dialogue between the researcher and the client. Cooley and Bickel presented case evidence to document the importance of being client-oriented.

In a major review of evaluation use in nonprofit organizations, the Independent Sector concluded that attending to "the human side of evaluation" makes all the difference. "Independent Sector learned that evaluation means task, process, *and* people. It is the people side—the human resources of the organization—who make the "formal" task and process work and will make the results work as well" (Moe 1993:19).

The evaluation literature contains substantial additional evidence that working with intended users can increase use (e.g., Bedell et al. 1985; Dawson and D'Amico 1985; King 1985; Lawler et al. 1985; Siegel and Tuckel 1985; Cole 1984; Evans and Blunden 1984; Hevey 1984; Rafter 1984; Bryk 1983; Campbell 1983; Glaser, Abelson, and Garrison 1983; Lewy and Alkin 1983; Stalford 1983; Barkdoll 1982; Beyer and Trice 1982; Canadian Evaluation Society 1982; King and Pechman 1982; Saxe and Koretz 1982; Dickey and Hampton 1981; Leviton and Hughes 1981; Alkin and Law 1980; Braskamp and Brown 1980; Studer 1978).

Support for the importance of the personal factor also emerged from the work of the Stanford Evaluation Consortium, one of the leading places of ferment and reform in evaluation during the late 1970s and early 1980s. Cronbach and associates in the Consortium identified major reforms needed in evaluation by publishing a provocative set of 95 theses, following the precedent of Martin Luther. Among their theses was this observation on the personal factor: "Nothing makes a larger difference in the use of evaluations than *the personal factor*—the interest of officials in learning from the evaluation and the desire of the evaluator to get attention for what he knows" (Cronbach et al. 1980:6; emphasis added).

Evaluation's Premier Lesson

The importance of the personal factor in explaining and predicting evaluation use leads directly to the emphasis in utilization-focused evaluation on working with intended users to specify intended uses. The personal factor directs us to attend to specific people who understand, value, and care about evaluation and further directs us to attend to their interests. This is the primary lesson the profession has learned about enhancing use, and it is wisdom now widely acknowledged by practicing evaluators, as evidenced by research on evaluators' beliefs and practices conducted by Cousins et al. (1995).

Cousins and his colleagues (1995) surveyed a sample of 564 evaluators and 68 practitioners drawn from the membership lists of professional evaluation associations in the United States and Canada. The survey included a list of possible beliefs that respondents could agree or disagree with. Greatest consensus centered on the statement "Evaluators should formulate recommendations from the study." (I'll discuss recommendations in a later chapter.) The item eliciting the next highest agreement was "The evaluator's primary function is to maximize intended uses by intended users of evaluation data" (p. 19). Given widespread agreement about the desired outcome of evaluation, namely, intended uses by intended users, let's now examine some of the practical implications of this perspective.

Practical Implications of the Personal Factor

First, in order to work with primary intended users to achieve intended uses, the evaluation process must surface people who want to know something. This means locating people who are able and willing to use information. The number may vary from one prime user to a fairly large group representing several constituencies, for example, a task force of program staff, clients, funders, administrators, board members, community representatives, and officials or policymakers (see Exhibit 3.1). Cousins et al. (1995) surveyed evaluators and found that they reported six stakeholders as the median number typically involved in a project. While stakeholders' points of view may vary on any number of issues, what they should share is a genuine interest in

EXHIBIT 3.1

A Statewide Evaluation Task Force

The Personal Factor means getting key influentials together, face-to-face, to negotiate the design. Here's an example.

In 1993, the Minnesota Department of Transportation created eight Area Transportation Partnerships to make decisions about roads and other transportation investments in a cooperative fashion between state and local interests. To design and oversee the study of how the partnerships were working, a technical panel was created to represent the diverse interests involved. Members of the technical panel included:

- The District Engineer from District 1 (Northeast)
- The Planning Director from District 6 (Southeast)
- The District Planner from District 7 (South central)
- Planner for a Regional Development Council (Northwest)
- Department of Transportation Director of Economic Analysis and Special Studies, State Office of Investment Management
- An influential county commissioner
- Director of a regional transit operation
- Director of a regional metropolitan Council of Governments (Western part of the state)
- Member of the Metropolitan Council Transportation Advisory Committee (Greater Minneapolis/Saint Paul)
- A county engineer
- A private transportation consultant
- A city engineer from a small town
- A metropolitan planning and research engineer
- The State Department of Transportation Interagency Liaison
- A University of Minnesota researcher from the University's Center for Transportation Studies
- An independent evaluation consultant (not the project evaluator)
- Five senior officials from various offices of the State Department of Transportation
- The evaluator and two assistants

This group met quarterly throughout the study. The group made substantive improvements in the original design, gave the study credibility with different stakeholder groups, participated in interpreting findings, and laid the groundwork for use.

using evaluation, an interest manifest in a willingness to take the time and effort to work through their information needs and interests. Thus, the first challenge in evaluation is to answer seriously and searchingly the question posed by Marvin Alkin (1975a): "Evaluation: Who Needs It? Who Cares?" Answering this question, as we shall see, is not always easy, but it is always critical.

Second, formal position and authority are only partial guides in identifying primary users. Evaluators must find strategically located people who are enthusiastic, committed, competent, interested, and assertive. Our data suggest that more may be accomplished by working with a lower-level person displaying these characteristics than by working with a passive, uninterested person in a higher position.

Third, quantity, quality, and timing of interactions with intended users are all important. A large amount of interaction between evaluators and users with little substance may backfire and actually reduce stakeholder interest. Evaluators must be strategic and sensitive in asking for time and involvement from busy people, and they must be sure they're interacting with the right people around relevant issues. Increased contact by itself is likely to accomplish little. Nor will interaction with the wrong people (i.e., those who are not oriented toward use) help much. It is the nature and quality of interactions between evaluators and decision makers that is at issue. My own experience suggests that where the right people are involved, the amount of direct contact can sometimes be reduced because the interactions that do occur are of such high quality. Later, when we review the decisions that must be made in the evaluation process, we'll return to the issues of quantity, quality, and timing of interactions with intended users.

Fourth, evaluators will typically have to work to build and sustain interest in evaluation use. Identifying intended users is part selection and part nurturance. Potential users with low opinions of or little interest in evaluation may have had bad prior experiences or just not have given much thought to the benefits of evaluation. The second chapter discussed ways of cultivating interest in evaluation and building commitment to use. Even people initially inclined to value evaluation will still often need training and support to become effective information users.

Fifth, evaluators need skills in building relationships, facilitating groups, managing conflict, walking political tightropes, and effective interpersonal communications to capitalize on the importance of the personal factor. Technical skills and social science knowledge aren't sufficient to get evaluations used. People skills are critical. Ideals of rational decision making in modern organizations notwithstanding, personal and political dynamics affect what really happens. Evaluators without the savvy and skills to deal with people and politics will find their work largely ignored, or, worse yet, used inappropriately.

Sixth, a particular evaluation may have multiple levels of stakeholders and therefore need multiple levels of stakeholder involvement. For example, funders, chief executives, and senior officials may constitute the primary users for overall effectiveness results, while lower-level staff and participant stakeholder groups may be involved in using implementation and monitoring data for program improvement. Exhibit 3.2 provides an example of such a multiple level structure for different levels of stakeholder involvement and evaluation use.

Menu 3.1 summarizes these practical implications of the personal factor for use.

Diversions Away From Intended Users

To appreciate some of the subtleties of the admonition to focus on intended use by intended users, let's consider a few of the

EXHIBIT 3.2

A Multilevel Stakeholder Structure and Process

The Saint Paul Foundation formed a Donor Review Board of several philanthropic foundations in Minnesota to fund a project, Supporting Diversity in Schools (SDS). The project established local school-community partnerships with communities of color: African Americans, Hispanics, Native Americans, and Southeast Asians. The evaluation had several layers based on different levels of stakeholder involvement and responsibility.

Stakeholder Group	*Evaluation Focus*	*Nature of Involvement*
Donor Review Board (Executives and Program Officers from contributing Foundations and School Superintendent)	Overall effectiveness; policy implications; sustainability	Twice-a-year meetings to review the design and interim evaluation results Final report directed to this group
District Level Evaluation Group (Representatives from participating schools, social service agencies, community organizations, and project staff)	Implementation monitoring in early years; district-level outcomes in later years	An initial full-day retreat with 40 people from diverse groups; annual retreat sessions to update, refocus, and interpret interim findings
Partnership Level Evaluation Teams (Teachers, community representatives, and evaluation staff liaisons)	Documenting activities and outcomes at the local partnership level: one school, one community of color	Annual evaluation plan; completing evaluation documents for every activity; quarterly review of progress to use findings for improvement

temptations evaluators face that lure them away from the practice of utilization-focused evaluation.

First, and most common, evaluators are tempted to make themselves the major decision makers for the evaluation. This can happen by default (no one else is willing to do it), by intimidation (clearly, the evaluator is the expert), or simply by failing to think about or seek primary users (why make life difficult?). The tip-off that evaluators have become the primary intended users (either by intention or default) is that the evaluators are answering their own questions according to their own interests, needs, and priorities. Others may have occasional input here and there, but what emerges is an evaluation by the evaluators, for the evaluators, and of the evaluators. Such studies are seldom of use to other stakeholders, whose reactions are likely to be, "Great study. Really well done. Shows lots of work, but doesn't tell us anything *we* want to know."

A less innocent version of this scenario occurs when academics pursue their basic research agendas under the guise of evaluation research. The tip-off here is that the

MENU 3.1

Implications of the Personal Factor for Planning Use

- Find and cultivate people who want to learn.
- Formal position and authority are only partial guides in identifying primary users. Find strategically located people who are enthusiastic, committed, competent, and interested.
- Quantity, quality, and timing of interactions with intended users are all important.
- Evaluators will typically have to work to build and sustain interest in evaluation use. Building effective relationships with intended users is part selection, part nurturance, and part training.
- Evaluators need *people skills* in how to build relationships, facilitate groups, manage conflict, walk political tightropes, and communicate effectively.
- A particular evaluation may have multiple levels of stakeholders and therefore need multiple levels of stakeholder involvement. (See Exhibit 3.2.)

evaluators insist on designing the study in such a way as to test some theory they think is particularly important, whether or not people involved in the program see any relevance to such a test.

A second temptation that diverts evaluators from focusing on specific intended users is to fall prey to the seemingly stakeholder-oriented "identification of audience" approach. Audiences turn out to be relatively passive groups of largely anonymous faces: the "feds," state officials, the legislature, funders, clients, the program staff, the public, and so forth. If specific individuals are not identified from these audiences and organized in a manner that permits meaningful involvement in the evaluation process, then, by default, the evaluator becomes the real decision maker and stakeholder ownership suffers, with a corresponding threat to utility. This is my critique of "responsive evaluation" as advocated by Stake (1975) and Guba and Lincoln (1981). Responsive evaluation "takes as its organizer the *concerns and issues of stakeholding audiences*" (Guba and Lincoln 1981:23; emphasis in the original). The evaluator interviews and observes stakeholders, then designs an evaluation that is responsive to stakeholders' issues. The stakeholders, however, are no more than sources of data and an audience for the evaluation, not real partners in the evaluation process.

The 1994 revision of the Joint Committee Standards for Evaluation moved to language about "intended users" and "stakeholders" in place of earlier references to "audiences." Thus, in the new version, "the Utility Standards are intended to ensure that an evaluation will serve the information needs of *intended users*," as opposed to "given audiences" in the original 1981 version (Joint Committee 1994, 1981; emphasis added). The first standard was changed to "Stakeholder Identification" rather than the original "Audience Identification." Such changes in language are far from trivial. They indicate how the knowledge base of the profession has evolved. The language we use shapes how we think. The nuances and connotations reflected in these language changes are fundamental to the philosophy of utilization-focused evaluation.

A third diversion from intended users occurs when evaluators target organizations rather than specific individuals. This appears to be more specific than targeting general audiences, but really isn't. Organizations as targets can be strangely devoid of real people. Instead, the focus shifts to positions and the roles and authority that attach to positions. Since Max Weber's (1947) seminal essay on bureaucracy gave birth to the study of organizations, sociologists have viewed the interchangeability of people in organizations as the hallmark of institutional rationality in modern society. Under ideal norms of bureaucratic rationality, it doesn't matter who's in a position, only that the position be filled using universalistic criteria. Weber argued that bureaucracy makes for maximum efficiency precisely because the organization of role-specific positions in an unambiguous hierarchy of authority and status renders action calculable and rational without regard to personal considerations or particularistic criteria. Such a view ignores the personal factor. Yet, it is just such a view of the world that has permeated the minds of evaluators when they say that their evaluation is for the federal government, the state, the agency, or any other organizational entity. But organizations do not consume information; people do—individual, idiosyncratic, caring, uncertain, searching people. *Who* is in a position makes all the difference in the world to evaluation use. To ignore the personal factor is to diminish utilization potential from the outset. To target evaluations at organizations is to target them at nobody in particular—and, in effect, not to really target them at all.

A fourth diversion away from intended users is to focus on decisions instead of on decision makers. This approach is epitomized by Mark Thompson (1975), who defined evaluation as "marshalling of information for the purposes of improving decisions" (p. 26) and made the first step in an evaluation "identification of the decision or decisions for which information is required" (p. 38). The question of who will make the decision remains implicit. The decision-oriented approach stems from a rational social scientific model of how decision making occurs:

1. A clear-cut decision is expected to be made.
2. Information will inform the decision.
3. A study supplies the needed information.
4. The decision is then made in accordance with the study's findings.

The focus in this sequence is on data and decisions rather than people. But people make decisions and, it turns out, most "decisions" accrete gradually and incrementally over time rather than getting made at some concrete, decisive moment (Weiss 1990, 1977; Allison 1971; Lindblom 1965, 1959). It can be helpful, even crucial, to orient evaluations toward future decisions, but identification of such decisions, and the implications of those decisions for the evaluation, are best made in conjunction with intended users who come together to decide what data will be needed for what purposes, including, but not limited to, decisions.

Utilization-focused evaluation is often confused with or associated with decision-oriented approaches to evaluation, in part, I presume, because both approaches are concrete and focused and both are considered "utilitarian." Ernest House (1980) wrote an important book categorizing various approaches to evaluation in which he included utilization-focused evaluation among the "decision-making models" he reviewed. The primary characteristic of a decision-making model is that "the evaluation be structured by the actual decisions to be made" (p. 28). I believe he incorrectly categorized utilization-focused evaluation because he failed to appreciate the distinct and critical nature of the personal factor. While utilization-focused evaluation includes the option of focusing on decisions, it can also serve a variety of other purposes, depending on the information needs of primary intended users. That is, possible intended uses include a large menu of options, which we'll examine in Chapters 4 and 5. For example, the evaluation process can be important in directing and focusing how people *think about* the basic policies involved in a program, what has come to be called conceptual use; evaluations can help in fine-tuning program implementation; the process of designing an evaluation may lead to clearer, more specific, and more meaningful program goals; and evaluations can provide information on client needs and assets that will help inform general public discussions about public policy. These and other outcomes of evaluation are entirely compatible with utilization-focused evaluation but do not make a formal decision the driving force behind the evaluation.

Nor does utilization-focused evaluation really fit within any of House's other seven categories, though any of them could be an option in a utilization-focused evaluation if that's the way intended users decided to orient the evaluation: (1) *systems analysis*, which quantitatively measures program inputs and outcomes to look at effectiveness and efficiency; (2) *the behavioral objectives approach*, which measures attainment of clear, specific goals; (3) *goal-free evaluation*, which examines the extent to which actual client needs are being met by the program; (4) *the art criticism approach*, which makes the evaluator's own expertise-derived standards of excellence a criterion against which programs are judged; (5) *the accreditation model*, where a team of external accreditors determines the extent to which a program meets professional standards for a given type of program; (6) *the adversary approach*, in which two teams do battle over the summative question of whether a program should be continued; and (7) *the transaction model*, which concentrates on program processes.

What is omitted from the House classification scheme is an approach to evaluation that focuses on and is driven by the information needs of specific people who will use the evaluation processes and findings. The point is that the evaluation is *user-focused*. Utilization-focused evaluation, then, in my judgment, falls within a category of evaluations that I would call, following Marvin Alkin (1995), user-oriented. This is a distinct alternative to the other models identified by House. In the other models, the content of the evaluation is determined by the *evaluator's* presuppositions about what constitutes an evaluation: a look at the relationship between inputs and outcomes; the measurement of goal attainment; advice about a specific programmatic decision; description of program processes; a decision about future or continued funding; or judgment according to some set of expert or professional standards. In contrast to these models, user-focused evaluation describes an evaluation process for making decisions about the content of an evaluation—but the content itself is not specified or implied in advance.

Thus, any of the eight House models, or adaptations and combinations of those models, might emerge as the guiding direction in user-focused evaluation, depending on the information needs of the people for whom the evaluation information was being collected. Let's continue, now, examining three other temptations that divert evaluators from being user focused.

A fifth temptation is to assume that the funders of the evaluation are the primary intended users, that is, those who pay the fiddler call the tune. In some cases, this is accurate. Funders are hopefully among those most interested in using evaluation. But there may be additional important users. Moreover, evaluations are funded for reasons other than their perceived utility, for example, wanting to give the appearance of supporting evaluation; because legislation or licensing requires evaluation; or because someone thought it had to be written into the budget. Those who control evaluation purse strings may not have any specific evaluation questions. Often, they simply believe that evaluation is a good thing that keeps people on their toes. They may not care about the content of a specific evaluation; they may care only that evaluation—any evaluation—takes place. They mandate the process, but not the substance. Under such conditions (which are not unusual), there is considerable opportunity for identifying and working with additional interested stakeholders to formulate relevant evaluation questions and a correspondingly appropriate design.

A sixth temptation is to put off attending to and planning for use from the beginning. It's tempting to wait until findings are in to worry about use, essentially not planning for use by waiting to see what happens. In contrast, planned use occurs when the intended use by intended users is identified at the beginning. Unplanned use can occur in any evaluation, but relying on the hope that something useful will turn up is a risky strategy. Eleanor Chelimsky (1983) has argued that the most important kind of accountability in evaluation is use that comes from "designed tracking and follow-up of a predetermined use to predetermined user" (p. 160). She calls this a "closed-looped feedback process" in which "the policymaker wants information, asks for it, and is interested in and informed by the response" (p. 160). This perspective solves the problem of defining use, addresses the question of whom the evaluation is for, and builds in evaluation accountability since the predetermined use becomes the criterion against which the success of the evaluation can be judged. Such a process has to be *planned.*

A seventh and final temptation (seven use-deadly sins seem sufficient, though certainly not exhaustive of the possibilities) is to convince oneself that it is unseemly to enter the fray and thereby run the risks that come with being engaged. I've heard academic evaluators insist that their responsibility is to ensure data quality and design rigor in the belief that the scientific validity of the findings will carry the day. The evidence suggests this seldom happens. An academic stance that justifies the evaluator standing above the messy fray of people and politics is more likely to yield scholarly publications than improvements in programs. Fostering use requires becoming engaged in building relationships and sorting through the politics that enmesh any program. In so doing, the evaluator runs the risks of getting entangled in changing power dynamics, having the rug pulled out by the departure of a key intended user, having relationships go bad, and/or being accused of bias. Later we'll discuss strategies for dealing with these and other risks, but the only way I know to avoid them

MENU 3.2

Temptations Away From Being User-Focused: Seven Use-Deadly Sins

1. Evaluators make themselves the primary decision makers and, therefore, the primary users.
2. Identifying vague, passive audiences as users instead of real people.
3. Targeting organizations as users (e.g., "the feds") instead of specific persons.
4. Focusing on decisions instead of decision makers.
5. Assuming the evaluation's funder is automatically the primary stakeholder.
6. Waiting until the findings are in to identify intended users and intended uses.
7. Taking a stance of standing above the fray of people and politics.

altogether is to stand aloof; that may provide safety, but at the high cost of utility and relevance.

Menu 3.2 summarizes these seven use-deadly temptations that divert evaluators from clearly specifying and working with intended users.

User-Focused Evaluation in Practice

Lawrence Lynn Jr., Professor of Public Policy at the Kennedy School of Government, Harvard University, has provided excellent evidence for the importance of a user-focused way of thinking in policy analysis and evaluation. Lynn was interviewed by Michael Kirst for *Educational Evaluation and Policy Analysis*. He was asked, "What would be a test of a 'good policy analysis'?"

> One of the conditions of a good policy analysis is that it is helpful to a decision maker. A decision maker looks at it and finds he or she understands the problem better, understands the choices better, or understands the implications of choice better. The decision maker can say that this analysis helped me. (Lynn 1980a:85)

Notice here that the emphasis is on informing the decision maker, not the decision. Lynn argues in his casebook on policy analysis (Lynn 1980b) that a major craft skill needed by policy and evaluation analysts is the ability to understand and make accommodations for a specific decision maker's cognitive style and other personal characteristics. His examples are exemplars of the user-focused approach.

> Let me take the example of Elliot Richardson, for whom I worked, or Robert MacNamara, for that matter. These two individuals were perfectly capable of understanding the most complex issues and absorbing details—absorbing the complexity, fully considering it in their own minds. Their intellects were not limited in terms of what they could handle. . . . On the other hand,

you will probably find more typical the decision makers who do not really like to approach problems intellectually. They may be visceral, they may approach issues with a wide variety of preconceptions, they may not like to read, they may not like data, they may not like the appearance of rationality, they may like to see things couched in more political terms, or overt value terms. And an analyst has got to take that into account. There is no point in presenting some highly rational, comprehensive piece of work to a Secretary or an Assistant Secretary of State who simply cannot or will not think that way. But that does not mean the analyst has no role; that means the analyst has to figure out how he can usefully educate someone whose method of being educated is quite different.

We did a lengthy case on the Carter administration's handling of the welfare reform issue, and, in particular, the role of Joe Califano and his analysts. Califano was very different in the way he could be reached than an Elliot Richardson, or even Casper Weinberger. Califano is a political animal and has a relatively short attention span—highly intelligent, but an action-oriented person. And one of the problems his analysts had is that they attempted to educate him in the classical, rational way without reference to any political priorities, or without attempting to couch issues and alternatives in terms that would appeal to a political, action-oriented individual. And so there was a terrible communications problem between the analysts and Califano. I think a large part of that had nothing to do with Califano's intellect or his interest in the issues; it had a great deal to do with the fact that his cognitive style and the analyst's approach just did not match.

Lynn also used the example of Jerry Brown, former Governor of California. Brown liked policy analyses framed as a debate—thesis, antithesis—because he had been trained in the Jesuitical style of argument. The challenge for a policy analyst or evaluator, then, becomes grasping the decision maker's cognitive style and logic. President Ronald Reagan, for example, liked *Reader's Digest* style stories and anecdotes. From Lynn's perspective, an analyst presenting to Reagan would have to figure out how to communicate policy issues through stories. He admonished analysts and evaluators to "discover those art forms by which one can present the result of one's intellectual effort" in a way that can be heard, appreciated and understood:

> In my judgment, it is not as hard as it sounds. I think it is not that difficult to discover how a Jerry Brown or a Joe Califano or a George Bush or a Ted Kennedy thinks, how he reacts. All you have got to do is talk to people who deal with them continuously, or read what they say and write. And you start to discover the kinds of things that preoccupy them, the kinds of ways they approach problems. And you use that information in your policy analyses. I think the hang-up most analysts or many analysts have is that they want to be faithful to their discipline. They want to be faithful to economics or faithful to political science and are uncomfortable straying beyond what their discipline tells them they are competent at dealing with. The analyst is tempted to stay in that framework with which he or she feels most comfortable.
>
> And so they have the hang-up, they cannot get out of it. They are prone to say that my tools, my training do not prepare me to deal with things that are on Jerry Brown's mind, therefore, I cannot help him. That is wrong. They can help, but they have got to be willing to use the information they have about how these individuals think and then begin to craft their work, to take that into account. (Lynn 1980a: 86-87).

Lynn's examples document the importance of the personal factor at the highest levels of government. Alkin et al. (1979) have shown how the personal factor operates in evaluation use at state and local levels. Focusing on the personal factor provides direction about what to look for and how to proceed in planning for use.

Beyond Just Beginning

In this chapter, we've discussed the personal factor as a critical consideration in enhancing evaluation use. The importance of the personal factor explains why utilization-focused evaluators begin by identifying and organizing primary intended evaluation users. They then interact with these primary users throughout the evaluation to nurture and sustain the commitment to use. **For there is an eighth deadly-use sin: identifying primary intended users at the outset of the study, then ignoring them until the final report is ready.**

Attending to primary intended users is not just an academic exercise performed for its own sake. Involving specific people who can and will use information enables them to establish direction for, commitment to, and ownership of the evaluation every step along the way, from initiation of the study through the design and data collection stages right through to the final report and dissemination process. If decision makers have shown little interest in the study in its earlier stages, our data suggest that they are not likely to show a sudden interest in using the findings at the end. They won't be sufficiently *prepared* for use.

The remainder of this book examines the implications of focusing on intended use by intended users. We'll look at the implications for how an evaluation is conceptualized and designed (Chapters 4 through 10), methods decisions (Chapters 11 and 12), and analysis approaches (Chapter 13). We'll also look at the political and ethical implications of utilization-focused evaluation (Chapter 14).

Throughout, we'll be guided by attention to the essence of utilization-focused evaluation: **focusing on intended use for specific intended users.** Focus and specificity are ways of coming to grips with the fact that no evaluation can serve all potential stakeholders' interests equally well. Utilization-focused evaluation makes explicit whose interests are served. For, as Baltasar Gracian observed in 1647 in *The Art of Worldly Wisdom:*

> It is a great misfortune to be of use to nobody; scarcely less to be of use to everybody.

Notes

1. At the time of the study in 1976, I was Director of the Evaluation Methodology Program in the Humphrey Institute of Public Affairs, University of Minnesota. The study was conducted through the Minnesota Center for Social Research, University of Minnesota. Results of the study were first published under the title "In Search of Impact: An Analysis of the Utilization of Federal Health Evaluation Research" (Patton, Grimes, et al. 1977). For details on the study's design and methods, see Patton 1986:30-39. The 20 cases in the study included 4 mental health evaluations, 4 health training programs, 2 national assessments of laboratory proficiency, 2 evaluations of neighborhood health center programs, studies of 2 health services delivery systems programs, a training program on alcoholism, a health regulatory program, a federal loan-forgiveness program, a training workshop evaluation, and 2 evaluations of specialized health facilities. The types of evaluations ranged from a three-week program

review carried out by a single internal evaluator to a four-year evaluation that cost $1.5 million. Six of the cases were internal evaluations and 14 were external.

Because of very limited resources, it was possible to select only three key informants to be contacted and intensively interviewed about the utilization of each of the 20 cases in the final sample. These key informants were (a) the government's internal project officer (PO) for the study, (b) the person identified by the project officer as being either the decision maker for the program evaluated or the person most knowledgeable about the study's impact, and (c) the evaluator who had major responsibility for the study. Most of the federal decision makers interviewed had been or now are office directors (and deputy directors), division heads, or bureau chiefs. Overall, these decision makers represented over 250 years of experience in the federal government.

The evaluators in our sample were a rather heterogeneous group. Six of the 20 cases were internal evaluations, so the evaluators were federal administrators or researchers. In one case, the evaluation was contracted from one unit of the federal government to another, so the evaluators were also federal researchers. The remaining 13 evaluations were conducted by private organizations or nongovernment employees, although several persons in this group either had formerly worked for the federal government or have since come to do so. Evaluators in our sample represented over 225 years of experience in conducting evaluative research.

2. Citations for quotes taken from the interview transcripts use the following format: [DM367:13] refers to the transcript of an interview with a decision maker about evaluation study number 367; this quote was taken from page 13 of the transcript. The study numbers and page numbers have been systematically altered to protect the confidentiality of the interviewees. EV201:10 and P0201:6 refer to interviews about the same study, the former being an interview with the evaluator, the latter an interview with the project officer.

4

Intended Uses of Findings

If you don't know where you're going, you'll end up somewhere else.

—Yogi Berra

When Alice encounters the Cheshire Cat in Wonderland, she asks, "Would you tell me, please, which way I ought to walk from here?"

"That depends a good deal on where you want to get to," said the Cat.

"I don't much care where—" said Alice.

"Then it doesn't matter which way you walk," said the Cat.

"—so long as I get somewhere," Alice added as an explanation.

"Oh, you're sure to do that," said the Cat, "if you only walk long enough."

—Lewis Carroll

This story carries a classic evaluation message: To evaluate how well you're doing, you must have some place you're trying to get to. For programs, this has meant having goals and evaluating goal attainment. For evaluators, this means clarifying the intended uses of a particular evaluation.

In utilization-focused evaluation, the primary criterion by which an evaluation is judged is *intended use by intended users*. The previous chapter discussed identifying intended users. This chapter will offer a menu of intended uses.

Identifying Intended Uses From the Beginning

The last chapter described a follow-up study of 20 federal health evaluations that assessed use and identified factors related to varying degrees of use. A major finding from that study was that **none of our interviewees had carefully considered intended use prior to getting the evaluation's findings.** We found that decision makers, program officers, *and* evaluators typically devoted little or no attention to intended uses prior to data collection. The goal of those evaluations was to produce findings, then they'd worry about how to use whatever was found. Findings would determine use, so until findings were generated, no real attention was paid to use.

Utilization-focused evaluators, in contrast, work with intended users to determine priority uses early in the evaluation process. The agreed-on, intended uses then become the basis for subsequent design decisions. This increases the likelihood that an evaluation will have the desired impact. Specifying intended uses is evaluation's equivalent of program goal setting.

Intended uses vary from evaluation to evaluation. There can be no generic or absolute definition of evaluation use because "use" depends in part on the values and goals of primary users. As Eleanor Chelimsky (1983) has observed, "The concept of usefulness . . . depends upon the perspective and values of the observer. This means that one person's usefulness may be another person's waste" (p. 155). To help intended users deliberate on and commit to intended uses, evaluators need a menu of potential uses to offer. Utilization-focused evaluation is a menu-oriented approach. **It's a process for matching intended uses and intended users.** Here, then, is a menu of three different evaluation purposes based on varying uses for evaluation *findings*. In the next chapter, we'll add to this menu a variety of uses of evaluation *processes*.

Three Uses of Findings

The purpose of an evaluation conditions the use that can be expected of it.

—Eleanor Chelimsky (1997)

You don't get very far in studying evaluation before realizing that the field is characterized by enormous diversity. From large-scale, long-term, international comparative designs costing millions of dollars to small, short evaluations of a single component in a local agency, the variety is vast. Contrasts include internal versus external evaluation; outcomes versus process evaluation; experimental designs versus case studies; mandated accountability systems versus voluntary management efforts; academic studies versus informal action research by program staff; and published, polished evaluation reports versus oral briefings and discussions where no written report is ever generated. Then there are combinations and permutations of these contrasting approaches. The annual meetings of the American Evaluation Association, the Canadian Evaluation Society, and the Australasian Evaluation Society offer an awesome cornucopia of variations in evaluation practice (and ongoing debate about which approaches are *really* evaluation). In the midst of such splendid diversity, any effort to reduce the complexity of evaluation options to a few major categories will inevitably oversimplify. Yet, some degree of simplification is needed to make the evaluation design process manageable. So let us attempt to heed Thoreau's advice:

> Simplicity, simplicity, simplicity! I say, let your affairs be as two or three, and not a hundred or a thousand. (*Walden*, 1854)

A Menu for Using Findings: Making Overall Judgments, Facilitating Improvements, and Generating Knowledge

Evaluation findings can serve three primary purposes: rendering judgments, facilitating improvements, and/or generating knowledge. Chelimsky (1997) distinguishes these three purposes by the perspective that undergirds them: judgments are undergirded by the accountability perspective; improvements are informed by a developmental perspective; and generation knowledge operates from the knowledge perspective of academic values. These are by no means inherently conflicting purposes, and some evaluations strive to incorporate all three approaches, but, in my experience, one is likely to become the dominant motif and prevail as the *primary* purpose informing design decisions and priority uses; or else, different aspects of an evaluation are designed, compartmentalized, and sequenced to address these contrasting purposes. I also find that confusion among these quite different purposes, or failure to prioritize them, is often the source of problems and misunderstandings along the way and can become disastrous at the end when it turns out that different intended users had different expectations and priorities. I shall discuss each, offering variations and examples.

Judgment-Oriented Evaluation

Evaluations aimed at determining the overall merit, worth, or value of something are judgment-oriented. Merit refers to the intrinsic value of a program, for example, how effective it is in meeting the needs of those it is intended to help. Worth refers to extrinsic value to those outside the program, for example, to the larger community or society. A welfare program that gets jobs for recipients has *merit* for those who move out of poverty and *worth* to society by reducing welfare costs. Judgment-oriented evaluation approaches include performance measurement for public accountability; program audits; summative evaluations aimed at deciding if a program is sufficiently effective to be continued or replicated; quality control and compliance reports; and comparative ratings or rankings of programs à la *Consumer Reports*.

The first clue that intended users are seeking an overall judgment is when you hear the following kinds of questions: Did the program work? Did it attain its goals? Should the program be continued or ended? Was implementation in compliance with funding mandates? Were funds used appropriately for the intended purposes? Were desired client outcomes achieved? Answering these kinds of evaluative questions requires a data-based judgment that some need has been met, some goal attained, or some standard achieved.

Another clue that rendering judgment will be a priority is lots of talk about "accountability." Funders and politicians like to issue calls for accountability (notably for others, not for themselves), and managing for accountability has become a rallying cry in both private and public sectors (Kearns 1996). Program and financial audits are aimed at ensuring compliance with intended purposes and mandated procedures. The program evaluation units of legislative audit offices, offices of comptrollers and inspectors, and federal agencies like the General Accounting Office (GAO) and the Office of Management and Budget (OMB) have government oversight responsibilities to make sure programs are properly implemented and effective. The U.S. Government Performance and Results Act of 1993 required annual performance measurement to "justify" program decisions and budgets. Political leaders in Canada, the United Kingdom, and Australia have been active and vocal in attempting to link performance measurement to budgeting for purposes of accountability (Auditor General of Canada 1993), and these efforts greatly influenced the U.S. federal approach to accountability (Breul 1994).

Rhetoric about accountability can become particularly strident in the heat of political campaigns. Everyone campaigns against ineffectiveness, waste, and fraud. Yet, one person's waste is another's jewel. For years, U.S. Senator William Proxmire of Wisconsin periodically held press conferences in which he announced Golden Fleece Awards for government programs he considered especially wasteful. I had the dubious honor of being the evaluator for one such project ridiculed by Proxmire, a project to take higher education administrators into the wilderness to experience, firsthand, experiential education. The program was easy to make fun of: Why should taxpayer dollars be spent for college deans to hike in the woods? Outrageous! What was left out of Proxmire's press release was that the project, supported by the Fund for the Improvement of Postsecondary Education, had been selected in a competitive process and funded because of its innovative approach to rejuvenating burned-out and discouraged administrators, and that many of those administrators returned to their colleges to spearhead curriculum reform. There was lots of room for debate about the merit or worth of the program *depending on one's values and priorities*, but our evaluation found that the funds were spent in accordance with the agency's innovative mandate and many, though not all, participants followed through on the project's goal of providing leadership for educational change. The funding agency found sufficient merit and worth that the project was awarded a year-long dissemination grant.

In judgment-oriented evaluations, specifying the criteria for judgment is central and critical. Different stakeholders will bring different criteria to the table (or apply them without coming to the table, as in Proxmire's case). The funding agency's criterion was whether participants developed personally and professionally in ways that led them to subsequently exercise innovative leadership in higher education; Proxmire's criterion was whether, on the surface, the project would sound wasteful to the ordinary taxpayer.

During design discussions and negotiations, evaluators may offer additional criteria for judgment beyond those initially thought of by intended users. As purpose and design negotiations conclude, the standard to be met by the evaluation has been articulated in the Joint Committee Program Evaluation Standards:

> *Values Identification:* The perspectives, procedures, and rationale used to interpret the findings should be carefully described, *so that the bases for value judgments are clear.* (Joint Committee 1994:U4; emphasis added)

Some criteria, such as fraud and gross incompetence, are sufficiently general and agreed-on that they may remain implicit as bases for value judgments when the explicit focus is on goal attainment. Yet, finding criminal, highly unethical, or grossly incompetent actions will quickly overwhelm other effectiveness criteria. One of my favorite examples comes from an audit of a weatherization program in Kansas as reported in the newsletter of Legislative Program Evaluators.

> Kansas auditors visited several homes that had been weatherized. At one home, workers had installed 14 storm windows to cut down on air filtration in the house. However, one could literally see through the house because some of the siding had rotted and either pulled away from or fallen off the house. The auditors also found that the agency had nearly 200 extra storm windows in stock. Part of the problem was that the supervisor responsible for measuring storm windows was afraid of heights; he would "eyeball" the size of second-story windows from the ground. . . . If these storm windows did not fit, he ordered new ones. (Hinton 1988:3)

The auditors also found fraud. The program bought windows at inflated prices from a company secretly owned by a program employee. A kickback scheme was uncovered. "The workmanship on most homes was shoddy, bordering on criminal. . . . [For example], workers installing a roof vent used an ax to chop a hole in the roof." Some 20% of beneficiaries didn't meet eligibility criteria. Findings like these are thankfully rare, but they grab headlines when they become public, and they illustrate why accountability will remain a central purpose of many evaluations.

The extent to which concerns about accountability dominate a specific study varies by the role of the evaluator. For auditors, accountability is always primary. Public reports on performance indicators for government programs are accountability-driven. As we shall see, however, many evaluations of private sector programs aimed at internal program improvement have no public accountability purpose. First, however, let's review *summative evaluation* as a major form of judgment-oriented evaluation.

Summative evaluation constitutes an important purpose distinction in any menu of intended uses. Summative evaluations judge the overall effectiveness of a program and are particularly important in making decisions about continuing or terminating an experimental program or demonstration project. As such, summative evaluations are often requested by funders. Summative evaluation contrasts with *formative evaluation*, which focuses on ways of improving and enhancing programs rather than rendering definitive judgment about effectiveness. Michael Scriven (1967: 40-43) introduced the summative-formative distinction in discussing evaluation of educational curriculum. The distinction has since become a fundamental evaluation typology.

With widespread use of the summative-formative distinction has come misuse, so it is worth examining Scriven's (1991a) own definition:

> Summative evaluation of a program (or other evaluand) is conducted *after* completion of the program (for ongoing programs that means after stabilization) and *for* the benefit of some *external* audience or decision-maker (for example, funding agency, oversight office, historian, or future possible users). . . . The decisions it services are most often decisions between these options: export (generalize), increase site support, continue site support, continue with conditions (probationary status), continue with modifications, discontinue. . . . The aim is to

> report *on* it [the program], not to report *to* it. (p. 340)

Summative evaluation provides data to support a judgment about the program's worth so that a decision can be made about the merit of continuing the program. While Scriven's definition focuses on a single program, summative evaluations of multiple programs occur when, like the products in a *Consumer Reports* test, programs are ranked on a set of criteria such as effectiveness, cost, sustainability, quality characteristics, and so on. Such data support judgments about the comparative merit or worth of different programs.

In judgment-oriented evaluations, what Scriven (1980) has called "the logic of valuing" rules. Four steps are necessary: (1) select criteria of merit; (2) set standards of performance; (3) measure performance; and (4) synthesize results into a judgment of value (Shadish, Cook, and Leviton 1991:73, 83-94). This is clearly a deductive approach. In contrast, improvement-oriented evaluations often use an inductive approach in which criteria are less formal as one searches openly for whatever areas of strengths or weaknesses may emerge from looking at what's happening in the program.

Improvement-Oriented Evaluation

Using evaluation results to improve a program turns out, in practice, to be fundamentally different from rendering judgment about overall effectiveness, merit, or worth. Improvement-oriented forms of evaluation include formative evaluation, quality enhancement, responsive evaluation, learning organization approaches, humanistic evaluation, and Total Quality Management (TQM), among others. What these approaches share is a focus on improvement—making things better—rather than rendering summative judgment. Judgment-oriented evaluation requires preordinate, explicit criteria and values that form the basis for judgment. Improvement-oriented approaches tend to be more open ended, gathering varieties of data about strengths and weaknesses with the expectation that both will be found and each can be used to inform an ongoing cycle of reflection and innovation. Program management, staff, and sometimes participants tend to be the primary users of improvement-oriented findings, while funders and external decision makers tend to use judgmental evaluation, though I hasten to add that these associations of particular categories of users with specific types of evaluations represent utilization tendencies, not definitional distinctions; any category of user may be involved in any kind of use.

Improvement-oriented evaluations ask the following kinds of questions: What are the program's strengths and weaknesses? To what extent are participants progressing toward the desired outcomes? Which types of participants are making good progress and which types aren't doing so well? What kinds of implementation problems have emerged and how are they being addressed? What's happening that wasn't expected? How are staff and clients interacting? What are staff and participant perceptions of the program? What do they like? dislike? want to change? What are perceptions of the program's culture and climate? How are funds being used compared to initial expectations? How is the program's external environment affecting internal operations? Where can efficiencies be realized? What new ideas are emerging that can be tried out and tested?

The flavor of these questions—their nuances, intonation, feel—communicate improvement rather than judgment. Bob Stake's metaphor explaining the difference between summative and formative evaluation can be adapted more generally to the distinction between judgmental evaluation and improvement-oriented evaluation: "When the cook tastes the soup, that's formative; when the guests taste the soup, that's summative" (quoted in Scriven 1991a:169). More generally, anything done to the soup during preparation in the kitchen is improvement oriented; when the soup is served, judgment is rendered, including judgment rendered by the cook that the soup was ready for serving (or at least that preparation time had run out).

The metaphor also helps illustrate that one must be careful to stay focused on intent rather than activities when differentiating purposes. Suppose that those to whom the soup is served are also cooks, and the purpose of their tasting the soup is to offer additional recipe ideas and consider potential variations in seasoning. Then the fact that the soup has moved from kitchen to table does not mean a change in purpose. Improvement remains the primary agenda. Final judgment awaits another day, a different serving—unless, of course, the collection of cooks suddenly decides that the soup as served to them is already perfect and no further changes should be made. Then what was supposed to be formative would suddenly have turned out to be summative. And thus are purposes and uses often confounded in real-world evaluation practice.

Formative evaluation typically connotes collecting data for a specific period of time, usually during the start-up or pilot phase of a project, to improve implementation, solve unanticipated problems, and make sure that participants are progressing toward desired outcomes. Improvement-oriented evaluation more generally, however, includes using information systems to monitor program efforts and outcomes regularly over time to provide feedback for fine-tuning a well-established program. That's how data are meant to be used as part of a Total Quality Management (TQM) approach. It also includes the "decision-oriented educational research" of Cooley and Bickel (1985), who built a classroom-based information system aimed at "monitoring and tailoring." For example, by systematically tracking daily attendance patterns for individuals, classrooms, and schools, educational administrators could quickly identify attendance problems and intervene before the problems became chronic or overwhelming. Attendance could also be treated as an early warning indicator of other potential problems.

Again, I want to reiterate that we are focusing on distinctions about intended and actual use of findings. A management information system that routinely collects data can be used for monitoring progress and reallocating resources for increased effectiveness in a changing environment; that's improvement-oriented use. However, if that same system is used for public accountability reporting, that's judgment-oriented use. These contrasting purposes often come into conflict because the information needed for management is different from the data needed for accountability; or knowing that the data will be used for accountability purposes, the system is set up and managed for that purpose and becomes useless for ongoing improvement-oriented decision making. Exhibit 4.1 provides an example of how formative evaluation can prepare a program for summative evaluation by connecting these separate and distinct evaluation purposes

EXHIBIT 4.1

Formative and Summative Evaluation of the Saint Paul Technology for Literacy Center (TLC): A Utilization-Focused Model

TLC was established as a three-year demonstration project to pilot-test the effectiveness of an innovative, computer-based approach to adult literacy. The pilot project was funded by six Minnesota Foundations and the Saint Paul Schools at a cost of $1.3 million. The primary intended users of the evaluation were the school superintendent, senior school officials, and School Board Directors, who would determine whether to continue and integrate the project into the district's ongoing community education program. School officials and foundation donors participated actively in designing the evaluation. The evaluation cost $70,300.

After 16 months of formative evaluation, the summative evaluation began. The formative evaluation, conducted by an evaluator hired to be part of the TLC staff, used extensive learner feedback, careful documentation of participation and progress, and staff development activities to specify the TLC model and bring implementation to a point of stability and clarity where it could be summatively evaluated. The summative evaluation, conducted by two independent University of Minnesota social scientists, was planned as the formative evaluation was being conducted.

The summative evaluation began by validating that the specified model was, in fact, being implemented as specified. This involved interviews with staff and students and observations of the program in operation. Outcomes were measured using the Test of Adult Basic Education administered on a pre-post basis to participant and control groups. The test scores were analyzed for all students who participated in the program for a three month period. Results were compared to data available on other adult literacy programs. An extensive cost analysis was also conducted by a university educational economist. The report was completed six months prior to the end of the demonstration, in time for decision makers to use the results to determine the future of the program. Retention and attrition data were also analyzed and compared with programs nationally.

to separate and distinct stages in the program's development.

Knowledge-Oriented Evaluation

Both judgment-oriented and improvement-oriented evaluations involve the *instrumental* use of results (Leviton and Hughes 1981). Instrumental use occurs when a decision or action follows, at least in part, from the evaluation. Evaluations are seldom the sole basis for subsequent summative decisions or program improvements, but they contribute, often substantially, if a utilization-focused approach is used at the design stage.

Conceptual use of findings, on the other hand, contrasts with instrumental use in that no decision or action is expected; rather, it "is the use of evaluations to influence thinking about issues in a general way" (Rossi and Freeman 1985:388). The evaluation findings contribute by increasing knowledge. This knowledge can be as specific as clarifying a program's model, test-

Comparisons showed significant gains in reading comprehension and math for the participant group versus no gains for the control group. Adult learners in the program advanced an average of one grade level on the test for every 52.5 hours spent in TLC computer instruction. However, the report cautioned that the results showed great variation: high standard deviations, significant differences between means and medians, ranges of data that included bizarre extremes, and very little correlation between hours spent and progress made. The report concluded: "Each case is relatively unique. TLC has created a highly individualized program where learners can proceed at their own pace based on their own needs and interests. The students come in at very different levels and make very different gains during their TLC work . . . , thus the tremendous variation in progress" (Council on Foundations 1993:142).

Several years after the evaluation, the Council on Foundations commissioned a follow-up study on the evaluation's utility. The Saint Paul Public Schools moved the project from pilot to permanent status. The Superintendent of Schools reported that "the findings of the evaluation and the qualities of the services it had displayed had irrevocably changed the manner in which adult literacy will be addressed throughout the Saint Paul Public Schools" (Council on Foundations, 1993:148). TLC also became the basis for the District's new Five-Year Plan for Adult Literacy. The evaluation was so well-received by its original philanthropic donors that it led the Saint Paul Foundation to begin and support an Evaluation Fellows program with the University of Minnesota. The independent Council on Foundations follow-up study concluded: "Everyone involved in the evaluation—TLC, funding sources, and evaluators—regards it as a "utilization-focused evaluation. . . . The organization and its founders and funders decided what they wanted to learn and instructed the evaluators accordingly" (Council on Foundations, 1993:154-55). The formative evaluation was used extensively to develop the program and get it ready for the summative evaluation. The summative evaluation was then used by primary intended users to inform a major decision about the future of computer-based adult literacy. Ten years later, Saint Paul's adult literacy effort continues to be led by TLC's original developer and director.

SOURCES: Turner and Stockdill 1987; Council on Foundations (1993:129-55).

ing theory, distinguishing types of interventions, figuring out how to measure outcomes, generating lessons learned, and/or elaborating policy options. In other cases, conceptual use is more vague, with users seeking to understand the program better; the findings, then, may reduce uncertainty, offer illumination, enlighten funders and staff about what participants really experience, enhance communications, and facilitate sharing of perceptions. In early studies of utilization, such uses were overlooked or denigrated. In recent years, they have come to be more appreciated and valued (Weiss 1990:177).

We found conceptual use to be widespread in our follow-up study of federal health evaluations. As one project manager reported:

> The evaluation led us to redefine some target populations and rethink the ways we connected various services. This rethinking happened over a period of months as we got a

> better perspective on what the findings meant. But we didn't so much change what we were doing as we changed how we thought about what we were doing. That has had big pay-offs over time. We're just a lot clearer now. [DM248:19]

This represents an example of conceptual use that is sometimes described as *enlightenment*. Carol Weiss (1990) has used this term to describe the effects of evaluation findings being disseminated to the larger policy community "where they have a chance to affect the terms of debate, the language in which it is conducted, and the ideas that are considered relevant in its resolution" (p. 176). She continued,

> Generalizations from evaluation can percolate into the stock of knowledge that participants draw on. Empirical research has confirmed this. . . . Decision makers indicate a strong belief that they are influenced by the ideas and arguments that have their origins in research and evaluation. Case studies of evaluations and decisions tend to show that generalizations and ideas that come from research and evaluation help shape the development of policy. The phenomenon has come to be known as "enlightenment" . . . , an engaging idea. The image of evaluation as increasing the wattage of light in the policy arena brings joy to the hearts of evaluators. (pp. 176-77)

While Weiss has emphasized the informal ways in which evaluation findings provide, over time, a knowledge base for policy, Chen (1990, 1989; Chen and Rossi 1987) has focused on a more formal knowledge-oriented approach in what he has called *theory-driven evaluation*. While theory-driven evaluations can provide program models for summative judgment or ongoing improvement, the connection to social science theory tends to focus on increasing knowledge about how effective programs work in general. For example, Shadish (1987) has argued that the understandings gleaned from evaluations ought to contribute to *macrotheories* about "how to produce important social change" (p. 94). Scheirer (1987) has contended that evaluators ought to draw on and contribute to *implementation theory* to better understand the "what and why of program delivery" (p. 59). Such knowledge-generating efforts focus beyond the effectiveness of a particular program to future program designs and policy formulation in general.

As the field of evaluation has matured and a vast number of evaluations has accumulated, the opportunity has arisen to look across findings about specific programs to formulate generalizations about effectiveness. This involves synthesizing findings from different studies. (It is important to distinguish this form of synthesis evaluation, that is, synthesizing across different studies, from what Scriven [1994] calls "the final synthesis," which refers to sorting out and weighing the findings in a single study to reach a summative judgment.) Cross-study syntheses have become an important contribution of the GAO (1992c) in providing accumulated wisdom to Congress about how to formulate effective policies and programs. An example is GAO's (1992b) report on *Adolescent Drug Use Prevention: Common Features of Promising Community Programs*. (See Exhibit 4.2.)

An excellent and important example of synthesis evaluation is Lisbeth Schorr's (1988) *Within Our Reach*, a study of programs aimed at breaking the cycle of poverty. She identified "the lessons of successful programs" as follows (pp. 256-83):

EXHIBIT 4.2
An Example of a Knowledge-Oriented Evaluation

The U.S. General Accounting Office (GAO 1992a) identified "Common Features of Promising Community Programs" engaged in adolescent drug use prevention. The evaluation was aimed at enlightening policymakers, in contrast to other possible uses of findings, namely, judging the effectiveness of or improving specific programs.

Six features associated with high levels of participant enthusiasm and attachment:

1. a comprehensive strategy
2. an indirect approach to drug abuse prevention
3. the goal of empowering youth
4. a participatory approach
5. a culturally sensitive orientation
6. highly structured activities

Six common program problems:

1. maintaining continuity with their participants
2. coordinating and integrating their service components
3. providing accessible services
4. obtaining funds
5. attracting necessary leadership and staff
6. conducting evaluation

- offering a broad spectrum of services;
- regularly crossing traditional professional and bureaucratic boundaries, that is, organizational flexibility;
- seeing the child in the context of family and the family in the context of its surroundings, that is, holistic approaches;
- coherent and easy-to-use services;
- committed, caring, results-oriented staff;
- finding ways to adapt or circumvent traditional professional and bureaucratic limitations to meet client needs;
- professionals redefining their roles to respond to severe needs; and
- overall, intensive, comprehensive, responsive and flexible programming.

These kinds of "lessons" constitute accumulated wisdom—principles of effectiveness or "best practices"—that can be adapted, indeed, must be adapted, to specific programs, or even entire organizations (Wray and Hauer 1996). For example, the Ford Foundation commissioned an evaluation of its Leadership Program for Community Foundations. This study of 27 community foundations over five years led to a guide for *Building Community Capacity* (Mayer 1996, 1994, n.d.) that incorporates lessons learned and generalizable development strategies for community foundations—a distinguished and useful example of a knowledge-generating evaluation. Other examples include a special evaluation issue of *Marriage and Family Review* devoted to "Exemplary Social Intervention Programs" (Guttman and Sussman 1995) and a special issue of *The Future of Children* (CFC 1995) devoted to "Long-Term Outcomes of Early Childhood Programs."

In the philanthropic world, a related approach has come to be called *cluster evaluation* (Millett 1996; Council on Foundations 1993:232-51). A cluster evaluation team visits a number of different grantee projects with a similar focus (e.g., grassroots leadership development) and draws on individual grant evaluations to identify patterns across and lessons from the whole cluster (Campbell 1994; Sanders 1994; Worthen 1994; Barley and Jenness 1993; Kellogg Foundation n.d.). The McKnight Foundation commissioned a cluster evaluation of 34 separate grants aimed at aiding families in poverty. One lesson learned was that "effective programs have developed processes and strategies for learning about the *strengths* as well as the needs of families in poverty" (Patton et al. 1993:10). This lesson takes on added meaning when connected with the finding of Independent Sector's review of "Common Barriers to Effectiveness in the Independent Sector":

> The deficits model holds that distressed people and communities are "needy"; they're a collection of problems, pathologies, and handicaps; they need doctoring, rehabilitation, and fixing of the kind that professionalized services are intended to provide.
>
> The assets model holds that even the most distressed person or community has strengths, abilities, and capacities; with investment, their strengths, abilities, and capacities can increase. This view is only barely allowed to exist in the independent sector, where organizations are made to compete for funds on the basis of "needs" rather than on the basis of "can-do."
>
> The deficit model—seeing the glass half empty—is a barrier to effectiveness in the independent sector. (Mayer 1993:7-8)

The McKnight Foundation cluster evaluation and the Independent Sector study reached similar conclusions concurrently and independently. Such generalizable evaluation findings about principles of effective programming have become the knowledge base of our profession. Being knowledgeable about patterns of program effectiveness allows evaluators to provide guidance about development of new initiatives, policies, and strategies for implementation. Such contributions constitute the **conceptual use** of evaluation findings. Efforts of this kind may be considered *research* rather than evaluation, but such research is ultimately evaluative in nature and important to the profession.

Synthesis evaluations also help us generate knowledge about conducting useful evaluations. The premises of utilization-focused evaluation featured in this book originally emerged from studying 20 federal evaluations (Patton, Grimes, et al. 1977). Those premises have been affirmed by Alkin et al. (1979) in the model of evaluation use they developed by analyzing evaluations from different education districts in California and by Wargo (1989) in his "characteristics of successful program evaluations" identified by studying three "unusually successful evaluations of national food and nutrition programs" (p. 71). The Council on Foundations commissioned a synthesis evaluation based on nine case studies of major foundation evaluations to learn lessons about "effective evaluating." (A summary of one of those case studies is presented as Exhibit 4.1 in this chapter.) Among the Council's 35 key lessons learned is this utilization-focused evaluation premise: "Key 6. *Make sure the people who can make the most use of the evaluation are involved as stakeholders in planning and carrying out the evaluation*" (Council on Foundations 1993:255).

Applying Purpose and Use Distinctions

By definition, the three kinds of uses we've examined—making overall judgments, offering formative improvements, or generating generic knowledge—can be distinguished clearly. Menu 4.1 presents these three uses with examples of each. Although conceptually distinct in practice, these uses can become entangled. Let me illustrate with an evaluation of an innovative educational program.

Some years ago, the Northwest Regional Educational Laboratory (NWREL) contracted with the Hawaii State Department of Education to evaluate Hawaii's experimental "3-on-2 Program," a team teaching approach in which three teachers worked with two regular classrooms of primary-age children, often in multi-age groupings. Walls between classrooms were removed so that three teachers and 40 to 60 children shared one large space. The program was aimed at creating greater individualization, increasing cooperation among teachers, and making more diverse resources available to students.

The laboratory (NWREL 1977) proposed an advocacy-adversary model for summative evaluation. Two teams were created; by coin toss, one was designated the advocacy, the other the adversary team. The task of the advocacy team was to gather and present data supporting the proposition that Hawaii 's 3-on-2 Program was effective and ought to be continued. The adversaries were charged with marshalling all possible evidence demonstrating that the program ought to be terminated.

The advocacy-adversary model was a combination debate/courtroom approach to evaluation (Wolf 1975; Kourilsky 1974; Owens 1973). I became involved as a resource consultant on fieldwork as the two teams were about to begin site visits to observe classrooms. When I arrived on the scene, I immediately felt the exhilaration of the competition. I wrote in my journal,

> No longer staid academic scholars, these are athletes in a contest that will reveal who is best; these are lawyers prepared to use whatever means necessary to win their case. The teams have become openly secretive about their respective strategies. These are experienced evaluators engaged in a battle not only of data, but also of wits. The prospects are intriguing.

As the two teams prepared their final reports, a concern emerged among some about the narrow focus of the evaluation. The summative question concerned whether the Hawaii 3-on-2 program should be continued or terminated. Some team members also wanted to offer findings about how to change the program or how to make it better without terminating it. Was it possible that a great amount of

MENU 4.1

Three Primary Uses of Evaluation Findings

Uses	*Examples*
Judge merit or worth	Summative evaluation Accountability Audits Quality control Cost-benefit decisions Decide a program's future Accreditation/licensing
Improve programs	Formative evaluation Identify strengths and weaknesses Continuous improvement Quality enhancement Being a learning organization Manage more effectively Adapt a model locally
Generate knowledge	Generalizations about effectiveness Extrapolate principles about what works Theory building Synthesize patterns across programs Scholarly publishing Policy making

NOTE: Menu 5.1 (Chapter 5) presents a corresponding menu, "Four Primary Uses of Evaluation Logic and Processes," which includes Enhancing shared understandings, Reinforcing program interventions, Engagement (participatory and empowerment evaluation), and Developmental evaluation. Menu 5.1 presents uses where the impact on the program comes primarily from application of evaluation thinking and engaging in an evaluation process in contrast to impacts that come from using the content of evaluation findings, the focus of this menu.

time, effort, and money was directed at answering the wrong question? Two participating evaluators summarized the dilemma in their published post mortem of the project:

> As we became more and more conversant with the intricacies, both educational and political, of the Hawaii 3-on-2 Program, we realized that Hawaii's decision makers should not be forced to deal with a simple save-it-or-scrap-it choice. Middle ground positions were more sensible. Half-way measures, in this instance, probably made more sense. But there we were, obliged to do battle with our adversary colleagues on the

> unembellished question of whether to maintain or terminate the 3-on-2 Program. (Popham and Carlson 1977:5)

In the course of doing fieldwork, the evaluators had encountered many stakeholders who favored a formative evaluation approach. These potential users wanted an assessment of strengths and weaknesses with ideas for improvement. Many doubted that the program, given its popularity, could be terminated. They recognized that changes were needed, especially cost reductions, but that fell in the realm of formative not summative evaluation. I had a conversation with one educational policymaker that highlighted the dilemma about appropriate focus. He emphasized that, with a high rate of inflation, a declining school-age population, and reduced federal aid, the program was too expensive to maintain. "That makes it sound like you've already made the decision to terminate the program before the evaluation is completed," I suggested.

"Oh, no!" he protested. "All we've decided is that the program has to be changed. In some schools the program has been very successful and effective. Teachers like it; parents like it; principals like it. How could we terminate such a program? But in other schools it hasn't worked very well. The two-classroom space has been redivided into what is essentially three self-contained classrooms. We know that. It's the kind of program that has some strong political opposition and some strong political support. So there's no question of terminating the program and no question of keeping it the same."

I felt compelled to point out that the evaluation was focused entirely on whether the program should be continued or terminated. "And that will be very interesting," he agreed. "But afterwards we trust you will give us answers to our practical questions, like how to reduce the size of the program, make it more cost effective, and increase its overall quality."

Despite such formative concerns from some stakeholders, the evaluation proceeded as originally planned with the focus on the summative evaluation question. But was that the right focus? The evaluation proposal clearly identified the primary intended users as state legislators, members of the State Board of Education, and the superintendent. In a follow-up survey of those education officials (Wright and Sachse 1977), most reported that they got the information they wanted. But the most important evidence that the evaluation focused on the right question came from actions taken following the evaluation when the decision makers decided to eliminate the program.

After it was all over, I had occasion to ask Dean Nafziger, who had directed the evaluation as director of evaluation, research, and assessment for NWREL, whether a shift to a formative focus would have been appropriate. He replied,

> We maintained attention to the information needs of the *true* decision makers, and adhered to those needs in the face of occasional counter positions by other evaluation audiences. . . . If a lesson is to be learned it is this: an evaluator must determine who is making the decisions and keep the information needed by the decision makers as the highest priority. In the case of the Hawaii "3 on 2" evaluation, the presentation of program improvement information would have served to muddle the decision-making process. (Personal correspondence 1979)

Choosing Among Alternatives

As the Hawaii case illustrates, the formative-summative distinction can be critical. Formative and summative evaluations involve significantly different research foci. The same data seldom serve both purposes well. Nor will either a specific formative or summative evaluation necessarily yield generic knowledge (lessons learned) that can be applied to effective programming more generally. It is thus important to identify the primary purpose of the evaluation at the outset: overall judgment of merit or worth, ongoing improvement, or knowledge generation? Other decisions about what to do in the evaluation can then be made in accordance with how best to support that primary purpose. One frequent reaction to posing evaluation alternatives is: "We want to do it all." A comprehensive evaluation, conducted over time and at different levels, may include all three uses, but for any given evaluation activity, or any particular stage of evaluation, it's critical to have clarity about the priority use of findings.

Consider the evaluation of a leadership program run by a private philanthropic foundation. The original evaluation contract called for three years of formative evaluation followed by two years of summative evaluation. The program staff and evaluators agreed that the formative evaluation would be for staff and participant use; however, the summative evaluation would be addressed to the foundation's board of directors. The formative evaluation helped shape the curriculum, brought focus to intended outcomes, and became the basis for the redesign of follow-up activities and workshops. As time came to make the transition from formative to summative evaluation, the foundation's president got cold feet about having the evaluators meet directly with the board of directors. The evaluators insisted on interacting directly with these primary users to lay the groundwork for genuinely summative decision making. Senior staff decided that no summative decision was imminent, so the evaluation continued in a formative mode, and the design was changed accordingly. As a matter of ethics, the evaluators made sure that the chair of the board was involved in these negotiations and that the board agreed to the change in focus. There really was no summative decision on the horizon because the foundation had a long-term commitment to the leadership program.

Now, consider a different case, the evaluation of an innovative school, the Saturn School, in Saint Paul, Minnesota.

Again, the original evaluation design called for three years of formative evaluation followed by two, final years with a summative focus. The formative evaluation revealed some developmental problems, including lower than desired scores on district-mandated standardized tests. The formative evaluation report, meant only for internal discussion aimed at program improvement, got into the newspapers with glaring headlines about problems and low test scores. The evaluation's visibility and public reporting put pressure on senior district officials to make summative decisions about the program, despite earlier assurances that the program would have a full five years before such decisions were made. The formative evaluation essentially became summative when it hit the newspapers, much to the chagrin of staff.

Sometimes, however, program staff like such a reversal of intended use when, for example, evaluators produce a formative report that is largely positive and staff want to disseminate the results as if they were summative, even though the methods of the formative evaluation were aimed only at capturing initial perceptions of program progress, not at rendering an overall judgment of merit or worth. Keeping formative evaluations formative, and summative evaluations summative, is an ongoing challenge, not a one-time decision. When contextual conditions merit or mandate a shift in focus, evaluators need to work with intended users to fully understand the consequences of such a change. We'll discuss these issues again in the chapter on situational responsiveness and evaluator roles. Let me close this section with one final example.

A national foundation funded a cluster evaluation in which a team of evaluators would assemble data from some 30 different projects and identify lessons for effective community-based health programming—essentially a knowledge-generating evaluation. The cluster evaluation team had no responsibility to gather data to improve specific programs nor make summative judgments. Each separate project had its own evaluation for those purposes. The cluster evaluation was intended to look for patterns of effectiveness (and barriers to same) across projects. Yet, during site visits, individual projects provided cluster evaluators with a great deal of formative feedback that they wanted communicated to the foundation, and individual grantees were hungry for feedback and comparative insights about how well they were doing and ways they might improve. As the evaluation approached time for a final report, senior foundation officials and trustees asked for summative conclusions about the overall effectiveness of the entire program area as part of rethinking funding priorities and strategies. Thus, a knowledge-generating evaluation got caught up in pressures to adapt to meet demands for both formative and summative uses.

Evaluation Use and Decision Making: Being Realistic About Impact

All three uses of evaluation findings—to render judgment, to improve programs, and to generate knowledge—support decision making. The three kinds of decisions, however, are quite different.

1. Rendering judgment about overall merit or worth for summative purposes supports decisions about whether a program should be continued, enlarged, disseminated, or terminated—all major decisions.
2. Decisions about how to improve a program tend to be made in small, incremental steps based on specific evaluation findings aimed purposefully at instrumental use.
3. Policy decisions informed by cumulative knowledge from evaluations imply a weak and diffuse connection between specific evaluation findings and the eventual decision made—thus the term *enlightenment use*.

Trying to sort out the influence of evaluations on decisions has been a major focus of researchers studying use. Much of the early literature on program evaluation defined use as immediate, concrete, and observable influence on specific decisions and program activities resulting *directly* from evaluation findings. For example, Carol Weiss (1972c), one of the pioneers in studying use, stated, "Evaluation research is meant for immediate and direct use in improving the quality of social programming" (p. 10). It was with reference to immediate and direct use that Weiss was speaking when she concluded that "a review of evaluation experience suggests that evaluation results have generally not exerted significant influence on program decisions" (p. 11). Weiss (1988, 1990) reaffirmed this conclusion in her 1987 keynote address at the American Evaluation Association: "The influence of evaluation on program decisions has not noticeably increased" (p. 7). The evaluation literature reviewed in the first chapter was likewise overwhelming in concluding that evaluation studies exert little influence in decision making.

It was in this gloomy context that I set out with a group of students in search of evaluations that had actually been used to help us identify factors that might enhance use in the future. (Details about this follow-up study of the use of federal health evaluations were presented in Chapter 3 and in Patton, Grimes, et al. 1977). Given the pessimistic picture of most writings on use, we began our study fully expecting our major problem would be finding even one evaluation that had had a significant impact on program decisions. What we found was considerably more complex and less dismal than our original impressions had led us to expect. Our results provide guidance in how to work with intended users to set *realistic* expectations about how much influence an evaluation will have.

Views From the Field on Evaluation Impact

Our major question on use was as follows:

> We'd like to focus on the actual impact of this evaluation study . . . , to get at any ways in which the study may have had an impact—an impact on program operations, on planning, on funding, on policy, on decisions, on thinking about the program, and so forth. From your point of view, what was the impact of this evaluation study on the program we've been discussing?

After coding responses for the nature and degree of impact (Patton 1986:33), we found that 78% of responding decision makers and 90% of responding evaluators felt that *the evaluation had an impact on the program*. We asked a follow-up question about the nonprogram impacts of the evaluations:

> We've been focusing mainly on the study's impact on the program itself. Sometimes studies have a broader impact on things beyond an immediate program, things like general thinking on issues that arise from a study, or position papers, or legislation. To what extent and in what ways did this evaluation have an impact on any of these kinds of things?

We found that 80% of responding decision makers and 70% of responding evaluators felt these specific evaluation studies had identifiable nonprogram impacts.

The positive responses to the questions on impact are quite striking considering the predominance of the impression of nonuse in the evaluation literature. The main difference here, however, was that **the actual participants in each specific evaluation process were asked to define *impact* in terms that were meaningful to them and their situations.** None of the evaluations we studied led directly and immediately to the making of a major, concrete program decision. The more typical impact was one in which the evaluation provided additional pieces of information in the difficult puzzle of program action, permitting some reduction in the uncertainty within which any decision maker inevitably operates. In most such cases, though the use was modest, those involved considered the evaluation worthwhile.

The most dramatic example of use reported in our sample was evaluation of a pilot program. The program administrator had been favorable to the program in principle, was uncertain what the evaluation results would be, but was "hoping the results would be positive." The evaluation proved to be negative. The administrator was "surprised, but not alarmingly so. . . . We had expected a more positive finding or we would not have engaged in the pilot studies" [DM367:13]. The program was subsequently ended, with the evaluation carrying "about a third of the weight of the total decision" [DM367:8]. Thus, the evaluation served a summative purpose but was one of only several factors (politics, impressions already held, competing priorities and commitments) that influenced the decision.

Contrast such summative use with the experiences of a different decision maker we interviewed, one who had 29 years of experience in the federal government, much of that time directing research. He reported the impact of the evaluation about which he was interviewed as follows:

> It served two purposes. One is that it resolved a lot of doubts and confusions and misunderstandings that the advisory committee had . . . and the second was that it gave me additional knowledge to support facts that I already knew, and, as I say, broadened the scope more than I realized. In other words, the perceptions of where the organization was going and what it was accomplishing were a lot worse than I had anticipated . . . but I was somewhat startled to find out that they were worse, yet it wasn't very hard because it partly confirmed things that I was observing. [DM232:17]

He went on to say that, following the evaluation:

> We changed our whole functional approach to looking at the identification of what we should be working on. But again I have a hard time because these things, *none of these things occurred overnight, and in an evolutionary process it's hard to say, you know, at what point it made a significant difference or did it merely verify and strengthen the resolve that you already had.* [DM232:17]

As in this example of conceptual use, respondents frequently had difficulty assessing the degree to which an evaluation actually affected decisions made after completion of the evaluation. This was true, for example, in the case of a large-scale evaluation conducted over several years at considerable cost. The findings revealed some deficiencies in the program but overall were quite positive. Changes corresponding to those recommended in the study occurred when the report was published, but those changes could not be directly and simply attributed to the evaluation:

> A lot of studies like this confirmed what close-by people knew and they were already taking actions before the findings. *So you can't link the finding to the action, that's just confirmation. . . . The direct link between the finding and the program decision is very diffuse.* [DM361:12, 13]

In essence, we found that evaluations provided some additional information that was judged and used in the context of other available information to help reduce the unknowns in the making of incremental program changes. The impact ranged from "it sort of confirmed our impressions . . . , confirming some other anecdotal information or impression that we had" [DM209:7, 1] to providing a new awareness that carried over to other programs.

This kind of conceptual use to stimulate thinking about what's going on and reduce uncertainty emerged as highly important to decision makers. In some cases, it simply made them more confident and determined. On the other hand, where a need for change was indicated, an evaluation study could help speed up the process of change or provide a new impetus for finally getting things rolling. Reducing uncertainty, speeding things up, and getting things finally started are real impacts—not revolutionary—but real, important impacts in the opinion of the people we interviewed. We found few major, direction-changing decisions in most programs—few really summative decisions. Rather, evaluation findings were used as one piece of information that fed into a slow, evolutionary process of program development. Program development is typically a process of "muddling through" (Allison 1971; Lindblom 1965, 1959), and program evaluation is part of that muddling. Or, as Weiss (1980) has observed, even major decisions typically accrete gradually over time through small steps and minor adjustments rather than getting decided all at once at some single moment at the end of a careful, deliberative, and rational process.

The impacts of evaluation have most often been felt as ripples, not waves. The question is whether such limited impact is sufficient to justify the costs of evaluation. The decision makers and evaluators we interviewed 20 years ago were largely satisfied with the type and degree of use they experienced. But times have changed. The stakes are higher. There's more sophistication about evaluation and, I think, higher expectations for accountability. However, the point of a utilization-focused approach is not to assume either high or low expectations. The point is to find out what the expectations of intended users are and negotiate a shared understanding of realistic, intended use—a mutual commitment that can be met. In negotiating the nature and degree of evaluation use, that is, setting goals for the evaluation, it is important to challenge intended users to be both optimistic and realistic—the twin tensions in any goal-setting exercise. Whether the expected type and degree of use hoped for actually occurs can then be followed up as a way of evaluating the evaluation.

In part, we need to distinguish a goals-oriented, up-front definition of use from an after-the-fact, follow-up definition of use. King and Pechman (1984, 1982) defined use as "intentional and serious consideration of evaluation information by an individual with the potential to act on it" (1984:244). This definition recognizes that evaluation is only one influence among many in the taking of an action or making of a decision; therefore, it is reasonable to consider an evaluation used if it has been seriously considered and the findings genuinely taken into account. Such a definition makes sense when evaluators are trying to study use after the fact and sort out relative influences. But the question utilization-focused evaluation asks is: What are the expected uses by intended users before and during the evaluation? Maybe serious consideration is what they expect as well; but maybe they expect more, or less.

Evaluators need to push intended users to be clear about what, if any, decisions are expected to be influenced by an evaluation. It is worth repeating that none of the federal health decision makers we interviewed about evaluation use had been involved in a utilization-focused process. That is, none of them had carefully considered how the

EXHIBIT 4.3

Questions to Ask of Intended Users to Establish an Evaluation's Intended Influence on Forthcoming Decisions

What decisions, if any, are the evaluation findings expected to influence?

(There may not be any, in which case the evaluation's purpose may be simply to generate knowledge for conceptual use and future enlightenment. If, however, the evaluation is expected to influence decisions, clearly distinguish summative decisions about program funding, continuation, or expansion from formative decisions about program improvement and ongoing development.)

When will decisions be made? By whom? When, then, must the evaluation findings be presented to be timely and influential?

What is at stake in the decisions? For whom? What controversies or issues surround the decisions?

What's the history and context of the decision-making process?

What other factors (values, politics, personalities, promises already made) will affect the decision making? What might happen to make the decision irrelevant or keep it from being made? In other words, how volatile is the decision making environment?

How much influence do you expect the evaluation to have—*realistically?*

To what extent has the outcome of the decision already been determined?

What data and findings are needed to support decision making?

What needs to be done to achieve that level of influence?

(Include special attention to which stakeholders to involve for the evaluation to have the expected degree of influence.)

How will we know afterward if the evaluation was used as intended?

(In effect, how can use be measured?)

evaluation would be used in advance of data collection. My experiences in pushing decision makers and intended users to be more intentional and prescient about evaluation use *during the design phase* have taught me that it is possible to significantly increase the degree of influence evaluations have. Doing so, however, requires persistence in asking the following kinds of questions: What decisions, if any, is the evaluation expected to influence? What is at stake? When will decisions be made? By whom? What other factors (values, politics, personalities, promises already made) will affect the decision making? How much influence do you expect the evaluation to have? What needs to be done to achieve that level of influence? How will we know afterward if the evaluation was used as intended? (In effect, how can use

be measured?) Exhibit 4.3 offers a number of questions to ask of intended users to establish an evaluation's intended influence on forthcoming decisions.

Connecting Decisions to Uses

Where the answers to the evaluator's questions indicate a major decision about program merit, worth, continuation, expansion, dissemination, and/or funding is at stake, then the evaluation should be designed to render overall judgment—summative judgment. The design should be sufficiently rigorous and the data collected should be sufficiently credible that a summative decision can be made. The findings must be available in time to influence this kind of major decision.

Where the dialogue with primary intended users indicates an interest in identifying strengths and weaknesses, clarifying the program's model, and generally working at increased effectiveness, the evaluation should be framed to support improvement-oriented decision making. Skills in offering formative feedback and creating an environment of mutual respect and trust between the evaluator and staff will be as important as actual findings.

Where the intended users are more concerned about generating knowledge for formulating future programs than with making decisions about current programs, then some form of synthesis or cluster evaluation will be most appropriate to discover generic principles of effectiveness.

In helping intended users select from the evaluation menu, and thereby focus the evaluation, evaluators may encounter some reluctance to make a commitment. I worked with one director who proudly displayed this sign on his desk: "My decision is maybe—and that's final." Unfortunately, the sign was all too accurate. He wanted me to decide what kind of evaluation should be done. After several frustrating attempts to narrow the evaluation's focus, I presented what I titled a "MAYBE DESIGN." I laid out cost estimates for an all-encompassing evaluation that included formative, summative, and knowledge-generating components looking at all aspects of the program. Putting dollars and time lines to the choices expedited the decision making considerably. He decided not to undertake any evaluation "at this time."

I was relieved. I had become skeptical about the potential for doing anything useful. Had I succumbed to the temptation to become the decision maker, an evaluation would have been done, but it would have been my evaluation, not his. I'm convinced he would have waffled over using the findings as he waffled over deciding what kind of evaluation to do.

Thus, in utilization-focused evaluation, the choice of not dining at all is always on the menu. It's better to find out before preparing the meal that those invited to the banquet are not really hungry. Take your feast elsewhere, where it will be savored.

5

Intended Process Uses

Impacts of Evaluation Thinking and Experiences

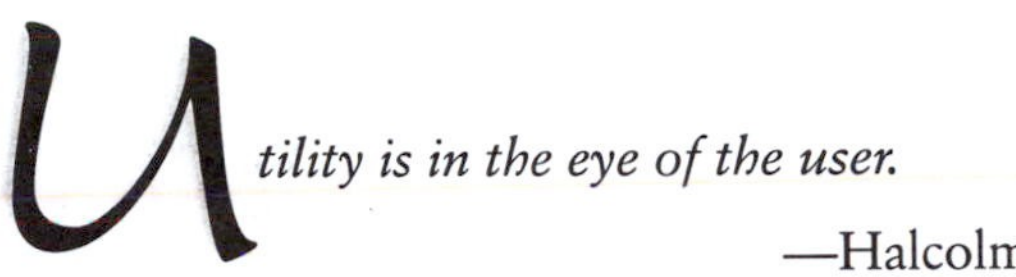

Utility is in the eye of the user.

—Halcolm

In the past, the search for use has often been conducted like the search for contraband in the famous Sufi story about Nasrudin[1] the smuggler.

Nasrudin used to take his donkey across a frontier every day with the panniers loaded with straw. Since he admitted to being a smuggler, when he trudged home every night, the frontier guards searched him carefully. They searched his person, sifted the straw, steeped it in water, even burned it from time to time. Meanwhile, he was becoming visibly more and more prosperous.

Eventually, he retired to another country, very wealthy. Years later one of the customs officials encountered him there. "You can tell me now, Nasrudin," he said. "Whatever was it that you were smuggling, that we could never catch you at?"

"Donkeys," replied Nasrudin grinning.

—Adapted from Shah 1964:59

Process as Outcome

In this chapter, we'll consider ways in which being engaged in the processes of evaluation can be useful quite apart from the findings that may emerge from those processes. Reasoning processes are evaluation's donkeys; they carry the load. Reasoning like an evaluator and operating according to evaluation's values have impacts. When I refer to *process use*, then, I mean using the logic, employing the reasoning, and being guided by the values that undergird the profession (Fournier 1995; Whitmore 1990; House 1980). Exhibit 5.1 provides examples of evaluation logic and values.

Those of us trained in the methods of research and evaluation can easily take for granted the logic that undergirds those methods. Like people living daily inside any culture, the way of thinking of our culture—the research culture—seems natural and easy. However, to practitioners, decision makers, and policymakers, our logic can be hard to grasp and quite unnatural. I'm talking about what appear to be very simple, even simplistic, notions that have profound effects on how one views the world. Thinking in terms of what's clear, specific, concrete, and observable does not come easily to people who thrive on, even depend on, vagueness, generalities, and untested beliefs as the basis for action. They're in the majority. Practitioners of evaluation logic are a small minority. The good news is that our way of thinking, once experienced, is often greatly valued. That's what creates demand for our services. Learning to see the world as an evaluator sees it often has a lasting impact on those who participate in an evaluation—an impact that can be greater and last longer than the findings that result from that same evaluation.

How do I know this? Because that's often what intended users tell me when I follow up the evaluations I conduct to evaluate use. Months after an evaluation, I'll talk with clients (intended users) to get their assessments of whether the evaluation achieved its intended uses and to find out what other impacts may have resulted. They often say some version of the following, a response from an experienced and wise program director:

> We used the findings to make some changes in our intake process and improvements in the treatment program. We reorganized parts of the program and connected them together better. But you know, the big change is in our staff's attitude. They're paying more attention to participant reactions on a daily basis. Our staff meetings are more outcomes oriented and reflective. Staff exchanges about results are more specific and data based. We're more focused. And the fear of evaluation is gone. Doing the evaluation had a profound impact on our program culture. It really did.

Any evaluation can, and often does, have these kinds of effects. What's different about utilization-focused evaluation is that the process of actively involving intended users increases these kinds of evaluation impacts. Furthermore, the possibility and desirability of learning from evaluation processes as well as findings can be made intentional and purposeful. In other words, instead of treating process use as an informal offshoot, explicit and up-front attention to the potential impacts of evaluation logic and processes can increase those impacts and make them a planned purpose for undertaking the evaluation. In that way the evaluation's overall utility is increased.

EXHIBIT 5.1

Examples of the Logic and Values of Evaluation That Have Impact on and Are Useful to Participants Who Experience Evaluation Processes

The logic and values of evaluation derive from research methods and communications. These admonitions constitute a "logic" in the sense that they represent a particular mode of reasoning viewed as valid within the culture of evaluation. They are values in the sense that they are what evaluators generally believe. The guidelines and principles below are meant to be illustrative rather than exhaustive of all possibilities.

Be clear	Be clear about goals and purposes; about what's being evaluated, what data will be collected, what judgments are to be made, how results will be used—indeed, be clear about everything.
Be specific	A favorite evaluation clarifying question: "What *exactly* do you mean by that?"
Focus and prioritize	You can't do or look at everything. Be intentional and purposeful in deciding what's worth doing and knowing.
Be systematic	Plan your work; work your plan. Carefully document what occurs at every stage of decision making and data collection.
Make assumptions explicit	Determine what can and cannot be subjected to empirical test.
Operationalize program concepts, ideas, and goals	The fundamental evaluation challenge is determining how to measure and observe, what is important. Reality testing becomes real at this point.
Distinguish inputs and processes from outcomes	Confusing processes with outcomes is common.
Have data to provide empirical support for conclusions	This means a commitment to reality testing in which logic and evidence are valued over strength of belief and intensity of emotions.
Separate data-based statements of fact from interpretations and judgments	Interpretations go beyond the data and must be understood as what they are: interpretations. Judgments involve values, determining what is desirable or undesirable.
Make criteria and standards for judgments explicit	The logical mandates to be clear and specific apply to making criteria and standards explicit.
Limit generalizations and causal explanations to what data support	Overgeneralizations and overly definitive attributions of causality are epidemic outside the culture of research and evaluation.
Distinguish deductive from inductive processes	Both are valued but involve different reasoning sequences.

Process Use Defined

> Process use refers to and is indicated by individual changes in thinking and behavior, and program or organizational changes in procedures and culture, that occur among those involved in evaluation as a result of the learning that occurs during the evaluation process. Evidence of process use is represented by the following kind of statement after an evaluation: "The impact on our program came not just from the findings but from going through the thinking process that the evaluation required."

An Analogy

Before looking in detail at how evaluation processes can affect users, let me suggest an analogy to clarify the distinction between process use versus findings use. I hike the Grand Canyon annually. During the days there, my body hardens and my thoughts soften. I emerge more mellow, peaceful, and centered. It doesn't matter which part of the Canyon I hike: the South Rim or North; whether I descend all the way to the Colorado River or stay on the Tonto to explore a side canyon; whether I push strenuously to cover as much territory as possible or plan a leisurely journey; whether I ascend some interior monument like Mount Huethawali or traverse the Supai platform that runs the length of the Canyon—I return different from when I entered. Not always different in the same way. But different.

Let me suggest that the specifics of place are like the findings of an evaluation report. The different places provide different content. From the rim, one can view magnificent vistas. Deep within a side canyon, one can see little and feel completely alone. Much of the Canyon is desert, but rare streams and even rarer waterfalls offer a stark contrast to the ancient, parched rock. Each place offers different content for reflection. The substantive insights one receives may well vary by place, time, and circumstance. But quite beyond those variations is the impact that comes from the very act of reflection—regardless of content and place. The impacts of reflection and meditation on one's inner sense of self are, for me, analogous to the impacts of engaging in the processes of evaluation, quite apart from the content of the evaluation's findings. In this same sense, for certain developmental purposes—staff development, program development, organization development—it doesn't matter so much what the focus of an evaluation is, or what its findings, some impact will come from engaging thoughtfully and seriously in the process.

A Menu: Uses of Evaluation Logic and Processes

In working with intended users, it's important to help them think about the potential and desired impacts of *how* the evaluation will be conducted. Questions about who will be involved take on a different degree of importance when considering that those most directly involved will not only play a critical role in determining the content of the evaluation, and therefore the focus of findings, but they also will be the people most affected by exposure to evaluation logic and processes. The degree of internal involvement, engagement, and ownership will affect the nature and degree of impact on the program's culture. How funders and users of evaluation think about and calculate the costs and benefits of evaluation also are affected. The cost-benefit ratio changes on both sides of the equation when the evaluation produces not only findings but also serves immediate programmatic needs such as staff development or participant empowerment.

I differentiate four primary uses of evaluation logic and processes: (1) enhancing shared understandings, especially about results; (2) supporting and reinforcing the program through intervention-oriented evaluation; (3) increasing participants' engagement, sense of ownership, and self-determination (participatory and empowerment evaluation); and (4) program or organizational development. I'll discuss each of these, with examples, then consider the controversies engendered by using evaluation in these ways.

Using Evaluation to Enhance Shared Understandings

Evaluation both depends on and facilitates clear communications. Shared understandings emerge as evaluation logic pushes the senders of messages to be as specific as possible and challenges listeners to reflect on and feed back to senders what they think they've heard. Shared understandings are especially important with regard to expected results. For example, board members and program staff often have different notions of what an agency or program is supposed to accomplish. The processes of clarifying desired ends and focusing staff efforts on accomplishing those ends by evaluating actual accomplishments ought to be primary board functions, but few boards fulfill these functions effectively (Carver 1990).

I'm often asked to facilitate board or staff retreats to help them learn and apply the logic and discipline of evaluation to formulating the organization's mission and goals. The feedback I get is that the questions I pose as an evaluator (e.g., What specific results are you committed to achieving and how would you know if you accomplished them?) are different from what they are asked by non-evaluators. It's not so much that other facilitators don't ask these questions, but they don't ask them with the same seriousness and pursue the answers with the same rigor and intensity. The very process of formulating a mission and goals so they can be evaluated will usually have an impact, long before data are actually collected to measure effectiveness.

A parallel use of evaluation is to increase shared understandings between program managers and line staff. Following the admonition that "what gets measured gets done," managers can work with staff under the guidance of an evaluator to establish a monitoring system to help everyone involved stay focused on desired outcomes. While the data from such a system may ultimately support decision making, in the short run, the impact is to focus staff attention and energy on priority outcomes. The process needs to be facilitated in such a way that staff can speak openly about whether board and administrative expectations are meaningful, realistic, and attainable. In other words, done properly, evaluation facilitates shared commitments to results from top to bottom *and* bottom to top for "improved communication between staff at different levels of program implementation" (Aubel 1993:13).

You may have experienced both the presence and absence of evaluation logic in your education. When a teacher announces a test and says, "Here's what will be on the test and here's what I'll be looking for," that teacher is manifesting the evaluation principle that **what gets measured gets done.** Making criteria explicit and communicating them to all concerned is equitable and fair. In contrast, I've observed teachers refuse to tell their class what will be on a test, then later, in individual, informal conversations, they reveal the test's focus to persistent and inquiring students. Telling everyone would have been more fair.

The logic and principles of evaluation also can be useful in negotiations between parties with different perspectives. For example, a major foundation was interested in funding an effort to make schools more racially equitable. The school district expressed great interest in such funding but resisted committing to explicit school changes that might undermine building-level autonomy or intrude into personnel evaluations of principals. Over a period of several months, the funder and school officials negotiated the project. The negotiations centered on expected evaluation outcomes. The funder and school district eventually agreed to focus the project and evaluation on community-based, school-specific action plans, activities, and changes rather than a standardized and prescribed set of district-determined mandates. Case studies were chosen as the most appropriate evaluation method, rather than standardized instruments for measuring school climate. The design of the entire project was changed and made more focused as a result of these negotiations. Applying the logic of evaluation had a major impact on the project's design without any data collection, findings, or a report. Everyone came out of the negotiations clear about what was to happen in the project and how it would be evaluated.

Inadequate specification of desired results reduces the likelihood of attaining those results. Consider how adding a results orientation changed the Request for Proposals announcement of a major environment-oriented philanthropic foundation. In the initial announcement, the foundation wanted to cast the net wide, so it issued a general invitation:

> We seek grant proposals that will enhance the health of specific ecosystems.

The responses varied greatly with many completely missing the mark in the opinion of the foundation staff. But what was the mark? A great deal of time and effort was wasted by hopeful proposal writers who didn't know what criteria to address, and staff spent a lot of time sifting through proposals that had no hope of being funded. The process created frustration on both sides. After a planning session focused on specifying desired results and explicit evaluation criteria, the second announcement was quite a bit more focused:

> We seek grant proposals that will enhance the health of specific ecosystems. Proposals will be judged on the following criteria:
>
> - clarity and meaningfulness of ecosystem definition
> - private-public sector cooperation
> - action orientation and likelihood of demonstrable impact
> - incorporation of a prevention orientation
> - regional coordination

This set of criteria eliminates basic research proposals, of which a large number were received from universities in the first round, and makes it clear that those seeking grants must submit as cooperative groups rather than as single individuals or entities, also characteristic of a large number of initial proposals. Subsequent announcements became even more specific when focused on specific action priorities, such as pollution prevention. The staff, with training and facilitation, learned to use evaluation logic to articulate desired results, enhance communications, and increase responsiveness.

A different use of evaluation to enhance mutual understanding involves designing the evaluation to "give voice" to the disenfranchised, underprivileged, poor, and others outside the mainstream (Weiss and Greene 1992:145). In the evaluation of a diversity project in the Saint Paul Schools, a major part of the design included capturing and reporting the experiences of people of color. Providing a way for African American, Native American, Chicano-Latino, and Hmong parents to tell their stories to mostly white, corporate funders was an intentional part of the design, one approved by those same white corporate funders. Rather than reaching singular conclusions, the final report was a multivocal, multicultural presentation of different experiences with and perceptions of the program's impacts. The medium of the report carried the message that multiple voices needed to be heard and valued as a manifestation of diversity (Stockdill et al., 1992). The findings were used for both formative and summative purposes, but the parents and many of the staff were most interested in using the evaluation processes to make themselves heard by those in power. **Being heard was an end in itself, quite separate from use of findings.**

Wadsworth (1995) has reported that evaluation processes can facilitate interactions between service providers and service users in a way that leads to "connectedness" and "dialogue across difference" (p. 9). Each learns to see the service through the others' eyes. In the process, what began as opposing groups with opposing truths is transformed into "an affinity-based community of inquiry" with shared truths.

Using evaluation to enhance shared understandings is a relatively traditional use of evaluation logic. Let's turn now to a different and more controversial use of evaluation processes: intervention-oriented evaluation.

Evaluation as an Integral Programmatic Intervention

Textbooks on measurement warn that measuring the effects of a treatment (e.g., a social program) should be independent of and separate from the treatment itself. For example, participants who take a pretest may perform better in the program than those who do not take the pretest because the pretest increases awareness, stimulates learning, and/or enhances preparation for program activities. To account for such test effects, evaluation researchers in the past have been advised to use experimental designs that permit analysis of differences in performance for those who took the pretest compared to a group that did not take the pretest. Integrating data collection into program implementation would be considered a problem—a form of treatment contamination—under traditional rules of research.

Departing from defining evaluation as rigorous application of social science methods opens a different direction in evaluation (Patton 1988), one that supports integration of evaluation into program processes. Making data collection integral rather than separate can reinforce and strengthen the program intervention. Such an approach also can be cost-effective and efficient since, when evaluation becomes integral to the program, its costs aren't an add-on. This enhances the sustainability of evaluation because, when it's built in rather than added on, it's not viewed as a temporary effort or luxury that can be easily dispensed with when cuts are necessary.

To illustrate this approach, consider the case of a one-day workshop. A traditional evaluation design, based on standard social science standards of rigor, would typically include a pretest and posttest to assess changes in participants' knowledge, skills, and attitudes. As the workshop opens, participants are told,

> Before we begin the actual training, we want you to take a pretest. This will provide a baseline for our evaluation so we can find out how much you already know and then measure how much you've learned when you take the posttest.

At the end of the day, participants are administered the same instrument as a posttest. They are told,

> Now the workshop is over, but before you leave, we need to have you take the posttest to complete the evaluation and find out how much you have benefited from the training.

The desired design for high internal validity would include, *in addition to* the pre-post treatment group, (1) a control group that takes the pre- and posttests without experiencing the workshop, (2) a control group that gets the posttest only, and (3) a treatment group that gets the posttest only. All groups, of course, should be randomly selected and assigned, and the administration of the test should be standardized and take place at the same time. Such a design would permit measurement of and control for instrumentation effects.

Let me now pose a contrary example of how the evaluation might be handled, a design that fully integrates the evaluation data collection into the program delivery, that is, a design that makes the data collection part of the workshop rather than separate from and independent of the workshop. In this scenario, the workshop begins as follows:

> The first part of the workshop involves your completing a self-assessment of your knowledge, skills, and attitudes. This will help you prepare for and get into thinking about the things we will be covering today in your training.

The workshop then proceeds. At the end of the day, the workshop presenter closes as follows:

> Now the final workshop activity is for you to assess what you have learned today. To that end, we are going to have you retake the self-assessment you took this morning. This will serve as a review of today and let you see how much you've learned.

In this second scenario, the word *evaluation* is never mentioned. The pre- and post-assessments are explicitly and intentionally part of the workshop in accordance with adult learning principles (Brookfield 1990; Knox 1987; Schön 1987; Knowles et al. 1985). We know, for example, that when participants are told what they will learn, they become prepared for the learning; learning is further enhanced when it is reinforced both immediately and over the long term. In the second scenario, the self-assessment instrument serves *both* the function of preparing people for learning and as baseline data. The posttest serves the dual functions of learning reinforcement and evaluation. Likewise, a six-month follow-up to assess retention can serve the dual functions of learning reinforcement and longitudinal evaluation.

The methodological specialist will note that the second scenario is fraught with threats to validity. However, the purpose of data collection in this second scenario is not only assessment of the extent to which change has occurred, but increasing the likelihood that change will occur. It does not matter *to these particular intended users (the workshop instructors)* how much of the measured change is due to pretest sensitization versus actual learning activities, or both, as long as the instrument items are valid indicators of desired outcomes. Moreover, in the second scenario, the data collection is so well integrated into the program that there are no separate evaluation costs except for the data analysis itself. Under the second scenario, the administration of the pretest and posttest is a part of the program such that **even if the data were not analyzed for evaluation purposes, the data collection would still take place,** making evaluation data collection highly cost-effective.

Principles of Intervention-Oriented Evaluation

I have called this process *intervention-oriented evaluation* to make explicit the direct and integral connection between data collection and program results. A program is an intervention in the sense that it is aimed at changing something. The evaluation becomes part of the programmatic intervention to the extent that the way it is conducted supports and reinforces accomplishing desired program goals.

The primary principle of *intervention-oriented evaluation* is to build a program delivery model that logically and meaningfully interjects data collection in ways that enhance achievement of program outcomes, while also meeting evaluation information needs. We followed this principle in evaluating a wilderness program that aimed to turn college administrators into leaders in *experiential education.* Participants hiked 10 days in the Gila Wilderness of New Mexico in the fall, climbed the Kofa Mountains of Arizona in the winter, and rafted the San Juan River in Utah in the spring. During these trips, participants kept journals for reflection. The program's philosophy was, "One doesn't just learn from experience; one learns from *reflection* on experience." The process of journaling was part of the program intervention, but also a prime source of qualitative evaluation data capturing how participants reacted to and were changed by project participation. In addition, participants were paired together to interview each other before, during, and after each wilderness experience. These interviews were part of the project's reflection process, but also a source of case data for evaluation. The evaluation process thus became part of the intervention in providing participants with experiences in *reflective practice* (Schön 1987, 1983). Indeed, it was on this project that I first learned how profoundly in-depth interviews can affect people. Such personal, intensive, and reflective data collection is an intervention. In intervention-oriented evaluation, such data collection is designed to reinforce and strengthen the program's impact.

Another, quite different, example comes from an intervention-designed evaluation of an international development effort called the Caribbean Agricultural Extension Project, funded by the U.S. Agency for International Development (U.S. AID). The project aimed to improve national agricultural extension services in eight Caribbean countries. The project began with a rapid reconnaissance survey to identify the farming systems in each participating island. This involved an interdisciplinary team of agricultural researchers, social scientists, and extension staff doing fieldwork and interviewing farmers for a period of 10 days to identify extension priorities for a specific agro-ecological zone. This process served as the basis for needs assessment and program development. It was also, quite explicitly and intentionally, an intervention in and of itself in that the process garnered attention from both farmers and agricultural officials, thereby beginning the extension mobilization process. In addition, the rapid reconnaissance survey served the critical evaluation function of establishing baseline data. Subsequent data on the effects of extension and agricultural development in the zone were compared against this baseline for evaluation purposes. Yet, it would have been much too expensive to undertake this kind of intensive team fieldwork simply for purposes of evaluation. Such data collection was practical and cost-effective because it was fully integrated into other critical program processes.

Once the various farming systems were identified and the needs of farmers had been specified within those systems, the extension staff began working with individual farmers to assess their specific production goals. This process included gathering data about the farmer's agricultural enterprises and household income flows. With these data in hand, extension agents worked with farmers to set realistic goals for change and to help farmers monitor the effects of recommended interventions. The program purpose of using this approach, called a *farm management approach*, was to individualize the work of extension agents with farmers so that the agent's recommendations were solidly grounded in knowledge of the farm and household situation, including labor availability, land availability, income goals, and past agricultural experiences. These data were necessary for the extension agent to do a good job of advising farm families about increasing their productivity.

These same data were the baseline for measuring the program's impact on individual farmers for evaluation purposes. The collection of such data for farm management purposes required training of agents, and a great deal of time and effort. It would have been enormously expensive to collect such data independently, solely for purposes of evaluation. However, by establishing a record-keeping system for individual farmers that served a primary extension purpose, the project also established a record-keeping system for evaluation purposes. By aggregating the data from individual households, it was possible to analyze system-level impact over time. The data aggregation and comparative analysis were above and beyond the main program purpose of collecting the data. However, without that program purpose, the data would have been much too expensive to collect solely for evaluation of the system.

The program staff also used the evaluation design formulated by the external evaluators as the framework for their plan of work, which set the agenda for monthly staff meetings and quarterly staff reports (an example of using evaluation to enhance and focus communications). As such, the evaluation priorities were kept before the staff at all times. As a result, the evaluation process improved program implementation from the very beginning by focusing staff implementation efforts.

Still another powerful example of intervention-oriented evaluation comes from the Hazelden Foundation, a chemical dependency treatment program in Minnesota. Part of the program intervention includes helping clients and their significant others identify their chemical abuse patterns. A self-assessment instrument serves this purpose while also providing baseline data on chemical use. After residency treatment, all clients and significant others receive follow-up surveys at six months, one year, and two years. The follow-up surveys provide outcomes data on program effectiveness, but they also remind clients and their significant others to assess their current chemical use behaviors. Clients who have relapsed into abusive behaviors are invited to contact Hazelden for support, assessment, and possible reentry into treatment. Thus, the follow-up survey is a mechanism for reinforcing treatment and extending an offer of new help. Many clients respond to this contact and seek additional help. For that reason, the survey is sent to all former clients, not just the small random sample that would be sufficient if the survey provided only evaluation data.

In my experience, program funders, managers, and staff can become very excited about the creative possibilities for integrating evaluation into a program in such a way that it supports and reinforces the program intervention. Not only does this make the evaluation process more useful, it often makes the evaluation findings more relevant, meaningful, accessible, and useful. Yet, this approach can be controversial because the evaluation's credibility may be undercut by concerns about whether the data are sufficiently independent of the treatment to be meaningful and trustworthy; the evaluator's independence may be suspect when the relations with staff and/or participants become quite close; and the capacity to render an independent, summative judgment may be diminished. These are considerations to discuss with intended users and evaluation funders in deciding the relative priority of different potential uses of evaluation and in reviewing the principles of intervention-oriented evaluation (Exhibit 5.2). Now, let's examine the use of evaluation processes to engage participants more fully.

Supporting Engagement, Self-Determination, and Ownership: Participatory, Collaborative, and Empowerment Evaluation

Early in my career, I was commissioned by a Provincial Deputy Minister in Canada to undertake an evaluation in a school division he considered mediocre. I asked what he wanted the evaluation to focus on.

"I don't care what the focus is," he replied. "I just want to get people engaged in some way. Education has no life there. Parents aren't involved. Teachers are just putting in time. Administrators aren't leading. Kids are bored. I'm hoping evaluation can stir things up and get people involved again." That's how the evaluation of the Frontier School Division, described in Chapter 2, began.

The processes of participation and collaboration have an impact on participants and collaborators quite beyond whatever they may accomplish by working together. In the process of participating in an evaluation, participants are exposed to and have the opportunity to learn the logic of evaluation and the discipline of evaluation reasoning. Skills are acquired in problem identification, criteria specification, and data collection, analysis, and interpretation. Acquisition of evaluation skills and ways of thinking can have a longer-term impact than the use of findings from a particular evaluation study.

EXHIBIT 5.2

Principles of Intervention-Oriented Evaluation

- The evaluation is designed to support, reinforce, and enhance attainment of desired program outcomes.
- Evaluation data collection and use are integrated into program delivery and management. Rather than being separate from and independent of program processes, the evaluation is an integral part of those processes.
- Program staff and participants know what is being evaluated and know the criteria for judging success.
- Feedback of evaluation findings is used to increase individual participant goal attainment as well as overall program goal attainment.
- There are no or only incidental add-on costs for data collection because data collection is part of program design, delivery, and implementation.
- Evaluation data collection, feedback, and use are part of the program model, that is, evaluation is a component of the intervention.

Moreover, people who participate in creating something tend to feel more ownership of what they have created, make more use of it, and take better care of it. Active participants in evaluation, therefore, are more likely to feel ownership not only of *their* evaluation findings, but also of the evaluation process itself. Properly, sensitively, and authentically done, it becomes *their* process.

Participants and collaborators can be staff and/or program participants (e.g., clients, students, community members, etc.). Sometimes administrators, funders, and others also participate, but the usual connotation is that the primary participants are "lower down" in the hierarchy. Participatory evaluation is bottom up.

In 1995, evaluators interested in "Collaborative, Participatory, and Empowerment Evaluation" formed a Topical Interest Group within the American Evaluation Association. What these approaches have in common is a style of evaluation in which the evaluator becomes a facilitator, collaborator, and teacher in support of program participants and staff engaging in their own evaluation. While the findings from such a participatory process may be useful, the more immediate impact is to use the evaluation process to increase participants' sense of being in control of, deliberative about, and reflective on their own lives and situations.

The labels *participatory evaluation* and *collaborative evaluation* mean different things to different evaluators. Some use these phrases interchangeably or as mutually reinforcing concepts (e.g., Dugan 1996; Powell, Jeffries, and Selby 1989; Whitmore and Kerans 1988). Wadsworth (1993b) distinguishes "research on people, for people, or *with* people" (p. 1). Whitmore (1988) has defined the participatory approach as combining "social investigation, education, and action with the ultimate purpose of engendering broad community and social change" (p. 3).

Whitmore worked with a community-based team and contended that, through the evaluation process, participants not only gained new knowledge and skills but also created a support network among themselves and gained a greater sense of self-efficacy.

In the mid-1980s, several international grassroots development organizations advocated participatory evaluation as a tool for community and local leadership development, not only as a management tool (PACT 1986). In advocating for participatory evaluation, the *Evaluation Sourcebook* of the American Council of Voluntary Agencies for Foreign Service (ACVAFS 1983) asserted, "Participation is what development is about: gaining skills for self-reliance" (p. 12). Thus, in developing countries, participatory evaluation has been linked to community development and empowerment; industrialized countries, where notions of "value-free" social science have long been dominant, have come to this idea of linking evaluation participation with empowerment more slowly, and, as we shall see later, the notion remains controversial.

Norman Uphoff (1991) has published *A Field Guide for Participatory Self-Evaluation,* aimed at grassroots community development projects. After reviewing a number of such efforts, he concluded,

> If the process of self-evaluation is carried out regularly and openly, with all group members participating, the answers they arrive at are in themselves not so important as what is learned from the discussion and from the process of reaching consensus on what questions should be used to evaluate group performance and capacity, and on what answers best describe their group's present status. (p. 272)

Here is clear support for the central premise of this chapter: The process of engaging in evaluation can have as much or more impact than the findings generated. It was not a group's specific questions or answers that Uphoff found most affected the groups he observed. It was the process of reaching consensus about questions and engaging with each other in the meaning of the answers turned up. The process of participatory self-evaluation, in and of itself, provided useful learning experiences for participants.

Since no definitive definitions exist for *participatory* and *collaborative* evaluation, these phrases must be defined and given meaning in each setting where they're used. Exhibit 5.3 presents what I consider the primary principles of participatory evaluation. This list can be a starting point for working with intended participants to decide what principles they want to adopt for their own process.

Cousins and Earl (1995, 1992) have advocated participatory and collaborative approaches primarily to increase use of findings: "Unlike emancipatory forms of action research, the rationale for participatory evaluation resides not in its ability to ensure social justice or to somehow even the societal playing field but in the utilization of systematically collected and socially constructed knowledge" (p. 10). Yet, the authors go beyond increased use of findings when they discuss how participation helps create a learning organization. Viewing participatory evaluation as a means of creating an organizational culture committed to ongoing learning has become an important theme in recent literature linking evaluation to *learning organizations* (e.g., King 1995; Aubel 1993; Leeuw, Rist, and Sonnichsen 1993; Sonnichsen 1993) "The goal of a participatory evaluator is eventually to put him or herself out of work when

EXHIBIT 5.3
Principles of Participatory Evaluation

- The evaluation process involves participants in learning evaluation logic and skills, for example, goal setting, establishing priorities, focusing questions, interpreting data, data-based decision making, and connecting processes to outcomes.
- Participants in the process *own* the evaluation. They make the major focus and design decisions. They draw and apply conclusions. Participation is real, not token.
- Participants focus the evaluation on process and outcomes they consider important and to which they are committed.
- Participants work together as a group and the evaluation facilitator supports group cohesion and collective inquiry.
- All aspects of the evaluation, including the data, are understandable and meaningful to participants.
- Internal, self-accountability is highly valued. The evaluation, therefore, supports participants' accountability to themselves and their community first, and external accountability secondarily, if at all.
- The evaluator is a facilitator, collaborator, and learning resource; participants are decision makers and evaluators.
- The evaluation facilitator recognizes and values participants' perspectives and expertise and works to help participants recognize and value their own and each other's expertise.
- Status differences between the evaluation facilitator and participants are minimized.

the research capacity of the organization is self-sustaining" (King 1995:89). Indeed, the *self-evaluating organization* (Wildavsky 1985) constitutes an important direction in the institutionalization of evaluation logic and processes.

Utilization-focused evaluation is inherently participatory and collaborative in actively involving primary intended users in all aspects of the evaluation. Evidence presented in earlier chapters has demonstrated the effectiveness of this strategy for increasing use of findings. The added emphasis of this chapter is how participation and collaboration can lead to an ongoing, longer-term commitment to using evaluation logic and building a culture of learning in a program or organization. Making this kind of process use explicit enlarges the menu of potential evaluation uses. How important this use of evaluation should be in any given evaluation is a matter for negotiation with intended users. The practical implication of an explicit emphasis on creating a learning culture as part of the process will mean building into the evaluation attention to and training in evaluation logic and skills.

Not all references to participatory or collaborative evaluation make the link to participant learning. Levin (1993) distinguished three purposes for collaborative research: (1) the pragmatic purpose of increasing use, (2) the philosophical or methodological purpose of grounding data in practitioner's perspectives, and (3) the political purpose of mobilizing for social action. A fourth purpose, identified here, is teaching evaluation logic and skills. In the next section, we'll examine in greater depth the political uses of evaluation to mobilize for social action and support social justice.

Empowerment Evaluation

The theme of the 1993 American Evaluation Association national conference was "Empowerment Evaluation." David Fetterman (1993), AEA President that year, defined empowerment evaluation as "the use of evaluation concepts and techniques to foster self-determination. The focus is on helping people help themselves" (p. 115).

> Self-determination, defined as the ability to chart one's own course in life, forms the theoretical foundation of empowerment evaluation. It consists of numerous interconnected capabilities that logically follow each other . . . : the ability to identify and express needs, establish goals or expectations and a plan of action to achieve them, identify resources, make rational choices from various alternative courses of action, take appropriate steps to pursue objectives, evaluate short- and long-term results (including reassessing plans and expectations and taking necessary detours), and persist in pursuit of those goals. (Fetterman 1994a:2)

These skills are used to realize the group's own political goals; through self-assessment and a group's knowledge of itself, it achieves accountability unto itself as well as to others (Fetterman, Kaftarian, and Wandersman 1996). In so doing, community capacity can also be enhanced as a group realizes and builds on its assets (Mayer 1996, n.d.).

Empowerment evaluation is most appropriate where the goals of the program include helping participants become more self-sufficient and personally effective. In such instances, empowerment evaluation is also intervention oriented in that the evaluation is designed and implemented to support and enhance the program's desired outcomes. Weiss and Greene (1992) have shown how *empowerment partnerships* between evaluators and program staff were particularly appropriate in the family support movement because that movement emphasized participant and community empowerment.

I facilitated a cluster team evaluation of 34 programs serving families in poverty (Patton et al. 1993). A common and important outcome of those programs was *increased intentionality*—having participants end up with a plan, a sense of direction, an assumption of responsibility for their lives, and a commitment to making progress. Increased intentionality began with small first steps. Families in poverty often feel stuck where they are or are experiencing a downward spiral of worsening conditions and ever greater hopelessness. These programs commonly reported that it was a major achievement to give people a sense of hope manifest in a concrete plan that participants had developed, understood, and believed they could accomplish. Increased intentionality is a commitment to change for the better and a belief that such a change is possible. Thus, the programs collectively placed a great deal of emphasis on developing such skills as goal setting, learning to map out strategies for attaining goals, and monitoring progress in attaining personal goals. The programs' evaluations were built around these family plans and supported them. Developing family plans was not an end in itself, but the ability and willingness to work on a plan emerged as a leading indicator of the likelihood of success in achieving longer-term outcomes. Creating and taking ownership of a plan became milestones of progress. The next milestone was putting the plan into action.

Another empowering outcome of participatory evaluation is forming effective groups for collective action and reflection. For example, social isolation is a common characteristic of families in poverty. Isolation breeds a host of other problems, including family violence, despair, and alienation. Bringing participants together to establish mutual goals of support and identifying ways of evaluating (reality-testing) goal attainment is a process of community development. The very process of working together on an evaluation has an impact on the group's collective identity and skills in collaborating and supporting each other. Participants also learn to use expert resources, in this case, the facilitating evaluator, but inquiry is democratized (IQREC 1997). One poverty program director explained to me the impact of such a process as she observed it:

> It's hard to explain how important it is to get people connected. It doesn't sound like a lot to busy middle-class people who feel their problem is too many connections to too many things. But it's really critical for the people we work with. They're isolated. They don't know how the system works. They're discouraged. They're intimidated by the system's jargon. They don't know where to begin. It's just so critical that they get connected, take action, and start to feel effective. I don't know how else to say it. I wish I could communicate what a difference it makes for a group of poor people who haven't had many years of formal education to share the responsibility to evaluate their own program experiences, learn the language of evaluation, deal with data, and report results. It's very empowering.

Empowerment and Social Justice

The phrase "empowerment evaluation" can bridle. It comes across to some like a trendy buzzword. Others experience it as oxymoronic or disingenuous. Still others find the phrase offensive and condescending. Few people, in my experience, react neutrally. Like the strategic planning term *proactive*, the word *empowerment* can create hostile reactions and may fall on hard times.

Empowerment carries an activist, social change connotation, as does a related idea, using evaluation for social justice. Vera, the main character in Nadine Gordimer's (1994) novel, *None to Accompany Me*, exclaims, after a lengthy exchange about empowerment of South African Blacks, "Empowerment, what is this new thing? What happened to what we used to call justice?" (p. 285). Perhaps Vera would have been pleased by the theme chosen by President Karen Kirkhart for the American Evaluation Association national conference in 1994 (the year after Empowerment Evaluation was the theme): "Evaluation and Social Justice."

The first prominent evaluation theorist to advocate valuing based on principles of social justice was Ernest House (1990b, 1980). He has consistently voiced concern for democratizing decision making. In that context, he has analyzed the ways in which evaluation inevitably becomes a political tool in that it affects "who gets what" (distributive justice). Evaluation can enhance fair and just distribution of benefits and responsibilities, or it can distort such distributions and contribute to inequality. In rendering judgments on programs, the social justice evaluator is guided by such principles as equality, fairness, and concern for the common welfare (Sirotnik 1990).

Both social justice and empowerment evaluation change the role of the evaluator from the traditional judge of merit or worth to a social change agent. Many evaluators surveyed by Cousins et al. (1995) were hostile to or at least ambivalent about whether participatory evaluation can or should help bring about social justice. Certainly, evaluators undertaking such an approach need to be comfortable with and committed to it, and such an activist agenda must be explicitly recognized by, negotiated with, and formally approved by primary intended users.

From a utilization-focused perspective, the important point is this: **Using evaluation to mobilize for social action, empower participants, and support social justice are options on the menu of evaluation process uses.** Since how these options are labeled will affect how they are viewed, when discussing these possibilities with primary intended users, evaluation facilitators will need to be sensitive to the language preferences of those involved.

Now, we turn to a conceptually different use of evaluation processes, what I'll call here *developmental evaluation*.

Program and Organization Development: Developmental Evaluation

The profession of program evaluation has developed parallel to the professions of management consulting and organization development (OD). OD consultants advise on and facilitate a variety of change processes (O'Toole 1995; Kanter, Stein, and Jick 1992; Fossum 1989; McLean 1982), including solving communications problems (D'Aprix 1996); conflict resolution (Kottler 1996); strategic planning (Bryson 1995); leadership development (Kouzes and Posner 1995; Terry 1993; Bryson and Crosby 1992; Schein 1985; Argyris 1976); teamwork (Parker 1996); human resources (Argyris 1974); diversity training (Morrison 1995); shaping organizational culture (Hampden-Turner 1990; Schein 1989); organizational learning (Aubrey and Cohen 1995; Watkins and Marsick 1993; Senge 1990; Morgan 1989; Argyris 1982); and defining mission, to name but a few OD arenas of action (Handy 1993; Massarik 1990; Morgan 1986; Azumi and Hage 1972). Sometimes their methods include organizational surveys and field observations, and they may facilitate *action research* as a basis for problem solving (Whyte 1991; Schön 1987; Argyris, Putnam, and Smith 1985; Wadsworth 1984) or even evaluation (King 1995; Prideaux 1995; Wadsworth 1993a, 1993b; Patton 1990:157-62). Program evaluation can be viewed as one approach on the extensive menu of organization and program development approaches. Evaluation's niche is defined by its emphasis on reality testing based on systematic data collection for improvement, judging merit and worth, or generating knowledge about effectiveness. The processes of evaluation support change in organizations by getting people engaged in reality testing, that is, helping them think empirically, with attention to specificity and clarity, and teaching them the methods and utility of data-based decision making. Bickman (1994), in an article entitled "An Optimistic View of Evaluation," predicted that evaluators in the future would become more involved in program development, especially "front end" assistance as part of a development team.

For example, *evaluability assessment* (Wholey 1994; Smith 1989) has emerged as a process for evaluators to work with program managers to help them get ready for evaluation. It involves clarifying goals, finding out various stakeholders' views of important issues, and specifying the model or intervention to be assessed. From my perspective, this is really a fancy term that gives evaluators a credible niche for doing program and organizational development. Time and time again, evaluators are asked to undertake an evaluation only to find that goals are muddled, key stakeholders have vastly different expectations of the program, and the model that the program supposedly represents, that is, its intervention, is vague at best. In other words, the program has been poorly designed, conceptualized, or developed. In order to do an evaluation, the evaluator has to make up for these deficiencies. Thus, by default, the evaluator becomes a program or organizational developer. Rog (1985) studied the use of evaluability assessments and found that many of them precipitated substantial program change but did not lead to a formal evaluation. The programs realized through the process of evaluability assessment that they had a lot more development to do before they could or should undertake a formal evaluation, especially a summative evaluation. In such cases, the processes and logic of evaluation have impact on program staff quite beyond the use of findings from the assessment.

Mission-oriented evaluation is an organizational development approach that involves assessing the extent to which the various units and activities of the organization are consistent with its mission. For example, I evaluated the extent to which 550 grants made by the Northwest Area Foundation over five years were congruent with its mission. The board used that assessment at a retreat to review and then revise the organization's mission. The process of clarifying the foundation's mission with staff and board directors had at least as much impact as the findings (Hall 1992).

Action research (King and Lonnquist 1994a, 1994b), evaluability assessment, and mission-oriented evaluation facilitate organizational change through the processes staff experience as much as through any findings generated. That is also the case for a type of evaluation partnership aimed explicitly at development: developmental evaluation.

Developmental Evaluation

I introduced the term *developmental evaluation* (Patton 1994a) to describe certain long-term, partnering relationships with clients who are themselves engaged in ongoing program or organizational development. (See Exhibit 5.4 for a formal definition of developmental evaluation.) These clients incorporate me into their decision-making process as part of their design teams because they value the logic and conceptual rigor of evaluation thought, as well as the knowledge I've picked up about effective programming based on accumulated evaluation wisdom. My role is to ask evaluative questions and hold their feet to the fire of reality testing. Evaluation data are collected and used as part of this process, to be sure, but quite above and beyond the use of findings, these development-oriented decision makers want to have their ideas examined in the glaring light of evaluation logic.

EXHIBIT 5.4
Developmental Evaluation Defined

Developmental evaluation refers to evaluation processes undertaken for the purpose of supporting program, project, staff and/or organizational *development*, including asking evaluative questions and applying evaluation logic for developmental purposes. The evaluator is part of a team whose members collaborate to conceptualize, design, and test new approaches in a long-term, ongoing process of continuous improvement, adaptation, and intentional change. The evaluator's primary function in the team is to elucidate team discussions with evaluative questions, data, and logic and to facilitate data-based decision making in the developmental process.

Developmentally oriented programs have as their purpose the sometimes vague, general notion of ongoing development. The process is the outcome. They eschew clear, specific, and measurable goals up front because clarity, specificity, and measurability are limiting. They've identified an issue or problem and want to explore some potential solutions or interventions, but they realize that where they end up will be different for different participants—and that participants themselves should play a major role in goal setting. The process often includes elements of participatory evaluation, for example, engaging staff and participants in setting personal goals and monitoring goal attainment, but those goals aren't fixed—they're milestones for assessing progress, subject to change as learning occurs—so the primary purpose is program and organizational development rather than individual or group empowerment. As the evaluation unfolds, program designers observe where they end up and make adjustments based on dialogue about what's possible and what's desirable, though the criteria for what's "desirable" may be quite situational and always subject to change.

Developmentally oriented leaders in organizations and programs don't expect (or even want) to reach the state of "stabilization" required for summative evaluation. Staff don't aim for a steady state of programming because they're constantly tinkering as participants, conditions, learning, and context change. They don't aspire to arrive at a fixed model that can be generalized and disseminated. At most, they may discover and articulate principles of intervention and development, but not a replicable model that says "do X and you'll get Y." Rather, they aspire to continuous progress, ongoing adaptation, and rapid responsiveness. No sooner do they articulate and clarify some aspect of the process than that very awareness becomes an intervention and acts to change what they do. They don't value traditional characteristics of summative excellence, such as standardization of inputs, consistency of treatment, uniformity of outcomes, and clarity of causal linkages. They assume a world of multiple causes, diversity of outcomes, inconsistency of interventions, interactive effects at every level—and they find such a world exciting and desirable. They never expect to conduct a summative evaluation because they don't expect the program—or world—to hold still long enough for summative review. They expect to be forever developing and changing—and they want an evaluation approach that supports development and change.

Moreover, they don't conceive of development and change as necessarily improvements. In addition to the connotation that formative evaluation is ultimately meant to lead to summative evaluation (Scriven 1991a), formative evaluation carries a bias about making something better rather than just making it different. From a developmental perspective, you do something different because something has changed—your understanding, the characteristics of participants, technology, or the world. Those changes are dictated by your current perceptions, but the commitment to change doesn't carry a judgment that what was done before was inadequate or less effective. Change is not necessarily progress. Change is adaptation. As one design team member said,

> We did the best we knew how with what we knew and the resources we had. Now we're at a different place in our development—doing and thinking different things. That's development. That's change. But it's not necessarily improvement.

Developmental programming calls for developmental evaluation in which **the evaluator becomes part of the design team helping to shape what's happening, both processes and outcomes, in an evolving, rapidly changing environment of constant interaction, feedback, and change.** The developmental perspective, as I experience it, feels quite different from the traditional logic of programming in which goals are predetermined and plans are carefully made for achieving those goals. Development-focused relationships can go on for years and, in many cases, never involve formal, written reports.

The evaluator becomes part of the program design team or an organization's management team, not apart from the team or just reporting to the team, but fully participating in decisions and facilitating discussion about how to evaluate whatever happens. All team members, together, interpret evaluation findings, analyze implications, and apply results to the next stage of development. The purpose of the evaluation is to help develop the intervention; the evaluator is committed to improving the intervention and uses evaluative approaches to facilitate ongoing development.

Five Examples of Developmental Evaluation

1. **A community leadership program.** With two evaluation colleagues, I became part of the design team for a community leadership program in rural Minnesota. The design team included a sociologist, a couple of psychologists, a communications specialist, some adult educators, a funder, and program staff. All design team members had a range of expertise and experiences. What we shared was an interest in leadership and community development.

The relationship lasted over six years and involved different evaluation approaches each year. During that time, we engaged in participant observation, several different surveys, field observations, telephone interviews, case studies of individuals and communities, cost analyses, theory of action conceptualizations, futuring exercises, and training of participants to do their own evaluations. Each year, the program changed in significant ways and new evaluation questions emerged. Program goals and strategies evolved. The evaluation evolved. No final report was ever written. The program continues to evolve —and continues to rely on developmental evaluation.

2. **Supporting diversity in schools.** A group of foundations agreed to support multicultural education in the Saint Paul Public Schools for 10 or more years. Community members identified the problem as low levels of success for children of color on virtually every indicator they examined, for example, attendance, test scores, and graduation. The "solution" called for a high degree of community engagement, especially by people of color, in partnering with schools. The nature of the partnering and interim outcomes were to emerge from the process. Indeed, it would have been "disempowering" to local communities to predetermine the desired strategies and outcomes prior to their involvement. Moreover, different communities of color —African Americans, Native Americans, Hispanics, and Southeast Asians—could be expected to have varying needs, set differing goals, and work with the schools in different ways. All of these things had to be *developed.*

The evaluation documented developments, provided feedback at various levels from local communities to the overall district, and facilitated the process of community people and school people coming together to develop evaluative criteria and outcome claims. Both the program design and evaluation changed at least annually, sometimes more often. In the design process, lines between participation, programming, and evaluation were ignored as everyone worked together to develop the program. As noted earlier in this chapter, the evaluation reports took the form of multiple voices presenting multiple perspectives. These voices and perspectives were facilitated and organized by the evaluation team, but the evaluator's voice was simply one among many. The developmental evaluation and process are still ongoing as this is being written. No summative evaluation is planned or deemed appropriate, though a great deal of effort is going into publicly communicating the developmental processes and outcomes.

3. **Children's and families' community initiative.** A local foundation made a 20-year commitment to work with two inner-city neighborhoods to support a healthier environment for children and families. The communities are poor and populated by people of diverse ethnic and racial backgrounds. The heart of the commitment was to provide funds for people in the community to set their own goals and fund projects they deemed worthwhile. A community-based steering committee became, in effect, a decision-making group for small community grants. Grant-making criteria, desired outcomes, and evaluation criteria all had to be developed by the local community. The purpose of the developmental process was to support internal, community-based accountability (as opposed to external judgment by the affluent and distant board of the sponsoring foundation). My role, then, was facilitating sessions with local community leaders to support their developing their own evaluation process and sense of shared accountability. The evaluation process had to be highly flexible and responsive. Aspects of participatory and empowerment evaluation also were incorporated. Taking a 20-year developmental perspective, where the locus of accountability is community-based rather than funder-based, changes all the usual parameters of evaluation.

4. **A reflective practice process in adult education.** I've been working for several years with a suburban adult and community education program in facilitating a reflective practice process for staff development and organizational change. We meet monthly to get reports from staff about their action research observations for the last month. The focus of these observations is whatever issue the group has chosen the previous month. The reflective practice process involves: (1) identifying an issue, interest, or concern; (2) agreeing to try something; (3) agreeing to observe some things about what is tried; (4) reporting back to the group individually; (5) identifying patterns of experience or themes across the separate reports; (6) deciding what to try next, that is, determining the action implications of the findings, and (7) repeating the process with the new commitment to action. Over several years, this process has supported major curricular and organizational change. Evaluation is ongoing and feedback is immediate. The process combines staff and organizational development and evaluation. My role as facilitator is to keep them focused on data-based observations and help them interpret and apply findings. There are no formal reports and no formative or summative judgments in the usual evaluation sense. There is only an ongoing developmental process of incremental change, informed by data and judgment, which has led to significant cumulative evolution of the entire program. This has become a learning organization.

5. **Wilderness education for college administrators.** Earlier in this chapter, I described briefly the use of journals and interviews in a wilderness education program as an example of intervention-oriented evaluation. That same project provides an example of developmental evaluation. As evaluation participant observers, my evaluation partner and I provided daily feedback to program staff about issues surfacing in our interviews and observations. Staff used that feedback to shape the program, not just in the formative sense of improvement, but in a developmental way, actually designing the program as it unfolded. My evaluation partner and I became part of the decision-making staff that conceptualized the program. Our evaluative questions, quite apart from the data we gathered and fed back, helped shape the program.

An example will illustrate our developmental role. Early in the first trip, we focused staff attention on our observation that participants were struggling with the transition from city to wilderness. After considerable discussion and input from participants, staff decided to have evening discussions on this issue. Out of those discussions, a group exercise evolved in which, each morning and evening, we threw our arms about, shook our legs, and tossed our heads in a symbolic act of casting off the toxins that had surfaced from hidden places deep inside. The fresh air, beauty, quiet, fellowship, periods of solitude, and physical activity combined to "squeeze out the urban poisons." Participants left the wilderness feeling cleaner and purer than they had felt in years. They called that being "detoxified." Like the drunk who is finally sober, they took their leave from the wilderness committed to staying clear of the toxins.

No one was prepared for the speed of retoxification. Follow-up interviews revealed that participants were struggling with reentry. As evaluators, we worked with staff to decide how to support participants in dealing with reentry problems. When participants came back together three months later, they carried the knowledge that detox faded quickly and enduring purification couldn't be expected. Then the wilderness again salved them with its cleansing power. Most left the second trip more determined than ever to resist retoxification, but the higher expectations only made the subsequent falls more distressing. Many came to the third trip skeptical and resistant. It didn't matter. The San Juan River didn't care whether participants embraced or resisted it. After 10 days rowing and floating, participants, staff, *and* evaluators abandoned talking about detox as an absolute state. We came to understand it as a matter of degree and a process: an ongoing struggle to monitor the poisons around us, observe carefully their effects on our minds and bodies, and have the good sense to get to the wilderness when being poisoned started to feel normal. This understanding became part of the program model developed jointly by participants, staff, and evaluators—but as evaluators we led the discussions and pushed for conceptual clarity beyond what staff and participants would likely have been able to do without an evaluation perspective.

Commentary on Developmental Evaluation

It will be clear to the reader, I trust, that my evaluation role in each of the programs just reviewed involved a degree of engagement that went beyond the independent data collection and assessment that have traditionally defined evaluation functions. Lines between evaluation and development became blurred as we worked together collaboratively in teams. I have found these relationships to be substantially different from the more traditional evaluations I conducted earlier in my practice. My role has become more *developmental.*

But, once again, a note of caution about language. The term *development* carries negative connotations in some settings. Miller (1981), in *The Book of Jargon*, defines development as "a vague term used to euphemize large periods of time in which nothing happens" (p. 208). Evaluators are well advised to be attentive to what specific words mean in a particular context to specific intended users—and to choose their terms accordingly.

One reaction I've had from colleagues is that the examples I've shared above aren't "evaluations" at all but rather organizational development efforts. I won't quarrel with that. There are sound arguments for defining evaluation narrowly in order to distinguish genuinely evaluative efforts from other kinds of organizational mucking around. But, in each of the examples I've shared, and there are many others, **my participation, identity, and role were considered evaluative by those with whom I was engaged (and by whom I was paid).** There was no pretense of external independence. My role varied from being evaluation facilitator to full team member. In no case was my role *external* reporting and accountability.

Developmental evaluation certainly involves a role beyond being solely an evaluator, but I include it among the things we evaluators can do because organizational development is a legitimate use of evaluation processes. What we lose in conceptual clarity and purity with regard to a narrow definition of evaluation that focuses only on judging merit or worth, we gain in appreciation for evaluation expertise. When Scriven (1995) cautions against crossing the line from rendering judgments to offering advice, I think he underestimates the valuable role evaluators can play in design and program improvement based on cumulative knowledge. Part of my value to a design team is that I bring a reservoir of knowledge (based on many years of practice and having read a great many evaluation reports) about what kinds of things tend to work and where to anticipate problems. Young and novice evaluators may be well advised to stick fairly close to the data. However, experienced evaluators have typically accumulated a great deal of knowledge and wisdom about what works and doesn't work. More generally, as a profession, we know a lot about patterns of effectiveness, I think—and will know more over time. That knowledge makes us valuable partners in the design process. Crossing that line, however, can reduce independence of judgment. The costs and benefits of such a role change must be openly acknowledged and carefully assessed.

Concerns, Controversies, and Caveats

Menu 5.1 summarizes the four primary uses of evaluation logic and processes discussed in this chapter. As I noted in opening this chapter, any evaluation can, and often does, have these kinds of effects unintentionally or as an offshoot of using findings.

What's different about utilization- focused evaluation is that the possibility and desirability of learning from evaluation processes, as well as from findings, can be made intentional and purposeful—an option for intended users to consider building in from the beginning. In other words, instead of treating process use as an informal ripple effect, explicit and up-front attention to the potential impacts of evaluation logic and processes can increase those impacts and make them a planned purpose for undertaking the evaluation. In this way the evaluation's overall utility is increased.

The four kinds of process use identified and discussed here—(1) enhancing shared understandings, (2) reinforcing interventions, (3) supporting participant engagement, and (4) developing programs and organizations—have this in common: They all go beyond the traditional focus on findings and reports as the primary vehicles for evaluation impact. As such, these new directions have provoked controversy. Six kinds of objections—closely interrelated, but conceptually distinct—arise most consistently:

1. **Definitional objection.** Evaluation should be narrowly and consistently defined in accordance with the "common sense meaning of evaluation," namely, "the systematic investigation of the merit or worth of an object" (Stufflebeam 1994: 323). Anything other than that isn't evaluation. Adding terms such as *empowerment* or *developmental* to evaluation changes focus and undermines the essential nature of evaluation as a phenomenon unto itself.

2. **Goals confusion objection.** The goal of evaluation is to render judgment. "While . . . 'helping people help themselves' is a worthy goal, it is not the fundamental goal of evaluation" (Stufflebeam 1994:323).

3. **Role confusion objection.** Evaluators as people may play various roles beyond being an evaluator, such as training clients or helping staff develop a program, but in taking on such roles, one moves beyond being an evaluator and should call the role what it is, for example, trainer or developer, not evaluator.

> While one might appropriately assist clients in these ways, such services are not evaluation. . . . The evaluator must not confuse or substitute helping and advocacy roles with

MENU 5.1

Four Primary Uses of Evaluation Logic and Processes

For the uses below, the impact of the evaluation comes from application of evaluation thinking and engaging in evaluation processes (in contrast to impacts that come from using specific findings).

Uses	*Examples*
Enhancing shared understandings	Specifying intended uses to provide focus and generate shared commitment Managing staff meetings around explicit outcomes Sharing criteria for equity/fairness Giving voice to different perspectives and valuing diverse experiences
Supporting and reinforcing the program intervention	Building evaluation into program delivery processes Having participants monitor their own progress Specifying and monitoring outcomes as integral to working with program participants
Increasing engagement, self-determination, and ownership	Participatory and collaborative evaluation Empowerment evaluation Reflective practice Self-evaluation
Program and organizational development	Developmental evaluation Action research Mission-oriented, strategic evaluation Evaluability assessment Model specification

NOTE: Menu 4.1 (Chapter 4) presents a corresponding menu, "Three Primary Uses of Evaluation Findings," which addresses making judgments (e.g., summative evaluation), improving programs (formative evaluation), and generating knowledge (e.g., meta-analyses and syntheses).

> rendering of assessments of the merit and/or worth of objects that he/she has agreed to evaluate. (Stufflebeam 1994:324)

Scriven (1991a) has been emphatic in arguing that being able to identify that something is or is not working (an evaluator's role) is quite different from knowing how to fix or improve it (a designer's role).

4. **Threat to data validity objection.** Quantitative measurement specialists teach

that data collection, in order for the results to be valid, reliable, and credible, should be separate from the program being evaluated. Integrating data collection in such a way that it becomes part of the intervention contaminates both the data and the program.

5. **Loss of independence objection.** Approaches that depend on close relationships between evaluators and other stakeholders undermine the evaluator's neutrality and independence. "It's quite common for younger evaluators to 'go native,' that is, psychologically join the staff of the program they are supposed to be evaluating and become advocates instead of evaluators" (Scriven 1991a:41). This can lead to overly favorable findings and an inability to give honest, negative feedback.

6. **Corruption and misuse objection.** Evaluators who identify with and support program goals, and develop close relationships with staff and/or participants, can be inadvertently co-opted into serving public relations functions or succumb to pressure to distort or manipulate data, hide negative findings, and exaggerate positive results. Even if they manage to avoid corruption, they may be suspected of it, thus undermining the credibility of the entire profession. Or these approaches may actually serve intentional misuse and foster corruption, as Stufflebeam (1994) worries:

> What worries me most about . . . empowerment evaluation is that it could be used as a cloak of legitimacy to cover up highly corrupt or incompetent evaluation activity. Anyone who has been in the evaluation business for very long knows that many potential clients are willing to pay much money for a "good, empowering evaluation," one that conveys the particular message, positive or negative, that the client/interest group hopes to present, irrespective of the data, or one that promotes constructive, ongoing, and nonthreatening group process. . . .
>
> Many administrators caught in political conflicts would likely pay handsomely for such friendly, nonthreatening, empowering evaluation service. Unfortunately, there are many persons who call themselves evaluators who would be glad to sell such service. (p. 325)

These are serious concerns that have sparked vigorous debate (e.g., Fetterman 1995). In Chapter 14 on the politics and ethics of utilization-focused evaluation, I'll address these concerns with the seriousness they deserve. For the purpose of concluding this chapter, it is sufficient to note that the utilization-focused evaluator who presents to intended users options that go beyond narrow and traditional uses of findings has an obligation to disclose and discuss objections to such approaches. As evaluators explore new and innovative options, they must be clear that **dishonesty, corruption, data distortion, and selling out are not on the menu.** Where primary intended users want and need an independent, summative evaluation, that is what they should get. Where they want the evaluator to act independently in bringing forward improvement-oriented findings for formative evaluation, that is what they should get. But those are no longer the only options on the menu of evaluation uses. New participatory, collaborative, intervention-oriented, and developmental approaches are already being used. The utilization-focused issue is not whether such approaches should exist. They already do. The issues are understanding when such approaches are appropriate and helping intended users make informed decisions about their appropriateness. That's what the next chapter addresses.

Note

1. Sufi stories, particularly those about the adventures and follies of the incomparable Mulla (Master) Nasrudin, are a means of communicating ancient wisdom:

Nasrudin is the classical figure devised by the dervishes partly for the purpose of halting for a moment situations in which certain states of mind are made clear. . . . Since Sufism is something which is lived as well as something which is perceived, a Nasrudin tale cannot in itself produce complete enlightenment. On the other hand, it bridges the gap between mundane life and a transmutation of consciousness in a manner which no other literary form yet produced has been able to attain. (Shah 1964:56)

PART 2

Focusing Evaluations: Choices, Options, and Decisions

Desiderata for the Indecisive and Complacent

Go placidly amid the noise and haste, and remember what peace there may be in avoiding options. As far as possible, without surrender, be on good terms with the indecisive. Avoid people who ask you to make up your mind; they are vexations to the spirit. Enjoy your indecisiveness as well as your procrastinations. Exercise caution in your affairs lest you be faced with choices, for the world is full of menus. Experience the joys of avoidance.

You are a child of the universe, no less than the trees and the stars; you have a right to do and think absolutely nothing. And if you want merely to believe that the universe is unfolding as it should, avoid evaluation, for it tests reality. Evaluation threatens complacency and undermines the oblivion of fatalistic inertia. In undisturbed oblivion may lie happiness, but therein resides neither knowledge nor effectiveness.

—Halcolm's *Indesiderata*

6

Being Active-Reactive-Adaptive

Evaluator Roles, Situational Responsiveness, and Strategic Contingency Thinking

Human propensities in the face of evaluation: feline curiosity; stultifying fear; beguiling distortion of reality; ingratiating public acclamation; inscrutable selective perception; profuse rationalization; and apocalyptic anticipation. In other words, the usual run-of-the-mill human reactions to uncertainty.

Once past these necessary initial indulgences, it's possible to get on to the real evaluation issues: What's worth knowing? How will we get it? How will it be used?

Meaningful evaluation answers begin with meaningful questions.

—Halcolm

A young hare, born to royal-rabbit parents in a luxury warren, showed unparalleled speed. He won races far and wide, training under the world's best coach. He boasted that he could beat anyone in the forest.

The only animal to accept the hare's challenge was an old tortoise. This first amused, then angered the arrogant hare, who felt insulted. The hare agreed to the race, ridiculing the tortoise to local sports columnists. The tortoise said simply, "Come what may, I will do my best."

A course was created that stretched all the way through and back around the forest. The day of the race arrived. At the signal to start, the hare sped away, kicking dust in the tortoise's eyes. The tortoise slowly meandered down the track.

Halfway through the race, rain began falling in torrents. The rabbit hated the feel of cold rain on his luxuriously groomed fur, so he stopped for cover under a tree. The tortoise pulled his head into his shell and plodded along in the rain.

When the rain stopped, the hare, knowing he was well ahead of the meandering tortoise and detesting mud, decided to nap until the course dried. The track, however, was more than muddy; it had become a stream. The tortoise turned himself over, did the backstroke, and kept up his progress.

By and by, the tortoise passed the napping hare and won the race. The hare blamed his loss on "unfair and unexpected conditions," but observant sports columnists reported that the tortoise had beaten the hare by adapting to conditions as he found them. The hare, it turned out, was only a "good conditions" champion.

Evaluation Conditions

What are good evaluation conditions? Here's a wish list (generated by some colleagues over drinks late one night at the annual conference of the American Evaluation Association). The program's goals are clear, specific, and measurable. Program implementation is standardized and well managed. The project involves two years of formative evaluation working with open, sophisticated, and dedicated staff to improve the program; this is followed by a summative evaluation for the purpose of rendering independent judgment to an interested and knowledgeable funder. The evaluator has ready access to all necessary data and enthusiastic cooperation from all necessary people. The evaluator's role is clear and accepted. There are adequate resources and sufficient time to conduct a comprehensive and rigorous evaluation. The original evaluation proposal can be implemented as designed. No surprises turn up along the way, like departure of the program's senior executive or the report deadline moved up six months.

How often had this experienced group of colleagues conducted an evaluation under such ideal conditions? Never. (Bring on another round of drinks.)

The real world doesn't operate under textbook conditions. Effective evaluators learn to adapt to changed conditions. This requires situational responsiveness and strategic, contingency thinking—what I've come to call being active-reactive-adaptive in working with primary intended users.

By way of example, let me begin by describing how the focus of an evaluation can change over time. To do so, I'll draw on the menu of uses offered in the previous two chapters. In Chapter 4, we considered three uses for findings: rendering summative judgments; improving programs formatively; and generating knowledge about generic patterns of effectiveness. In Chapter 5, we considered four uses of evaluation processes and logic: enhancing communications and understanding; reinforcing a program intervention; supporting participant engagement, ownership, and empowerment; and program or organizational development. The following example will illustrate how these uses can be creatively combined in a single project to build on and reinforce each other over time as conditions and needs change. Then we'll consider a menu of evaluator roles and examine some of the situations and contingencies that influence the choice of evaluator roles and type of evaluation.

Changing Uses Over Time

Since the 1970s, Minnesota has been at the forefront in implementing Early Childhood Family Education programs through school districts statewide. These programs offer early screening for children's health and developmental problems; libraries of books, toys, and learning materials; and parent education classes that include parent-only discussions as well as activities with their infants, toddlers, and preschoolers. Parents learn about child development; ways of supporting their child's intellectual, emotional, and physical growth; and how to take care of themselves as parents. Some programs include home visits. A hallmark of the program has been universal access and outreach; that is, the program is not targeted selectively to low-income families or those deemed at risk. The program serves over 260,000 young children and their parents annually. It is the nation's largest and oldest program of its kind.

Evaluation has been critical to the program's development, acceptance, and expansion over the years. Evaluation methods have included parent surveys, field observations of programs, standardized instruments measuring parenting knowledge and skills, interviews with staff and parents, pre-post assessments of parent-child interactions, and videotapes of parent-child interaction (Mueller 1996). I have been involved with these statewide evaluation efforts for over 20 years, so I want to use this case to illustrate the menus of evaluation uses, both use of findings and use of evaluation logic and processes.

Formative evaluation. Parent feedback surveys have been used from the beginning to make the programs responsive to parent needs and interests. More recently, a large-scale, statewide evaluation involving 29 programs has used pre-post interviews and videotapes with parents to share information and results across programs. Staff have discussed program variations, identified populations with which they are more and less successful, and shared materials. The evaluation has become a vehicle for staff throughout the state to share ideas about everything from recruitment to outcomes assessment. Every program in the state can identify improvements made as a result of this evaluation-centered sharing and staff development.

Summative evaluation. Periodically the program has produced formal evaluation reports for the state legislature. A great deal is at stake. For example, in 1992, the program was funded by over $26 million in state aid and local levies. At a time of severe funding cuts for all kinds of programs, the universal access philosophy and operations of the program came under attack. Why should the state fund parent education and parent-child activities for middle-class parents? To save money and more narrowly focus the program, some legislators and educators proposed targeting the program for low-income and at-risk parents. The program's statewide evaluation played a major role in that debate. The summative report, entitled *Changing Times, Changing Families* (MECFE 1992), was distributed widely both within and outside the legislature. It described parent outcomes in great detail, showing that middle-class parents had a great deal to learn about parenting. Pre-post interviews with 183 parents showed how parent knowledge, skills, behaviors, and feelings changed. Smaller samples examined effects on single parents and teen parents. The report also included recommendations for program improvement, for example, working harder and more effectively to get fathers involved. The summative evaluation contributed to the legislature's decision to maintain universal access and expand support for early childhood parent education programming. State staff felt that, without a summative evaluation, the program would have been especially vulnerable to questions about the value of serving middle-class parents. The summative report anticipated that policy question, because legislators were identified as primary intended users.

Knowledge-generating evaluation. The fact that program offerings and implementation vary from district to district throughout the state has offered opportunities to synthesize lessons learned. For example, using comparative data about varying degrees of effectiveness in changing parent-child interactions, staff analyzed different ways of working with parents. One theme that emerged was the importance of directly engaging and training parents in how to observe their children. Early in the program, staff trained in child development underestimated the skills and knowledge involved in observing a child. New parents lacked a context or criteria for observing their own children. Having parents and children come together in groups provided opportunities to make observational skills a focus of parent education. This understanding has a number of programmatic implications, but at the level of cross-program synthesis, it represents knowledge generation. The lessons learned by Minnesota staff have been shared with programs in other states, and vice versa. One kind of important lesson learned has been how to use evaluation processes to enhance program effectiveness. We turn, then, to uses of evaluation logic and processes.

Using evaluation to enhance mutual understanding. All evaluation instruments for 20 years have been developed with full staff participation. At full-day sessions involving program directors from all over the state, rural, urban, and state staff have shared understandings about program priorities and challenges as they have operationalized outcomes. State staff have shared legislators' priorities. Rural staff have shared parents' concerns. All have discussed, and sometimes debated, what kinds of changes are possible, important, and/or crucial. The evaluation became a mechanism for formalizing, sharing, and communicating the program's philosophy, priorities, and approaches among diverse directors separated sometimes by hundreds of miles.

Intervention-oriented evaluation. In each program, a sample of parents was selected for pre-post interviews and videotapes of parent-child interactions. Staff, after evaluation training, conducted the interviews and made the videotapes. Staff soon discovered that the processes of interviewing and videotaping were powerful interventions. In the course of data collection, staff and parents got to know each other, developed rapport and trust, and discussed parents' concerns. Soon, parents not included in the study design were asking to be interviewed and videotaped. Some programs have decided to continue pre-post interviews with all parents and are routinely videotaping and reviewing the results with parents. The interviews and videotapes support and reinforce the program's goal of making parents more reflective and observant about their parentingo.

Data collection has become a valued intervention.

Participation, collaboration, and empowerment. The staff has had complete ownership of the evaluation from the beginning. From determining the focus of each subsequent evaluation through data collection and analysis, staff have participated fully. My role, and that of my evaluation colleagues, has been to support and facilitate the process. Program directors have reported feeling affirmed by the research knowledge they have gained. Most recently, they have been interpreting factor analysis and regression coefficients generated from the latest statewide effort. They have learned how to interpret other evaluation and research studies in the course of working on their own evaluations. They have taken instruments developed for statewide evaluation and adapted them for ongoing local program use. They feel competent to discuss the results with school superintendents and state legislators. They're also able to engage with confidence in discussions about what can and can't be measured.

Developmental evaluation. I've been involved with many of these program directors for 20 years. Over the years, we've wrestled with questions of how knowledge change relates to behavior change, how much importance to attach to attitudinal change and increases in parent confidence, and what outcomes to monitor among children. In so doing, we've been engaged in a long-term process of model specification and program development that go well beyond and have a larger impact than simply deciding what data to collect in the next round of evaluation. The evaluation deliberation process has become a vehicle for program development beyond use of findings about effectiveness.

Variable Evaluator Roles Linked to Variable Evaluation Purposes

Different types of and purposes for evaluation call for varying evaluator roles. Gerald Barkdoll (1980), as associate commissioner for planning and evaluation of the U.S. Food and Drug Administration, identified three contrasting evaluator roles. His first type, evaluator as scientist, he found was best fulfilled by aloof academics who focus on acquiring technically impeccable data while studiously staying above the fray of program politics and utilization relationships. His second type he called "consultative" in orientation; these evaluators were comfortable operating in a collaborative style with policymakers and program analysts to develop consensus about their information needs and decide jointly the evaluation's design and uses. His third type he called the "surveillance and compliance" evaluator, a style characterized by aggressively independent and highly critical auditors committed to protecting the public interest and ensuring accountability (e.g., Walters 1996). These three types reflect evaluation's historical development from three different traditions: (1) social science research; (2) pragmatic field practice, especially by internal evaluators and consultants; and (3) program and financial auditing.

When evaluation research aims to generate generalizable knowledge about causal linkages between a program intervention and outcomes, rigorous application of social science methods is called for and the evaluator's role as methodological expert will be primary. When the emphasis is on determining a program's overall merit or worth, the evaluator's role as judge takes center stage. If an evaluation has been commissioned because of and is driven by public accountability concerns, the evaluator's role as independent auditor, inspector, or investigator will be spotlighted for policymakers and the general public. When program improvement is the primary purpose, the evaluator plays an advisory and facilitative role with program staff. As a member of a design team, a developmental evaluator will play a consultative role. If an evaluation has a social justice agenda, the evaluator becomes a change agent.

In utilization-focused evaluation, the evaluator is always a negotiator—negotiating with primary intended users what other roles he or she will play. Beyond that, all roles are on the table, just as all methods are options. Role selection follows from and is dependent on intended use by intended users.

Consider, for example, a national evaluation of food stamps to feed low-income families. For purposes of accountability and policy review, the primary intended users are members of the program's oversight committees in Congress (including staff to those committees). The program is highly visible, costly, and controversial, especially because special interest groups differ about its intended outcomes and who should be eligible. Under such conditions, the evaluation's credibility and utility will depend heavily on the evaluators' independence, ideological neutrality, methodological expertise, and political savvy.

Contrast such a national accountability evaluation with an evaluator's role in helping a small, rural leadership program of the Cooperative Extension Service increase its impact. The program operates in a few local communities. The primary intended users are the county extension agents, elected county commissioners, and farmer representatives who have designed the program. Program improvement to increase participant satisfaction and behavior change is the intended purpose. Under these conditions, the evaluation's use will depend heavily on the evaluator's relationship with design team members. The evaluator will need to build a close, trusting, and mutually respectful relationship to effectively facilitate the team's decisions about evaluation priorities and methods of data collection and then take them through a consensus-building process as results are interpreted and changes agreed on.

These contrasting case examples illustrate the range of contexts in which program evaluations occur. The evaluator's role in any particular study will depend on matching her or his role with the context and purposes of the evaluation as negotiated with primary intended users.

Academic Versus Service Orientations

One of the most basic role divisions in the profession is that between academic and service-oriented evaluators, a division identified by Shadish and Epstein (1987) when they surveyed a stratified random sample of the members of the Evaluation Network and the Evaluation Research Society, the two organizations now merged as the American Evaluation Association. The authors inquired about a variety of issues related to evaluators' values and practices. They found that responses clustered around two contrasting views of evaluation. *Academic evaluators* tend to be at universities and emphasize the research purposes of evaluation, traditional standards of methodological rigor, summative outcome studies, and contributions to social science theory. *Service evaluators* tend to be independent consultants or internal evaluators and emphasize serving stakeholders' needs, program improvement, qualitative methods, and assisting with program decisions. According to Shadish and Epstein, "The general discrepancy between service-oriented and academically oriented evaluators seems warranted on both theoretical and empirical grounds" (p. 587).

In addition, Shadish and Epstein (1987) found that 31% of the respondents described their *primary* professional identity as that of "evaluator" (p. 560). Others thought of themselves first as a psychologist, sociologist, economist, educator, and so on, with identity as an evaluator secondary. Evaluators whose primary professional identity was evaluation were more likely to manifest the service/stakeholder orientation, with an emphasis on formative evaluation and commitment to improved program decision making. Those who did not identify primarily as evaluators (but rather took their primary identity from a traditional academic discipline) were significantly more likely to be engaged in academic evaluative research emphasizing research outcomes and summative judgments (p. 581).

Enter Morality: Activist Versus Academic Evaluation

The profession of evaluation remains very much split along these lines, but with new twists and, perhaps, deeper antagonisms. The schism erupted openly, and perhaps deepened, in the early 1990s, when the American Evaluation Association elected successive presidents who represented two quite divergent perspectives. While on the surface the debate was partly about methods—quantitative versus qualitative, a fray we shall enter in Chapter 12—the more fundamental conflict centered on vastly different images of the profession.

Yvonna Lincoln (1991), in her 1990 presidential address, advocated what I would call an activist role for evaluators, one that goes beyond just being competent applied researchers who employ traditional scientific methods to study programs—the academic perspective. She first lamented and then disputed the notion that " 'science' is about knowing and 'art' is about feeling and spiritual matters" (p. 2). She went on to talk about the need for an "*arts* and *sciences* of evaluation as plurals" (emphasis in the original) in which she identified four new sciences and six new arts for evaluation (pp. 2-6).

Lincoln's New Sciences of Evaluation

1. The science of locating interested stakeholders
2. The science of getting information—good, usable information—to those same stakeholders
3. The science of teaching various stakeholder groups how to use information to empower themselves
4. A science of communicating results

Lincoln's New Arts of Evaluation

1. The art of judgment, not only our own, but eliciting the judgments of stakeholders
2. The art of "appreciating" in our stakeholders and in ourselves, that is, comprehending meaning within a context . . . , seeing something fully

3. The art of cultural analysis
4. The art of hearing secret harmonies, that is, listening for meanings
5. The art of negotiating, not only our contracts, but the worlds in which our target populations and audiences live
6. The art of dealing with people different from ourselves

Lincoln (1991) closed her speech by asserting that "my message is a moral one." Because evaluators are a powerful group, these new arts and sciences have profound moral implications, she argued, including speaking truth to power,

> and to make that truth grounded in lived experience and in multiple voices. . . . We need to move beyond cost-benefit analyses and objective achievement measures to interpretive realms . . . to begin talking about what our programs mean, what our evaluations tell us, and what they contribute to our understandings as a culture and as a society. We need literally to begin to shape—as a shaman would—the dreams of all of us into realities. (p. 6)

The following year, the American Evaluation Association president was Lee Sechrest, who by his own definition represented the traditional, academic view of evaluation. He objected to Lincoln's metaphorical call for a new generation of evaluators. "I ask myself," Sechrest (1992) mused, "could we of the preceding generations possibly have given rise to this new, Fourth Generation? Where in our makeup are the origins of this new creature so unlike us. . . . I sense a very real and large generational gap" (p. 2). He went on to argue the merits of traditional scholarly approaches to evaluation, especially the use of quantitative and experimental methods.

But what alienated Sechrest the most was the tone of moral superiority he heard in Lincoln's call for a new arts and sciences of evaluation. Referring to a notice he had seen, presumably inspired by Lincoln's perspective, that invited organizing "the New Power Generation" into a group that might be called The Moral Evaluators, he replied,

> The most offensive part of the text, however, is the arrogation of the term "moral" by these new generation, rebellious evaluators. As constructionists, they should know that morality, like so many other things, is in the eye of the beholder. They do not look so extraordinarily moral to me. (p. 5)

Sechrest (1992) closed by implying that the activist stance advocated by Lincoln, presumably based on commitment to shaping a better world, could be viewed as corrupt. Noting that academic evaluators who use traditional quantitative methods also care about finding programs that work, he chided, "They are simply not willing to fudge very much to do so" (p. 6).

What Shadish and Epstein (1987) originally distinguished as academic versus service orientations has evolved, I believe, into different conceptions of evaluator activism that continue to split the profession. The Lincoln-Sechrest debate foreshadowed a no less rancorous exchange between two more evaluation luminaries, Dan Stufflebeam (1994) and David Fetterman (1995), about the morality of empowerment evaluation. Stufflebeam fears that such an activist orientation will undermine the credibility and integrity of the field. Fetterman sees evaluator activism as realizing the full potential of the profession to contribute to creating a better world, especially for the disempowered.

The degree of evaluator activism is a continuum, the endpoints of which have been defined by Lincoln and Fetterman on the activist side and by Sechrest and Stufflebeam on the academic side. One perspective places evaluators in the fray, even arguing that we have a moral obligation to acknowledge our power and use it to help those in need who lack power. The other perspective argues that evaluation's integrity and long-term contribution to shaping a better world depend on not being perceived as advocates, even though we push for use. Eleanor Chelimsky (1995a), a longtime champion of evaluation use and the person who conceived the goal "intended use by intended users," took the occasion of her 1995 presidential address to the American Evaluation Association to warn against being perceived as taking sides.

> What seems least well understood, in my judgment, is the dramatically negative and long-term impact on credibility of the appearance of advocacy in an evaluation. There is a vast cemetery out there of unused evaluation findings that have been loudly or quietly rejected because they did not "seem" objective. In short, evaluators' survival in a political environment depends heavily on their credibility, as does the use of their findings in policy. (p. 219)

My own view, focused as always on utility, is that these different stances, indeed the whole continuum of evaluator activism, constitute options for discussion and negotiation with primary intended users. Chelimsky's primary intended users were members of Congress. Fetterman's were, among others, disenfranchised and oppressed Blacks in South African townships.

Both national policymakers and people in poverty can benefit from evaluation, but not in the same ways and not with the same evaluator roles.

Neither more nor less activism, in my judgment, is morally superior. Various degrees of activism involve different ways to practice as an evaluator, often in different arenas. Indeed, how activist to be involves consideration of an evaluation's purpose, decisions about intended users and uses, and the evaluator's own values and commitments, all of which need to be made explicit. The challenge will be to create appreciation for such diversity among those both within and outside the profession who have a single and narrow view of evaluation and its practice. The debate will, and should, go on, for that's how we discover the implications and ramifications of diverse approaches, but I foresee and desire no turning back of the clock to a single dominant perspective.

In their original research on the emerging schism in evaluation, Shadish and Epstein (1987) anticipated that, while the profession's diversity can help make the field unique and exciting, it also has the potential for increasing tensions between activist and academic interests, "tensions that arise because of the different demands and reward structures under which the two groups often operate" (p. 587). They went on to note that such tensions could lead to polarization, citing as evidence the debate within psychology between practicing versus academic clinical psychologists, which has led to a major schism there. They concluded,

> To the extent that the underlying causes are similar—and there are indeed some important relevant similarities in the political and economic characteristics of the two professions—the lesson to evaluation is clear. Program evaluation must continue its efforts to accommodate diverse interests in the same profession. . . . In the long run, evaluation will not be well served by parochialism of any

kind—in patterns of practice or anything else. (p. 588)

As the professional practice of evaluation has become increasingly diverse, the potential roles and relationships have multiplied. Menu 6.1 offers a range of dimensions to consider in defining the evaluator's relationship to intended users. Menu 6.2 presents options that can be considered in negotiations with intended users. The purpose of these menus is to elaborate the multiple roles now available to evaluators and the kind of strategic, contingency thinking involved in making role decisions.

I would hope that these menus help communicate the rich diversity of the field, for I agree with Shadish and Epstein (1987) that "in the long run, evaluation will not be well served by parochialism of any kind—in patterns of practice or anything else" (p. 588). A parochial practice is one that repeats the same patterns over and over. A pluralistic and cosmopolitan practice is one that adapts evaluation practices to new situations.

Situational Evaluation

There is no one best way to conduct an evaluation.

This insight is critical. The design of a particular evaluation depends on the people involved and their situation. *Situational evaluation* is like situational ethics (Fletcher 1966) situational leadership (Blanchard 1986; Hersey 1985), or situated learning: "Action is grounded in the concrete situation in which it occurs" (Anderson et al. 1996:5). The standards and principles of evaluation (see Chapters 1 and 2) provide overall direction, a foundation of ethical guidance, and a commitment to professional competence and integrity, but there are no absolute rules an evaluator can follow to know exactly what to do with specific users in a particular situation. That's why Newcomer and Wholey (1989) concluded in their synthesis of knowledge about evaluation strategies for building high-performance programs: "Prior to an evaluation, evaluators and program managers should work together to define the ideal final product" (p. 202). This means *negotiating* the evaluation's intended and expected uses.

Every evaluation situation is unique. A successful evaluation (one that is useful, practical, ethical, and accurate) emerges from the special characteristics and conditions of a particular situation—a mixture of people, politics, history, context, resources, constraints, values, needs, interests, and chance. Despite the rather obvious, almost trite, and basically commonsense nature of this observation, it is not at all obvious to most stakeholders, who worry a great deal about whether an evaluation is being done "right." Indeed, one common objection stakeholders make to getting actively involved in designing an evaluation is that they lack the knowledge to do it right. The notion that there is one right way to do things dies hard. The right way, from a utilization-focused perspective, is the way that will be meaningful and useful to the specific evaluators and intended users involved, and finding that way requires interaction, negotiation, and situational analysis.

Alkin (1985) identified some 50 factors associated with use. He organized them into four categories:

1. *Evaluator characteristics*, such as commitment to make use a priority, willingness

MENU 6.1

DIMENSIONS AFFECTING EVALUATOR AND USER ENGAGEMENT

1. Relationship with primary intended users

Distant from/ noninteractive	————————	Close to/ highly interactive

2. Control of the evaluation process

Evaluator directed and controlled; evaluator as primary decision maker	————————	Directed by primary intended users; evaluator consults

3. Scope of intended user involvement

Very narrow; primarily as audience for findings	—— Involved /in some parts (usually focus but not methods or analysis) ——	Involved in all aspects of the evauation from start to finish

4. Number of primary intended users and/or stakeholders—engaged

None	—— One —— A few —— Many ——	All constituencies represented

5. Variety of primary intended users engaged

Homogenous	————————	Heterogeneous

Dimensions of heterogeneity:

(a) Position in program (funders, board executives, staff, participants, community members, media, onlookers)
(b) Background variables: cultural/racial/ethnic/gender/social class
(c) Regional: geographically near or far
(d) Evaluation: sophistication and experience
(e) Ideology (political perspective/activism)

6. Time line for the evaluation

Tight deadline; little time for processing with users	————————	Long developmental timeline; time for processing with users

MENU 6.2

Optional Evaluator Roles

Most Likely Primary Users	*Primary Evaluator Roles*	*Dominant Style of Evaluator*	*Most Likely Evaluation Purpose*	*Primary Evaluator Characteristics Affecting Use*
1. Funders Officials Decision makers	Judge	Authoritative	Summative determination of overall merit or worth	Perceived independence Methodological expertise Substantive expertise Perceived neutrality
2. Funders Policymakers Board members	Auditor Inspector Investigator	Independent	Accountability Compliance Adherence to rules	Independence Perceived toughness Detail-oriented Thoroughness
3. Academics Planners Program designer Policy specialists	Researcher	Knowledgeable	Generate generalizable knowledge; truth	Methodological expertise Academic credentials Scholarly status Peer review support
4. Program staff Program executives and administrators Participants	Consultant for program improvement	Interactive Perceptive Insightful	Program improvement Trust	Perceived understanding of program Rapport Insightfulness
5. Diverse stakeholders	Evaluation facilitator	Available Balanced Empathic	Facilitate judgments and recommendations by non-evaluators	Interpersonal skills Group facilitation skills Evaluator knowledge Trust Consensus-building skills

6. Program design team	Team member with evaluation perspective	Participatory Questioning Challenging	Program development	Contribution to team Insightfulness Ability to communicate evaluation perspective Flexibility Analytical leadership
7. Program staff and participants	Collaborator	Involved Supportive Encouraging	Action research and evaluation on groups' own issues; participatory evaluation	Accepting of others Mutual respect Communication skills Enthusiasm Perceived genuineness of collaborative approach
8. Program participants/ community members	Empowerment facilitator	Resource person	Participant self-determination; pursuit of political agenda	Mutual respect Participation Engagement Enabling skills Political savvy
9. Ideological adherents	Supporter of cause	Co-leader Committed	Social justice	Engagement Commitment Political expertise Knowledge of "the system" Integrity Values
10. Future evaluation planners and users	Synthesizer Meta-evaluator Cluster leader	Analytical	Synthesize findings from multiple evaluations Judge quality of evaluations	Professionalism Analytical insightfulness Conceptual brilliance Integrity Adherence to standards

to involve users, political sensitivity, and credibility

2. *User characteristics*, such as interest in the evaluation, willingness to commit time and energy, and position of influence
3. *Contextual characteristics*, such as size of organization, political climate, and existence of competing information
4. *Evaluation characteristics*, such as nature and timing of the evaluation report, relevance of evaluation information, and quality of the data and evaluation

Menu 6.3 offers examples of situations that pose special challenges to evaluation use and the evaluator's role.

Exhibit 6.1 (pages 132-3) is a look at a few of the many situational variables an evaluator may need to be aware of and take into account in conducting a utilization-focused, feasibility-conscious, propriety-oriented, and accuracy-based evaluation.

The situational variables in Exhibit 6.1 are presented in no particular order. Most of them could be broken down into several additional variables. I have no intention of trying to operationalize these dimensions (that is, make them clear, specific, and measurable). The point of presenting them is simply to emphasize and reiterate this: **Situational evaluation means that evaluators have to be prepared to deal with a lot of different people and situations.** If we conceive of just three points (or situations) on each of these dimensions—the two endpoints and a midpoint—then the combinations of these 20 dimensions represent 8,000 unique evaluation situations.

Nor are these static situations. The program you thought was new at the first session turns out to have been created out of and to be a continuation of another program; only the name has been changed to protect the guilty. You thought you were dealing with only one primary decision maker at the outset, and suddenly you have stakeholders coming out your ears, or vice versa. With some programs, I've felt like I've been through all 8,000 situations in the first month.

And, in case 8,000 situations to analyze, be sensitive to, and design evaluations for doesn't seem challenging enough, just add two more points to each dimension—a point between each endpoint and the midpoint. Now, combinations of the five points on all 20 dimensions yield 3,200,000 potentially different situations. Perhaps such complexity helps explain why the slogan that won the hearts of evaluators in attendance at the 1978 Evaluation Network conference in Aspen, Colorado, was Jim Hennes's lament:

> Evaluators do **IT**
> under difficult circumstances.

Of course, one could make the same analysis for virtually any area of decision making, couldn't one? Life is complex, so what's new? First, let's look at what's old. **The evidence from social and behavioral science is that in other areas of decision making, when faced with complex choices and multiple situations, we fall back on a set of rules and standard operating procedures that predetermine what we will do, that effectively short-circuit situational adaptability.** The evidence is that we are running most of the time on preprogrammed tapes. That has always been the function of rules of thumb and scientific paradigms. Faced with a new situation, the evaluation researcher (unconsciously) turns to old and comfortable patterns. This may help explain why so many eval- uators who have rhetorically embraced the philosophy of situational evaluation find that the approaches in which they are trained

MENU 6.3

Examples of Situations That Pose Special Challenges to Evaluation Use and the Evaluator's Role

Situation	*Challenge*	*Special Evaluator Skills Needed*
1. Highly controversial issue	Facilitating different points of view	Conflict resolution skills
2. Highly visible program	Dealing with publicity about the program; reporting findings in a media-circus atmosphere	Public presentation skills Graphic skills Media handling skills
3. Highly volatile program environment	Rapid change in context, issues, and focus	Tolerance for ambiguity Rapid responsiveness Flexibility Being a "quick study"
4. Cross-cultural or international	Including different perspectives, values Being aware of cultural blinders and biases	Cross-culture sensitivity Skills in understanding and incorporating different perspectives
5. Team effort	Managing people	Identifying and using individual skills of team members; team-building skills
6. Evaluation attacked	Preserving credibility	Calm; staying focused on evidence and conclusions
7. Corrupt program	Resolving ethical issues/ upholding standards	Integrity Clear ethical sense Honesty

and with which they are most comfortable *just happen* to be particularly appropriate in each new evaluation situation they confront—time after time after time. Sociologists just happen to find doing a survey appropriate. Economists just happen to feel the situation needs cost-benefit analysis. Psychologists study the situation and decide that—surprise!—testing would be appropriate. And so it goes.

Utilization-focused evaluation is a problem-solving approach that calls for creative adaptation to changed and changing conditions, as opposed to a technical approach, which attempts to mold and define conditions to fit preconceived models of how things should be done. Utilization-focused evaluation involves overcoming what Brightman and Noble (1979) have identified as "the ineffective education of decision scientists." They portray the typical decision scientist (a generic term for evaluators, policy analysts, planners, and so on) as follows:

EXHIBIT 6.1

Examples of Situational Factors in Evaluation That Can Affect Users' Participation and Use

One primary decision maker	*1. Number of stakeholders to be dealt with*	Large number
Formative purpose (improvement)	*2. Purpose of the evaluation*	Summative purpose (funding decision)
New program	*3. History of the program*	Long history
Enthusiasm	*4. Staff attitude toward evaluation*	Resistance
Knows virtually nothing	*5. Staff knowledge about evaluation*	Highly knowledgeable
Cooperative	*6. Program interaction patterns (administration-staff, staff-staff, staff-client)*	Conflict-laden
First time ever	*7. Program's prior evaluation experience*	Seemingly endless experience
High	*8. Staff and participants education levels*	Low
Homogeneous groups	*9. Staff and/or participants' characteristics (pick any 10 you want)*	Heterogeneous groups

hopelessly naive and intellectually arrogant. Naive because they believe that problem solving begins and ends with analysis, and arrogant because they opt for mathematical rigor over results. They are products of their training. Decision science departments appear to have been more effective at training technocrats to deal with structured problems than problem solvers to deal with ill-structured ones. (p. 150)

Narrow technocratic approaches emphasize following rules and standard operating procedures. Creative problem-

One site	*10. Program location*	Multiple sites
No money to speak of	*11. Resources available for evaluation*	Substantial funding
One funding source	*12. Number of sources of program funding*	Multiple funding sources
Simple and unidimensional	*13. Nature of the program treatment*	Complex and multidimensional
Highly standardized and routine	*14. Standardization of treatment*	Highly individualized and nonroutine
Horizontal, little hierarchy, little stratification	*15. Program organizational decision-making structure*	Hierarchical, long chain of command, stratified
Well-articulated, specifically defined	*16. Clarity about evaluation purpose and function*	Ambiguous, broadly defined
Operating information system	*17. Existing data on program*	No existing data
External	*18. Evaluator(s)' relationship to the program*	Internal
Voluntary, self-initiated	*19. Impetus for the evaluation*	Required, forced on program
Long time line, open	*20. Time available for the evaluation*	Short time line, fixed deadline

solving approaches, in contrast, focus on what works and what makes sense in the situation. Standard methods recipe books aren't ignored. They just aren't taken as the final word. New ingredients are added to fit particular tastes. Homegrown or locally available ingredients replace the processed foods of the national supermarket chains, with the attendant risks of both greater failure and greater achievement.

Lawrence Lynn's (1980a) ideal policy analyst bears a striking resemblance to my idea of a creative and responsive utilization-focused evaluator.

Individuals really do have to be interdisciplinary; they have to be highly catholic in their taste for intellectual concepts and ideas and tools. I do not think we are talking so much about acquiring a specific kind of knowledge or a specialist's knowledge in order to deal with environmental issues or energy issues. One does not have to know what a petroleum engineer knows, or what an air quality engineer knows, or what a chemist knows. Rather, *one simply has to be able to ask questions of many disciplines and many professions and know how to use the information.* And what that says is, I think, *one has to be intellectually quite versatile.*

It is not enough to be an economist . . . , an operations research specialist, [or] a statistician. One has to be a little bit of all of those things. One has to have an intuitive grasp of an awful lot of different intellectual approaches, different intellectual disciplines or traditions so that one can range widely in doing one's job of crafting a good analysis, so that you are not stuck with just the tools you know. I think, then, the implication is versatility and an intuitive grasp of a fairly wide range of different kinds of skills and approaches. (p. 88; emphasis added)

Learning to Be Situationally Responsive

Expert evaluators are sophisticated at situation recognition. Such expertise does not develop overnight, nor is it an outcome of training. Expertise comes from practice. Consider expertise in chess as a metaphor for developing situationally responsive expertise in evaluation.

It takes at least 15 years of hard work for even the most talented individuals to become world-class chess masters: what they seem to learn is a repertoire for recognizing types of situations or scripts or intuitive sensibilities and understandings about how these situations will largely unfold. Simon estimates a differential repertoire of 50,000 situation recognitions at the world-class chess level. There is also some increase in overall long-range strategic planning ability—beginners typically are hard pressed to go beyond one move deep; world-class players often anticipate 3 or sometimes 5 future moves in calculating alternative reactions to their moves. . . . One further learning is the capacity to diagnose not just specific game situations but to model or "psyche out" different opponents. (Etheredge 1980:243)

I suggest there's a parallel here to anticipating potential use and knowing how to facilitate it. Etheredge (1980) also found that experienced players develop efficient scanning techniques and the ability to discard unnecessary information. They cultivate what seems like an intuitive sense but is really a practiced sense of where to devote attention. You will be hard-pressed, in my view, to find a better description of evaluation expertise in working with intended users. Effective facilitation involves situation recognition and responsiveness, anticipation, and the ability to analyze people—knowing where, when, and how to focus attention. These are learned and practiced behaviors, a view I assert when someone suggests that utilization-focused evaluation only works for certain personality types.

Being Active-Reactive-Adaptive

In the title of this chapter, I used the phrase "active-reactive-adaptive" to suggest the nature of the consultative interactions that go on between evaluators and intended users. The phrase is meant to be

both descriptive and prescriptive. It describes how real-world decision making actually unfolds. Yet, it is prescriptive in alerting evaluators to consciously and deliberately act, react, and adapt in order to increase their effectiveness in working with stakeholders.

Utilization-focused evaluators are, first of all, active in deliberately and calculatedly identifying intended users and focusing useful questions. They are reactive in listening to intended users and responding to what they learn about the particular situation in which the evaluation unfolds. They are adaptive in altering evaluation questions and designs in light of their increased understanding of the situation and changing conditions. Active-reactive-adaptive evaluators don't impose cookbook designs. They don't do the same thing time after time. They are genuinely immersed in the challenges of each new setting and authentically responsive to the intended users of each new evaluation.

It is the paradox of decision making that effective action is born of reaction. Only when organizations and people take in information from the environment and react to changing conditions can they act on that same environment to reduce uncertainty and increase discretionary flexibility (see Thompson 1967). The same is true for the individual decision maker or for a problem-solving group. Action emerges through reaction and leads to adaptation. The imagery is familiar: thesis-antithesis-synthesis; stimulus-response-change.

This active-reactive-adaptive stance characterizes all phases of evaluator-user interactions, from initially identifying primary intended users to focusing relevant questions, choosing methods, and analyzing results. All phases involve collaborative processes of action-reaction-adaptation as evaluators and intended users consider their options. The menu of choices includes a broad range of methods, evaluation ingredients from bland to spicy, and a variety of evaluator roles: collaborator, trainer, group facilitator, technician, politician, organizational analyst, internal colleague, external expert, methodologist, information broker, communicator, change agent, diplomat, problem solver, and creative consultant. The roles played by an evaluator in any given situation will depend on the evaluation's purpose, the unique constellation of conditions with which the evaluator is faced, **and the evaluator's own personal knowledge, skills, style, values, and ethics.**

The mandate to be active-reactive-adaptive in role-playing provokes protest from those evaluators and intended users who advocate only one narrow role, namely, that the evaluator renders judgment about merit or worth—*nothing else* (Stufflebeam 1994; Scriven 1991a). Clearly, I have a more expansive view of an evaluator's role possibilities and responsibilities. Keeping in mind that the idea of multiple evaluator roles is controversial, let's turn to look at what the evaluator brings to the utilization-focused negotiating table.

Multiple Evaluator Roles and Individual Style

The evaluator as a person in his or her own right is a key part of the situational mix. Each evaluation will be unique in part because individual evaluators are unique. Evaluators bring to the negotiating table their own style, personal history, and professional experience. All of the techniques and ideas presented in this book must be adapted to the style of the individuals using them.

Cousins, Donohue, and Bloom (1996) surveyed North American evaluators to find out what variables correlated with a collaborative style of practice. Organizational affiliation, gender, and primary job responsibility did not differentiate practice and opinion responses. Canadian evaluators reported greater depth of stakeholder involvement than Americans. Most telling, however, were years and depth of experience with collaborative approaches. More experienced evaluators expected more use of their evaluations and reported a greater sense of satisfaction from the collaborative process and greater impacts of the resulting evaluations. In essence, evaluators get better at the active-reactive-adaptive process the more they experience it; and the more they use it, the more they like it and the more impact they believe it has.

Being active-reactive-adaptive explicitly recognizes the importance of the individual evaluator's experience, orientation, and contribution by placing the mandate to be active first in this consulting triangle. Situational responsiveness does not mean rolling over and playing dead (or passive) in the face of stakeholder interests or perceived needs. Just as the evaluator in utilization-focused evaluation does not unilaterally impose a focus and set of methods on a program, so, too, the stakeholders are not set up to impose their initial predilections unilaterally or dogmatically. Arriving at the final evaluation design is a negotiated process that allows the values and capabilities of the evaluator to intermingle with those of intended users.

The utilization-focused evaluator, in being active-reactive-adaptive, is one among many at the negotiating table. At times there may be discord in the negotiating process; at other times harmony. Whatever the sounds, and whatever the themes, the utilization-focused evaluator does not sing alone. He or she is part of a choir made up of primary intended users. There are solo parts, to be sure, but the climatic theme song of utilization-focused evaluation is not Frank Sinatra's "I Did It My Way." Rather, it's the full chorus joining in a unique, situationally specific rendition of "We Did It Our Way."

User Responsiveness and Technical Quality

User responsiveness should not mean a sacrifice of technical quality. Later chapters will discuss in detail the utilization-focused approach to ensuring technical quality. A beginning point is to recognize that standards of technical quality vary for different users and varying situations. The issue is not meeting some absolute research standards of technical quality but, rather, making sure that methods and measures are *appropriate* to the validity and credibility needs of a particular evaluation purpose and specific intended users.

Jennifer Greene (1990) examined in depth the debate about technical quality versus user responsiveness. She found general agreement that both are important but disagreement about the relative priority of each. She concluded that the debate is really about how much to recognize and deal with evaluation's political inherency:

> Evaluators should recognize that tension and conflict in evaluation practice are virtually inevitable, that the demands imposed by most if not all definitions of responsiveness and technical quality (not to mention feasibility and propriety) will characteristically reflect the competing politics and values of the setting. (p. 273)

She then recommended that evaluators "explicate the politics and values" that undergird decisions about purpose, audience, design, and methods. Her recommendation is consistent with utilization-focused evaluation.

Respect for Intended Users

One central value that should undergird the evaluator's active-reactive-adaptive role is respect for all those with a stake in a program or evaluation. In their seminal article on evaluation use, Davis and Salasin (1975) asserted that evaluators were involved inevitably in facilitating change and that "any change model should . . . generally *accommodate* rather than *manipulate* the view of the persons involved" (p. 652). Respectful utilization-focused evaluators do not use their expertise to intimidate or manipulate intended users. Egon Guba (1977) has described in powerful language an archetype that is the antithesis of the utilization-focused evaluator:

> It is my experience that evaluators sometimes adopt a very supercilious attitude with respect to their clients; their presumptuousness and arrogance are sometimes overwhelming. We treat the client as a "child-like" person who needs to be taken in hand; as an ignoramus who cannot possibly understand the tactics and strategies that we will bring to bear; as someone who doesn't appreciate the questions he *ought* to ask until we tell him—and what we tell him often reflects our own biases and interests rather than the problems with which the client is actually beset. The phrase "Ugly American" has emerged in international settings to de-

> scribe the person who enters into a new culture, immediately knows what is wrong with it, and proceeds to foist his own solutions onto the locals. In some ways I have come to think of evaluators as "Ugly Americans." And if what we are looking for are ways to manipulate clients so that they will fall in with *our* wishes and cease to resist our blandishments, I for one will have none of it. (p. 1; emphasis in original)

For others who "will have none of it," there is the alternative of undertaking a utilization-focused evaluation process based on mutual respect between evaluators and intended users.

Internal and External Evaluators

One of the most fundamental issues in considering the role of the evaluator is the location of the evaluator inside or outside the program and organization being evaluated, what has sometimes been called the "in-house" versus "outhouse" issue. The early evaluation literature was aimed primarily at external evaluators, typically researchers who conducted evaluations under contract to funders. External evaluators come from universities, consulting firms, and research organizations or work as independent consultants. The defining characteristic of external evaluators is that they have no long-term, ongoing position within the program or organization being evaluated. They are therefore not subordinated to someone in the organization and not directly dependent on the organization for their job and career.

External evaluators are valuable precisely because they are outside the organization. It is typically assumed that their external status permits them to be more independent, objective, and credible than internal evaluators. Internal evaluations are suspect because, it is presumed, they can be manipulated more easily by administrators to justify decisions or pressured to present positive findings for public relations purposes (House 1986). Of course, external evaluators who want future evaluation contracts are also subject to pressure to produce positive findings. In addition, external evaluators are also typically more costly, less knowledgeable about the nuances and particulars of the local situation, and less able to follow through to facilitate the implementation of recommendations. When external evaluators complete their contract, they may take with them a great deal of knowledge and insight that is lost to the program. That knowledge stays "in-house" with internal evaluators. External evaluators have also been known to cause difficulties in a program through insensitivity to organizational relationships and norms, one of the reasons the work of external evaluators is sometimes called "outhouse" work.

One of the major trends in evaluation during the 1980s was a transition from external to internal evaluation, with Canadian Arnold Love (1991, 1983) documenting and contributing to the development of internal evaluation. At the beginning of the 1970s evaluation was just emerging as a profession. There were fewer distinct evaluation units within government bureaus, human service agencies, and private sector organizations than there are now. School districts had research and evaluation units, but even they contracted out much of the evaluation work mandated by the landmark 1965 Elementary and Secondary Education Act in the United States. As evaluation became more pervasive in the 1970s, as the mandate for evaluation was added to more and more legislation, and as training for evaluators became more available and widespread, internal evaluation units became more common. Now, most federal, state, and local agencies have internal evaluation units; international organizations also have internal evaluation divisions; and it is clear that "internal evaluators can produce evaluations of high quality that meet rigorous standards of objectivity while still performing useful service to administrators if they have previously established an image of an independent but active voice in the organizational structure" (Sonnichsen 1987: 34-35).

Over the years, I have had extensive contact with internal evaluators through training and consulting, working closely with several of them to design internal monitoring and evaluation systems. For the second edition of this book, I interviewed 10 internal evaluators who I knew used a utilization-focused approach. Their comments about how they have applied utilization-focused principles offer insights into the world of the internal evaluator and illuminate research findings about effective approaches to internal evaluation (Winberg 1991; Lyon 1989; Huberty 1988; Kennedy 1983).

Themes From Internal Evaluators

1. **Actively involving stakeholders within the organization can be difficult** because evaluation is often perceived by both superiors and subordinates as the job of the evaluator. The internal evaluator is typically expected to *do* evaluations, not facilitate an evaluation process involving others. Internal evaluators who have had success involving others have had to work hard at finding special incentives to attract participation in the evaluation process. One internal evaluator commented,

> My director told me he doesn't want to spend time thinking about evaluation. That's why he hired me. He wants me to "anticipate his information needs." I've had to find ways to talk with him about his interests and information needs without explicitly telling him he's helping me focus the evaluation. I guess you could say I kind of involve him without his really knowing he's involved.

2. **Internal evaluators are often asked by superiors for public relations information rather than evaluation.** The internal evaluator may be told, "I want a report for the legislature proving our program is effective." It takes clear conviction, subtle diplomacy, and an astute understanding of how to help superiors appreciate evaluation to keep internal evaluation responsibilities from degenerating into public relations. One mechanism used by several internal evaluators to increase support for real evaluation rather than public relations is establishing an evaluation advisory committee, including influential people from outside the organization, to provide independent checks on the integrity of internal evaluations.

3. **Internal evaluators get asked to do lots of little data-gathering and report-writing tasks** that are quite time consuming but too minor to be considered meaningful evaluation. For example, if someone in the agency wants a quick review of what other states are doing about some problem, the internal evaluator is an easy target for the task. Such assignments can become so pervasive that it's difficult to have time for longer-term, more meaningful evaluation efforts.

4. **Internal evaluators are often excluded from major decisions** or so far removed from critical information networks that they don't know about new initiatives or developments in time to build in an evaluation perspective up front. One internal evaluator explained,

> We have separate people doing planning and evaluation. I'm not included in the planning process and usually don't even see the plan until it's approved. Then they expect me to add on an evaluation. It's a real bitch to take a plan done without any thought of evaluation and add an evaluation without screwing up or changing the plan. They think evaluation is something you do at the end rather than think about from the start. It's damn hard to break through these perceptions. Besides, I don't want to do the planners' job, and they don't want to do my job, but we've got to find better ways of making the whole thing work together. That's my frustration. . . . It takes me constantly bugging them, and sometimes they think I'm encroaching on their turf. Some days I think, "Who needs the hassle?" even though I know it's not as useful just to tack on the evaluation at the end.

5. **Getting evaluation used takes a lot of follow-through.** One internal evaluator explained that her job was defined as data gathering and report writing without consideration of following up to see if report recommendations were adopted. That's not part of her job description, and it takes time and some authority. She commented,

> How do I get managers to use a report if my job is just to write the report? But they're above me. I don't have the authority to ask them in six months what they've done. I wrote a follow-up memo once reminding managers about recommendations in an evaluation and some of them didn't like it at all, although a couple of the good ones said they were glad I reminded them.

Another internal evaluator told me he had learned how to follow up informally. He has seven years' experience as an internal human services evaluator. He said,

> At first I just wrote a report and figured my job was done. Now, I tell them when we review the initial report that I'll check back in a few months to see how things are going. I find I have to keep pushing, keep reminding, or they get busy and just file the report. We're gradually getting some understanding that our job should include some follow-up. Mostly it's on a few things that we decide are really important. You can't do it all.

Internal Role Definitions

The themes from internal evaluators indicate the importance of carefully defining the job to include attention to use. When and if the internal evaluation job is defined primarily as writing a report and filling out routine reporting forms, the ability of the evaluator to influence use is quite limited. When and if the internal evaluator is organizationally separated from managers and planners, it is difficult to establish collaborative arrangements that facilitate use. Thus, a utilization-focused approach to internal evaluation will often require a redefinition of the position to include responsibility for working with intended users to develop strategies for acting on findings.

One of the most effective internal evaluation units I've encountered was in the U.S. Federal Bureau of Investigation (FBI). This unit reported directly to the bureau's deputy director. The evaluation unit director had direct access to the director of the FBI in both problem identification and discussion of findings. The purpose of the unit was program improvement. Reports were written *only* for internal use; there was no public relations use of reports. Public relations was the function of a different unit. The internal evaluation staff was drawn from experienced FBI agents. They thus had high credibility with agents in the field. They also had the status and authority of the director's office behind them. The evaluation unit had an operations handbook that clearly delineated responsibilities and procedures. Evaluation proposals and designs were planned and reviewed with intended users. Multiple methods were used. Reports were written with use in mind. Six months after the report had been written and reviewed, follow-up was formally undertaken to find out if recommendations had been implemented. The internal evaluators had a strong commitment to improving FBI programs and clear authority to plan, conduct, and report evaluations in ways that would have an impact on the organization, including follow-up to make sure recommendations approved by the director were actually implemented.

Based on his experience directing the FBI's internal evaluation unit, Dick Sonnichsen (1988) formulated what he has called *internal advocacy evaluation* as a style of organizational development:

> Internal evaluators have to view themselves as change agents and participants in policy formulation, migrating from the traditional position of neutrality to an activist role in the organizational decision-making process. The practice of *Advocacy Evaluation* positions internal evaluators to become active participants in developing and implementing organizational improvements. Operating under an advocacy philosophy, evaluation becomes a tool for change and a vehicle for evaluators to influence the organization. (p. 141; emphasis in original)

An evaluation advocate is not a cheerleader for the program, but rather, a champion of evaluation use. This is sometimes called *persuasive use* in which "advocates work actively in the politics of the organization to get results used" (Caracelli and Preskill 1996).

> The new evaluator is a program advocate—not an advocate in the sense of an ideologue willing to manipulate data and to alter findings to secure next year's funding. The new evaluator is someone who believes in and is interested in helping programs and organizations succeed. At times the program advocate evaluator will play the traditional critic role: challenging basic program assumptions, reporting lackluster performance, or identifying inefficiencies. The difference, however, is that criticism is not the end of performance-oriented evaluation; rather, it is part of a larger process of program and organizational improvement, a process that receives as much of the evaluator's attention and talents as the criticism function. (Bellavita et al. 1986:289)

The roles of champion, advocate, and change agent (Sonnichsen 1994) are just some of the many roles open to internal evaluators. Love (1991) has identified a number of both successful and unsuccessful roles for internal evaluators (see Exhibit 6.2). Carefully defining the role of internal evaluator is a key to effective and credible internal evaluation use.

Part of defining the role is labeling it in a meaningful way. Consider this reflection from internal school district evaluator Nancy Law (1996), whose office was re-

EXHIBIT 6.2
Successful and Unsuccessful Roles of Internal Evaluators

Successful Roles	*Unsuccessful Roles*
Management consultant	Spy
Decision support	Hatchet carrier
Management information resource	Fear-inspiring dragon
Systems generalist	Number cruncher
Expert troubleshooter	Organizational conscience
Advocate for/champion of evaluation use	Organizational memory
Systematic planner	Public relations officer

SOURCE: Adapted and expanded from Love 1991:9.

named from Research and Evaluation to Accountability Department.

> This title change has become meaningful for me personally. It was easy to adopt the name, but harder to live up to it. . . .
>
> Now, I am learning that *I* am the one accountable—that my job doesn't end when the report is finished and presented. My role continues as I work with others outside research to create changes that I have recommended. Oh, yes, we still perform the types of research/evaluation tasks done previously, but there is a greater task still to be done—that of convincing those who need to make changes to move ahead! Put simply, when we took a different name, we became something different and better. (p. 1)

Internal-External Evaluation Combinations

In workshops, I am often asked to compare the relative advantages and disadvantages of internal versus external evaluations. After describing some of the differences along the lines of the preceding discussion, I like to point out that the question is loaded by implying that internal and external approaches are mutually exclusive. Actually, there are a good many possible combinations of internal *and* external evaluations that may be more desirable and more cost-effective than either a purely internal *or* purely external evaluation.

Accreditation processes are a good example of an internal-external combination. The internal group collects the data and arranges them so that the external group can come in, inspect the data collected by the internal group, sometimes collect additional information on their own, and pass judgment on the program.

There are many ways in which an evaluation can be set up so that some external group of respected professionals and evaluators guarantees the validity and fairness of the evaluation process while the people internal to the program actually collect and/or analyze the evaluation data. The cost savings of such an approach can be substantial while still allowing the evaluation to have basic credibility and legitimacy through the blessing of the external review committee.

I worked for several years with one of the leading chemical dependency treatment centers in the country, the Hazelden Foundation of Minnesota. The foundation has established a rigorous evaluation process that involves data collection at the point of entry into the program and then follow-up questionnaires 6 months, 12 months, and 24 months after leaving the program. Hazelden's own research and evaluation department collects all of the data. My responsibility as an external evaluator was to monitor that data collection periodically to make sure that the established procedures were being followed correctly. I then worked with the program decision makers to identify the kind of data analysis that was desirable. They performed the data analysis with their own computer resources. They sent the data to me, and I wrote the annual evaluation report. They participated in analyzing, interpreting, and making judgments about the data, but for purposes of legitimacy and credibility, the actual writing of the final report was done by me.

This internal/external combination is sometimes extended one step further by having still another layer of external professionals and evaluators pass judgment on the quality and accuracy of the evaluation final report through a *meta-evaluation* process—evaluating the evaluation based on the profession's standards and principles. Indeed, the revised standards for evaluation (Joint Committee 1994:A12) prescribe meta-evaluation so that stakeholders have an independent credible review of an evaluation's strengths and weaknesses. Such an effort will be most meaningful and cost-beneficial for large-scale summative evaluations of major policy importance.

When orchestrating an internal-external combination, one danger to watch for is that the external group may impose unmanageable and overwhelming data collection procedures on the internal people. I saw this happen in an internal-external model with a group of school districts in Canada. The external committee set as the standard doing "comprehensive" data collection at the local school level, including data on learning outcomes, staff morale, facilities, curriculum, the school lunch program, the library, parent reactions, the perceptions of local businesspeople, analysis of the school bus system, and so on. After listening to all of the things the external committee thought should be done, the internal folks dubbed it the Internal-External-*Eternal* model of evaluation.

The point is that a variety of internal-external combinations are possible to combine the lower costs of internal data collection with the higher credibility of external review. In working out the details of internal-external combinations, care will need to be taken to achieve an appropriate and mutually rewarding balance based on a collaborative commitment to the standards of utility, feasibility, propriety, and accuracy.

Evaluation as Results-Oriented Leadership

Most writings about internal evaluation assume a separate unit or specialized position with responsibility to conduct evaluations. An important new direction in evaluation is to treat evaluation as a leadership function of all managers and program directors in the organization. The person responsible for internal evaluation then plays a facilitative, resource, and training function in support of managers rather

EXHIBIT 6.3
Four Functions of Results-Oriented, Reality-Testing Leadership

- Create and nurture a results-oriented, reality-testing culture.
- Lead in deciding what outcomes to commit to and hold yourselves accountable for.
- Make measurement of outcomes thoughtful, meaningful, and credible.
- Use the results—and model for others serious use of results.

than spending time actually conducting evaluations. The best example of this approach I've worked with and observed up close was the position of Associate Administrator for Performance Measurement and Evaluation in Hennepin County, Minnesota (Minneapolis). The county had no internal evaluation office. Rather, this senior position, as part of the County Executive team, had responsibility to infuse evaluation systems throughout the county, in every department and program. The framework called for a results-oriented approach that was "thoughtful, useful, and credible" (Knapp 1995). Every manager in the county received training in how to build outcomes evaluation into ongoing program processes. Performance measurement was tied to reporting and budgeting systems. What made this approach to internal evaluation work, in my judgment, was threefold: (1) Results-oriented performance measurement was defined as a leadership function of every county manager, not just a reporting function to be delegated as far down as possible in the department; (2) the overall responsibility for evaluation resided at the highest level of the organization, in the executive team, with direct access to the County Board of Commissioners backed up by public commitments to use evaluation for decision making and budgeting; and (3) because of the prior two commitments, a person of great competence and dedication was selected to fill the Associate Administrator Performance Measurement and Evaluation position, after a national search.

These patterns of effectiveness stand out because so often internal evaluation is delegated to the lowest level in an organization and treated as a clerical function. Indeed, being given an evaluation assignment is often a form of punishment agency directors use, or a way of giving deadwood staff something meaningless to occupy themselves with. It is clear that, for internal evaluators to be useful and credible, they must have high status in the organization and real power to make evaluation meaningful.

Elevating the status of evaluation in this way is most likely to occur when evaluation is conceived of as a leadership function rather than a low-level clerical or data management task. Exhibit 6.3 presents the four functions of results-oriented leadership. In this framework, evaluation becomes a senior management responsibility focused on decision-oriented use rather than a data-collection task focused on routine internal reporting.

There is a downside to elevating the status and visibility of internal evaluators: They become more politically vulnerable. To complete the example cited above, when the county administrator of Hennepin County departed, the Associate Administrator for Performance Measurement and Evaluation position was terminated. Politically, the position was dependent on the county's chief executive officer. When that person left, the internal evaluation position became expendable as part of the subsequent political shakeout. As Chapter 15 will discuss, the Achilles' heel of utilization-focused evaluation is turnover of primary intended users.

Going Bananas

Before closing this chapter, it seems appropriate to provide a situation for situational analysis, a bit of a practice exercise, if you will. Consider, then, the evaluation relevance of the following story repeated from generation to generation by schoolchildren.

> *A man walking along the street notices another man on the other side with bananas in his ears. He shouts, "Hey, mister, why do you have bananas in your ears?" Receiving no response, he pursues the man, calling again as he approaches, "Pardon me, but why have you got bananas in your ears?" Again there is no response.*
>
> *He catches up to the man, puts his hand on his shoulder, and says "Do you realize you have bananas in your ears?"*
>
> *The gentleman in question stops, looks puzzled, takes the bananas out of his ears, and says, "I'm sorry, what did you ask? I couldn't hear you because I have bananas in my ears."*

Now for the situational analysis. How might you use this story with a group of intended users to make a point about the nature of evaluation? What point(s) could the story be used to illustrate (metaphorically)?

What are the implications of the story for evaluation under four different conditions:

1. If the man with the bananas in his ears is a stakeholder and the man in pursuit is an evaluator
2. If the banana man is an evaluator, and the man in pursuit is a stakeholder
3. If both are primary stakeholders and the evaluator observes this scene
4. Both are evaluators observed by a stakeholder

It is just such situational variations that make strategic, contingency thinking and evaluator responsiveness so important — and so challenging.

7

Beyond the Goals Clarification Game

Focusing on Outcomes

Mulla Nasrudin was a Sufi guru. A king who enjoyed Nasrudin's company, and also liked to hunt, commanded him to accompany him on a bear hunt. Nasrudin was terrified.

When Nasrudin returned to his village, someone asked him: "How did the Hunt go?"

"Marvelously!"

"How many bears did you see?"

"None."

"How could it have gone marvelously, then?"

"When you are hunting bears, and you are me, seeing no bears at all is a marvelous experience."

—Shah 1964:61

Evaluation of the Bear Project

If this tale were updated by means of an evaluation report, it might read something like this:

Under the auspices of His Majesty's Ministry of the Interior, Department of Natural Resources, Section on Hunting, Office of Bears, field observers studied the relationship between the number of bears sighted on a hunt and the number of bears shot on a hunt. Having hypothesized a direct, linear relationship between the sighting of bears and killing of bears, data were collected on a recent royal hunting expedition. The small sample size limits generalizability, but the results support the hypothesis at the 0.001 level of statistical significance. Indeed, the correlation is perfect. The number of bears sighted was zero and the number killed was zero. In no case was a bear killed without first being sighted. We therefore recommend new Royal regulations requiring that bears first be sighted before they are killed.

Respectfully submitted,
The Incomparable Mulla Nasrudin
Royal Evaluator

Whose Goals Will Be Evaluated?

Although Nasrudin's evaluation bares certain flaws, it shares one major trait with almost all other reports of this genre: Namely, it is impossible to tell whether it answers anyone's question. Who decided that the goal evaluated should be the number of bears killed? Perhaps the hunt's purpose was a heightened sensitivity to nature, or a closer relationship between Nasrudin and the king, or reducing Nasrudin's fear of bears, or an increase in the king's power over Nasrudin. It may even be possible (likely!) that different participants in the hunt had different goals. Nasrudin perceived a "marvelous" outcome. Other stakeholders, with different goals, might have concluded otherwise.

In utilization-focused evaluation, the primary intended users determine whose goals will be evaluated if they decide that evaluating goal attainment will be the focus of the evaluation. There are other ways of focusing an evaluation, as we'll see, but first, let's review the traditional centrality of goal attainment in evaluation.

The Centrality of Goals in Evaluation

Traditionally, evaluation has been synonymous with measuring goal attainment (Morris and Fitz-Gibbon 1978). Peter Rossi (1972) has stated that "a social welfare program (or for that matter any program) which does not have clearly specified goals cannot be evaluated without specifying some measurable goals. This statement is obvious enough to be a truism" (p. 18). In a major review of the evaluation literature in education, Worthen and Sanders (1973) concluded that "if evaluators agree in anything, it is that program objectives written in unambiguous terms are useful information for any evaluation study" (p. 231). Carol Weiss (1972b) observed that

> the traditional formulation of the evaluation question is: To what extent is the program succeeding in reaching its goals? . . . The goal must be clear so that the evaluator knows what to look for. . . . Thus begins the long, often painful process of getting people to state goals in terms that are *clear, specific*, and *measurable*. (pp. 74-76; emphasis in original)

As the preceding quotes illustrate, the evaluation literature is replete with serious treatises on the centrality of program goals, and this solemnity seems to carry over into evaluators' work with program staff. There may be no more deadly way to begin an evaluation effort than assembling program staff to identify and clarify program goals and objectives. If evaluators are second only to tax collectors in the hearts of program staff, I suspect that it is not because staff fear evaluators' judgments about program success, but because they hate constant questioning about goals.

The Goals Clarification Game

Evaluators frequently conduct goals clarification meetings like the Twenty Questions game played at parties. Someone thinks of an object in the room and then the players are allowed 20 questions to guess what it is. In the goals clarification game, the evaluator has an object in mind (a clear, specific, and measurable goal). Program staff are the players. The game begins with the staff generating some statement they think is a goal. The evaluator scrutinizes the statement for clarity, specificity, and measurability, usually judging the staff's effort inadequate. This process is repeated in successive tries until the game ends in one of three ways: (1) The staff gives up (so the evaluator wins and writes the program goals for staff); (2) the evaluator gives up (so the staff gets by with vague, fuzzy, and unmeasurable goals); or (3) in rare cases, the game ends when staff actually stumbles on a statement that reasonably approximates what the evaluator had in mind.

Why do program staff typically hate this game so much?

1. They have played the game hundreds of times, not just for evaluators, but for funders and advisory boards, in writing proposals, and even among themselves.

2. They have learned that, when playing the game with an evaluator, the evaluator almost always wins.
3. They come out of the game knowing that they appear fuzzy-minded and inept to the evaluator.
4. It is a boring game.
5. It is an endless game because each new evaluator comes to the game with a different object in mind. (Clarity, specificity, and measurability are not clear, specific, and measurable criteria, so each evaluator can apply a different set of rules in the game.)

Among experienced program staff, evaluators may run into countering strategies like the goals clarification shuffle. Like many dance steps (e.g., the Harlem shuffle, the hustle) this technique has the most grace and style when executed simultaneously by a group. The goals clarification shuffle involves a sudden change in goals and priorities after the evaluator has developed measuring instruments and a research design. The choreography is dazzling. The top-priority program goal is moved two spaces to either the right or left and four spaces backward. Concurrently, all other goals are shuffled with style and subtlety, the only stipulation being that the first goal end up somewhere in the middle, with other goals reordered by new criteria.

The goals clarification shuffle first came into national prominence in 1969 when it was employed as a daring counterthrust to the Westinghouse-Ohio State University Head Start Evaluation. That study evaluated cognitive and affective outcomes of the Head Start Program and concluded that Head Start was largely ineffective (Cicarelli 1971; Westinghouse Learning Corporation 1969). However, as soon as the final report was published, the goals clarification shuffle was executed before enthusiastic Congressional audiences, showing that Head Start's health, nutrition, resource redistribution, cultural, and community goals ought to have been in the spotlight (see Evans 1971:402; Williams and Evans 1969). Thus, despite negative evaluation findings, Congress expanded the Head Start program, and the evaluators were thrown on the defensive. (It was about this same time that serious concerns over nonuse of evaluation findings started to be heard on a national scale.)

Conflict Over Goals and the Delphi Counter

Not all goals clarification exercises resemble dances. Often, the more fitting metaphor is war. Conflict over program goals among different stakeholder groups is common. For example, in criminal justice programs, battles are waged over whether the purpose of a program is punitive (punish criminal offenders for wrongdoing), custodial (keep criminal offenders off the streets), or rehabilitative (return offenders to society after treatment). In education and training programs, conflicts often emerge over whether the priority goal is attitude change or behavior change. In welfare agencies, disagreements can be found over whether the primary purpose is to get clients off welfare or out of poverty, and whether the focus should be long-term change or short-term crisis intervention (Conte 1996). In health settings, staff dissension may emerge over the relative emphasis to be placed on preventive versus curative medical practice. Chemical dependency programs are often enmeshed in controversy over whether the desired outcome is sobriety or responsible use. Even police and fire departments can get caught in controversy about the purposes and actual effects of sirens, with critics arguing that they're more a nuisance than a help (Perlman 1996). Virtually any time a group of people assemble to determine program goals, conflict can emerge, resulting in a lengthy, frustrating, and inconclusive meeting.

For inexperienced evaluators, conflicts among stakeholders can be unnerving. Once, early in my career, a goals clarification session erupted into physical violence between a school board member and the district's internal evaluator. The novice evaluator can lose credibility by joining one side or the other. More experienced evaluators have learned to remain calm and neutral, sometimes suggesting that multiple goals be evaluated, thereby finessing the need for consensus about program priorities.

A more elaborate counter to goals conflict is the use of some kind of formal ranking approach such as the Delphi Technique (Dalkey 1969; Helmer 1966), especially where there are large numbers of stakeholders and many possible priorities.

> The Delphi technique, a method of developing and improving group consensus, was originally used at the Rand Corporation to arrive at reliable prediction about the future of technology; hence its oracular name. . . . Delphi essentially refers to a series of intensive interrogations of samples of individuals (most frequently, experts) by means of mailed questionnaires concerning some important problem or question; the mailings are interspersed with controlled feedback to the participants. The responses in each round of questioning are gathered by an intermediary, who summarizes and returns the information to each participant, who may then revise his own opinions and ratings. . . . However antagonistic the initial positions and complex the questions under analysis—competing opinions apparently converge and synthesize when this technique is used. (Rosenthal 1976:121)

The trick to managing conflict with this technique is that the stakeholders never meet face to face. Thus, disagreements and arguments never get a chance to surface on an interpersonal level. Individual responses remain confidential.

> The technique has proved so successful in producing consensus . . . it is now often adopted in many kinds of situations where convergence of opinion is advisable or desirable . . . avoiding as it does the sundry prima donna behaviors that may vitiate roundtable discussions. (Rosenthal 1976:121-22)

The strength of the Delphi approach—lack of face-to-face interaction—is also its weakness. The process fails to deal with real stakeholder power issues and divergent interests. If those issues aren't dealt with early in the evaluation, they will likely resurface later and threaten the evaluation's credibility and utility.

In some instances, an evaluator may encounter open warfare over goals and values. A "goals war" usually occurs when two or more strong coalitions are locked in battle to determine which group will control the future direction of some public policy or program. Such wars involve highly emotional issues and deeply held values, such as conflicting views on abortion or sex education for teenagers.

Evaluation of school busing programs to achieve racial balance offers an example rich with conflict. By what criteria ought busing programs be evaluated? Changed racial attitudes? Changed interracial behaviors? Improved student achievement? Degree of parent involvement? Access to educational resources? All are candidates for

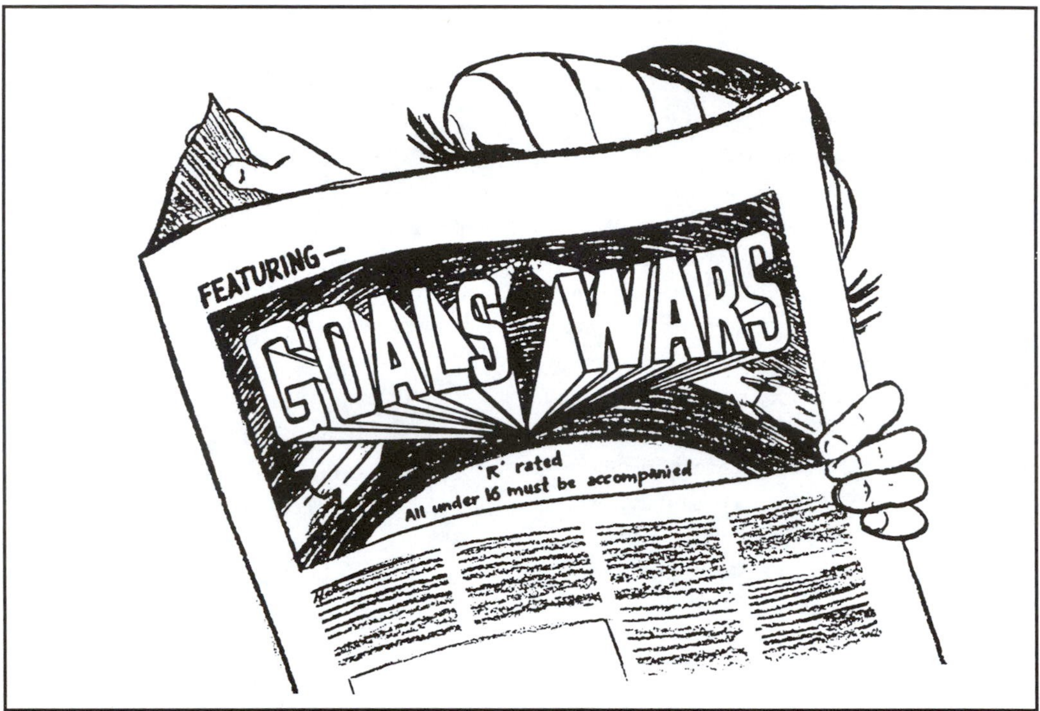

the honor of primary program goal. Is school busing supposed to achieve desegregation (representative proportions of minority students in all schools) or integration (positive interracial attitudes, cooperation, and interaction)? Many communities, school boards, and school staffs are in open warfare over these issues. Central to the battles fought are basic disagreements about what evaluation criteria to apply (see Cohen and Weiss 1977; Cohen and Garet 1975).

Evaluability Assessment and Goals Clarification

Evaluators have gotten heavily involved in goals clarification because, when we are invited in, we seldom find a statement of clear, specific, prioritized, and measurable goals. This can take novice evaluators by surprise if they think that their primary task will be formulating an evaluation design for already established goals. Even where goals exist, they are frequently unrealistic, having been exaggerated to secure funding. One reason evaluability assessment has become an important preevaluation tool is that, by helping programs get ready for evaluation, it acknowledges the common need for a period of time to work with program staff, administrators, funders, and participants on clarifying goals—making them realistic, meaningful, agreed on, and evaluable (Wholey 1994; Smith 1989). Evaluability assessment often includes fieldwork and interviews to determine how much consensus there is among various stakeholders about goals and to identify where differences lie. Based on this kind of contextual analysis, an evaluator can work with primary intended users to plan a strategy for goals clarification.

When an evaluability assessment reveals broad aims and fuzzy goals, it's important to understand what role goals are understood to play in the program. Fuzzy goals actually characterize much human cognition and reasoning (Zadeh et al. 1975:ix). Laboratory experiments suggest that fuzzy conceptualizing may be typical of half the population (Kochen 1975:407). No wonder evaluators have so much trouble getting clear, specific, and measurable goals! Carol Weiss (1972b) has commented in this regard:

> Part of the explanation [for fuzzy goals] probably lies in practitioners' concentration on concrete matters of program functioning and their pragmatic mode of operation. They often have an intuitive rather than an analytical approach to program development. But there is also a sense in which ambiguity serves a useful function; it may mask underlying divergences in intent . . . glittering generalities that pass for goal statements are meant to satisfy a variety of interests and perspectives. (p. 27)

Thus, evaluators have to figure out if administrators and staff are genuinely fuzzy about what they're attempting to accomplish, or if they're simply being shrewd in not letting the evaluator (or others) discover their *real* goals, or if they're trying to avoid conflict through vagueness.

Fuzzy goals, then, may be a conscious strategy for avoiding an outbreak of goals wars among competing or conflicting interests. In such instances, the evaluation may be focused on important questions, issues, and concerns without resort to clear, specific, and measurable objectives. However, more often than not in my experience, the difficulty turns out to be a conceptual problem rather than deviousness.

From a utilization-focused point of view, the challenge is to calculate how early interactions in the evaluation process will affect later use. Typically, it's not useful to ignore goals conflict, accept poorly formulated or unrealistic goals, or let the evaluator assume responsibility for writing clear, specific, and measurable goals. Primary intended users need to be involved in assessing how much effort to put into goals clarification. In doing so, both evaluators and primary intended users do well to heed the *evaluation standard on political viability*:

> The evaluation should be planned and conducted with anticipation of the different positions of various interest groups, so that their cooperation may be obtained, and so that possible attempts by any of these groups to curtail evaluation operations or to bias or misapply the results can be averted or counteracted. (Joint Committee on Standards 1994:F2)

There are alternatives to goals-based evaluation, alternatives we'll consider in the next chapter. First, let's examine how to work with intended users who want to focus on goals and results.

Communicating About Goals and Results

Part of the difficulty, I am convinced, is the terminology: *goals and objectives*. These very words can intimidate staff. Goals and objectives have become daunting weights that program staff feel around their necks, burdening them, slowing their efforts, and impeding rather than advancing their progress. Helping staff clarify their purpose and direction may mean avoiding use of the term *goals and objectives*.

I've found program staff quite animated and responsive to the following kinds of questions: What are you trying to achieve with your clients? If you are successful, how will your clients be different after the program than they were before? What kinds of changes do you want to see in your clients? When your program works as you want it to, how do clients *behave* differently? What do they say differently? What would I see in them that would tell me they are different? Program staff can often provide quite specific answers to these questions, answers that reveal their caring and involvement with the client change process, yet when the same staff are asked to specify their goals and objectives, they freeze.

After querying staff about what results they hope to accomplish with program participants, I may then tell them that what they have been telling me constitutes their goals and objectives. This revelation often brings considerable surprise. They often react by saying, "But we haven't said anything about what we would count." This, as clearly as anything, I take as evidence of how widespread the confusion is between the conceptualization of goals and their measurement. Help program staff and other intended users be realistic and concrete about goals and objectives, but don't make them hide what they are really trying to do because they're not sure how to write a formally acceptable statement of goals and objectives, or because they don't know what measurement instruments might be available to get at some of the important things they are trying to do. Instead, take them through a process that focuses on achieving outcomes and results rather than writing goals. The difference, it turns out, can be huge.

Focusing on Outcomes and Results

In the minds of many program people, from board members to front-line staff and participants, goals are abstract statements of ideals written to secure funding—meant to inspire, but never achieved. Consider this poster on the wall of the office of a program I evaluated: **The greatest danger is not that we aim too high and miss, but that our goal is too low and we attain it.** For the director of this program, goals were something you put in proposals and plans, and hung on the wall, then went about your business.

Let me illustrate the difference between traditional program goals and a focus on participant outcomes with plans submitted by county units to the Minnesota Department of Human Services (MDHS).[1] The plans required statements of outcomes. Each statement below promises something, but that something is not a change in client functioning, status, or well-being. These statements reveal how people in social services have been trained to think about program goals. My comments, following each goal, are meant to illustrate how to help program leaders and other intended evaluation users reframe traditional goals to focus on participant outcomes.

Problematic Outcome Examples

1. To continue implementation of a case management system to maintain continued contact with clients before, during, and after treatment.

   Comment: Continued implementation of the system is the goal. And what is promised for the client? "Continued contact."

2. Case management services will be available to all persons with serious and persistent mental illness who require them.

   Comment: This statement aims at availability—a service delivery improvement. Easily accessible services could be available 24 hours a day, but with what outcomes?

3. To develop needed services for chronically chemically dependent clients.

   Comment: This statement focuses on program services rather than the client outcomes. My review of county plans revealed that most managers focus planning at the program delivery level, that is, the program's goals, rather than how clients' lives will be improved.

4. To develop a responsive, comprehensive crisis intervention plan.

   Comment: A plan is the intended outcome. I found that many service providers confuse planning with getting something done. The characteristics of the plan—"responsive, comprehensive"— reveal nothing about results for clients.

5. Develop a supportive, family-centered, empowering, capacity-building intervention system for families and children.

   Comment: This goal statement has all the latest human services jargon, but, carefully examined, the statement doesn't commit to empowering any families or actually enhancing the capacity of any clients.

6. Expand placement alternatives.

   Comment: More alternatives is the intended result, but to what end? Here is another system-level goal that carries the danger of making placement an end in itself rather than a means to client improvement.

7. County clients will receive services which they value as appropriate to their needs and helpful in remediating their concerns.

   Comment: Client satisfaction can be an important outcome, but it's rarely sufficient by itself. Especially in tax-supported programs, taxpayers and policymakers want more than happy clients. They want clients to have jobs, be productive, stay sober, parent effectively, and so on. Client satisfaction needs to be connected to other desired outcomes.

8. Improve ability of adults with severe and persistent mental illness to obtain employment.

   Comment: Some clients remain for years in programs that enhance their ability to obtain employment—without ever getting a job.

9. Adults with serious and persistent mental illness will engage in a process to function effectively in the community.

   Comment: Engaging in the process is as much as this aims for, in contrast to clients actually functioning effectively in the community.

10. Adults with developmental disabilities will participate in programs to begin making decisions and exercising choice.

    Comment: Program participation is the stated focus. This leads to counting how many people show up rather than how many make meaningful decisions and exercise real choice. A client can participate in a program aimed at teaching decision-making skills, and can even learn those skills, yet never be permitted to make real decisions.

11. Each developmentally disabled consumer (or their substitute decision maker) will identify ways to assist them to remain connected, maintain, or develop natural supports.

 Comment: This goal is satisfied, as written, if each client has a list of potential connections. The provider, of course, can pretty much guarantee composition of such a list. The real outcome: Clients who are connected to a support group of people.

12. Adults in training and rehab will be involved in an average of 120 hours of community integration activities per quarter.

 Comment: Quantitative and specific, but the outcome stated goes only as far as being involved in *activities*, not actually being integrated into the community.

13. Key indicators of intended results and client outcomes for crisis services:
 - Number of patients served
 - Number of patient days and the average length of stay
 - Source of referrals to the crisis unit and referrals provided to patients at discharge

 Comment: Participation numbers, not client outcomes.

14. Minimize hospitalizations of people with severe and persistent mental illness.

 Comment: This is a system level outcome that is potentially dangerous. One of the premises of results-oriented management reviewed in Chapter 1 is that "what gets measured gets done." An easy way to attain this desired outcome is simply not to refer or admit needy clients to the hospital. That will minimize hospitalizations (a system-level outcome) but may not help clients in need. A more appropriate outcome focus would be that these clients function effectively. If that outcome is attained, they won't need hospitalizations.

15. Improve quality of child protection intervention services.

 Comment: I found a lot of outcome statements aimed at enhancing quality. Ironically, quality can be enhanced by improving services without having an impact on client outcomes. Licensing and accrediting standards often focus on staff qualifications and site characteristics (indicators of quality), but seldom require review of what program participants achieve.

The point of reviewing these examples has been to show the kinds of goal statements an evaluator may encounter when beginning to work with a program. A utilization-focused evaluator can help intended users review plans and stated goals to see if they include an outcomes focus. There's nothing wrong with program level (e.g., improve access or quality) or system level (e.g., reduce costs) goals, but such goals ought to connect to outcomes for clients. An evaluator can facilitate discussion of why, in the current political environment, one hears increased demand for "outcomes-based" management and program funding (MDHS 1996; Behn 1995; ICMA 1995; Knapp 1995; Schalock 1995; Schorr 1993; Brizius and Campbell 1991; Williams, Webb, and Phillips 1991; Carver 1990). Evaluators need to provide technical assistance in helping program planners, managers, and other potential evaluation users understand the difference between a participant outcomes approach and traditional program or system goals approaches. In particular, they need assistance understanding the difference between service-focused goals versus client-focused outcome goals. Exhibit 7.1 com-

EXHIBIT 7.1
Service-Focused Versus Client-Focused Outcome Evaluation: Examples From Parenting Programs

Service-Focused	*Client-Focused Outcome*
Provide coordinated case management services with public health to pregnant adolescents	Pregnant adolescents will give birth to healthy babies and care for the infants and themselves appropriately
Improve the quality of child protection intervention services	Children will be safe; they will not be abused or neglected
Develop a supportive, family-centered, capacity-building intervention system for families and children	Parents will adequately care and provide for their children
Provide assistance to parents to make employment-related child care decisions	Parents who wish to work will have adequate child care

pares these two kinds of goals. Both can be useful, but they place emphasis in different places.

Leading a Horse to Water Versus Getting It to Drink

The shift from service goals to outcomes often proves difficult in programs and agencies that have a long history of focusing on services and activities. But even where the difference is understood and appreciated, some fear or resistance may emerge. One reason is that service providers are well schooled in the proverbial wisdom that "you can lead a horse to water, but you can't make it drink."

This familiar adage illuminates the challenge of committing to outcomes. The desired outcome is that the horse drink the water. Longer-term outcomes are that the horse stays healthy and works effectively. But because program staff know they can't make a horse drink water, they focus on the things they can control: leading the horse to water, making sure the tank is full, monitoring the quality of the water, and keeping the horse within drinking distance of the water. In short, they focus on the *processes* of water delivery rather than the outcome of water drunk. Because staff can control processes but cannot guarantee attaining outcomes, government rules and regulations get written specifying exactly how to lead a horse to water. Funding is based on the number of horses led to water. Licenses are issued to individuals and programs that meet the qualifications for leading horses to water. Quality awards are made for improving the path to the water—and keeping the horse happy along the way.

Whether the horse drinks the water gets lost in all this flurry of lead-to-water-ship. Most reporting systems focus on how many horses get led to the water, and how difficult it was to get them there, but never quite get around to finding out whether the horses drank the water and stayed healthy.

One point of resistance to outcomes accountability, then, is the fear among providers and practitioners that they're being asked to take responsibility for, and will be judged on, something over which they have little control. The antidote to this fear is building into programming incentives for attaining outcomes and establishing a results-oriented culture in an organization or agency. Evaluators have a role to play in such efforts by facilitating a process that helps staff, administrators, and other stakeholders think about, discuss the implications of, and come to understand both the advantages and limitations of an outcomes approach. There's a lot of managerial and political rhetoric about being results oriented, but not much expertise in how to set up a results-oriented system. The next section presents a framework for conceptualizing outcomes that are meaningful and measurable for use in facilitating an outcomes-oriented management and evaluation system.

Utilization-Focused Outcomes Framework

This framework distinguishes six separate elements that need to be specified for focusing an evaluation on participant or client outcomes:

- a specific participant or client target group
- the desired outcome(s) for that target group
- one or more indicators for each desired outcome
- details of data collection
- how results will be used
- performance targets

I'll discuss each of these elements and offer illustrations from actual programs to show how they fit together. Evaluators can use this framework to work with primary intended users.

Identifying Specific Participant or Client Target Groups

I'll use the generic term *client* to include program participants, consumers of services, beneficiaries, students, and customers, as well as traditional client groups. The appropriate language varies, but for every program, there is some group that is expected to benefit from and attain outcomes as a result of program participation. However, the target groups identified in enabling legislation or existing reporting systems typically are defined too broadly for meaningful outcomes measurement. Intended outcomes can vary substantially for subgroups within general eligible populations. The trick is to be as specific as necessary to conceptualize meaningful outcomes. Some illustrations may help clarify why this is so.

Consider a program aimed at supporting the elderly to continue living in their homes, with services ranging from "meals on wheels" to home nursing. Not all elderly people can or want to stay in their homes. Therefore, if the desired outcome is "continuing to live in their own home," it would be inappropriate to specify that outcome for all elderly people. A more appropriate target population, then, would be people over the age of 55 who want to and can remain safely in their homes. For this group, it is appropriate to aim to keep them in their homes. It is also clear that some kind of screening process will be necessary to identify this subpopulation of the elderly.

A different example comes from programs serving people with developmental disabilities (DD). Many programs exist to prepare DD clients for work and then support them in maintaining employment. However, not all people with developmental disabilities can or want to work. In cases where funding supports the right of DD clients to choose whether to work, the appropriate subpopulation become people with developmental disabilities who can and want to work. For that specific subpopulation, then, the intended outcome could be that they obtain and maintain satisfying employment.

There are many ways of specifying subpopulation targets. Outcomes are often different for young, middle-aged, and elderly clients in the same general group (e.g., persons with serious and persistent mental illness). Outcomes for pregnant teens or teenage mothers may be different from outcomes for mothers receiving welfare who have completed high school. Outcomes for first-time offenders may be different from those for repeat offenders. The point is that categories of funding eligibility often include subgroups for whom different outcomes are appropriate. Similarly, when identifying groups by services received, for example, counseling services or jobs training, the outcomes expected for generic services may vary by subgroups. It is important, then, to make sure an intended outcome is meaningful and appropriate for everyone in the identified target population.

Specifying Desired Outcomes

The choice of language varies under different evaluation approaches. Some models refer to *expected outcomes* or *intended outcomes*. Others prefer the language of *client goals* or *client objectives*. What is important is not the phrase used but that there be a clear statement of the targeted change in circumstances, status, level of functioning, behavior, attitude, knowledge, or skills. Other outcome types include maintenance and prevention. Exhibit 7.2 provides examples of outcomes.

Outcome Indicators

An indicator is just that, an indicator. It's not the same as the phenomenon of interest, but only an indicator of that phenomenon. A score on a reading test is an indicator of reading ability but should not be confused with a particular person's true ability. All kinds of things affect a test score on a given day. Thus, indicators are inevitably approximations. They are imperfect and vary in validity and reliability.

The resources available for evaluation will greatly affect the kinds of data that can be collected for indicators. For example, if the desired outcome for abused children is that there be no subsequent abuse or neglect, a periodic in-home visitation and observation, including interviews with the child, parent(s), and knowledgeable others, would be desirable, but such data collection is expensive. With constrained resources, one may have to rely on routinely collected data, that is, official substantiated reports of abuse and neglect over time. Moreover, when using such routine data, privacy and confidentiality restrictions may limit the indicator to aggregate results quarter by quarter rather than one that tracks specific families over time.

As resources change, the indicator may change. Routine statistics may be used by an agency until a philanthropic foundation

EXHIBIT 7.2
Outcome Examples

Type of Change	*Illustration*
Change in circumstances	Children safely reunited with their families of origin from foster care
Change in status	Unemployed to employed
Change in behavior	Truants will regularly attend school
Change in functioning	Increased self-care; getting to work on time
Change in attitude	Greater self-respect
Change in knowledge	Understand the needs and capabilities of children at different ages
Change in skills	Increased reading level; able to parent appropriately
Maintenance	Continue to live safely at home (e.g., the elderly)
Prevention	Teenagers will not use drugs

funds a focused evaluation to get better data for a specific period of time. In such a case, the indicator would change, but the desired outcome would not. This is the advantage of clearly distinguishing the desired outcome from its indicator. As the state of the art of measurement develops or resources change, indicators may improve without changing the desired outcome.

Time frames also affect indicators. The ultimate goal of a program for abused children would be to have them become healthy, well-functioning, and happy adults, but policymakers cannot wait 10 to 15 years to assess the outcomes of a program for abused children. Short-term indicators must be relied on, things like school attendance, school performance, physical health, and the psychological functioning of a child. These short-term indicators provide sufficient information to make judgments about the likely long-term results. It takes 30 years for a forest to grow, but you can assess the likelihood of ending up with a forest by evaluating how many saplings are still alive a year after the trees are planted.

Another factor affecting indicator selection is the demands data collection will put on program staff and participants. Short-term interventions such as food shelves, recreational activities for people with developmental disabilities, drop-in centers, and one-time community events do not typically engage participants intensely enough to justify collection of much, if any, data. Many programs can barely collect data on end-of-program status, much less follow-up data.

In short, a variety of factors influence the selection of indicators, including the importance of the outcome claims being made, resources available for data collection, the state of the art of measurement of human functioning, the nature of decisions to be made with the results, and the willingness of staff and participants to engage in assessment. Some kind of indicator is necessary, however, to measure degree of outcome attainment. **The key is to make**

sure that the indicator is a reasonable, useful, and meaningful measure of the intended client outcome.

The framework offered here will generate outcome statements that are *clear, specific*, and *measurable*, but getting clarity and specificity is separated from selecting measures. The reason for separating the identification of a desired outcome from its measurement is to ensure the utility of both. This point is worth elaborating. The following is a classic goal statement:

> Student achievement test scores in reading will increase one grade level from the beginning of first grade to the beginning of second grade.

Such a statement mixes together and potentially confuses the (1) specification of a desired outcome with (2) its measurement and (3) the desired performance target. The desired outcome is increased student achievement. The indicator is a norm-referenced standardized achievement test. The performance target is one year's gain on the test. These are three separate decisions that primary intended evaluation users need to discuss. For example, there are ways other than standardized tests for measuring achievement, for example, student portfolios or competency-based tests. The desired outcome should not be confused with its indicator. In the framework offered here, outcome statements are clearly separated from operational criteria for measuring them.

Another advantage of separating outcomes identification from indicator selection is to encourage program staff to be serious about the process. A premature focus on indicators may be heard as limiting a program to attempt only those things that staff already know how to measure. Such a limitation is too constraining. It is one thing to establish a purpose and direction for a program. It is quite another thing to say how that purpose and direction are to be measured. By confusing these two steps and making them one, program goals can become detached from what program staff and funders are actually working to accomplish. Under such a constraint, staff begin by figuring out what can be measured. Given that they seldom have much expertise in measurement, they end up counting fairly insignificant behaviors and attitudes that they can somehow quantify.

When I work with groups on goals clarification, I have them state intended outcomes **without regard to measurement.** Once they have stated as carefully and explicitly as they can what they want to accomplish, then it is time to figure out what indicators and data can be collected to monitor outcome attainment. They can then move back and forth between conceptual level statements and operational (measurement) specifications, attempting to get as much precision as possible in both.

To emphasize this point, let me overstate the trade-off. **I prefer to have soft or rough measures of important goals rather than highly precise, quantitative measures of goals that no one much cares about.** In too many evaluations, program staff are forced to focus on the latter (meaningless but measurable goals) instead of on the former (meaningful goals with soft measures).

Of course, this trade-off, stated in stark terms, is only relative. It is desirable to have as much precision as possible. By separating the process of goals clarification from the process of selecting goal indicators, it is possible for program staff to focus first on what they are really trying to accomplish and to state their goals and objectives as explicitly as possible **without regard to measurement,** and then to worry about how one would measure actual attainment of those goals and objectives.

Performance Targets

A performance target specifies the amount or level of outcome attainment that is expected, hoped for, or, in some kinds of performance contracting, required. What percentage of participants in employment training will have full-time jobs six months after graduation: 40%? 65%? 80%? What percentage of fathers failing to make child support payments will be meeting their full child support obligations within six months of intervention? 15%? 35%? 60%?

The best basis for establishing future performance targets is past performance. "Last year we had 65% success. Next year we aim for 70%." Lacking data on past performance, it may be advisable to wait until baseline data have been gathered before specifying a performance target. Arbitrarily setting performance targets without some empirical baseline may create artificial expectations that turn out unrealistically high or embarrassingly low. One way to avoid arbitrariness is to seek norms for reasonable levels of attainment from other, comparable programs, or review the evaluation literature for parallels.

As indicators are collected and examined over time, from quarter to quarter, and year to year, it becomes more meaningful and useful to set performance targets. The relationship between resources and outcomes can also be more precisely correlated longitudinally, with trend data, all of which increases the incremental and long-term value of an outcomes management approach.

The challenge is to make performance targets meaningful.

In a political environment of outcomes mania, meaningfulness and utility are not necessarily priorities. Consider this example and judge for yourself. The 1995 Annual Management Report from the Office of the New York City Mayor included this performance target: The average daytime speed of cars crossing from one side of midtown Manhattan to the other will increase from 5.3 to 5.9 miles per hour. Impressed by this vision of moving from a "brisk 5.3" to a "sizzling 5.9," *The New Yorker* magazine interviewed Ruben Ramirez, Manhattan's Department of Transportation Traffic Coordinator, to ask how such a feat could be accomplished in the face of downsizing and budget cuts. Ramirez cited better use of resources. Asked what could he accomplish with adequate resources, he replied: "I think we could do six or seven, and I'm not being outrageous." *The New Yorker* found such a performance target a "dreamy future," one in which it might actually be possible to drive across midtown Manhattan faster than you can walk ("Speed" 1995:40).

Is such a vision visionary? Is a performance increase from 5.3 to 5.9 miles per hour meaningful? Is 6 or 7 worth aiming for? For a noncommuting Minnesotan, such numbers fail to impress. But, converted into annual hours and dollars saved for commercial vehicles in Manhattan, the increase may be valued in hundreds of thousands of dollars, perhaps even millions. It's for primary stakeholders in Manhattan, not Minnesota, to determine the meaningfulness of such a performance target.

Details of Data Collection

The details of data collection are a distinct part of the framework; they must be attended to, but they shouldn't clutter the focused outcome statement. Unfortunately, I've found that people can get caught up in the details of refining methods and lose sight of the outcome. The details typically get worked out after the other parts of the framework have been conceptualized. Details include answering the following kinds of questions:

- What existing data will be used and how will they be accessed? Who will collect new indicators data?
- Who will have oversight and management responsibility for data collection?
- How often will indicators data be collected? How often reported?
- Will data be gathered on all program participants or only a sample? If a sample, how selected?
- How will findings be reported? To whom? In what format? When? How often?

These pragmatic questions put flesh on the bones of the outcomes framework. They are not simply technical issues, however. How these questions get answered will ultimately determine the credibility and utility of the entire approach. Primary intended users need to be involved in making decisions about these issues to ensure that they feel ownership of and responsibility for all aspects of the evaluation.

How Results Will Be Used

The final element in the framework is to make sure that the data collected on the outcomes identified will be useful. This means engaging intended users in a simulation exercise in which they pretend that they have results and are interpreting and using those results. The evaluation facilitator asks: If the results came out this way, what would you do? If the findings came out this other way, what would that tell you, and what actions would you take? Given what you want the evaluation to accomplish, have we focused on the right outcomes and useful indicators? At every stage of a utilization-focused evaluation, the evaluator facilitator pushes intended users to think seriously about the implications of design and measurement decisions for use.

Interconnections Among the Distinct Parts of the Framework

The utilization-focused outcomes framework, as just reviewed, consists of six parts: a specific participant target group; a desired outcome for that group; one or more outcome indicators; a performance target (if appropriate and desired); details of data collection; and specification of how findings will be used. While these are listed in the order in which intended users and staff typically conceptualize them, the conceptualization process is not linear. Groups often go back and forth in iterative fashion. The target group may not become really clear until the desired outcome is specified or an indicator designated. Sometimes formulating the details of data collection will give rise to new indicators, and those indicators force a rethinking of how the desired outcome is stated. The point is to end up with all elements specified, consistent with each other, and mutually reinforcing. That doesn't necessarily mean marching through the framework lockstep.

Exhibit 7.3 provides an example of all the elements specified for a parenting program aimed at high school-age mothers.

Completing the framework often takes several tries. Exhibit 7.4 shows three versions of the utilization-focused outcomes

EXHIBIT 7.3
Example of a Fully Specified Utilization-Focused Outcome Framework

Target subgroup:	Teenage mothers at Central High School
Desired outcome:	Appropriate parenting knowledge and practices
Outcome indicator:	Score on Parent Practice Inventory (knowledge and behavior measures)
Data collection:	Pre- and post-test, beginning and end of program; six-month follow-up; district evaluation office will administer and analyze results
Performance target:	75% of entering participants will complete the program and attain a passing score on both the knowledge and behavior scales
Use:	The evaluation advisory task force will review the results (principal, two teachers, two participating students, one agency representative, one community representative, an associate superintendent, one school board member, and the district evaluator). The task force will decide if the program should be continued at Central High School and expanded to other district high schools. A recommendation will be forwarded to the superintendent and school board.

framework as it emerged from the work of a developmental disabilities staff group. Their first effort yielded a service-oriented goal. They revised that with a focus on skill enhancement. Finally, they agreed on a meaningful client outcome: functioning independently.

A Utilization-Focused Process for Developing Outcomes

A central issue in implementing an outcomes evaluation approach is who will be involved in the process of developing the outcomes. When the purpose is ongoing management by outcomes, the program's executives and staff must buy into the process. Who else is involved is a matter of political judgment. Those involved will feel the most ownership of the resulting system.

Some processes involve only managers and directors. Other processes include advisory groups from the community. Collaboration between funders and service providers in determining outcomes is critical where contracts for services are involved. Advice from some savvy foundation funders is to match outcomes evaluation to the stage of a program's development (Daniels 1996), keep the context long-term (McIntosh 1996) and "turn outcome 'sticks' into carrots" (Leonard 1996:46).

Exhibit 7.5 shows the stages of a utilization-focused approach to developing an outcomes-based management system for a program (MDHS 1996). Critical issues and

EXHIBIT 7.4
Three Versions of an Outcome-Focused Framework

	Target Population: Children With Developmental Disabilities		
	Desired Outcome	*Outcome Indicator*	*Method*
First draft (Service-oriented)	Children with developmental disabilities will receive supportive services for improved functioning in basic daily living skills	Track hours of supportive services received, and levels and amounts of client participation in training	Case records monitoring services and participation will be aggregated quarterly
Revised (Skills-focused; interim outcome)	Children with developmental disabilities will increase their skills for functioning independently	Changes in skills on a staff assessment form	Quarterly administration of skills assessment form as part of the ongoing training
Final version (Primary desired outcome)	Children with developmental disabilities will function independently in their activities of daily living	Activities of Daily Living (ADL) behavioral assessment instrument	Quarterly administration of ADL to all children in the program. Compare scores over time. Do both individual case profiles and aggregate results by categories of severity and age

SOURCE: MDHS 1996:20.

EXHIBIT 7.5

Developing a Utilization-Focused System for Managing Outcomes: Stages, Issues, and Activities

	1	2	3	4	5	6	7	8	9	10	11	12	13
Stages	Identify and engage key actors and leaders whose commitment and support will be needed for transition to management and accountability based on client outcomes	Key actors and leaders: Commit to establish a client outcome approach. Understand principles, purposes, and implications of change	Agree on intended use by intended users	Conceptualize client outcomes; select indicators; set targets	Engage line staff: facilitate their understanding and buy-in	Design data collection system; finalize methods; pilot establish baselines	Implement data collection; train staff and managers for data collection and use	Prepare for use: Determine management uses; potential actions; decision options and parameters, and accountability report format	Analyze results: Compare results to baseline and targets	Involve key stakeholders in processing the findings	Judge performance and effectiveness	Make management decisions. Report results	Review and evaluate the outcome-based management system.
Issues	Who are the key actors and leaders who must buy in? How wide-spread should initial involvement be?	What level of commitment and under-standing is needed? By whom? How to distinguish real commitment from mere rhetoric?	What uses are possible? What uses are doable?	What target groups? How many outcomes? What are the really important, bottom-line outcomes?	What is staff's perspective/ history/ concerns/ incentives?	What can be done with existing data? What new data will be needed? How can the system be integrated?	What resources will be available to support data collection? How will validity and reliability be addressed?	What incentives exist for managers to participate? How will managers be brought along? trained? rewarded? Who determines accountability reporting approaches?	Who will do the analysis? What additional data are needed to interpret the outcome results (e.g., demographics)	How do you keep key stakeholders engaged?	How clear are the data to support solid judgments?	What are the links between internal and external uses and audiences?	What should the system accomplish? Who determines success?
Activities	Establish leadership group	Leadership group makes strategic decision about how best to proceed and who to involve	Map out users and uses. Set priorities	Establish work team to determine outcomes; involve advisory to bring them along	Conduct staff workshops/ training	Work team to make design decisions	Collect data; pilot-test and monitor data collection	Conduct training and management team sessions based on data use and simulations and mock scenarios	Analyze data; prepare graphics	Facilitate meeting of key stake-holders	Facilitate key stakeholders in judging and interpreting	Write report; present data; facilitate management decision making	Assemble a review team of based management system users and key stakeholders

SOURCE: Minnesota Department of Human Services (MDHS) 1996:22-23.

parallel activities are shown for each stage. Those to be involved will need training and support. I've found it helpful to begin with an overview of the purpose of an outcomes-focused programming approach: history, trends, the political climate, and potential benefits. Then I have participants work in small groups working on the elements of the utilization-focused outcomes framework (see Exhibit 7.3) for an actual program with which they're familiar. Facilitation, encouragement, and technical assistance are needed to help such groups successfully complete the task. Where multiple groups are involved, I like to have them share their work and the issues that emerged in using the outcomes framework.

It's important that those involved get a chance to raise their concerns openly. There's often suspicion about political motives. Providers worry about funding cuts and being held accountable for things they can't control. Administrators and directors of programs worry about how results will be used, what comparisons will be made, and who will control the process. Line staff worry about the amount of time involved, paperwork burdens, and the irrelevancy of it all. State civil servants responsible for reporting to the Legislature worry about how data can be aggregated at the state level. These and other concerns need to be aired and addressed. Having influential leaders visibly involved in the process enhances their own understanding and commitment while also sending signals to others about the importance being placed on outcomes.

Meaningful and Useful Goals

With the utilization-focused outcomes framework as background, here are 10 guidelines for working with intended users to identify meaningful and useful goals.

1. **Distinguish between outcome goals and activities.** Outcomes describe desired impacts of the program on participants: Students will read with understanding. Participants will stop smoking. Activities goals describe *how* outcome goals will be achieved: Students will read two hours a day. Participants will openly discuss their dependence on cigarettes. People in the program will be treated with respect.

2. **Outcome goals should be clearly outcome oriented.** Program staff often write activity goals thinking that they have stated desired outcomes. An agricultural extension agent told me his goal was "to get 50 farmers to participate in a farm tour." But what, I asked, did he want to result from the farm tour? After some dialogue, it became clear that the outcome goal was this: "Farmers will adopt improved milking practices in their own farm operations."

A corporation stated one of its goals for the year as "establishing a comprehensive energy conservation program." After we discussed that it was perfectly possible to establish such a program without ever saving any energy, they rewrote the goal: "The corporation will significantly reduce energy consumption."

3. **It should be possible to conceptualize either the absence of the desired outcome or an alternative to it.** Some goal statements are amazingly adept at saying nothing. I worked with a school board whose overall goal was "Students will learn." There is no way *not* to attain this goal. It is the nature of the species that young people learn. Fortunately, they can learn in spite of the schools. The issues are *what* and *how much* they will learn.

Another favorite is "increasing awareness." It's fairly difficult to put people through two weeks of training on some topic (e.g., chemical dependency) and *not* increase awareness. Under these conditions, the goal of "increasing awareness of chemical dependency issues" is hardly worth aiming at. Further dialogue revealed that the program staff wanted to change knowledge, attitudes, and behavior.

4. **Each goal and objective should contain only one idea.** There is a tendency in writing goal statements to overload the content.

5. **The statement of goals and objectives should be understandable.** Goals should communicate a clear sense of direction. Avoid difficult grammatical constructions and complex interdependent clauses. Goal statements should also avoid internal program or professional jargon. The general public should be able to make sense of goals. Consider these two versions of goal statements for what amount to the *same* outcome:

(a) To maximize the capabilities of professional staff and use taxpayer resources wisely while engaging in therapeutic interventions and case management processes so that children's developmental capacities are unencumbered by adverse environmental circumstances or experiences.
(b) Children will be safe from abuse and neglect.

Now, see if you can make sense of this beauty from the National Council of Teachers of English and the International Reading Association: "Students employ a wide range of strategies as they write and use different writing process elements appropriately to communicate with different audiences for a variety of purposes." The *New York Times* (1996) found this goal less than inspiring or user-friendly, and editorialized: "a fog of euphemism and evasion" (p. A24). Bumper sticker: Honk if you use *writing process elements* appropriately.

6. **Formal goals statements should focus on the most important program outcomes.** Writing goals should not be a marathon exercise in seeing how long a document one can produce. As human beings, our attention span is too short to focus on long lists of goals and objectives. Limit them to outcomes that matter and for which the program intends to be held accountable.

7. **Keep goal statements separate from statements of how goals are to be attained.** An agricultural extension program had this goal: "Farmers will increase yields through the educational efforts of extension including farm tours, bulletins, and related activities." Everything after the word *yields* describes how the goal is to be attained. Keep the goal focused, clear, and crisp.

8. **Separate goals from indicators.** Advocates of *management by objectives* and *behavioral objectives* often place more emphasis on measurement than on establishing a clear sense of direction (Combs 1972). The two are related, but not equivalent.

9. **Make the writing of goals a positive experience.** Goals clarification exercises are so often approached as pure drudgery that staff hate not only the exercise itself but also the resulting goals. Goals clarification should be an invigorating process of prioritizing what those involved care about and hope to accomplish. Goals should not

become a club for assaulting staff but a tool for helping staff focus and realize their ideals.

10. **Thou shalt not covet thy neighbor's goals and objectives.** Goals and objectives don't travel very well. They often involve matters of nuance. It is worth taking the time for primary stakeholders to construct their own goals so that they reflect their own values, expectations, and intentions in their own language.

There are exceptions to all of these guidelines, particularly the last one. One option in working with groups is to have them review the goals of other programs, both as a way of helping stakeholders clarify their own goals and to get ideas about format and content. Evaluators who work with behavioral objectives often develop a repertoire of potential objectives that can be adopted by a variety of programs. The evaluator has already worked on the technical quality of the goals so program staff can focus on selecting the content they want. Where there is the time and inclination, however, I prefer to have a group work on its own goals statement so that participants feel ownership and understand what commitments have been made. This can be part of the training function served by evaluators, increasing the likelihood that staff will have success in future goals clarification exercises.

Levels of Goal Specification

From Overall Mission to Specific Objectives

To facilitate framing evaluation questions in complex programs, evaluators may have to work with primary stakeholders to clarify purposes at three levels: the overall mission of the program or organization, the goals of specific programmatic units (or subsystems), and the specific objectives that specify desired outcomes. The mission statement describes the general direction of the overall program or organization in long-range terms. The peacetime mission of the U.S. Army is simply "readiness." A mission statement may specify a target population and a basic problem to be attacked. For example, the mission of the Minnesota Comprehensive Epilepsy Program was to "improve the lives of people with epilepsy."

The terms *goals* and *objectives* have been used interchangeably up to this point, but it is useful to distinguish between them as representing different levels of generality. Goals are more general than objectives and encompass the purposes and aims of program subsystems (i.e., research, education, and treatment in the epilepsy example). Objectives are narrow and specific, stating what will be different as a result of program activities, that is, the concrete outcomes of a program. To illustrate these differences, a simplified version of the mission statement, goals, and objectives for the Minnesota Comprehensive Epilepsy Program is presented in Exhibit 7.6. This outline was developed after an initial discussion with the program director. The purpose of the outline was to establish a context for later discussions aimed at more clearly framing specific evaluation questions. In other words, we used this goals clarification and objectives *mapping exercise* as a means of focusing the evaluation question rather than as an end in itself.

The outline of goals and objectives for the Epilepsy Project (Exhibit 7.6) illustrates several points. First, the only dimension that consistently differentiates goals and objectives is the relative degree of specificity of each: objectives narrow the focus of goals. There is no absolute criterion for distinguishing goals from objectives; the distinction is always a relative one.

Second, this outline had a specific evaluation purpose: to facilitate priority setting as I worked with primary intended users to focus the evaluation. Resources were insufficient to fully evaluate all three component parts of the program. Moreover, different program components faced different contingencies. Treatment and research had more concrete outcomes than education. The differences in the specificity of the objectives for the three components reflect real differences in the degree to which the content and functions of those program subsystems were known at the beginning of the evaluation. Thus, with limited resources and variations in goal specificity, it was necessary to decide which aspects of the program could best be served by evaluation.

Third, the outline of goals and objectives for the Comprehensive Epilepsy Program is not particularly well written. I constructed the outline from notes taken during my first meeting with the director. At this early point in the process, the outline was a tool for posing this question to evaluation decision makers: **Which program components, goals, and objectives should be evaluated to produce the most useful information for program improvement and decision making?** That is the question. To answer it, one does not need technically perfect goal statements. Once the evaluation is focused, relevant goals and objectives can be reworked as necessary. The point is to avoid wasting time in the construction of grandiose, complex models of program goals and objectives just because the folklore of evaluation prescribes such an exercise. In complex programs, evaluators can spend so much time working on goals statements that considerable momentum is lost.

Establishing Priorities: Importance Versus Utility

Let me elaborate the distinction between writing goals for the sake of writing goals and writing them to use as tools in narrowing the focus of an evaluation. In utilization-focused evaluation, goals are prioritized in a manner quite different from that usually prescribed. The usual criterion for prioritizing goals is ranking or rating in terms of *importance* (Edwards, Guttentag, and Snapper 1975; Gardiner and Edwards 1975). The reason seems commonsensical: Evaluations ought to focus on important goals. But, from a utilization-focused perspective, what appears to be most sensible may not be most useful.

The most important goal may not be the one that decision makers and intended users most need information about. In utilization-focused evaluation, goals are also prioritized on the basis of what information is most needed and likely to be most useful, given the evaluation's purpose. For example, a summative evaluation would likely evaluate goals in terms of overall importance, but a formative evaluation might focus on a goal of secondary importance because it is an area being neglected or proving particularly troublesome.

Ranking goals by importance is often quite different from ranking them by the utility of evaluative information needed. Exhibit 7.7 provides an example from the Minnesota Comprehensive Epilepsy Program, contrasting goals ranked by importance and utility. Why the discrepancy? The

EXHIBIT 7.6

Minnesota Comprehensive Epilepsy Program: Mission Statement, Goals, and Objectives

Program Mission: Improve the lives of people with epilepsy

Research Component

Goal 1: Produce high quality, *scholarly research* on epilepsy

Objective 1: Publish research findings in high-quality, refereed journals

Objective 2: Contribute to knowledge about:
a. neurological aspects of epilepsy
b. pharmacological aspects of epilepsy
c. epidemiology of epilepsy
d. social and psychological aspects of epilepsy

Goal 2: Produce interdisciplinary research

Objective 1: Conduct research projects that *integrate* principal investigators from different disciplines

Objective 2: Increase meaningful *exchanges* among researchers from different disciplines

Education Component

Goal 3: Health professionals will know the nature and effects of epilepsy behaviors

Objective 1: Increase the *knowledge* of health professionals who serve people with epilepsy so that they know:
a. what to do if a person has a seizure
b. the incidence and prevalence of epilepsy

Objective 2: Change the attitudes of health professionals so that they:
a. are sympathetic to the needs of people with epilepsy
b. believe in the importance of identifying the special needs of people with epilepsy

Goal 4: Educate persons with epilepsy about their disorder

Goal 5: Inform the general public about the nature and incidence of epilepsy.

Treatment Component

Goal 6: Diagnose, treat, and rehabilitate persons with severe, chronic, and disabling seizures

Objective 1: Increase seizure control in treated patients

Objective 2: Increase the functioning of patients

EXHIBIT 7.7

Minnesota Comprehensive Epilepsy Program: Goals Ranked by Importance to Program Versus Goals Ranked by Utility of Evaluative Information Needed by Primary Users

Ranking of Goals by Importance	*Ranking Goals by Usefulness of Evaluative Information to Intended Users*
1. Produce high-quality scholarly research on epilepsy	1. Integrate the separate program components into a comprehensive whole that is greater than the sum of its parts
2. Produce interdisciplinary research	2. Educate health professionals about epilepsy
3. Integrate the separate components into a whole	3. Diagnose, treat, and rehabilitate people with chronic and disabling seizures
4. Diagnose, treat, and rehabilitate people with chronic and disabling seizures	4. Produce interdisciplinary research

staff did not feel they needed a formal evaluation to monitor attainment of the most important program goal. The publishing of scholarly research in refereed journals was so important that the director was committed to personally monitor performance in that area. Moreover, he was relatively certain about how to achieve that outcome, and he had no specific evaluation question related to that goal that he needed answered. By contrast, the issue of comprehensiveness was quite difficult to assess. It was not at all clear how comprehensiveness could be facilitated, although it was third on the importance list. Data on comprehensiveness had high formative utility.

The education goal, second on the usefulness list, does not even appear among the top four goals on the importance list. Yet, information about educational impact was ranked high on the usefulness list because it was a goal area about which the program staff had many questions. The education component was expected to be a difficult, long-term effort. Information about how to increase the educational impact of the Comprehensive Epilepsy Program had high use potential. In a utilization-focused approach, the primary intended users make the final decision about evaluation priorities.

In my experience, the most frequent reason for differences in importance and usefulness rankings is variation in the degree to which decision makers already have what they consider good information about performance on the most important goal. At the program level, staff members may be so involved in trying to achieve their most important goal that they are relatively well informed about performance on that goal. Performance on less important goals may involve less certainty for staff; information about performance in that goal area is therefore more useful because it tells staff members something they do not already know.

What I hope is emerging through these examples is an image of the evaluator as an active-reactive-adaptive problem solver. The evaluator actively solicits information about program contingencies, organizational dynamics, environmental uncertainties, and decision makers' goals in order to focus the evaluation on questions of real interest and utility to primary intended users.

Evaluation of Central Versus Peripheral Goals

Prioritizing goals on the basis of perceived evaluative utility means that an evaluation might focus on goals of apparent peripheral importance rather than more central program goals. This is a matter of some controversy. In her early work, Weiss (1972b) offered the following advice to evaluators:

> The evaluator will have to press to find out priorities—which goals the staff sees as critical to its mission and which are subsidiary. But since the evaluator is not a mere technician for the translation of a program's stated aims into measurement instruments, he has a responsibility to express his own interpretation of the relative importance of goals. *He doesn't want to do an elaborate study on the attainment of minor and innocuous goals,* while some vital goals go unexplored. (pp. 30-31; emphasis added)

Contrast that advice with the perspective of an evaluator from our study of use of federal health evaluations:

> I'd make this point about minor evaluation studies. If you have an energetic, conscientious program manager, he's always interested in improving his program around the periphery, because that's where he usually can. And an evaluation study of some minor aspect of his program may enable him to significantly improve. [EV52:171]

In our study, we put the issue to decision makers and evaluators as follows:

> Another factor sometimes believed to affect use has to do with whether the central objectives of a program are evaluated. Some writers argue that evaluations can have the greatest impact if they focus on major program objectives. What happened in your case?

The overwhelming consensus was that, at the very least, central goals ought to be evaluated and, where possible, both central and peripheral goals should be studied. As they elaborated, nine decision makers and eight evaluators said that utilization had probably been increased by concentrating on **central issues**. This phrase reflects an important shift in emphasis. As they elaborated their answers about evaluating central versus peripheral goals, they switched from talking about goals to talking about "issues." Utilization is increased by focusing on central issues. **And what is a central issue? It is an evaluation question that someone really cares about.** The subtle distinction here is critical. Evaluations are useful to decision makers if they focus on central *issues*—which may or may not include evaluating attainment of central goals.

The Personal Factor Revisited

Different people will have different perceptions of what constitutes central program goals or issues. Whether it is the evaluator's opinion about centrality, the funder's, some special interest group's perspective, or the viewpoints of program staff and participants, the question of what constitutes central program goals and objectives remains an intrinsically subjective one. It cannot be otherwise. The question of central versus peripheral goals cannot really be answered in the abstract. The question thus becomes: central from whose point of view? The personal factor (Chapter 3) intersects the goals clarification process in a utilization-focused evaluation. Increasing use is largely a matter of matching: getting information about the right questions, issues, and goals to the right people.

Earlier in this chapter, I compared the goals clarification process to the party game of Twenty Questions. Research indicates that different individuals behave quite differently in such a game (and, by extension, in any decision-making process). Worley (1960), for example, studied subjects' information-seeking endurance in the game under experimental conditions. Initially, each subject was presented with a single clue and given the option of guessing what object the experimenter had in mind or of asking for another clue. This option was available after each new clue, but a wrong guess would end the game. Worley found large and consistent individual differences in the amount of information players sought. Donald Taylor (1965) cites the research of Worley and others as evidence that decision-making and problem-solving behavior is dynamic, highly variable, and contingent upon both situational and individual characteristics. This does not make the evaluator's job any easier. It does mean that the personal factor remains the key to evaluation use. The careful selection of knowledgeable, committed, and information-valuing people makes the difference. The goals clarification game is most meaningful when played by people who are searching for information because it helps them focus on central issues without letting the game become an end in itself or turning it into a contest between staff and evaluators.

The Goals Paradox

This chapter began with an evaluation of Nasrudin's hunting trip in search of bears. For Nasrudin, that trip ended with the "marvelous" outcome of seeing no bears. Our hunting trip in search of the role of goals in evaluation has no conclusive ending because the information needs of primary intended users will vary from evaluation to evaluation and situation to situation. Focusing an evaluation on program goals and objectives is clearly not the straightforward, logical exercise depicted by the classical evaluation literature because decision making in the real world is not purely rational and logical. This is the paradox of goals. They are rational abstractions in nonrational systems. Statements of goals emerge at the interface between the ideals of human rationality and the reality of diverse human values and ways of thinking. Therein lies their strength and their weakness. Goals provide direction for action and evaluation, but only for those who share in the values expressed by the goals. Evaluators live inside that paradox.

One way out of the paradox is to focus the evaluation without making goal attainment the central issue. The next chapter considers alternatives to goals-based evaluation.

Note

1. This material, and related information in the chapter, has been adapted and used with permission from the Minnesota Department of Human Services.

8

Focusing an Evaluation

Alternatives to Goals-Based Evaluation

Creative thinking may mean simply the realization that there's no particular virtue in doing things the way they always have been done.

—Rudolf Flesch

If you can see in any given situation only what everybody else can see, you can be said to be so much a representative of your culture that you are a victim of it.

—S. I. Hayakawa

More Than One Way to Manage a Horse

Here is a story about the young Alexander from Plutarch (1952):

There came a day when Philoneicus the Thessalian brought King Philip a horse named Bucephalus, which he offered to sell for 13 talents. The king and his friends went down to the plain to watch the horse's trials and came to the conclusion that he was wild and quite unmanageable, for he would allow no one to mount him, nor would he endure the shouts of Philip's grooms, but reared up against anyone who approached. The king became angry at being offered such a vicious unbroken animal and ordered it led away. But Alexander, who was standing close by, remarked, "What a horse they are losing, and all because they don't know how to handle him, or dare not try!"

King Philip kept quiet at first, but when he heard Alexander repeat these words and saw that he was upset, he asked him: "Do you think you know more than your elders or can manage a horse better?"

"I could manage this one better," retorted Alexander.

"And if you cannot," said his father, "what penalty will you pay for being so impertinent?"

"I will pay the price of the horse," answered the boy. At this, the whole company burst out laughing. As soon as the father and son had settled the terms of the bet, Alexander went quickly up to Bucephalus, took off his bridle, and turned him towards the sun, for he had noticed that the horse was shying at the sight of his own shadow, as it fell in front of him and constantly moved whenever he did. He ran alongside the animal for a little way, calming him down by stroking him, and then, when he saw he was full of spirit and courage, he quietly threw aside his cloak and with a light spring vaulted safely onto his back. For a little while, he kept feeling the bit with the reins, without jarring or tearing his mouth, and got him collected. Finally, when he saw that the horse was free of his fears and impatient to show his speed, he gave him his head and urged him forward, using a commanding voice and touch of the foot.

King Philip held his breath in an agony of suspense until he saw Alexander reach the end of his gallop, turn in full control, and ride back triumphant, exulting in his success. Thereupon the rest of the company broke into loud applause, while his father, we are told, actually wept for joy. When Alexander had dismounted, he kissed him and said: "My boy, you must find a kingdom big enough for your ambitions. Macedonia is too small for you."

More Than One Way to Focus an Evaluation

Young Alexander, later to be Alexander the Great, showed that there was more than one way to manage a horse. What I like most about this story, as a metaphor for managing an evaluation, is that he based his approach to the horse on careful observations of the horse and situation. He noticed that the horse was afraid of its shadow, so he turned him toward the sun. He established a relationship with the wild animal before mounting it. He was sensitive to the horse's response to the bit and reins. Alexander exemplified being active, reactive, and adaptive.

The last chapter focused on goals and outcomes as traditional ways to focus an evaluation. A program with clear, specific, and measurable goals is like a horse already trained for riding. Programs with multiple, conflicting, and still developing or ever-changing goals can feel wild and risky to an evaluator whose only experience is with seasoned and trained horses. This chapter will examine why goals-based evaluation often doesn't work and offer alternatives for focusing an evaluation. Just as there's more than one way to manage a wild horse, there's more than one way to manage evaluation of a seemingly chaotic program.

Problems With Goals-Based Evaluation

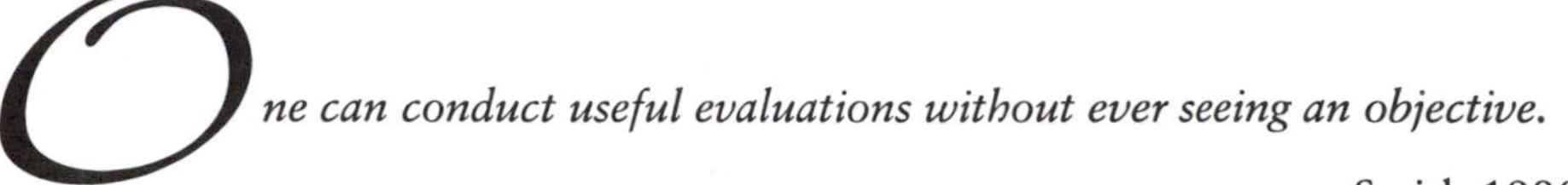

One can conduct useful evaluations without ever seeing an objective.

—Smith 1980:39

Alternatives to goals-based evaluation have emerged because of the problems evaluators routinely experience in attempting to focus on goals. In addition to fuzzy goals and conflicts over goals—problems addressed in the previous chapter—measuring goal attainment can overpoliticize goals. In this regard, Lee J. Cronbach and associates (1980) at the Stanford Evaluation Consortium have warned about the distortions that result when program staff pay too much attention to what an evaluator decides to measure, essentially giving the evaluator the power to determine what activities become primary in a program.

> It is unwise for evaluation to focus on whether a project has "attained its goals." Goals are a necessary part of political rhetoric, but all social programs, even supposedly targeted ones, have broad aims. Legislators who have sophisticated reasons for keeping goal statements lofty and nebulous unblushingly ask program administrators to state explicit goals. Unfortunately, whatever the evaluator decides to measure tends to become a primary goal of program operators. (p. 5)

In other words, what gets measured gets done. An example is when teachers focus on whether students can pass a reading test rather than on whether they learn to read. The result can be students who pass mandated competency tests but are still functionally illiterate.

Another critique of goals is that they're often unreal. Since I've argued that evaluation is grounded in reality testing, it behooves us to examine the reality of goals. To "reify" is to treat an abstraction as if it were real. Goals have been a special target of social scientists concerned with concept reification. For example, Cyert and March (1963:28) have asserted that **individual people have goals, collectivities of people do not.** They likewise assert that only individuals can act; organizations or programs, as such, cannot be said to take action. The future state desired by an organization (its goals) is nothing but a function of individual "aspirations."

Azumi and Hage (1972) reviewed the debate about whether organizations have goals and concluded, "Organizational sociologists have found it useful to assume that organizations are purposive. . . . However, it has been much more difficult to actually measure the goals of an organization. Researchers find the purposive image helpful but somehow elusive" (p. 414).

In brief, **social scientists who study goals are not quite sure what they are studying. Goals analysis as a field of study is complex, chaotic, controversial, and confusing.** In the end, most researchers follow the pragmatic logic of organizational sociologist Charles Perrow (1970):

> For our purposes we shall use the concept of an organizational goal as if there were no question concerning its legitimacy, even

> though we recognize that there are legitimate objections to doing so. Our present state of conceptual development, linguistic practices, and ontology (knowing whether something exists or not) offers us no alternative. (p. 134)

Like Perrow, evaluators are likely to come down on the side of practicality. The language of goals will continue to dominate evaluation. By introducing the issue of goals reification, I have hoped merely to induce a modicum of caution and compassion among evaluators before they impose goals clarification exercises on program staff. Given the way organizational sociologists have gotten themselves tangled up in the question of whether program-level goals actually exist, it is just possible that **difficulties in clarifying a program's goals may be due to problems inherent in the notion of goals rather than staff incompetence, intransigence, or opposition to evaluation.** Failure to appreciate these difficulties and proceed with sensitivity and patience can create staff resistance that is detrimental to the entire evaluation process.

I have also hoped that reviewing the conceptual and operational problems with goals would illuminate why utilization-focused evaluation does not depend on clear, specific, and measurable objectives as the sine qua non of evaluation research. Clarifying goals is neither necessary nor appropriate in every evaluation.

Turbulent Environments and Goals

The extent to which evaluators should seek clarity about goals will depend, among other things, on the program's developmental status and environment. Organizational sociologists have discovered that the clarity and stability of goals are contingent on the organization's environment. Emery and Trist (1965) identified four types of organizational environments characterized by varying degrees of uncertainty facing the organization. Uncertainty includes things like funding stability, changes in rules and regulations, mobility and transience of clients and suppliers, and political, economic, or social turbulence. What is important about their work from an evaluation perspective is the finding that **the degree of uncertainty facing an organization directly affects the degree to which goals and strategies for attaining goals can be made concrete and stable.** The less certain the environment, the less stable and less concrete the organization's goals will be. Effective organizations in turbulent environments adapt their goals to changing demands and conditions.

In practical terms, this means that the more unstable and turbulent the environment of a program, the less likely it is that the evaluator will be able to generate concrete and stable goals. Second, few evaluations can investigate and assess all the many programmatic components and special projects of an agency, organization, or program. The clarity, specificity, and measurability of goals will vary throughout a program, depending on the environmental turbulence faced by specific projects and program subparts. As an evaluator works with primary intended users to focus the evaluation, the degree to which it is useful to labor over writing a goals statement will vary for different parts of the program. It will not be efficient or useful to force developing and adapting programs into a static and rigid goals model. Developmental evaluation, discussed in Chapter 5, is one way of being a useful form of evaluation in innovative settings where goals are emergent and changing rather than predetermined and fixed. Another alternative is goal-free evaluation.

Goal-Free Evaluation

Philosopher-evaluator Michael Scriven has been a strong critic of goals-based evaluation and, as an alternative, an advocate of what he has called *goal-free evaluation*. Goal-free evaluation involves gathering data on a broad array of *actual effects* and evaluating the importance of these effects in meeting demonstrated needs. The evaluator makes a deliberate attempt to avoid all rhetoric related to program goals. No discussion about goals is held with staff, and no program brochures or proposals are read; only the program's actual outcomes and measurable effects are studied, and these are judged on the extent to which they meet *demonstrated participant needs*.

Scriven (1972b) has offered four reasons for doing goal-free/needs-based evaluation:

1. To avoid the risk of narrowly studying stated program objectives and thereby missing important unanticipated outcomes
2. To remove the negative connotations attached to the discovery of unanticipated effects, because "the whole language of 'side-effect' or 'secondary effect' or even 'unanticipated effect' tended to be a put-down of what might well be the crucial achievement, especially in terms of new priorities" (pp. 1-2)
3. To eliminate the perceptual biases introduced into an evaluation by knowledge of goals
4. To maintain evaluator objectivity and independence through goal-free conditions

In Scriven's (1972b) own words:

> It seemed to me, in short, that consideration and evaluation of goals was an unnecessary but also a possibly contaminating step. I began work on an alternative approach—simply the emulation of *actual* effects against a profile of *demonstrated* needs. I call this Goal-Free Evaluation. . . .
>
> The less the external evaluator hears about the goals of the project, the less tunnel vision will develop, the more attention will be paid to *looking* for *actual* effects (rather than checking on *alleged* effects). (p. 2; emphasis in original)

Scriven (1972b) distrusted the grandiose goals of most projects. Such great and grandiose proposals "assume that a gallant try at Everest will be perceived more favorably than successful mounting of molehills. That may or may not be so, but it's an unnecessary noise source for the evaluator" (p. 3). He saw no reason to get caught up in distinguishing alleged goals from real goals: "Why should the evaluator get into the messy job of trying to disentangle that knot?" He would also avoid goals conflict and goals war: "Why try to decide which goal should supervene?" He even countered the goals clarification shuffle:

> Since almost all projects either fall short of their goals or overachieve them, why waste time rating the goals, which usually aren't what is achieved? Goal-free evaluation is unaffected by—and hence does not legislate against—the shifting of goals midway in a project.

Scriven (1991b) also dealt with the fuzziness problem: "Goals are often stated so vaguely as to cover both desirable and undesirable activities, by almost anyone's standards. Why try to find out what was really intended—if anything?" Finally, he has argued that "if the program *is* achieving its stated goals and objectives, then these will show up" in the goal-free interviews with and observations of program participants done to determine actual impacts (p. 180).

Sometimes the result of goal-free evaluation is a statement of goals; that is, rather than being the initial focus of the evaluation process, a statement of operating goals becomes its outcome. Scriven, however, considers this inappropriate:

> It often happens in goal-free evaluation that people use this as a way of working out what the goals are, but I discourage them from trying to do that. That's not the point of it. The outcome is an assessment of the merit of the program.
>
> A better way to put the trouble with the name goal-free is to say that you might put it better by saying it is *needs-based instead of goal-based*. It is based on something, namely the needs of the client or recipient, but it isn't based on the goals of the program people and you never need to know those and you shouldn't ever look at them. As far as the idea that you finally come up with them as a conclusion, you'd be surprised the extent to which you don't. (Scriven and Patton 1976: 13-14; emphasis added)

Some critics of Scriven have countered that goal-free evaluation only appears to get rid of goals. The only goals really eliminated are those of local project staff. Scriven replaces staff objectives with more global goals based on societal needs and basic standards of morality. Under a goal-free approach, only the evaluator knows for sure what those needs and standards are, although Scriven (1972b) considers such standards to be as obvious as the difference between soap and cancer:

> Another error is to think that all standards of merit are arbitrary or subjective. There's nothing subjective about the claim that we need a cure for cancer more than a new brand of soap. The fact that some people have the opposite preference (if true) doesn't even weakly undermine the claim about which of these alternatives the *nation* needs most. So the Goal-Free Evaluation may use needs and not goals, or the goals of the consumer or the funding agency. Which of these is appropriate depends on the case. But in no case is it proper to use *anyone's* as the standard unless they can be *shown* to be the appropriate ones *and* morally defensible. (pp. 3-4)

As a philosopher, Scriven may feel comfortable specifying what "the nation needs" and designating standards as "morally defensible." But from a utilization-focused perspective, this simply begs the question of who is served by the information collected. The issue is not which goals are better or worse, moral or immoral, appropriate or inappropriate, in any objective sense. The issue is whose goals will be evaluated. Scriven's goal-free model eliminates only one group from the game: local project staff. He directs data in only one clear direction—away from the stated concerns of the people who run the program. He addresses an external audience, such as legislative funders. But, inasmuch as these audiences are ill defined and lack organization, I am unconvinced that the standards he applies are none other than his very own preferences about what program effects are appropriate and morally defensible. Scriven's denial notwithstanding (cf. Scriven 1972b:3), goal-free evaluation carries the danger of substituting the evaluator's goals for those of the project. Marv Alkin (1972) has made essentially the same point:

> This term "Goal-Free Evaluation" is not to be taken literally. The Goal-Free Evaluation *does* recognize goals (and not just idiosyncratic ones), but they are to be wider context goals rather than the specific *objectives* of a program. . . . By "goal-free" Scriven simply means that the evaluator is free to choose a wide context of goals. By his description, he implies that a goal-free evaluation is always free of the goals of the specific program and *sometimes* free of the goals of the program sponsor. In reality, then, goal-free evaluation is not really goal-free at all, but is simply directed at a different and usually wide decision audience. The typical goal-free evaluator must surely think (especially if he rejects the goals of the sponsoring agency) that his evaluation will extend at least to the level of "national policy formulators." The question is whether this decision audience is of the highest priority. (p. 11)

It should be noted that Scriven's goal-free proposal assumes both internal and external evaluators. Thus, part of the reason the external evaluators can ignore program staff and local project goals is because the internal evaluator takes care of all that. Thus, again, goal-free evaluation is only partially goal-free. Someone has to stay home and mind the goals while the external evaluators search for any and all effects. As Scriven (1972b) has argued,

> Planning and production require goals, and formulating them in testable terms is absolutely necessary for the manager as well as the internal evaluator who keeps the manager informed. That has nothing to do with the question of whether the external evaluator needs or should be given any account of the project's goals. (p. 4)

In later reflections, Scriven (1991b: 181) proposed "hybrid forms" in which one part of a comprehensive evaluation includes a goal-free evaluator working parallel to a goals-based evaluator. This solves the potential problem that, if evaluators need not know where a program is headed to evaluate where it ends up, then program staff might embrace this logic and, likewise, decide to eschew goals. Under a pure goal-free approach, program staff need only wait until the goal-free evaluator determines what the program has accomplished and then proclaim those accomplishments as their original goals. Ken McIntyre (1976) has described eloquently just such an approach to evaluation in a poem addressed to program staff.

> Your program's goals you need a way of knowing.
> You're sure you've just about arrived,
> But where have you been going?
>
> So, like the guy who fired his rifle at a 10-foot curtain
> And drew a ring around the hole to make a bull's-eye certain,
>
> It's best to wait until you're through
> And then see where you are:
> Deciding goals before you start is riskier by far.
>
> So, if you follow my advice in your evaluation,
> You'll start with certainty
> And end with self-congratulation. (p. 39)

There have been several serious critiques of goal-free evaluation (see Alkin 1972; Kneller 1972; Popham 1972; Stufflebeam 1972), much of it focused on the label as much as the substance. Scriven's critique of goals-based evaluation, however, is useful in affirming why evaluators need more than one way of focusing an evaluation.

Evaluation will not be well served by dividing people into opposing camps: pro-goals versus anti-goals evaluators. I am reminded of an incident at the University of Wisconsin during the student protests over the Vietnam War. Those opposed to the war were often labeled communists. At one demonstration, both anti-war and pro-war demonstrators got into a scuffle, so police began making arrests indiscriminately. When one of the pro-war demonstrators was apprehended, he began yelling, "You've got the wrong person. I'm *anti-communist*!" To which the police officer replied, "I don't care what kind of communist you are, you're going to jail."

Well, I don't care what kind of evaluator you are, to be effective you need the flexibility to evaluate with or without goals. **The utilization-focused evaluation issue is what information is needed by primary intended users, not whether goals are clear, specific, and measurable.** Let's consider, then, some other alternatives to goals-based evaluation.

A Menu Approach to Focusing Evaluations

Menu 8.1 at the end of this chapter offers an extensive list of alternative ways of focusing an evaluation. I'll elaborate on only a few of these here.

Focusing on future decisions. An evaluation can be focused on information needed to inform future decisions. Proponents and opponents of school busing for desegregation may never agree on educational goals, but they may well agree on what information is needed to inform future debate, for example, data about who is bused, at what distances, from what neighborhoods, and with what effects.

Focusing on critical issues or concerns. When the Minnesota Legislature first initiated Early Childhood Family Education programs, some legislators were concerned about what instruction and advice were being given to parents. The evaluation focused on this issue, and the evaluators became the eyes and ears for the Legislature and general public at a time of conflict about "family values" and anxiety about values indoctrination. The evaluation, based on descriptions of what actually occurred and data on parent reactions, helped put this issue to rest. Now, 20 years later, the latest evaluation of this program (Mueller 1996) has focused on the issue of universal access. Should the program be targeted to low-income parents or continue to be available to all parents, regardless of income? What are the effects on parents of a program that integrates people of different socioeconomic backgrounds? And, as before, this issue has been raised in the Legislature. Both these evaluations, then, were issue-based more than goals-based, although attention to differential parent outcomes was subsumed within the issues.

The "responsive approach" to evaluation. Stake (1975) advocates incorporating into an evaluation the various points of view of constituency groups under the assumption that "each of the groups associated with a program understands and experiences it differently and has a valid perspective" (Stecher and Davis 1987:56-57). The focus, then, is on informing each group of the perspective of other groups.

Focusing on questions. In Chapter 2, I described focusing an evaluation in Canada by having primary intended users generate questions that they wanted answered—without regard to methods, measurement, design, resources, precision—just 10 basic questions, real questions that they considered important.

After working individually and in small groups, we pulled back together and generated a single list of 10 basic evaluation questions—answers to which, they agreed, could make a real difference to the operations of the school division. The questions were phrased in *their* terms, incorporating important local nuances of meaning and circumstance. Most important, they had discovered that they had questions they cared about—not my questions but their questions, because during the course of the exercise it had become their evaluation. Generating a list of real and meaningful evaluation questions played a critical part in getting things started. Exhibit 2.4 in Chapter 2 offers criteria for good utilization-focused questions.

It is worth noting that formulating an appropriate and meaningful question involves considerable skill and insight. In her novel, *The Left Hand of Darkness*, science fiction author Ursula K. Le Guin (1969) reminds us that questions and answers are precious resources, not to be squandered or treated casually. She shows us that how one poses a question frames the answer one gets—and its utility. In the novel, the character Herbor makes an arduous journey to fortune tellers who convene rarely and, when they do, permit the asking of only a single question. His mate is obsessed with death, so Herbor asks them how long his mate will live. Herbor returns home to tell his mate the answer, that Herbor will die before his mate. His mate is enraged: "You fool! You had a question of the Foretellers, and did not ask them when I am to die, what day, month, year, how many days are left to me—you asked *how long?* Oh you fool, you staring fool, longer than you, yes, longer than you!" And with that his mate struck him with a great stone and killed him, fulfilling the prophecy and driving the mate into madness. (pp. 45-46)

A "Seat-of-the-Pants" Approach

In our follow-up study of how federal health evaluations were used, we came across a case example of using issues and questions to focus an evaluation. The decision makers in that process, for lack of a better term, called how they designed the evaluation a "seat-of-the-pants" approach. I would call it focusing on critical issues. The results influenced major decisions about the national Hill-Burton Hospital Construction Program. This evaluation illustrates some key characteristics of utilization-focused evaluation.

The evaluation was mandated in federal legislation. The director of the national Hill-Burton program established a permanent committee on evaluation to make decisions about how to spend evaluation funds. The committee included representatives from various branches and services in the division: people from the state Hill-Burton agencies, from the Comprehensive Health Planning agencies, from the health care industry, and regional Hill-Burton people. The committee met at regular intervals to "kick around" evaluation ideas. Everyone was free to make suggestions. Said the director, "If the committee thought a suggestion was worthwhile, we would usually give the person that suggested it an opportunity to work it up in a little more detail" [DM159:3]. The program officer commented that the final report *looked* systematic and goals-based, but

> that's not the kind of thinking we were actually doing at that time . . . We got started by brainstorming: "Well, we can look at the funding formula and evaluate it." And someone said, "Well, we can also see what state agencies are doing." See? And it was this kind of seat-of-the-pants approach. That's the way we got into it. [PO159:4]

The evaluation committee members were carefully selected on the basis of their knowledge of central program issues. While this was essentially an internal evaluation, the committee also made use of outside experts. The director reported that the committee was the key to the evaluation's use: "I think the makeup of the committee was such that it helped this study command quite a lot of attention from the state agencies and among the federal people concerned" [DM159:18].

Here, then, we have a case example of the first two steps in utilization-focused evaluation: (1) identifying and organizing primary intended users of the evaluation and (2) focusing the evaluation on their interests and what they believe will be useful. And how do you keep a group like this working together?

Director: Well, I think this was heavily focused toward the major aspects of the program that the group was concerned about.

Interviewer: Did the fact that you focused on major aspects of the program make a difference in how the study was used?

Decision maker: It made a difference in the interest with which it was viewed by people. . . . I think if we hadn't done that, if the committee hadn't been told to go ahead and proceed in that order, and given the freedom to do that, the committee itself would have lost interest. The fact that they felt that they were going to be allowed to pretty well free-wheel and probe into the most important things *as they saw them*, I think that had a lot to do with the enthusiasm with which they approached the task. [DM159:22]

The primary intended users began by brainstorming issues ("seat-of-the-pants approach") but eventually framed the evaluation question in the context of major policy concerns that included, but were not limited to, goal attainment. They negotiated back and forth—acting, reacting, adapting—until they determined and agreed on the most relevant focus for the evaluation.

Changing Focus Over Time: Stage Models of Evaluation

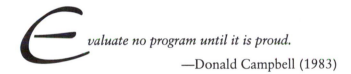

Evaluate no program until it is proud.

—Donald Campbell (1983)

Important to focusing an evaluation can be matching the evaluation to the program's stage of development, what Tripodi, Felin, and Epstein (1971) called *differential evaluation*. Evaluation priorities can vary at the *initiation stage* (when resources are being sought), the *contact stage* (when the program is just getting under way), and the full implementation stage.

In a similar vein, Jacobs (1988) has conceptualized a "five-tier" approach: (1) the preimplementation tier focused on needs assessment and design issues; (2) the accountability tier to document basic functioning to funders; (3) the program clarification tier focused on improvement and feedback to staff; (4) the "progress toward objectives" tier, focused on immediate, short-term outcomes and differential effectiveness among clients; and (5) the "program impact" tier, which focuses on overall judgments of effectiveness, knowledge about what works, and model specification for replication.

The logic of these stage models of evaluation is that, not only do the questions evolve as a program develops, but the stakes go up. When a program begins, all kinds of things can go wrong, and, as we'll see in the next chapter on implementation evaluation, all kinds of things typically do go wrong. It is rare that a program unfolds as planned. Before committing major resources to overall effectiveness evaluation, then, a stage model begins by making sure the groundwork was carefully laid during the needs assessment phase; then basic implementation issues are examined and formative evaluation for improvement becomes the focus; if the early results are promising, then *and only then*, are the stakes raised by conducting rigorous summative evaluation. It was to this kind of staging of evaluation that Donald Campbell (1983), one of the most distinguished social scientists of the twentieth century, was referring when he implored that no program should be evaluated before it is "proud." Only when program staff have reached a point where they and others close to the program believe that they're on to something, "something special that we know works here and we think others ought to borrow," should rigorous summative evaluation be done to assess the program's overall merit and worth (Schorr 1988:269-70).

An example may help clarify why it's so important to take into account a program's stage of development. The Minnesota State Department of Education funded a "human liberation" course in the Minneapolis public schools aimed at enhancing communication skills around issues of sexism and racism. Funding was guaranteed for three years, but a renewal application with evaluation findings had to be filed each year. To ensure rigorous evaluation, an external, out-of-state evaluator was hired. When the evaluator arrived on the scene, virtually everything about the program was uncertain: curriculum content, student reaction, staffing, funding, relationship to the school system, and parent support. The evaluator insisted on beginning at what Jacobs (1988) called the fourth of five tiers: assessing progress toward objectives. He forced staff, who were just beginning course development (so they were at the initiation or preimplementation stage, tier one) to articulate clear, specific, and measurable goals in behavioral terms. The staff had no previous experience writing behavioral objectives, nor was program conceptualization sufficiently advanced to concretize goals, so the evaluator formulated the objectives for the evaluation.

To the evaluator, the program seemed chaotic. How can a program operate if it doesn't know where it's going? How can it be evaluated if there are no operational objectives? His first-year evaluation rendered a negative judgment with special emphasis on what he perceived as the staff's failure to seriously attend to the behavioral objectives he had formulated. The teaching staff reacted by dismissing the evaluation as irrelevant. State education officials were also disappointed because they understood the problems of first-year programs and found the evaluation flawed in failing to help staff deal with those problems. The program staff refused to work with the same evaluator the second year and faced the prospect of a new evaluator with suspicion and hostility.

When a colleague and I became involved the second year, staff made it clear that they wanted nothing to do with behavioral objectives. The funders and school officials agreed to a formative evaluation with staff as primary users. The evaluation focused on the staff's need for information to inform ongoing, adaptive decisions aimed at program development and improvement. This meant confidential interviews with students about strengths and weaknesses of the course, observations of classes to describe interracial dynamics and student reactions, and beginning work on measures of racism and sexism. On this latter point, program staff were undecided as to whether they were really trying to change student attitudes and behaviors or just make students more "aware." They needed time and feedback to work out satisfactory approaches to the problems of racism and sexism.

By the third year, uncertainties about student reaction and school system support had been reduced by the evaluation. Initial findings indicated support for the program. Staff had become more confident and experienced. They decided to focus on instruments to measure student changes. They were ready to deal with program outcomes as long as they were viewed as experimental and flexible.

The results of the third-year evaluation showed that students' attitudes became more racist and sexist because the course experience inadvertently reinforced students' prejudices and stereotypes. Because they helped design and administer the tests used, teachers accepted the negative findings. They abandoned the existing curriculum and initiated a whole new approach to dealing with the issues involved. By working back and forth between specific information needs, contextual goals, and focused evaluation questions, it was possible to conduct an evaluation that was used to improve the program in the second year and make an overall decision about effectiveness at the end of the third year. The key to use was matching the evaluation to the program's stage of development and the information needs of designated users as those needs changed over time.

Focusing an Evaluation

Focusing an evaluation is an interactive process between evaluators and the primary intended users of the evaluation. It can be a difficult process because deciding what will be evaluated means deciding what will not be evaluated. Programs are so complex and have so many levels, goals, and functions that there are always more potential study foci than there are resources to examine them. Moreover, as human beings, we have a limited capacity to take in data and juggle complexities. We can deal effectively with only so much at one time. The alternatives have to be narrowed and decisions made about which way to go. That's why I've emphasized the menu metaphor throughout this book. The utilization-focused evaluation facilitator is a chef offering a rich variety of choices, from full seven-course feasts to fast-food preparations (but never junk). The stage approach to evaluation involves figuring out whether, in the life of the program, it's time for breakfast, lunch, a snack, a light dinner, or a full banquet.

This problem of focus is by no means unique to program evaluation. Management consultants find that a major problem for executives is focusing their energies on priorities. The trick in meditation is learning to focus on a single mantra, koan, or image. Professors have trouble getting graduate students to analyze less than the whole of human experience in their dissertations. Time-management specialists find that people have trouble setting and sticking with priorities in both their work and personal lives. And evaluators have trouble getting intended users to focus evaluation issues.

Focusing an evaluation means dealing with several basic concerns. What is the purpose of the evaluation? How will the information be used? What will we know after the evaluation that we don't know now? What actions will we be able to take based on evaluation findings? These are not simply rote questions answered once and then put aside. The utilization-focused evaluator keeps these questions front and center throughout the design process. The answers to these and related questions will determine everything else that happens in the evaluation. As evaluators and primary users interact around these questions, the evaluation takes shape.

The challenge is to find those "vital few" facts among the "trivial many" that are high in payoff and information load (MacKenzie 1972). The 20-80 rule expresses the importance of focusing on the right information. The 20-80 rule states that, in general, 20% of the facts account for 80% of what's worth knowing (Anderson 1980:26).

In working with intended users to understand the importance of focus, I often do a short exercise. It goes like this:

> Let me ask you to put your right hand out in front of you with your arm fully extended and the palm of your hand open. Now, focus on the center of the palm of your hand. Really look at your hand in a way that you haven't looked at it in a long time. Study the lines—some of them long, some short; some of them deep, some shallow; some relatively straight, some nicely curved, and some of them quite jagged and crooked. Be aware of the colors in your hand: reds, yellows, browns, greens, blues, different shades and hues. And notice the textures, hills and valleys, rough places and smooth. Become aware of the feelings in your hand, feelings of warmth or cold, perhaps tingling sensations.
>
> Now, keeping your right hand in front of you, extend your left arm and look at your left palm in the same way, not comparatively, but just focus on the center of your left palm, studying it, seeing it, feeling it. . . . Really allow your attention to become concentrated on the center of your left palm, getting to know your left hand in a new way. (Pause.)
>
> Now, with both arms still outstretched I want you to *focus*, with the same intensity that you've been using on each hand, I want you to focus on the center of *both* palms at the *same* time. (Pause while they try.) Unless you have quite unusual vision, you're not able to do that. There are some animals who can move their eyes independently of each other, but humans do not have that capability. We can look back and forth between the two hands, or we can use peripheral vision and glance at both hands at the same time, but we can't focus intensely on the center of both palms simultaneously.

Focusing involves a choice. The decision to look at something is also a decision not to look at something. A decision to see something means that something else will not be seen, at least not with the same acuity. Looking at your left hand or looking at your right hand or looking more generally at both hands provides you with different information and different experiences.

The same principle applies to evaluation. Because of limited time and limited resources, it is never possible to look at everything in great depth. Decisions have to be made about what's worth looking at. Choosing to look at one area in depth is also a decision not to look at something else in depth. Utilization-focused evaluation suggests that the criterion for making those choices of focus be the likely utility of the resulting information. Findings that would be of greatest use for program improvement and decision making focus the evaluation.

A Cautionary Note and Conclusion

Making use the focus of evaluation decision making enhances the likelihood of, but does not guarantee, actual use. There are no guarantees. All one can really do is increase the likelihood of use. Utilization-focused evaluation is time consuming, frequently frustrating, and occasionally exhausting. The process overflows with options, ambiguities, and uncertainties. When things go wrong, as they often do, you may find yourself asking a personal evaluation question: How did I ever get myself into this craziness?

But when things go right; when decision makers care; when the evaluation question is important, focused, and on target; when you begin to see programs changing even in the midst of posing questions—then evaluation can be exhilarating, energizing, and fulfilling. The challenges yield to creativity, perseverance, and commitment as those involved engage in that most splendid of human enterprises—the application of intellect and emotion to the search for answers that will improve human effort and activity. It seems a shame to waste all that intellect and emotion studying the wrong issues. That's why it's worth taking the time to carefully focus an evaluation for optimum utility.

MENU 8.1

Alternative Ways of Focusing Evaluations

Different types of evaluations ask different questions and focus on different purposes. This menu is meant to be illustrative of the many alternatives available. These options by no means exhaust all possibilities. Various options can be and often are used together within the same evaluation, or options can be implemented in sequence over a period of time, for example, doing implementation evaluation before doing outcomes evaluation, or formative evaluation before summative evaluation.

Focus or Type of Evaluation	*Defining Question or Approach*
Accreditation focus	Does the program meet minimum standards for accreditation or licensing?
Causal focus	Use rigorous social science methods to determine the relationship between the program (as a treatment) and resulting outcomes
Cluster evaluation	Synthesizing overarching lessons and/or impacts from a number of projects within a common initiative or framework
Collaborative approach	Evaluators and intended users work together on the evaluation
Comparative focus	How do two or more programs rank on specific indicators, outcomes, or criteria?
Compliance focus	Are rules and regulations being followed?
Connoisseurship approach	Specialists or experts apply their own criteria and judgment, as with a wine or antiques connoisseur
Context focus	What is the environment within which the program operates politically, socially, economically, culturally, and scientifically? How does this context affect program effectiveness?
Cost-benefit analysis	What is the relationship between program costs and program outcomes (benefits) expressed in dollars?
Cost-effectiveness analysis	What is the relationship between program costs and outcomes (where outcomes are *not* measured in dollars)?
Criterion-focused evaluation	By what criteria (e.g., quality, cost, client satisfaction) shall the program be evaluated?
Critical issues focus	Critical issues and concerns of primary intended users focus the evaluation
Decisions focus	What information is needed to inform specific future decisions?
Descriptive focus	What happens in the program? (No "why" questions or cause/effect analyses)
Developmental evaluation	The evaluator is part of the program design team, working together over the long term for ongoing program development
Diversity focus	The evaluation gives voice to different perspectives on and illuminates various experiences with the program. No single conclusion or summary judgment is considered appropriate.
Effectiveness focus	To what extent is the program effective in attaining its goals? How can the program be more effective?
Efficiency focus	Can inputs be reduced and still obtain the same level of output or can greater output be obtained with no increase in inputs?

Effort focus	What are the inputs into the program in terms of number of personnel, staff/client ratios, and other descriptors of levels of activity and effort in the program?
Empowerment evaluation	The evaluation is conducted in a way that affirms participants' self-determination and political agenda
Equity focus	Are participants treated fairly and justly?
Ethnographic focus	What is the program's culture?
Evaluability assessment	Is the program ready for formal evaluation? What is the feasibility of various evaluation approaches and methods?
Extensiveness focus	To what extent is the program able to deal with the total problem? How does the present level of services and impacts compare to the needed level of services and impacts?
External evaluation	The evaluation is conducted by specialists outside the program and independent of it to increase credibility
Formative evaluation	How can the program be improved?
Goal-free evaluation	What are the *actual* effects of the program on clients (without regard to what staff say they want to accomplish)? To what extent are real needs being met?
Goals-based focus	To what extent have program goals been attained?
Impact focus	What are the direct and indirect program impacts, not only on participants, but also on larger systems and the community?
Implementation focus	To what extent was the program implemented as designed? What issues surfaced during implementation that need attention in the future?
Inputs focus	What resources (money, staff, facilities, technology, etc.) are available and/or necessary?
Internal evaluation	Program employees conduct the evaluation
Intervention-oriented evaluation	Design the evaluation to support and reinforce the program's desired results
Judgment focus	Make an overall judgment about the program's merit or worth (see also summative evaluation)
Knowledge focus (or Lessons Learned)	What can be learned from this program's experiences and results to inform future efforts?
Logical framework	Specify goals, purposes, outputs, and activities, and connecting assumptions; for each, specify indicators and means of verification
Longitudinal focus	What happens to the program and to participants over time?
Meta-evaluation	Was the evaluation well done? Is it worth using? Did the evaluation meet professional standards and principles?
Mission focus	To what extent is the program or organization achieving its overall mission? How well do outcomes of departments or programs within an agency support the overall mission?
Monitoring focus	Routine data collected and analyzed routinely on an ongoing basis, often through a management information system
Needs assessment	What do clients need and how can those needs be met?
Needs-based evaluation	See Goal-free evaluation

(continued)

MENU 8.1 Continued

Focus or Type of Evaluation	*Defining Question or Approach*
Norm-referenced approach	How does this program population compare to some specific norm or reference group on selected variables?
Outcomes evaluation	To what extent are desired client/participant outcomes being attained? What are the effects of the program on clients or participants?
Participatory evaluation	Intended users, usually including program participants and/or staff, are directly involved in the evaluation
Personnel evaluation	How effective are staff in carrying out their assigned tasks and in accomplishing their assigned or negotiated goals?
Process focus	What do participants experience in the program? What are strengths and weaknesses of day-to-day operations? How can these processes be improved?
Product evaluation	What are the costs, benefits, and market for a specific product?
Quality assurance	Are minimum and accepted standards of care being routinely and systematically provided to patients and clients? How can quality of care be monitored and demonstrated?
Questions focus	What do primary intended users want to know that would make a difference to what they do? The evaluation answers questions instead of making judgments
Reputation focus	How the program is perceived by key knowledgeables and influentials; ratings of the quality of universities are often based on reputation among peers
Responsive evaluation	What are the various points of view of different constituency groups and stakeholders? The responsive evaluator works to capture, represent, and interpret these varying perspectives under the assumption each is valid and valuable
Social and community indicators	What routine social and economic data should be monitored to assess the impacts of this program? What is the connection between program outcomes and larger-scale social indicators, for example, crime rates?
Social justice focus	How effectively does the program address social justice concerns?
Summative evaluation	Should the program be continued? If so, at what level? What is the overall merit and worth of the program?
Theory-driven focus	On what theoretical assumptions and model is the program based? What social scientific theory is the program a test of and to what extent does the program confirm the theory?
Theory of action approach	What are the linkages and connections between inputs, activities, immediate outcomes, intermediate outcomes, and ultimate impacts?
Utilization-focused evaluation	What information is needed and wanted by primary intended users that will actually be used for program improvement and decision making? (Utilization-focused evaluation can include any of the other types above.)

Implementation Evaluation: What Happened in the Program?

If your train's on the wrong track, every station you come to is the wrong station.

—Bernard Malamud

An old story is told that through a series of serendipitous events, much too convoluted and incredible to sort out here, four passengers found themselves together in a small plane—a priest; a young, unemployed college dropout; the world's smartest person; and the President of the United States. At 30,000 feet, the pilot suddenly announced that the engines had stalled, the plane was crashing, and he was parachuting out. He added as he jumped, "I advise you to jump too, but I'm afraid there are only three parachutes left. . . . " With that dire news, he was gone.

The world's smartest person did the fastest thinking, grabbed a parachute, and jumped. The President of the United States eyed the other two, put on a parachute, and said as he jumped, "You understand, it's not for myself but for the country."

The priest looked immensely uneasy as he said, "Well, my son, you're young, and after all I am a priest, and, well, it seems only the right thing to do, I mean, if you want, um, just, um, go ahead, and um, well. . . ."

The college dropout smiled and handed the priest a parachute. "Not to worry, Reverend. There's still a parachute for each of us. The world's smartest person grabbed my backpack when he jumped."

Checking the Inventory

Programs, like airplanes, need all their parts to do what they're designed to do and accomplish what they're supposed to accomplish. Programs, like airplanes, are supposed to be properly equipped to carry out their assigned functions and guarantee passenger (participant) safety. Programs, like airplanes, are not always so equipped. Regular, systematic evaluations of inventory and maintenance checks help avoid disasters in both airplanes and programs.

Implementation evaluation focuses on finding out if the program has all its parts, if the parts are functional, and if the program is operating as it's supposed to be operating. Implementation evaluation can be a major evaluation focus. It involves finding out what actually is happening in the program. Of what does the program consist? What are the program's key characteristics? Who is participating? What do staff do? What do participants experience? What's working and what's not working? What is the program? Menu 9.1 at the end of this chapter provides additional implementation questions. (For a larger menu of over 300 implementation evaluation questions, see King, Morris, and Fitz-Gibbon 1987:129-41.)

An Exemplar

Our follow-up study of federal health evaluations turned up one quite dramatic case of evaluation use with important implementation lessons. A state legislature established a program to teach welfare recipients the basic rudiments of parenting and household management. Under this mandate, the state welfare department was charged with conducting workshops, distributing brochures, showing films, and training caseworkers on how low-income people could better manage their meager resources and become better parents. A single major city was selected for pilot-testing the program, with a respected independent research institute contracted to evaluate the program. Both the state legislature and the state welfare department committed themselves publicly to using the evaluation findings for decision making.

The evaluators interviewed a sample of welfare recipients before the program began, collecting data about parenting, household management, and budgetary practices. Eighteen months later, they interviewed the same welfare recipients again. The results showed no measurable change in parenting or household management behavior. The evaluators judged the program ineffective, a conclusion they reported to the state legislature and the newspapers. Following legislative debate and adverse publicity, the legislature terminated funding for the program—a dramatic case of using evaluation results to inform a major decision.

Now suppose we want to know why the program was ineffective. The evaluation as conducted shed no light on what went wrong because it focused entirely on measuring the attainment of intended program outcomes: changed parenting and household management behaviors of welfare recipients. As it turns out, there is a very good reason why the program didn't attain the desired outcomes. It was never implemented.

When funds were allocated from the state to the city, the program immediately became embroiled in the politics of urban welfare. Welfare rights organizations questioned the right of government to tell poor people how to spend their money or rear their children: "You have no right to tell us we have to run our houses like the white middle-class parents. And who's this Frenchman Piaget who's going to tell us how to raise American kids?"

These and other political battles delayed program implementation. Procrastination being the better part of valor, no parenting brochures were ever printed; no household management films were ever shown; no workshops were held; and no caseworkers were ever hired or trained.

In short, **the program was never implemented. But it was evaluated!** It was found to be ineffective—and was killed.

The Importance of Implementation Analysis

It is important to know the extent to which a program attains intended outcomes and meets participant needs, but to answer those questions it is essential to know what occurred in the program that can reasonably be connected to outcomes. The primer *How to Assess Program Implementation* (King et al. 1987) puts it this way:

> To consider *only* questions of program outcomes may limit the usefulness of an evaluation. Suppose the data suggest emphatically that the program was a success. You can say, "It worked!" But unless you have taken care to describe the details of the program's operations, you may be unable to answer a question that logically follows such a judgment of success: **"What worked?"** If you

> cannot answer that, you will have wasted the effort measuring the outcomes of events that cannot be described and therefore remain a mystery. . . .
>
> If this happens to you, you will not be alone. As a matter of fact, you will be in good company. Few evaluation reports pay enough attention to describing the processes of a program that helped participants achieve its outcomes. (p. 9; emphasis in the original)

Not knowing enough about implementation limits the usefulness of findings about effective programs and compounds misunderstandings about what is often called "the human services shortfall: the large and growing gap between what we expect from government-supported human service systems and what these systems in fact deliver" (Lynn and Salasin 1974:4). The human services shortfall is made up of two parts: (1) failure of implemented programs to attain desired outcomes and (2) failure to actually implement policy in the form of operating programs. In the early days of evaluation, evaluators directed most of their attention to the first problem by conducting outcomes evaluations. That practice began to change in the face of evidence that the second problem was equally, if not even more, critical. In a classic study of social program implementation, Walter Williams concluded, "The lack of concern for implementation is currently *the* crucial impediment to improving complex operating programs, policy analysis, and experimentation in social policy areas" (Williams and Elmore 1976:267; emphasis in original).

> The fundamental implementation question remains whether or not what has been decided actually can be carried out in a manner consonant with that underlying decision. More and more, we are finding, the answer is no.
>
> It is not just that the programs fall short of the early rhetoric that described them; they often barely work at all. . . . *Indeed, it is possible that past analysis and research that ignored implementation issues may have asked the wrong questions, thereby producing information of little or no use to policy making.* (Williams and Elmore 1976:xi-xii; emphasis in the original)

The notion that asking the wrong questions will result in useless information is fundamental to utilization-focused evaluation. To avoid gathering useless information about outcomes, it is important to frame evaluation questions in the context of program implementation. Data on why this is critical come from many sources. At the international level, studies collected and edited by John C. de Wilde (1967) demonstrated that program implementation and administration were *the* critical problems in developing countries. Organizational sociologists have documented the problems that routinely arise in implementing programs that are new and innovative alongside or as part of existing programs (e.g., Kanter 1983; Corwin 1973; Hage and Aiken 1970). Researchers studying diffusion of innovations have thoroughly documented the problems of implementing new ideas in new settings (e.g., Brown 1981; Havelock 1973; Rogers and Shoemaker 1971; Rogers and Svenning 1969). Then there's the marvelous case study of the Oakland Project by Pressman and Wildavsky (1984). Now a classic on the trials and tribulations of implementation, this description of a Great Society urban development effort is entitled:

IMPLEMENTATION

How Great Expectations in Washington Are Dashed in Oakland; Or, Why It's Amazing That Federal Programs Work at All, This Being a Saga of the Economic Development Administration as Told by Two Sympathetic Observers Who Seek to Build Morals on a Foundation of Ruined Hopes

Focus on Utility: Information for Action and Decisions

The problem with pure outcomes evaluation is that the results give decision makers little information to guide action. Simply learning that outcomes are high or low doesn't tell decision makers much about what to do. They also need to understand the nature of the program. In the example that opened this chapter, legislators learned that targeted welfare parents showed no behavioral changes, so they terminated the program. The evaluators failed to include data on implementation that would have revealed the absence of any of the mandated activities that were supposed to bring about the desired changes. By basing their decision only on outcomes information, the legislators terminated a policy approach that had never actually been tried. This was not a unique case.

> Although it seems too obvious to mention, it is important to know whether a program actually exists. Federal agencies are often inclined to assume that, once a cash transfer has taken place from a government agency to a program in the field, a program exists and can be evaluated. Experienced evaluation researchers know that the very existence of a program cannot be taken for granted, even after large cash transfers have taken place. Early evaluations of Title I programs in New York City provide an illustration of this problem. (Guttentag and Struening 1975b:3-4)

Terminating a policy inappropriately is only one possible error when outcomes data are used without data about implementation. Expanding a successful program inappropriately is also possible when decision makers lack information about the basis for the program's success. In one instance, a number of drug addiction treatment centers in a county were evaluated based on rates of readdiction for treated patients. All had relatively mediocre success rates except one program that reported a 100% success rate over two years. The county board immediately voted to triple the budget of that program. Within a year, the readdiction rates for that program had fallen to the same mediocre level as other centers. By enlarging the program, the county board had eliminated the key elements in the program's success—its small size and dedicated staff. It had been a six-patient, halfway house with one primary counselor who ate, slept, and lived that program. He established such a close relationship with each addict that he knew exactly how to keep each one straight. When the program was enlarged, he became administrator of three houses and lost personal contact with the clients. The successful program became mediocre. A highly effective program was lost because the county board acted without understanding the basis for the program's success.

Renowned global investor and philanthropist George Soros tells a similar story. Through a foundation he established in Moscow when the Cold War thawed, he funded a successful program aimed at transforming the education system. "I wanted to make it bigger, so I threw a lot of money at it—and in so doing, I destroyed it, effectively. It was too much money" (quoted by Buck 1995:76-77).

If, because of limited time and evaluation resources, one had to choose between implementation evaluation and outcomes measurement, there are instances in which implementation assessment would be of greater value. Decision makers can use implementation monitoring to make sure that a policy is being put into operation according to design or to test the very feasibility of the policy.

For example, Leonard Bickman (1985) has described a statewide evaluation of early childhood interventions in Tennessee that began by asking stakeholders in state government what they wanted to know. The evaluators were prepared to undertake impact studies, and they expected outcomes data to be the evaluation priority. However, interviews with stakeholders revealed a surprising sophistication about the difficulties and expenses involved in getting good, generalizable outcomes data in a timely fashion. Moreover, it was clear that key policymakers and program managers "were more concerned about the allocation and distribution of resources than about the effectiveness of projects" (p. 190). They wanted to know whether every needy child was being served. What services were being delivered to whom? State agencies could use this kind of implementation and service delivery information to "redistribute their resources to unserved areas and populations or encourage different types of services" (p. 191). They could also use descriptive information about programs to increase communications among service providers about what ideas were being tried and to assess gaps in services. Before "the more sophisticated (and expensive) questions about effectiveness" were asked, "policymakers wanted to know simpler descriptive information. . . . If the currently funded programs could not even be described, how could they be improved?" (Bickman 1985:190-91).

Unless one knows that a program is operating according to design, there may be little reason to expect it to produce the desired outcomes. Furthermore, until the program is implemented and a "treatment" is believed to be in operation, there is little reason to evaluate outcomes. This is another variation on Donald Campbell's (1983) admonition to evaluate no program until it is proud, by which he meant that demanding summative outcomes evaluation should await program claims and supporting evidence that something worth rigorous evaluation is taking place.

Ideal Program Plans and Actual Implementation

Why is implementation so difficult? Part of the answer appears to lie with how programs are legislated and planned. Policymakers seldom seem to analyze the feasibility of implementing their ideas during decision making (W. Williams 1976:270). This ends up making the task of evaluation all the more difficult because implementation is seldom clearly conceptualized. As a result, either as part of evaluability assessment or in early interactions with primary intended users, the evaluator will often have to facilitate discussion of what the program should look like before it can be said to be fully implemented and operational. Criteria for evaluating implementation will have to be developed.

Implementation evaluation is further complicated by the finding that programs are rarely implemented by single-mindedly adopting a set of means to achieve predetermined ends. The process simply isn't that rational or logical. More common is some degree of incremental implementation in which a program takes shape slowly and adaptively in response to the emerging situation and early experiences. For example, Jerome Murphy (1976:96) found, in studying implementation of Title V of the Elementary and Secondary Education Act, that states exhibited great variation in implementation. He found no basis for the widespread assumption that competently led bureaucracies would operate like goal-directed, unitary decision makers. Instead, implementers at the field level did what made sense to them rather then simply following mandates from higher up; moreover, the processes of implementation were more political and situational than rational and logical.

Sociologists who study formal organizations, social change, and diffusion of innovations have carefully documented the substantial slippage in organizations between plans and actual operations. Design, implementation, and routinization are stages of development during which original ideas are changed in the face of what's actually possible (Kanter 1983; Hage and Aiken 1970; Mann and Neff 1961; Smelser 1959). Even where planning includes a trial period, what gets finally adopted typically varies from what was tried out in the pilot effort (Rogers 1962). Social scientists who study change and innovation emphasize two points: (1) **routinization or final acceptance is never certain at the beginning;** and (2) **the implementation process always contains unknowns that change the ideal so that it looks different when and if it actually becomes operational.**

Barriers to Implementation

Understanding some of the well-documented barriers to implementation can help evaluators ask appropriate questions and generate useful information for program adaptation and improvement. For example, organizational conflict and disequilibrium often increase dramatically during the implementation stage of organizational change. No matter how much planning takes place, "people problems" will arise.

> The human element is seldom adequately considered in the implementation of a new product or service. There will be mistakes that will have to be corrected. . . . In addition, as programs take shape power struggles develop. The stage of implementation is thus the stage of conflict, especially over power. . . . Tempers flare, interpersonal animosities develop, and the power structure is shaken. (Hage and Aiken 1970:100, 104)

Odiorne (1984:190-94) dissected "the anatomy of poor performance" in managing change and found gargantuan human obstacles including staff who give up when they encounter trivial obstacles, people who hang onto obsolete ideas and outmoded ways of doing things, emotional outbursts when asked to perform new tasks, muddled communications, poor anticipation of problems, and delayed action when problems arise so that once manageable problems become major management crises.

Meyers (1981:37-39) has argued that much implementation fails because program designs are "counterintuitive"—they just don't make sense. He adds to the litany of implementation hurdles the following: undue haste, compulsion to spend all allotted funds by the end of the fiscal year, personnel turnovers, vague legislation, severe understaffing, racial tensions, conflicts between different levels of government, and the divorce of implementation from policy.

The difference between the ideal, rational model of program implementation and the day-to-day, incrementalist, and conflict-laden realities of program implementation is explained without resort to jargon in this notice found by Jerome Murphy (1976) in the office of a state education agency:

> NOTICE
>
> The objective of all dedicated
> department employees should
> be to thoroughly analyze all
> situations, anticipate all problems
> prior to their occurrence,
> have answers for these problems,
> and move swiftly to solve these
> problems when called upon. . . .
>
> However . . .
>
> When you are up to your ass in
> alligators, it is difficult to remind
> yourself that your initial objective
> was to drain the swamp. (p. 92)

The Case of Project Follow Through

Failing to understand that implementation of program ideals is neither automatic nor certain can lead to evaluation disaster, not only resulting in lack of use, but discrediting the entire evaluation effort. The national evaluation of Follow Through is a prime example. Follow Through was introduced as an extension of Head Start for primary-age children. It was a "planned variation experiment" in compensatory education featuring 22 different models of education to be tested in 158 school districts on 70,000 children throughout the nation. The evaluation employed 3,000 people to collect data on program effectiveness.

The evaluation started down the path to trouble when the designers "simply assumed in the evaluation plan that alternative educational models could and would be implemented in some systematic, uniform fashion" (Alkin 1970:2). This assumption quickly proved fallacious.

> Each sponsor developed a large organization, in some instances larger than the entire federal program staff, to deal with problems of model implementation. Each local school system developed a program organization consisting of a local director, a team of teachers and specialists, and a parent advisory group. The more the scale and complexity of the program increased, the less plausible it became for Follow Through administrators to control the details of program variations, and the more difficult it became to determine whether the array of districts and sponsors represented "systematic" variations in program content. (Williams and Elmore 1976: 108)

The Follow Through results revealed greater variation within models than between them; that is, the 22 models did not show systematic treatment effects as such. Most effects were null, some were negative, but "of all our findings, the most pervasive, consistent, and suggestive is probably this: *The effectiveness of each Follow Through model depended more on local circumstances than on the nature of the model*" (Anderson 1977:13; emphasis in original). In reviewing these findings, Eugene Tucker (1977) of the U.S. Office of Education suggested that, in retrospect, the Follow Through evaluation should have begun as a formative effort with greater focus on implementation strategies:

> It is safe to say that evaluators did not know what was implemented in the various sites. Without knowing what was implemented, it is virtually impossible to select valid effectiveness measures. . . . Hindsight is a marvelous teacher and in large-scale experimentations an expensive one. (pp. 11-12)

Ideals and Discrepancies

Provus (1971:27-29) had warned against the design used in the Follow Through evaluation at a 1966 conference on educational evaluation of national programs:

> An evaluation that begins with an experimental design denies to program staff what it needs most: information that can be used to make judgments about the program while it is in its dynamic stages of growth. . . . Evaluation must provide administrators and program staff with the information they need and the freedom to act on that information. . . .
>
> We will not use the antiseptic assumptions of the research laboratory to compare children receiving new program assistance with those not receiving such aid. We recognize that the comparisons have never been productive, nor have they facilitated corrective action. The overwhelming number of evaluations conducted in this way show no significant differences between "experimental" and "control" groups. (pp. 11-12)

Instead, Provus (1971) advocated "discrepancy evaluation," an approach that compares the actual with the ideal and places heavy emphasis on implementation evaluation. He argued that evaluations should begin by establishing the degree to which programs are actually operating as desired. Conceptualization of ideals "may arise from any source, but under the Discrepancy Evaluation Model they are derived from the values of the program staff and the client population it serves" (p. 12). Data to compare actual practices with ideals would come from local fieldwork "of the process assessment type" in which evaluators systematically collect and weigh data descriptive of ongoing program activity (p. 13).

Given the reality that actual implementation will typically look different from original ideas, a primary evaluation challenge is to help identified decision makers determine **how far from the ideal the program can deviate, and in what ways it can deviate, while still constituting the original idea (as opposed to the original ideal).** In other words, a central evaluation question is: How different can an actual program be from its ideal and still be said to have been implemented? The answer must be clarified between primary intended users and evaluators as part of the process of specifying criteria for assessing implementation.

> At some point, there should be a determination of the degree to which an innovation has been implemented successfully. What should the implemented activity be expected to look like in terms of the underlying decision? For a complex treatment package put in different local settings, decision makers usually will not expect—or more importantly, *not want* —a precise reproduction of every detail of the package. The objective is performance, not conformance. To enhance the probability of achieving the basic program or policy objectives, implementation should consist of a realistic development of the underlying decision in terms of the local setting. In the ideal situation, those responsible for implementation would take the basic idea

> and modify it to meet special local conditions. There should be a reasonable resemblance to the basic idea, as measured by inputs and expected outputs, incorporating the best of the decision and the best of the local ideas. (Williams and Elmore 1976: 277-78)

The implementation of the Oregon Community Corrections Act offers an excellent illustration of how local people can adapt a statewide mandate to fit local needs and initiatives. In studying variations in implementation of this legislation, Palumbo, Maynard-Moody, and Wright (1984) found a direct relationship between higher levels of implementation and success in attaining goals. Yet, "the implementation factors that lead to more successful outcomes are not things that can easily be transferred from one locale to another" (p. 72).

Local Variations in Implementing National Programs

I would not belabor these points if it were not so painfully clear that implementation processes have been ignored so frequently in evaluations. Edwards et al. (1975) lamented that "we have frequently encountered the idea that a [national] program is a fixed, unchanging object, observable at various times and places" (p. 142). Because this idea seems so firmly lodged in so many minds and spawns so many evaluation designs with reduced utility, I feel compelled to offer one more piece of evidence to the contrary.

Rand Corporation, under contract to the U.S. Office of Education, studied 293 federal programs supporting educational change—one of the largest and most comprehensive studies of educational change ever conducted. The study concluded that implementation "dominates the innovative process and its outcomes":

> In short, where implementation was successful, and where significant change in participant attitudes, skills, and behavior occurred, implementation was characterized by a process of mutual adaptation in which project goals and methods were modified to suit the needs and interests of the local staff and in which the staff changed to meet the requirements of the project. This finding was true even for highly technological and initially well-specified projects; unless adaptations were made in the original plans or technologies, implementation tended to be superficial or symbolic, and significant change in participants did not occur. (McLaughlin 1976:169)

The Change Agent Study found that the usual emphasis in federal programs on the *delivery system* is inappropriate. McLaughlin (1976) recommended

> a shift in change agent policies from a primary focus on the *delivery system* to an emphasis on the *deliverer*. An important lesson that can be derived from the Change Agent Study is that unless the developmental needs of the users are addressed, and unless projects are modified to suit the needs of the user and the institutional setting, the promise of new technologies is likely to be unfulfilled. (p. 180; emphasis in original)

The emphasis on the "user" in the Rand study brings us back to the importance of the personal factor and attention to primary intended users in evaluation of implementation processes. Formative, improvement-oriented evaluations can help users make the kinds of program adaptations to local conditions that Rand found so effective. That is, evaluation can be a powerful tool for guiding program development during implementation; it can facilitate initial judgments about the connections between program activities and outcomes. But implementation evaluation, like program innovation, must also be adaptive and focused on users if the process and results are to be relevant, meaningful, and useful. Utilization-focused criteria for evaluating implementation must be developed through interaction with primary intended users. Evaluation facilitators will have to be active-reactive-adaptive in framing evaluation questions in the context of program implementation.

Variations and Options in Implementation Evaluation

In working with intended users to focus evaluation questions, several alternative types of implementation evaluation can be considered, many of which can be used in combination. These options deal with different issues. Over time, a comprehensive evaluation might include all five types of implementation evaluation reviewed below.

Effort Evaluation

Effort evaluations focus on documenting "the quantity and quality of activity that takes place. This represents an assessment of input or energy regardless of output. It is intended to answer the questions 'What did you do?' and 'How well did you do it?' " (Suchman 1967:61). Effort evaluation moves up a step from asking if the program exists to asking how active the program is. If relatively inactive, it is unlikely to be very effective.

Effort questions include: Have sufficient staff been hired with the proper qualifications? Are staff-client ratios at desired levels? How many clients with what characteristics are being served by the program? Are necessary materials available? An effort evaluation involves making an inventory of program operations.

Tripodi et al. (1971) have linked effort evaluations to stages of program development. At initiation of a program, evaluation questions focus on getting services under way. Later, questions concerning the appropriateness, quantity, and quality of services become more important.

Monitoring Programs: Routine Management Information

Monitoring has become an evaluation specialization (Grant 1978). An important way of monitoring implementation over time is to establish a management information system (MIS). This provides routine data on client intake, participation levels, program completion rates, caseloads, client characteristics, and program costs. The hardware and software decisions for an MIS have long-term repercussions, so the development of such a routine data collection system must be approached with special attention to questions of use and problems of managing management information systems (Patton 1982b). Establishing and using an MIS are often primary responsibilities of internal evaluators. This has been an important growth area in the field of evaluation as demands for accountability have increased in human services (Attkisson et al. 1978; Broskowski, Driscoll, and Schulberg 1978; Elpers and Chapman 1978). The "monitoring and tailoring" approach of Cooley and Bickel (1985) demonstrates how an MIS can be client oriented and utilization focused.

Problems in implementing an MIS can lead to a MIS-match (Dery 1981). While there have been no shortage of documented MIS problems and disasters (Lucas 1975), computers and data-based management information systems have brought high technology and statistical process control to programs of all kinds (Cranford 1995; Posavac 1995; Richter 1995). The trick is to design them to be useful—and then actually get them used. Utilization-focused evaluators can play an important facilitative role in such efforts.

Process Evaluation

Process evaluation focuses on the internal dynamics and actual operations of a program in an attempt to understand its strengths and weaknesses. Process evaluations ask: What's happening and why? How do the parts of the program fit together? How do participants experience and perceive the program? This approach takes its name from an emphasis on looking at how a product or outcome is produced rather than looking at the product itself; that is, it is an analysis of the processes whereby a program produces the results it does. Process evaluation is developmental, descriptive, continuous, flexible, and inductive (Patton 1980a).

Process evaluations search for explanations of the successes, failures, and changes in a program. Under field conditions in the real world, people and unforeseen circumstances shape programs and modify initial plans in ways that are rarely trivial. The process evaluator sets out to understand and document the day-to-day reality of the setting or settings under study. This means unraveling what is actually happening in a program by searching for the major patterns and important nuances that give the program its character. A process evaluation requires sensitivity to both qualitative and quantitative changes in programs throughout their development; it means becoming intimately acquainted with the details of the program. Process evaluations not only look at formal activities and anticipated outcomes, but also investigate informal patterns and unanticipated consequences in the full context of program implementation and development.

Finally, process evaluations usually include perceptions of people close to the program about how things are going. A variety of perspectives may be sought from people inside and outside the program. For example, process data for a classroom can be collected from students, teachers, parents, staff specialists, and administrators. These differing perspectives can provide unique insights into program processes as experienced and understood by different people.

A process evaluation can provide useful feedback during the developmental phase of a program as well as later, in providing details for diffusion and dissemination of an effective program. One evaluator in our utilization of federal health evaluations reported that process information had been particularly useful to federal officials in expanding a program nationwide. Process data from early pilot efforts were used to inform the designs of subsequent centers as the program expanded.

Process evaluation is one of the four major components of the CIPP (context, input, process, product) model of evaluation developed by Stufflebeam et al. (1971; Stufflebeam and Guba 1970). It involves (1) gathering data to detect or predict defects in the procedural design or its implementation during the implementation stages, (2) providing information for program decision, and (3) establishing a record of program development as it occurs.

Component Evaluation

The component approach to implementation involves a formal assessment of distinct parts of a program. Programs can be conceptualized as consisting of separate operational efforts that may be the focus of a self-contained implementation evaluation. For example, the Hazelden Foundation Chemical Dependency Program typically includes the following components: detoxification, intake, group treatment, lectures, individual counseling, release, and outpatient services. While these components make up a comprehensive chemical dependency treatment program that can be and is evaluated on the outcome of continued sobriety over time (Laundergan 1983; Patton 1980b), there are important questions about the operation of any particular component that can be the focus of evaluation, either for improvement or to decide if that component merits continuation. In addition, linkages between one or more components may become the focus of evaluation.

Bickman (1985) has argued that one particularly attractive feature of the component approach is the potential for greater generalizability of findings and more appropriate cross-program comparisons:

> The component approach's major contribution to generalizability is its shift from the program as the unit of analysis to the component. By reducing the unit of analysis to a component instead of a program, it is more likely that the component as contrasted to entire programs can be generalized to other sites and other providers. The more homogeneous units are, the more likely one can generalize from one unit to another. In principle, the smaller the unit of analysis within a hierarchy, the more homogeneous it will be. By definition, as programs are composed of components, programs are more heterogeneous than components. It should be easier to generalize from one component to another than to generalize from one program to another.
>
> An example of this process might clarify the point. Any two early childhood programs may consist of a variety of components implemented in several different ways. Knowledge of the success of one program would not tell us a great deal about the success of the other unless they were structurally similar. However, given the diversity of programs, it is unlikely that they would have the same type and number of components. In contrast, if both had an intake component, it would be possible to compare them just on that component. A service provider in one part of the state can examine the effectiveness of a particular component in an otherwise different program in a different part of the state and see its relevance to the program he or she was directing. (p. 199)

Treatment Specification

Treatment specification involves identifying and measuring precisely what it is about a program that is supposed to have an effect. It means conceptualizing the program as a carefully defined intervention or treatment—or at least finding out if there's enough consistency in implementation to permit such a conceptualization. This requires elucidation of the "theory" program staff hold about what they have to do in order to accomplish the results they want. In technical terms, this means identifying independent variables that are expected to affect outcomes (the dependent variables). Treatment specification reveals the causal assumptions undergirding program activity.

Measuring the degree to which conceptualized treatments actually occur can be a tricky and difficult task laden with methodological and conceptual pitfalls:

> Social programs are complex undertakings. Social program evaluators look with something akin to jealousy at evaluators in agriculture who evaluate a new strain of wheat or evaluators in medicine who evaluate the effects of a new drug. . . . The same stimulus can be produced again, and other researchers can study its consequences—under the same or different conditions, with similar or different subjects, but with some assurance that they are looking at the effects of the same *thing*.
>
> Social programs are not nearly so specific. They incorporate a range of components, styles, people, and procedures. . . . The content of the program, what actually goes on, is much harder to describe. There are often marked internal variations in operation from day to day and from staff member to staff member. When you consider a program as large and amorphous as the poverty program or the model cities program, it takes a major effort to just describe and analyze the program inputs. (Weiss 1972b:43)

Yet, unless basic data are generated about the program as an intervention, the evaluator does not know to what to attribute the outcomes observed. This is the classic problem of treatment specification in social science research and, of course, takes us into the arena of trying to establish causality.

> Any new program or project may be thought of as representing a theory or hypothesis in that—to use experimental terminology—the decision maker wants to put in place a treatment expected to *cause* certain predicted effects or outcomes. (Williams and Elmore 1976:274; emphasis in original)

From this perspective, one task of implementation evaluation is to identify and operationalize the program treatment.

Some comparative or experimental design evaluations fall into the trap of relying on the different names programs call themselves—their labels or titles—to distinguish different treatments. Because this practice yields data that can easily be misunderstood and misused, the next section explores the problem in greater depth.

The Challenge of Truth-in-Labeling

Warning: This section sermonizes on the Pandorian folly attendant upon those who believe program titles and names. What a program calls its intervention is no substitute for gathering actual data on program implementation. Labels are not treatments.

I suspect that overreliance on program labels is a major source of null findings in evaluation research. Aggregating results under a label can lead to mixing effective with ineffective programs that have nothing in common except their name. An evaluation of Residential Community Corrections Programs in Minnesota offers a case in point. The report, prepared by the Evaluation Unit of the Governor's Commission on Crime Prevention and Control, compared recidivism rates for three "types" of programs: (1) halfway houses, (2) PORT (Probationed Offenders Rehabilitation and Training) projects, and (3) juvenile residences. The term *halfway house* referred to a "residential facility designed to facilitate the transition of paroled adult ex-offenders returning to society from institutional confinement." This distinguished halfway houses from *juvenile residences*, which served only juveniles. Offenders on probation were the target of the PORT projects (GCCPC 1976:8). What we have, then, are three different target groups, not three different treatments.

The report presented aggregated outcome data for each type of community corrections program, thereby combining the results for projects about which they had no systematic implementation data. In effect, they compared the outcomes of three labels: halfway houses, PORT projects, and juvenile residences. Nowhere in the several hundred pages of the report was there any systematic data about the activities offered in these programs. People went in and people came out; what happened in between was ignored by the evaluators.

The evaluation concluded that "the evidence presented in this report indicates that residential community corrections programs have had little, if any, impact on the recidivism of program clients" (GCCPC 1976:289). These preliminary findings resulted in a moratorium on funding of new residential community corrections, and the final report recommended maintaining that moratorium. With no attention to the meaningfulness of their analytical labels, and with no treatment specifications, the evaluators passed judgment on the effectiveness of an $11 million program.

The aggregated comparisons were essentially meaningless. When I interviewed staff in a few of these community corrections projects, it became clear that halfway houses varied tremendously in treatment modality, clientele, and stage of implementation. The report's comparisons were based on averages within the three types of programs, but the averages disguised important variations within each type. No "average" project existed, yet, the different programs of like name were combined for comparative purposes. Within types, the report obscured individual sites that were doing excellent work as well as some of dubious quality.

One has only to read the journals that publish evaluation findings to find similar studies. There are comparisons between "open" schools and "traditional" schools that present no data on relative openness. There are comparisons of individual therapy with group therapy where no attention is paid to the homogeneity of either category of treatment.

> A common administrative fiction, especially in Washington, is that because some money associated with an administrative label (e.g., Head Start) has been spent at several places and over a period of time, that the entities spending the money are comparable from time to time and from place to place. Such assumptions can easily lead to evaluation-research disasters. (Edwards et al. 1975:142).

Treatment Specification: An Alternative to Labeling

A newspaper cartoon showed several federal bureaucrats assembled around a table in a conference room. The chair of the group was saying, "Of course the welfare program has a few obvious flaws . . . but if we can just think of a catchy enough name for it, it just might work!" (Dunagin 1977).

Treatment specification means getting behind labels to state what is going to happen in the program that is expected to make a difference. For example, one theory undergirding community corrections has been that integration of criminal offenders into local communities is the best way to rehabilitate those offenders and thereby reduce recidivism. It is therefore important to gather data about the degree to which each project actually integrates offenders into the community. Halfway houses and juvenile residences can be run like small-scale prisons, completely isolated from the environment. Treatment specification tells us what to look for in each project to find out if the program's causal theory is actually being put to the test. (At this point we are not dealing with the question of how to measure the relevant independent variables in a program theory, but only attempting to specify the intended treatment in nominal terms.)

Here's an example of how treatment specification can be useful. A county Community Corrections Department in Minnesota wanted to evaluate its foster group-home program for juvenile offenders. The primary information users lacked systematic data about what the county's foster group homes were actually like. The theory undergirding the program was that juvenile offenders would be more likely to be rehabilitated if they were placed in warm, supportive, and nonauthoritarian environments where they were valued by others and could therefore learn to value themselves. The goals of the program included helping juveniles feel good about themselves and become capable of exercising independent judgment, thereby reducing subsequent criminal actions (recidivism).

The evaluation measured both outcomes and implementation with special attention to *treatment environment*. What kind of treatment is a youth exposed to in a group home? What are the variations in group homes? Do certain types of foster group homes attain better results, both providing positive experiences for youth and reducing recidivism?

The findings revealed that the environments of the sample of 50 group homes could be placed along a continuum from highly supportive and participatory home environments to nonsupportive and authoritarian ones. Homes were about evenly distributed along the continua of support versus nonsupport and participatory versus authoritarian patterns; that is, about half the juveniles experienced homes with measurably different climates. Juveniles from supportive-participatory group homes showed significantly lower recidivism rates than juveniles from nonsupportive-authoritarian ones ($r = .33, p < .01$). Variations in type of group-home environment were also correlated significantly with other outcome variables (Patton, Guthrie, et al. 1977).

In terms of treatment specification, these data demonstrated two things: (1) in about half of the county's group homes, juveniles were not experiencing the kind of treatment that the program design called for; and (2) outcomes varied directly with the nature and degree of program implementation. Clearly it would make no sense to conceptualize these 50 group homes as a homogeneous treatment. We found homes that were run like prisons and homes in which juveniles were physically abused. We also found homes where young offenders were loved and treated as members of the family. Aggregating recidivism data from all 50 homes into a single average rate would disguise important environmental variations. By specifying the desired treatment and measuring implementation compliance, the program's theory could be examined in terms of both feasibility and effectiveness.

EXHIBIT 9.1

Format for Connecting Goals With Implementation Plans and Measurement

	Goals: Expected Client Outcomes	*Indicators: Outcome Data/Measurement Criteria*	*How Goals Will Be Attained (Implementation Strategies)*	*Data on Implementation Criteria*
1.				
2.				
3.				
4.				

(For an in-depth discussion of how to measure treatment environments for different kinds of programs—mental health institutions, prisons, family environments, military units, classrooms, businesses, schools, hospitals, and factories—see Conrad and Roberts-Gray 1988; Moos 1979, 1975, 1974.)

The process of specifying the desired treatment environment began with identified evaluation users, not with a scholarly literature search. The theory tested was that held by primary decision makers. Where resources are adequate and the design can be managed, the evaluators may prevail upon intended users to include tests of those theories the evaluators believe are illuminative. But first priority goes to providing intended users with information about the degree to which their own implementation ideals and treatment specifications have actually been realized in program operations. Causal models are sometimes forced on program staff when they bear no similarity to the models on which that staff bases its program activities. The evaluators' research interests are secondary to the information needs of primary intended information users in utilization-focused evaluation.

Connecting Goals and Implementation

In complex programs with multiple goals, it can be useful to engage staff in an exercise that links activities to outcomes and specifies measures for each. Exhibit 9.1 offers a matrix to guide this exercise. Once completed, the matrix can be used to focus the evaluation and decide what information would be most useful for program improvement and decision making.

Implementation Overview

This chapter has reviewed five evaluation approaches to implementation: (1) effort evaluation, (2) ongoing program monitoring, (3) process evaluation, (4) component evaluation, and (5) treatment specification. Depending on the nature of the issues involved and the information needed, any one, two, or all five approaches might be employed. The point is that without information about actual program operations, decision makers are limited in interpreting performance data for program improvement. These different evaluations answer different questions and focus on different aspects of program implementation. The key is to match the type(s) of evaluation to the information needs of specific stakeholders and primary intended users. One of the decision makers we interviewed in our utilization study was emphatic on this point:

> Different types of evaluations are appropriate and useful at different times. . . . We tend to talk about evaluation as if it's a single thing. The word *evaluation* should not be used generically. It's harmful. We ought to stop talking about evaluation as if it's a single homogenous thing. [DM111:29]

Implementation is one possible focus for an evaluation. Not all designs will include a lot of implementation data. Other information may be more important, relevant, and useful to inform pending decisions. What is crucial is that during the process of framing the evaluation, the issue of implementation analysis is raised. Evaluators have a responsibility in their active-reactive-adaptive interactions with stakeholders to explore options with intended users to decide jointly what will be useful in the particular circumstances at hand.

Sometimes what primary users need and want varies from the evaluator's initial expectations.

Former Ambassador to China Winston Lord was once driving in the Chinese countryside with his wife. They stopped at an ancient Buddhist temple, where the senior monk greeted them enthusiastically. "Would you do this temple a great honor and favor for our future visitors, to guide and instruct them? Would you write something for us in English?"

Ambassador Lord felt quite flattered because he knew that, traditionally, only emperors and great poets were invited to write for the temple. The monk returned shortly carrying two wooden plaques and said: "To guide and instruct future English visitors, would you write on this plaque the word 'Ladies' and on this plaque the word 'Gentlemen'?"

May the writings of evaluators be as useful.

MENU 9.1

Sample Implementation Evaluation Questions

Feasibility and Compliance Issues

1. What was originally proposed and intended for implementation?
2. What needs assessment or situation analysis informed program design?
3. What was the program's expected model?
4. What theory and assumptions undergirded the proposed model, if any?
5. Who has a stake in the program being implemented as proposed and originally designed?
6. What resources were anticipated for full implementation?
7. What staff competencies and roles were anticipated?
8. What were the original intended time lines for implementation?
9. What aspects of implementation, if any, involve meeting legal mandates?
10. What potential threats to implementation were anticipated during design?

Formative Evaluation Questions

1. What are the program's key characteristics as perceived by various stakeholders, for example, participants, staff, administrators, funders? How similar or different are those perceptions? What's the basis of differences?
2. What are the characteristics of program participants and how do those compare to the intended target population for the program?
3. How do actual resources, staff competencies and experiences, and time lines compare to what was expected?
4. What's working as expected? What's not working as expected? What challenges and barriers have emerged? How has staff responded to those challenges and barriers?
5. What assumptions have proved true? What assumptions are problematic?
6. What do participants actually do in the program? What are their primary activities (in detail)? What do they experience?
7. What do participants like and dislike? What are their perceptions of what's working and not working? Do they know what they're supposed to accomplish as participants? Do they "buy into" the program's goals and intended outcomes?

(continued)

MENU 9.1 Continued

8. How well are staff functioning together? What are their perceptions about what's working and not working? Do they know what outcomes they're aiming for? Do they "buy into" the program's goals and intended outcomes? What are their perceptions of participants? of administrators? of their own roles and effectiveness?
9. What has changed from the original design and why? On what basis are adaptations from the original design being made? Who needs to "approve" such changes?
10. What monitoring system has been established to assess implementation on an ongoing basis and how is it being used?

Summative Implementation Questions

1. As the program has been implemented, what model has emerged? That is, can the program be modeled as an intervention or treatment with clear connections between inputs, activities, and outcomes?
2. To what extent and in what ways was the original implementation design feasible? What was not feasible? Why? Were deviations from the original design great enough that what was actually implemented constitutes a different model, treatment, or intervention from what was originally proposed? In other words, has the feasibility and viability of the original design actually been tested in practice, or was something else implemented?
3. How stable and standardized has the implementation become both over time and, if applicable, across different sites?
4. To what extent is the program amenable to implementation elsewhere? What aspects of implementation were likely situational? What aspects are likely generalizable?
5. What are the start-up and continuing costs of implementation?
6. Has implementation proved sufficiently effective and consistent that the program merits continuation?

Lessons Learned Implementation Questions

1. What has been learned about implementation of this specific program that might inform similar efforts elsewhere?
2. What has been learned about implementation in general that would contribute to scholarly and policy research on implementation?

NOTE: For a larger menu of over 300 implementation evaluation questions, see King et al. 1987:129-41.

10

The Program's Theory of Action

Conceptualizing Causal Linkages

All the World's a Stage for Theory

In Tony Kushner's Pulitzer Prize-winning play, *Angels in America*, Part Two opens in the Hall of Deputies, the Kremlin, where Aleksii Antedilluvianovich Prelapsarianov, the World's Oldest Living Bolshevik, speaks with sudden, violent passion, grieving a world without theory:

> *How are we to proceed without Theory? What System of Thought have these Reformers to present to this mad swirling planetary disorganization, to the Inevident Welter of fact, event, phenomenon, calamity? Do they have, as we did, a beautiful Theory, as bold, as Grand, as comprehensive a construct. . . ? You can't imagine, when we first read the Classic Texts, when in the dark vexed night of our ignorance and terror the seed-words sprouted and shoved incomprehension aside, when the incredible bloody vegetable struggled up and through into Red Blooming gave us Praxis, True Praxis, True Theory married to Actual Life. . . . You who live in this Sour Little Age cannot imagine the grandeur of the prospect we gazed upon: like standing atop the highest peak in the mighty Caucasus, and viewing in one all-knowing glance the mountainous, granite order of creation. You cannot imagine it. I weep for you.*
>
> *And what have you to offer now, children of this Theory? What have you to offer in its place? Market Incentives? American Cheeseburgers? Watered-down Bukharinite stopgap makeshift Capitalism! NEPmen! Pygmy children of a gigantic race!*
>
> *Change? Yes, we must change, only show me the Theory, and I will be at the barricades, show me the book of the next Beautiful Theory, and I promise you these blind eyes will see again, just to read it, to devour that text. Show me the words that will reorder the world, or else keep silent.*
>
> —Kushner 1994:13-14[1]

Mountaintop Inferences

That evil is half-cured whose cause we know.

—Shakespeare

Causal inferences flash as lightning bolts in stormy controversies. While philosophers of science serve as meteorologists for such storms—describing, categorizing, predicting, and warning, policymakers seek to navigate away from the storms to safe harbors of reasonableness. When studying causality as a graduate student, I marveled at the multitude of mathematical and logical proofs necessary to demonstrate that the world is a complex place (e.g., Nagel 1961; Bunge 1959). In lieu of rhetoric on the topic, I offer a simple Sufi story to introduce this chapter's discussion of the relationship between means and ends, informed and undergirded by theory.

The incomparable Mulla Nasrudin was visited by a would-be disciple. The man, after many vicissitudes, arrived at the hut on the mountain where the Mulla (teacher) was sitting. Knowing that every single action of the illuminated Sufi was meaningful, the newcomer asked Nasrudin why he was blowing on his hands. "To warm myself in the cold, of course," Nasrudin replied.

Shortly afterward, Nasrudin poured out two bowls of soup, and blew on his own. "Why are you doing that, Master?" asked the disciple. "To cool it, of course," said the teacher.

At that point, the disciple left Nasrudin, unable to trust any longer a man who used the same process to cause different effects—heat and cold.

—Adapted from Shah 1964: 79-80

Reflections on Causality in Evaluation

In some cases, different programs use divergent processes to arrive at the same outcome; in others, various programs use similar means to achieve different outcomes. Sometimes, competing treatments with the same goal operate side by side in a single program. Sorting out causal linkages challenges both theoretically and methodologically.

Stated quite simply, the causal question in evaluation is this: Did the implemented program lead to the desired outcomes? However, in the previous chapters, it has become clear that delineating either program implementation or outcomes can lead us into conceptual and empirical labyrinths unto themselves. Now we must consider how to find openings where they connect to each other. To what extent and in what ways do the processes, activities, and treatments of a program cause or affect the behaviors, attitudes, skills, knowledge, and feelings of targeted participants? Such questions are complex enough in small, local programs, but imagine for a moment the complexity of attributing effects to causes in evaluating an entire multilayered, multisite initiative to integrate human services (Knapp 1996:25-26; Marquart and Konrad 1996).

One need know little about research to appreciate the elusiveness of definitive, pound-your-fist-on-the-table conclusions about causality. Our aim is more modest: reasonable estimations of the likelihood that particular activities have contributed in concrete ways to observed effects—emphasis on the word *reasonable*. Not definitive conclusions. Not absolute proof. Evaluation offers reasonable estimations of probabilities and likelihood, enough to provide useful guidance in an uncertain world (Blalock 1964). Policymakers and program decision makers, I find, typically understand and appreciate this. Hard-core academics and scientists often don't. As always, the question of primary intended users is . . . *primary*.

The Theory Option in Evaluation: Constructing a Means-Ends Hierarchy

Causation. The relation between mosquitos and mosquito bites.

—Michael Scriven (1991b:77)

To venture into the arena of causality is to undertake the task of theory construction. This chapter suggests some simple conceptual approaches to theory construction aimed at elucidating and testing the theory upon which a program is based. A theory links means and ends. The construction of a means-ends hierarchy for a program constitutes a comprehensive description of the program's model. For example, Suchman (1967) recommended building a *chain of objectives* by trichotomizing objectives into immediate, intermediate, and ultimate goals. The linkages between these levels make up a continuous series of actions wherein immediate objectives (focused on implementation) logically precede intermediate goals (short-term outcomes) and therefore must be accomplished before higher-level goals (long-term impacts). Any given objective in the chain is the outcome of the successful attainment of the preceding objective and, in turn, is a precondition to attainment of the next higher objective.

> Immediate goals refer to the results of the specific act with which one is momentarily concerned, such as the formation of an obesity club; the intermediate goals push ahead toward the accomplishment of the specific act, such as the actual reduction in weight of club members; the ultimate goal then examines the effect of achieving the intermediate goal upon the health status of the members, such as reduction in the incidence of heart disease. (Suchman 1967:51-52)

The means-ends hierarchy for a program often has many more than three links. In Chapter 7, I presented the mission statement, goals, and objectives of the Minnesota Comprehensive Epilepsy Program. This three-tier division—mission, goals, and objectives—was useful to get an overview of the program as an initial step in identifying what evaluation information might be most useful. Once that initial focus was determined, a more detailed, multitiered chain of objectives could be constructed. For example, the epilepsy program had educational, research, treatment, and administrative goals. Once the research goal was selected by decision makers as the evaluation priority, a more thorough means-ends hierarchy was constructed. Exhibit 10.1 illustrates the difference between the initial three-tier conceptualization and the more refined multitier chain of objectives developed later. To have constructed such a detailed, multitier chain of objectives for all seven epilepsy goals would have taken a great deal of time and effort. By using the simple, three-tier approach initially, it was possible to then focus on those goal areas in which conceptualizing a full chain of objectives (or means-ends hierarchy) was worth the time and effort.

The full chain of objectives that links inputs to activities, activities to immediate outputs, immediate outputs to intermediate outcomes, and intermediate outcomes to ultimate goals constitutes a program's theory. Any particular paired linkage in the theory displays an action and reaction: a hypothesized cause and effect. As one constructs a hierarchical/sequential model, it becomes clear that there is only a relative distinction between ends and means: "Any end or goal can be seen as a means to another goal, [and] one is free to enter the 'hierarchy of means and ends' at any point" (Perrow 1968:307). **In utilization-focused evaluation, the decision about where to enter the means-ends hierarchy for a particular evaluation is made on the basis of what information would be most useful to the primary intended evaluation users.** In other words, a formative evaluation might focus on the connection between inputs and activities (an implementation evaluation) and not devote resources to measuring outcomes higher up in the hierarchy until implementation was ensured. Elucidating the entire hierarchy does not incur an obligation to evaluate every linkage in the hierarchy. The means-ends hierarchy displays a series of choices for more focused evaluations while also establishing a context for such narrow efforts.

Suchman (1967:55) used the example of a health education campaign to show how a means-ends hierarchy can be stated in terms of a series of measures or evaluation findings. Rather than linking a series of objectives, in Exhibit 10.2, he displayed the theoretical hierarchy as a series of evaluative measurements.

How theory-driven an evaluation should be is a matter of debate, as is the question of what sources to draw on in theory construction (Bickman 1990; Chen and Rossi 1989). Evaluators who gather purely descriptive data about implementation or outcomes without connecting the two in some framework risk being attacked as atheoretical technicians. Yet, a program must have achieved a certain level of maturity to make the added effort involved in theory-driven evaluation fruitful. At times, all decision makers need and want is descriptive data for monitoring, fine-tuning, or improving program operations. However, attention to program theory can yield important insights and, in recent years, thanks especially to Chen's (1990) advocacy of *theory-driven evaluation* and the

EXHIBIT 10.1
Initial and Refined Epilepsy Program Means-Ends Theory

Initial Conceptualization of Epilepsy Program

Program Mission:	To improve the lives of people with epilepsy through research
Program Goal:	To publish high-quality, scholarly research on epilepsy
Program Objective:	To conduct research on neurological, pharmacological, epidemiological, and social psychological aspects of epilepsy

Refined Conceptualization of Epilepsy Chain of Objectives

1. People with epilepsy lead healthy, productive lives
2. Provide better medical treatment for people with epilepsy
3. Increase physicians' knowledge of better medical treatment for epileptics
4. Disseminate findings to medical practitioners
5. Publish findings in scholarly journals
6. Produce high-quality research findings on epilepsy
7. Establish a program of high-quality research on epilepsy
8. Assemble necessary resources (personnel, finances, facilities) to establish a research program
9. Identify and generate research designs to close knowledge gaps
10. Identify major gaps in knowledge concerning causes and treatment of epilepsy

work of Connell et al. (1995) on using *theories of change* to frame evaluations of community initiatives, evaluators have been challenged to take a more active role in looking for opportunities to design evaluations on a solid foundation of theory.

Three Approaches to Program Theory

Three major approaches to program theory development for evaluation are:

1. The *deductive approach*—drawing on scholarly theories from the academic literature
2. The *inductive approach*—doing fieldwork on a program to generate grounded theory
3. The *user-focused approach*—working with intended users to extract and specify their implicit theory of action

The deductive approach draws on dominant theoretical traditions in specific scholarly disciplines to construct models of the relationship between program treatments and outcomes. For example, an evaluation of whether a graduate school teaches students to think critically could be based on the theoretical perspective of *a phenomenography of adult critical reflection*, as articulated by the Distin-

EXHIBIT 10.2
Theoretical Hierarchy of Evaluation Measures for a Health Education Campaign

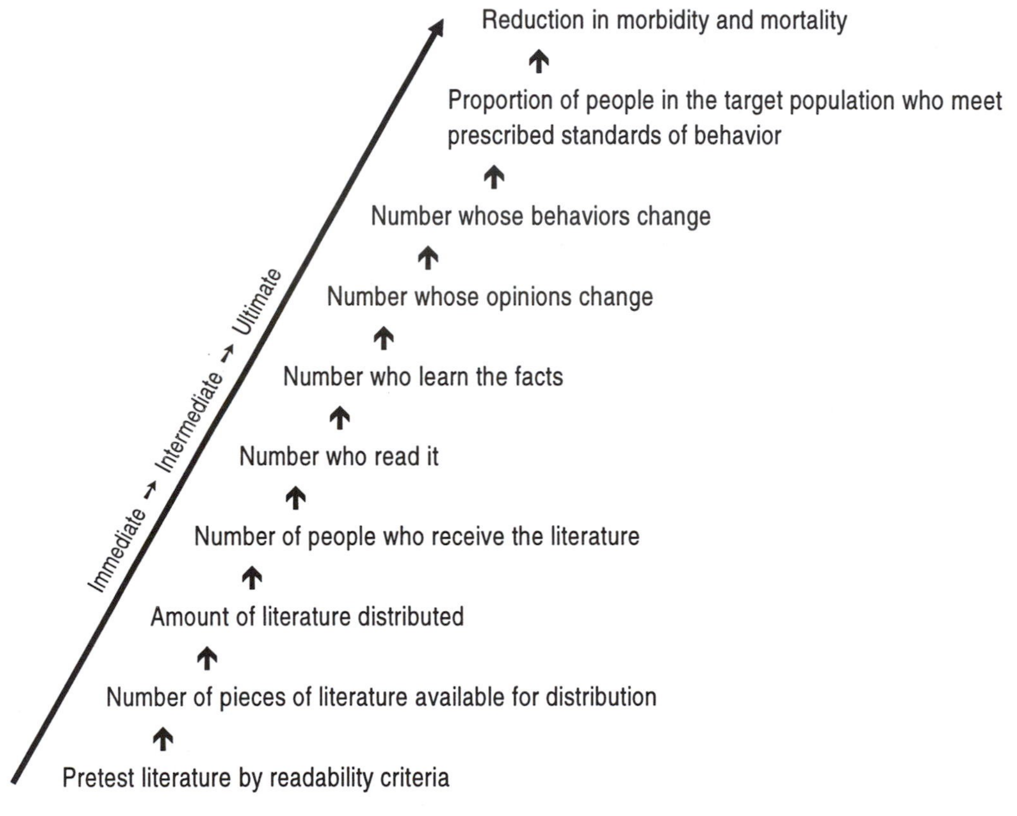

SOURCE: Adapted from Suchman 1967:55.

guished Professor of Education Stephen Brookfield (1994), an approach that emphasizes the visceral and emotional dimensions of critical thought as opposed to purely intellectual, cognitive, and skills emphases. Illustrations of the deductive approach to evaluation are chronicled in Rossi and Freeman (1993) and Boruch, McSweeny, and Soderstrom (1978). However, the temptation in the deductive approach is to make the study more research than evaluation, that is, to let the literature review and theory testing take over the evaluation. Testing social science theories may be a by-product of an evaluation in which the primary purpose is knowledge generation (see Chapter 4), but the primary focus in this chapter is on testing practitioner theories about why they do what they do and what they think results from what they do. Utilization-focused evaluation involves primary intended users in specifying the program's theory and in deciding how much attention to give to testing the theory generated, including how much to draw on social science theory as a framework for the evaluation (Patton 1989).

The inductive approach involves the evaluator in doing fieldwork to generate theory. Staying with the example of evaluating whether graduate students learn to think critically, the inductive approach would involve assessing student work, observing students in class, and interviewing students and professors to determine what model of education undergirds efforts to impart critical thinking skills. Such an effort could be done as a study unto itself, for example, as part of an early evaluability assessment process, or it could be done in conjunction with a deductive effort based on a literature review. The product of the inductive approach, and therefore a major product of the evaluation, would be an empirically derived theoretical model of the relationship between program activities and outcomes framed in terms of important contextual factors.

User-Focused Theory of Action Approach

In the user-focused approach, the evaluator's task is to facilitate intended users, including program personnel, in articulating their operating theory. Continuing with the critical thinking example, this would mean bringing together students and professors to make explicit *their* educational assumptions and generate a model that could then be tested as part of the evaluation. In the purely inductive approach above, by way of contrast, the evaluator builds the theory from observations and fieldwork rather than from discussion and group facilitation with those involved.

What makes the user-focused approach challenging is that practitioners are seldom aware of their theory of action. The notion that people in programs operate on the basis of theories of action derives from the work of organizational development scholars Chris Argyris and Donald Schön (1978, 1974). They studied the connection between theory and practice as a means of increasing professional effectiveness:

> We begin with the proposition that people hold theories of action about how to produce consequences they intend. Such theories are theories about human effectiveness. By *effectiveness* we mean the degree to which people produce their intended consequences in ways that make it likely that they will continue to produce intended consequences. Theories of action, therefore, are theories about effectiveness, and because they contain propositions that are falsifiable, they are also theories about truth. *Truth* in this case means truth about how to behave effectively. (Argyris 1982:83)

The phrase *theories of action* refers specifically to how to produce desired results in contrast to theories in general, which explain why some phenomenon of interest occurs. Deductive and inductive approaches to theory make use of programs as manifestations of some larger phenomenon of interest while theories of action are quite specific to a particular program or organization. Argyris and Schön (1978) distinguish two kinds of theories of action: (1) espoused theories—what people say or believe is their theory; and (2) theories-in-use—the bases on which people actually act. They drew on a great body of research showing the following:

> People do not always behave congruently with their beliefs, values, and attitudes (all part of espoused theories). . . . Although people do not behave congruently with their espoused theories, they do behave congruently with their theories-in-use, *and* they are unaware of this fact. (Argyris 1982:85)

In this conundrum of dissonance between belief and practice lies a golden opportunity for reality testing: the heart of evaluation.

The user-focused theory of action approach can involve quite a bit of work, since few front-line practitioners in programs are schooled to think systematically in terms of theoretical constructs and relationships. Moreover, the idea of making their assumptions explicit and then testing them can be frightening. The user-focused evaluator, as facilitator of this process, must do at least five things:

1. Make the process of theory articulation understandable.
2. Help participants be comfortable with the process intellectually and emotionally.
3. Provide direction for how to articulate espoused theories that participants believe undergird their actions.
4. Facilitate a commitment to test espoused theories in the awareness that actual theories-in-use, as they emerge, may be substantially different from espoused theories.
5. Keep the focus on doing all this to make the evaluation useful.

The causal model to be tested in the user-focused evaluation is the causal model upon which program activities are based, not a model extracted from academic sources or fieldwork. First priority goes to providing primary stakeholders with information about the degree to which their own implementation ideals and treatment specifications actually achieve desired outcomes through program operations. The evaluator's own theories and academic traditions can be helpful in discovering and clarifying the program's theories of action, but testing intended users' and decision makers' theories of programmatic action is primary; the evaluator's scholarly interests are secondary.

The importance of understanding the program's theory of action as perceived by key stakeholders is explained in part by basic insights from the sociology of knowledge and work on *the social construction of reality* (Holzner and Marx 1979; Berger and Luckman 1967; Schutz 1967). This work is built on the observation of W. I. Thomas that **what is perceived as real is real in its consequences.** In this case, espoused theories are what practitioners perceive to be real. Those espoused theories, often implicit and only espoused when asked for, have real consequences for what practitioners do. Elucidating the theory of action held by primary users can help them be more deliberative about what they do and more willing to put their beliefs and assumptions to an empirical test through evaluation. In short, the user-focused approach challenges decision makers, program staff, funders, and other users to engage in reality testing, that is, to test whether what they believe to be true (their espoused theory of action) is what actually occurs (theory-in-use).

A Reality-Testing Example

Let me offer a simple example of user-focused, theory-of-action reality testing. A State Department of Energy allocated conservation funds through 10 regional districts. An evaluation was commissioned by the department to assess the impact of local involvement in priority setting. State and regional officials articulated the following *equitable and uniform model* of decision making as their espoused theory of action:

1. State officials establish funding targets for each district based on needs assessments and available funds.
2. District advisory groups develop proposals to meet the state targets with broad citizen input.
3. The State approves the budgets based on the merit of the proposals within the guidelines, rules, and targets provided.
4. Expected result: Approved funds equal original targets.

In short, the espoused theory of action was that decisions are made equitably based on explicit procedures, guidelines, and rules. The data showed this to be the case in 6 of the 10 districts. In the other 4 districts, however, proposals from the districts exceeded the assigned target amounts by 30% to 55%; that is, a district assigned a target of $100 million submitted proposals for $140 million (despite a "rule" that said proposals could not exceed targets). Moreover, the final, approved budgets exceeded the original targets by 20% to 40%. The district with a target of $100 million and proposals for $140 million received $120 million. Four of the districts, then, were not engaged in a by-the-book equitable process; rather, their process was negotiated, personal, and political. Needless to say, when these data were presented, the six districts that followed the guidelines and played the funding game by what they thought were uniform rules—the districts whose proposals equaled their assigned targets—were outraged. Testing the espoused theory of uniformity and fairness revealed that the reality (theory-in-use) in four districts did not match the espoused theory in ways that had significant consequences for all concerned.

This is a simple, commonsense example of a user-focused approach to articulating and testing a program's theory of action. Nothing elegant. No academic trappings. The espoused theory of action is a straightforward articulation of what is supposed to happen in the process that is intended to achieve desired outcomes. The linkages between processes and outcomes are made explicit. Evaluative data then reveal the theory-in-use, that is, what actually happens. Program staff, other intended users, *and* evaluators can learn a great deal from engaging in this collaborative process (e.g., Layzer 1996).

A Menu of Theory-Based Approaches

Each of the three approaches to program theory—deductive, inductive, and user-focused—has advantages and disadvantages. These are reviewed in Menu 10.1, drawing on the work of Lipsey and Pollard (1989) and Chen (1989). The strategic calculations a utilization-focused evaluator must make include determining how useful it will be to spend time and effort elucidating a theory of action (or more than one where different perspectives exist); how to keep theory generation from becoming esoteric and overly academic; how formal to be in the process; and what combinations of the three approaches, or relative emphasis, should be attempted. Factors to consider in making these calculations will be clearer after some more examples, which follow, but the focus here is on the user-focused, theory-of-action approach.

MENU 10.1

Approaches to Generating Program Theory

Approach	*Potential Advantages*	*Potential Disadvantages*	*Pitfalls to Avoid*
User-focused approach: working with intended users to extract and specify their implicit theory of action to make it explicit action to make it explicit	Intended users understand the theory of action Intended users own the theory of action	As users struggle to articulate their theory, they may be defensive Formal explicit model may not reflect program realities	Don't oversimplify to the point of esoteric meaninglessness in an effort to manage conflict or varying perceptions Don't force articulation of a single theory. Different users may well have different theories of action
Inductive approach: doing fieldwork on a program to generate grounded theory	Theory grounded in real world practice High relevance because theory is generated from actual program activities and observed outcomes Can focus an evaluability assessment effort	Fieldwork takes time and resources for evaluation and program Likely that different program people operate with different theories in large, multilevel, or complex programs	Don't force a single theory or model on the program where multiple theories of action are operating Don't let generating theory take on a life of its own and become a higher priority than generating useful results
Deductive approach: drawing on scholarly theories from the academic literature	Draws on existing knowledge and literature High academic credibility Connects to larger issues	May not be relevant to specific program May feel esoteric to practitioners Literature search takes time and resources	Don't force program into a theory pigeonhole Don't let theory testing become higher priority than generating useful results

Getting at Assumptions and Causal Connections

Identifying Critical Validity Assumptions

The purpose of thoroughly delineating a program's theory of action is to assist practitioners in making explicit their assumptions about the linkages between inputs, activities, immediate outputs, intermediate outcomes, and ultimate goals. Suchman (1967) called beliefs about cause-effect relationships the program's *validity assumptions*. For example, many education programs are built on the validity assumptions that (1) new information leads to attitude change and (2) attitude change affects behavior. These assumptions are testable. Does new knowledge change attitudes? Do changed attitudes lead to changed behaviors?

As validity assumptions are articulated in a means-ends hierarchy, the evaluator can work with intended users to focus the evaluation on those critical linkages where information is most needed at that particular point in the life of the program. It is seldom possible or useful to test all the validity assumptions or evaluate all the means-ends linkages in a program's theory of action. The question is one of how freely such validity assumptions are made and how much is at stake in testing the validity of critical assumptions (Suchman 1967:43). **In a utilization-focused evaluation, the evaluator works with the primary intended users to identify the critical validity assumptions where reduction of uncertainty about causal linkages could make the most difference.**

The evaluator's beliefs about the validity of assumptions is less important than what staff and decision makers believe. An evaluator can have greater impact by helping program staff and decision makers empirically test their causal hypotheses than by telling them such causal hypotheses are nonsense. Not only does the wheel have to be re-created from time to time, its efficacy has to be restudied and reevaluated to demonstrate its usefulness. Likewise, the evaluator's *certain belief* that square wheels are less efficacious than round ones may have little impact on those who believe that square wheels are effective. The utilization-focused evaluator's task is to delineate the belief in the square wheel and then assist the believers in designing an evaluation that will permit them to *test for themselves* their own perceptions and hypotheses.

This does not mean that the evaluator is passive. In the active-reactive-adaptive process of negotiating the evaluation's focus and design, the evaluation facilitator can suggest alternative assumptions and theories to test, but first priority goes to evaluation of validity assumptions held by primary intended users.

Filling in the Conceptual Gaps

Helping stakeholders identify conceptual gaps in their theory of action is another task for the user-focused evaluation facilitator. The difference between identifying validity assumptions and filling in conceptual gaps can be illustrated as follows. Rutman (1977) has argued that the idea of using prison guards as counselors to inmates ought never have been evaluated (Ward, Kassebaum, and Wilner 1971) because, on the face of it, the idea is nonsense. Why would anyone ever believe that such a program could work? But clearly, whether they should have or not, many people did believe that the program would work. The evaluator's task is to fill in the conceptual gaps in this theory of action so that critical evaluative information needs can be identified. For example, are there initial selection processes and training programs for guards? Are guards supposed to be changed during such training? The first critical evaluation issue may be whether prison guards can be trained to exhibit desired counselor attitudes and behaviors. Whether prison guards can learn and practice human relations skills can be evaluated without ever implementing a full-blown program.

Filling in the gaps in the program's theory of action goes to the heart of the implementation question. What series of activities must take place before there is reason even to hope that impact will result? If activities and objectives lower in the means-ends hierarchy will not or cannot be implemented, then evaluation of ultimate outcomes is problematic.

> There are only two ways one can move up the scale of objectives in an evaluation: (a) by proving the intervening assumptions through research, that is, changing an assumption to a fact, or (b) by assuming their validity without full research proof. When the former is possible, we can then interpret our success in meeting a lower-level objective as automatic progress toward a higher one. . . .
>
> When an assumption cannot be proved . . . we go forward at our peril. To a great extent, the ultimate worth of evaluation for public service programs will depend upon research proof of the validity of assumptions involved in the establishment of key objectives. (Suchman 1967:57)

The National Clean Air Act and its amendments in the mid-1970s provide a good example of legislation in which policy and planning activity focused on initial objectives and ultimate goals but failed to delineate crucial intervening objectives. The ultimate goal was cleaner air; the target of the legislation was a handful of engines that each auto manufacturer tested before going to mass production. Authorization for mass production was given if these prototypes operated under carefully controlled conditions for 50,000 miles. Cars that failed pollution tests as they left the assembly line were not withheld from dealers. Cars on the road were not inspected to make sure that pollution control equipment was still in place and functioning properly. Prototypes were tested for 50,000 miles, but most cars are eventually used for 100,000 miles, with pollution in older cars being much worse than that in new ones. In short, there are many intervening steps between testing prototype automobiles for pollution control compliance and improving air quality. As Bruce Ackerman (1977) predicted,

> Over a period of time, the manufacturers will build cleaner and cleaner prototypes. Billions of dollars will be spent on the assembly line to build devices that *look* like these prototypes. But until Congress, the EPA, and the states require regular inspections of all cars on the road, very little will come of all this glittering machinery.
>
> Indeed, we could save billions if we contented ourselves with dirtier prototypes, but insisted on cleaner cars. . . . Congressmen themselves woefully exaggerate the importance of their votes for cleaner prototypes. They simply have no idea of the distance between prototype and reality. They somehow imagine that the hard job is technological innovation and that the easy job is human implementation. (p. 4)

Delineating an espoused theory of action involves identifying critical assumptions, conceptual gaps, and information gaps. The conceptual gaps are filled by logic, discussion, and policy analysis. The information gaps are filled by evaluation research.

Using the Theory of Action to Focus the Evaluation: The New School Case

Once an espoused theory of action is delineated, the issue of evaluation focus remains. This involves more than mechanically evaluating lower-order validity assumptions and then moving up the hierarchy. Not all linkages in the hierarchy are amenable to testing; different validity assumptions require different resources for evaluation; data-gathering strategies vary for different objectives. In a summative evaluation, the focus will be on outcomes attainment and causal attribution. For formative evaluation, the most important factor is determining what information would be most useful at a particular point in time. This means selecting what Murphy (1976) calls *targets of opportunity* in which additional information could make a difference to the direction of incremental, problem-oriented, program decision making:

> In selecting problems for analysis, targets of opportunity need to be identified, with political considerations specifically built into final choices. Planning activity in a certain area might be opportune because of expiring legislation, a hot political issue, a breakdown in standard operation procedures, or new research findings. At any time, certain policies are more susceptible to change than others. (p. 98)

Targets of opportunity are those evaluation questions about which primary information users care the most and most need evaluative information for decision making. Having information about and answers to those select questions can make a difference in what is done in the program. An example from an evaluation of the New School of Behavioral Studies in Education, University of North Dakota, illustrates this.

The New School of Behavioral Studies in Education was established as a result of a statewide study of education conducted between 1965 and 1967. The New School was to provide leadership in educational innovations with an emphasis on individualized instruction, better teacher-pupil relationships, an interdisciplinary approach, and better use of a wide range of learning resources (Statewide Study 1967:11-15). In 1970, the New School had gained national recognition when Charles Silberman described the North Dakota Experiment as a program that was resolving the "crisis in the classroom" in favor of open education.

The New School established a master's degree, teaching-intern program in which interns replaced teachers without degrees so that the latter could return to the university to complete their baccalaureates. The cooperating school districts released those teachers without degrees who volunteered to return to college and accepted the master's degree interns in their place. Over four years, the New School placed 293 interns in 48 school districts and 75 elementary schools, both public and parochial. The school districts that cooperated with the New School in the intern program contained nearly one third of the state's elementary school children.

The Dean of the New School formed a task force of teachers, professors, students, parents, and administrators to evaluate the program. In working with that task force, I constructed the theory of action shown in Exhibit 10.3. The objectives stated in the first column are a far cry from being clear, specific, and measurable, but they were quite adequate for discussions aimed at focusing the evaluation question. The second column lists validity assumptions underlying each linkage in the theory of action. The third column shows the measures that could be used to evaluate objectives at any level in the hierarchy. Ultimate objectives are not inherently more difficult to operationalize. Operationalization and measurement are separate issues to be determined after the focus of the evaluation has been decided.

When the Evaluation Task Force discussed Exhibit 10.3, members decided they already had sufficient contact with the summer program to assess the degree to which immediate objectives were being met. They also felt they had sufficient experience to be comfortable with the validity assumption linking objectives six and seven. With regard to the ultimate objectives, the task force members said that they needed no further data at that time in order to document the outcomes of open education (objectives one and two), nor could they do much with information about the growth of the open education movement (objective three). However, a number of critical uncertainties surfaced at the level of intermediate objectives. Once students left the summer program for the one-year internships, program staff were unable to carefully and regularly monitor intern classrooms. They didn't know what variations existed in the openness of the classrooms, nor did they have reliable information about how local parents and administrators were reacting to intern classrooms. These were issues about which information was wanted and needed. Indeed, for a variety of personal, political, and scholarly reasons, these issues made quite good evaluation targets of opportunity. The evaluation therefore focused on three questions: (1) To what extent are summer trainees conducting open classrooms during the regular year? (2) What factors are related to variations in openness? (3) What is the relationship between variations in classroom openness and parent/administrator reactions to intern classrooms?

At the onset, nothing precluded evaluation at any of the seven levels in the hierarchy of objectives. There was serious discussion of all levels and alternative foci. In terms of the educational literature, the issue of the outcomes of open education could be considered most important; in terms of university operations, the summer program would have been the appropriate focus; but in terms of the information needs of the primary decision makers and primary intended users on the task force, evaluation of the intermediate objectives had the highest potential for generating useful, formative information.

In order to obtain the resources necessary to conduct this evaluation, Vito Perrone, dean of the New School, had to make unusual demands on the U.S. Office of Education (OE). The outcomes of the New School teaching program were supposed to be evaluated as part of a national OE study. Perrone argued that the national study, as designed, would be useless to the New School. He talked the OE people into allowing him to spend the New School's portion of the national evaluation money on a study designed and conducted locally. The subsequent evaluation was entirely the creation of the local task force described above, and it produced instruments and data that became an integral part of the North Dakota program (see Pederson 1977).

The national study produced large volumes of numbers (with blanks entered on the lines for North Dakota) and, as far as I can tell, was of no particular use to anyone.

Developing a Theory of Action as Process Use

Thus far, this discussion of theory of action has been aimed at demonstrating the value of this conceptual strategy as a way of focusing evaluation questions and identifying the information needs of primary stakeholders. At times, helping program staff or decision makers to articulate their programmatic theory of action is an end in itself. Evaluators are called on, not only to gather data, but also to assist in program design. Knowing how to turn a vague discussion of the presumed linkages between program activities and expected outcomes into a formal written theory of action can be an important service to a program. This is an example of **using the evaluation process to improve a program**, as discussed in Chapter 5.

Evaluation use takes many forms, not only use of findings. The work of Palumbo, Musheno, and Maynard-Moody (1985) on the Community Corrections Act of Oregon nicely illustrates the use of evaluation to (1) conceptualize a major piece of statewide legislation from vague policies into a formal implementation-outcomes hierarchy; (2) design practical, programmatic linkages; and (3) construct a viable, streetwise theory of action.

On many occasions, then, the evaluation data collection effort may include discovering and formalizing a program's theory of action. In such cases, rather than being a means of facilitating the process of focusing evaluation questions, the theory of action can be the primary focus of analysis in the evaluation. This means moving beyond discussing the theory of action to gathering data on it. Such was the case in an evaluation of a multifaceted home nursing program for the elderly. Facilitating articulation of the program's theory of action helped staff sort out which of the many things they did were really central to the outcomes they wanted. As a member of an evaluation task force for farming systems research, I worked with colleagues to identify the critical elements of "a farming systems approach" and place those elements in a hierarchy that constituted a developmental theory of action. In these and many other cases, my primary contributions were program design and conceptualization skills that combined stakeholder discussions with observations of the program to develop a theory of action. Once developed, the theory of action served to focus future program development efforts as well as evaluation questions.

Targets of Opportunity Over Time: Theory as a Road Map

Evaluation can make an ongoing contribution to program improvement as program staff and other primary stakeholders learn to use evaluation concepts to shape and test program ideas. This ongoing, developmental role for evaluation is particularly important for internal evaluators to cultivate. The theory of action can be a road map to plan different evaluation efforts over time.

Unlike most external evaluators, who encounter a program at a particular point in time, make their contribution, and leave, perhaps never to have contact with the program again, internal evaluators are there for the long haul. They need to be particularly sensitive to how evaluation can serve different needs over time, including

EXHIBIT 10.3

The New School Theory of Action: A Hierarchy of Objectives, Validity Assumption Linkages, and Evaluation Criteria

Hierarchy of Objectives	*Validity Assumption Linkages*	*Evaluative Criteria*
I. Ultimate Objectives		
1. Prepare children to live full, rich, satisfying lives as adults.		1. Longitudinal measures of child and adult satisfaction, happiness, and success.
	Children whose affective and cognitive needs are met will lead fuller, richer, more satisfying lives as adults.	
2. Meet the affective and cognitive needs of individual children in North Dakota and the United States.		2. Measures of student affective and cognitive growth in open and traditional schools.
	More open classrooms will better meet the affective and cognitive needs of individual children.	
3. Facilitate and legitimize the establishment and maintenance of a larger number of more open classrooms in North Dakota and the United States.		3. Measures of increases in the number of open classrooms in North Dakota and the United States over time and measures of the influence of the New School on the number of open classrooms.
	Parents and administrators will favor and expand open education once they have experienced it firsthand.	

II. Intermediate Objectives

4. Provide parents and administrators in North Dakota with a firsthand demonstration of the advantages of open education.

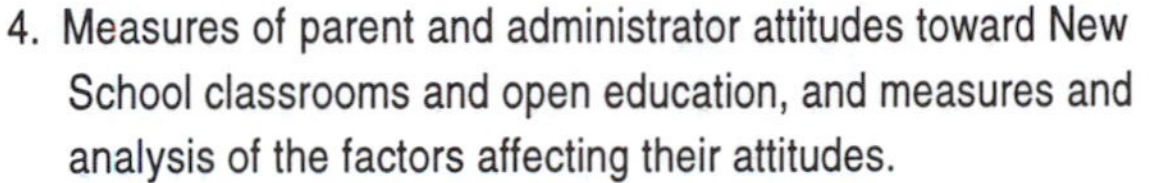

4. Measures of parent and administrator attitudes toward New School classrooms and open education, and measures and analysis of the factors affecting their attitudes.

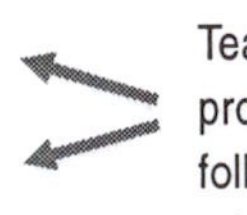

Teachers who have experienced the New School summer program can and will conduct open classrooms during the following intern year that are visible to local parents and administrators.

5. Provide teachers and teachers-in-training with a one-year classroom experience in conducting an open classroom.

5. Measures of the degree of openness of New School teaching intern classrooms and the factors affecting the degree of openness of these classrooms.

Teachers who have experienced the summer program can and will conduct open classrooms.

III. Immediate Objectives

6. Provide teachers and teachers-in-training with a summer program in how to conduct an open classroom.

6. Measures of teacher attitudes, teacher understanding, and teacher competency before and after the New School Program.

In order to learn about open education it is best to experience it. Teachers teach the way they are taught.

7. Provide teachers and teachers-in-training with a personalized and individualized learning experience in an open learning environment.

7. Measures of the degree to which the New School training program is individualized and personalized, and measures of the cognitive and affective growth of teachers in the New School Program.

NOTE: The validity assumptions (middle column) link objectives (left column). Arrows indicate to which objectives the assumptions apply.

both program design and accountability functions. In this way internal evaluators help build an **institutional memory** for a program or organization, a memory made up of lessons learned, ideas cultivated, and skills developed over time. This means that internal evaluators need to understand and take into consideration the "social learning" (Stone 1985) that comes from evaluation within organizations over time.

A theory of action is at least partially temporal in conceptualization because it progresses from immediate objectives to ultimate goals. Part of the test of a theory of action is the temporal logic of the hierarchy. In causal language, it is impossible for an effect or outcome to precede its cause. It is important, however, that temporal logic not become rigid. Once a program is in operation, the relationships between links in the causal hierarchy are likely to be recursive rather than unidirectional. The implementation and attainment of higher-level objectives interact with the implementation and attainment of lower-order objectives through feedback mechanisms, interactive configurations, and cybernetic systems. Program components may be conceptually distinct in the formal version of a theory of action, but in practice these analytically distinct components, links, and stages are highly interdependent and dynamically interrelated. In short, the cause-effect relationships may be mutual, multidirectional, and multilateral. For example, open classrooms affect the opinions and actions of parents, but parent reactions also affect the degree of openness of classrooms; classroom climate and school curriculum affect student achievement, but variations in student achievement also affect school climate and curriculum. Once again, the means-ends distinction proves to be somewhat arbitrary and simplified, but there is no avoiding such simplification: "Put simply, the basic dilemma faced in all sciences is that of how much to oversimplify reality" (Blalock 1964:8). The challenge is to construct simplifications that pass the dual tests of usefulness and accuracy.

Theory Informing Practice, Practice Informing Theory

Comparing Theories of Action

Much evaluation involves comparing different programs to determine which is more effective or efficient. Evaluations can be designed to compare the effectiveness of two or more programs with the same goal, but if those goals do not bear the same importance in the two programs' theories of action, the comparisons may be misleading. Before undertaking a comparative evaluation, it is useful to compare programmatic theories of action in order to understand the extent to which apparently identical or similarly labeled programs are in fact comparable.

Programs with different goals cannot be fairly compared to each other on a unidimensional basis. Teacher centers established to support staff development and resource support for school teachers provide an example. The U.S. Office of Education proposed that teacher centers be evaluated according to a single set of universal outcomes. But evaluator Sharon Feiman (1977) found that teacher centers throughout the country varied substantially in both program activities and goals. Feiman described three types of teacher centers: behavioral, humanistic, and developmental. Exhibit 10.4 summarizes the variations among these types of centers.

Different teacher centers were trying to accomplish different outcomes. Compari-

EXHIBIT 10.4
Variations in Types of Teacher Centers

Type of Center	*Primary Process of Affecting Teachers*	*Primary Outcomes of the Process*
1. Behavioral centers	Curriculum specialists directly and formally instruct administrators and teachers.	Adoption of comprehensive curriculum systems, methods, and packages by teachers.
2. Humanistic centers	Informal, nondirected teacher exploration; "teachers select their own treatment."	Teachers feel supported and important; pick up concrete and practical ideas and materials for immediate use in their classroom.
3. Developmental centers	Advisers establish warm, interpersonal, and directive relationship with teachers working with them over time.	Teachers' thinking about what they do and why they do it is changed over time; teacher personal development.

sons to determine which one was most effective became problematic because they were trying to do different things. Evaluation could help determine the extent to which outcomes have been attained for each specific program, but empirical data could not determine which outcome was most desirable. That is a values question. An evaluation facilitator can help users clarify their value premises, but because the three teacher-center models were different, evaluation criteria for effectiveness varied for each type. In effect, three quite different theories of teacher development were operating in quite different educational environments. Attention to divergent theories of action helped avoid inappropriate comparisons and reframed the evaluation question from *Which model is best?* to *What are the strengths and weaknesses of each approach, and which approach is most effective for what kinds of educational environments?* Very different evaluation questions!

Matching a Theory of Action With Levels of Evidence

Claude Bennett (1982, 1979) has conceptualized a relationship between the "chain of events" in a program and the "levels of evidence" needed for evaluation. Although his work was aimed specifically at evaluation of cooperative extension programs (agriculture, home economics, and 4-H/youth), his ideas are generally applicable to any program. Exhibit 10.5 depicts a general adaptation of Bennett's model.

The model suggests a typical chain of program events:

1. Inputs (resources) must be assembled to get the program started.
2. Activities are undertaken with available resources.
3. Program participants (clients, students, beneficiaries) engage in program activities.
4. Participants react to what they experience.

5. As a result of what they experience, changes in knowledge, attitudes, and skills occur (if the program is effective).
6. Behavior and practice changes follow knowledge and attitude change.
7. Overall impacts result, both intended and unintended.

This model explicitly and deliberately places highest value on attaining ultimate social and economic goals (e.g., increased agricultural production, increased health, and a higher quality of community life). Actual adoption of recommended practices and specific changes in client behaviors are necessary to achieve ultimate goals and are valued over knowledge, attitude, and skill changes. People may learn about some new agricultural technique (knowledge change), believe it's a good idea (attitude change), and know how to apply it (skill change)—but the higher-level criterion is whether they actually begin **using** the new technique (i.e., change their agricultural practices). Participant reactions (satisfaction, likes, and dislikes) are lower still on the hierarchy. All of these are outcomes, but they are not equally valued outcomes. The bottom part of the hierarchy identifies the means necessary for accomplishing higher-level ends; namely, in descending order, (3) getting people to participate, (2) providing program activities, and (1) organizing basic resources and inputs to get started.

Utilization-Focused Evaluation Theory of Action

Interestingly, this same hierarchy can be applied to evaluating evaluations. Exhibit 10.6 shows a hierarchy of evaluation accountability. In utilization-focused evaluation, the purpose is to improve programs and increase the quality of decisions made.

To accomplish this ultimate end, a chain of events must unfold.

1. Resources must be devoted to the evaluation, including stakeholder time and financial inputs.
2. Working with intended users, important evaluation issues are identified and questions focused; based on those issues and questions, the evaluation is designed and data are collected.
3. Key stakeholders and primary users are involved throughout the process.
4. Intended users react to their involvement (hopefully in positive ways).
5. The evaluation process and findings provide knowledge and new understandings.
6. Intended users interpret results, generate and adopt recommendations, and use evaluation results.
7. The program improves and decisions are made.

Each step in this chain can be evaluated. Exhibit 10.6 shows the evaluation question that corresponds to each level in the utilization-focused theory of action hierarchy.

Logical Framework

The *Logical Framework Approach* (Sartorius 1996a, 1991) offers a format for connecting levels of impact with evidence. Used widely by international development agencies as a comprehensive map in designing projects, the framework begins by requiring specification of the overall goal and purposes of the project. Short-term outputs are linked logically to those purposes, and activities are identified that are expected to produce the outputs. (The language of this model can be confusing because what the

EXHIBIT 10.5

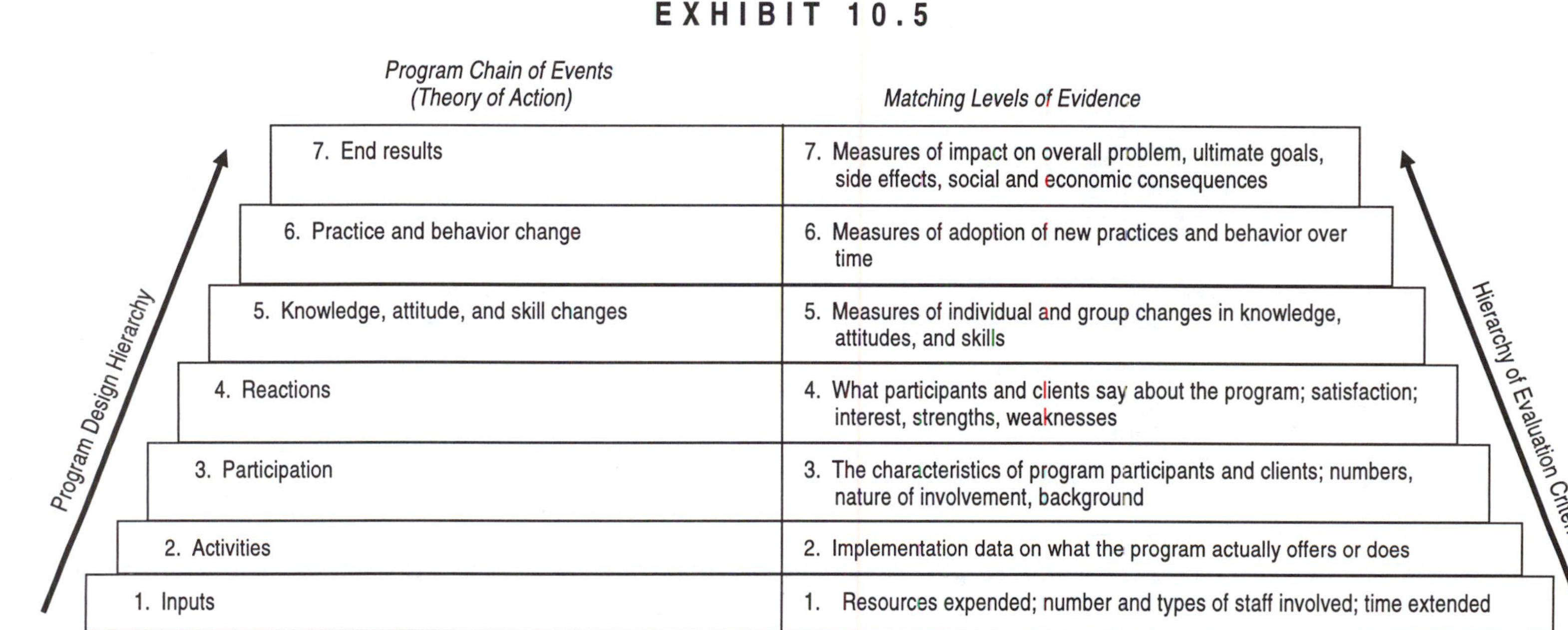

Program Chain of Events
(Theory of Action)
Matching Levels of Evidence
7. End results
7. Measures of impact on overall problem, ultimate goals, side effects, social and economic consequences
6. Practice and behavior change
6. Measures of adoption of new practices and behavior over time
5. Knowledge, attitude, and skill changes
5. Measures of individual and group changes in knowledge, attitudes, and skills
4. Reactions
4. What participants and clients say about the program; satisfaction; interest, strengths, weaknesses
3. Participation
3. The characteristics of program participants and clients; numbers, nature of involvement, background
2. Activities
2. Implementation data on what the program actually offers or does
1. Inputs
1. Resources expended; number and types of staff involved; time extended
Program Design Hierarchy
Hierarchy of Evaluation Criteria

SOURCE: Adapted from Bennett 1979.

EXHIBIT 10.6

Hierarchy of Evaluation Accountability: Evaluating Evaluation

Evaluation Action Hierarchy	Hierarchy Utilization Questions
7. Program and decision impacts	7. To what extent and in what ways was the program improved? To what extent were informed, high-quality decisions made?
6. Practice and program change	6. To what extent did intended use occur? Were recommendations implemented?
5. Stakeholders' knowledge and attitude changes	5. What did intended users learn? How were users' attitudes and ideas affected?
4. Reactions of primary intended users	4. What do intended users think about the evaluation? What's the evaluation's credibility? believability? relevance? accuracy? potential utility?
3. Stakeholder participation	3. Who was involved? To what extent were key stakeholders and primary decision makers involved throughout?
2. Evaluation activities	2. What data were gathered? What was the focus, the design, the analysis? What happened in the evaluation?
1. Inputs	1. To what extent were resources for the evaluation sufficient and well managed? Was time sufficient?

logical framework calls a *goal* is what other models more commonly call *mission;* and *purposes* are similar to objectives or outcomes; outputs are short-term, end-of-project deliverables. For every goal, purpose, output, and activity, the framework requires specification of *objectively verifiable indicators*, means of verification (types of data), and important assumptions about the linkage between activities and outputs, outputs to purposes, and purposes to goals. A software program called PC/LogFRAME© supports completing the logical framework (Sartorius 1996b).

Causal Theorizing in Perspective

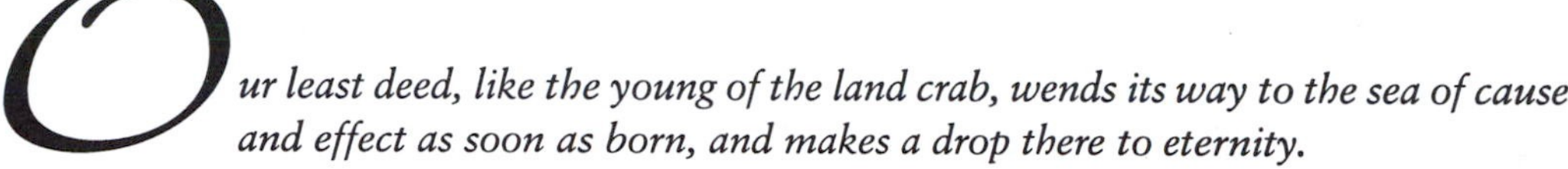

Our least deed, like the young of the land crab, wends its way to the sea of cause and effect as soon as born, and makes a drop there to eternity.

—Thoreau (*Journal*, March 14, 1838)

While causal linkages may never be established with certainty, the delineation of assumed causal relationships in a chain of hierarchical objectives can be a useful exercise in the process of focusing an evaluation. It is not appropriate to construct a detailed theory of program action for every evaluation situation, but it is important to consider the option. Therefore, the skills of a utilization-focused evaluation facilitator include being able to help intended users construct a means-ends hierarchy, specify validity assumptions, link means to ends, and lay out the temporal sequence of a hierarchy of objectives.

Attention to theoretical issues can provide useful information to stakeholders when *their* theories are formulated and reality-tested through the evaluation process. Theory construction is also a mechanism by which evaluators can link particular program evaluation questions to larger social scientific issues for the purpose of contributing to scientific knowledge through empirical generalizations. But in a utilization-focused approach to evaluation research, the initial theoretical formulations originate with primary stakeholders and intended users; scholarly interests are adapted to the evaluation needs of relevant decision makers, not vice versa.

Theory-driven evaluations can seduce researchers away from answering straightforward formative questions or determining the merit or worth of a program into the ethereal world of academic theorizing. In this regard, Scriven (1991b) asserts that theory testing is "a luxury for the evaluator." He considers it "a gross though frequent blunder to suppose that 'one needs a theory of learning to evaluate teaching' " (p. 360). One does not need to know anything at all about electronics, he observes, to evaluate computers.

On the other hand, a theory can be the key that unlocks the door to effective action.

How much to engage stakeholders and intended users in articulating their theories of action is a matter for negotiation. Helping practitioners test their espoused theories and discover real theories-in-use can be a powerful learning experience, both individually and organizationally. At a simpler level, without constructing a fully specified theory, the evaluator may pose basic causal questions about the relationship between program activities and outcomes. Even for these more modest questions (more modest in the sense that they don't involve testing a fully specified theory), evaluation data can seldom provide more than an approximation of the likelihood of causal connections. It is important to interpret results about causal linkages with prudence and care. In that regard, consider the wisdom of this Buddhist story.

> *One day an old man approached Zen Master Hyakujo. The old man said, "I am not a human being. In ancient times I lived on this mountain. A student of the Way asked me if the enlightened were still affected by causality. I replied saying that they were not affected. Because of that, I was degraded to lead the life of a wild fox for five hundred years. I now request you to answer one thing for me. Are the enlightened still affected by causality?"*
>
> *Master Hyakujo replied, "They are not deluded by causality."*
>
> *At that the old man was enlightened.*
>
> —Adapted from Hoffman 1975:138

Causal evaluation questions can be enlightening; they can also lead to delusions. Unfortunately, there is no clear way of telling the difference. So among the many perils evaluators face, we can add that of being turned into a wild fox for five hundred years!

Note

1. Reprinted from *Angels in America, Part Two: Perestroika* by Tony Kushner. Copyright 1992 and 1994 by the author. Published by Theatre Communications Group. Used by permission.

PART 3

Appropriate Methods

Blowhard Evaluation

This is the story of three little pigs who built three little houses for protection from the BIG BAD WOLF.

The first pig worked without a plan, building the simplest and easiest structure possible with whatever materials happened to be laying around, mostly straw and sticks.

When the BIG BAD WOLF appeared, he had scarcely to huff and puff to blow the house down, whereupon the first pig ran for shelter and protection to the second pig's house.

The second pig's house was prefabricated in a most rigorous fashion with highly reliable materials. Architects and engineers had applied the latest techniques and most valid methods to the design and construction of these standardized, prefabricated models. The second pig had a high degree of confidence that his house could withstand any attack.

The BIG BAD WOLF followed the first pig to the house of the second pig and commanded, "Come out! Come out! Or by the hair on my chinny-chin-chin, I'll huff and I'll puff and I'll blow your house down."

The second pig laughed a scornful reply: "Huff and puff all you want. You'll find no weaknesses in this house, for it was designed by experts using the latest and best scientific methods guaranteed not to fall apart under the most strenuous huffing and puffing."

So the BIG BAD WOLF huffed and puffed, and he huffed and puffed some more, but the structure was solid, and gave not an inch.

In catching his breath for a final huffing and puffing, the BIG BAD WOLF noticed that the house, although strong and well built, was simply sitting on top of the ground.

It had been purchased and set down on the local site with no attention to establishing a firm connecting foundation that would anchor the house in its setting. Different settings require very different site preparation with appropriately matched foundations, but the prefabricated kit came with no instructions about how to prepare a local foundation. Understanding all this in an instant, the sly wolf ceased his huffing and puffing. Instead, he confidently reached down, got a strong hold on the underside of the house, lifted, and tipped it over. The second pig was shocked to find himself uncovered and vulnerable. He would have been easy prey for the BIG BAD WOLF had not the first pig, being more wary and therefore more alert, dashed out from under the house, pulling his flabbergasted brother with him. Together they sprinted to the house of the third pig, crying "wee wee wee" all the way there.

The house of the third pig was the source of some controversy in the local pig community. Unlike any other house, it was constructed of a hodgepodge of local materials and a few things borrowed from elsewhere. It incorporated some of the ideas seen in the prefabricated houses designed by experts, but those ideas had been altered to fit local conditions and the special interests and needs of the third pig. The house was built on a strong foundation, well anchored in its setting and carefully adapted to the specific conditions of the spot on which the house was built. Although the house was sometimes the object of ridicule because it was unique and different, it was also the object of envy and praise, for it was evident to all that it fit quite beautifully and remarkably in that precise location.

The BIG BAD WOLF approached the house of the third pig confidently. He huffed and puffed his best huffs and puffs. The house gave a little under these strenuous forces, but it did not break. Flexibility was part of its design, so it could sway and give under adverse and changed conditions without breaking and falling apart. Being firmly anchored in a solid foundation, it would not tip over. The BIG BAD WOLF soon knew he would have no pork chops for dinner that night.

Following the defeat of the BIG BAD WOLF, the third pig found his two brother pigs suddenly very interested in how to build houses uniquely adapted to and firmly grounded in a specific location with a structure able to withstand the onslaughts of the most persistent blowhards. They opened a consulting firm to help other pigs. The firm was called "Wee wee wee, all the way home."

—From Halcolm's "Evaluation Fairy Tales"

11

Evaluations Worth Using

Utilization-Focused Methods Decisions

They say there was method to his madness. Perhaps so. It is easier to select a method for madness than a single best method for evaluation, though attempting the latter is an excellent way of achieving the former.

—Halcolm

The three pigs story that precedes this chapter and introduces this part of the book on Appropriate Methods can be interpreted as an evaluation parable. The first pig built a house that was the equivalent of what is disparagingly called a "quick and dirty evaluation." They are low-budget efforts that give the outward appearance of evaluation, but their value and utility are fleeting. They simply do not stand up under scrutiny. The second pig replicated a high-quality design that met uniform standards of excellence as specified by distant experts. Textbook designs have the advantage of elegance and sophistication, but they don't travel well. Prefabricated structures brought in from far away are vulnerable to unanticipated local conditions. Beware the evaluator who offers essentially the same design for every situation.

The third pig, then, exemplifies the utilization-focused evaluator, one who designs an evaluation to fit a specific set of circumstances, needs, and interests. The third pig demonstrated situational adaptability and responsiveness, a strategic stance introduced in Chapter 6. In this chapter, we'll examine how situational responsiveness affects methods decisions.

Methods to Support Intended Uses, Chosen by Intended Users

In utilization-focused evaluation, methods decisions, like decisions about focus and priority issues, are guided and informed by our evaluation goal: intended use by intended users. Attaining this goal is enhanced by having intended users actively involving in methods decisions, an assertion I shall substantiate in depth throughout this chapter. It remains, however, a controversial assertion, evidence about its desirability and effectiveness notwithstanding. The source of the controversy, I'm convinced, is territorial.

I've had some success persuading colleagues and students that use can be enhanced by actively involving intended users in decisions about the evaluation's purpose, scope, and focus to ensure relevance and buy-in. In other words, they can accept playing a consultative and collaborative role during the conceptual phase of the evaluation. Where we often part company is in the role to be played by intended users in making measurement and design decisions. "The evaluator is nothing," they argue, "if not an expert in methods and statistics. Clearly social scientists ought to be left with full responsibility for operationalizing program goals and determining data collection procedures." Edwards and Guttentag (1975) articulated the classic position, one that I find still holds sway today: "The decision makers' values determine on what variables data should be gathered. The researcher then decides how to collect the data" (p. 456).

Utilization-focused evaluation takes a different path.

Beyond Technical Expertise

The common perception of methods decisions among nonresearchers is that such decisions are primarily technical in nature. Sample size, for example, is determined by a mathematical formula. The evaluation methodologist enters the values of certain variables, makes calculations, and out pops the right sample size to achieve the desired level of statistical robustness, significance, power, validity, reliability, generalizability, and so on—all technical terms that dazzle, impress, and intimidate practitioners and nonresearchers. Evaluation researchers have a vested interest in maintaining this technical image of scientific expertise, for it gives us prestige, inspires respect, and, not incidentally, it leads nonresearchers to defer to us, essentially giving us the power to make crucial methods decisions and then interpret the meaning of the resulting data. It is not in our interest, from the perspective of maintaining prestige and power, to reveal to intended users that methods decisions are far from purely technical. But, contrary to public perception, evaluators know that methods decisions are never purely technical. Never. Ways of measuring complex phenomena involve simplifications that are inherently somewhat arbitrary, are always constrained by limited resources and time, inevitably involve competing and conflicting priorities, and rest on a foundation of values preferences that are typically resolved by pragmatic considerations, disciplinary biases, and measurement traditions.

The only reason to debunk the myth that methods and measurement decisions are primarily technical is if one wants to enhance use. For we know that use is enhanced when practitioners, decision makers, and other users fully understand the strengths and weaknesses of evaluation data, and that such understanding is increased by being involved in making methods decisions. We know that use is enhanced when intended users participate in making sure that, when trade-offs are considered, as they inevitably are because of limited resources and time, the path chosen is informed by relevance. We know that use is enhanced when users buy into the design

EXHIBIT 11.1
Reasons Primary Users Should Be Involved in Methods Decisions

1. Intended use affects methods choices. Intended users can and should judge the utility of various design options and kinds of data.

2. Limited time and resources necessitate trade-offs—more of this, less of that. Primary users have the greatest stake in such decisions since findings are affected.

3. Methods decisions are never *purely* technical. Practical considerations constrain technical alternatives. Everything from how to classify participants to how to aggregate data has utility implications that deserve users' consideration.

4. No design is perfect. Intended users need to know the strengths and weaknesses of an evaluation to exercise informed judgment.

5. Different users may have different criteria for judging methodological quality. These should be made explicit and negotiated during methods discussions.

6. Credibility of the evidence and the perceived validity of the overall evaluation are key factors affecting use. These are matters of subjective user judgment that should inform methods decisions.

7. Intended users learn about and become more knowledgeable and sophisticated about methods and using data by being involved in methods decisions. This benefits both the current and future evaluations.

8. Methods debates should take place *before* data collection, as much as possible, so that findings are not undercut by bringing up concerns that should have been addressed during design. Methods debates among intended users after findings are reported distract from using evaluation results.

and find it credible and valid within the scope of its intended purposes as determined by them. And we know that when evaluation findings are presented, the substance is less likely to be undercut by debates about methods if users have been involved in those debates prior to data collection.

As in all other aspects of the evaluation, then, the utilization-focused evaluator advises intended users about options; points out the consequences of various choices; offers creative possibilities; engages with users actively, reactively, and adaptively to consider alternatives; and facilitates *their* methods decisions. At the stage of choosing methods, the evaluator remains a technical adviser, consultant, and teacher. The primary intended users remain decision makers about the evaluation. Exhibit 11.1 summarizes reasons why primary intended users should be involved in methods decisions. In the pages that follow, I'll elaborate on these rationales, explore the implications of this approach, and provide examples. Let's begin with an example.

The Million Man March

On October 16, 1995, some number of African American men marched on Washington, D.C., as a call to action. The number of men in the march mattered a great deal to both its organizers and critics. Disputes about the number subsequently led to major lawsuits against the National Park Service, which provides the government's official estimates of demonstrations on the Capitol Mall. For weeks after the march, newspaper commentators, television journalists, policymakers, activists, academics, and pundits debated the number. The size of the march overshadowed its substance and intended message. Varying estimates of the number of marchers led to charges and countercharges of racism and bigotry.

Could this controversy have been anticipated, avoided, or at least tempered? Let's consider how the evaluation was conducted and then how a utilization-focused approach would have been different.

First, let's examine what made this march a focus for evaluation. The organizer of the march, Nation of Islam leader Louis Farrakhan, was a controversial figure often accused of being anti-Semitic and fomenting hatred against whites. Some Black congressmen and the leadership of the National Association for the Advancement of Colored People (NAACP) refused to join the march. Many other Black leaders worked to make it a success. From the moment the march was announced, through the months leading up to it, debate about the legitimacy and purpose of the march received high-visibility media coverage. As the day of the march approached, the central question became: How many will show up?

Why was the number so important? Because the target number became the name of the march: The Million Man March. The goal was unusually clear, specific, and measurable. The march's leaders staked their prestige on attaining *that* number. The march's detractors hoped for failure. The number came to symbolize the unity and political mobilization of African American men.

In time for the evening news on the day of the march, the National Park Service released its estimate: 400,000. This ranked the march as one of the largest in the history of the United States, but the number was far short of the 1 million goal. March advocates reacted with disbelief and anger. March critics gloated at Farrakhan's "failure." Who made the estimate? A white man, a career technician, in the National Park Service. He used the method he always used, a sample count from photographs. Leaders of the march immediately denounced the official number as racist. The debate was on. A week later, independent researchers at Boston University, using different counting methods, estimated the number at 800,000—double the National Park Service estimate. Others came in with other estimates. The leaders of the march continued to insist that more than a million participated. The significance of this historically important event remains clouded by rancorous debate over the seemingly simplest of all evaluation questions: How many people participated in the "program"?

Suppose, now, for the sake of illustration, that the responsible National Park official—a white male, remember—had taken a utilization-focused approach. As the visibility of the march increased leading up to it, and as its potential historical significance became apparent, he could have identified and convened a group of primary stakeholders: one or more representatives of the march's organizers, representatives of other national Black organizations, academics with expertise in crowd estimates, and perhaps police officials from other cities who had experience estimating the size of large crowds. A couple of respected newsprint and television journalists could have been added to the group. Indeed, and this is surely a radical proposal, a professional evaluator might have been asked to facilitate the group's work.

Once such a group was assembled, consider the challenging nontechnical decisions that have to be made to figure out the size of the march. These questions are in addition to technical questions of aerial photography sampling and computer programs designed to count heads in a crowd. To answer these questions requires some combination of common sense, political savvy, appreciation of different perspectives, and pragmatism. Here, then, are some questions that would occur to me if I had been asked to facilitate such a discussion:

1. Who gets counted? It's the million *man march* aimed at *Black men*. Do women count? Do children count? Do whites count?
2. Do spectators and onlookers get counted as well as marchers?
3. When during the daylong event will counts be made? Is there one particular time that counts the most; for example, Farrakhan's speech? (His speech was three hours long, so when or how often during his speech?)
4. Should the final number account for people who came and went over the course of the day, or only people present at some single point in time?
5. What geographical boundary gets included in the count? What are the boundaries of the Capitol Mall for purposes of sampling?
6. Sympathy and support marches are scheduled to take place in other cities. Do their numbers count in the one million total?
7. Should we report a single number, such as 1 million, or communicate the variability of any such count by reporting a range, for example 900,000 to 1.1 million?
8. Who are the most credible people to actually engage in or supervise the actual analysis?
9. What reviews should the analysis undergo, by whom, before being released officially?
10. Who do we say determined the counting methods and under whose name, or combination of named sponsors, should the result be publicized?

I certainly don't assert that convening a group of primary stakeholders to negotiate answers to these questions would have ended all controversy, but I do believe it could have tempered the rancorous tone of the debate, diffused the racial overtones of the counting process, and permitted more focus on the substantive societal issues raised by the march, issues about family values, community involvement, social responsibility, economic opportunity, and justice. The evaluation task force, once convened to decide how to count from one to one million, might even have decided to prepare methods of following up the march to determine its longer term impacts on Black men, families, and communities—evaluation questions overshadowed by the controversy about the number of participants.

Parallel Evaluation Decisions

I like the Million Man March example because it shows how complex a simple question like "how many" can become. Parallel complexities can be found in any program evaluation. For example, in most programs the dropout rate is an important indicator of how participants are reacting to a program. But when has someone dropped out? This typically turns out to involve some arbitrary cutoff. School districts vary widely on how they define, count, and report dropouts, as do chemical dependency, adult literacy, parent education, and all kinds of other programs.

No less vague and difficult are concepts like *in the program* and *finished the program*. Many programs lack clear beginning and ending points. For example, a job training program aimed at chronically unemployed minority men has a monthlong assessment process, including testing for drug use and observing a potential participant's persistence in staying with the process. During this time, the participant, with staff support and coaching, develops a plan. The participant is on probation until he or she completes enough of the program to show seriousness and commitment, but the program is highly individualized so different people are involved in the early assessment and probation processes over very different time periods. There is no clear criterion for when a person has begun probation or completed probation and officially *entered* the program. Yet, that decision, in aggregate, will determine the denominator for dropout and completion rates and will be the numerator for the program's "acceptance" rate. Making sure that such categories are meaningful and valid, so that the numbers are credible and useful, involves far more than statistics. Careful thought must be given, with primary intended users, to how the numbers and reported rates will be calculated and used.

Nor are these kinds of categorical decisions only a problem when measuring human behavior. The Minnesota Department of Transportation categorizes road projects as *preservation, replacement*, and *new or expansion*. How dollars are allocated and distributed in these three categories to regions throughout the state has enormous implications. Now, consider the Lake Street Bridge, which connects Minneapolis and Saint Paul. Old and in danger of being condemned, the bridge was torn down and a new one built. The old bridge had only two lanes and no decorative flourishes. The new bridge has four lanes and attractive design features. Should this project be categorized as replacement or expansion? (In a time of economic optimism and expanding resources, such as the 1960s, new and expansion projects were favored. In a time of downsizing and reduced resources, like the 1990s, replacement projects are more politically viable.) Perhaps, you might argue, the Lake Street Bridge illustrates the need for a new category: Part replacement/part expansion. But no replacements are pure replacements when new materials are used and updated codes or standards are followed. And few expansions are done without replacing something. How much mix, then, would have to occur for a project to fall into the new, combined part replacement/part expansion category? A doctoral degree in research and statistics provides no more guidance in answering this question than thoughtful consideration of how the data will be used, grounded in common sense and pragmatism—a decision that should be made by intended users with intended uses in mind. Such inherently arbitrary measurement decisions determine what data will emerge in findings.

Methods and Measurement Options

There can be acting or doing of any kind, till it be recognized that there is a thing to be done; the thing once recognized, doing in a thousand shapes becomes possible.

—Thomas Carlyle,
philosopher and historian
(1795-1881)

Mail questionnaires, telephone interviews, or personal face-to-face interviews? Individual interviews or focus groups? Even-numbered or odd-numbered scales on survey items? Opinion, knowledge, and/or behavioral questions? All closed questions or some open-ended? If some open-ended, how many? Norm-referenced or criterion-referenced tests? Develop our own instruments or adopt measures already available? Experimental design, quasi-experimental design, or case studies? Participant observation or spectator observation? A few in-depth observations or many shorter observations? Single or multiple observers? Standardized or individualized protocols? Fixed or emergent design? Follow up after two weeks, three months, six months, or a year? Follow up everyone or a sample? What kind of sample: simple random, stratified, and/or purposeful? What size sample? Should interviewers have the same characteristics as program participants: gender? age? race? What comparisons to make: past performance? intended goals? hoped-for goals? other programs? I won't list a thousand such options à la Thomas Carlyle, but I've no doubt it could be done. I would certainly never try the patience of primary stakeholders with a thousand options, but I do expect to work with them to consider the strengths and weaknesses of major design and measurement possibilities.

The primary focus in making evaluation methods decisions should be on getting the best possible data to adequately answer primary users' evaluation questions given available resources and time. The emphasis is on *appropriateness and credibility* — measures, samples, and comparisons that are appropriate and credible to address key evaluation issues. The Joint Committee's (1994) evaluation standards provide the following guidance:

> Utility Standard on
> Information Scope and Selection
>
> Information collected should be broadly selected to address pertinent questions about the program and be responsive to the needs and interests of clients and other specified stakeholders (U3).

In my judgment, the best way to ensure pertinence and responsiveness is through direct interaction with evaluation clients and primary stakeholders, facilitating their making decisions to represent their needs and interests.

Assuring Methodological Quality and Excellence

I am easily satisfied with the very best.

—Winston Churchill,
British prime minister during
World War II (1874-1965)

One of the myths believed by nonresearchers is that researchers have agreed among themselves about what constitutes methodological quality and excellence. This belief can make practitioners and other nonacademic stakeholders understandably reluctant to engage in methods discussions. In fact, researchers disagree with each other vehemently about what constitutes good research and, with a little training and help, I find that nonresearchers can grasp the basic issues involved and make informed choices.

To increase the confidence of nonresearchers that they can and should contribute to methods discussions—for example, to consider the merits of telephone interviews versus face-to-face interviews or mail questionnaires—I'll often share the results of research on how researchers rate research quality. In a seminal study for the National Science Foundation, McTavish et al. (1975) used eminent social scientists to judge and rate the research quality of 126 federal studies. They found "important and meaningful differences between raters in their professional judgments about a project's methodology" (p. 63). Eva Baker, Director of the UCLA Center for the Study of Evaluation and former editor of *Educational Evaluation and Policy Analysis (EEPA)*, established a strong system of peer review for *EEPA*, requiring three independent reviewers for every article. Eva has told me that in several years as editor, **she has never published an article on which all three reviewers agreed the article was good!** I edited the peer-reviewed *Journal of Extension* for three years and had the same experience. Robert Donmoyer (1996), new features editor of *Educational Researcher*, reported that "peer reviewers' recommendations often conflict and their advice is frequently contradictory. . . . There is little consensus about what research and scholarship are and what research reporting and scholarly discourse should look like" (p. 19).

This kind of inside look at the world of research can be shocking to people who think that there surely must be consensus regarding what constitutes "good" research. The real picture is more chaotic and warlike, what Donmoyer (1996) portrays as "a diverse array of voices speaking from quite different, often contradictory perspectives and value commitments" (p. 19). Perspectives and value commitments? Not just rules and formulas? Perspectives and value commitments imply stakes, which leads to stakeholders, which leads to involving stakeholders to represent their stakes, even in methods decisions, or should we say, *especially* in methods decisions, then those decisions determine what findings will be available for interpretation and use.

The evidence of dissensus about research standards and criteria for judging quality will not surprise those inside science who understand that a major thrust of methodological training in graduate school is learning how to pick apart and attack any study. There are no perfect studies. And there cannot be, for there is no agreement on what constitutes perfection.

This has important implications for methods decisions in evaluation. There are no universal and absolute standards for judging methods. The consensus that has emerged within evaluation, as articulated by the Joint Committee on Standards (1994) and the American Evaluation Association's Guiding Principles (Shadish et al. 1995) is that evaluations are to be judged on the basis of appropriateness, utility, practicality, accuracy, propriety, credibility, and relevance. These criteria are necessarily situational and context bound. One cannot judge the adequacy of methods used in a specific evaluation without knowing the purpose of the evaluation, the intended uses of the findings, the resources available, and the trade-offs negotiated. Judgments about validity and reliability, for example, are necessarily and appropriately relative rather than absolute in that the rigor and quality of an evaluation's design and measurement depend on the purpose and *intended use* of the evaluation. The Accuracy Standards of the Joint Committee on Standards (1994) make it clear that validity and reliability of an evaluation depend on the intended use(s) of the evaluation.

> *Valid Information:* The information-gathering procedures should be chosen or developed and then implemented so that they will assure that the interpretation arrived at is valid *for the intended use*. (A5; emphasis added)
>
> *Reliable Information:* The information-gathering procedures should be chosen or developed and then implemented so that they will assure that the information obtained is sufficiently reliable *for the intended use*. (A6; emphasis added)

The Art of Making Methods Decisions

Lee J. Cronbach (1982), an evaluation pioneer and author of several major books on measurement and evaluation, observed that designing an evaluation is as much art as science: "Developing an evaluation is an exercise of the dramatic imagination" (p. 239). This metaphor, this perspective, can help free practitioners and other primary users who are nonresearchers to feel they have something important to contribute. It can also, hopefully, open the evaluator to hearing their contributions and facilitating their "dramatic imaginations." The art of evaluation involves creating a design that is appropriate for a specific situation and particular action or policymaking context. In art there is no single, ideal standard. Beauty is in the eye of the beholder, and the evaluation beholders include decision makers, policymakers, program managers, practitioners, participants, and the general public. Thus, for Cronbach (1982), any given design is necessarily an interplay of resources, possibilities, creativity, and personal judgments by the people involved. "There is no single best plan for an evaluation, not even for an inquiry into a particular program, at a particular time, with a particular budget" (p. 231).

Hard Versus Soft Data

The next chapter will explore in depth the "paradigms debate" involving quantitative/experimental methods versus qualitative/naturalistic approaches. This is sometimes framed as "hard data" versus "soft data." At this point it suffices to say that the issue is not hard versus soft, but relevant and appropriate versus irrelevant and inappropriate. Participants in the Stanford Evaluation Consortium (Cronbach et al. 1980) observed that "merit lies not in form of inquiry but in relevance of information" (p. 7). My experience with stakeholders suggests that they would rather have soft data about an important question than hard data about an issue of minor relevance.

Obviously, the ideal is hard data about important questions, whatever hard data may mean in a particular context. But, in the real world of trade-offs and negotiations, the evaluation researcher too often determines what is evaluated according to his or her own expertise or preference in what to measure, rather than by deciding first what intended users determine is worth evaluating and then doing the best he or she can with methods. Relevance and utility are the driving forces in utilization-focused evaluation; methods are employed in the service of relevance and use, not as their master.

One implication of this perspective—that quality and excellence are situational, that design combines the scientific and artistic—is that it is futile to attempt to design studies that are immune from methodological criticism. There simply is no such immunity. Intended users who participate in making methods decisions should be prepared to be criticized regardless of what choices they make. Especially futile is the desire, often articulated by nonresearchers, to conduct an evaluation that will be accepted by and respected within the academic community. As we demonstrated above, in discussing peer review research, the academic community does not speak with one voice. Any particular academics whose blessings are particularly important for evaluation use should be invited to participate in the evaluation design task force and become, explicitly, intended users. Making no pretense of pleasing the entire scientific community (an impossibility), utilization-focused evaluation strives to attain the more modest and attainable goal of pleasing primary intended users. This does not mean that utilization-focused evaluations are less rigorous. It means the criteria for judging rigor must be articulated for each evaluation.

Credibility and Use

Credibility affects use. Credibility is a complex notion that includes the perceived accuracy, fairness, and believability of the evaluation *and* the evaluator. In the Joint Committee's (1994) standard on Evaluator Credibility, evaluators are admonished to be "both trustworthy and competent" so that findings achieve "maximum credibility and acceptance" (p. U2). Report clarity, full and frank disclosure of data strengths and weaknesses, balanced reporting, defensible information sources, valid and reliable measurement, justified conclusions, and impartial reporting are all specific standards aimed at credibility as a foundation for use. The American Evaluation Association's Guiding Principles (Shadish et al. 1995) likewise emphasize systematic inquiry, competence, and honesty and integrity to ensure credibility and utility.

For information to be useful and to merit use, it should be as accurate and believable as possible. Limitations on the degree of accuracy should be stated clearly. Research by Weiss and Bucuvalas (1980) found that decision makers apply *both* truth tests (whether data are believable and accurate) and utility tests (whether data are relevant) in deciding how seriously to weigh findings. Decision makers want highly accurate and trustworthy data. This means they want data that are valid and reliable. But in the politically charged environment of evaluation, these traditional scientific concepts have taken on some new and broader meanings.

Overall Evaluation Validity

The government ministries are very keen on amassing statistics. They collect them, raise them to the nth power, take the cube root, and prepare wonderful diagrams. But you must never forget that every one of these figures comes in the first place from the village watchman, who just puts down what he damn well pleases.

—Sir Josiah Stamp, 1911,
English economist (1880-1941)

House (1980:249) has suggested that validity means "worthiness of being recognized:" For the typical evaluation this means being "true, credible, and right" (p. 250). Different approaches to evaluation establish validity in different ways. The important part of House's contribution from the point of view of utilization-focused evaluation is that he applies the notion of validity to *the entire evaluation*, not just the data. An *evaluation* is perceived as valid in a global sense that includes the overall approach used, the stance of the evaluator, the nature of the process, the design, data gathering, and the way in which results are reported. Both the evaluation *and* the evaluator must be perceived as trustworthy for the evaluation to have high validity.

Alkin et al. (1979) studied use and found that "for evaluations to have impact, users must believe what evaluators have to say" (p. 245). The believability of an evaluation depends on much more than the perceived scientific validity of the data and findings. Believability depends on the users' perceptions of and experiences with the program being evaluated, users' prior knowledge and prejudices, the perceived adequacy of evaluation procedures, and the users' trust in the evaluator (Alkin et al. 1979:245-47). Trust, believability, and credibility are the underpinnings of *overall* evaluation validity.

It is important to understand how overall evaluation validity differs from the usual, more narrow conception of validity in scientific research. Validity is usually focused entirely on data collection procedures, design, and technical analysis, that is, whether measures were valid or whether the design allows drawing inferences about causality (internal design validity).

A measure is scientifically valid to the extent that it captures or measures the concept (or thing) it is intended to measure. For example, asking if an IQ test really measures native intelligence (rather than education and socioeconomic advantage) is a validity question. Validity is often difficult to establish, particularly for new instruments. Over time, scientists develop some consensus about the relative validity of often-used instruments, such as major norm-referenced standardized educational tests. Rossi, Freeman, and Wright (1979) discuss three common criteria for validity of quantitative instruments.

> 1. *Consistency with usage:* A valid measurement of a concept must be consistent with past work that used that concept. Hence, a measure of adoption must not be in contradiction to the usual ways in which that term had been used in previous evaluations of interventions.
> 2. *Consistency with alternative measures:* A valid measure must be consistent with alternative measures that have been used effectively by other evaluators. Thus, a measure must produce roughly the same results as other measures that have been proposed, or, if different, have sound conceptual reasons for being different.
> 3. *Internal consistency:* A valid measure must be internally consistent. That is, if several questions are used to measure adoption, the answers to those questions should be related to each other as if they were alternative measures of the same thing. (pp. 170-71)

Qualitative data collection (e.g., such techniques as participant observation and in-depth, open-ended interviewing) poses different validity challenges. In qualitative methods, validity hinges to a greater extent on the skill, competence, and rigor of the researcher because the observer or interviewer is the instrument.

> Since as often as not the naturalistic inquirer is himself the instrument, changes resulting from fatigue, shifts in knowledge, and cooptation, as well as variations resulting from differences in training, skill, and experience among different "instruments," easily occur. But this loss in rigor is more than offset by the flexibility, insight, and ability to build on tacit knowledge that is the peculiar province of the human instrument. (Guba and Lincoln 1981:113)

Validity concerns also arise in using official statistics such as health or crime statistics. Joe Hudson (1977) has cautioned about the care that must be taken in using crime statistics because of validity problems:

> First, officially collected information used as measures of program outcomes are, by their very nature, indirect measures of behavior. For example, we have no practical or direct way of measuring the actual extent to which graduates of correctional programs commit new crimes. Second, the measurements provided are commonly open to serious problems. For example, the number of crimes known to authorities in most situations is only a fraction of the number of crimes committed, although that fraction varies from crime to crime. . . . The growing willingness of victims of sexual assault to report their crimes to the police and actively cooperate in prosecution is an example of the manner in which public attitudes can affect officially recorded rates of crime.
>
> Of the various criteria used to measure recidivism, that of arrest appears to be especially problematic. Recidivism rates based on arrest do not tell us whether those arrested have, in fact, returned to criminal behavior but only that they are presumed to have done so. . . .
>
> The widespread discretion exercised by the police to arrest is a further source of invalidity. For example, it is probably reasonable to expect that the number of individuals arrested for a particular type of crime within a jurisdiction is to some extent a direct reflection of changing police policies and not totally the function of changing patterns of

law-violating behavior. In addition to the power of deciding when to arrest, police also have discretionary authority to determine which of a number of crimes an individual will be arrested for in a particular situation. Thus, if policy emphasis is placed upon combating burglary, this may affect decisions as to whether an arrestee is to be arrested for burglary, simple larceny, or criminal damage to property. In short, the discretion of the police to control both the number and types of arrests raises serious validity problems in evaluations which attempt to use this measure of program outcome. (pp. 88-89)

In summary, then, validity problems, along with the trustworthiness of the evaluator, affect the overall credibility of the evaluation, and this is true for all kinds of data collection—quantitative measures, questionnaires, qualitative observations, government statistics, and social indicators. The precise nature of the validity problem varies from situation to situation, but evaluators must always be concerned about the extent to which the data collected are credible and actually measure what is supposed to be measured; they must also make sure that intended users understand validity issues. In addition, a validity issue of special, though not unique, concern to utilization-focused evaluators is face validity.

Believable and Understandable Data

Face Validity in Utilization-Focused Measurement

Face validity concerns "the extent to which an instrument looks as if it measures what it is intended to measure" (Nunnally 1970:149). An instrument has face validity if stakeholders can look at the items and understand what is being measured. Face validity, however, is generally held in low regard by measurement experts. Predictive validity, concurrent validity, construct validity—these technical approaches are much preferred by psychometricians. Nunnally (1970) considers face validity to have occasional public relations value when data are gathered for the general public: "Less logical is the reluctance of some administrators in applied settings, e.g., industry, to permit the use of predictor instruments which lack face validity" (p. 149). Yet, from a utilization perspective, it is perfectly logical for decision makers to want to understand and believe in data they are expected to use. Nunnally disagrees: "Although one could make a case for the involvement of face validity in the measurement of constructs, to do so would probably serve only to confuse the issues" (p. 150). It is little wonder that evaluators, many of whom cut their measurement teeth on Nunnally's textbooks, have little sympathy for the face validity needs of stakeholders. Nor is it surprising that such evaluators complain that their findings are not used. Consider the following case.

The board of directors of a major industrial firm decided to decentralize organizational decision making in hopes of raising worker morale. The president of the company hired an organizational consultant to monitor and evaluate the decentralization program and its effects. From the literature on the sociology of organizations, the evaluator selected a set of research instruments designed to measure decentralization, worker autonomy, communication patterns, and worker satisfaction. The scales had been used by sociologists to measure organizational change in a number of different settings, and the factorial composition of the scales had been validated. The instruments had high predictive and construct validity, but low face validity.

The evaluator found no statistically significant changes between pretest and posttest so, when he met with the board of directors, he dutifully reported that the decentralization program had failed and that worker morale remained low. The president of the company had a considerable stake in the success of the program; he did not have a stake in the evaluation data. He did what decision makers frequently do in such cases—he attacked the data.

President: How can you be so sure that the program failed?

Evaluator: We collected data using the best instruments available. I won't go into all the technical details of factor analysis and Cronbach's alpha. Let me just say that these scales have been shown to be highly valid and reliable. Take this 10-item scale on *individual autonomy*. The best predictor item in this particular scale asks respondents: (a) "Do you take coffee breaks on a fixed schedule?" or (b) "Do you go to get coffee whenever you want to?"

President: [visibly reddening and speaking in an angry tone] Am I to understand that your entire evaluation is based on some kind of questionnaire that asks people how often they get coffee, that you never personally talked to any workers or managers, that you never even visited our operations? Am I to understand that we paid you $20,000 to find out how people get their coffee?

Evaluator: Well, there's a lot more to it than that, you see . . .

President: That's it! We don't have time for this nonsense. Our lawyers will be in touch with you about whether we want to press fraud and malpractice charges!

Clearly the president was predisposed to dismiss any negative findings. But suppose the evaluator had reviewed the instrument and survey design with the president before gathering data. Suppose he had explained what the items were supposed to indicate and then asked,

> Now, if we survey employees with these items measuring these factors, will they tell you what you want to know? Does this make sense to you? Are you prepared to act on this kind of data? Would you believe the results if they came out negative?

Such an exchange might not have made a difference. It's not easy to get busy executives to look carefully at instruments in advance, nor do evaluators want to waste time explaining their trade. Many decision makers are just as happy not being bothered with technical decisions. After all, that's why they hired an evaluator in the first place, to design and conduct the evaluation! But the costs of such attitudes to use can be high. Utilization-focused evaluators check out the face validity of instruments before data are collected. Subsequent data analysis, interpretation and use are all facilitated by attention to face validity—making sure users understand and believe in the data.

Useful Designs

Face validity criteria can also be applied to design questions. Do intended users understand the design? Does it make sense to them? Do they appreciate the implications of comparing Program A with Program B? Do they know why the design includes, or does not include, a control group? Is the sample size sufficiently large to be believable? You can be sure that decision makers will have opinions about these issues when results are presented, particularly if findings turn out negative. By asking these questions before data collection, potential credibility problems can be identified and dealt with, and users' insights can help shape the design to increase its relevance. Consider the following case.

At an evaluation workshop I conducted, the marketing director for a major retail merchandising company attended to find out how to get more mileage out of his marketing research department. He told this story.

Two years earlier he had spent a considerable sum researching the potential for new products for his company's local retail distribution chain. A carefully selected representative sample of 285 respondents had been interviewed in the Minneapolis-Saint Paul greater metropolitan area. The results indicated one promising new line of products for which there appeared to be growing demand. He took this finding to the board of directors with a recommendation that the company make a major capital investment in the new product line. The board, controlled by the views of its aging chairman, vetoed the recommendation. The reason: "If you had presented us with opinions from at least a thousand people, we might be able to move on this item. But we can't make a major capital commitment on the basis of a couple of hundred interviews."

The marketing director tactfully tried to explain that increased sample size would have made only a marginal reduction in possible sampling error. The chairperson remained unconvinced, the findings of an expensive research project were ignored, and the company missed out on a major opportunity. A year later, the item they rejected had become a fast-selling new product for a rival company.

It is easy to laugh at the board's mistake, but the marketing director was not laughing. He wanted to know what to do. I suggested that next time, he check out the research design with the board before collecting data, going to them and saying,

> Our statistical analysis shows that a sample of 285 respondents in the Twin Cities area will give us an accurate picture of market potential. Here are the reasons they recommend this sample size. . . . Does that make sense to you? If we come in with a new product recommendation based on 285 respondents, will you believe the data?

If the board responds positively, the potential for use will have been enhanced, though not guaranteed. If the board says the sample is too small, then the survey might as well include more respondents—or be canceled. There is little point in implementing a design that is known in advance to lack credibility.

Reliability and Error

Reliability has to do with consistency. A measure is reliable to the extent that essentially the same results can be reproduced repeatedly, as long as the situation does not change. For example, in measuring the height of an adult, one should get the same results from one month to the next. Measuring attitudes and behavior is more complex because one must determine whether measured change means the attitude has changed or the data collection is unreliable.

Inconsistent data collection procedures, for example, asking interview questions in different sequence to different respondents, can change results and introduce errors. Nonresearchers will often have unrealistic expectations about evaluation instruments, expecting no errors. For many reasons, all data collection is subject to some measurement error. Henry Dyer, a former president of the highly respected Educational Testing Service (ETS), tells of trying to explain to a government official that test scores, even on the most reliable tests, have enough measurement error that they must be used with understanding of their limitations. The high-ranking official responded that test makers should "get on the ball" and start producing tests that "are 100% reliable under all conditions."

Dyer's (1973) reflections on this conversation are relevant to an understanding of error in all kinds of measures. He asked,

> How does one get across the shocking truth that 100% reliability in a test is a fiction that, in the nature of the case, is unrealizable? How does one convey the notion that the test-reliability problem is not one of reducing measurement error to absolute zero, but of minimizing it as far as practicable and doing one's best to estimate whatever amount of error remains, so that one may act cautiously and wisely in a world where all knowledge is approximate and not even death and taxes are any longer certain? (p. 87)

Sources of error are many. For example, consider sources of error in an individual test score. Poor health on the day of the test can affect the score. Whether the student had breakfast can make a difference. Noise in the classroom, a sudden fire drill, whether or not the teacher or a stranger gives the test, a broken pencil, and any number of similar disturbances can change a test score. The mental state of the child—depression, boredom, elation, a conflict at home, a fight with another student, anxiety about the test, a low self-concept—can affect how well the student performs. Simple mechanical errors such as marking the wrong box on the test sheet by accident, inadvertently skipping a question, or missing a word while reading are common problems for all of us. Students who have trouble reading will perform poorly on reading tests, but they are also likely to perform poorly on social studies, science, and math tests.

Some children perform better on tests because they have been taught how to take written tests. Some children are simply better test takers than other children because of their background or personality or because of how seriously they treat the idea of the test. Some schools make children sit all day taking test after test, sometimes for an entire week. Other schools give the test for only a half-day or two hours at a time to minimize fatigue and boredom. Some children like to take tests; some don't. Some teachers help children with difficult words, or even read the tests along with the children; others don't. Some schools devote their curriculum to teaching students what is on the tests. Others place little emphasis on test taking and paper-and-pencil skills, thus giving students less experience in the rigor and tricks of test taking.

All these sources of error—and I have scarcely scratched the surface of possibilities

—can seriously affect an individual score. Moreover, they have virtually nothing to do with how good the test is, how carefully it was prepared, or how valid its content is for a given child or group. Intrinsic to the nature of testing, these errors are always present to some extent and are largely uncontrollable. They are the reason that statisticians can never develop a test that is 100% reliable.

The errors are more or less serious depending on how a test is used. When looking at test scores for large groups, we can expect that, because of such errors, some students will perform above their true level and other students will perform below their true score. For most groups, statisticians believe that these errors cancel each other. The larger the group tested, the more likely this is to be true.

Different evaluation instruments are subject to different kinds of errors. Whether the evaluation includes data from tests, questionnaires, management information systems, government statistics, or whatever—the analysis should include attention to potential sources of error, and, where possible, calculate and report the degree of error. The point is that evaluators need not be defensive about errors. Rather, they need to explain the nature of errors, help intended users decide what level of precision is needed, consider the costs and benefits of undertaking procedures to reduce error (for instance, a larger sample size), and help users to understand the implications for interpreting findings. Primary intended users can be helpful in identifying potential sources of error. In my experience, their overall confidence in their ability to correctly and appropriately use evaluation data is increased when there has been a frank and full discussion of *both* the data's strengths and weaknesses. In this way, evaluators are helping to make evaluation clients more knowledgeable so they will understand what Dyer's government official did not: The challenge is not reducing measurement error to absolute zero, but rather minimizing it as far as practicable and doing one's best to estimate whatever amount of error remains, so that one may act cautiously and wisely in a world where all knowledge is approximate and not even death and taxes are any longer certain.

Trade-Offs

Different evaluation purposes affect how much error can be tolerated. A summative evaluation to inform a major decision that will affect the future of a program, perhaps touching the lives of thousands of people and involving allocations of millions of dollars, will necessarily and appropriately involve considerable attention to and resources for minimizing error. In contrast, a small-scale, fairly informal, formative evaluation aimed at stimulating staff to think about what they're doing will raise fewer concerns about error. There is a lot of territory between these extremes. How precise and robust findings need to be, given available resources, are matters for discussion and negotiation. The next two sections look at additional concerns that commonly involve negotiation and trade-offs: (1) breadth versus depth and (2) the relative generalizability of findings.

Breadth Versus Depth

Deciding how much data to gather involves trade-offs between depth and breadth. Getting more data usually takes longer and costs more, but getting less data usually reduces confidence in the findings. Studying a narrow question or very specific problem in great depth may produce clear results but leave other important issues and problems unexamined. On the other hand, gathering information on a large variety of issues and problems may leave the evaluation unfocused and result in knowing a little about a lot of things, but not knowing a lot about anything.

During methods deliberations, some boundaries must be set on data collection. Should all parts of the program be studied or only certain parts? Should all participants be studied or only some subset of clients? Should the evaluator aim at describing all program processes and outcomes or only certain priority areas?

In my experience, determining priorities is challenging. Once a group of primary stakeholders gets turned on to learning evaluative information, they want to know everything. The evaluator's role is to help them move from a rather extensive list of potential questions to a much shorter list of realistic questions and finally to a focused list of essential and necessary questions. This process moves from divergence to convergence, from generating many possibilities (divergence) to focusing on a few worthwhile priorities (convergence).

This applies to framing overall evaluation questions as well as to narrowing items in a particular instrument, such as a survey or interview. Many questions are interesting, but which are crucial? These end up being choices not between good and bad, but among alternatives, all of which have merit.

Internal and External Validity in Design

Trade-offs between internal and external validity have become a matter of debate in evaluation since Campbell and Stanley (1963) asserted that "internal validity is the sine qua non" (p. 175). Internal validity in its narrowest sense refers to certainty about cause and effect. Did X cause Y? Did the program cause the observed outcomes? In a broader sense, it refers to the "trustworthiness of an inference" (Cronbach 1982:106). External validity, on the other hand, refers to the degree of confidence one has in generalizing findings beyond the situation studied.

Internal validity is increased by exercising rigorous control over a limited set of carefully defined variables. However, such rigorous controls create artificialities that limit generalizability. The highly controlled situation is less likely to be relevant to a greater variety of more naturally occurring, less controlled situations. In the narrowest sense, this is the problem of going from the laboratory into the real world. By contrast, increasing variability and sampling a greater range of experiences or situations typically reduces control and precision, thereby reducing internal validity. The ideal is high internal validity and high external validity. In reality, there are typically trade-offs involved in the relative emphasis placed on one or the other.

Cronbach's (1982) discussion of these issues for evaluation is quite comprehensive and insightful. He emphasized that "both external validity and internal validity are matters of degree and external validity does not depend directly on internal validity" (p. 170). Being able to apply findings to future decisions and new settings is often more important than establishing rigorous causal relations under rigid experimental conditions. He introduced the idea of *extrapolation* rather than generalization. Extrapolation involves logically and cretively thinking about what specific findings mean for other situations, rather than the statistical process of generalizing from a sample to a larger population. He advocated that findings be interpreted in light of stakeholders' and evaluators' experiences and knowledge, and then applied/extrapolated using all available insights, including understandings about quite different situations. This focuses interpretation away from trying to determine truth in some absolute sense (a goal of basic research) to a concern with conclusions that are reasonable, justifiable, plausible, warranted, and useful.

The contrasting perspectives of Campbell and Cronbach have elucidated the trade-offs between designs that give first priority to certainty about causal inference (internal validity) versus those that better support extrapolations to new settings (external validity). These evaluation pioneers formulated fundamentally different theories of practice (Shadish et al. 1991). In working with primary stakeholders to design evaluations that are credible, the evaluator will need to consider the degree to which internal and external validity are of concern, and to emphasize each in accordance with stakeholder priorities. Choices are necessitated by the fact that no single design is likely to attain internal and external validity equally well.

Truth and Utility

Stakeholders want accurate information; they apply truth tests (Weiss and Bucuvalas 1980) in deciding how seriously to pay attention to an evaluation. They also want useful and relevant information. The ideal, then, is both truth and utility. In the real world, however, there are often choices to be made between the extent to which one maximizes truth and the degree to which data are relevant.

The simplest example of such a choice is time. The time lines for evaluation are often ridiculously short. A decision maker may need whatever information can be obtained in three months, even though the researcher insists that a year is necessary to get data of reasonable quality and accuracy. This involves a trade-off between truth and utility. Highly accurate data in a year are less useful to this decision maker than data of less precision and validity obtained in three months.

Decision makers regularly face the need to take action with limited and imperfect information. They prefer more accurate information to less accurate information, but they also prefer some information to no information. This is why research quality and rigor are "much less important to utilization than the literature might suggest" (Alkin et al. 1979:24).

The effects of methodological quality on use must be understood in the full context of a study, its political environment, the degree of uncertainty with which the decision maker is faced, and thus his or her relative need for any and all clarifying information. If information is scarce, then new information, even of dubious quality, may be somewhat helpful.

The scope and importance of an evaluation greatly affect the emphasis that will be placed on technical quality. Eleanor Chelimsky (1987a, 1987b), former President of the American Evaluation Association and founding Director of the Program Evaluation and Methodology Division of the U.S. General Accounting Office, has insisted that technical quality is paramount in policy evaluations to Congress. The technical quality of national policy research matters, not only in the short term, when findings first come out, but over the long term as policy battles unfold and evaluators are called on to explain and defend important findings (Chelimsky 1995a).

On the other hand, debates about technical quality are likely to be much more center stage in national policy evaluations than in local efforts to improve programs at the street level, where the policy rubber hits the day-to-day programming road. One evaluator in our study of the use of federal health studies linked the issue of technical quality to the nature of uncertainty in organizational decision making. He acknowledged inadequacies in the data he had collected, but he had still worked with his primary users to apply the findings, fully recognizing their problematic nature:

> You have to make the leap from very limited data. I mean, that's what a decision's like. You make it from a limited data base; and, damn it, when you're trying to use quantitative data and it's inadequate, you supposedly can't make a decision. Only you're not troubled by that. You can use impressionistic stuff. Yeah, your intuition is a lot better. I get a gestalt out of this thing on every program.
>
> This may come as a great shock to you, but that is what you use to make decisions. In Chester Barnard's definition, for example, the function of the executive is to make a decision in the absence of adequate information. [EV148:11]

He went on to express some pride in the cost-benefit ratio of his evaluation, despite admitted methods inadequacies:

> It was a pretty small investment on the part of the government—$47,000 bucks. In the evaluation business that's not a pile of money. The questions I had to ask were pretty narrow and the answers were equally narrow and relatively decisive, and the findings were put to use immediately and in the long term. So, can you beat that? [EV148:8]

Another evaluator expressed similar sentiments about a study that had to be completed in only three months.

> There are a million things I'd do differently. We needed more time. . . . At the time, it was probably the best study we could do. . . . I'm satisfied in the sense that some people found it useful. It wasn't just kept on a shelf. People paid attention to that study and it had an impact. Now, I've done other studies that I thought were methodologically really much more elegant that were kind of ignored, just sitting on somebody's shelf.
>
> My opinion is that this really modest study probably has had impact all out of proportion to the quality of the research. It happened to be at a certain place at a certain time, where it at least talked about some of the things that people were interested in talking about, so it got some attention. And many other studies that I know of that have been done, that I would consider of higher quality, haven't really gotten used. [EV145:34]

Technical quality (truth tests) may get less attention than researchers desire because many stakeholders are not very sophisticated about methods. Yet, they know (almost intuitively) that **the methods and measurements used in any study are open to question and attack,** a point emphasized earlier in this chapter. They know that researchers don't agree among themselves about technical quality. As a result, experienced decision makers apply less rigorous standards than academics and, as long as they find the evaluation effort credible and serious, they're more interested in discussing the substance of findings than in debating methods. Credibility involves more than technical quality, though that is an important contributing factor. Credibility, and therefore utility, are affected by "the steps we take to make and explain our evaluative decisions, [and] also intellectually, in the effort we put forth to look at all sides and all stakeholders of an evaluation" (Chelimsky 1995a:219). The perception of impartiality is at least as important as methodological rigor in highly political environments.

Another factor that can reduce the weight decision makers give to technical quality is skepticism about the return on investment of large-scale, elaborately designed, carefully controlled, and expensive studies. Cohen and Weiss (1977) reviewed 20 years of policy research on race and schools, finding progressive improvement in research methods (i.e., increasingly rigorous designs and ever more sophisticated analytical techniques). Sample sizes increased, computer technology was introduced, multiple regression and path analytic techniques were employed, and more valid and reliable data-gathering instruments were developed. After reviewing the findings of studies produced with these more rigorous methods, as well as the uses made of their findings, they concluded that "these changes have led to more studies that disagree, to more qualified conclusions, more arguments, and more arcane reports and unintelligible results" (Cohen and Weiss 1977:78). In light of this finding, simple, understandable, and focused evaluations have great appeal to practitioners and action-oriented evaluation users.

In utilization-focused evaluation, attention to technical quality is tied to and balanced by concern for relevance and timeliness. As one decision maker in our federal health evaluations study put it:

> You can get so busy protecting yourself against criticism that you develop such an elaborate methodology that by the time your findings come out, who cares? So, I mean, you get a balance—the validity of the data against its relevance. And that's pretty tough stuff. I mean, that's hard business. [DM111:26]

As no study is ever methodologically perfect, it is important for primary stakeholders to know firsthand what imperfections exist—and to be included in deciding which imperfections they are willing to live with in making the inevitable leaps from limited data to incremental action.

The Dynamics of Measurement and Design Decisions

Research quality and relevance are not set in stone once an evaluation proposal has been accepted. A variety of factors emerge throughout the life of an evaluation that require new decisions about methods. Actively involving intended users in making methods decisions about these issues means more than a one-point-in-time acquiescence to a research design.

In every one of the 20 federal health studies we investigated, significant methods revisions and redesigns had to be done after data collection began. While little attention has been devoted in the evaluation literature to the phenomenon of slippage between methods as originally proposed and methods as actually implemented, the problem is similar to that of program implementation, where original specifications typically differ greatly from what finally gets delivered (see Chapter 9).

McTavish et al. (1975) studied implementation of 126 research projects funded across seven federal agencies. All 126 projects were rated by independent judges along seven descriptive methodological scales. Both original proposals and final reports were rated; the results showed substantial instability between the two. The researchers concluded,

> Our primary conclusion from the Predictability Study is that the quality of final report methodology is essentially not predictable from proposal or interim report documentation. This appears to be due to a number of factors. First, research is characterized by significant change as it develops over time. Second, unanticipated events force shifts in direction. Third, the character and quality of information available early in a piece of research makes assessment of some features of methodology difficult or impossible. (pp. 62-63)

Earlier in the report, they had pointed out that

> among the more salient reasons for the low predictability from early to late documentation is the basic change which occurs during the course of most research. It is, after all, a risky pursuit rather than a pre-programmed product. Initial plans usually have to be altered once the realities of data or opportunities and limitations become known. Typically, detailed plans for analysis and reporting are postponed and revised. External events also seem to have taken an expected toll in the studies we examined. . . . Both the context of research and the phenomena being researched are typically subject to great change. (p. 56)

If intended users are involved only at the stage of approving research proposals, they are likely to be surprised when they see a final report. Even interim reports bear only moderate resemblance to final reports. Thus, making decisions about methods is a continuous process that involves checking out changes with intended users as they are made. While it is impractical to have evaluator-stakeholder discussions about every minor change in methods, utilization-focused evaluators prefer to err in the direction of consultative rather than unilateral decision making, when there is a choice. Stakeholders also carry a responsibility to make sure they remain committed to the evaluation. One internal evaluator interviewed in our federal utilization study, still smarting from critiques of his evaluation as methodologically weak, offered the following advice to decision makers who commission evaluations:

> Very, very often those of us who are doing evaluation studies are criticized for poor methodology, and the people who levy the criticism sometimes are the people who pay for the study. Of course, they do this more often when the study is either late or it doesn't come up with the answers that they were looking for. But I think that a large share of the blame or responsibility belongs to the project monitor, sponsor, or funder for not maintaining enough control, direct hands-on contact with the evaluation as it's ongoing.
>
> I don't think that it's fair to blame an [evaluation] contractor for developing a poor study approach, a poor methodology, and absolve yourself, if you're the sponsor because it's your role as a project monitor to be aware of what those people that you're paying are doing all the time, and to guide them.
>
> We let contracts out and we keep our hands on these contractors all the time. And when we see them going down a road that we don't think is right, we pull them back and we say, "Hey, you know, we disagree." We don't let them go down the road all the

way and then say, "Hey fella, you went down the wrong road." [EV32:15]

I have found this a useful quote to share with primary stakeholders who have expressed reluctance to stay involved with the evaluation as it unfolds. *Caveat emptor.*

Threats to Data Quality

Evaluators have an obligation to think about, anticipate, and provide guidance about how threats to data quality will affect interpreting and using results. Threats to internal validity, for example, affect any conclusion that a program produced an observed outcome. The observed effect could be due to larger societal changes (history), as when generally increased societal awareness of the need for exercise and proper nutrition contaminates the effects of specific programs aimed at encouraging exercise and proper nutrition. Maturation is a threat to validity when it is difficult to separate the effects of a program from the effects of growing older; this is a common problem in juvenile delinquency programs, as delinquency has been shown to decline naturally with age. Reactions to gathering data can affect outcomes independent of program effects, as when students perform better on a posttest simply because they are more familiar with the test the second time; or there can be interactions between the pretest and the program when the experience of having taken a pretest increases participants' sensitivity to key aspects of a program. Losing people from a program (experimental mortality) can affect findings since those who drop out, and therefore fail to take a posttest, are likely to be different in important ways from those who stay to the end.

However, it is impossible to anticipate all potential threats to data quality. Even when faced with the reality of particular circumstances and specific evaluation problems, it is impossible to know in advance precisely how a creative design or measurement approach will affect results. For example, having program staff do client interviews in an outcomes evaluation could (1) seriously reduce the validity and reliability of the data, (2) substantially increase the validity and reliability of the data, or (3) have no measurable effect on data quality. The nature and degree of effect would depend on staff relationships with clients, how staff were assigned to clients for interviewing, the kinds of questions being asked, the training of the staff interviewers, attitudes of clients toward the program, and so on. Program staff might make better or worse interviewers than external evaluation researchers, depending on these and other factors.

An evaluator must grapple with these kinds of data quality questions for all designs. No automatic rules apply. There is no substitute for thoughtful analysis based on the specific circumstances and information needs of a particular evaluation, both initially and as the evaluation unfolds.

Threats to Utility

Whereas traditional evaluation methods texts focus primarily on threats to validity, this chapter has focused primarily on threats to utility. Threats to utility include the following:

- failure to focus on intended use by intended users
- inadequate involvement of primary intended users in making methods decisions

- focusing on unimportant issues—low relevance
- inappropriate methods and measures given stakeholder questions and information needs
- poor stakeholder understanding of the evaluation generally and findings specifically
- low user belief and trust in the evaluation process and findings
- low face validity
- failure to design the evaluation to fit the context and situation
- unbalanced data collection and reporting
- perceptions that the evaluation is unfair or that the evaluator is biased or less than impartial
- low evaluator credibility
- political naïveté
- failure to keep stakeholders adequately informed and involved along the way as design alterations are necessary

We now have substantial evidence that paying attention to and working to counter these threats to utility will lead to evaluations that are worth using—and are actually used.

Designing Evaluations Worth Using: Reflections on the State of the Art

This chapter has described the challenges evaluators face in working with intended users to design evaluations worth using. My consulting brings me into contact with hundreds of evaluation colleagues and users. I know from direct observation that many evaluators are meeting these challenges with great skill, dedication, competence, and effectiveness. Much important and creative work is being done by evaluators in all kinds of difficult and demanding situations as they fulfill their commitment to do the most and best they can with the resources available, the short deadlines they face, and the intense political pressures they feel. They share a belief that doing something is better than doing nothing, so long as one is realistic and honest in assessing and presenting the limitations of what is done.

This last caveat is important. I have not attempted to delineate all possible threats to validity, reliability, and utility. This is not a design and measurement text. My purpose has been to stimulate thinking about how attention to intended use for intended users affects all aspects of evaluation practice, including methods decisions.

Pragmatism undergirds the utilitarian emphasis of utilization-focused evaluation. In designing evaluations, it is worth keeping in mind World War II General George S. Patton's Law: **A good plan today is better than a perfect plan tomorrow.**

Then there is Halcolm's evaluation corollary to Patton's law: **Perfect designs aren't.**

12

The Paradigms Debate and a Utilitarian Synthesis

Lady, I do not make up things. That is lies. Lies is not true. But the truth could be made up if you know how. And that's the truth.

—Lily Tomlin as character "Edith Ann,"
Rolling Stone, October 24, 1974

Training

A former student sent me the following story, which she had received as an e-mail chain letter, a matter of interest only because it suggests widespread distribution.

Once upon a time, not so very long ago, a group of statisticians (hereafter known as quants) and a party of qualitative methodologists (quals) found themselves together on a train traveling to the same professional meeting. The quals, all of whom had tickets, observed that the quants had only one ticket for their whole group.

"How can you all travel on one ticket?" asked a qual.

"We have our methods," replied a quant.

Later, when the conductor came to punch tickets, all the quants slipped quickly behind the door of the toilet. When the conductor knocked on the door, the head quant slipped their one ticket under the door, thoroughly fooling the conductor.

On their return from the conference, the two groups again found themselves on the same train. The qualitative researchers, having learned from the quants, had schemed to share a single ticket. They were chagrined, therefore, to learn that, this time, the statisticians had boarded with no tickets.

"We know how you traveled together with one ticket," revealed a qual, "but how can you possibly get away with no tickets?"

"We have new methods," replied a quant.

Later, when the conductor approached, all the quals crowded into the toilet. The head statistician followed them and knocked authoritatively on the toilet door. The quals slipped their one and only ticket under the door. The head quant took the ticket and joined the other quants in a different toilet. The quals were subsequently discovered without tickets, publicly humiliated, and tossed off the train at its next stop.

Methodological Respectability

This story offers a remnant of what was once a great paradigms debate about the relative merits of quantitative/experimental methods versus qualitative/naturalistic methods. That debate has run out of intellectual steam and is now relegated to comedy on the Internet. As Thomas Cook, one of evaluation's luminaries—the Cook of Cook and Campbell (1979), the bible of quasi-experimentation, and of Shadish, Cook, and Leviton (1991), the definitive work on evaluation theorists—pronounced in his keynote address to the 1995 International Evaluation Conference in Vancouver, "Qualitative researchers have won the qualitative-quantitative debate."

Won in what sense?

Won acceptance.

The validity of experimental methods and quantitative measurement, appropriately used, was never in doubt. Now, qualitative methods have ascended to a level of parallel respectability. That ascendance was not without struggle and sometimes acrimonious debate, as when Lee Sechrest, American Evaluation Association president in 1991, devoted his presidential address to alternatively defending quantitative methods and ridiculing qualitative approaches. He lamented what he perceived as a decline in the training of evaluators, especially in conducting rigorous quantitative studies. He linked this to a more general "decline of numeracy" and increase in "mathematical illiteracy" in the nation. "My opinion," he stated, "is that qualitative evaluation is proving so attractive because it is, superficially, so easy" (Sechrest 1992:4). Partly tongue in cheek, he cited as evidence of qualitative evaluators' mathematical ineptitude a proposal he had reviewed from a qualitative researcher that contained a misplaced decimal point and, as another piece of evidence, an invitation to a meeting of "qualitative research types" that asked for a February 30 reply (p. 5). He concluded, "If we want to have the maximum likelihood of our results being accepted and used, we will do well to ground them, not in theory and hermeneutics, but in the dependable rigor afforded by our best science and accompanying quantitative analyses" (p. 3).

Beyond the rancor, however, Sechrest joined other eminent researchers in acknowledging a role for qualitative methods, especially in combination with quantitative approaches. He was preceded in this regard by distinguished methodological scholars such as Donald Campbell and Lee J. Cronbach. Ernest House (1977), describing the role of *qualitative argument* in evaluation, observed that "when two of the leading scholars of measurement and experimental design, Cronbach and Campbell, strongly support qualitative studies, that is strong endorsement indeed" (p. 18). In my own work, I have found increased interest in and acceptance of qualitative methods in particular and multiple methods in general.

A consensus has emerged in the profession that evaluators need to know and use a variety of methods in order to be responsive to the nuances of particular evaluation questions and the idiosyncrasies of specific stakeholder needs. As noted in the previous chapter, the issue is the appropriateness of methods for a specific evaluation purpose and question, not adherence to some absolute orthodoxy that one or the other approach is inherently preferred. The field has come to recognize that, where possible, using multiple methods—both quantitative and qualitative—can be valuable, since each has strengths and one approach can often overcome weaknesses of the other.

The problem is that this ideal of evaluators being situationally responsive, methodologically flexible, and sophisticated in using a variety of methods runs headlong into the realities of the evaluation world. Those realities include limited resources, political considerations of expediency, and the narrowness of disciplinary training available to most evaluators—training that imbues them with varying degrees of methodological prejudice. Moreover, while I believe that the paradigms debate has lost its acerbic edge among most evaluators, many users of evaluation—practitioners, policymakers, program managers, and funders—remain mired in the simplistic worldview that statistical results (hard data) are more scientific and valid than qualitative case studies (soft data). Therefore, to involve intended users in methods decisions, utilization-focused evaluators need to understand the paradigms debate and be able to facilitate choices that are appropriate to the evaluation's purpose. This will often require educating primary stakeholders about the legitimate options available, the potential advantages of multiple methods, and the strengths and weaknesses of various approaches. Toward that end, this chapter reviews the paradigms debate and then offers a utilization-focused synthesis.

The Paradigms Debate

A paradigm is a worldview built on implicit assumptions, accepted definitions, comfortable habits, values defended as truths, and beliefs projected as reality. As such, paradigms are deeply embedded in the socialization of adherents and practitioners: Paradigms tell them what is important, legitimate, and reasonable. Paradigms are also normative, telling the practitioner what to do without the necessity of long existential or epistemological consideration. But it is this aspect of paradigms that constitutes both their strength and their weakness—their strength in that it makes action possible, their weakness in that the very reason for action is hidden in the unquestioned assumptions of the paradigm.

> Scientists work from models acquired through education and through subsequent exposure to the literature, often without quite knowing or needing to know what characteristics have given these models the status of community paradigms. . . . That

> scientists do not usually ask or debate what makes a particular problem or solution legitimate tempts us to suppose that, at least intuitively, they know the answer. But it may only indicate that neither the question nor the answer is felt to be relevant to their research. Paradigms may be prior to, more binding, and more complete than any set of rules for research that could be unequivocally abstracted from them. (Kuhn 1970:46)

Evaluation was initially dominated by the natural science paradigm of hypothetico-deductive methodology, which values quantitative measures, experimental design, and statistical analysis as the epitome of "good" science. Influenced by philosophical tenets of logical positivism, this model for evaluation came from the tradition of experimentation in agriculture, the archetype of applied research.

> The most common form of agricultural-botany type evaluation is presented as an assessment of the effectiveness of an innovation by examining whether or not it has reached required standards on prespecified criteria. Students—rather like plant crops—are given pretests (the seedlings are weighed or measured) and then submitted to different experiments (treatment conditions). Subsequently, after a period of time, their attainment (growth or yield) is measured to indicate the relative efficiency of the methods (fertilizer) used. Studies of this kind are designed to yield data of one particular type, i.e., "objective" numerical data that permit statistical analyses. (Parlett and Hamilton 1976:142)

By way of contrast, the alternative to the dominant quantitative/experimental paradigm was derived from the tradition of anthropological field studies and undergirded by the philosophical tenets of phenomenology. Using the techniques of in-depth, open-ended interviewing and personal observation, the alternative paradigm relies on qualitative data, naturalistic inquiry, and detailed description derived from close contact with people in the setting under study.

In utilization-focused evaluation, neither of these paradigms is intrinsically better than the other. They represent alternatives from which the utilization-focused evaluator can choose; both contain options for primary stakeholders and information users. **Issues of methodology are issues of strategy, not of morals.** Yet, it is not easy to approach the selection of evaluation methods in this adaptive fashion. The paradigmatic biases in each approach are quite fundamental. Great passions have been aroused by advocates on each side. Kuhn (1970) has pointed out that this is the nature of paradigm debates:

> To the extent that two scientific schools disagree about what is a problem and what is a solution, they will inevitably talk through each other when debating the relative merits of their respective paradigms. In the partially circular arguments that regularly result, each paradigm will be shown to satisfy more or less the criteria that it dictates for itself and to fall short of a few of those dictated by its opponent. . . . Since no paradigm ever solves all problems it defines, and since no two paradigms leave all the same problems unanswered, paradigm questions always involve the question: Which problem is it more significant to have solved? (pp. 109-10)

The countering positions that sparked the debate in evaluation remain relevant because much social science training is still quite narrow. Evaluators and those who commission or use evaluation will naturally be most comfortable with those methods in which they have been trained and to which they have most often been exposed. A particular way of viewing the world, based on disciplinary training and specialization, becomes so second-nature that it takes on the characteristics of a paradigm. The paradigms debate has been a prominent and persistent topic in evaluation and has generated a substantial literature, only a sample of which is referenced here (Donmoyer 1996; Moss 1996; Cook 1995; Phillips 1995; Denzin and Lincoln 1994; Guba and Lincoln 1994, 1989, 1981; Fishman 1992; Eisner 1991; House 1991; Rizo 1991; Cochran-Smith and Lytle 1990; Patton 1990, 1978, 1975a; Howe 1988; J. K. Smith 1988; Lincoln and Guba 1985; Cronbach 1982, 1975; Heilman 1980; Reichardt and Cook 1979; Rist 1977). Paradigm discussions and debates have also been a regular feature at meetings of professional evaluators worldwide.

The Quantitative/Experimental Paradigm in Its Days of Domination

Evidence of the early dominance of the quantitative/experimental (hypothetico-deductive) paradigm as *the* method of choice in evaluation research can be found in the meta-evaluation work of Bernstein and Freeman (1975). The purpose of their study was to assess the quality of evaluative research at the time. What is of interest to us here is the way Bernstein and Freeman defined *quality*. Exhibit 12.1 shows how they coded their major indicators of quality; a higher number represents higher-quality research. The highest quality rating was reserved for completely quantitative data obtained through an experimental design and analyzed with sophisticated statistical techniques. Bernstein and Freeman did not concern themselves with whether the evaluation findings were important or used, or even whether the methods and measures were appropriate to the problem under study. They judged the quality of evaluation research entirely by its conformance with the dominant, hypothetico-deductive paradigm.

Documenting the consensus that existed for how they defined evaluation quality, Bernstein and Freeman cited major texts of the time, for example, Suchman (1967), Caro (1971), and Rossi and Williams (1972). Representative of the dominant perspective at the time is that of Wholey et al. (1970): "Federal money generally should not be spent on evaluation of individual local projects unless they have been developed as field experiments, with equivalent treatment and control groups" (p. 93). The Social Science Research Council (Reicken and Boruch 1974) took a similar position, as did eminent evaluation pioneer Peter Rossi (1972) in reporting general consensus about the most desired evaluation research methods at a conference on evaluation and policy research sponsored by the American Academy of Arts and Sciences in 1969.

A cursory skimming of major educational and social science research journals would confirm the dominance of the hypothetico-deductive paradigm. In their widely used methodological primer, Campbell and Stanley (1963) called this paradigm "the only available route to cumulative progress" (p. 3). It was this belief in and commitment to the natural science model on the part of the most prominent academic researchers that made experimental designs and statistical measures dominant. As Kuhn (1970) has explained, "A paradigm governs, in the first instance, not a subject matter but rather a group of practitioners" (p. 80). Those practitioners

EXHIBIT 12.1

Dominant Paradigm: Operational Definition of Evaluation Quality in the 1970s

Dimension of Evaluation Quality	*Coding Scheme (higher number = higher quality)*
Sampling	1 = Systematic random
	0 = Nonrandom, cluster, or nonsystematic
Data analysis	2 = Quantitative
	1 = Qualitative and quantitative
	0 = Qualitative
Statistical procedures	4 = Multivariate
	3 = Descriptive
	2 = Ratings from qualitative data
	1 = Narrative data only
	0 = No systematic material
Impact Procedures Design	3 = Experimental or quasi-experimental randomization and control groups
	2 = Experimental or quasi-experimental without both randomization and control groups
	1 = Longitudinal or cross-sectional without control or comparison groups
	0 = Descriptive, narrative

SOURCE: Bernstein and Freeman 1975.

most committed to the dominant paradigm were found in universities, where they employed the scientific method in their own evaluation research and nurtured students in a commitment to that same methodology.

In our mid-1970s study of how federal health evaluations were used, every respondent answered methodological questions with reference to the dominant paradigm. If a particular evaluation being reviewed had departed from what were implicitly understood to be the ideals of "good science," long explanations about practical constraints were offered, usually defensively, under the assumption that since we were from a university, we would be critical of such departures. Studies were described as hard or soft along a continuum in which harder was clearly better and didn't even need explicit definition.

The problem from a utilization-focused perspective was that the very dominance of the quantitative/experimental paradigm had cut off the great majority of evaluators and stakeholders from serious consideration of any alternative paradigm or methods. The label *research* had come to mean the equivalent of employing *the* scientific method: testing hypotheses, formulated deductively, through random assignment of program participants to treatment and control controls, and measuring outcomes quantitatively. Nothing else was really worthy of serious attention *by definition.*

An alternative existed, however, another way of studying program processes and outcomes that began to attract a following from evaluators and practitioners who found that the dominant paradigm failed to answer—or even ask—their questions.

The importance of having an alternative is captured powerfully by the distinguished adult educator Malcolm Knowles (1989), who, in his autobiography, *The Making of an Adult Educator*, listed discovery of an alternative way of evaluating adult learning as one of the eight most important episodes of his life, right there alongside his marriage.

The Emergence of the Alternative Qualitative/Naturalistic Paradigm

The alternative methods paradigm was derived most directly from anthropological field methods and more generally from qualitative sociology and phenomenology. It was undergirded by the *doctrine of Verstehen* (understanding):

> Advocates of some version of the *verstehen* doctrine will claim that human beings can be understood in a manner that other objects of study cannot. Humans have purposes and emotions, they make plans, construct cultures, and hold certain values, and their behavior is influenced by such values, plans, and purposes. In short, a human being lives in a world which has "meaning" to him, and, because his behavior has meaning, human actions are intelligible in ways that the behavior of nonhuman objects is not. (Strike 1972:28)

In essence, the Verstehen doctrine asserted that applied social sciences need methods different from those used in agriculture because human beings are different from plants. The alternative paradigm emphasized attention to the meaning of human behavior, the context of social interaction, and the connections between subjective states and behavior. The tradition of Verstehen places emphasis on the human capacity to know and understand others through empathic introspection and reflection based on detailed description gathered through direct observation, in-depth, open-ended interviewing, and case studies. Evaluation came to have advocates for and users of alternative methods. Robert Stake's (1975) *responsive approach* was one such early alternative.

> Responsive evaluation is an alternative, an old alternative, based on what people do naturally to evaluate things; they observe and react. The approach is not new. But this alternative has been avoided in district, state, and federal planning documents and regulations because it is subjective and poorly suited to formal contracts. It is also capable of raising embarrassing questions. (p. 14)

Stake recommended responsive evaluation because "it is an approach that trades off some measurement precision in order to increase the usefulness of the findings to persons in and around the program" (p. 14). Stake influenced a new generation of evaluators to think about the connection between methods and use, and his book on *The Art of Case Research* (1995), published two decades later, promises to extend that influence.

Another window into alternative methods came from what Parlett and Hamilton (1976) called *illuminative evaluation*, an approach they developed for schools.

> Illuminative evaluation takes account of the wider contexts in which educational programs function. Its primary concern is with description and interpretation rather than measurement and prediction. It stands unambiguously within the alternative anthropological paradigm. The aims of illuminative evaluation are to study the innovatory program: how it operates; how it is influenced by the various school situations in which it is applied; what those directly concerned regard as its advantages and disadvantages; and how students' intellectual tasks and academic experiences are most affected. It aims to discover and document what it is like to be participating in the scheme, whether as teacher or pupil, and, in addition, to discern and discuss the innovation's most significant features, recurring concomitants, and critical processes. In short, it seeks to address and illuminate a complex array of questions. (p. 144)

I joined the fray at about the same time when, after being thoroughly indoctrinated into the dominant paradigm as a quantitative sociologist, I became involved in evaluating an open education program whose practitioners objected to the narrow and standardized outcomes measured by standardized tests. Because they advocated an educational approach that they considered individualized, personal, humanistic, and nurturing, they wanted evaluation methods with those same characteristics. In attempting to be responsive to my intended users (open educators) and do an evaluation that was credible and useful to them, I discovered qualitative methods. That led me to write a monograph comparing alternative paradigms (Patton 1975a), reactions to which embroiled me directly and personally in the passions and flames of the great paradigms debate. At the time it was exhilarating. Looking back from today's vantage point of methodological eclecticism, the barbs traded by opposing camps would appear silly but for the fact that, in circles not yet touched by the light that eventually emerged from the debate, friction and its attendant heat still burn evaluators who encounter true believers in the old orthodoxies. It is to prepare for such encounters, and be able to rise gently above the acrimony they can inspire, that students of evaluation need to understand the dimensions and passions of the debate.

Dimensions of the Competing Paradigms

By the end of the 1970s, then, the evaluation profession had before it the broad outlines of two competing research paradigms.

Exhibit 12.2 displays the contrasting emphases of the two methodological paradigms. Beyond differences in basic philosophical assumptions about the nature of reality (e.g., singular reality versus multiple realities), in its details the paradigms debate included the relative merits of a number of dimensions, like the relative merits of being close to versus distant from program participants during an evaluation. While reviewing these dimensions will illuminate the nature of the paradigms debate, they also can be thought of as options that might be offered to intended users during methods deliberations and negotiations. We'll begin with the division about the relative merits of numbers versus narrative.

EXHIBIT 12.2
Dimensions of Competing Methodological Paradigms

Qualitative/Naturalistic Paradigm	*Quantitative/Experimental Paradigm*
Qualitative data (narratives, descriptions)	Quantitative data (numbers, statistics)
Naturalistic inquiry	Experimental designs
Case studies	Treatment and control groups
Inductive analysis	Deductive hypothesis testing
Subjective perspective	Objective perspective
Close to the program	Aloof from the program
Holistic contextual portrayal	Independent and dependent variables
Systems perspective focused on interdependencies	Linear, sequential modeling
Dynamic, ongoing view of change	Pre-post focus on change
Purposeful sampling of relevant cases	Probabilistic, random sampling
Focus on uniqueness and diversity	Standardized, uniform procedures
Emergent, flexible designs	Fixed, controlled designs
Thematic content analysis	Statistical analysis
Extrapolations	Generalizations

Quantitative and Qualitative Data: Different Perspectives on the World

Quantitative measures strive for precision by focusing on things that can be counted and, when gathering data from human beings, conceptualizing predetermined categories that can be treated as ordinal or interval data and subjected to statistical analysis. The experiences of people in programs and the important variables that describe program outcomes are fit into these standardized categories to which numerical values are attached. Quantitative data come from questionnaires, tests, standardized observation instruments, and program records.

In contrast, the evaluator using a qualitative approach seeks to capture what a program experience means to participants in their own words, through interviews, and in their day-to-day program settings, through observation. Qualitative data consist of detailed descriptions of situations, events, people, interactions, and observed behaviors; direct quotations from people about their experiences, attitudes, beliefs, and thoughts; and excerpts or entire passages from documents, correspondence, records, and case histories. The data are collected as open-ended narrative without predetermined, standardized categories such as the response choices that make up typical questionnaires or tests.

Numbers are parsimonious and precise; words provide detail and nuance. Each way of turning the complexities of the world into data has strengths and weaknesses. Qualitative data offer detailed, rich description, capturing variations between cases; quantitative data facilitate comparisons because all program participants respond to the same questions on standardized scales within predetermined response categories. Standardized tests and surveys make it possible to measure the reactions of many respondents to a limited set of questions; statistical aggregation and analysis are relatively straightforward, following established rules and procedures. By contrast, qualitative methods typically produce a wealth of detailed data about a much smaller number of people and cases; analysis can be painstaking, time-consuming, and uncertain.

Sociologist John Lofland (1971) suggested that there are four elements in collecting qualitative data. First, the qualitative evaluator must get close enough to the people and situation being studied to be able to understand the depth and details of what goes on. Second, the qualitative evaluator must aim at capturing what actually takes place and what people actually say: the perceived facts. Third, qualitative data consist of a great deal of pure description of people, activities, and interactions. Fourth, qualitative data consist of direct quotations from people, both what they speak and what they write down.

> The commitment to get close, to be factual, descriptive, and quotive, constitutes a significant commitment to represent the participants in their own terms. This does not mean that one becomes an apologist for them, but rather that one faithfully depicts what goes on in their lives and what life is like for them, in such a way that one's audience is at least partially able to project themselves into the point of view of the people depicted. They can "take the role of the other" because the reporter has given them a living sense of day-to-day talk, day-to-day activities, day-to-day concerns and problems. . . .
>
> A major methodological consequence of these commitments is that the qualitative study of people in situ is a process of discovery. It is of necessity a process of learning what is happening. Since a major part of what is happening is provided by people in their own terms, one must find out about those terms rather than impose upon them a preconceived or outsider's scheme of what they are about. It is the observer's task to find out what is fundamental or central to the people or world under observation. (p. 4)

So what is there to debate about quantitative versus qualitative when each can contribute in important ways to our understanding of programs? The debate stems from underlying connotations and deeply held values. "If you can't measure it, if you can't quantify it, it doesn't exist," is a refrain many program staff have heard from evaluators seeking "clear, specific, and measurable goals" (see Chapter 7 on the goals clarification game). "What gets measured gets done," the mantra of management by objectives and performance contracting, communicates that only what can be quantified is important. Statistical presentations tend to have more credibility, to seem more like "science," whereas qualitative narratives tend to be associated with "mere" journalism. A certain assertiveness, even machismo, often accompanies the demand that outcomes be quantified: hard data connote virility; soft data are flaccid. (Sexual innuendo works in science no less than in advertising, or so it would seem.)

Kuhn (1970), a philosopher and historian of science, observed that the values scientists hold "most deeply" concern predictions: "quantitative predictions are preferable to qualitative ones" (pp. 184-85). It's a short distance from a preference for quantitative data to the virtual exclusion of other types of data. Bernstein and Freeman (1975) even ranked evaluations that gathered *both* quantitative and qualitative data as lower in methodological quality than those that gathered only quantitative data. This is an example of what sociologist C. Wright Mills (1961) called "abstracted empiricism: . . . a methodological inhibition [that] seizes upon one juncture in the process of work and allows it to dominate the mind" (p. 50).

Valuing quantitative measures to the exclusion of other data limits not only what one can find out but also what one is even willing to ask. It is easy to count the words a child spells correctly, but what about that same child's ability to use those words in a meaningful way? It is easy to count the minutes a student spends reading in class, but what does reading mean to that student? **Different kinds of problems require different types of data.** If we only want to know the frequency of interactions between children of different races in desegregated schools, then statistics are appropriate. However, if we want to understand the meanings of interracial interactions, open-ended, in-depth interviewing will be more appropriate.

> If the problems upon which one is at work are readily amenable to statistical procedures, one should always try them first. . . . No one, however, need accept such procedures, when generalized, as the only procedures available. Certainly no one need accept this model as a total canon. It is not the only empirical manner.
>
> It is a choice made according to the requirements of our problems, not a "necessity" that follows from an epistemological dogma. (Mills 1961:73-74)

One evaluator in our federal utilization study told of struggling with this issue. He was evaluating community mental health programs and reported that statistical measures frequently failed to capture real differences among programs. For example, he found a case in which community mental health staff cooperated closely with the state hospital. On one occasion, he observed a therapist from the community mental health center accompany a seriously disturbed client on the "traumatic, fearful, anxiety-ridden trip to the state hospital." The therapist had been working with the client on an outpatient basis. After commitment to the state facility, the therapist continued to see the client weekly and assisted that person in planning toward and getting out of the state institution and back into the larger community as soon as possible. The evaluator found it very difficult to measure this aspect of the program quantitatively.

> This actually becomes a *qualitative* aspect of how they were carrying out the mental health program, but there's a problem of measuring the impact of that qualitative change from when the sheriff used to transport the patients from that county in a locked car with a stranger in charge and the paraphernalia of the sheriff's personality and office. The qualitative difference is obvious in the possible effect on a disturbed patient, but the problem of measurement is very, very difficult. So what we get here in the report is a portrayal of some of the qualitative differences and a very limited capacity of the field at that time to measure those qualitative differences. *We could describe some of them better than we could measure them.* [EV5:3]

A more extended example will help illustrate the importance of seeking congruence between the phenomenon studied and the data gathered for an evaluation. Edna Shapiro (1973) found no achievement test differences between (1) children in an enriched Follow Through program modeled along the lines of open education and (2) children in comparison schools not involved in Follow Through or other enrichment programs. **When the children's responses in the test situation were compared, no differences of any consequence were found. However, when observations of the children in their classrooms were made, there were striking differences between the Follow Through and comparison classes.** First, the environments were observedly different (implementation evaluation).

> The Follow Through (FT) classrooms were characterized as lively, vibrant, with a diversity of curricular projects and children's products, and an atmosphere of friendly, cooperative endeavor. The non-FT classrooms were characterized as relatively uneventful, with a narrow range of curriculum, uniform activity, a great deal of seat work, and less equipment; teachers as well as children were quieter and more concerned with maintaining or submitting to discipline. (Shapiro 1973:529)

Observations also revealed that the children performed differently in the two environments on important dimensions that standardized achievement tests failed to detect. Shapiro found factors operating against the demonstration of differences, factors that called into question, for her, traditional ways of gauging the impact and effectiveness of different kinds of school experiences. **The testing methodology, in fact, narrowed the nature of the questions that were being asked and predetermined nonsignificant statistical results.**

> I assumed that the internalized effects of different kinds of school experience could be observed and inferred only from responses in test situations, and that the observation of teaching and learning in the classroom should be considered auxiliary information, useful chiefly to document the differences in the children's group learning experiences.
>
> The rationale of the test, on the contrary, is that each child is removed from the classroom and treated equivalently, and differences in response are presumed to indicate differences in what has been taken in, made one's own, that survives the shift to a different situation.
>
> The findings of this study, with the marked disparity between classroom responses and test responses, have led me to reevaluate this rationale. This requires reconsideration of the role of classroom data, individual test situation data, and the relation between them. *If we minimize the importance of the child's behavior in the classroom because it is influenced by situational variables, do we not have to apply the same logic to the child's responses in the test situation, which is also influenced by situational variables?* (Shapiro 1973:532-34; emphasis added)

Shapiro (1973) elaborated and illustrated these points at length. Her conclusion went to the heart of the problem posed by the previous dominance of a single methodological paradigm in evaluation research: **"Research methodology must be suited to the particular characteristics of the situations under study. . . . An omnibus strategy will not work"** (p. 543).

At first, some evaluators were willing to recognize that qualitative data might be useful at an exploratory stage to design quantitative instruments. What they denied was that qualitative data could be a legitimate basis for drawing conclusions and making judgments. But, as Shapiro found, certain processes and outcomes are more amenable to qualitative observation. It is worth remembering in this regard that one of the functions of scientific paradigms is to provide criteria for choosing problems that can be assumed to have solutions: "Changes in the standards governing permissible problems, concepts, and explanations can transform a science" (Kuhn 1970:106). It was the failure of the quantitative paradigm to answer important questions like those raised by Shapiro that gradually made serious consideration of the qualitative paradigm so crucial for evaluation research.

A consensus has emerged that *both* qualitative and quantitative data can contribute to all aspects of evaluative inquiries (Cook 1995; Sechrest 1992). Evaluators must be able to use a variety of tools if they are to be sophisticated and flexible in matching research methods to the nuances of particular evaluation questions and the idiosyncrasies of specific decision-maker needs. There are no logical reasons why qualitative and quantitative methods cannot be used together (Patton 1982a). *Qualitative Evaluation and Research Methods* (Patton 1990) describes conditions under which qualitative methods are particularly appropriate in evaluation research. Sometimes quantitative methods alone are most appropriate. But in many cases, both qualitative and quantitative methods should be used together. Where multiple methods are used, the contributions of each kind of data should be fairly assessed. In many cases, this means that evaluators working in teams will need to work hard to overcome their tendency to dismiss certain kinds of data without first considering seriously and fairly the merits of those data.

The Program Evaluation Standards (Joint Committee 1994) provide useful guidance in this regard, in that they give equal attention, weight, and credence to qualitative and quantitative analyses. Indeed, the Joint Committee was absolutely diligent and precise about this equality of treatment by formulating a standard for each type of data with identical wording except for the words *quantitative* and *qualitative*.

> *Standard on Analysis of Quantitative Information*
>
> Quantitative information in an evaluation should be appropriately and systematically analyzed so that evaluation questions are effectively answered. (p. A8)
>
> *Standard on Analysis of Qualitative Information*
>
> Qualitative information in an evaluation should be appropriately and systematically analyzed so that evaluation questions are effectively answered. (p. A9)

Naturalistic and Experimental Inquiry Options

The paradigms debate was in part a debate about the relative importance of causal questions in evaluation. Those evaluation researchers who believe that the most important and central function of evaluation is to measure the effects of programs on participants in order to make valid causal inferences are strong advocates of randomized experiments as "the standard against which other designs for impact evaluation are judged" (Boruch and Rindskopf 1984:121). In advocating experimental designs, evaluation researchers such as Campbell and Boruch (1975) and Lipsey (1990) have demonstrated the power and feasibility of randomized experiments for a variety of programs (Boruch et al. 1978). The concerns that permeate these writings are concerns about increased rigor, well-controlled settings, reduction of threats to internal validity, precise estimates of program effects, and statistical power.

Naturalistic inquiry, in contrast, involves observing ongoing programs as they unfold without attempting to control or manipulate the setting, situation, people, or data. Naturalistic inquiry investigates "phenomena within and in relation to their naturally occurring context" (Willems and Raush 1969:3). The extent to which any particular investigator engages in naturalistic inquiry varies along a continuum (Guba 1978). It is certainly possible to enter a field situation and try to control what happens, just as it is possible for the experimentalist to control only the initial assignment to groups, then to watch what happens "naturally." The important distinction is between relative degrees of calculated manipulation. A naturalistic inquiry strategy is selected when the investigator wants to minimize research manipulation by studying natural field settings; experimental conditions and designs are selected when the evaluator wants to introduce a considerable amount of control and reduce variation in extraneous variables.

Guba and Lincoln (1981) identified two dimensions along which types of scientific inquiry can be described: the extent to which the scientist manipulates some phenomenon in advance in order to study it, and the extent to which constraints are placed on output measures; that is, the extent to which predetermined categories or variables are used to describe the phenomenon under study. They then define *naturalistic inquiry* as a "discovery-oriented" approach that minimizes investigator manipulation of the study setting and places no prior constraints on what the outcomes of the research will be. Naturalistic inquiry is thus contrasted to experimental research, in which, ideally, the investigator attempts to control conditions of the study completely by manipulating, changing, or holding constant external influences and in which a very limited set of outcome variables is measured.

> Naturalistic inquiry aims at understanding actualities, social realities, and human perceptions that exist untainted by the obtrusiveness of formal measurement or preconceived questions. It is a process geared to the uncovering of many idiosyncratic but nonetheless important stories told by real people, about real events, in real and natural ways. The more general the provocation, the more these stories will reflect what respondents view as salient issues, meaningful evidence, and appropriate inferences. . . . Naturalistic inquiry attempts to present "slice-of-life" episodes documented through natural language and representing as closely as possible how people feel, what they know, and what their concerns, beliefs, perceptions, and understandings are. (Wolf and Tymitz (1976-77:6)

Where the evaluator wants to know about day-to-day life and work in program settings, naturalistic inquiry replaces the static snapshots of traditional survey research with a dynamic, process orientation. To capture dynamic processes, the naturalistic inquiry evaluator eschews the fixed comparisons of pre-post experimental designs, instead making observations periodically and systematically from beginning to end of participants' experiences.

Qualitative data can be collected in experimental designs in which participants have been randomly divided into treatment and control groups. Likewise, some quantitative data may be collected in naturalistic inquiry approaches. Such combinations and flexibility are still rather rare, however. Experimental designs predominantly aim for statistical analyses, whereas qualitative data are the primary focus in naturalistic inquiry.

Deductive and Inductive Approaches

Another point of friction in the paradigms debate has been the relative value and feasibility of deductive and inductive research strategies. With an inductive strategy, the evaluator attempts to make sense of a program without imposing preexisting expectations on the program setting. Inductive designs begin with specific observations and build toward general patterns. Categories or dimensions of analysis emerge from open-ended observations as the evaluator comes to understand program patterns that exist in the empirical world under study. Goal-free evaluation, discussed in Chapter 7, is inductive in the sense that the evaluator enters the program with no knowledge of program goals, then observes the program and studies participants to determine the extent to which participants' needs are being met.

This contrasts with the hypothetico-deductive approach of experimental designs, which requires the specification of main variables and the statement of specific research hypotheses before data collection begins. Specifying hypotheses based on an explicit theoretical framework means that general principles provide the framework for understanding specific observations or cases, as in theory-driven evaluation (Chen 1990. The evaluator must decide in advance what variables are important and what relationships among those variables are to be tested. The classic deductive approach to evaluation involves measuring relative attainment of predetermined goals in a randomized experiment that permits precise attribution of goal attainment to identifiable program treatments.

Qualitative researchers ask questions rather than test hypotheses. Inductive designs allow the important analysis dimensions to emerge from patterns found in the cases under study without presupposing what the important dimensions will be. Theories that may emerge about what is happening in a program are grounded in direct program experience rather than imposed on the basis of predetermined, deductively derived constructs.

Evaluation can be inductive in two ways.

1. Within a particular program, induction means describing the experiences of individual participants, without pigeonholing or delimiting what those experiences will be in advance of fieldwork.

2. Between programs, inductive inquiry involves looking for unique institutional characteristics that make each setting a case unto itself. At either level, patterns across cases emerge from thematic content analysis, but the initial focus is on full understanding of individual cases, before those unique cases are combined or aggregated.

At the simplest level, closed-ended questionnaires require deductive construction while open-ended interviews depend on inductive analysis. A structured, multiple-choice question requires predetermining response categories based on some theory or preordinate criteria about what is important to measure. An open-ended interview, on the other hand, asks the respondent to describe what is meaningful and salient without being pigeonholed into standardized categories. In practice, these approaches are often combined, not only in the same study, but in the same instrument. Some evaluation questions are determined deductively while others are left sufficiently open to permit inductive analyses based on direct observations.

The paradigms debate has sharpened our understanding of the strengths and weaknesses of each strategy, and an evaluation can include elements of both as, for example, when the evaluation flows from inductive inquiry—to find out what the important questions and variables are (exploratory work)—to deductive hypothesis testing aimed at confirming exploratory findings, then back again to inductive analysis to look for rival explanations and unanticipated or unmeasured factors.

From Objectivity Versus Subjectivity to Fairness and Balance

Qualitative evaluators are accused frequently of *subjectivity*—a term with the power of an epithet in that it connotes the very antithesis of scientific inquiry. Objectivity has been considered the sine qua non of the scientific method. To be subjective has meant to be biased, unreliable, and nonrational. Subjectivity implies opinion rather than fact, intuition rather than logic, and impression rather than rigor. Evaluators are advised to avoid subjectivity and make their work "objective and value-free."

In the paradigms debate, the means advocated by scientists for controlling subjectivity through the scientific method were the techniques of the dominant quantitative experimental paradigm. Yet, the previous section observed that quantitative methods can work in practice to limit and even bias the kinds of questions that are asked and the nature of admissible solutions.

Michael Scriven (1972a), evaluation's long-time resident philosopher, has insisted that quantitative methods are no more synonymous with objectivity than qualitative methods are synonymous with subjectivity:

> Errors like this are too simple to be explicit. They are inferred confusions in the ideological foundations of research, its interpretations, its application. . . . It is increasingly clear that the influence of ideology on methodology and of the latter on the training and behavior of researchers and on the identification and disbursement of support is staggeringly powerful. Ideology is to research what Marx suggested the economic factor was to politics and what Freud took sex to be for psychology. (p. 94)

The possibility that "ideological" preconceptions can lead to dual perspectives about a single phenomenon goes to the very heart of the contrasts between paradigms. Two scientists may look at the same thing, but because of different theoretical perspectives, assumptions, or ideology-based methodologies, **they may literally not see the same thing** (Petrie 1972:48). Indeed, Kuhn (1970) has pointed out,

> Something like a paradigm is prerequisite to perception itself. What a man sees depends both upon what he looks at and also upon what his previous visual-conceptual experience has taught him to see. In the absence of such training there can only be, in William James's phrase, "a bloomin' buggin' confusion." (p. 113)

A child's parable, the story of Han and the Dragon, illustrates this point at another level of simplicity. Han, a small boy, lived in a city threatened by wild horsemen from the north. The Mandarin ruler and his advisers decided that only the Great Cloud Dragon could save the city, so they prayed for the Dragon's intervention. As he prayed, the Mandarin envisioned a dragon that looked like a proud lord—a Mandarin. The captain of the army imagined and prayed to a dragon that looked like a warrior. The merchant thought that a dragon would appear rich and splendid, as he was. The chief workman was convinced that a dragon would be tough and strong. The wise man conceived of the dragon as "the wisest of all creatures," which meant it must look like a wise man. In the midst of the crisis, a small fat man with long beard and bald head arrived and announced that he was the Great Cloud Dragon. The Mandarin and his advisers ridiculed the old man and dismissed him rudely. Only because of Han's kindness did the old man save the city, transforming himself into a magnificent dragon the color of sunset shining through rain, scales scattering the light, claws and teeth glittering like diamonds, beautiful and frightening at the same time, and most important, beyond any possibility of preconception because the dragon was beyond prior human experience. But, only Han saw the dragon, because only he was open to seeing it.

Qualitative researchers prefer to describe themselves as open rather than subjective. They enter a setting without prejudgment, including no preconceived hypotheses to test.

Scriven (1991a) has defined objectivity as being "unbiased or unprejudiced," literally, not having "prejudged." This definition

> misleads people into thinking that anyone who comes into a discussion with strong views about an issue can't be unprejudiced. The key question is whether the views are justified. The fact that we all have strong views about the sexual abuse of small children and the importance of education does not show prejudice, only rationality. (p. 248)

The debate about objectivity versus subjectivity includes different assumptions about whether it is possible for us to view the complexities of the real world without somehow filtering and simplifying those complexities. The qualitative assumption is that, at even the most basic level of sensory data, we are always dealing with perceptions, not "facts" in some absolute sense. "The very categories of things which comprise the 'facts' are theory dependent" (Petrie 1972:49) or, in this case, paradigm dependent. It was this recognition that led the distinguished qualitative sociologist Howard Becker (1970) to argue that "the question is not whether we should take sides, since we inevitably will, but rather whose side we are on" (p. 15).

The paradigms offer differ perspectives on the nature of "human reality" and thus have different conceptions of the role of research in predicting human reality. The quantitative/experimental paradigm conceives of science as the search for truth about a singular reality, thus the importance of objectivity. The qualitative/naturalistic paradigm searches for perspective and understanding in a world of multiple "realities," thus the inevitability of subjectivity. Although the possibility of attaining objectivity and truth in any absolute sense has become an untenable position in evaluation, the negative connotations associated with the term *subjectivity* make it an unacceptable alternative. There is a solution.

As a utilization-focused evaluator, being practical in orientation, I prefer to replace the traditional scientific search for objective truth with a search for useful and balanced information. For the classic mandate to be objective, I substitute the mandate to be fair and conscientious in taking account of multiple perspectives, multiple interests, and multiple realities. In this regard, Egon Guba (1981) has suggested that evaluators could learn from investigative journalists.

> Journalism in general and investigative journalism in particular are moving away from the criterion of objectivity to an emergent criterion usually labeled "fairness." . . . Objectivity assumes a single reality to which the story or evaluation must be isomorphic; it is in this sense a one-perspective criterion. It assumes that an agent can deal with an object (or another person) in a nonreactive and noninteractive way. It is an absolute criterion.
>
> Journalists are coming to feel that objectivity in that sense is unattainable. . . .
>
> Enter "fairness" as a substitute criterion. In contrast to objectivity, fairness has these features:
>
> - It assumes multiple realities or truths—hence a test of fairness is whether or not "both" sides of the case are presented, and there may even be multiple sides.
> - It is adversarial rather than one-perspective in nature. Rather than trying to hew the line with *the* truth, as the objective reporter does, the fair reporter seeks to present each side of the case in the manner of an advocate—as, for example, attorneys do in making a case in court. The presumption is that the public, like a jury, is more likely to reach an equitable decision after having heard each side presented with as much vigor and commitment as possible.
> - It is assumed that the subject's reaction to the reporter and interaction between them heavily determines what the reporter perceives. Hence one test of fairness is the length to which the reporter will go to test his own biases and rule them out.
> - It is a relative criterion that is measured by *balance* rather than by isomorphism to enduring truth.
>
> Clearly, evaluators have a great deal to learn from this development. (pp. 76-77)

The Program Evaluation Standards reflect this change in emphasis:

> *Propriety Standard on Complete and Fair Assessment:* The evaluation should be complete and fair in its examination and recording of strengths and weaknesses of the program being evaluated, so that strengths can be built upon and problem areas addressed. (Joint Committee 1994:P5)

> *Accuracy Standard on Impartial Reporting:* Reporting procedures should guard against distortion caused by personal feelings and biases of any party to the evaluation, so that evaluation reports fairly reflect the evaluation findings. (Joint Committee 1994:A11)

Words such as *fairness, neutrality*, and *impartiality* carry less baggage than *objectivity* and *subjectivity*. To stay out of arguments about objectivity, I talk with intended users about balance, fairness, and being explicit about what perspectives, values, and priorities have shaped the evaluation, both the design and findings. Others choose to use the term *objective* because of its political power. At the national policy level, 1995 American Evaluation Association President Eleanor Chelimsky (1995a) recommended thus:

> Although all of us realize that we can never be entirely objective, that is hardly an excuse for skewed samples, or grandiloquent conclusions or generalizations that go beyond the evaluator's data, or for any of 101 indications to a careful reader that a particular result is more desired than documented.
>
> There are, in fact, a great many things that we can do to foster objectivity and its appearance, not just technically, in the steps we take to make and explain our evaluative decisions, but also intellectually, in the effort we put forth to look at all sides and all stakeholders of an evaluation. (p. 219)

The Continuum of Distance From Versus Closeness to the Program

Here are the opposing paradigm positions: Too much closeness may compromise objectivity. Too much distance may diminish insight and understanding.

Quantitative researchers depend on distance to guarantee neutrality and academic integrity. Scholarly comportment connotes calm and detached analysis without personal involvement or emotion. The qualitative paradigm, in contrast, assumes that without empathy and sympathetic introspection derived from direct experience, one cannot fully understand a program. Understanding comes from trying to put oneself in the other person's shoes, thereby discerning how others think, act, and feel. Qualitative methodologist John Lofland (1971) has explained that methodologically this means getting close to the people being studied through attention to details, by being where they are over a period of time, and through development of closeness in the social sense of intimacy and confidentiality. "The commitment to get close, to be factual, descriptive, and quotive, constitutes a significant commitment to represent the participants *in their own terms*" (p. 4).

The desire for closeness derives from the assumption that the inner states of people are important and can be known. From this flows a concern with meaning, mental states, and worldview. Attention to inner perspectives does not mean administering attitude surveys. "The inner perspective assumes that understanding can only be achieved by actively participating in the life of the observed and gaining insight by means of introspection" (Bruyn 1966: 226). For evaluators, this can even mean undertaking observation by being a program participant, where possible and appropriate.

> In order to capture the participants "in their own terms" one must learn *their* analytic ordering of the world, *their* categories for rendering explicable and coherent the flux of raw reality. That, indeed, is the first principle of qualitative analysis. (Lofland 1971:7; emphasis in original)

In the Shapiro study of Follow Through open classrooms, her presence in classrooms over an extended period of time and her closeness to the children allowed her to see things that were not captured by standardized tests. She could see what they were learning. She could feel their tension in the testing situation and their spontaneity in the more natural classroom setting. Had she worked solely with data collected by others or only at a distance, she would never have discovered the crucial differences she uncovered between Follow Through and non-Follow Through classrooms—differences that allowed her to evaluate the innovative program in a meaningful and relevant way.

In a similar vein, one evaluator in our utilization of federal health evaluations expressed frustration at trying to make sense out of data from over 80 projects when site visit funds were cut out of the evaluation: "There's no way to understand something that's just data, you know. You have to go look" [EV111:3]. Lofland (1971) concluded likewise,

> In everyday life, statistical sociologists, like everyone else, assume that they do not know or understand very well people they do not see or associate with very much. They assume that knowing and understanding other people require that one see them reasonably often and in a variety of situations relative to a variety of issues. Moreover, statistical sociologists, like other people, assume that in order to know or understand others, one is well-advised to give some conscious attention to that effort in face-to-face contacts. They assume, too, that the internal world of sociology—or any other social world—is not understandable unless one has been part of it in a face-to-face fashion for quite a period of time. How utterly paradoxical, then, for these same persons to turn around and make, by implication, precisely the opposite claim about people they have never encountered face-to-face—those people appearing as numbers in their tables and as correlations in their matrices! (p. 3)

It is instructive to remember that many major contributions to our understanding of the world have come from scientists' personal experiences—Piaget's closeness to his children, Freud's proximity to and empathy with his patients, Darwin's closeness to nature, and even Newton's intimate encounter with an apple.

On the other hand, closeness is not the only way to understand human behavior. For certain questions and for situations involving large groups, distance is inevitable. But, where possible, face-to-face interaction can deepen insight, especially in program evaluation. This returns us to the recurrent theme of matching evaluation methods to intended use by intended users.

Of Variables and Wholes

The quantitative/experimental paradigm operationalizes independent and dependent variables, then measures their relationships statistically. Outcomes must be identified and measured as specific variables. Treatments and programs must also be conceptualized as discrete, independent variables. Program participants are also described along standardized, quantified dimensions. Sometimes a program's goals are measured directly, for example, student achievement test scores, recidivism statistics for a group of juvenile delinquents, or sobriety rates for participants in chemical dependency treatment programs. Evaluation measures can also be indicators of a larger construct, for example, "community well-being" as a general construct measured by indicators such as crime rates, fetal deaths, divorce, unemployment, suicide, and poverty (Brock, Schwaller, and Smith 1985).

Adherents of the qualitative paradigm argue that the variables-based approach (1) oversimplifies the interconnected complexities of real-world experiences, (2) misses major factors of importance that are not easily quantified, and (3) fails to capture a sense of the program and its impacts as a "whole." The qualitative/naturalistic paradigm strives to be *holistic* in orientation. It assumes that the whole is greater than the sum of its parts; that the parts cannot be understood without a sense of the whole; and that a description and understanding of a program's context is essential to an understanding of program processes and outcomes. This, of course, follows the wisdom of the fable about the blind children and the elephant. As long as each felt only a part—a fan-like ear, the rope-like tail, a tree-like leg, the snake-like trunk—they could not make sense of the whole elephant. The qualitative, systems-oriented paradigm goes even further. Unless they could see the elephant at home in the African wilderness, they would not understand the elephant's ears, legs, trunk, and skin in relation to how the elephant has evolved in the context of its ecological niche.

Philosopher and educator John Dewey (1956a) advocated a holistic approach to both teaching and research, if one was to reach into and understand the world of the child.

> The child's life is an integral, a total one. He passes quickly and readily from one topic to another, as from one spot to another, but is not conscious of transition or break. There is no conscious isolation, hardly conscious distinction. The things that occupy him are held together by the unity of the personal and social interests which his life carries along. . . . [His] universe is fluid and fluent; its contents dissolve and re-form with amazing rapidity. But after all, it is the child's own world. It has the unity and completeness of his own life. (pp. 5-6)

Again, Shapiro's (1973) work in evaluating innovative Follow Through classrooms is instructive. She found that test results could not be interpreted without understanding the larger cultural and institutional context in which the individual child was situated. Deutscher (1970) adds that despite our personal experiences as living, working human beings, we have focused in our research on parts to the virtual exclusion of wholes:

> We knew that human behavior was rarely if ever directly influenced or explained by an isolated variable; we knew that it was impossible to assume that any set of such variables was additive (with or without weighting); we knew that the complex mathematics of the interaction among any set of variables was incomprehensible to us. In effect, although we knew they did not exist, we defined them into being. (p. 33)

Although most scientists would view this radical critique of variable analysis as too extreme, I find that teachers and practitioners often voice the same criticisms. Innovative teachers complain that experimental results lack relevance for them because they have to deal with the whole in their classrooms; they can't manipulate just a couple of factors in isolation from everything else going on. The reaction of many program staff to scientific research is like the reaction of Copernicus to the astronomers of his day: "With them," he observed,

> it is as though an artist were to gather the hands, feet, head, and other members for his images from diverse models, each part excellently drawn, but not related to a single body, and since they in no way match each other, the result would be monster rather than man. (quoted in Kuhn 1970:83)

How many program staff have complained of the evaluation research monster?

Yet, it is no simple task to undertake holistic evaluation, to search for the Gestalt in programs. The challenge for the participant observer is "to seek the essence of the life of the observed, to sum up, to find a central unifying principle" (Bruyn 1966:316).

The advantages of using variables and indicators are parsimony, precision, and ease of analysis. Where key program elements can be quantified with validity, reliability, and credibility, and where necessary statistical assumptions can be met (e.g., linearity, normality, and independence of measurement), statistical portrayals can be quite powerful and succinct. The advantage of qualitative portrayals of holistic settings and impacts is that attention can be given to nuance, setting, interdependencies, complexities, idiosyncracies, and context. In combination, the two approaches can be powerful and comprehensive; they can also be contradictory and divisive.

Two Views of Change

The paradigms debate is in part about how best to understand and study change. The quantitative/experimental paradigm typically involves gathering data at two points in time, pretest and posttest, then comparing the treatment group to the control group statistically. Ideally, participants are assigned to treatment and control groups randomly, or, less ideally, are matched on critical background variables. Such designs assume an identifiable, coherent, and consistent treatment. Moreover, they assume that, once introduced, the treatment remains relatively constant and unchanging. In some designs, time series data are gathered at several predetermined points rather than just at pretest and posttest. The purpose of these designs is to determine the extent to which the program (treatment) accounts for measurable changes in participants in order to make a summative decision about the value and effectiveness of the program in producing desired change (Lipsey 1990; Boruch and Rindskopf 1984; Mark and Cook 1984).

In contrast, the qualitative/naturalistic paradigm conceives of programs as dynamic and ever developing, with "treatments" changing in subtle but important ways as staff learn, as clients move in and out, and as conditions of delivery are altered. Qualitative/naturalistic evaluators seek to describe these dynamic program processes and understand their holistic effects on participants. Thus, part of the paradigms debate has been about the relative utility, desirability, and possibility of understanding programs from these quite different perspectives for different purposes.

The quantitative/experimental/summative approach is most relevant for fairly established programs with stable, consistent, and identifiable treatments and clearly quantifiable outcomes, in which a major decision is to be made about the effectiveness of one treatment in comparison to another (or no) treatment.

The qualitative/naturalistic/formative approach is especially appropriate for developing, innovating, or changing programs in which the focus is improving the program, facilitating more effective implementation, and exploring a variety of effects on participants. This can be particularly important early in the life of a program or at major points of transition. As an innovation or program change is implemented, it frequently unfolds in a manner quite different from what was planned or conceptualized in a proposal. Once in operation, innovative programs are often changed as practitioners learn what works and what does not, and as they experiment, grow, and change their priorities.

Changing developmental programs can frustrate evaluators whose design approach depends on specifiable unchanging treatments to relate to specifiable predetermined outcomes. Evaluators have been known to do everything in their power to stop program adaptation and improvement so as to maintain the rigor of their research design (see Parlett and Hamilton 1976). The deleterious effect this may have on the program itself, discouraging as it does new developments and redefinitions in midstream, is considered a small sacrifice made in pursuit of higher-level scientific knowledge. But there is a distinct possibility that such artificial evaluation constraints will contaminate the program treatment by affecting staff morale and participant response.

Were some science of planning and policy or program development so highly evolved that initial proposals were perfect, one might be able to sympathize with these evaluators' desire to keep the initial program implementation intact. In the real world, however, people and unforeseen circumstances shape programs, and initial implementations are modified in ways that are rarely trivial.

Under conditions in which programs are subject to change and redirection, the naturalistic evaluation paradigm replaces the static underpinnings of the experimental paradigm with a dynamic orientation. A dynamic evaluation is not tied to a single treatment or to predetermined outcomes but, rather, focuses on the actual operations of a program over a period of time, taking as a given the complexity of a changing reality and variations in participants' experiences over the course of program participation.

Again, the issue is one of matching the evaluation design to the program, of meshing evaluation methods with decision-maker information needs. The point of contrasting fixed experimental designs with dynamic process designs in the paradigms debate was to release evaluators "from unwitting captivity to a format of inquiry that is taken for granted as the naturally proper way in which to conduct scientific inquiry" (Blumer 1969:47).

Nowhere is this unwitting captivity better illustrated than in those agencies that insist, in the name of science, that all evaluations must employ experimental designs. Two examples will illustrate this problem. In Minnesota, the Governor's Commission on Crime Prevention and Control required experimental evaluation designs of *all* funded projects. A small Native American alternative school was granted funds to run an innovative crime prevention project with parents and students. The program was highly flexible; participation was irregular and based on self-selection. The program was designed to be sensitive to Native American culture and values. It would have been a perfect situation for formative responsive evaluation. Instead, program staff were forced to create the illusion of an experimental pretest and posttest design. The evaluation design interfered with the program, alienated staff, wasted resources, and collected worthless information, unrelated to evolving program operations, under the guise of maintaining scientific consistency. The evaluators refused to alter or adapt the design and data collection in the face of a program dramatically different from the preconceptions on which they had based the design.

The second example is quite similar but concerns the Minnesota Department of Education. The state monitor for an innovative arts program in a free school for at-risk students insisted on quantitative, standardized test measures collected in pretest and posttest situations; a control group was also required. The arts program was being tried out in a free school as an attempt to integrate art and basic skills. Students were self-selected and participation was irregular; the program had multiple goals, all of them vague; even the target population was fuzzy; and the treatment depended on who was in attendance on a given day. The free school was a highly fluid environment for which nothing close to a reasonable control or comparison group existed. The teaching approach was highly individualized, with students designing much of their program of study. Both staff and students resented the imposition of rigid, standardized criteria that gave the appearance of a structure that was not there. Yet, the Department of Education insisted on a static, hypothetico-deductive evaluation approach because "it's departmental evaluation policy."

On the other hand, the direction of the design error is not always the imposition of overly rigid experimental formats. Campbell and Boruch (1975) have shown that many evaluations suffer from an underutilization of more rigid designs. They have made a strong case for randomized assignment to treatments by demonstrating six ways in which quasi-experimental evaluations in compensatory education tend to underestimate effects.

Matching methods to programs and decision-maker needs is a creative process that emerges from a thorough knowledge of the organizational dynamics and information uncertainties of a particular context. Regulations to the effect that all evaluations must be of a certain type serve neither the cause of increased scientific knowledge nor that of greater program effectiveness.

Alternative Sampling Logics

The quantitative paradigm employs random samples sufficient in size to permit valid generalizations and appropriate tests of statistical significance. Qualitative inquiry involves small "purposeful samples" of information-rich cases (Patton 1990: 169-86. Differences in logic and assumptions between these sampling strategies illuminate paradigm differences.

When the evaluation or policy question is aimed at generalizations, some form of random, probabilistic sampling is the design of choice. A needs assessment, for example, aimed at determining how many residents in a county have some particular problem would suggest the need for a random sample of county residents.

Case studies, on the other hand, become particularly useful when intended users need to understand a problem, situation, or program in great depth, and they can identify cases rich in needed information—rich in the sense that a great deal can be learned from a few exemplars of the phenomenon of interest. For example, much can be learned about how to improve a program by studying dropouts or select successes. Such case studies can provide detailed understanding of what is going on and solid grounds for making improvements.

The best-selling management book *In Search of Excellence* (Peters and Waterman 1982), studied 50 corporations with outstanding reputations for excellence to learn lessons about what these exemplars were doing right. The problem with this approach is yielding to the temptation to inappropriately generalize case study findings to the entire population, as when management consultants generalized the lessons from *In Search of Excellence* to all of corporate America—indeed, to all organizations of all kinds in the world! It is precisely such overgeneralizations that have led advocates of randomized, probabilistic sampling to be suspicious of case studies and purposeful sampling.

On the other hand, qualitative methodologists are suspicious of generalizations based on statistical inference at a single point in time. Findings based on samples, however large, are often stripped of their context when generalizations are made across time and space. Cronbach (1975) has observed that generalizations decay over time; that is, they have a half-life much like radioactive materials. Guba and Lincoln (1981) were particularly critical of the dependence on generalizations in quantitative methods because, they ask, "What can a generalization be except an assertion that is context free? . . . [Yet] *It is virtually impossible to imagine any human behavior that is not heavily mediated by the context in which it occurs*" (p. 62; emphasis in original).

Cronbach and colleagues in the Stanford Evaluation Consortium (1980) offered a middle ground in the paradigms debate with regard to the problem of generalizability and the relevance of evaluations. They criticized experimental designs that were so focused on controlling cause and effect that the results were largely irrelevant beyond the experimental situation. On the other hand, they were equally concerned that entirely idiosyncratic case studies yield little of use beyond the case study setting. They suggested, instead, that designs balance depth and breadth, realism and control, so as to permit reasonable extrapolation (pp. 231-35). Unlike the usual meaning of the term *generalization*, an *extrapolation* connotes that one has gone beyond the narrow confines of the data to think about other applications of the findings. Extrapolations are modest speculations on the likely applicability of findings to other situations under similar, but not identical, conditions. Extrapolations are logical, thoughtful, and problem-oriented rather than purely empirical, statistical, and probabilistic. Evaluation users often expect evaluators to thoughtfully extrapolate from their findings in the sense of pointing out lessons learned and potential applications to future efforts.

Designs that combine probabilistic and purposeful sampling have the advantage of extrapolations supported by quantitative and qualitative data. Larger samples of statistically meaningful data can address questions of incidence and prevalence (generalizations), while case studies add depth and detail to make interpretations more meaningful and grounded. Such designs can also introduce a balance between concerns about individualization and standardization, the distinction in the next section.

Standardization or Diversity: Different Emphases

The quantitative paradigm requires the variety of human experience to be captured along standardized scales. Individuals and groups are described as exhibiting more or less of some trait (self-esteem, satisfaction, competence, knowledge), but everyone is rated or ranked on a limited set of predetermined dimensions. Statistical analyses of these dimensions present central tendencies (averages and deviations from those averages). Critics of standardized instrumentation and measurement are concerned that such an approach only captures quantitative differences, thereby missing significant qualitative differences and important idiosyncrasies. Critics of statistics are fond of telling about the person who drowned in a creek with an average depth of six inches; what was needed was some in-depth information about the six-foot pool in the middle of the creek.

The qualitative paradigm pays particular attention to uniqueness, whether this be an individual's uniqueness or the uniqueness of program, community, home, or other unit of analysis. When comparing programs, the qualitative evaluator begins by trying to capture the unique, holistic character of each program with special attention to context and setting. Patterns across individuals or programs are sought only after the uniqueness of each case has been described.

For program staff in innovative programs aimed at individualizing treatments, the central issue is how to identify and deal with individual differences among participants. Where the emphasis is on individualization of teaching or on meeting the needs of individual clients in social action programs, an evaluation strategy of case studies is needed that focuses on the individual, one that is sensitive both to unique characteristics in people and programs and to similarities among people and commonalities across treatments. Case studies can and do accumulate. Anthropologists have built up an invaluable wealth of case study data that includes both idiosyncratic information and patterns of culture.

Using both quantitative and qualitative approaches can permit the evaluator to address questions about quantitative differences on standardized variables and qualitative differences reflecting individual and program uniquenesses. **The more a program aims at individualized outcomes, the greater the appropriateness of qualitative methods. The more a program emphasizes common outcomes for all participants, the greater the appropriateness of standardized measures of performance and change.**

Whither the Evaluation Methods Paradigms Debate? The Debate Has Withered

Evaluation is much too important to be left to the methodologists.

—Halcolm

The history of the paradigms debate parallels the history of evaluation. The earliest evaluations focused largely on quantitative measurement of clear, specific goals and objectives. With the widespread social and educational experimentation of the 1960s and early 1970s, evaluation designs were aimed at comparing the effectiveness of different programs and treatments through rigorous controls and experiments. This was the period when the quantitative/experimental paradigm dominated, as represented by the Bernstein and Freeman (1975) critique of evaluation quality and such popular texts as Campbell and Stanley (1963), Weiss (1972b), Suchman (1972), Rutman (1977), and the first edition of *Evaluation* (Rossi et al. 1979).

By the middle 1970s, the paradigms debate was becoming a major focus of evaluation discussions and writings (Cronbach 1975; Patton 1975a; Parlett and Hamilton 1972). By the late 1970s, the alternative qualitative/naturalistic paradigm had been fully articulated (Guba 1978; Patton 1978; Stake 1978). During this period, concern about finding ways to increase use became predominant in evaluation (see Chapter 1), and evaluators began discussing standards. A period of pragmatism and dialogue followed, during which calls for and experiences with multiple methods and a synthesis of paradigms became more common (House 1980; Reichardt and Cook 1979; Rist 1977).

The advice of Cronbach et al. (1980), in their important book on reform of program evaluation, was widely taken to heart:

> The evaluator will be wise not to declare allegiance to either a quantitative-scientific-summative methodology or a qualitative-naturalistic-descriptive methodology. (p. 7)

Signs of detente and pragmatism now abound. Methodological tolerance, flexibility, eclecticism, and concern for appropriateness rather than orthodoxy now characterize the practice, literature, and discussions of evaluation. Ten developments seem to me to explain the withering of the methodological paradigms debate.

1. **Evaluation has emerged as a genuinely interdisciplinary and multimethod field of professional practice.** Evaluation began as a specialization within separate social science and educational disciplines. The methods expertise of evaluators was closely tied to the methodological focus of their discipline of origin. In recent years, however, courses and programs have emerged for training evaluators that focus attention on evaluation as an interdisciplinary, practical, professional, and problem-solving effort (Altschuld and Engle 1994). This has permitted more balanced training and a more balanced approach to methods, which emphasizes methodological appropriateness rather than disciplinary orthodoxy.

2. **The utilization crisis focused attention on the need for methodological flexibility.** When the utilization crisis emerged in the 1960s, there were two major kinds of recommendations for increasing evaluation use. One kind focused on upgrading methodological rigor as a way of increasing the accuracy, reliability, and validity of evaluation data, and thereby increasing use. The second set of recommendations focused on evaluation processes: increasing attention to stakeholder needs, acting with greater political savvy, championing findings among intended users, and matching methods to questions. Methodological rigor alone has not proven an effective strategy for increasing use. Direct attention to issues of use, as in utilization-focused evaluation, has proven effective.

3. **The articulation of professional standards by evaluation associations has emphasized methodological appropriateness rather than paradigm orthodoxy.** The Program Evaluation Standards (Joint Committee 1994, 1981), the Guiding Principles of the American Evaluation Association (Shadish et al. 1995), and the earlier standards of the Evaluation Research Society (1980) before it merged into the American Evaluation Association all emphasize accuracy and systematic data collection within a context that takes into account varying evaluation purposes, stakeholders, and uses—and, therefore, varying methods. The standards and AEA guiding principles provide a basis other than methodological rigor for judging the excellence of evaluations. This has made it possible to employ a variety of methods, including qualitative ones, and still do an evaluation judged of high quality.

4. **The accumulation of practical evaluation experience during the last two dec-**

ades has reduced paradigms polarization. The practical experience of evaluators in attempting to work with programs to improve their effectiveness has led evaluators to become pragmatic in their approaches to methods issues, and in that pragmatism has emerged a commitment to do what works rather than a commitment to methodological rigor as an end in itself.

5. **The strengths and weaknesses of both quantitative/experimental methods and qualitative/naturalistic methods are now better understood.** In the original debate, quantitative methodologists tended to attack some of the worst examples of qualitative evaluations while the qualitative evaluators tended to hold up for critique the worst examples of quantitative/experimental approaches. With the accumulation of experience and confidence, exemplars of both qualitative and quantitative approaches have emerged with corresponding analyses of the strengths and weaknesses of each. This has permitted more balance and a better understanding of the situations for which various methods are most appropriate as well as grounded experience in how to combine methods.

6. **A broader conceptualization of evaluation, and of evaluator training, has directed attention to the relation of methods to other aspects of evaluation, such as use, and has therefore reduced the intensity of the methods debate as a topic unto itself.** Early evaluation texts defined evaluation narrowly as the application of social science methods to measure goal attainment. More recent definitions of evaluation, including the one in this book (Chapter 2), emphasize providing useful information for program improvement and decision making. This broader conceptualization has directed attention to the political nature of evaluation, the need to integrate evaluation into program processes, working with stakeholders throughout the evaluation process and laying a solid foundation for the use of evaluation. While high quality *and* appropriate methods remain important, methods decisions are now framed in a broader context of use which, I believe, has reduced the intensity of the paradigms debate, a debate that often went on in absolute terms—context-free.

7. **Advances in methodological sophistication and diversity within both paradigms have strengthened diverse applications to evaluation problems.** The proliferation of books and journals in evaluation, including but not limited to methods contributions, has converted the field into a rich mosaic that cannot be reduced to quantitative versus qualitative in primary orientation. This is especially true of qualitative methods, which had more catching up to do, in which a great deal of important work has been published addressing questions of validity, reliability, and systematic analysis (Coffey and Atkinson 1996; Maxwell 1996; Stake 1995; Denzin and Lincoln 1994; Miles and Huberman 1994; Patton 1990; Williams 1986). The paradigms debate, in part, increased the amount of qualitative work being done, created additional opportunities for training in qualitative methods, and brought attention by methodologists to problems of increasing the quality of qualitative data. As the quality of qualitative methods has increased, as training in qualitative methods has improved (e.g., Levine et al. 1980), and as claims about qualitative methods have become more balanced, the attacks on qualitative methods have become less strident. Moreover, the upshot of all the developmental work in qualitative

methods is that "today there is as much variation among qualitative researchers as there is between qualitatively and quantitatively oriented scholars" (Donmoyer, 1996:21). The same can be said of developments in quantitative-experimental methods, as methodologists have focused on fine-tuning and adapting social science methods to evaluation and public policy situations (e.g., Davidson 1996; Folz 1996; Yates 1996; Fink 1995; Conrad 1994; Cordray 1993; Sechrest and Scott 1993; Lipsey 1990; Trochim 1986; Boruch and Wothke 1985; and the extensive Sage series on Quantitative Applications in the Social Sciences). Lipsey (1988), whose quantitative credentials are impeccable, epitomized the emergent commitment to matching methods to problems and situations when he concluded:

> Much less evaluation research in the quantitative-comparative mode should be done. Though it is difficult to ignore the attractiveness of assessing treatment effects via formal measurement and controlled design, it is increasingly clear that doing research of this sort well is quite difficult and should be undertaken only under methodologically favorable circumstances, and only then with extensive prior pilot-testing regarding measures, treatment theory, and so forth. The field of evaluation research and the individual treatments evaluated would generally be better served by a thorough descriptive, perhaps qualitative, study as a basis for forming better concepts about treatment, or a good management information system that provides feedback for program improvement, or a variety of other approaches rather than by a superficially impressive but largely invalid experimental study. (pp. 22-23)

8. **Support for methodological eclecticism from major figures and institutions in evaluation has increased methodological tolerance.** Early in this chapter, I noted that when eminent measurement and methods scholars such as Donald Campbell and Lee J. Cronbach, their commitment to rigor never being in doubt (see Shadish et al. 1991 for their pioneering contributions to evaluation theory and practice), began publicly recognizing the contributions that qualitative methods could make, the acceptability of qualitative/naturalistic approaches was greatly enhanced. Another important endorsement of multiple methods has come from the Program Evaluation and Methodology Division of the United States General Accounting Office (GAO), which arguably did the most important and influential evaluation work at the national level (until it was disbanded in 1996). Under the leadership of Assistant Comptroller General and former American Evaluation Association President (1995) Eleanor Chelimsky, GAO published a series of methods manuals, including *Quantitative Data Analysis* (GAO 1992d), *Case Study Evaluations* (GAO 1990a), *Prospective Evaluation Methods* (GAO 1990b), and *The Evaluation Synthesis* (GAO 1992c). The GAO manual on *Designing Evaluations* (1991) puts the paradigms debate to rest as it describes what constitutes a strong evaluation. Strength is not judged by adherence to a particular paradigm. It is determined by use and technical adequacy, whatever the method, within the context of purpose, time, and resources.

> Strong evaluations employ methods of analysis that are appropriate to the question, support the answer with evidence, document the assumptions, procedures, and modes of analysis, and rule out the competing evidence. Strong studies pose questions clearly, address them appropriately, and draw inferences commensurate with the power of the

design and the availability, validity, and reliability of the data. Strength should not be equated with complexity. Nor should strength be equated with the degree of statistical manipulation of data. Neither infatuation with complexity nor statistical incantation makes an evaluation stronger.

The strength of an evaluation is not defined by a particular method. Longitudinal, experimental, quasi-experimental, before-and-after, and case study evaluations can be either strong or weak. . . . That is, the strength of an evaluation has to be judged within the context of the question, the time and cost constraints, the design, the technical adequacy of the data collection and analysis, and the presentation of the findings. A strong study is technically adequate and useful—in short, it is high in quality. (GAO 1991:15-16)

9. **Evaluation professional societies have supported exchanges of views and high-quality professional practice in an environment of tolerance and eclecticism.** The evaluation professional societies and journals serve a variety of people from different disciplines who operate in different kinds of organizations at different levels, in and out of the public sector, and in and out of universities. This diversity, and opportunities to exchange views and perspectives, have contributed to the emergent pragmatism, eclecticism, and tolerance in the field. A good example is the volume of *New Directions for Program Evaluation* on "The Qualitative-Quantitative Debate: New Perspectives" (Reichardt and Rallis 1994a). The tone of the eight distinguished contributions in that volume is captured by such phrases as "peaceful coexistence," "each tradition can learn from the other," "compromise solution," "important shared characteristics," and "a call for a new partnership" (Datta 1994; Reichardt and Rallis 1994b, 1994c; Rossi 1994; Yin 1994).

10. **There is increased advocacy of and experience in combining qualitative and quantitative approaches.** The volume of *New Directions for Program Evaluation* on "The Qualitative-Quantitative Debate: New Perspectives" (Reichardt and Rallis 1994a) included these themes: "blended approaches," "integrating the qualitative and quantitative," "possibilities for integration," "qualitative plus quantitative" and "working together" (Datta 1994; Hedrick 1994; House 1994; Reichardt and Rallis 1994c; Smith 1994). As evaluators have worked to focus evaluation questions and gather useful information, they have begun using multiple methods and a variety of data sources to elucidate evaluation questions (e.g., Mark and Shotland 1987). Initial efforts at merging quantitative and qualitative perspectives often proved difficult. For example, Kidder and Fine (1987) found that qualitative methods may not triangulate easily with quantitative methods because qualitative questions and designs can change during the study so that the two kinds of data end up addressing different issues. Synthesizing qualitative and quantitative data has often proved challenging, and when doubts have been raised or conflicts emerged, it was often the qualitative data that bore the larger burden of proof. An excellent article by M. G. Trend (1978) described the difficulties of getting fair consideration of qualitative data in a major study.

The 1980 meetings of the Society of Applied Anthropology in Denver included a symposium on the problems encountered by anthropologists participating in teams in which both quantitative and qualitative data were being collected. The problems they shared were stark evidence that qualitative methods were typically perceived as exploratory and secondary when used in conjunction with quantitative/experimental approaches. When qualitative data supported quantitative findings, that was icing on the cake. When qualitative data conflicted with quantitative data, the qualitative data were often dismissed or ignored.

Despite these difficulties, there have now emerged positive examples in which qualitative and quantitative data have been used together. Fetterman (1984, 1980) has had considerable success in reporting and integrating both kinds of data. He used qualitative data to understand quantitative findings and quantitative data to broaden qualitative interpretations. Maxwell, Bashook, and Sandlow (1985) demonstrated how an ethnographic approach can be combined with an experimental design within a single-study framework. Another area of integration has emerged in evaluations that include a large number of case sites in a large-scale study; Firestone and Herriott (1984) have demonstrated how quantitative logic can contribute to the interpretation of qualitative data as the number of sites in a study grows. The theoretical basis for combining qualitative and quantitative methods has been well articulated (House 1994; Patton 1982a; Reichardt and Cook 1979). Sechrest (1992), while attacking those few whom he perceived advocated qualitative methods to the exclusion of quantitative approaches, offered high-quality examples where both had been integrated.

Thus, there are positive signs that evaluators have become much more sophisticated about the complexities of methodological choices and combinations. However, although concrete examples of methods integration are increasing, the evidence also suggests that integrating qualitative and quantitative methods continues to be a difficult task requiring great sensitivity and respect for the strengths of each approach and recognition of the weaknesses of each kind of data. Moreover, some intended users whom a utilization-focused evaluator encounters may hold strong views about the value of certain kinds of methods. Understanding the evolution of the paradigms debate in evaluation should help evaluators work through the biases of primary stakeholders.

Withered But Not Dead

The trends and factors just reviewed suggest that the paradigms debate has withered substantially. The focus has shifted to methodological appropriateness rather than orthodoxy, methodological creativity rather than rigid adherence to a paradigm, and methodological flexibility rather than conformity to a narrow set of rules. However, paradigm discussions have not disappeared, and are not likely to. What has changed, I believe, is that those discussions are now primarily about philosophy rather than methods. The connection between philosophical paradigms and methods has been broken. Philosophical paradigm debates concern the nature of reality (e.g., Bednarz 1985): Is it singular or multiple? Is there even such a thing as truth? Is the world knowable in any absolute sense? Is all knowledge relative to time and place? These are interesting and important philosophical questions, but, I find, they have little bearing on the practicalities of designing a useful evaluation with specific intended users.

Let's examine the pragmatic implications of logically incompatible philosophical views of the world. Guba and Lincoln (1981) have argued that the scientific and naturalistic paradigms contain incompatible assumptions about the inquirer/subject relationship and the nature of truth. For example, the scientific paradigm assumes that reality is "singular, convergent, and fragmentable," while the naturalistic paradigm holds a view of reality that is "multiple, divergent, and inter-related" (Guba and Lincoln 1981:57). These opposite assumptions are not about methods alternatives; they are fundamental assumptions about the nature of reality. An evaluator can conduct interviews and observations under either set of assumptions, and the data will stand on their own.

I disagree, then, that philosophical assumptions necessarily require allegiance by evaluators to one paradigm or the other. Pragmatism can overcome seemingly logical contradictions. I believe that the flexible, responsive evaluator can shift back and forth between paradigms within a single evaluation setting. In so doing, such a flexible and open evaluator can view the same data from the perspective of each paradigm and can help adherents of either paradigm interpret data in more than one way.

This kind of flexibility begins at the design stage. Consider the following situation. An evaluator is working with a group of educators, some of whom are "progressive, open education" adherents and some of whom are "back-to-basics" fundamentalists. The open education group wants to frame the evaluation of a particular program within a naturalistic framework. The basic skills people want a rigorous, scientific approach. Must the evaluator make an either/or choice to frame the evaluation within either one or the other paradigm? Must an either/or choice be made about the kind of data to be collected? Are the views of each group so incompatible that each must have its own evaluation?

I've been in precisely this situation a number of times. I do not try to resolve the paradigms debate. Rather, I try to establish an environment of tolerance and respect for different, competing viewpoints, and then focus the discussion on the actual information that is needed by each group: test scores? interviews? observations? The design and measures must be negotiated. Multiple methods and multiple measures will give each group some of what they want. The naturalistic paradigm educators will want to be sure that test scores are interpreted within a larger context of classroom activities, observations, and outcomes. The scientific paradigm educators will likely use interview and observational data to explain and justify test score interpretations. My experience suggests that both groups can agree on an evaluation design that includes multiple types of data and that each group will ultimately pay attention to and use "the other group's data." In short, a particular group of people can arrive at agreement on an evaluation design that includes both qualitative and quantitative data without resolving ultimate paradigmatic issues. Such agreement is not likely, however, if the evaluator begins with the premise that the paradigms are incompatible and that the evaluation must be conducted within the framework of either one or the other.

Perhaps an analogy will help here. A sensitive, practical evaluator can work with a group to design a meaningful evaluation that integrates concerns from both paradigms in the same way that a skillful teacher can work with a group of Buddhists, Christians, Jews, and Muslims on issues of common empirical concern without resolving which religion has the correct worldview.

Another example: an agricultural project in the Caribbean that included social scientists and government officials of varying political persuasions. Despite their theoretical differences, the Marxist and Keynesian economists and sociologists had little difficulty agreeing on what data were needed to understand agricultural extension needs in each country. Their interpretations of those data also differed less than I expected.

Thus, the point I'm making about the paradigms debate extends beyond methodological issues to embrace a host of potential theoretical, philosophical, religious, and political perspectives that can separate the participants in an evaluation process. I am arguing that, from a practical perspective, the evaluator need not even attempt to resolve such differences. By focusing on and negotiating data collection alternatives in an atmosphere of respect and tolerance, the participants can come together around a commitment to an empirical perspective, that is, bringing data to bear on important program issues. As long as the empirical commitment is there, the other differences can be negotiated in most instances.

Debating paradigms with one's clients, and taking sides in that debate, is different from debating one's colleagues about the nature of reality. I doubt that evaluators will ever reach consensus on the ultimate nature of reality. But the paradigms debate can go on among evaluators without paralyzing the practice of practical evaluators who are trying to work responsively with primary stakeholders to get answers to relevant empirical questions. The belief that evaluators must be true to only one paradigm in any given situation underestimates the human capacity for handling ambiguity and duality, shifting flexibly between perspectives. In short, I'm suggesting that evaluators would do better to worry about understanding and being sensitive to the worldviews and evaluation needs of their clients than to maintain allegiance to or work within only one perspective.

Beyond Paradigm Orthodoxies

The paradigms debate helped elucidate the complexity of choices available in evaluation. It also demonstrated the difficulty of moving beyond narrow disciplinary training to make decisions based on utility. It is premature to characterize the practice of evaluation as completely flexible and focused on methodological appropriateness rather than disciplinary orthodoxy, but it is fair to say that the goals have shifted dramatically in that direction. The debate over which paradigm was the right path to *truth* has been replaced, at the level of methods, by a paradigm of choices.

Utilization-Focused Synthesis: A Paradigm of Choices

Exhibit 12.3 summarizes the contrasting themes of the paradigms debate and describes the synthesis that is emerging with the shift in emphasis from methodological orthodoxy to methodological appropriateness and utility. *Utilization-focused evaluation* offers a paradigm of choices. Today's evaluator must be sophisticated about matching research methods to the nuances of particular evaluation questions and the idiosyncrasies of specific decision-maker needs. The evaluator must have a large repertoire of research methods and techniques available to use on a variety of problems.

The utilization-focused evaluator works with intended users to include any and all data that will help shed light on evaluation questions, given constraints of resources and time. Such an evaluator is committed to research designs that are relevant, rigorous, understandable, and able to produce useful results that are valid, reliable, and believable. The paradigm of choices recognizes that different methods are appropriate for different situations and purposes.

Sometimes the paradigm of choice is a simple set of questions. Once, early in my

career, working on a school evaluation, I was asked by the superintendent what evaluation model I worked from and, without waiting for a response, he listed several possibilities to let me know he had taken an evaluation course in graduate school. The first edition of *Utilization-Focused Evaluation* (Patton 1978) had only recently been published and was not among the frameworks he offered. Nor did I recognize all the models he listed or know which he preferred. The evening before I had been helping my young son memorize a poem for school, so I said, smiling: "Actually, I find Kipling's model most helpful." "Kipling?" he asked, bemused. I quoted:

I keep six honest serving men
They taught me all I knew:
Their names are What and Why and When
And How and Where and Who."

He laughed and said. "I was an English major in college. Kipling will do just fine." I wish I could tell you how to add luck and a little chutzpa to your evaluation design kit, because both can come in quite handy—luck always, chutzpa sometimes. What I can offer is the framework for a Kipling-inspired, utilization-focused paradigm of choices that I prepared and gave to the superintendent the next day. These questions guided the discussions of the evaluation task force he convened for me to work with.

Who . . . ?	Who is the evaluation for?
What . . . ?	What do we need to find out?
Why . . . ?	Why do we want to find that out?
When . . . ?	When will the findings be needed?
Where . . . ?	Where should we gather information?
How . . . ?	How will results be used?

EXHIBIT 12.3

The Evaluation Methods Paradigms Debate
Summary of Emphases: Thesis, Antithesis, Synthesis

	Thesis: Originally Dominant "Scientific" Paradigm	*Antithesis: Originally Competing "Alternative" Paradigm*	*Synthesis: Utilization-Focused Evaluation, a Paradigm of Choices*
Purpose	Summative	Formative	Intended use for intended users
Measurement	Quantitative data	Qualitative data	Appropriate, credible, useful data
Design	Experimental designs	Naturalistic inquiry	Creative, practical, situationally responsive designs
Researcher stance	Objectivity	Subjectivity	Fairness and balance
Inquiry mode	Deduction	Induction	Either or both
Conceptualization	Independent and dependent variables	Holistic interdependent system	Stakeholder questions and issues
Relationships	Distance, detachment	Closeness, involvement	Collaboration, consultative
Approach to study of change	Pre-post measures, time series, static portrayals at discrete points in time	Process-oriented, evolving, capturing ongoing dynamism	Developmental, action-oriented. What needs to be known to get program from where it is to where it wants to be?
Relationship to prior knowledge	Confirmatory, hypothesis testing	Exploratory, hypothesis generating	Either or both
Sampling	Random, probabilistic	Purposeful, key informants	Combinations, depending on what information is needed
Primary approach to variations	Quantitative differences on uniform, standardized variables	Qualitative differences, uniquenesses	Flexible: Focus on comparisons most relevant to intended users and evaluation questions
Analysis	Descriptive and inferential statistics	Case studies, content and pattern analysis	Answers to stakeholders' questions
Types of statements	Generalizations	Context-bound	Extrapolations
Contribution to theory	Validating theoretical propositions from scientific literature	Grounded theory	Describing, exploring, and testing stakeholders' and program's theory of action
Goals	Truth, scientific acceptance	Understanding, perspective	Utility, relevance: Acceptance by intended users

13

Deciphering Data and Reporting Results

Analysis, Interpretations, Judgments, and Recommendations

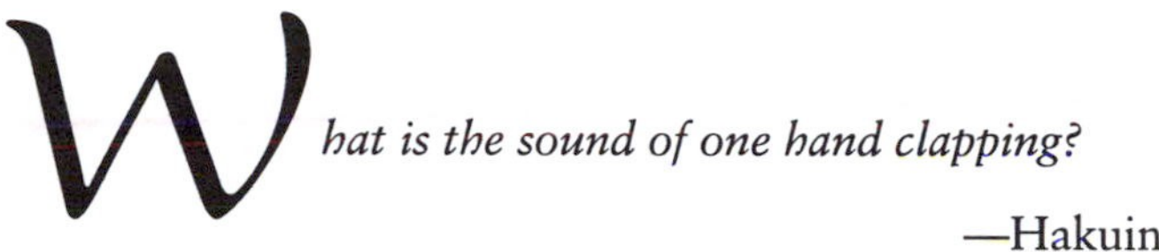

What is the sound of one hand clapping?

—Hakuin

This question was first posed by the Japanese Zen Master Hakuin (1686-1769) as a means of facilitating enlightenment. "The disciple, given a Koan [riddle] to see through, was encouraged to put his whole strength into the single-minded search for its solution, to be 'like a thirsty rat seeking for water . . . ,' to carry the problem with him everywhere, until suddenly, if he were successful, the solution came" (Hoffman 1975:22). Solving a Koan is a technique originated by the Zen masters to shake their students out of routine ways of thinking and acting, open up new possibilities, and help individual students realize their full potential. The evaluator is engaged in some of these same processes. Utilization-focused evaluation helps decision makers and intended users stand outside the program and look at what is happening; evaluations can help shake staff out of routine ways of doing things, open up new possibilities, and help programs realize their full potential.

This allusion to Zen and the Enlightenment of Evaluation is not frivolous. Religion and philosophy are ultimately personal, perceptual, and interpretive mechanisms for establishing the meaning of life; evaluation is ultimately a personal, perceptual, and interpretive approach to establishing the meaning—and meaningfulness—of programs. The Zen search through Koans consists of three basic parts: a question, an answer, and interpretation/assimilation of the answer in terms of the student's own life; evaluation involves a question, an empirical answer, and interpretation/utilization of the answer in the context of the program's own dynamics. A fundamental tenet of the Koanic method is that the question is as important as the answer; the same principle applies to utilization-focused evaluation. The Zen Master carefully matches the Koan to the student; the responsive evaluator focuses on questions that are relevant to specific intended users. In Zen, many pathways lead to enlightenment; in paradigm-flexible evaluation, multiple methods offer divergent paths in the search for utility. Finally, the Zen student must struggle to make sense out of the answer to the Koanic riddle; in evaluation, the meaning of empirical data emerges from interpretation, dialogue, and situational application. Consider the following Koanic exchange, entitled "A Flower in Bloom."

A monk asked Master Ummon, "What is the pure body of truth?"
Master Ummon said, "A flower in bloom."
Monk: " 'A flower in bloom'—what's it mean?"
Master: "Maggot in the shit hole, pus of leprosy, scab over a boil."

—Hoffman 1975:119

"What's it mean?" may be a philosophical, religious, or epistemological question. It can also be the very concrete practical question of program staff laboring over pages of statistical tables and reams of computer printout. For any given set of data, meaning depends on who is interpreting the data.

The truism that where some people see flowers, others see maggots is regularly and consistently ignored in the design and interpretation of evaluation studies. Evaluators and decision makers can deceive themselves into believing that once data have been collected, it will be clear whether or not the program works. But data simply do not exist outside the context of a specific group of people with a particular perspective. That's why utilization-focused evaluation begins with identification and organization of intended information users. That's also why data analysis and interpretation depend on the active participation of primary users, because, in the end, they are the ones who must translate data into decisions and action.

Setting the Stage for Use

Mock Data Application Scenarios

The stage can be set for analysis and use before data are ever collected. Once instruments have been designed—but before data collection—I like to conduct a mock or simulated use session. This involves fabricating possible results and interpreting the action implications of the made-up data.

cating possible results and interpreting the action implications of the made-up data.

The evaluator prepares some possible "positive" results and some negative on the most important issues. For example, suppose primary users have chosen the job placement rate as the priority outcome variable for a vocational training program. The evaluator might construct data showing a placement rate of 40% for black participants and 75% for white participants. The evaluator facilitates analysis by asking such questions as: "What do these results mean? What actions would you take based on these results? How would you use these data?"

Such a discussion accomplishes four things:

1. The simulated analysis is a check on the design to make sure that all the relevant data for interpretation and use are going to be collected. All too often at the analysis stage, evaluators and stakeholders realize that they forgot to ask an important question.
2. The mock use session trains stakeholders for the real analysis later. They learn how to interpret data and apply results.
3. Working through a use scenario prior to data collection helps set realistic expectations about what the results will look like. Strengths and limitations of the design emerge. This helps prepare users for the necessity of interpreting findings in relation to possible actions and likely ambiguities.
4. Use scenarios help build the commitment to use—or reveal the lack of such commitment. When intended users are unable to deal with how they would use findings prior to data collection, a warning flag goes up that they may be unable, or unwilling, to use findings after data collection. The commitment to use can be cultivated by helping intended users think realistically and concretely about how findings might be applied before data collection gets under way. The relatively safe, even fun, exercise of analyzing mock data can help strengthen the resolve to use before being confronted with real findings and decisions.

Quantitative data are fairly easy to fabricate once instruments have been developed. With qualitative data, it's necessary to construct imaginary quotations and case examples. This extra work can pay large dividends as decision makers develop a utilization-focused mind-set based on an actual experience struggling with data. Athletes, performing artists, astronauts, and entertainers spend hundreds of hours preparing for events that take only a few hours. Is it too much to ask intended users to spend a couple of hours practicing use to get mentally and analytically ready for the climax of an evaluation?

Standards of Desirability

A simulated use session also offers a prime opportunity to think about and formalize criteria for making judgments before data collection. With quantitative data, this can be done quite precisely by establishing standards of desirability. I like to have users set at least three levels of attainment:

1. Level at which the program is considered highly effective
2. Level at which the program is considered adequate
3. Level at which the program is considered inadequate

Such standards can be established for implementation targets (e.g., program

EXHIBIT 13.1

Intensity of Teachers' Use of a Teacher Center

Category of Visits by a Teacher	*Number of Visits*	*Percentage of Total Visitors*
1 or 2	185	80.4
3 or more	45	19.6

NOTE: Data are for visits between January 10 and February 28.
SOURCE: Feiman 1977:19-21.

pants have changed). Suppose one is collecting satisfaction data on a workshop. At what level of satisfaction is the workshop a success? At what level is it merely adequate? At what level of participant satisfaction is the workshop to be judged ineffective? It's better to establish these kinds of standards of desirability in a calm and deliberative manner before actual results are presented. This exercise, done before data collection, may also reveal that satisfaction data alone are an inadequate indicator of effectiveness while there's still time to measure additional outcomes.

The process of specifying objectives sometimes involves setting performance targets, for example, 75% of workshop participants will be satisfied. However, this doesn't tell us what constitutes an outstanding accomplishment; it doesn't distinguish adequacy from excellence. Nor does it make it clear whether 65% satisfaction is inadequate or merely "lower than we hoped for but acceptable." Moreover, objectives are often set a long time before the program is under way or well before an actual evaluation has been designed. Reviewing objectives and establishing precise standards of desirability just before data collection increases the likelihood that judgment criteria will be up to date, realistic, and meaningful.

During the early conceptual stage of an evaluation, questions of use are fairly general and responses may be vague. The evaluator asks, "What would you do if you had an answer to your evaluation question? How would you use evaluation findings?" These general questions help focus the evaluation, but once the context has been delineated, the priority questions focused, and methods selected, the evaluator can pose much more specific use questions based on what the results might actually look like. For example, if recidivism in a community corrections program is 55%, is that high or low? Does it mean the program was effective or ineffective? The program had some impact, but what level of impact is desirable? What level spells trouble?

Consider evaluation of a teacher center. One of the implementation issues concerns the extent to which teachers use the center intensively (three or more times) versus superficially (once or twice). Actual data from such a study are shown in Exhibit 13.1. Now, suppose the staff assembles to discuss the actual results without having set standards of desirability or performance targets.

EXHIBIT 13.2
Teacher Center Standards of Desirability

Judgment	*Percentage and Number of Teachers Who Have Contact With the Center Three or More Times*
We're doing an *outstanding* job of engaging teachers at this level.	
We're doing an *adequate* job of engaging teachers at this level.	
We're doing a *poor* job of engaging teachers at this level.	

First staff speaker: That's about what I anticipated.

Second staff speaker: Plus, remember, the data don't include teachers in our workshops and special classes.

Third staff speaker: I think the observation time was really too short.

Fourth staff speaker: I agree. January and February are bad months, you know, everyone is depressed with winter, and . . .

Soon it becomes apparent that either the data don't tell staff much, at least not without other data, or that staff are not prepared to deal with what the data do show. Such resistance and defensiveness are not unusual as aspects of a postevaluation scenario.

Now, let's try a different scenario. At the outset of the evaluation, the program staff discuss their notions of what their task is and how teacher change occurs. They decide that the kind of impact they want to have cannot occur in one or two visits to the teacher center: "If teachers don't return after one or two visits, we must be doing something wrong." The period of time in question is a full 12-month period. Before the data are collected, the staff fill in the table shown in Exhibit 13.2.

A record-keeping system must then be established, which staff agree to and believe in so that the data have credibility. The teacher center staff have committed themselves to actively engaging teachers on a multiple-contact basis. The data will provide clear feedback about the effectiveness of the program. The key point is that if staff are unwilling or unable to set expectancy levels before data collection, there is no reason to believe they can do so afterward. In addition, going through this process ahead of time alerts participants to additional data they need in order to make sense of and act on the results; clearly, measuring frequency of visits is only a starting place.

Many of the most serious conflicts in evaluation are rooted in the failure to clearly specify standards of desirability in advance of data collection. This can lead both to collection of the wrong data and to intense disagreement about criteria for judging effectiveness. Without explicit criteria, data can be interpreted to mean almost anything about a program—or to mean nothing at all.

Making Findings Interesting

Another way of setting the stage for analysis and use is having stakeholders speculate about results prior to seeing the real data. This can be done prior to data collection or after data collection but prior to actual presentation of findings. Stakeholders are given an analysis table with all the appropriate categories but no actual data (a dummy table). They then fill in the missing data with their guesses of what the results will be.

This kind of speculation prepares users for how the results will be formatted and increases interest by building a sense of anticipation. I've even had stakeholders establish a betting pool on the results. Each person puts in a dollar or more and the person closest to the actual results on the major outcome wins the pot. That creates interest! And the winner must be present at the unveiling of the findings to win. Strange how attendance at the presentation of findings is increased under these conditions.

A second function of having stakeholders write down their guesses is to provide a concrete basis for determining the extent to which actual results come close to expectations. Program staff, for example, sometimes argue that they don't need formal evaluations because they know their clients, students, or program participants so well that evaluation findings would just confirm what they already know. I've found that when staff commit their guesses to paper in advance of seeing actual results, the subsequent comparison often calls into question just how well some staff do know what is happening in the program. At least with written guesses on paper, program staff and other stakeholders can't just say, "That's just what I expected." A database (in the form of their guesses) exists to determine how much new has been learned. This can be useful in documenting the extent to which an evaluation has provided new insights and understandings.

You can combine establishing standards of desirability and speculating on results. Give stakeholders a page with two columns. The first column asks them to specify what outcome they consider desirable, and the second column asks them to guess what result they believe will be obtained. Having specified a standard of desirability and guessed at actual results, users have a greater stake in and a framework for looking at the actual findings. When real results are presented, the evaluator facilitates discussion on the implications of the data falling below, at, or above the desired response, and why the actual findings were different from or the same as what they guessed. In my experience, animated interactions among users follow as they fully engage and interpret the results.

The amount of data presented must be highly focused and limited to major issues. This is not a data-dredging exercise. Carefully constructed tables and spotlighted analysis can make such presentations lively and fruitful.

I find that, given the time and encouragement, stakeholders with virtually no methods or statistics training can readily identify the strengths, weaknesses, and implications of the findings. The trick is to move people from passive reception—

from audience status—to active involvement and participation (Greene 1988a).

A Framework for Reviewing Data

Four distinct processes are involved in making sense out of evaluation findings.

1. **Description and analysis:** Describing and analyzing findings involves organizing raw data into a form that reveals basic patterns. The evaluator presents, in user-friendly fashion, the factual findings as revealed in actual data.

2. **Interpretation:** What do the results mean? What's the significance of the findings? Why did the findings turn out this way? What are possible explanations of the results? Interpretations go beyond the data to add context, determine meaning, and tease out substantive significance based on deduction or inference.

3. **Judgment:** Values are added to analysis and interpretations. Determining merit or worth means resolving to what extent and in what ways the results are positive or negative. What is good or bad, desirable or undesirable, in the outcomes? Have standards of desirability been met?

4. **Recommendations:** The final step (if agreed to be undertaken) adds action to analysis, interpretation, and judgment. What should be done? What are the action implications of the findings? Only recommendations that follow from and are grounded in the data ought to be formulated.

Primary intended users should be actively involved in all four of these processes so that they fully explore the findings and their implications. Facilitating these processes, especially helping stakeholders understand these four fundamental distinctions, requires skills that go well beyond what is taught in statistics courses. Working with stakeholders to analyze and interpret findings is quite different from doing it on one's own as a researcher (Greene 1988a). Let's consider each of these processes in greater depth.

Arranging Data for Ease of Interpretation: Focusing the Analysis

They say that figures rule the world. I do not know if this is true, but I do know that figures tell us if it is well or poorly ruled.

—Goethe, German philosopher and author (1749-1832), 1814

Providing descriptive statistics in a report means more than simply reproducing the results in relatively raw form. Data need to be arranged, ordered, and organized in some reasonable format that permits decision makers to detect patterns. Consider the three presentations of data shown in Exhibit 13.3. Each presents data from the

EXHIBIT 13.3

Three Presentations of the Same Data (in percentages)

Presentation 1: Raw results presented in the same order as items appeared in the survey

Expressed Needs of 478 Physically Disabled People	*Great Need for This*	*Much Need*	*Some Need*	*Little Need*
Transportation	35	36	13	16
Housing	33	38	19	10
Educational opportunities	42	28	9	21
Medical care	26	45	25	4
Employment opportunities	58	13	6	23
Public understanding	47	22	15	16
Architectural changes in buildings	33	38	10	19
Direct financial assistance	40	31	12	17
Changes in insurance regulations	29	39	16	16
Social opportunities	11	58	17	14

Presentation 2: Results combined into two categories; no priorities emerge

	Great or Much Need	*Some or Little Need*
Transportation	71	29
Housing	71	29
Educational opportunities	70	30
Medical care	71	29
Employment opportunities	71	29
Public understanding	69	31
Architectural changes in buildings	71	29
Direct financial assistance	71	29
Changes in insurance regulations	68	32
Social opportunities	69	31

Presentation 3: Utilization-focused results arranged in rank order by "great need" to highlight priorities

Rank order	*Great Need for This*
Employment opportunities	58
Public understanding	47
Educational opportunities	42
Direct financial assistance	40
Transportation	35
Housing	33
Architectural changes in buildings	33
Changes in insurance regulations	29
Medical care	26
Social opportunities	11

same survey items, but the focus and degree of complexity are different in each case.

The first presentation reports items in the order in which they appeared on the survey, with percentages for every category of response. It is difficult to detect patterns with 40 numbers to examine. The second presentation simplifies the results by dividing the scale at the midpoint and reducing the four categories to two. Sometimes, such an analysis would be very revealing, but, in this case, no priorities emerge. Since determining priorities was the purpose of the survey, decision makers would conclude from the second presentation that the survey had not been useful.

The third presentation arranges the data so that decision makers can immediately see respondents' priorities. Support for employment programs now ranks first as a great need (58%) in contrast to social programs (11%), rated lowest in priority. Users can go down the list and decide where to draw the line on priorities, perhaps after *direct financial assistance* (40%). Failure to arrange the data as displayed in the third presentation places decision makers at an analytical disadvantage. Presentation 3 is utilization focused.

Simplicity in Data Presentations

> *Unless one is a genius, it is best to aim at being intelligible.*
>
> —Anthony Hope,
> British novelist (1863-1933)

William of Occam with his razor would have made an excellent analyst of evaluation data. Look first for the simplest presentation that will handle the facts. Evaluators may need and use sophisticated and complex statistical techniques to enhance analytic power or uncover nuances in data, but simple and straightforward statistical presentations are needed to give decision makers access to evaluation findings.

Eminent economic historian Robert Heilbroner (1996) has lamented what he considers the decline of economics from an applied policy science to an abstract and arcane exercise in mathematical navel gazing. Current economics, he charged, displays "a degree of unreality that can be matched only by medieval scholasticism. . . . Economics is in retreat from political reality. It's embracing mathematics and elaborate models—an enormous loss of relevance" (pp. 65-66). His reflections reminded me that, when I first entered evaluation, distinguished social scientists were advocating more sophistication in evaluation designs and data analysis, for example, multiple regression, path analysis, and log-linear techniques. At the same time, most decision makers I encountered at the federal, state, and local levels were intimidated by simple percentages, unsure of correlation coefficients, and wary of what they considered to be statistical gobbledygook. Few decision makers understand sophisticated procedures or the assumptions on which they rest.

I am not implying that sophisticated techniques, where appropriate and helpful, should not be used. I am suggesting that it is the height of folly to center one's public presentations and decision-making discussions around complex statistical findings. I have been told by some of my colleagues that they make such presentations to educate public officials about statistics. From my observations, I would suggest that they are contributing to a sense that social science research is useless and convincing policymakers that researchers can't communicate.

Evaluation, if it is to be accessible to and understandable by key stakeholders, must depart from the trends of the various social science disciplines and return to simplicity as a virtue in data presentations. Certainly, an evaluator can use sophisticated techniques to confirm the strength and meaningfulness of discovered patterns, but the next step is to think creatively about how to translate those findings into simple, straightforward, and understandable presentations. This means, for example, that the results of a regression analysis might be reduced to nothing more complex than a chi-square table or a set of descriptive statistics (percentages and means). This need not distort the presentation. Quite the contrary, it will usually focus and highlight the most important findings while allowing the investigators to explain in a footnote and/or an appendix that more sophisticated techniques have been used to confirm the simple statistics here presented.

Simplicity as a virtue means that we seek clarity, not complexity. Our presentations must be like the skilled acrobat who makes the most dazzling moves look easy, the audience being unaware of the long hours of practice and the sophisticated calculations involved in what appear to be simple movements. Likewise, evaluators must find ways of so perfecting their public performances that those participating will understand the results, though unaware of the long hours of arduous work involved in sifting through the data, organizing it, arranging it, testing out relationships, taking the data apart, and creatively putting it back together to arrive at that moment of public unveiling.

Simplicity as a virtue means that we are rewarded not for how much we confuse or impress, but for how much we enlighten. It means that we make users feel they can master what is before them, rather than intimidating them with our own expertise, knowledge, and sophistication. It means distinguishing the complexity of analysis from the clarity of presentation and using the former to inform and guide the latter. Simplicity as a virtue is not simple. It often involves more work and creativity to simplify than to rest content with a presentation of complex statistics as they originally emerged from analysis. Simplicity as a virtue is not simple, but it can be effective.

Strive for Balance

The counterpoint to my sermonette on simplicity is that evaluation findings are seldom really simple. In striving for simplicity, one must be careful to avoid simplemindedness. It is simpleminded to present only one point of view. This happens most often in evaluation when results are boiled down, in the name of simplicity, to some single number—a single percentage, a single cost/benefit ratio, or a single proportion of the variance explained. Striving for simplicity means making the data understandable, but balance and fairness need not be sacrificed in the name of simplicity. Achieving balance may mean that multiple perspectives have to be represented

EXHIBIT 13.4
Illustrative Data (Constructed)

	Beginning Level	*Level Four Years Later*	*Absolute Amount of Change*	*Percentage Change*
Median white income	$10,100	$10,706	$606	6%
Median black income	$ 5,500	$ 6,050	$550	10%

through several different numbers, all of them presented in an understandable fashion. Much advertising is based on the deception of picking the one number that puts a product in the best light, for example, gas mileage instead of price. Politicians often do likewise, picking the statistic that favors their predetermined analysis. An example may help clarify what I mean.

In his 1972 presidential campaign, Richard Nixon made the claim that under his administration, black incomes had risen faster than white incomes. In the same campaign the Democratic nominee, George McGovern, made the claim that after four years of Nixon, blacks were worse off than whites in terms of income. Both statements were true. Each statement represented only part of the picture. To understand what was happening in the relationship between black and white incomes, one needed to know, at a minimum, both absolute income levels and percentage changes. Consider the data in Exhibit 13.4 to illustrate this point. These data illustrate that black incomes rose faster than white incomes, but blacks were worse off than whites at the end of the four-year period under study. A balanced view requires both the absolute changes and the percentage changes. When a report gives only one figure or the other (i.e., only absolute changes or only percentage changes), the reader has cause to suspect that the full picture has not been presented.

Another example comes from a study of Internal Revenue Service audits conducted by the U.S. General Accounting Office (GAO 1979). The cover page of the report carried the sensational headline that IRS audits in five selected districts missed $1 million in errors in four months: "These districts assessed incorrect tax estimated to total $1.0 million over a 4-month period because of technical errors, computation errors, or failure to make automatic adjustments."

The IRS response to the GAO report pointed out that the same audit cases with $1 million in overlooked errors had revealed over $26 million in errors that led to adjustments in tax. Thus, the $1 million represented only about 4% of the total amount of money involved. Moreover, the IRS disputed the GAO's $1 million error figure because the GAO included all potential audit items whereas the IRS ignored differences of $100 or less. In the data presented by the GAO, it is impossible to tell what proportion of the $1 million involved errors of under $100, which are routinely ignored by the IRS as not worth the costs of pursuing. Finally, a detailed reading of the report shows that the $1 million error involves cases of two types: instances in which additional tax would be due to the IRS and instances in which a refund would be due the taxpayer from the IRS. In point of fact, the $1 million error would result in virtually no additional revenue to the government, had all the errors been detected and followed up, because the two kinds of errors would cancel each other out.

The gross simplification of the evaluation findings and the headlining of the $1 million error represent considerable distortion of the full picture. Simplicity at the expense of accuracy is no virtue; complexity in the service of accuracy is no vice. The point is to make complex matters understandable without distortion. The omitted information from the GAO report could not be justified on the basis of simplification. The omissions constituted distortions rather than simplification.

Striving for balance means thinking about how to present the full picture without getting bogged down in trivia or extraneous details. It can mean providing both absolute changes and percentage changes; reporting the mean, median, and mode in order to fully represent the distribution of data; providing multiple measures of an attitude or behavior; categorizing data more than one way to see what differences those categorical distributions make; providing information about mean, range, and standard deviations (represented as straightforward and understandable confidence limits); presenting both positive and negative quotes from interviewees; and finding ways to show the same thing in more than one way to increase understanding.

Be Clear About Definitions

Confusion or uncertainty about what was actually measured or studied can lead to misinterpretations. In workshops on data analysis, I give the participants statistics on farmers, on families, and on recidivism. In small groups, the participants interpret the data. Almost invariably, they jump right into analysis without asking how *farmer* was defined, how *family* was defined, or what *recidivism* actually meant in the data at hand. A simple term like *farmer* turns out to be enormously variant in its use and definition. When does the weekend gardener become a farmer, and when does the large commercial farmer become an *agribusinessperson?* A whole division of the Census Bureau wrestles with this problem.

Defining *family* is no less complex. There was a time, not so long ago, when Americans may have shared a common definition of family. Now, there is real question about who has to be together under what arrangement before we call them a family. Single-parent families, foster families, same-sex marriages, and extended families are just a few of the possible complications. Before interpreting any statistics on families it would be critical to know how family was defined.

Measuring recidivism is common in evaluation, but the term offers a variety of different definitions and measures. Recidivism may mean (1) a new arrest, (2) a new appearance in court, (3) a new conviction, (4) a new sentence, (5) or actually committing a new crime regardless of whether the offender is apprehended. The statistics will vary considerably, depending on which definition of recidivism is used.

A magazine cartoon showed a group of researchers watching a television cartoon and debating the question: "When the coyote bounces after falling off the cliff, does the second time he hits the ground count as a second incidence of violence?" Of such decisions are statistics made.

DEFINITIONAL DILEMMAS

A "study" was published by the National Federation of Decency concerning the decadent content of the Phil Donahue television talk show. One of the categories of analysis included Donahue programs that encouraged "abnormal sex." The author of the report later acknowledged that it was probably a bit excessive of the federation to have included breast feeding in this category (*Boulder Daily Camera*, September 30, 1981:2). But, then, definitions of abnormal sex do seem to vary somewhat. Any reader of a research report on the subject would be well advised to look with care at the definition used by the researcher. Of course, any savvy evaluator involved in such a study would be careful to make sure that his or her own sexual practices were categorized as normal.

In the 1972 presidential campaign, President Nixon gained considerable press attention for making a major budget shift from defense spending to more funds for social services. One had to listen quite attentively to learn that Veterans Administration expenditures had simply been moved from the defense side of the ledger to the social services side of the ledger. The statistical changes in proportion of expenditures for different purposes were entirely an artifact of a change in categorical definition.

Such examples are not meant to make people cynical about statistics. Many distortions of this kind are inadvertent, due to sloppiness of thinking, unexamined assumptions, or the rush to complete a final report. Sometimes, of course, they're the result of incompetence, or the old adage that "figures lie, and liars figure." Widespread skepticism about statistics is all the more reason for evaluators to exercise care in making sure that data are useful, accurate, and understandable. Clear definitions provide the foundation for utility, accuracy, and understandability. A Sufi story reinforces the importance of being clear about definitions before drawing conclusions.

The wise fool Mulla Nasrudin and a friend went to the circus together. They were dazzled by the tightrope walker. Afterward, Nasrudin's friend kept raving about the performance of the tightrope walker. Nasrudin tired of the conversation, but his companion resisted all attempts to change the subject. Finally, in frustration, Nasrudin asserted, "It wasn't really such a great feat as all that. I myself can walk a tightrope."

Angry at Nasrudin's boasting, the friend challenged him with a substantial wager. They set a time for the attempt in the town center so that all the villagers could be witness. At the appointed hour Mulla Nasrudin appeared with the rope, stretched it out on the ground, walked along it, and demanded his money.

"But the tightrope must be in the air for you to win the wager!" exclaimed the companion.

"I wagered that I could walk a tightrope," replied Nasrudin. "As everyone can see, I have walked the tightrope."

The village judicial officer ruled in Nasrudin's favor. "Definitions," he explained to the assembled villagers, "are what make laws."

They also make evaluations.

MENU 13.1

Menu of Program Comparisons

The outcomes of a program can be compared to

1. The outcomes of selected "similar" programs
2. The outcomes of the same program the previous year (or any other trend period, e.g., quarterly reports)
3. The outcomes of a representative or random sample of programs in the field
4. The outcomes of special programs of interest, for example, those known to be exemplary models or those having difficulty (purposeful sample comparison, Patton 1990:169-86)
5. The stated goals of the program
6. Participants' goals for themselves
7. External standards of desirability as developed by the profession
8. Standards of minimum acceptability (e.g., basic licensing or accreditation standards)
9. Ideals of program performance
10. Guesses by staff or other decision makers about what the outcomes would be

Combinations of any of these comparisons are also possible.

Make Comparisons Carefully and Appropriately

Virtually all analysis ends up being in some way comparative. Numbers in isolation, standing alone without a frame of reference or basis of comparison, seldom make much sense. A recidivism rate of 40% is a meaningless statistic. Is that high or low? Does that represent improvement or deterioration? An error of $1 million in IRS audits is a meaningless number. Some basis of comparison or standard of judgment is needed in order to interpret such statistics. The challenge lies in selecting the appropriate basis of comparison. In the example of the IRS audit, the GAO believed that the appropriate comparison was an error of zero dollars—absolute perfection in auditing. The IRS considered such a standard unrealistic and suggested, instead, comparing errors against the total amount of corrections made in all audits.

Skepticism can undermine evaluation when the basis for the comparison appears arbitrary or contrived. Working with users to select appropriate comparisons involves considering a number of options. Menu 13.1 presents 10 possibilities plus combinations. Evaluators should work with stakeholders to decide which comparisons are appropriate and relevant to give a full and balanced view of what is happening in the program.

Consider the new jogger or running enthusiast. At the beginning, runners are likely to use as a basis for comparison their previously sedentary lifestyle. By that standard, the initial half-mile run appears pretty good. Then the runner discovers that there are a lot of other people running, many of them covering 3 miles, 4 miles, 5 or 10 miles a week. Compared to seasoned joggers, the runner's half-mile doesn't look so good. On days when new runners want to feel particularly good, they may compare themselves to all the people who don't run at all. On days when they need some incentive to push harder, they may compare themselves to people who run twice as far as they do. Some adopt medical standards for basic conditioning, something on the order of 30 minutes of sustained and intense exercise at least three times a week. Some measure their progress in miles, others in minutes and hours. Some compare themselves to friends; others get involved in official competitions and races. All these comparisons are valid, but each yields a different conclusion because the basis of comparison is different in each case.

In politics, it is said that conservatives compare the present to the past and see all the things that have been lost, while liberals compare the present to what could be in the future and see all the things yet to be attained. Each basis of comparison provides a different perspective. Fascination with comparisons undergirds sports, politics, advertising, management, and, certainly, evaluation. America's first president, George Washington, captured this fascination when he observed in the year 1791:

> Take two managers and give them the same number of laborers and let these laborers be equal in all respects. Let both managers rise equally early, go equally late to rest, be equally active, sober, and industrious, and yet, in the course of the year, one of them, without pushing the hands that are under him more than the other, shall have performed infinitely more work.

"Infinitely more" appears in this instance to be a rather crude estimate of difference, but by the time he posed this hypothetical experiment, Washington had given up surveying and become a politician. An evaluator would seek somewhat more precise measures for the comparison, then move on to interpretations (Why the differences?) and judgments (Are such differences good or bad?), as we shall now do.

Interpretations and Judgments

In resisting the temptation to bear alone the burden of analysis and interpretation, the utilization-focused evaluator views the collaborative process as a training opportunity through which users can become more sophisticated about data-based decision making. Science fiction author and futurist H. G. Wells (1866-1946) anticipated the importance of making statistical thinking accessible to nonstatisticians when he observed, "Statistical thinking will one day be as necessary for efficient citizenship as the ability to read and write."

For evaluation users, that day is now. Incorporating a training perspective into evaluation will mean being prepared to help users with statistical reasoning. The logic of qualitative analysis also needs to be made accessible to stakeholders.

Researchers have internalized the differences between analysis and interpretation, but that distinction will need reinforcement for nonresearchers. In working with stakeholders to understand interpretation, three themes deserve special attention.

1. **Numbers and qualitative data must be interpreted to have meaning.** Numbers are not bad or good, they're just numbers. Interpretation means thinking about what the data mean and how they ought to be applied. No magic formulas, not even those for statistical significance, can infuse meaning into data. Only thinking humans can do that. Interpretation is a human process, not a computer process. Statisticians have no corner on the ability to think and reason. The best guideline may be Nobel scientist Albert Einstein's dictum that "the important thing is to keep on questioning."

2. **Data are imperfect indicators or representations of what the world is like.** Just as a map is not the territory it describes, the statistical tables describing a program are not the program. That's why they have to be interpreted.

3. **Statistics and qualitative data contain varying degrees of error.** Research offers probabilities, not absolutes. The switch from absolute judgment (things are or are not) to probabilistic thinking (things are more or less likely) is fundamental to entry into empirical reasoning and careful interpretations.

Different stakeholders will bring varying perspectives to the evaluation. Those perspectives will affect their interpretations. The evaluator initially facilitates elaboration of possibilities, then begins the work of convergence—aiming to reach consensus, if possible, on the most reasonable and useful interpretations supported by the data. Where different perspectives prevail, those varying interpretations should be reported and their implications explored. Judgments follow analysis and interpretations.

Scriven (1994, 1991a, 1967) has advocated consistently and forcefully the evaluator's responsibility to draw conclusions and render independent judgment.

> It is still common [for evaluators] to try to avoid adopting any actual evaluation stance although they still call what they do evaluation. This approach is referred to here as "pseudoevaluative investigation," and it results in a description masquerading as evaluation. It is sometimes rationalized by appeal to the following claim: . . . that the professional evaluator's duty is to give clients the facts and let them assemble (interpret) these according to their own values or to give them the subevaluations and let them put these together.
>
> The first part of this fallacy creates the curious picture of the professional evaluator doing everything except what is normally called evaluating something. In reality, the situation is even worse. . . . Thus, balking at the last step—the overall evaluation—is like deciding you want to be a virgin after the orgy but before the Day of Judgment. [Such an evaluator] is nearly always guilty of inconsistency as well as misleading advertising. (Scriven 1991a:31)

In contrast to Scriven, others have argued that the evaluator's job can be limited to supplying the data and that stakeholders alone might make the final judgments (e.g., Stake 1996). **Utilization-focused evaluation treats these opposing views as options to be negotiated with primary users.** The evaluator's job can include offering interpretations, making judgments, and generating recommendations if, as is typical, that is what the evaluation users want. Even so, in order to facilitate direct engagement and increase users' ownership, prior to offering my interpretations, judgments, and recommendations, if they are requested, I first give decision makers and intended users an opportunity to arrive at their own conclusions unencumbered by my perspective but facilitated by me. In doing so, I find that I have to keep returning, sensitively and diplomatically, to the distinctions among analysis, interpretation, judgment, and recommendations.

While this kind of facilitation usually occurs with a small number of primary users, the process can be facilitated for very large groups. The following example involved over 200 people in a half-day process of analysis, interpretation, judgment, and generating recommendations—moving back and forth between small groups and full-session reporting and adopting conclusions.

An Example of Utilization-Focused Deliberations With Stakeholders

In an evaluation of foster group homes for juvenile offenders, we collected data from natural parents, foster parents, juveniles, and community corrections staff. The primary intended users, the Community Corrections Advisory Board, agreed to a findings review process that involved a large number of stakeholders from both the field and policy levels. We had worked closely with the board in problem identification, research design, and instrumentation. Once the data were collected, we employed a variety of statistical techniques, including alpha factor analysis and stepwise forward regression analysis. We then reduced these findings to a few pages in a simplified form and readable format for use at a half-day meeting with community corrections staff, welfare department staff, court services staff, and members of the county board. That meeting included some 40 of the most powerful elected and appointed officials in the county, as well as another 160 field professionals.

A major purpose of the evaluation was to describe and conceptualize effective foster group homes for juvenile delinquents so that future selection of homes and training of foster parents could be improved. The evaluation was also meant to provide guidance about how to achieve better matching between juvenile offenders and foster parents. We had data on how variations in recidivism, runaway rates, and juvenile attitudes varied by different kinds of group home environments. We had measured variations in homes with a 56-item instrument. Factor analysis of the 56 items uncovered a single major factor that explained 54% of the variance in recidivism, with 19 items loading above .45 on that factor. The critical task in data interpretation was to label that factor in such a way that its relationship to dependent variables would represent something meaningful to identified information users. We focused the half-day work session on this issue.

The session began with a brief description of the methods and data, which were then distributed. In randomly assigned groups of four, these diverse stakeholders were asked to look at the items in Exhibit 13.5 and label the factor or theme represented by those items in their own words. After the groups reported their labels, discussion followed. Consensus emerged around the terms *participation and support* as representing one end of the continuum and *authoritarian and nonsupportive* for the other end. We also asked the groups to describe the salient elements in the factor. These descriptions were combined with the labels chosen by the group. The resulting conceptualization—as it appeared in the final evaluation report—is shown in Exhibit 13.6.

EXHIBIT 13.5

Composition of the Group Home Treatment Environment Scale

The items that follow are juvenile interview items that are highly interrelated statistically in such a way that they can be assumed to measure the same environmental factor. The items are listed in rank order by factor loading (from .76 to .56 for a six-factor alpha solution). This means that when the scales were combined to create a single numerical scale, the items higher on the list received more weight in the scale (based on factor score coefficients).

From your perspective, what underlying factor or theme is represented by the combination of these questions? What do these different items have in common?

1. The [group home parent's names] went out of their way to help us.
   - almost always 30.9%
   - a lot of times 10.9%
   - just sometimes 34.5%
   - almost never 23.6% — Factor loading = .76
2. At . . . 's house, personal problems were openly talked about.
   - almost always 20.0%
   - a lot of times 9.1%
   - just sometimes 32.7%
   - almost never 38.2% — Factor loading = .76
3. Did you feel like the group home parents tried to help you understand yourself?
   - almost always 23.6%
   - a lot of times 29.1%
   - just sometimes 23.6%
   - almost never 23.6% — Factor loading = .74
4. How often did . . . take time to encourage you in what you did?
   - almost always 27.3%
   - a lot of times 20.0%
   - just sometimes 30.9%
   - almost never 21.8% — Factor loading = .73
5. At . . . 's house, how much were you each encouraged to make your own decisions about things? Would you say that you were encouraged . . .
   - almost always 18.9%
   - a lot of times 30.2%
   - just sometimes 30.2%
   - almost never 20.8% — Factor loading = .68
6. How often were you given responsibility for making your own decisions?
   - almost always 23.6%
   - a lot of times 20.0%
   - just sometimes 25.5%
   - almost never 30.9% — Factor loading = .67
7. We really got along well with each other at . . . 's.
   - almost always 23.6%
   - a lot of times 29.1%
   - just sometimes 32.7%
   - almost never 14.5% — Factor loading = .66

8. Would the group home parents tell you when you were doing well?

almost always	30.9%	
a lot of times	10.9%	
just sometimes	29.1%	
almost never	9.1%	Factor loading = .64

9. How often were you allowed to openly criticize the group home parents?

almost always	14.8%	
a lot of times	7.4%	
just sometimes	24.1%	
almost never	53.7%	Factor loading = .59

10. How much of the time would you say there was a feeling of "togetherness" at . . . 's?

almost always	27.3%	
a lot of times	23.6%	
just sometimes	32.7%	
almost never	16.4%	Factor loading = .59

11. How much did they help you make plans for leaving the group home and returning to your real home?

almost always	9.1%	
a lot of times	21.8%	
just sometimes	21.8%	
almost never	47.3%	Factor loading = .58

12. How often would they talk with you about what you'd be doing after you left the group home?

almost always	7.3%	
a lot of times	18.2%	
just sometimes	36.4%	
almost never	38.2%	Factor loading = .58

13. How much of the time did the kids have a say about what went on at . . . 's?

almost always	13.0%	
a lot of times	29.6%	
just sometimes	27.8%	
almost never	29.6%	Factor loading = .56

14. How much were decisions about what you all had to do at the group home made only by the adults without involving the rest of you?

almost always	30.9%	
a lot of times	18.2%	
just sometimes	32.7%	
almost never	18.2%	Factor loading = .56

15. How much of the time were discussions at . . . .'s aimed at helping you understand your personal problems?

almost always	23.6%	
a lot of times	23.6%	
just sometimes	18.2%	
almost never	34.5%	Factor loading = .56

EXHIBIT 13.6

Group Home Treatment Environment Continuum: Description of Group Home Ideal Types

Supportive-Participatory

In group homes nearer this end of the continuum, juveniles perceive group home parents as helpful, caring, and interested in them. Juveniles are encouraged and receive positive reinforcement. Juveniles are involved in decisions about what goes on in the home. Kids are encouraged to make their own decisions about the things they do personally. There is a feeling of togetherness, of being interested in each other, of caring about what happens now and in the future. Group home parents discuss the future with the kids and help them plan. There is a feeling of mutual support, and kids feel that they can openly express their feelings, thoughts, problems, and concerns.

Nonsupportive-Authoritarian

In group homes nearer this end of the continuum, juveniles report that group home parents are less helpful, less open with them, and less interested in them personally. Juveniles are seldom encouraged to make their own decisions, and the parents tend to make decisions without asking their opinions about things. There isn't much planning things together or talking about the future. Kids are careful about what they say, are guarded about expressing their thoughts and feelings. Kids get little positive reinforcement. There is not much feeling of togetherness, support, and mutual caring; group home parents kept things well under control.

NOTE: The descriptions presented here are based on stakeholders' interpretations of the factor analysis in Exhibit 13.5.

The groups then studied accompanying tables showing the relationships between this treatment environment factor and program outcome variables (see Exhibit 13.7). The relationships were statistically significant and quite transparent. Juveniles who reported experiencing more supportive-participatory corrections environments had lower recidivism rates, lower runaway rates, and more positive attitudes. Having established the direction of the data, we discussed the limitations of the findings, methodological weaknesses, and the impossibility of making firm causal inferences. Key decision makers were already well aware of these problems. Then, given those constraints, the group was asked for recommendations. The basic thrust of the discussion concerned ways to increase the supportive-participatory experiences of juvenile offenders. The people carrying on that discussion were the people who fund, set policy for, operate, and control juvenile offender programs. The final written evaluation report included the recommendations that emerged from that meeting as well as our own conclusions and recommendations as evaluators. But the final written report took another four weeks to prepare and print; the use process was already well under way as the meeting ended.

Four main points are illustrated here about a utilization-focused approach to findings. First, nonresearchers can under-

EXHIBIT 13.7
Relationship Between Different Home Environments and Recidivism

	No Recidivism	*Recidivism*	*Total*
Supportive-participatory homes	76% (N = 19)	24% (N = 6)	100% (N = 25)
Nonsupportive-authoritarian homes	44% (N = 11)	56% (N = 14)	100% (N = 25)

NOTE: Correlation r = .33; Significant at .009 level.

stand and interpret data when presented with clear, readable, and simplified statistical tables. Second, as experienced data analysts know, the only way to really understand a data set is to spend some time getting inside it; busy decision makers are unwilling or unable to spend days at such a task, but a couple of hours of structured time spent in facilitated analysis and interpretation can pay off in greater understanding of and commitment to using results. Third, evaluators can learn a great deal from stakeholder interpretations of data, if they are open and listen to what people knowledgeable about the program have to say. Just as decision makers do not spend as much time in data analysis as do evaluators, so evaluators do not spend as much time in program analysis, operations, and planning as do decision makers. Each can learn from the other in the overall effort to make sense out of the data and provide future direction for the program. Fourth, the transition from analysis to action is facilitated by having key actors involved in analysis. Use does not then depend on or have to wait for a written report.

Making Claims

One way I've found of focusing the attention of primary stakeholders, especially program administrators and staff, involves making claims. I ask: "Having reviewed the data, what can you claim about the program?" I then ask them to list possible claims, for example, (1) participants like the program, (2) participants get jobs as a result of the program, (3) the dropout rate is low, (4) changes in participants last over the long term, (5) the program is cost-effective, (6) the program does not work well with people of color, and so on. Having generated a list of possible claims, I then have them sort the claims into the categories (or cells) shown in Exhibit 13.8. This matrix distinguishes claims by their importance and rigor. Important claims speak to major issues of societal concern. Participants getting and keeping jobs as a result of a training program is a more important claim than that they're satisfied. Rigor concerns the amount and quality of evidence to support claims. The program might have strong evidence of participant satisfaction, but weak follow-up data about job reten-

EXHIBIT 13.8
Claims Matrix

		Importance of Claims	
		Major	*Minor*
Rigor of Claims	Strong	*	
	Weak		

*GOAL: *Strong claims of major importance.*

The most powerful, useful, and credible claims are those that are of major importance and have strong empirical support.

Characteristics of Claims of MAJOR IMPORTANCE

- Involves making a difference, having an impact, or achieving desirable outcomes
- Deals with a problem of great societal concern
- Affects large numbers of people
- Provides a sustainable solution (claim deals with something that lasts over time)
- Saves money
- Saves time, that is, accomplishes something in less time than is usually the case (an efficiency claim)
- Enhances quality
- Claims to be "new" or innovative
- Shows that something can actually be done about a problem, that is, claims the problem is malleable
- Involves a model or approach that could be used by others (meaning the model or approach is clearly specified and adaptable to other situations)

Characteristics of STRONG CLAIMS

- Valid, believable evidence to support the claim
- Follow-up data over time (longer periods of follow-up provide stronger evidence than shorter periods, and any follow-up is stronger than just end-of-program results)
- The claim is about a clear intervention (model or approach) with solid implementation documentation
- The claim is about clearly specified outcomes and impacts:
  — Behavioral outcomes are stronger than opinions, feelings, and knowledge

- The evidence for claims includes comparisons:
  - To program goals
  - Over time (pre-, post-, follow-up)
  - With other groups
  - With general trends or norms
- The evidence for claims includes replications:
  - Done at more than one site
  - More than one staff person attained outcomes
  - Different cohort groups of participants attained comparable outcomes over time
  - Different programs attained comparable results using comparable approaches
- Claims are based on more than one kind of evidence or data (i.e., triangulation of data):
  - Quantitative and qualitative data
  - Multiple sources (e.g., kids, parents, teachers, and staff corroborate results)
- There are clear logical and/or empirical linkages between the intervention and the claimed outcomes
- The evaluators are independent of the staff (or where internal evaluation data are used, an independent, credible person reviews the results and certifies the results)
- Claims are based on systematic data collection over time

CAVEAT: Importance and rigor are not absolute criteria. Different stakeholders, decision makers, and claims makers will have different definitions of what is important and rigorous. What staff deem to be of major importance may not be so to outside observers. What is deemed important and rigorous changes over time and across contexts. Making public claims is a political action. Importance and rigor are, to some extent, politically defined and dependent on the values of specific stakeholders.

Related Distinctions

1. Program *premises* are different from but related to and dependent on program *claims.*

   Premises are the basic assumptions on which a program is based, for example, that effective, attentive parenting is desirable and more likely to produce well-functioning children who become well-functioning adults. This premise is based on *research.* The program cannot "prove" the premise (though supporting research can and should be provided). The program's claims are about the program's actual implementation and concrete outcomes, for example, that the program yielded more effective parents who are more attentive to their children. The program does not have to follow the children to adulthood before claims can be made.

2. Evidence is different from claims—but claims depend on evidence.

   Claim: This program trains welfare recipients for jobs, places them in jobs, and, as a result, they become self-sufficient and leave the welfare rolls.

   Evidence: Numbers and types of job placements over time; pre-, post-, and follow-up data on welfare status; participant interview data about program effects; employer interview data about placements; and so on.

tion. The most powerful, useful, and credible claims are those of major importance that have strong empirical support.

This framework can also be useful in the design phase to help primary users and key stakeholders focus on gathering rigorous data about important issues so that, at the end, the evaluation will be able to report important and strong claims.

Useful Recommendations

Before looking specifically at the process of generating recommendations, it may be helpful to position recommendations within the overall evaluation process. Evaluations are useful in ways that go beyond a narrow focus on implementing recommendations or making concrete, specific decisions about immediate courses of action. Participation in an evaluation process affects ways of thinking about a program; it can clarify goals, increasing (or decreasing) particular commitments; and the process can stimulate insights, the consequences of which may not be evident until some time in the distant future. (Chapter 5 discusses this kind of process use in depth.) Recommendations, then, do not bear the full brunt of the hopes for evaluation use. Nevertheless, recommendations are often the most visible part of an evaluation report. Well-written, carefully derived recommendations and conclusions can be the magnet that pulls all the other elements of an evaluation together into a meaningful whole. Done poorly, recommendations can become the center of attack, discrediting what was otherwise a professional job because of hurried and sloppy work on a last-minute recommendations section. I suspect that one of the most common reasons evaluators get into trouble when writing recommendations is that they haven't allowed enough time to really think through the possibilities and discuss them with people who have a stake in the evaluation. I've known cases in which, after working months on a project, the evaluators generated recommendations just hours before a final reporting session, under enormous time pressure. In our follow-up study of federal health evaluations, we asked 20 decision makers about the usefulness of the recommendations they had received. The following reactions provide a flavor of typical reactions to recommendations:

- I don't remember the specific recommendations.
- The recommendations weren't anything we could do much with.
- It was the overall process that was useful, not the recommendations.
- I remember reading them, that's about all.
- The recommendations looked like they'd been added as an afterthought. Not impressive.

Useful and Practical Recommendations: Ten Guidelines

Recommendations, when they are included in a report, draw readers' attention like bees to a flower's nectar. Many report readers will turn to recommendations before anything else. Some never read beyond the recommendations. Given their importance, then, let me offer 10 guidelines for evaluation recommendations.

1. After the evaluation purpose is clarified and before data are collected, **the nature and content of the final report should be negotiated with stakeholders and evaluation funders.** Not all evaluation reports include recommendations. The kinds

of recommendations, if any, to be included in a report are a matter of negotiation.

2. **Recommendations should clearly follow from and be supported by the evaluation findings.** The processes of analysis, interpretation, and judgment should lead logically to recommendations.

3. **Distinguish different kinds of recommendations.** Recommendations that deal directly with central questions or issues should be highlighted and separated from recommendations about secondary or minor issues. Distinctions should be made between summative and formative recommendations. It may be helpful and important to distinguish between recommendations that can be implemented immediately, recommendations that can be implemented in the short term (within six months to a year), and recommendations aimed at the long-term development of the program. In still other cases, it may be appropriate to orient recommendations toward certain groups of people: recommendations for funders, recommendations for program administrators, recommendations for program staff, and recommendations for clients or program participants.

Another way of differentiating types of recommendations is to clearly specify which recommendations are strongly supported by the data and have the solid support of the evaluator and/or the evaluation task force versus those recommendations that are less directly supported by the data or about which there is dissension among members of the task force. In similar fashion, it is important to distinguish between recommendations that involve a firm belief that some action should be taken and recommendations that are meant merely to stimulate discussion or suggestions that might become part of an agenda for future consideration and action.

The basic point here is that long, indiscriminate lists of recommendations at the end of an evaluation report diffuse the focus and diminish the power of central recommendations. By making explicit the different amounts of emphasis that the evaluator intends to place on different recommendations, and by organizing recommendations so as to differentiate among different kinds of recommendations, the evaluator increases the usefulness of the recommendations as well as the likelihood of the implementation of at least some of them.

4. **Some decision makers prefer to receive multiple options rather than recommendations that advocate only one course of action.** This approach may begin with a full slate of possible recommendations: terminate the program; reduce funding for the program; maintain program funding at its current level; increase program funding slightly; and increase program funding substantially. The evaluator then lists pros and cons for each of these recommendations, showing which findings, assumptions, interpretations, and judgments support each option.

5. **Insofar as possible, when making recommendations, particularly major ones involving substantial changes in program operations or policies, evaluators should study, specify, and include in their reports some consideration of the benefits and costs of making the suggested changes, including the costs and risks of not making them.**

6. **Focus on actions within the control of intended users.** A major source of frustration for many decision makers is that the recommendations in evaluation reports relate mainly to things over which they have no control. For example, a school desegregation study that focuses virtually all its

recommendations on needed changes in housing patterns is not very useful to school officials, even though they may agree that housing changes are needed. Is the implication of such a recommendation that the schools can do nothing? Is the implication that anything the school does will be limited in impact to the extent that housing patterns remain unchanged? Or, again, are there major changes a school could make to further the aims of desegregation, but the evaluator got sidetracked on the issue of housing patterns and never got back to concrete recommendations for the school? Of course, the best way to end up with recommendations that focus on manipulable variables is to make sure that, in conceptualizing the evaluation, the focus was on manipulable variables and that focus is maintained right on through to the writing of recommendations.

7. **Exercise political sensitivity in writing recommendations.** Ask yourself the questions, If I were in their place with their responsibilities, their political liabilities, their personal perspectives, how would I react to this recommendation stated in this way? What arguments would I raise to counter the recommendations? Work with stakeholders to analyze the political implications of recommendations. This doesn't mean recommendations should be weak but, rather, that evaluators should be astute. Controversy may or may not serve the cause of getting findings used. But, at the very least, controversies should be anticipated.

8. Be **careful and deliberate in wording evaluations.** Important recommendations can be lost in vague and obtuse language. Powerful recommendations can be diluted by an overly meek style, while particularly sensitive recommendations may be dismissed by an overly assertive style. Avoid words that confuse or distract from the central message.

9. **Allow time to do a good job on recommendations,** time to develop recommendations collaboratively with stakeholders, and time to pilot-test recommendations for clarity, understandability, practicality, utility, and meaningfulness.

10. **Develop strategies for getting recommendations taken seriously.** Simply listing recommendations at the end of a report may mean they get token attention. Think about how to facilitate serious consideration of recommendations. Help decision makers make decisions on recommendations, including facilitating a working session that includes clear assignment of responsibility for follow-up action and time lines for implementation.

Controversy About Recommendations

n evaluation without a recommendation is like a fish without a bicycle.

—Michael Scriven (1993:53)

While evaluators such as Mike Hendricks and Elizabeth Handley (1990) have argued that "evaluators should almost always offer recommendations" (p. 110),

Michael Scriven has been persistent and vociferous in warning evaluators against the logical fallacy of thinking that judging the merit or worth of something leads directly to recommendations. He considers it one of the "hard-won lessons in program evaluation" that evaluators seldom have the expertise to make recommendations and that they are generally well advised to stop at what they are qualified to do: render judgment.

> It is widely thought that program evaluations should always conclude with a recommendations section, but this view is based on a misunderstanding of the logic of evaluation, and the misunderstanding has seriously unfortunate effects. The conclusion of an evaluation is normally a statement or set of statements about the merit, worth, or value of something, probably with several qualifications (for example, These materials on planetary astronomy are probably the best available, for middle-school students with well-developed vocabularies). There is a considerable step from the conclusion to the recommendations (for example, You should buy these materials for this school), and it is a step that evaluators are often not well-qualified to make. For example, in teacher evaluation, an evaluator, or, for that matter, a student, may be able to identify a bad teacher conclusively. But it does not follow that the teacher should be fired or remediated or even told about the result of the evaluation (which may be informal). In making one of those recommendations, the evaluator must have highly specific local knowledge (for example, about the terms of the teacher's contract, the possibility of early retirement, and temporary traumas in the teacher's home life) and special expertise (for example, about the legal situation), both of which go a long way beyond the skills necessary for evaluation. If the evaluator is looking at recommendations aimed not at actions but at improvement (for example, suggested changes in the way in which the teacher organizes the lesson and changes in the frequency of question-asking), then he or she moves into an area requiring still further dimensions of expertise. (Scriven 1993:53)

Scriven (1991b) offers a number of analogies to make his point. A doctor may diagnose without being able to prescribe a cure. Just as "a roadtester is not a mechanical engineer, a program evaluator is not a management troubleshooter, though both often suffer from delusions of grandeur in this respect" (p. 304).

Yet, doctors routinely strive to prescribe remedies, and a savvy mechanical engineer would most certainly confer with a roadtester before making design changes. Scriven's vociferousness about eschewing recommendations follows from his assertion that the evaluator's primary obligation is to render judgment. While Scriven's counsel to avoid making recommendations if one lacks expertise in remediation or design is wise as far as it goes, he fails to take the added step of making it part of the evaluator's responsibility to seek such expertise and facilitate experts' engagement with the data. Utilization-focused evaluation does offer a way of taking that extra step by actively involving primary intended users in the process of generating recommendations based on their knowledge of the situation and their shared expertise. Utilization-focused recommendations are not the evaluator's alone; they result from a collaborative process that seeks and incorporates the very expertise Scriven says is necessary for informed action.

A Futures Perspective on Recommendations

Show the future implications of recommendations.

—Hendricks and Handley (1990:114)

Recommendations have long struck me as the weakest part of evaluation. We have made enormous progress in ways of studying programs, in methodological diversity, and in a variety of data-collection techniques and designs. The payoff from those advances often culminates in recommendations, but we have made comparatively less progress in how to construct useful recommendations. I have found that teaching students how to go from data to recommendations is often the most challenging part of teaching evaluation. It's not a simple, linear process. A common complaint of readers of evaluation reports is that they cannot tell how the evaluators arrived at their recommendations. Recommendations can become lengthy laundry lists of undifferentiated proposals. They're alternatively broad and vague or pointed and controversial. But what recommendations always include, usually implicitly, are assumptions about the future.

The field of futures studies includes a broad range of people who use a wide variety of techniques to make inquiries about the nature of the future. Futurists study the future in order to alter perceptions and actions in the present. Evaluators, on the other hand, study the past (what programs have already done) in order to alter perceptions and actions in the present. In this sense, then, both futurists and evaluators are interested in altering perceptions and actions in the present, the impact of which will be a changed future. Evaluators do so by looking at what has already occurred; futurists do so by forecasting what may occur.

In effect, at the point where evaluators make recommendations, we become futurists. Recommendations constitute a forecast of what will happen if certain actions are taken. Those forecasts are based on our analysis of what has occurred in the past. The accuracy of such forecasts, as with any predictions about the future, is subject to error due to changed conditions and the validity of assumptions that are necessarily made. Futurists have developed approaches for dealing with the uncertainties of their forecasts. Some of these approaches, I think, hold promise for evaluation. For example, futurists have developed techniques for constructing alternative scenarios that permit decision makers to consider the consequences of different assumptions and trends. These are variations on "if → then . . . " constructions. There are often three to four different scenarios constructed: a pessimistic scenario, an optimistic scenario, and one or two middle-of-the-road, or most likely-case scenarios.

The very presentation of scenarios communicates that the future is uncertain and that the way one best prepares for the future is to prepare for a variety of possibilities. General Robert E. Lee is reputed to have said, "I am often surprised, but I am never taken by surprise." That is the essence of a futures perspective—to be prepared for whatever occurs by having reflected on different possibilities, even those that are unlikely.

The advantage of scenarios in evaluation presentations is threefold. First, they permit us to communicate that recommendations are based on assumptions and thus, should those assumptions prove unwarranted, the recommendations may need to be altered accordingly. Second, the presentation of scenarios directs attention to those trends and factors that should be monitored so that as future conditions become known, program actions can be altered in accordance with the way the world actually unfolds (rather than simply on the basis of how we thought the world would unfold). Third, they remind us, inherently, of our limitations, for "results of a program evaluation are so dependent on the setting that replication is only a figure of speech; the evaluator is essentially an historian" (Cronbach et al. 1980:7)

Utilization-Focused Reporting

In utilization-focused evaluation, use does not center on the final report. Traditionally, evaluators and users have viewed the final written report as the climax—the end of the evaluation—and the key mechanism for use. From an academic perspective, use is achieved through dissemination of a published report. Moreover, use often doesn't emerge as an issue until there is something concrete (a report) to use. By contrast, utilization-focused evaluation is concerned with use from the beginning, and a final written report is only one of many mechanisms for facilitating use. The Minnesota Group Home Evaluation reviewed earlier illustrates this point. Major use was under way well before the report was written, as a result of the half-day work session devoted to analyzing the results with major stakeholders. The final report was an anticlimax, and appropriately so.

The data from our study of federal health evaluations revealed that much important reporting is interpersonal and informal. In hallway conversations, in rest rooms, over coffee, before and after meetings, over the telephone, and through informal networks, the word gets passed along when something useful and important has been found. Knowing this, evaluators can strategize about how to inject findings into important informal networks.

Formal oral briefings, presented with careful preparation and skill, can have an immediate and dramatic impact. Michael Hendricks (1994, 1984, 1982) has studied effective techniques for executive summaries and oral briefings: The key is good charts and graphics to capture attention and communicate quickly. A trend line, for example, can be portrayed more powerfully in graphic form than in a table, as Exhibit 13.9 shows. I saw Mike Hendricks at a national meeting as I was writing this chapter. He said emphatically, "Emphasize graphics. Evaluators have got to learn graphics. I'm amazed at how bad the charts and graphics are that I see in reports. You can't emphasize it too much. Reporting means GRAPHICS! GRAPHICS! GRAPHICS!"

Report Menu

As with other stages in utilization-focused evaluation, the reporting stage offers a smorgasbord of options. Menu 13.2 displays alternatives for reporting format and

EXHIBIT 13.9
The Power of Graphics

Data in a Table

1990	43 graduates
1991	49
1992	56
1993	46
1994	85
1995	98
1996	115
1997	138

The Same Data in Graphic Form

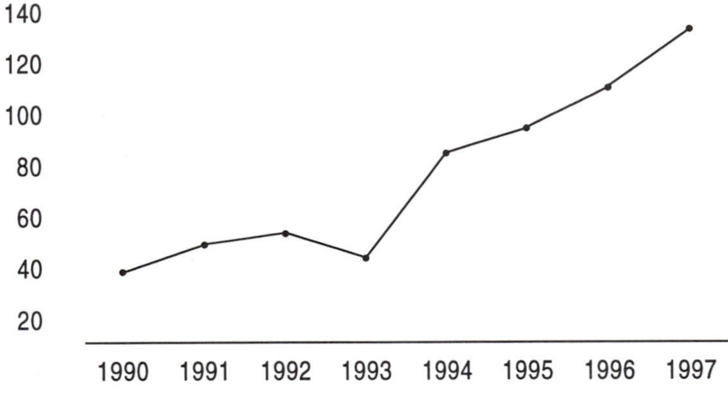

style, content, contributors, and perspectives. Selecting from the menu is affected by the purpose of the evaluation (see Chapter 4). A summative report will highlight an overall judgment of merit or worth with supporting data. A knowledge-generating report aimed at policy enlightenment may follow a traditional academic format. A formative report may take the form of an internal memorandum with circulation limited to staff. I am often asked by students to show them the standard or best format for an evaluation report. The point of Menu 13.2 is that there can be no standard report format, and the best format is the one that the fulfills the purposes of the evaluation and meets the needs of specific intended users. In many cases, multiple reporting strategies can be pursued to reach different intended users and dissemination audiences.

Utilization-Focused Reporting Principles

I've found the following principles helpful in thinking about how to make reporting useful: (1) Be intentional about reporting, that is, know the purpose of a report; (2) be user-focused; (3) avoid surprising primary stakeholders; (4) think positive about negatives; and (5) distinguish dissemination from use. Let me elaborate each of these principles.

Be Intentional and Purposeful About Reporting

Being intentional means negotiating a shared understanding of what it's going to mean to close the evaluation, that is, to achieve use. Use of the evaluation findings and processes is the desired outcome, not producing a report. A report is a means to an end—use. You need to communicate at every step in the evaluation your commitment to utility. One way to emphasize this point during early negotiations is to ask if a final report is expected. This question commands attention. "Will you want a final report?" I ask.

They look at me and they say, "Come again?"

I repeat. "Will you want a final report?"

They respond, "Of course. That's why we're doing this, to get a report."

And I respond. "I see it a little differently. I think we've agreed that we're doing this evaluation to get useful information to improve your programming and decision making. A final written report is one way of communicating findings, but there's substantial evidence now that it's not always the most effective way. Full evaluation reports don't seem to get read much, and it's very costly to write final reports. A third or more of the budget of an evaluation can be consumed by report writing. Let's talk about how to get the evaluation used, then we can see if a full written report is the most cost-effective way to do that." Then I share Menu 13.2 and we start talking reporting options.

Often, I find that, with this kind of interaction, my primary intended users really start to understand what utilization-focused evaluation means. They start to comprehend that evaluation doesn't have to mean producing a thick report that they can file under "has been evaluated." They start to think about use. Caveat: Whatever is agreed on, especially if there's agreement not to produce a traditional academic monograph, get the agreement in writing and remind them of it often. A commitment to alternative reporting approaches may need reinforcement, especially among stakeholders used to traditional formats.

Focus Reports on Primary Intended Users

A theme running throughout this book is that use is integrally intertwined with users. That's the thrust of the personal factor (Chapter 3). The style, format, content, and process of reporting should all be geared toward intended use by intended users. For example, we've learned, in general, that busy, big-picture policymakers and funders are more likely to read concise executive summaries than full reports, but detail-oriented users want—what else?—details. Some users prefer recommendations right up front at the beginning of the report; others want them at the end; and I had one group of users who wanted the recommendations in a separate document so that readers of the report had to reach their own conclusions without interpreting everything in terms of recommendations. Methods sections may be put in the body of the report, in an appendix, or omitted and shared only with the methodologically interested. Sometimes users can't articulate

MENU 13.2

Evaluation Reporting Menu

Style and Format Options: Written Report

Traditional academic research monograph
Executive summary followed by a full report
Executive summary followed by a few key tables, graphs, and data summaries
Executive summary only (data available to those interested)
Different reports (or formats) for different targeted users
Newsletter article for dissemination
Press release
Brochure (well crafted, professionally done)
No written report; only oral presentations

Style and Format Options: Oral and Creative

Oral briefing with charts
Short summary followed by questions (e.g., at a board meeting or legislative hearing)
Discussion groups based on prepared handouts that focus issues for interpretation and judgment based on data
Half-day or full-day retreat-like work session with primary intended users
Videotape or audiotape presentation
Dramatic, creative presentation (e.g., role-playing perspectives)
Involvement of select primary users in reporting and facilitating any of the above
Advocacy-adversary debate or court for and against certain conclusions and judgments
Written and oral combinations

Content Options

Major findings only; focus on data, patterns, themes, and results
Findings and interpretations with judgments of merit or worth (no recommendations)
(a) Summative judgment about overall program
(b) Judgments about program components

what they want until they see a draft. Then they know what they don't want and the responsive evaluator will have to do some rewriting. Consider this story from an evaluator in our federal use study.

Let me tell you the essence of the thing. I had almost no direction from the government [about the final report] except that the project officer kept saying, "Point 8 is really important. You've got to do point 8 on the contract."

Recommendations backed up by judgments, findings, and interpretations
- (a) Single, best-option recommendations
- (b) Multiple options with analysis of strengths, weaknesses, costs, and benefits of each
- (c) Options based on future scenarios with monitoring and contingency suggestions
- (d) Different recommendations for different intended users

Authors of and Contributors to the Report

Evaluator's report; evaluator as sole and independent author

Collaborative report coauthored by evaluator with others involved in the process

Report from primary users, written on their behalf by the evaluator as facilitator and adviser, but ownership of the report residing with others

Combinations:
- (a) Evaluator generates findings; collaborators generate judgments and recommendations
- (b) Evaluator generates findings and makes judgments; primary users generate recommendations
- (c) Separate conclusions, judgments, and recommendations by the evaluator and others in the same report

Perspectives Included

Evaluator's perspective as independent and neutral judge

Primary intended users only

Effort to represent all major stakeholder perspectives (may or may not be the same as primary intended users)

Program staff or administrators respond formally to the evaluation findings, (written independently by the evaluator); GAO approach

Review of the evaluation by an external panel; meta-evaluation (The Joint Committee 1994 standards prescribe that "the evaluation itself should be formatively and summatively evaluated against [the Evaluation Standards], so that its conduct is appropriately guided and, on completion, stakeholders can closely examine its strengths and weaknesses," p. A12).

So, when I turned in the draft of the report, I put points 1 through 9, without 8, in the first part of the report. Then I essentially wrote another report after that just on point 8 and made that the last half of the report. It was a detailed description of the activities of the program that came to very specific conclusions. It wasn't what had been asked for in proposal I responded to, but it was what they needed to answer their questions. The project officer read it and the comment back was, "It's a good report except for all that crap in the front."

OK, so I turned it around in the final version, and moved all that "crap" in the front into an appendix. If you look at the report, it has several big appendices. All of that, if you compare it carefully to the contract, all that "crap" in the appendix is what I was asked to get in the original request and contract. All the stuff that constitutes the body of the report was above and beyond the call, but that's what he wanted and that's what got used. [EV367:12]

Avoid Surprising Stakeholders: Share Findings First in Draft Form

The story just told emphasizes the importance of sharing draft reports with primary users in time to let them shape the final report. This doesn't mean fudging the results to make evaluation clients happy. It means focusing so that priority information needs get priority. Collaborating with primary users means that evaluators cannot wait until they have a highly polished final report prepared to share major findings. Evaluators who prefer to work diligently in the solitude of their offices until they can spring a final report on a waiting world may find that the world has passed them by. Formative feedback, in particular, is most useful as part of a process of thinking about a program rather than as a one-shot information dump. Even in the more formal environment of a major summative evaluation, surprises born of the public release of a final report are not likely to be particularly well received by primary stakeholders caught unawares.

In our study of the use of federal health evaluations, we asked the following question:

> Some suggest that the degree to which the findings of a study were expected can affect the study's impact. Arguments go both ways. Some say that surprise findings have the greatest impact because they bring to light new information and garner special attention. Others say that surprises will usually be rejected because they don't fit in with general expectations. What's your experience and opinion?

We found that minor surprises on peripheral questions created only minor problems, but major surprises on central questions were unwelcome. One decision maker we interviewed made the point that a "good" evaluation process should build in feedback mechanisms to primary users that guarantee the relative predictability of the content of the final report.

> Evaluation isn't a birthday party, so people aren't looking for surprises. If you're coming up with data that are different than the conventional wisdom, a good evaluation effort, I would suggest, would get those ideas floated during the evaluation process so that when the final report comes out, they aren't a surprise.
>
> Now, you could come up with findings contrary to the conventional wisdom, but you ought to be sharing those ideas with the people being evaluated during the evaluation process and working on acceptance. If you present a surprise, it will tend to get rejected. See, we don't want surprises. We don't like surprises around here. [DM346: 30-31]

The evaluator for this project expressed the same opinion: "Good managers are rarely surprised by the findings. If there's a surprising finding it should be rare. I mean, everybody's missed this insight except this great evaluator? Nonsense!" [EV364:13]. Surprise attacks may make for good war strategy, but in evaluation, the surprise attack does little to add credence to a study.

Think Positive About Negatives

John Sununu (while Governor of New Hampshire in 1988, discussing the economy and upcoming presidential election): "You're telling us that the reason things are so bad is that they are so good, and they will get better as soon as they get worse?"

James A. Baker (then President Reagan's Secretary of the Treasury): "You got it."

The program staff's fear of negative results can undermine an evaluation. On the other hand, the absence of negative findings can call into question the evaluator's independence, integrity, and credibility. Here, then, is where evaluation use can take a back seat to other agendas. Staff will resist being made to look bad and will often treat the mildest suggestions for improvements as deep criticisms. Evaluators, worried about accusations that they've lost their independence, emphasize negative findings. In the next chapter on politics and ethics, we'll revisit this confrontation of perspectives. In this section, I want to make two points: (1) one person's negative is another person's positive; and (2) evaluators can do much to increase staff receptivity by shifting the focus of reporting to learning and use rather than simply being judged as good or bad.

The context for these two points is a general belief that most evaluations have negative findings. Howard Freeman (1977), an evaluation pioneer, expressed the opinion that the preponderance of negative findings diminished use. He recommended, somewhat tongue-in-cheek, that "in view of the experience of the failure of most evaluations to come up with positive impact findings, evaluation researchers probably would do well to encourage the 'biasing' of evaluations in the direction of obtaining positive results" (p. 30). He went on to add that evaluators ought to play a more active role in helping design programs that have some hope of demonstrating positive impact, based on treatments that are highly specific and carefully targeted.

Freeman's colleague Peter Rossi, coauthor of one of the most widely used evaluation texts (Rossi and Freeman 1993), shared the view that most evaluations show zero impacts on targeted clients and problems. He asserted, also tongue-in cheek, that "only those programs likely to fail are evaluated." This led him to formulate Rossi's Plutonium Law of Evaluation: "Program operators will explode when exposed to typical evaluation research findings" (quoted in Shadish et al. 1991: 386-87).

On the other hand, Michael Scriven (1991b) has observed presumably the same scene and concluded that evaluations display a "General Positive Bias" such that there is a "strong tendency to turn in more favorable results than are justified" (p. 175).

The problem I have with either stereotype, that most evaluations are negative or most are positive, is that they impose a dichotomous win/lose, pass/fail, success/failure, and positive/negative construct on results that display considerable complexity. This seems born of a tendency I find common among evaluators and decision makers: to think of evaluation findings in monolithic, absolute, and purely summative terms. In my experience, evaluation findings are seldom either completely positive or completely negative. Furthermore, whether findings are interpreted as positive or negative depends on who is using and interpreting the findings. As the old adage observes: Whether the glass is half empty or half full depends on whether you're drinking or pouring.

Consider these data. In our 20 federal health evaluation case studies, respondents described findings as follows:

Basically positive findings	5
Basically negative findings	2
Mixed positive-negative findings	7
Evaluator-decision maker disagreement on nature of findings	6
Total	20

Our sample was not random, but it was as systematic and representative of federal evaluations as we could make it given the difficulty of identifying a "universe" of evaluations. Only 2 of 20 were basically negative; the most common pattern was a mix of positive and negative; and in 6 of 20 cases, the evaluator and primary decision maker disagreed about the nature of the judgment rendered. Moreover, in only one case did any of our respondents feel that the positive or negative nature of findings explained much about use. Because we encountered few summative decisions, the overall positive or negative nature of the evaluation was less important than how the findings could be used to improve programs. In addition, the positive or negative findings of a particular study constituted only one piece of information that fed into a larger process of deliberation and was interpreted in the larger context of other available information. Absolute judgments of a positive or negative nature were less useful than specific, detailed statements about levels of impact, the nature of relationships, and variations in implementation and effectiveness. This shifts the focus from whether findings are negative or positive to whether the evaluation results contain useful information that can provide direction for programmatic action.

Evaluators can shape the environment and context in which findings are reviewed so that the focus is on learning and improvement rather than absolute judgment. Placing emphasis on organizational learning, action research, participatory evaluation, collaborative approaches, developmental evaluation, and empowerment evaluation—approaches discussed in Chapter 5—can defuse fear of and resistance to negative judgment.

Finally, it's worth remembering, philosophically, that the positive or negative nature of evaluation findings can never be established with any absolute certainty. As Sufi wise-fool Mulla Nasrudin once advised, a heavy dose of humility should accompany judgments about what is good or bad. Nasrudin had the opportunity to render this caution at a teahouse. A monk entered and said:

"My Master taught me to spread the word that mankind will never be fulfilled until the man who has not been wronged is as indignant about a wrong as the man who actually has been wronged."

The assembly was momentarily impressed. Then Nasrudin spoke: "My Master taught me that nobody at all should become indignant about anything until he is sure that what he thinks is a wrong is in fact a wrong—and not a blessing in disguise."

—Shah 1964:58-59

Distinguish Dissemination From Use

Dissemination of findings to audiences beyond intended users deserves careful distinction from the kind of use that has been the focus of this book. Studies can have an impact on all kinds of audiences in all kinds of ways. As a social scientist, I value and want to encourage the full and free dissemination of evaluation findings. Each of us ought to be permitted to indulge in the fantasy that our evaluation reports will have impact across the land and through the years. But only a handful of studies will ever enjoy (or suffer) such widespread dissemination.

Dissemination efforts will vary greatly from study to study. The nature of dissemination, like everything else, is a matter for negotiation between evaluators and decision makers. In such negotiations, dissemination costs and benefits should be estimated. The questions addressed in an evaluation will have different meanings for people not directly involved in the painstaking process of focusing the evaluation. Different individuals and audiences will be interested in a given evaluation for reasons not always possible to anticipate. Effective dissemination involves skill in extrapolating the evaluation specifics of a particular study for use by readers in a different setting.

The problematic utility of trying to design an evaluation relevant to multiple audiences, each conceptualized in vague and general terms, was what led to the emphasis in utilization-focused evaluation on identification and organization of primary intended users. Dissemination can broaden and enlarge the impact of a study in important ways, but the nature of those long-term impacts is largely beyond the control of the evaluator. What the evaluator can control is the degree to which findings address the concerns of specific intended users. That is the use for which I take responsibility: intended use by intended users. Dissemination is not use, though it can be useful.

Final Reflections

Analyzing and interpreting results can be exciting processes. Many nights have turned into morning before evaluators have finished trying new computer runs to tease out the nuances in some data set. The work of months, sometimes years, finally comes to fruition as data are analyzed and interpreted, conclusions drawn, and alternative courses of action and recommendations considered.

This chapter has emphasized that the challenges and excitement of analysis, interpretation, and judgment ought not be the sole prerogative of evaluators. Stakeholders can become involved in struggling with data, too, increasing both their commitment to and understanding of the findings.

I remember fondly the final days of an evaluation when my co-evaluators and I were on the phone with program staff two or three times a day as we analyzed data on an educational project to inform a major decision about whether it met criteria as a valid model for federal dissemination funding. Program staff shared with us the process of watching the findings take final shape. Preliminary analyses appeared negative; as the sample became more complete, the findings looked more positive to staff; finally, a mixed picture of positive and negative conclusions emerged. Because the primary users had been intimately involved in designing the evaluation, we encountered no last-minute attacks on methods to explain away negative findings. The program staff understood the data, from whence it came, what it revealed, and how it could be used for program development. They didn't get the dissemination grant that year, but they got direction about how to implement the program more consistently and increase its impact. Two years later, with new findings, they did win recognition as a "best practices" exemplar, an award that came with a dissemination grant.

Figuring out what findings mean and how to apply them engages us in that most human of processes: making sense of the world. Utilization-focused evaluators invite users along on the whole journey, alternatively exciting and treacherous, from determining what's worth knowing to interpreting the results and following through with action. In that spirit, Marvin Alkin (1990:148) suggested a T-shirt that user-oriented evaluators could give to intended users:

COME ON INTO THE DATA POOL

PART 4

Realities and Practicalities of Utilization-Focused Evaluation

In Search of Universal Evaluation Questions

A long time ago, a young evaluator set out on a quest to discover the perfect evaluation instrument, one that would be completely valid, always reliable, and universally applicable. His search led to Halcolm, known far and wide for his wisdom.

Young Evaluator:	Great Master Halcolm, forgive this intrusion, but I am on a quest for the perfect evaluation instrument.
Halcolm:	Tell me about this perfect instrument.
Young Evaluator:	I seek an instrument that is valid and reliable in all evaluation situations, that can be used to evaluate all projects, all programs, all impacts, all benefits, all people. . . . I am seeking an evaluation tool that *anyone* can use to evaluate *anything*.
Halcolm:	What would be the value of such an instrument?
Young Evaluator:	Free of any errors, it would rid evaluation of politics and make evaluation truly scientific. It would save money, time, and frustration. We'd finally be able to get at the truth about programs.
Halcolm:	Where would you use such an instrument?
Young Evaluator:	Everywhere!

Halcolm:	With whom would you use it?
Young Evaluator:	Everyone!
Halcolm:	What, then, would become of the process of designing situationally specific evaluations?
Young Evaluator:	Who needs it?
Halcolm:	[Silence]
Young Evaluator:	Just help me focus. Am I on the right path, asking the most important questions?
Halcolm:	[Silence]
Young Evaluator:	What do I need to do to get an answer?
Halcolm:	[Silence]
Young Evaluator:	What's the use?
Halcolm:	[Silence]
Young Evaluator:	What methods can I use to find out what I want to know?
Halcolm:	What is universal in evaluation is not a secret. Your last five questions reveal that you already have what you seek in the very asking of those questions.

14

Power, Politics, and Ethics

theory of evaluation must be as much a theory of political interaction as it is a theory of how to determine facts.

—Lee J. Cronbach and Associates (1980:3)

Politics and Evaluation: A Case Example

During the mid-1970s, the Kalamazoo Education Association (KEA) in Michigan was locked in battle with the local school administration over the Kalamazoo Schools Accountability System. The accountability system consisted of 13 components, including teacher and principal performance, fall and spring standardized testing, teacher-constructed criterion-referenced tests in high school, teacher peer evaluations, and parent, student, and principal evaluations of teachers. The system had received considerable national attention, as when *The American School Board Journal* (in April 1974) editorialized that Kalamazoo Schools had designed "one of the most comprehensive computerized systems of personnel evaluation and accountability yet devised" (p. 40).

Yet, conflict enveloped the system as charges and countercharges were exchanged. The KEA, for example, charged that teachers were being demoralized; the superintendent responded that teachers didn't want to be accountable. The KEA claimed widespread teacher dissatisfaction; the superintendent countered that the hostility to the system came largely from a vocal minority of malcontent unionists. The newspapers hinted that the administration might be so alienating teachers that the system could not operate effectively. School board members, facing reelection, were nervous.

Ordinarily, a situation of this kind would continue to be one of charge and countercharge based entirely on selective perception, with no underlying data to clarify and test the reality of the opposing positions. But the KEA sought outside assistance from Vito Perrone, Dean of the Center for Teaching and Learning, University of North Dakota, who had a reputation for fairness and integrity. The KEA proposed that Dean Perrone conduct public hearings at which interested parties could testify on and be questioned about the operations and consequences of the Kalamazoo Accountability System. Perrone suggested that such a public forum might become a political circus; moreover, he was concerned that a fair and representative picture of the system could not be developed in such an openly polemical and adversarial forum. He suggested instead that a survey of teachers be conducted to describe their experiences with the accountability system and to collect a representative overview of teacher opinions about their experiences.

Perrone attempted to negotiate the nature of the accountability review with the superintendent of schools, but the administration refused to cooperate, arguing that the survey should be postponed until after the school board election when everyone could reflect more calmly on the situation. Perrone decided to go forward, believing that the issues were already politicized and that data were needed to inform public debate. The evaluation was limited to providing a review of the accountability program *from the perspective of teachers* based on a mail survey conducted independently by the Minnesota Center for Social Research (which is how I became involved). The evaluation staff of the school system previewed the survey instrument and contributed wording changes.

The results revealed intense teacher hostility toward and fear of the accountability system. Of the respondents, 93% believed that "accountability as practiced in Kalamazoo creates an undesirable atmosphere of anxiety among teachers," 90% asserted that "the accountability system is mostly a public relations effort," and 83% rated the "overall accountability system in Kalamazoo" either "poor" or "totally inadequate."

The full analysis of the data, including teachers' open-ended comments, suggested that the underlying problem was a hostile teacher-administration relationship created by the way in which the accountability system was developed (without teacher input) and implemented (forced on teachers from above). The data also documented serious misuse of standardized tests in Kalamazoo. The school board, initially skeptical of the survey, devoted a full meeting to discussion of the report.

The subsequent election eroded the school administration's support, and the superintendent resigned. The new superintendent and school board used the survey results as a basis for starting fresh with teachers. A year later, the KEA officials reported a new environment of teacher-administration cooperation in developing a mutually acceptable accountability system.

The evaluation report was only one of many factors that came into play in Kalamazoo at that time, but the results answered questions about the scope and nature of teachers' perspectives. Candidates for the position of superintendent called Dean Perrone to discuss the report. It became part of the political context within which administration-teacher relations developed throughout the following school year—information that had to be taken into account. The evaluation findings were used by teacher association officials to enhance their political position and increase their input into the accountability system.

The Political Nature of Evaluation

Scientists become uneasy when one group pushes a set of findings to further its own political purposes, as happened in Kalamazoo. They much prefer that the data serve all parties equally in a civilized search for the best answer. Research and experience suggest, however, that the Kalamazoo case, in which use was conditioned by political considerations, is quite common. In our study of how federal health evaluations were used, we found that use was affected by intra- and interagency rivalries, budgetary fights with the Office of Management and Budget and Congress, power struggles between Washington administrators and local program personnel, and internal debates about the purposes or accomplishments of pet programs. Budgetary battles seemed to be the most political, followed by turf battles over who had the power to act, but **political considerations intruded in some way into every evaluation we examined.**

The Program Evaluation Standards acknowledge the political nature of evaluation and offer guidance for making evaluations politically viable:

> The evaluation should be planned and conducted with anticipation of the different positions of various interest groups, so that their cooperation may be obtained, and so that possible attempts by any of these groups to curtail evaluation operations or to bias or misapply the results can be averted or counteracted. (Joint Committee 1994:F2)

A political perspective also informs the Guiding Principles of the American Evaluation Association (AEA Task Force 1995) as they address the "Responsibilities for General and Public Welfare: Evaluators should articulate and take into account the diversity of interests and values that may be related to the general and public welfare" (p. 20). This principle mandates a political responsibility that goes well beyond just collecting and reporting data.

Meeting the standard on political viability and the principle of general responsibility will necessitate some way of astutely identifying various stakeholders and their interests. *Stakeholder mapping* (Bryson and Crosby 1992:377-79) can be helpful in this regard. Exhibit 14.1 offers one kind of matrix for use in mapping stakeholders according to their initial inclination toward the program being evaluated (support, opposition, or neutrality) and how much they have at stake in the evaluation's outcome (a high stake, a moderate stake, or little stake).

Evaluation's Coming of Age: Beyond Political Innocence and Naivete

The article most often credited with raising evaluators' consciousness about the politics of evaluation was Carol Weiss's 1973 analysis of "Where Politics and Evaluation Research Meet." Reprinted 20 years later in *Evaluation Practice*, in recognition of its status as a classic, the article identified three major ways in which politics intrude in evaluation: (1) Programs and policies are "creatures of political decisions" so evaluations implicitly judge those decisions; (2) evaluations feed political decision making and compete with other perspectives in the political process; and (3) evaluation is inherently political by its very nature because of the issues it addresses and the conclusions it reaches. Weiss ([1973] 1993) concluded:

EXHIBIT 14.1
Mapping Stakeholders' Stakes

	Estimate of Various Stakeholders' Initial Inclination Toward the Program		
How high are the stakes for various primary stakeholders? ↓	*Favorable*	*Neutral or Unknown*	*Antagonistic*
High			
Moderate			
Low			

> Knowing that political constraints and resistances exist is not a reason for abandoning evaluation research; rather it is a precondition for useable evaluation research. Only when the evaluator has insight into the interests and motivations of other actors in the system, into the roles that he himself is consciously or inadvertently playing, the obstacles and opportunities that impinge upon the evaluative effort, and the limitations and possibilities for putting the results to work—only with sensitivity to the politics of evaluation research—can the evaluator be as creative and strategically useful as he should be. (p. 94)

Weiss showed that politics and use are joined at the hip. In this classic analysis, she made use directly contingent on the political sophistication of evaluators. How, then, can utilization-focused evaluators become politically sophisticated? The first step comes with being able to recognize what is political.

Often, in our interviews with evaluators about how federal health evaluations had been used, we found them uneasy about discussing the tensions between their research and politics; they were hesitant to acknowledge the ways in which the evaluation was affected by political considerations. We found that many evaluators disassociated themselves from the political side of evaluation, despite evidence throughout their interviews that they were enmeshed in politics. One interviewee, a research scientist with 12 years experience doing federal evaluations, described pressure from Congress to accelerate the evaluation, then added, "We really had no knowledge or feeling about political relationships. We are quite innocent on such matters. We may not have recognized [political factors]. We're researchers" [EV5:7].

In another case, the decision maker stated the evaluation was never used because program funding had already been terminated before the evaluation was completed. When asked about this in a later interview the evaluator replied, "I wasn't aware that the program was under any serious threat. Political matters related to the evaluation did not come up with us. It was not discussed to my recollection before, during, or after the study" [EV97: 12-13].

Part of evaluators' innocence or ignorance about political processes stemmed from a definition of politics that included only happenings of momentous consequences. Evaluators frequently answered our questions about political considerations only in terms of the overall climate of presidential or congressional politics and campaigns. They didn't define the day-to-day negotiations out of which programs and studies evolve as politics. One evaluator explained that no political considerations affected the study because "this was not a global kind of issue. There were vested interests all right, but it was not what would be considered a hot issue. Nobody was going to resign over whether there was this program or not" [EV145:12].

Failing to recognize that an issue involves power and politics reduces an evaluator's strategic options and increases the likelihood that the evaluator will be used unwittingly as some stakeholder's political puppet. It is instructive to look at cases in which the evaluators we interviewed described their work as nonpolitical. Consider, for example, the responses of an academic researcher who studied citizen boards of community mental health programs. At various points in the interview, he objected to the term *evaluation* and explained that he had conducted "basic research," not an evaluation, thus the nonpolitical nature of his work; this despite the fact that the study was classified by the funding agency as an evaluation and was used to make policy decisions about the processes studied. He was adamant throughout the interview that no political considerations or factors affected the study or its use in any way. He explained that he had demanded and received absolute autonomy so that no external political pressures could be brought to bear. In his mind, his work exemplified nonpolitical academic research. Consider, then, responses he gave to other questions.

Item: When asked how the study began, the evaluator admitted using personal connections to get funding for the project:

> We got in touch with some people [at the agency] and they were rather intrigued by this. . . . It came at year's end and, as usual, they had some funds left over. . . . I'm pretty certain we were not competing with other groups; they felt a sole bid kind of thing wasn't going to get other people angry. [EV4:1, 5-6]

Item: The purpose of the study?

> We were wondering about conflict patterns in citizen boards. At that time, the funding agency was concerned because many of their centers were in high-density ghetto areas, not only cutting across the black population, but with Mexican Americans or Puerto Ricans thrown in. Up until the time of the study, many agencies' boards were pretty middle-class. Now, you put in "poor people" and minorities—how is that going to work? Is that going to disturb the system as far as the middle-class people were concerned? Of course, some of them were pretty conservative, and they were afraid that we were rocking the boat by looking at this. [EV4:4]

Item: The study presented recommendations about how citizen boards should be organized and better integrated into programs, matters of considerable controversy.

Item: The results were used to formulate agency policy and, eventually, Congressional legislation.

> We kept people talking about citizen participation—What does it truly mean? You see, that generated a lot of thinking. [EV4:14]

Item: How did the results get disseminated?

> We released the results in a report. Now, the fascinating thing, like throwing a pebble in a pond, [was that] *Psychology Today* picked up this report and wrote a glowing little review. . . ; then they made some nasty comments about the cost of government research. [EV4:10-11]

Item: The researcher recounted a lengthy story about how a member of nationally visible consumer advocate Ralph Nader's staff got hold of the study, figured out the identity of local centers in the study's sample, and wrote a separate report. The researcher and his colleagues engaged lawyers but were unable to stop Nader's staff from using and abusing their data and sources, some of whom were identified incorrectly.

> We just didn't have the money to fight them, so we were furious. We thought that we would go to our lawyer friends and see if they couldn't do something, but they all came back with pretty much the same kind of negative response. What finally happened was that when [Nader's] big report came out, using our stuff, they gave it to the *New York Times* and various newspapers. [EV4:11-12]

Item: After the study, the researchers were involved in several regional and national meetings about their findings.

> We go to an enormous number of meetings. And so we talked . . . and we've become known in a limited circle as "the experts in this sort of thing." [EV4:20]

At one such meeting, the researcher became involved in an argument with local medical staff.

> The doctors and more middle-class people in mental health work said we were just making too much of a fuss, that things were really going along pretty well. And I remember distinctly in that room, which must have had 200 people that day, the blacks and some of the—you might call them militant liberals—were whispering to each other and I began to feel the tension and bickerings that were going on. [EV4:19]

Politics by Any Other Name

The researcher who conducted this study—a study of class and race conflict on mental health citizen boards that judged the effectiveness of such boards and included recommendations for improving their functioning—insisted that his work was nonpolitical academic research, not an evaluation. Yet, he revealed, by his own testimony, that personal influence was used to get funding. The research question was conceived in highly value-laden terms: *middle-class boards* versus *poor people's boards*. Concerns emerged about "rocking the boat." The study's controversial findings and recommendations were cited in national publications and used in policy formulation. The researchers became expert advocates for a certain view of citizen participation. **Personal contacts, value-laden definitions, rocking the boat, controversial recommendations, taking sides, defending positions—of such things are politics made.**

Sources of Evaluation's Political Inherency

The political nature of evaluation stems from several factors:

1. The fact that people are involved in evaluation means that the values, perceptions, and politics of everyone involved (scientists, decision makers, funders, program staff) impinge on the process from start to finish.

2. The fact that evaluation requires classifying and categorizing makes it political. Categories inevitably filter the data collected. One of the more politically sophisticated evaluators we interviewed described the politics of categories:

> Our decision to compare urban and rural reflected the politics of the time—concerns that city problems are different from rural problems. Since this was a national program, we couldn't concentrate solely on problems in the city and not pay any attention to rural areas. That wouldn't have been politically smart.
>
> And then our decision to report the percent nonwhite with mental illness, that certainly reflects attention to the whole political and socioeconomic distribution of the population. In that we used factors important in the politics of the nation, to that extent we were very much influenced by political considerations. We tried to reflect the political, social, and economic problems we thought were important at the time. [EV12:7-8]

3. The fact that empirical data undergird evaluation makes it political because data always require interpretation. Interpretation is only partly logical and deductive; it's also value laden and perspective dependent.

4. The fact that actions and decisions follow from evaluation makes it political.

5. The fact that programs and organizations are involved makes evaluation political. Organizations allocate power, status, and resources. Evaluation affects those allocation processes.

One of the weapons employed in organizational conflicts is evaluative information and judgments.

6. The fact that information is involved in evaluation makes it political. Information leads to knowledge; knowledge reduces uncertainty; reduction of uncertainty facilitates action; and action is necessary to the accumulation of power.

> Decision making, of course, is a euphemism for the allocation of resources—money, position, authority, etc. Thus, to the extent that information is an instrument, basis, or excuse for changing power relationships within or among institutions, evaluation is a political activity. (Cohen 1970:214)

The "Is" and the "Ought" of Evaluation Politics

We have not been discussing if evaluation should be political. The evidence indicates that whether researchers like it or not, evaluation will be influenced by political factors. The degree of politicalization varies, but it is never entirely absent. One astute decision maker we interviewed had made his peace with the inevitability of politics in evaluation as follows:

> [Government decision making] is not rational in the sense that a good scientific study would allow you to sit down and plan everybody's life. And I'm glad it's not because I would get very tired, very early, of something that ran only by the numbers. Somebody'd forget part of the numbers. So, I'm not fighting the system. But you do have to be careful what you expect from a rational study when you insert it into the system. It can have tremendous impact, but it's a political, not a rational process. . . . Life is not a very simple thing. [DM328:18-19]

In our interviews, evaluators tended to portray their findings as rational and objective while other inputs into the decision-making process were subjective and political. One evaluator lamented that his study wasn't used because "politics outweighed our results" [EV131:8]. Such a dichotomy between evaluation and politics fails to recognize the political and power-laden nature of evaluative information.

The Power of Evaluation

In this section, I want to briefly review a theory of power that I have found instructive in helping me appreciate what evaluation offers stakeholders and intended users. Understanding this has helped me explain to intended users how and why their involvement in a utilization-focused evaluation is in their own best interest. It provides a basis for understanding how knowledge is power.

Use of evaluation will occur in direct proportion to its power-enhancing capability. Power-enhancing capability is determined as follows: **The power of evaluation varies directly with the degree to which the findings reduce the uncertainty of action for specific stakeholders.**

This view of the relationship between evaluation and power is derived from the classic organizational theories of Michael Crozier (1964) and James Thompson (1967). Crozier studied and compared a French clerical agency and tobacco factory. He found that power relationships developed around uncertainties. Every group tried to limit its dependence on others and, correspondingly, enlarge its own areas of discretion. They did this by making their own behavior unpredictable in relation to other groups. Interpreting what he found, Crozier drew on Robert Dahl's (1957) definition of power: "The power of a person A over a person B is the ability of A to obtain that B do something he would not otherwise have done." Systems attempt to limit conflicts over power through rationally designed and highly routinized structures, norms, and tasks. Crozier (1964) found, however, that even in a highly centralized, routinized, and bureaucratic organization, it was impossible to eliminate uncertainties.

> In such a context, the power of A over B depends on A's ability to predict B's behavior and on the uncertainty of B about A's behavior. As long as the requirements of action create situations of uncertainty, the individuals who have to face them have power over those who are affected by the results of their choice. (p. 158)

Crozier (1964) found that supervisors in the clerical agency had no interest in passing information on to their superiors, the section chiefs. Section chiefs, in turn, competed with one another for attention from their superior—the division head. Section chiefs distorted the information they passed up to the division head to enhance their own positions. Section chiefs could get away with distortions because the lower-level supervisors, who knew the truth, were interested in keeping what they knew to themselves. The division head, on the other hand, used the information he received to schedule production and assign work. Knowing that he was dependent on information from others, and not being able to fully trust that information, his decisions were carefully conservative in the sense that he aimed only at safe, minimal levels of achievement because he knew he lacked sufficient information to narrow risks.

> The power of prediction stems to a major extent from the way information is distributed. The whole system of roles is so arranged that people are given information, the possibility of prediction and therefore control, precisely because of their position within the hierarchical pattern. (p. 158)

Whereas Crozier's analysis centered on power relationships and uncertainties between individuals and among groups within organizations, James Thompson (1967) found that a similar set of concepts could be applied to understand relationships between whole organizations. He argued that organizations are open systems that need resources and materials from outside, and that "with this conception the central problem for complex organizations is one of coping with uncertainty" (p. 13). He found that assessment and evaluation are used by organizations as mechanisms for reducing uncertainty and enhancing their control over the multitude of contingencies with which they are faced. They evaluate themselves to assess their fitness for the future, and they evaluate the effectiveness of other organizations to increase their control over the maintenance of crucial exchange relationships. **Information for prediction is information for control: thus the power of evaluation.**

The Kalamazoo Schools Accountability System case example with which this chapter opened offers a good illustration of evaluation's role in reducing uncertainty and, thereby, enhancing power. The accountability system was initiated, in part, to control teachers. Teachers' hostility to the system led to uncertainty concerning the superintendent's ability to manage. The superintendent tried to stop the study that would establish the degree to which teacher opposition was widespread and crystallized. The board members let the study proceed because, as politicians, they deplored uncertainty. Once the study confirmed widespread teacher opposition, union officials used the results to force the superintendent's resignation, mobilize public opinion, and gain influence in the new administration. In particular, teachers won the right to participate in developing the system that would be used to evaluate them. The Kalamazoo evaluation represents precisely the kind of political enterprise that Cohen (1970) has argued characterizes evaluation research: "To evaluate a social action program is to establish an information system in which the main questions involve the allocation of power, status, and other public goods" (p. 232).

Limits on Knowledge as Power

A perspective contrary to the notion that knowledge is power has been articulated by L. J. Sharpe (1977). In pondering how social scientists came to overestimate their potential influence on government decision making, he concluded that

> One important cause of this overoptimism is the widespread assumption that governments are always in need of, or actively seek, information. But it seems doubtful whether this is the case. It is more likely that government has too much information, not too little—too much, that is, by its own estimation. (p. 44)

Having information, Sharpe argued, delays and complicates government decision making. He cited distinguished British economist John Maynard Keynes (1883-1946) in support of the proposition that information avoidance is a central feature of government: "There is nothing a government hates more than to be well-informed; for it makes the process of arriving at decisions more complicated and difficult" (quoted in Sharpe 1977:44).

The perspectives of Keynes and Sharpe demonstrate the necessity of limiting the generalization that knowledge is power. Four qualifiers on this maxim derive from the premises of utilization-focused evaluation.

Political Maxims for Utilization-Focused Evaluators

1. *Not All Information Is Useful*

To be power laden, information must be relevant and in a form that is understandable to users. Crozier (1964) recognized this qualifier in linking power to reduced uncertainty: "One should be precise and specify *relevant* uncertainty. . . . People and organizations will care only about what they can recognize as affecting them and, in turn, what is possibly within their control" (p. 158).

Government, in the abstract, may well have too much irrelevant, trivial, and useless information, but individual stakeholders will tell you that they are always open to timely, relevant, and accurate information that can reduce uncertainty and increase their control.

2. *Not All People Are Information Users*

Individuals vary in their aptitude for handling uncertainty and their ability to exercise discretion. Differential socialization, education, and experience magnify such differences. In the political practice of evaluation, this means that information is power only in the hands (minds) of people who know to use it and are open to using it. The challenge of use remains one of matching: **getting the right information to the right people.**

One evaluator in our use study insisted on this point. Drawing on 35 years in government, 20 of those years directly involved in research and evaluation, and several years as a private evaluation contractor on some 80 projects, he opined that good managers are anxious to get useful information. In fact, they're hungry for it. The good manager "is interested in finding out what your views are, not defending his. . . . You know my sample is relatively small, but I'd say probably there are a quarter (25%) of what I'd call good managers" [EV346: 15]. **These, he believed, were the people who use evaluation.**

What of people who are not inclined to use information—people who are intimidated by, indifferent to, or even hostile to evaluation? A utilization-focused evaluator looks for opportunities and strategies for creating and training information users. Thus, the challenge of increasing use consists of two parts: (1) finding and involving those who are, by inclination, information users and (2) training those not so inclined. Just as in cards you play the hand you're dealt, in evaluation, you sometimes have to play the stakeholders you're dealt.

It's helpful is this regard to consider the 20-50-30 rule proffered by organizational change specialist Price Pritchett (1996). He estimates that 20% of people are change-friendly; another 50% are fence-sitters waiting to see which way the wind blows; and the remaining 30% are resisters. He counsels wooing the fence-sitters rather than the resisters while devoting generous attention to supporters of the process. "You must be willing to let squeaky wheels squeak. Save your grease for the quieter wheels that are carrying the load" (p. 4). Such political calculations undergird any change effort, and evaluation inherently holds the potential for change.

3. *Information Targeted at Use Is More Likely to Hit the Target*

It's difficult knowing in advance of a decision precisely what information will be most valuable. In the battle for control over uncertainty, one thing is certain—no one wants to be caught with less information than competitors for power. This fear leads to a lot of information being collected "just in case." One evaluator we interviewed explained the entire function of his office in these terms:

> I wouldn't want to be quoted by name, but there was a real question whether we were asked for these reports because they wanted them for decision making. We felt that the five-foot shelf we were turning out may have had no particular relevance to the real world. . . . But, this operation made it impossible for some Congressmen, or someone, to say that the issue had never been studied. Therefore, it would be a fairly standard administration ploy to study the issue so that it was not possible for somebody to insist you never even looked at the issue. [EV152:18]

Such a "just in case" approach to gathering data wastes scarce evaluation resources and fills shelves with neglected studies. It's impossible to study every possible future contingency. Utilization-focused evaluation requires a focus on real issues with real time lines aimed at real decisions—the opposite of "just in case" evaluation. In that way, utilization-focused evaluation aims at closing the gap between potential and actual use, between knowledge and action. Targeting an evaluation at intended use by intended users increases the odds of hitting the target.

4. *Only Credible Information Is Ultimately Powerful*

Eleanor Chelimsky, one of the profession's most experienced and successful evaluators in dealing with Congress, has reiterated at every opportunity that the foundation of evaluation use is credibility—not just information, but *credible* information. "Whether the issue is fairness, balance, methodological quality, or accuracy, no effort to establish credibility is ever wasted. The memory of poor quality lingers long" (Chelimsky 1987a:14).

Independent audits of evaluation quality offer one strategy for dealing with what Thomas Schwandt (1989a) called "the politics of verifying trustworthiness." The Program Evaluation Standards, in calling for *meta-evaluation* (Joint Committee 1994:A12; Schwandt and Halpern 1988) articulate an obligation to provide stake-

EXHIBIT 14.2
When Is Evaluation Not Political?

In 1988, my duties as President of the American Evaluation Association included posing a "Presidential Problem" to the membership, a tradition begun by Michael Scriven. The theme of the annual national meeting that year was The Politics of Evaluation. The problem I posed was: What is and is not politics in evaluation, and by what criteria does one judge the difference?

The winning entry from Robin Turpin (1989) asserted that "politics has a nasty habit of sneaking into all aspects of evaluation" (p. 55). All the other entries took essentially the same position; politics is omnipresent in evaluation.

This anonymous entry, my personal favorite, was unequivocal.

Evaluation is NOT political under the following conditions:

- No one cares about the program.
- No one knows about the program.
- No money is at stake.
- No power or authority is at stake.
- And, no one in the program, making decisions about the program, or otherwise involved in, knowledgeable about, or attached to the program, is sexually active.

holders with an independent assessment of an evaluation's strengths and weaknesses to guide stakeholders in judging an evaluation. Evaluation audits and meta-evaluation ensure evaluation credibility to users in the same way that independent financial audits ensure the credibility of profit reports to business investors. From a practical perspective, however, not every evaluation effort merits the resources required for full meta-evaluation. I would propose the following practical guideline: **The more politicized the context in which an evaluation is conducted and the more visible an evaluation will be in that politicized environment, the more important to credibility will be an independent assessment of evaluation quality.** This amounts to a form of matching in which safeguards of evaluation credibility are designed to anticipate and counter specific political intrusions within particular political environments. Political sophistication requires situational responsiveness. For guidance on how to anticipate the possible intrusion of politics into evaluation, see Exhibit 14.2.

The Political Foundations of Organizing Stakeholders Into an Evaluation Task Force

Where possible and practical, an evaluation task force can be organized to make major decisions about the focus, methods, and purpose of the evaluation. The task force is a vehicle for actively involving key stakeholders in the evaluation. Moreover, the very processes involved in making decisions about an evaluation will typically increase stakeholders' commitment to use results while also increasing their knowledge about evaluation, their sophistication in conducting evaluations, and their ability to interpret findings. The task force allows the evaluator to share responsibility for decision making by providing a forum for the political and practical perspectives that best come from those stakeholders who will ultimately be involved in using the evaluation.

Several things can be accomplished with a group or evaluation task force that are less likely to occur with individuals, assuming that participants are willing and the group is well facilitated.

1. An environment of openness can be established to reduce suspicions and fears about the evaluation. The key stakeholders who participate in the process know how decisions are made and who was involved in making them. This can reduce political paranoia.
2. Participants in the process become sensitized to the multiple perspectives that exist around any program. Their views are broadened as they are exposed to the varying agendas of people with different concerns. This increases the possibility of conducting an evaluation that is respectful of and responsive to different interests and values.
3. New ideas often emerge out of the dynamics of group interaction.
4. A sense of shared responsibility for the evaluation can be engendered that is often greater than the responsibility that would be felt by isolated individuals. Commitments made in groups, in front of others, are typically more lasting and serious than promises made to an evaluator in private.
5. An open forum composed of various stakeholders makes it difficult to suppress touchy questions or negative findings. Issues get raised and findings get publicized that otherwise might never see the light of day.
6. The evaluator has an opportunity to observe firsthand the interactions among various stakeholders and assess their interpersonal relationships. This can be very helpful in developing use strategies.
7. Momentum can be built through group processes that helps reduce delays or counter roadblocks resulting from the attitudes or actions of one person.
8. The evaluator(s) and stakeholders in a group process will often jell so that it's not the evaluator against the world. The other stakeholders share responsibility and ownership.
9. The group may continue to function after the evaluation is completed. Participants can develop a shared commitment to follow through on recommendations. After all, in most cases the evaluator is present for only a limited period. Stakeholders stay with the program after the evaluation is over. A task force can become a repository for evaluation knowledge and carry forward an appreciation of evaluation processes.
10. Groups, acting in concert, have more power than individuals.

Of course, all of these positive outcomes of group dynamics assume an effective group process. Success depends on: (1) who participates in that process and (2) the questions dealt with by the group, that is, the focus and quality of the process. Any group rapidly becomes greater than the sum of its parts. Bringing together a group of incompetents seems to increase geometrically the capacity for incompetent and misguided action. On the other hand, a group of competent, politically sensitive, and thoughtful people can create something that is more useful than any of them individually might have created. Shared decision making may mean compromise; it can also mean powerful chain reactions leading to increased energy and commitment, especially commitment to use evaluation findings in which group members have increased their "stake" through involvement in the evaluation decision-making process.

Political Considerations in Forming an Evaluation Task Force

Several criteria are important in forming an evaluation task force. Not all of these criteria can be met to the same degree in every case, but it is helpful to have in mind a basic framework for the composition of the group.

1. The members of the task force should represent the various groups and constituencies that have an interest and stake in the evaluation findings and their use, including the interests of program participants.
2. The task force members should either be people who have authority and power to use evaluation findings in decision making, or to influence others who do have such power and authority. Again, this includes representatives of the program's clients, who may be powerless as anonymous individuals but whose interests can be organized and taken into consideration for evaluation purposes.
3. The task force members should believe that the evaluation is worth doing.
4. The task force members should care how the results are used.
5. The task force members should be willing to make a firm commitment of time, including a commitment to attend all of the evaluation task force meetings. One of the common problems in working with an evaluation task force is having different people show up at different meetings. With inconsistent attendance, the process never really moves forward.

The composition and size of a task force is limited for practical reasons. Not every stakeholder can or should participate, though an attempt should be made to represent all major stakeholder constituencies and points of view. The evaluator should be fair, but practical, in working with program administrators, funders, clients, program staff, and public officials to establish a task force (and imbue it with the necessary authority to make decisions). In this regard, I find the advice of Guba and Lincoln (1981) to be impractical when they assert that "it is unethical for the evaluator . . . to fail to interact with any known audience in the search for concerns and issues." They direct the evaluator to address "the broadest possible array of persons interested in or affected by the evaluand [thing being evaluated, e.g., the program], including audiences that are unaware of the stakes they hold" (p. 37). While evaluators need to take care that the interests of program clients and the powerless are represented, there are practical limits to identification and organization of decision makers and information users. Fairness and a healthy regard for pluralism are guiding lights in this regard.

Chairing the Task Force

I prefer to have one of the task force participants act as chair of the group. The chair's responsibility is to convene meetings, see that agendas for meetings are followed, and keep discussions on the topic at hand. Having a stakeholder chair the task force helps symbolize the responsibility and authority of the group. The evaluator is a consultant to the group and is paid to do the nitty-gritty staff work for the evaluation, but the task force should assume responsibility for the overall direction of the process. As facilitator, trainer, and collaborator, the evaluator will command a good deal of floor time in task force sessions. However, an effective evaluator can accomplish everything needed by working with the chair, rather than being the chair.

Making the Process Work

Major stakeholders on an evaluation task force are likely to be busy people whose time constraints must be respected. The evaluator must be able to help focus the activities of the group so that time is used well, necessary decisions get made, and participants do not become frustrated with a meandering and ambiguous process. Minimize time spent on decisions about the group process and maximize the time spent on decisions about substantive evaluation issues. What follows is a description of a bare-bones process.

At a minimum, I expect to hold four two-hour meetings with the task force.

1. **Focus/conceptualization session.** The first meeting should establish the focus of the evaluation. The group considers alternative questions, issues, problems, and goals to decide the purpose and direction of evaluation.

2. **Methods and measurement options.** The second meeting considers different ways of conducting the evaluation, given the focus determined in the first meeting. The evaluator presents varying kinds of measurement approaches and different designs that might be used. Time considerations and intended uses are clarified so that methods can be selected that are manageable, credible, and practical. Issues of validity, reliability, generalizability, and appropriateness are also discussed in ways that are understandable and meaningful.

3. **Design and instrument review.** Between the second and third meetings the evaluator will design the instruments to be used and write a concrete methods proposal specifying units of analysis, control or comparison groups to be studied, sampling approaches and sample size, and the overall data collection strategy. In reviewing the proposed design and instruments, the task force members should understand what will be done and what will not be done, what findings can be generated and what findings cannot be generated, and what questions will be asked and what will not be asked. The third meeting will usually involve some changes in instrumentation —additions, deletions, revisions—and adjustments in the design. Basically, this meeting is aimed at providing final input into the research methods before data collection begins. The evaluator leaves the meeting with a clear mandate to begin data collection.

The third meeting is also a good time to do a mock use exercise in which task force members consider specifically how various kinds of findings might be used, given simulated results. If we get these answers to this question, what would that mean? What would we do with those results?

4. **Data interpretation session.** The fourth and final meeting in this minimum scenario focuses on data analysis, interpretation, judgment, and recommendations. The evaluator will have arranged the data

so that the task force members can understand and interpret the results.

Variations on a Political Theme

The bare-bones scenario of four focused meetings with primary intended users illustrates the minimum commitment (eight hours) one needs from busy stakeholders. Large-scale, complex evaluations with many stakeholders may involve more face-to-face sessions and different kinds of interactions. For example, in Chapter 12, I described a data interpretation session that involved some 200 criminal justice system stakeholders. Thus, the four-session outline above is *not* a recipe, but rather a beginning framework for thinking politically and instrumentally about how to make the stakeholder involvement process meaningful and practical.

Political Rules in Support of Use

The degree to which an evaluation becomes caught up in destructive power politics can be mitigated by savvy evaluators. By recognizing the inherently political nature of evaluation, evaluators can enter the political fray as power players in a game where the rules are subject to manipulation. The evaluator then works to negotiate rules in the power game that favor informed and intended use by intended users. Here are some rules of the power game that I find consistent with utilization-focused evaluation. These rules have been influenced by *Power: The Infinite Game* (Broom and Klein 1995) and adapted to fit evaluation.

1. **In working with stakeholders, seek to negotiate win/win scenarios.** For example, in an environment of controversy, with strong program advocates versus strong program adversaries, the evaluation question "Is the program effective?" frames a win/lose scenario. That is, the very way the question is posed—dichotomously—frames a win/lose scenario. In contrast, a strengths and weaknesses framing of the question focuses on learning and improvement rather than a good versus bad judgment: "For what kinds of participants under what conditions is the program most effective? And for whom is the program less effective?" Identifying strengths and acknowledging weaknesses is a win/win outcome. Forcing a judgment of effective/ineffective is a win/lose outcome.

2. **Help primary stakeholders avoid getting their egos attached to how the evaluation turns out.** When someone's ego or sense of esteem is at risk, the political stakes skyrocket. Emphasize the value of learning, regardless of what the results show, rather than being right or wrong. Help users derive ego strength from being astute information users rather than whether their a priori position is affirmed.

3. **Help users develop a long-term view of learning, improvement, and knowledge use.** Short-term "negative" results are less threatening when placed in a longer term context of ongoing development. If a short-term result becomes associated in a user's mind with ultimate success or failure, the stakes skyrocket, and the power games become potentially nastier.

4. **Create an environment of interpretation that values diverse perspectives.** Everyone doesn't have to reach the same

conclusion. Dialogue, discussion, and respect for differences enhance enlightenment. A focus on truth frames the results in a way that someone is right and someone else is wrong: again, win/lose instead of win/win.

5. **Seek to affirm and reaffirm that everyone is interested in what works best for intended beneficiaries.** Head off tendencies to lose sight of this high purpose when stakeholders are tempted to focus on power games such as who gains and loses resources or who gets credit or blame. Those issues are real and will need to be understood and negotiated, but within the context of a commitment to effectiveness. People do, in fact, respond to noble purposes—or can be forced to take such purposes into account even when pursuing their own selfish interests.

6. **Avoid getting entangled in group process rules, such as like Robert's Rules, or stifling voting procedures.** Seek consensus and shared ownership. Voting can lead to winners and losers. Consensus is inclusive of everyone. Of course, this isn't always possible. With large groups and cantankerous stakeholders, formal process rules and voting may become necessary, but I think it's worth striving for the ideal of operating by consensus.

7. **Diverge, then converge. Generate alternatives, then focus. Get diverse points of view, then prioritize.** Keep before the group that many possibilities exist. There's no single best approach or design. Utility and practicality are the order of the day, not rigid adherence to a preconceived notion of the best model. That's why this book has presented menus for the major decisions intended users must make.

8. **Keep in mind that what happens in a particular process aimed at making decisions for a specific evaluation has implications, not only for that evaluation, but for future evaluations.** Each evaluation process becomes part of one's evaluation legacy. Think long-term. The worst political abuses often occur in the name of short-term gain. Stay on the high road.

Fears of Political Co-optation

I encounter a lot of concern that in facilitating utilization-focused evaluation, the evaluator may become co-opted by stakeholders. How can evaluators maintain their integrity if they become involved in close, collaborative relationships with stakeholders? How does the evaluator take politics into account without becoming a political tool of only one partisan interest?

The nature of the relationship between evaluators and the people with whom they work is a complex and controversial one. On the one hand, evaluators are urged to maintain a respectful distance from the people they study to safeguard objectivity and minimize personal and political bias. On the other hand, the human relations perspective emphasizes that close, interpersonal contact is a necessary condition for building mutual understanding. Evaluators thus find themselves on the proverbial horns of a dilemma: Getting too close to decision makers may jeopardize scientific credibility; remaining distant may undermine use.

A program auditor at a workshop put the issue less delicately when he asked, "How can we get in bed with decision makers without losing our virginity?"

This is a fascinating and revealing metaphor, showing just how high the stakes can seem. The evaluator is portrayed as the innocent, the policymaker as the co-opting tempter planning a seduction. I once reported this metaphor to a group of policymakers who immediately reframed the question: How do we get in bed with evaluators without getting sadistically abused?" Different stakes, different fears.

Maintaining an Empirical Focus

One way to handle concerns about cooptation is to stay focused on evaluation's empirical foundation. In Chapter 2, I discussed the importance of and ways to engender a commitment to reality testing among intended users. The empirical basis of evaluation involves making assumptions and values explicit, testing the validity of assumptions and carefully examining a program to find out what is actually occurring. The integrity of an evaluation depends on its empirical orientation—that is, its commitment to systematic and credible data collection and reporting. Likewise, the integrity of an evaluation group process depends on helping participants adopt an empirical perspective. A commitment must be engendered to find out what is really happening, at least as nearly as one can, given the limitations of research methods and scarce resources. Engendering such commitment involves teaching and facilitating.

When stakeholders first begin discussing the purpose of an evaluation, they will often do so in nonempirical terms. "We want to prove the program's effectiveness." Proving effectiveness is a public relations job, not an evaluation task. This statement tells the evaluator about that person's attitude toward the program, and it indicates a need for diplomatically, sensitively, but determinedly, reorienting that stakeholder from a concern with public relations to a concern with learning about and documenting actual program activities and effects. The evaluator need not be frightened by such public relations statements. It's best to get such inclinations out in the open. Then the work begins of moving toward an empirical orientation.

Program Director: We want to prove the program's effectiveness.

Evaluator: What kind of information would do that?

Program Director: Information about how much people like the program.

Evaluator: Does everyone like the program?

Program Director: I think most everyone does.

Evaluator: Well, we could find out just how many do and how many don't. So there's a reasonable evaluation question: "What are participants' attitudes toward the program?" Later we'll need to get more specific about how to measure their attitudes, but first let's consider some other things we could find out. Assuming that some people don't like the program, what could be learned from them?

Program Director: I suppose we could find out what they don't like and why.

Evaluator: Would that kind of information be helpful in looking at the program, to find out about its strengths and weaknesses so that perhaps you could improve it in some ways? [This is a deliberately leading question, very hard to say "No" to.]

Program Director: Well, we know some of the reasons, but we can always learn more.

Evaluator: What other information would be helpful in studying the program to find out about its strengths and weaknesses? [Here the evaluator has carefully rephrased the original concern from "proving the program's effectiveness" to "finding out about the program's strengths and weaknesses."]

In this dialogue, the evaluator chips away at the program director's biased public relations perspective by carefully helping an empirical perspective emerge. At some point the evaluator may want to, or need to, address the public relations concern with a bit of a speech (or sermonette).

> I know you're concerned about proving the program's effectiveness. This is a natural concern. A major and common purpose of evaluation is to gather information so that judgments can be made about the value of a program. To what extent is it effective? To what extent is it worthwhile?
>
> If we only gathered and presented positive information, it would lack credibility. If you read a report that only says good things about a program, you figure something's been left out. In my experience, an evaluation has more credibility if it's balanced. No program is perfect. I've yet to see a program in which everyone was happy and all goals were achieved. You may find that it's more politically astute to study and report both strengths and weaknesses, and then show that you're serious about improving the program by presenting a strategy for dealing with areas of ineffectiveness. By so doing, you establish your credibility as serious program developers who can deal openly and effectively with inevitable difficulties.

Sometimes the opposite bias is the problem. Someone is determined to kill a program, to present only negative findings and to "prove" that the program is ineffective. In such cases, the evaluator can emphasize what can be learned by finding out about the program's strengths. Few programs are complete disasters. An empirical approach means gathering data on *actual* program activities and effects and then presenting those data in a fair and balanced way so that information users and decision makers can make their own judgments about goodness or badness, effectiveness or ineffectiveness. Such judgments, however, are separate from the data. In my experience, evaluation task force members will readily move into this kind of empirical orientation as they come to understand its utility and fairness. It's the evaluator's job to help them adopt that perspective.

I don't want to imply that shifting to an empirical orientation occurs easily or as the result of a single interaction. Quite the contrary, the empirical orientation of evaluation requires ongoing reinforcement. Some stakeholders never make the shift. Others do so enthusiastically. The savvy evaluator will monitor the empirical orientation of intended users and, in an active-reactive-adaptive mode of situational responsiveness, take appropriate steps to keep the evaluation on an empirical and useful path.

Evaluation Misuse

Evaluation processes and findings can be misused in the search for political advantage. Alkin and Coyle (1988) have made a critical distinction between *misevaluation*, in which an evaluator performs poorly or fails to adhere to standards and principles, and *misuse*, in which users manipulate the evaluation in ways that distort the findings or corrupt the inquiry.

The profession has become increasingly concerned about problems of misuse (Stevens and Dial 1994), whether the source be politics (Palumbo 1994), asking of the wrong questions (Posavac 1994), pressures on internal evaluators (Duffy 1994; Mowbray 1994), petty self-interest (Dial 1994), or ideology (Vroom, Columbo, and Nahan 1994). One emergent theme of these inquiries is that misuse, like use, is ultimately situational. Consider, for example, an illustrative case from Alkin and Coyle (1988).

> An administrator blatantly squashes several negative evaluation reports to prevent the results from reaching the general public. On the surface, such an action appears to be a prime case of misutilization. Now, consider the same action (i.e., suppressing negative findings) in a situation where the reports were invalid due to poor data collection. . . . Thus, misutilization in one situation may be conceived of as appropriate non-use in another. (p. 3)

King (1982) has argued, I think reasonably, that intentional non-use of poorly conducted studies should be viewed as appropriate and responsible. What complicates this position is the different perspectives on what constitutes a quality evaluation, as, for example, in the debate about methods reviewed in Chapter 12.

I would share the following thoughts about misuse:

1. **Misuse is not at the opposite end of a continuum from use.** Two dimensions are needed to capture the complexities of real-world practice. One dimension is a continuum from non-use to use. A second is a continuum from non-use to misuse. (See Exhibit 14.3.) Studying or avoiding misuse is quite different from studying or facilitating use.

2. **Having conceptualized two separate dimensions, it is possible to explore the relationship between them.** Therefore, permit me the following proposition: **As use increases, misuse will also increase.** (See Exhibit 14.3.) It seems to me that when people ignore evaluations, they ignore their potential uses as well as abuses. As we successfully focus greater attention on evaluation data, and as we increase actual use, we can also expect there to be a corresponding increase in abuse, often within the same evaluation experience. Donald T. Campbell (1988) made a similar prediction in formulating "a discouraging law that seems to be emerging: *the more any social indicator is used for social decision making, the greater the corruption pressures upon it*" (p. 306; emphasis in original).

3. **Misuse can be either intentional or unintentional.** Unintentional misuse can be corrected through the processes aimed at increasing appropriate and proper use. Intentional misuse is an entirely different matter, which invites active intervention to correct whatever has been abused, either the evaluation process or findings. As with most problems, correcting misuse is more expensive than preventing it in the first place.

4. **Working with multiple users who understand and value an evaluation is one of the best preventatives against misuse.** Allies in use are allies against misuse. Indeed, I work to have intended users take so much

EXHIBIT 14.3
Relation of Use to Misuse

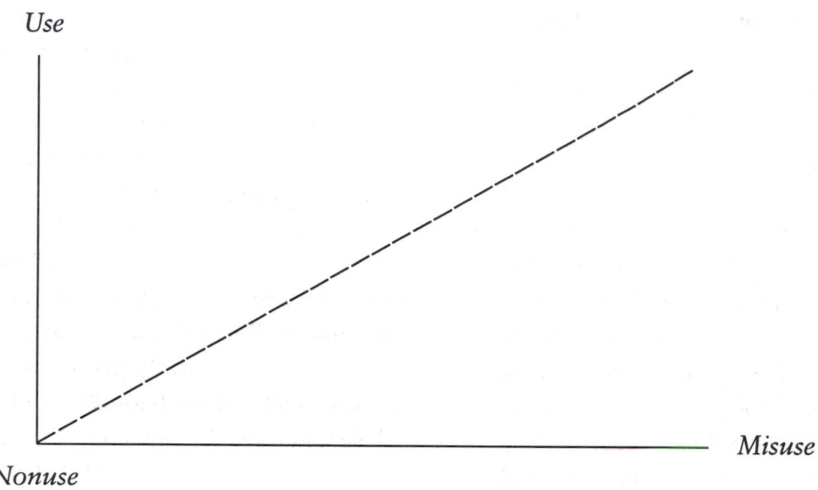

Hypothesis: **As use increases, misuse will also increase.**

ownership of the evaluation that they become the champions of appropriate use, the guardians against misuse, and the defenders of the evaluation's credibility when misuse occurs.

Policing misuse is sometimes beyond the evaluator's control, but what is always squarely within an evaluator's domain of direct responsibility and accountability is misevaluation: failures of conduct by the evaluator, which brings us to evaluation ethics.

Ethics of Being User-Focused

> *It is truly unethical to leave ethics out of program evaluation.*
>
> —Michael Scriven (1993:30)

> *Telling the truth to people who may not want to hear it is, after all, the chief purpose of evaluation.*
>
> —Eleanor Chelimsky (1995b:54)

Concern that utilization-focused evaluators may be co-opted by stakeholders, or become pawns in service of their political agendas, raises questions beyond how to be politically astute, strategic, and savvy, or how to prevent misuse. Underneath, decisions about one's relationships with intended users involve ethics. Speaking truth to power is risky—risky *business*. Not only is power involved, but money is involved. The Golden Rule of consulting is, "Know who has the gold." Evaluators work for paying clients. The jobs of internal evaluators depend on the pleasure of superiors, and future work for independent evaluators depends on client satisfaction. Thus, there's always the fear that "they who pay the piper call the tune," meaning not just determining the focus of the evaluation, but also prescribing the results. Evaluators can find themselves in conflict between their professional commitment to honest reporting and their personal interest in monetary gain or having future work. This conflict is so pervasive that Scriven (1991b) believes evaluation suffers from "General Positive Bias—a tendency to turn in more favorable results than are justified" (p. 174).

The quote below, also included at the end of Chapter 5, was aimed at empowerment evaluation, but the same concern is often expressed about any process of evaluation that involves close, responsive relationships between evaluators and clients.

> Anyone who has been in the evaluation business for very long knows that many potential clients are willing to pay much money for a "good, empowering evaluation," one that conveys the particular message, positive or negative, that the client/interest group hopes to present, irrespective of the data, or one that promotes constructive, ongoing, and nonthreatening group process. . . . Unfortunately, there are many persons who call themselves evaluators who would be glad to sell such service. (Stufflebeam 1994:325)

The Program Evaluation Standards provide general ethical guidance: Evaluation agreements should be in writing; rights of human subjects should be protected; evaluators should respect human dignity; assessments should be complete and fair; findings should be openly and fully disclosed; conflicts of interest should be dealt with openly and honestly; and sound fiscal procedures should be followed. The Propriety Standards "are intended to ensure that an evaluation will be conducted legally, ethically, and with due regard for the welfare of those involved in the evaluation, as well as those affected by the results" (Joint Committee 1994:P1-P8). Likewise, the "Guiding Principles" of the American Evaluation Association (1995) insist on integrity and honesty throughout the entire evaluation process, from initial negotiations with clients and stakeholders through reporting.

Newman and Brown (1996) have generated a framework for making ethical decisions in evaluation: (1) pay attention to one's intuition that something isn't quite right; (2) look for rules that provide guidance; (3) examine how the situation looks in terms of basic ethical principles: autonomy (rights involved), nonmaleficence (doing no harm), beneficence (doing good), justice (fairness), and fidelity (adhering to agreements); (4) examine your personal values—be in touch with your own beliefs and comfort levels; and (5) act, which can include consulting with colleagues, calculating trade-offs, and making and following a plan. They provide case problems, evaluation examples, and ethical challenges that illuminate how the framework can be applied in real situations.

Ethical Concerns Specific to Utilization-Focused Evaluation

The Program Evaluation Standards, the AEA Guiding Principles, the Newman/Brown Framework for Making Ethical Decisions, and a General Accounting Office (GAO 1996) report on the need for "continued vigilance" to protect human subjects provide general ethical guidance and make it clear that evaluators encounter all kinds of situations that require a strong grounding in ethics and may demand courage. Beyond general ethical sensitivity, however, the ethics of utilization-focused evaluators are most likely to be called into question around two essential aspects of utilization-focused evaluation: (1) limiting stakeholder involvement to primary intended users and (2) working closely with those users. The ethics of limiting and focusing stakeholder involvement concern who has access to the power of evaluation knowledge. The ethics of building close relationships concerns the integrity, neutrality, and corruptibility of the evaluator. Both of these concerns center on the fundamental ethical question: **Who does an evaluation —and an evaluator—serve?**

Consider the following exchange I had with Carol Weiss, who was arguing that findings must stand on their own rather than depend on interpersonal relationships, and Ernest House, who believes that evaluators are ethically obligated to consider the interests of the poorly educated or less powerful in society who are not in a position to advocate on their own behalf.

Carol Weiss: I think we limit ourselves too much if we think of interpersonal interaction as the critical component in utilization.

Michael Patton: From my perspective, I feel a great responsibility to serve my clients.

Ernest House: How far would you pursue this orientation? Surely you can't consider your only purpose to be meeting your client's interests?

Michael Patton: Tell me why I can't?

Ernest House: Why? It's an immoral position.

Michael Patton: I could argue. . . .

Ernest House: You can't. You can't. It would be a long argument which you'd lose.

Michael Patton: Let's go for it.

Ernest House: Who has the money to purchase evaluation? The most proper people in society. You would serve only the most proper people in society? You wouldn't condone that. . . . A doctor can't be concerned only with a particular patient and not concerned with the distribution of his or her services across society as a whole. . . . Medicine only for the richest? Surely you can't condone that kind of position. . . .

Michael Patton: What I am talking about is my responsibility to the specific set of people I work with, who will be different from case to case. What I take immediate responsibility for is what they do and the things that I do with them. I recognize that there's a broader set of things that are going to be of concern, but I can't take responsibility for all of what happens with that broader set of concerns.

Ernest House: Well, you must.

Michael Patton: But I can't.

Ernest House: Then you are immoral. Right? You'll back off that position. You cannot justify that position. You don't hold that position. I mean, you say it, but you can't hold it. . . . You have to have a concern that you're taking beyond the immediate welfare of the immediate client. I believe that you do that.

Michael Patton: I think I build that larger concern you're talking about into my interactions with that client. . . . There is a moral concern. There is a moral and value context that I bring to bear in that interaction with my clients.

Ernest House: You have to show concern for the rest of society. You can't just sell your services to whoever can purchase them. That would be an immoral position. . . . I say that you should be concerned about the interests of the less advantaged people in society. (Excerpted and edited from a transcription by Alkin 1990:101-105)

I've reproduced a portion of our discussion to offer a taste of its intensity. As the dialogue unfolded, three things were illuminated for me with regard to utilization-focused evaluation: (1) Evaluators need to be deliberative and intentional about their own moral groundings; (2) evaluators must exercise care, including ethical care, in selecting projects to work on and stakeholders to work with; and (3) evaluators must be clear about whose interests are more and less represented in an evaluation. Let me elaborate these points.

First, evaluators need to be deliberative and intentional about their own moral groundings. An evaluator, such as Ernest House, will and should bring moral concerns about social justice into negotiations over the design of an evaluation, including concerns about whose interests are represented in the questions asked and who will have access to the findings. The *active* part of being active-reactive-adaptive is bringing your own concerns, issues, and values to the table. The evaluator is also a stakeholder—not the primary stakeholder—but, **in every evaluation, an evaluator's reputation, credibility, and beliefs are on the line.** A utilization-focused evaluator is not passive in simply accepting and buying into whatever an intended user initially desires. The active-reactive-adaptive process connotes an obligation on the part of the evaluator to represent the standards and principles of the profession as well as his or her own sense of morality and integrity, while also attending to and respecting the beliefs and concerns of other primary users.

A second important point reinforced by the debate was the importance of project and stakeholder selection. At one point in the debate, Ross Connor, a former president of the American Evaluation Association, asked me, "You pick and choose clients, right?" I affirmed that I did. "My concern," he replied, "would be those who don't have the luxury of picking and choosing who they work with" (Quoted in Alkin 1990:104). One way in which I take into account the importance of the personal factor is by careful attention to whom I work with. Whether one has much choice in that, or not, it will affect the way in which ethical issues are addressed, especially what kinds of ethical issues are likely to be of concern. In challenging what he has called "clientism"—"the claim that whatever the client wants . . . is ethically correct," House (1995) asked: "What if the client is Adolph Eichmann, and he wants the evaluator to increase the efficiency of his concentration camps?" (p. 29).

A third issue concerns how the interests of various stakeholder groups are represented in a utilization-focused process. Despite House's admonitions, I'm reluctant, as a white, middle-class male, to pretend to represent the interests of people of color or society's disadvantaged. My preferred solution is to work to get participants in affected groups representing themselves as part of the evaluation negotiating process. As discussed in Chapter 3, user-focused evaluation involves real people, not just attention to vague, abstract audiences. Thus, where the interests of disadvantaged people are at stake, ways of hearing from or involving them directly should be explored, rather than having them represented in a potentially patronizing manner by the advantaged. Whether and how to do this may be part of what the evaluator attends to during active-reactive-adaptive interactions.

Guarding Against Corruption of an Evaluation

Ethics is not something for a special occasion; it is a part of daily practice.

—Newman and Brown (1996:187)

While House has raised concerns about how working with a selective group of intended users can serve the powerful and hurt the interests of the poor and less powerful, a different concern about utilization-focused evaluation is raised by Michael Scriven when he worries about undermining what he considers evaluation's central purpose—rendering independent judgments about merit or worth. If evaluators take on roles beyond judging merit or worth, such as creating learning organizations or empowering participants, or, alternatively, eschew rendering judgment in order to facilitate judgments by intended users, the opportunities for ethical slippage become so pervasive as to be overwhelming.

For Scriven, evaluators don't serve specific people. They serve truth. Truth may be a victim when evaluators form close working relationships with program staff. Scriven (1991b:182) admonishes evaluators to guard their independence scrupulously. Involving intended users would only risk weakening the hard-hitting judgments the evaluator must render. Evaluators, he has observed, must be able to deal with the loneliness that may accompany independence and guard against "going native," the tendency to be co-opted by and become an advocate for the program being evaluated. Going native leads to "incestuous relations" in which the "evaluator is 'in bed' with the program being evaluated" (p. 192). Scriven (1991a) has condemned any failure to render independent judgment as "the abrogation of the professional responsibility of the evaluator" (p. 32). He has derided what he mockingly called "a kinder, gentler approach" to evaluation (p. 39). His concerns stem from what he has experienced as the resistance of evaluation clients to negative findings and the difficulty evaluators have—psychologically—providing negative feedback. Thus, he has admonished evaluators to be uncompromising in reporting negative results. "The main reason that evaluators avoid negative conclusions is that they haven't the courage for it" (p. 42).

My experience has been different from Scriven's, so I reach different conclusions. Operating selectively, as I acknowledged earlier, I choose to work with clients who are hungry for quality information to improve programs. They are people of great competence and integrity who are able to use and balance both positive and negative information to make informed decisions. I take it as part of my responsibility to work with them in ways that they can hear the results, both positive and negative, and use them for intended purposes. I don't find them resistant. I find them quite eager to get quality information that they can use to develop the programs to which they have dedicated their energies. I try to render judgments, when we have negotiated my taking that role, in ways that can be heard, and I work with intended users to facilitate their arriving at their own conclusions. They are often harsher on themselves than I would be.

In my experience, it doesn't so much require courage to provide negative feedback as it requires skill. Nor do evaluation clients have to be unusually enlightened for negative feedback to be heard and used if, through skilled facilitation, the evaluator has built a foundation for such feedback so that it is welcomed for long-term effectiveness. Dedicated program staff don't want to waste their time doing things that don't work.

I have followed in the tracks of, and cleaned up the messes left by, evaluators who took pride in their courageous, hard-hitting, negative feedback. They patted themselves on the back for their virtues and went away complaining about program resistance and hostility. I watched them in action. They were arrogant, insensitive, and utterly unskilled in facilitating feedback as a learning experience. They congratulated themselves on their independence of judgment and commitment to "telling it like it is" and ignored their largely alienating and useless practices. They were closed to feedback about the ineffectiveness of their feedback.

It's from these kinds of experiences that I have developed a preference for constructive and utilization-focused feedback. In any form of feedback, it's hard to hear the substance when the tone is highly judgmental and demeaning. This applies to interactions between parents and children (in either direction), between lovers and spouses, among colleagues, and, most decidedly, between evaluators and intended users. Being kinder and gentler in an effort to be heard need not indicate cowardice or a loss of virtue. In this world of ever-greater diversity, sensitivity and respect are not only virtues, they're more effective and, in evaluation, more likely to lead to results being used.

Moral Discourse

Another attack on utilization-focused evaluation charges that it is void of and avoids moral discourse. Thomas Schwandt (1989b), in a provocative article, set out to "recapture the moral discourse in evaluation." He challenged the "bifurcation of value and fact;" he questioned my assertion that the integrity of an evaluation rests on its empirical orientation; and he expressed doubt about "the instrumental use of reason." He called for a rethinking of what it means to evaluate and invited us "to imagine what it would be like to practice evaluation without an instrumentalist conception of evaluation theory and practice" (p. 14).

In contrast to an instrumental and utilitarian approach, he advocated raising fundamental questions about the morality of programs, that is, not just asking if programs are doing things right, but are they doing right (moral) things? He argued for inquiry into the morals and values that undergird programs, not just whether programs work, but what their workings reveal about quality of life and the nature of society.

Such questions and such a focus for inquiry are compatible with a utilization-focus so long as intended users choose such an inquiry. The option to do so ought to be part of the menu of choices offered to primary stakeholders—and has been in this book. The process uses of evaluation discussed in Chapter 5 include participatory, collaborative, empowering, and social justice approaches, which emphasize the learning and development that derive from evaluative inquiry as an end in itself quite apart from the use of findings. Examining fundamental values, instrumental assumptions, and societal context are typically part of such processes.

Where I part company from Schwandt is in the superior position he ascribes to the moral questions he raises. Issues of morality do not shine brighter in the philosophical heavens than more mundane issues of effectiveness. He attacks methodological orthodoxy and narrowness, which deserve attack, but makes himself vulnerable to the counterattack that he is simply substituting his superior moral inquiry for others' superior methodological inquiry. He derides the technical expertise evaluators strive for and the arrogance attached to such expertise, yet he can be accused of merely offering another form of expertise and arrogance, this time in the trappings of moral discourse and those who know what questions are *really* important.

The fundamental value-premise of utilization-focused evaluation is that intended users are in the best position to decide for themselves what questions and inquiries are most important. From this perspective, moral inquiries and social justice concerns ought to be on the menu, not as greater goods, but as viable choices. Of course, as noted earlier, what intended users choose to investigate will be determined by how they are chosen, who they are, what they represent, and how the evaluator chooses to work with them—all decisions that involve both politics and ethics.

Exhibit 14.4 reproduces a letter from evaluator Yoland Wadsworth, recipient of the Churchill Fellowship, the Australian Mental Health Services Award, and the Australasian Evaluation Society's Pioneering Evaluation Literature Award. She writes concerning her own struggle to be true to her personal values as she engages in evaluation involving people in great need, many of whom are politically oppressed. Hers is an action-based inquiry into morality from the evaluation trenches, the source, I believe of her moral authority.

Standards and principles provide guidance for dealing with politics and ethics, but there are no absolute rules. These arenas of existential action are replete with dilemmas, conundrums, paradoxes, perplexities, quandaries, temptations, and competing goods. Utilization-focused evaluation may well exacerbate such challenges, so warnings about potential political corruption, ethical entrapments, and moral turpitude direct us to keep asking fundamental questions: What does it mean to be useful? Useful to whom? Who benefits? Who is hurt? Who decides? What values inform the selection of intended users and intended uses? Why? Or, why not?

EXHIBIT 14.4

Moral Discourse From Australia: Politics and Ethics in the Trenches

Evaluator Yoland Wadsworth spent a sabbatical year reflecting on working collaboratively with program staff and participants in evaluation and action research efforts aimed at mutual understanding and change. Her team's evaluation work at the front line in the psychiatric services system was recognized with a Gold Australian and New Zealand Mental Health Services Partnership Award in 1995, as well as the Australasian Evaluation Society's Pioneering Evaluation Literature award.

Wadsworth worked with a mental health program, one where staff would sometimes forcibly inject difficult patients with drugs to render them unconscious or strip them and lock them in a bare cell. Her concerns about how to engage in evaluation in such a setting led her to reflect on community-building efforts in politically oppressive regimes where practitioners of action research "have been known to die for their efforts" (Wildman 1995). In a letter to me, she pondered the politics and ethics of being an evaluator in such circumstances, excerpts of which, with her permission, I've reproduced here.

> In mutual inquiry efforts, under difficult political and interpersonal conditions, the most fragile thing of all is connectedness (or what some of us might call "love" if there wasn't such a powerful prohibition on mentioning such an emotive state!). What can thrive in its absence is fear—on both sides.
>
> How do we de-escalate—come together to speak our own truths within our own group, and then speak our truths together to each other's groups, no matter how uncomfortable? How do we learn to listen, communicate, heal things, collaborate, and then move on to new, more reflective and productive action? I want to use "inquiry"—small-scale research and evaluation methods—to facilitate these processes.
>
> Yet, when it comes to the more powerful partner ceding some real sovereignty to the less powerful "partner," suddenly fears may re-surface, defenses are re-built, "rational" objections are voiced, funds dry up, hard-won structures are dismantled until the "time is right," and old damaging-but-familiar practices resume. . . .

How difficult not to demonize. How difficult to stay firm. How difficult not to feel fearful and defeated, or alternatively "go over" to staff's way of thinking for a more peaceful life. How difficult to hold a line and keep respecting and trusting when suddenly such respect seems betrayed and trust seems naive. Yet, to draw attention to this attracts a howl of protest from sensitized staff.

And for staff, how difficult to stay open, retain professional or peer standing, not unwittingly exert power over consumers [mental health patients] yet again, and keep fears at bay—or well-debriefed. How difficult for staff not to allow feelings of being disempowered to blot out the knowledge of the profound power they hold over consumers. How difficult to remain in solidarity with staff at the same time as remaining working with and for and open to consumers. When the stakes are dangerously high—how difficult for everyone to avoid withdrawing and, eventually, taking up arms. . . . It needs courage.

Here's an articulation that guides me. An inpatient, who worked as a consultant to our project, wrote:

Poem for U&I[a]

In the cold of the dark
I see you stand before me
In a vision of Rage,
that neither you nor I
can control.
Weep for you and me.
Strangers, never more.
Time and place for you and I.

a. U&I was the acronym of Understanding and Involvement—the popular title selected by consumers for our Consumer Evaluation of Acute Psychiatric Hospital Practice project, 1993-1996. The *U* is staff or consumer, the *I* consumer or staff—depending on the direction of the gaze of the viewer.

15

Utilization-Focused Evaluation: Process and Premises

Asking questions about impact—that's evaluation.
Gathering data—that's evaluation.
Making judgments—that's evaluation.
Facilitating use—that's evaluation.
Putting all those pieces together in a meaningful whole that tells people something they want to know and can use about a matter of importance. **Now that's really evaluation!**

—Halcolm

A User's Perspective

This final chapter will provide an overview of utilization-focused evaluation. I want to set the stage by presenting the perspective of a very thoughtful evaluation user, distinguished educator Dr. Wayne Jennings. At the time of the following interview, he was actively reflecting on the role of evaluation in schools as principal of the innovative Saint Paul Open School, which had just been externally evaluated. Concerns such as those he expresses helped inspire utilization-focused evaluation.

Patton: You recently participated in a federal evaluation of your school. Why was it undertaken?

Jennings: It was mandated as part of federal funds we received. We hoped there would be some benefit to the school, that school staff would learn things to improve our program. We were interested in an evaluation that would address basic issues of education. Our school operates on the assumption that students learn from experience, and the more varied experiences they have, the more they learn. So, we hoped to learn what parts of the program made a contribution to and what parts maybe detracted from learning.

We hoped also to learn whether the program affected different groups of students differently, for instance, whether the program was more effective for younger children or older children. We wanted to know how well it worked for kids who have a lot of initiative and drive and are self-motivated learners versus the experiences and learnings of those who don't have that kind of attitude. And we were interested in determining what we should concentrate on more—as well as continue or discontinue. But we didn't get information to make those kind of basic decisions.

We asked the research firm for an evaluation that would help us with those kinds of questions. They came up with a design that seemed far off target—not at all what we had asked for. It takes a little imagination to do an evaluation that fits an innovative program. We got a standard recipe approach. I'm convinced that if we'd asked totally different questions, we'd have gotten the same design. It's as though they had a cookie cutter, and whether they were evaluating us or evaluating vocational education or anything—a hospital or a prison —it would have been the same design.

Patton: So why did you accept the design? Why participate in an evaluation you thought would be useless educationally?

Jennings: That's a good question. It happened like this. The first year, we worked with an out-of-state firm that had won the federal contract. The president came for the initial discussion in September, when school was getting started. He said he'd like to look around. Ten minutes later, I found him sitting in the front hall in a state of what appeared to be absolute shock. He was not prepared for our program, not in the least. He came and found kids running around. Students were noisy. They weren't seated in straight rows. We didn't resemble his conception of a school in any way, apparently. He just wasn't prepared for open education—for an alternative approach. That was the last we saw of him. He sent out a new researcher who didn't walk around the school. We simply met in the office and hashed out what data were required by funders. These people were not prepared to analyze a nonstandard school operation or adapt their design to our situation.

I think schools have operated pretty much in the same way for so long that all of us have a mind-set of what school is. So, to see something different can shock—culture shock. We've seen that in the eyes of several evaluators we've had in here. Now, I don't know how to prepare a standard educational evaluator to be open to an open school. Maybe we needed more of a participant observer, an anthropological type, someone who would come in and live here for a while and find out what the hell's going on.

Patton: You couldn't find that kind of evaluator?

Jennings: We did have, somewhere along the line, a proposal from a firm that had experience with our kind of schools. They were going to give us the kind of evaluation we were very much interested in, the kind we could learn from. We wanted to pursue that design, but State Department of Education officials said, "No, that won't provide us with concrete, comparable data for accountability."

Patton: The design approved by the State Department of Education, did that provide some "concrete, comparable data for accountability"? What were the findings?

Jennings: We knew politically that we had to achieve a certain degree of respectability with regard to standardized testing, so we looked at test results, reading scores, and all that sort of thing, and they seemed satisfactory. We didn't discover anything particularly startling to cause any serious problems with our Board of Education or the State Department of Education.

Patton: In what form did you receive the findings?

Jennings: In a report. I think it would have been helpful for the evaluators to meet with our staff and talk us through the report, elaborate a little on it, but that didn't happen—partly because the report came either during the summer or the following fall.

Patton: So, of what use was the evaluation?

Jennings: It served to legitimize us. Our local Board of Education, the district administration, and the State Department of Education were all interested in seeing an evaluation undertaken, but I don't think a single member of the board or administration read it. They may have glanced at the summary, and the summary said that the school was OK. That was it.

Patton: Any uses besides legitimization? Anything you learned?

Jennings: I suppose you could say we learned how difficult it is to get helpful evaluations.

Patton: What was staff reaction to the report?

Jennings: I doubt many bothered to read it. They were looking for something worthwhile and helpful, but it just wasn't there. Staff were interested in thinking through a good evaluation, but that would have required the evaluators to become thoroughly backgrounded in order to help us think it through and provide a proper evaluation. As it turned out, I think the staff have acquired a negative attitude about evaluation. I mean, they are interested in evaluation, but then the reports seem to lack anything that would help us with day-to-day decision making or give us a good mirror image of what's going on in the school, from an outsider's point of view, in terms of the growth and development of kids in all dimensions.

Patton: Let me broaden the question about use. Sometimes evaluations have an impact on things that go beyond immediate program improvements—things like general thinking on issues that arise from the study, or board policies, or legislation. Did the evaluation have an impact in any broader ways?

Jennings: I'm glad you're getting into that area, because that's of major interest to me. I had hoped that as the school got under way, it would become fairly clear, or would be evident to those interested in finding out, that this was a highly effective educational program that was making a considerable difference in the lives of most children. Well, the study didn't address that; the study simply said, "The program's OK." That's all it said. **Given the limited resources and imagination that were put into the evaluation, I'm not convinced they had enough knowledge to say even that—to say anything about the effectiveness of the program!**

Our major job is to educate 500 students, but we're engaged in a much larger struggle, at least I am, and that is to show that a less formal approach based on experiential education can be highly effective, including bringing students to the same level of achievement in a shorter time. We're concerned about achievement, but also about producing genuinely humane people for a complex, changing world.

Now, to be fair, the evaluation did provide something useful. When parents or other educators ask if the program has been evaluated and what the findings were, we say, "Yes, the evaluation shows the program is effective." On the other hand, anyone worth their salt, I suspect, if they read the evaluation carefully, would decide that it doesn't show much of anything, really, when you come right down to it. **We're left where we began, but we have the illusion of at least having been evaluated.**

Patton: I pulled some of the recommendations out of the study, and I'd just like to have you react to how those were received and used in any way by the school. The first one that's listed in the report is that objectives as they are related to the goals of the Open School should be written in performance-specific language. What was the reaction to that recommendation?

Jennings: I know that's the current popular view in education today, but I'm not sure it could be done. It would require an enormous amount of energy. Many of our objectives are not very specific subject-matter kinds of objectives. The general goals of the school are more philosophical in tone, and I guess we're just not willing to invest the time and energy to reduce those to the kinds of performance objectives they're speaking of, and I don't know if the end results would be particularly helpful.

Patton: Did it seem to you that that recommendation followed from the findings of the study?

Jennings: When I read that one, I thought—Where did that come from? You know, how did they arrive at that? Is that just some conventional wisdom in education today that can be plugged into any set of recommendations?

Patton: What, then, was your overall reaction to the recommendations?

Jennings: Each was simpleminded. They showed that the evaluators lacked depth of understanding of what the program was trying to accomplish. Each recommendation could have been a report in itself rather than some surface scratching and coming up with some conclusions that just weren't helpful.

Patton: Bottom line—what'd the evaluation accomplish?

Jennings: Legitimation. Just by existing, it served that function. With an impressive cover, even if it was filled with Chinese or some other language, as long as it was thick and had a lot of figures in it and people thought it was an evaluation and somewhere near the end it said that the school seemed to be doing a reasonably good job, that would be satisfactory for most people.

Patton: What about the evaluation supported the legitimation function?

Jennings: Its thickness. The fact that it's got numbers and statistics in it. It's authored by some Ph.D.s. It was done by an outside firm. Those things all lend credibility.

Patton: What would it have taken to make it more useful?

Jennings: I would say that to do the job right, we'd have to have people on our own staff who were free from most other responsibilities so that they could deal with designing the evaluation and work with the evaluators. Then I think that as the evaluation proceeded, there should probably have been regular interactions to adjust the evaluation—keep it relevant.

Patton: There's a side effect of evaluation studies that affects the way people like yourself, who are administrators and work in government and agencies and schools, feel about evaluation. How would you describe your general opinion of evaluation? Positive? Negative? Favorable? Unfavorable?

Jennings: We want careful evaluation. We want to know what we're doing well and not so well. We want data that will help us improve the program. We want that. We want the best that's available, and we want it to be accurate and we want the conclusions to be justified, and so on. **We just desperately want and need that information, to know if we're on the right track.** But we haven't gotten that so, by and large, my opinion of evaluation is not very good. Most reports look like they were written the last week before they're published, with hastily drawn conclusions and sometimes data that's manipulated for a preconceived conclusion fitting the evaluators' or funders' biases.

Patton: Have you given up on evaluation?

Jennings: I guess the reason hope springs eternal is that I have read carefully done evaluations that have informed my thinking about education and brought me to my present beliefs. I'd guess that 99% of evaluation is done on a model of education that I consider obsolete, like a factory trying to perfect its way of making wagon wheels. We need more relevant and useful approaches, something beyond wagon wheels evaluations.

The evaluators of the Open School were also interviewed, but when they read Jennings's comments, they asked that their interview not be used and that they not be named because their business might be hurt. The thrust of their comments was that they had viewed the state and federal education agencies as their primary audiences. They did what they were contracted to do. Once they submitted their reports, they had no further contacts with the funders of the evaluation and did not know how or if the reports had been useful. Federal and state officials we contacted said that they received hundreds of such evaluations and could not comment on specific case examples among the many they monitor.

A Utilization-Focused Alternative

Shortly after my interview with Jennings, he formed an evaluation task force made up of teachers, parents, students, community people, and graduate students trained in utilization-focused evaluation. With very limited resources, they designed an intensive study of Saint Paul Open School processes and outcomes using a variety of methods, both quantitative and qualitative. That evaluation provided useful information for incremental program development. Exhibit 15.1 contrasts their internal Open School Task Force evaluation with the earlier, mandated external evaluation. These contrasts highlight the critical elements of utilization-focused evaluation.

The three years of external, federally mandated evaluation at the Saint Paul Open School cost about $40,000—not a great deal of money as research goes. Yet, in the aggregate, evaluations on hundreds of programs like this cost millions of dollars. They constitute the major proportion of all evaluations conducted in the country. The benefit of those dollars is problematic. The internal, utilization-focused evaluation cost less than $1,000 in hard cash because the labor was all volunteer and release time. Due to the success of the internal task-force effort, the school continued the utilization-focused approach shown in Exhibit 15.1. Staff supported the evaluation with their own school resources because they found the process and results useful.

The Flow of a Utilization-Focused Evaluation Process

Exhibit 15.2 presents a flowchart of utilization-focused evaluation. First, intended users of the evaluation are identified (Chapter 3). These intended users are brought together or organized in some fashion, if possible (e.g., an evaluation task force of primary stakeholders), to work with the evaluator and share in making major decisions about the evaluation.

Second, the evaluator and intended users commit to the intended uses of the evaluation (Chapters 4 and 5) and determine the focus of the evaluation (Chapters 2 and 8). This can include considering the relative importance of focusing on attainment of goals (Chapter 7), program implementation (Chapter 9), and/or the program's theory of action (Chapter 10). The menu of evaluation possibilities is vast, so many different types of evaluations may need to be discussed. (See Menu 8.1 at the end of Chapter 8 for a suggestive list of different evaluation questions and types.) The evaluator works with intended users to determine priority uses with attention to political and ethical considerations (Chapter 14). In a style that is active-reactive-adaptive and situationally responsive, the evaluator helps intended users answer these questions: Given expected uses, is the evaluation worth doing? To what extent and in what ways are intended users committed to intended use?

The third part of the process as depicted in the flowchart involves methods, mea-

EXHIBIT 15.1
Contrasting Evaluation Approaches

Open School Utilization-Focused Evaluation	*Original External Mandated Evaluation*
1. A task force of primary intended users formed to focus evaluation questions.	1. The evaluation was aimed vaguely at multiple audiences: federal funders, the school board, State Department of Education staff, the general public, and Open School staff.
2. This group worked together to determine what information would be useful for program improvement and public accountability. The first priority was formative evaluation.	2. The evaluators unilaterally determined the evalution focus based on what they thought their audiences would want. Evaluators had minimal interactions with these audiences.
3. The evaluation included both implementation (process) data and outcomes data (achievement data and follow-up of Open School graduates).	3. The evaluation was a pure outcomes study. Evaluators collected data on presumed operational goals (i.e., scores on standardized achievement tests) based on a model that fit the evaluators' but not the programs assumptions.
4. The task force based their evaluation on an explicit statement of educational philosophy (a theory of action).	4. Evaluators ignored the program's philosophy and conceptualized the evaluation in terms of their own implicit educational theory of action.
5. A variety of methods were used to investigate a variety of questions. Methods were selected jointly by evaluators and intended users using multiple criteria: methodological appropriateness, face validity of instrumentation, believability, credibility, and relevance of the design and measuring instruments to information users and decision makers; and available resources. The task force was involved on a continual basis in making methods and measurement decisions as circumstances changed.	5. The major measurement technique was use of standardized tests that had low face validity, low credibility, and low relevance to program staff; other audiences, especially federal funders and state agency staff, appeared to want such instruments, but it was unclear who the evaluation was supposed to serve. Methods were determined largely by evaluators, based on available resources, with only initial review by program staff and federal and state officials.
6. Task force members worked together to analyze and interpret data as they were gathered. Data were discussed in rough form over a period of time before the evaluators wrote the final report. Findings and conclusions were known and being used before the final report was ready for dissemination.	6. Evaluators analyzed and interpreted data by themselves. A final report was the only form in which findings were presented. No interpretation sessions with program staff or any audience were ever held.
7. When the report was made public, the school principal and evaluators made presentations to parents, staff, and school officials.	7. The final report was mailed to funding agencies. No verbal presentations were made. No discussions of findings took place.
8. The evaluation was used by Open School staff for program development and shared with interested accountability audiences to show how the program was being improved.	8. No specific use was made of the evaluation though it may have helped legitimize the program by giving the "illusion" of outcomes evaluation.

EXHIBIT 15.2
Utilization-Focused Evaluation Flowchart

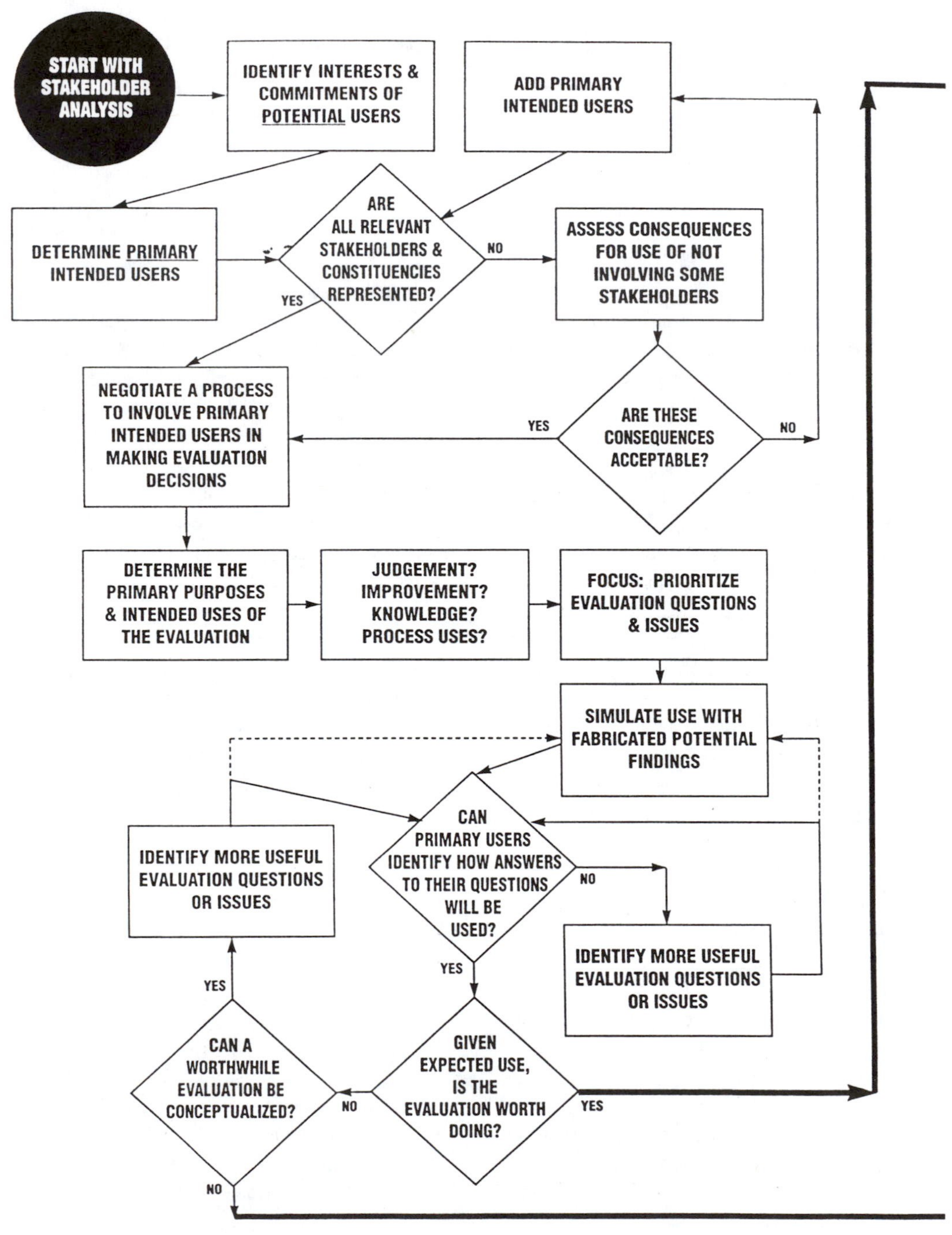

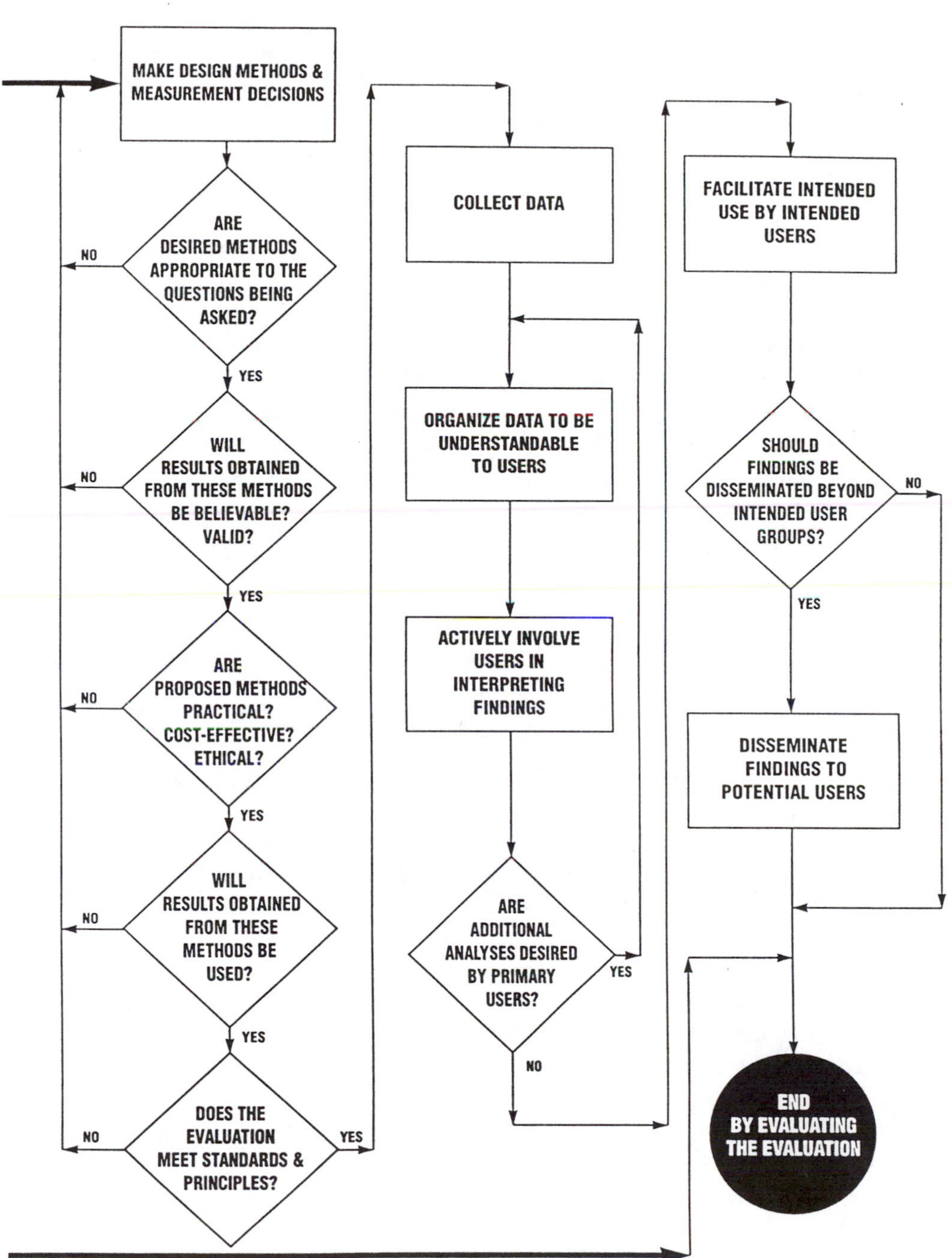
MAKE DESIGN METHODS & MEASUREMENT DECISIONS
ARE DESIRED METHODS APPROPRIATE TO THE QUESTIONS BEING ASKED?
NO
YES
WILL RESULTS OBTAINED FROM THESE METHODS BE BELIEVABLE? VALID?
NO
YES
ARE PROPOSED METHODS PRACTICAL? COST-EFFECTIVE? ETHICAL?
NO
YES
WILL RESULTS OBTAINED FROM THESE METHODS BE USED?
NO
YES
DOES THE EVALUATION MEET STANDARDS & PRINCIPLES?
NO
YES
COLLECT DATA
ORGANIZE DATA TO BE UNDERSTANDABLE TO USERS
ACTIVELY INVOLVE USERS IN INTERPRETING FINDINGS
ARE ADDITIONAL ANALYSES DESIRED BY PRIMARY USERS?
YES
NO
FACILITATE INTENDED USE BY INTENDED USERS
SHOULD FINDINGS BE DISSEMINATED BEYOND INTENDED USER GROUPS?
NO
YES
DISSEMINATE FINDINGS TO POTENTIAL USERS
END BY EVALUATING THE EVALUATION

surement, and design decisions (Chapters 11 and 12). A variety of options are considered: qualitative and quantitative data; naturalistic, experimental, and quasi-experimental designs; purposeful and probabilistic sampling approaches; greater and lesser emphasis on generalizations; and alternative ways of dealing with potential threats to validity, reliability, and utility. More specifically, the discussion at this stage will include attention to issues of methodological appropriateness, believability of the data, understandability, accuracy, balance, practicality, propriety, and cost. As always, the overriding concern will be utility. Will results obtained from these methods be useful—and actually used?

Once data have been collected and organized for analysis, the fourth stage of the utilization-focused process begins. Intended users are actively and directly involved in interpreting findings, making judgments based on the data, and generating recommendations (Chapter 13). Specific strategies for use can then be formalized in light of actual findings, and the evaluator can facilitate following through on actual use.

Finally, decisions about dissemination of the evaluation report can be made beyond whatever initial commitments were made earlier in planning for intended use. This reinforces the distinction between intended use by intended users (planned utilization) and more general dissemination for broad public accountability (where both hoped for and unintended uses may occur).

While the flowchart in Exhibit 15.2 depicts a seemingly straightforward, one-step-at-a-time logic to the unfolding of a utilization-focused evaluation, in reality the process is seldom simple or linear. The flowchart attempts to capture the sometimes circular and iterative nature of the process by depicting loops at the points where intended users are identified and again where evaluation questions are focused. For the sake of diagrammatic simplicity, however, many potential loops are missing. The active-reactive-adaptive evaluator who is situationally responsive and politically sensitive may find that new stakeholders become important or new questions emerge in the midst of methods decisions. Nor is there a clear and clean distinction between the processes of focusing evaluation questions and making methods decisions.

The real world of utilization-focused evaluation manifests considerably more complexity than a flowchart can possibly capture. The flowchart strives to outline the basic logic of the process, but applying that logic in any given situation requires flexibility and creativity.

The Achilles' Heel of Utilization-Focused Evaluation

Achilles' fame stemmed from his role as hero in Homer's classic, the *Iliad*. He was the Greeks' most illustrious warrior during the Trojan War, invulnerable because his mother had dipped him in the Styx, the river of the underworld across which Charon ferried the dead. His heel, where she held him in the river, was his sole point of vulnerability, and it was there that he was fatally wounded with an arrow shot by Paris.

The Achilles' heel of utilization-focused evaluation, its point of greatest vulnerability, is turnover of primary intended users. The process so depends on the active engagement of intended users that to lose users along the way to job transitions, reorganizations, reassignments, and elections can undermine eventual use. Replacement users who join the evaluation late in the process seldom come with the same agenda as those who were present at the beginning. The best antidote involves working with a task force of multiple intended users so that the departure of one or two is less critical. Still, when substantial turnover of primary intended users occurs, it may be necessary to reignite the process by renegotiating the design and use commitments with the new arrivals on the scene.

Previous chapters have discussed the challenges of selecting the right stakeholders, getting them to commit time and attention to the evaluation, dealing with political dynamics, building credibility, and conducting the evaluation in an ethical manner. All of these challenges revolve around the relationship between the evaluator and intended users. When new intended users replace those who depart, new relationships must be built. That may mean delays in original time lines, but such delays pay off in eventual use by attending to the foundation of understandings and relationships upon which utilization-focused evaluation is built.

Fundamental Premises of Utilization-Focused Evaluation

Articulating fundamental premises requires making assumptions and values explicit. What seems obvious to one person may not be at all obvious to another. Consider, for example, the Sufi story about Mulla Nasrudin standing in the center of the marketplace while a compatriot stopped passersby, whispering to them how they could entertain themselves by showing Nasrudin to be an idiot.

> *When offered a choice between two coins of different value, Nasrudin always chose the one worth less.*
>
> *One day, a kind man tried to enlighten the foolish Nasrudin. "You should take the coin of greater value," he urged, "then you'd have more money and people would no longer be able to make a fool of you."*
>
> *"But," replied Nasrudin, "if I take the more valuable coin, people will stop offering me money to prove that I'm more idiotic than they are. Then I would have no money at all."*
>
> —Adapted from Shah 1973:52

The premises of utilization-focused evaluation will seem obvious to some, of dubious merit to others, and controversial to many more. The rationales for and evidence supporting these various premises have been articulated throughout this book. Here, however, for the first time, as a summary of what has gone before, I have pulled together 14 fundamental premises of utilization-focused evaluation.

1. **Commitment to intended use by intended users should be the driving force in an evaluation.** At every decision point—whether the decision concerns purpose, focus, design, methods, measurement, analysis, or reporting—the evaluator asks intended users: How would that affect your use of this evaluation?

2. **Strategizing about use is ongoing and continuous from the very beginning of the evaluation.** Use isn't something one becomes interested in at the end of an evaluation. By the end of the evaluation, the potential for use has been largely determined. From the moment stakeholders and evaluators begin interacting and conceptualizing the evaluation, decisions are being made that will affect use in major ways.

3. **The personal factor contributes significantly to use.** The personal factor refers to the research finding that the personal interests and commitments of those involved in an evaluation undergird use. Thus, evaluations should be *specifically* user oriented—aimed at the interests and information needs of specific, identifiable people, not vague, passive audiences.

4. **Careful and thoughtful stakeholder analysis should inform identification of primary intended users,** taking into account the varied and multiple interests that surround any program, and therefore, any evaluation. Staff, program participants, directors, public officials, funders, and community leaders all have an interest in evaluation, but the degree and nature of their interests will vary. Political sensitivity and ethical judgments are involved in identifying primary intended users and uses.

5. **Evaluations must be focused in some way; focusing on intended use by intended users is the most useful way.** Resource and time constraints will make it impossible for any single evaluation to answer everyone's questions or to give full attention to all possible issues. Because no evaluation can serve all potential stakeholders' interests equally well, stakeholders representing various constituencies should come together to negotiate what issues and questions deserve priority.

6. **Focusing on intended use requires making deliberate and thoughtful choices.** Menu 4.1 in Chapter 4 identified three primary uses of findings: judging merit or worth (e.g., summative evaluation); improving programs (instrumental use); and generating knowledge (conceptual and formative use). Menu 5.1 in Chapter 5 presented four kinds of *process use:* enhancing shared understandings, reinforcing interventions, supporting participant engagement, and developing programs and organizations. Uses can change and evolve over time as a program matures.

7. **Useful evaluations must be designed and adapted situationally.** Standardized recipe approaches won't work. The relative value of a particular utilization focus (Premises 5 and 6) can only be judged in the context of a specific program and the interests of intended users. Situational factors affect use. As Exhibit 6.1 in Chapter 6 showed, these factors include community variables, organizational characteristics, the nature of the evaluation, evaluator credibility, political considerations, and resource constraints. In conducting a utilization-focused evaluation, the active-

reactive-adaptive evaluator works with intended users to assess how various factors and conditions may affect the potential for use.

8. **Intended users' commitment to use can be nurtured and enhanced by actively involving them in making significant decisions about the evaluation.** Involvement increases relevance, understanding, and ownership of the evaluation, all of which facilitate informed and appropriate use.

9. **High-quality participation is the goal, not high-quantity participation.** The quantity of group interaction time can be inversely related to the quality of the process. Evaluators conducting utilization-focused evaluations must be skilled group facilitators.

10. **High-quality involvement of intended users will result in high quality, useful evaluations.** Many researchers worry that methodological rigor may be sacrificed if nonscientists collaborate in making methods decisions. But, decision makers want data that are useful *and* accurate. Validity and utility are interdependent. Threats to utility are as important to counter as threats to validity. Skilled evaluation facilitators can help nonscientists understand methodological issues so that they can judge for themselves the trade-offs involved in choosing among the strengths and weaknesses of design options and methods alternatives.

11. **Evaluators have a rightful stake in an evaluation in that their credibility and integrity are always at risk, thus the mandate for evaluators to be active-reactive-adaptive.** Evaluators are active in presenting to intended users their own best judgments about appropriate evaluation focus and methods; they are reactive in listening attentively and respectful to others' concerns; and they are adaptive in finding ways to design evaluations that incorporate diverse interests, including their own, while meeting high standards of professional practice. Evaluators' credibility and integrity are factors affecting use as well as the foundation of the profession. In this regard, evaluators should be guided by the profession's standards and principles (see Exhibit 1.3 in Chapter 1 and Exhibit 2.1 in Chapter 2).

12. **Evaluators committed to enhancing use have a responsibility** ***to train users*** in evaluation processes and the uses of information. Training stakeholders in evaluation methods and processes attends to both short-term and long-term evaluation uses. Making decision makers more sophisticated about evaluation can contribute to greater use of evaluation over time.

13. **Use is different from reporting and dissemination.** Reporting and dissemination may be means to facilitate use, but they should not be confused with such intended uses as making decisions, improving programs, changing thinking, empowering participants, and generating knowledge (see Premise 6).

14. **Serious attention to use involves financial and time costs that are far from trivial.** The benefits of these costs are manifested in greater use. These costs should be made explicit in evaluation proposals and budgets so that utilization follow-through is not neglected for lack of resources.

A Vision of an Experimenting Society and Experimenting Evaluators

An experimenting society would vigorously try out possible solutions to recurrent problems and would make hard-headed, multidimensional evaluations of outcomes, and when the evaluation of one reform showed it to have been ineffective or harmful, would move on to try other alternatives.

—Donald T. Campbell (1988:291)

To be truly scientific we must be able to experiment. We must be able to advocate without that excess of commitment that blinds us to reality testing.

—Donald T. Campbell (1969:410)

Donald T. Campbell, one of the fathers of scientific evaluation, died in 1996 after nearly four-score years, many of them working to realize his vision of an Experimenting Society. His vision lives on. Its realization will depend on a shared commitment to engage in active reality testing by all those involved in and touched by programs and policies, not just researchers and evaluators. But evaluators must point the way. Utilization-focused evaluation invites stakeholders to join with evaluators as informed citizens of an Experimenting Global Society.

Utilization-focused evaluation combines style and substance, activism and science, personal perspective and systematic information. I have tried to capture the complexity and potential of utilization-focused evaluation with scenarios, case examples, findings from our study of federal evaluation use, Sufi parables, and children's stories. In the end, this approach to evaluation must also be judged by its usefulness.

I have presented research and theories that support the premises of utilization-focused evaluation. Still, skeptics will be skeptical—some who don't want to take the time to work with stakeholders, others who don't want to give up control of the process, and still others who are convinced that it probably works for certain kinds of evaluators (the personable, the human-relations types, whatever . . .), but that it won't work for them.

Certainly, I can offer no guarantees that a utilization-focused approach will always work. Just as decision makers live in a world of uncertainty, so too evaluators are faced with the ever-present possibility that, despite their best efforts, their work will be ignored or, worse, misused. Producing good evaluation studies that actually are used constitutes an enormous challenge. In many ways, the odds are all against use, and it's quite possible to become cynical about the futility of trying to have an impact in a world in which situation after situation seems impervious to change. Utilization-focused evaluators may be told, or may sometimes feel, that they are wasting their time. A final Sufi story provides, perhaps, something for skeptics to ponder.

Yogurt is made by adding a small quantity of old yogurt to a larger measure of milk. The action of the bacillus bulgaricus in the seeding portion of yogurt will in time convert the whole into a mass of new yogurt.

One day some friends saw Nasrudin down on his knees beside a warm forest spring adding a mass of yogurt to the water. One of the passers-by asked, "What are you trying to do, Nasrudin?"

"I'm trying to make yogurt."

"But you can't make yogurt like that," he scoffed.

"Perhaps not, but just supposing it works!"

The next day Nasrudin invited the entire village to taste his concoction. It wasn't like the yogurt they were used to, but all agreed it was unique and delicious.

The following day Nasrudin returned to the warm spring to make another batch. The result this time tasted acrid and made many who tried it sick.

For weeks thereafter, Nasrudin returned to the spring, each day trying to make again his original tasty creation. But, having failed to carefully observe and write down what he had done and what conditions prevailed at the time, he never succeeded in reproducing the original. He did, however, produce other tasty delicacies, but the villagers were reluctant to try them since they never knew for sure whether they would be delighted or made sick. Eventually, Nasrudin gave up, since he could never predict with certainty what would result in the changing conditions of the forest spring.

—Adapted from Shah 1964:90

Getting intended users to taste evaluation may, indeed, be a long shot in many situations. Many have been made "sick" by past concoctions called evaluation. The results of any particular effort cannot be guaranteed. Each evaluation being a blend of unique ingredients, no standardized recipe can ensure the outcome. We have only principles, premises, and utilization-focused processes to guide us, and we have much yet to learn. But the potential benefits merit the efforts and risks involved. At stake is improving the effectiveness of programs that express and embody the highest ideals of humankind. At stake is the vision of an Experimenting Society. It may be a long shot, "but just *supposing* it works!" And works for you. The only way to find out is to try it—and evaluate the results. Build the study of use into your evaluations and thereby help make not only programs, but also evaluations, accountable. Experiment with ways of making evaluation useful, for the vision of an Experimenting Society ultimately depends on experimenting and innovating evaluators and evaluation users working together.

References

Abramson, M. A. 1978. *The Funding of Social Knowledge Production and Application: A Survey of Federal Agencies*. Washington, DC: National Academy of Sciences.

Ackerman, Bruce A. 1977. "Illusions About New Cars, Clean Air." *Minneapolis Tribune*, August 29, p. 4A.

ACVAFS. 1983. *Evaluation Sourcebook*. New York: American Council of Voluntary Agencies for Foreign Service.

AEA Task Force on Guiding Principles for Evaluators. 1995. "Guiding Principles for Evaluators." *New Directions for Program Evaluation*, Summer, pp. 19-34.

AES (Australasian Evaluation Society). 1995. "Evaluation! Are You Being Served? How well are evaluation practices serving customers, clients, and other stakeholders." Presented at the 1995 Annual Conference, Sydney, Australia.

Alkin, Marvin. 1995. "Lessons Learned About Evaluation Use." Panel presentation at the International Evaluation Conference, American Evaluation Association, November 2, Vancouver, British Columbia.

———, ed. 1990. *Debates on Evaluation*. Newbury Park, CA: Sage.

———. 1985. *A Guide for Evaluation Decision Makers*. Beverly Hills, CA: Sage.

———. 1975a. "Evaluation: Who Needs It? Who Cares? *Studies in Educational Evaluation* 1(3):201-12.

———. 1975b. "Framing the Decision Context." In *AERA Cassette Series in Evaluation*. Washington, DC: American Educational Research Association.

———. 1972. "Wider Context Goals and Goal-Based Evaluators." *Evaluation Comment: The Journal of Educational Evaluation* (Center for the Study of Evaluation, UCLA) 3(4):10-11.

———. 1970. "A Review of the Evaluation of the Follow Through Program." Working Paper 10, Center for the Study of Evaluation, UCLA.

Alkin, Marvin and Karin Coyle. 1988. "Thoughts on Evaluation Misutilization." Presented at the Annual Meeting of the American Educational Research Association, April 5, New Orleans. See also, *Studies in Educational Evaluation* 14:331-40.

Alkin, Marvin C., Richard Daillak, and Peter White. 1979. *Using Evaluations: Does Evaluation Make a Difference?* Beverly Hills, CA: Sage.

Alkin, Marvin C., with P. Jacobson, J. Burry, P. White, and L. Kent. 1985. *Organizing for Evaluation Use. A Handbook for Administrators*. Los Angeles: Center for the Study of Evaluation, UCLA.

Alkin, Marvin and Alex Law. 1980. "A Conversation on Evaluation Utilization." *Educational Evaluation and Policy Analysis* 2(3):73-79.

Allison, Graham T. 1971. *Essence of Decision: Explaining the Cuban Missile Crisis*. Boston: Little, Brown.

Altschuld, James W. and Molly Engle, eds. 1994. *The Preparation of Professional Evaluators: Issues, Perspectives, and Programs* (New Directions for Program Evaluation, No. 62, Summer). San Francisco: Jossey-Bass.

Anderson, Barry F. 1980. *The Complete Thinker*. Englewood Cliffs, NJ: Prentice Hall.

Anderson, John R., Lynne M. Reder, and Herbert Simon. 1996. "Situated Learning and Education." *Educational Researcher* 25(4): 5-21.

Anderson, Richard B. 1977. "The Effectiveness of Follow Through: What Have We Learned?" Presented at the annual meeting of the American Educational Research Association, New York.

Argyris, Chris. 1982. *Reasoning, Learning, and Action*. San Francisco: Jossey-Bass.

———. 1976. *Increasing Leadership Effectiveness*. New York: John Wiley.

———. 1974. *Theory in Practice: Increasing Professional Effectiveness*. San Francisco: Jossey-Bass.

Argyris, Chris, R. Putnam, and D. M. Smith. 1985. *Action Science*. San Francisco: Jossey-Bass.

Argyris, Chris and Donald Schön. 1978. *Organizational Learning*. Reading, MA: Addison-Wesley.

———. 1974. *Theory in Practice: Increasing Professional Effectiveness*. San Francisco: Jossey-Bass.

Attkisson, C. Clifford, W. A. Hargreaves, M. J. Horowitz, and J. E. Sorenson, eds. 1978. *Evaluation of Human Service Programs*. New York: Academic Press.

Aubel, Judi. 1993. *Participatory Program Evaluation: A Manual for Involving Stakeholders in the Evaluation Process*. Dakar, Senegal: Catholic Relief Services under a U.S. AID grant.

Aubrey, Robert and Paul Cohen. 1995. *Working Wisdom: Learning Organizations*. San Francisco: Jossey-Bass.

Auditor General of Canada. 1993. *Program Evaluation*, Report to the House of Commons on Program Evaluation. Ottawa: Office of the Auditor General of Canada.

Australian Development Assistance Bureau. 1982. *Summaries and Review of Ongoing Evaluation Studies, 1975-80*. Canberra: Australian Government Publishing Service.

Azumi, Koya and Jerald Hage, eds., 1972. *Organizational Systems*. Lexington, MA: D. C. Heath.

Barkdoll, Gerald L. 1982. "Increasing the Impact of Program Evaluation by Altering the Working Relationship Between the Program Manager and the Evaluator." Ph.D. dissertation, University of Southern California.

———. 1980. "Type III Evaluations: Consultation and Consensus." *Public Administration Review* (March/April):174-79.

Barley, Zoe A. and Mark Jenness. 1993. "Cluster Evaluation: A Method to Strengthen Evaluation in Smaller Programs with Similar Purposes." *Evaluation Practice* 14(2): 141-47.

Becker, Howard. 1970. "Whose Side Are We On?" Pp. 15-26 in *Qualitative Methodology*, edited by William J. Filstead. Chicago: Markham.

Bedell, J. R., J. C. Ward, Jr., R. P. Archer, and M. K. Stokes. 1985. "An Empirical Evaluation of a Model of Knowledge Utilization." *Evaluation Review* 9(2):109-26.

Bednarz, D. 1985. "Quantity and Quality in Evaluation Research: A Divergent View." *Evaluation and Program Planning* 8:289-386.

Behn, Robert D. 1995. "The Management of Reinvented Federalism." *Governing* (February):54.

Bellavita, C., J. S. Wholey, and M. A. Abramson. 1986. "Performance-Oriented Evaluation: Prospects for the Future." Pp. 286-92 in *Performance and Credibility: Developing Excellence in Public and Nonprofit Organizations*, edited by J. S. Wholey, M. A. Abramson, and C. Bellavita. Lexington, MA: Lexington.

Bennett, Claude F. 1982. *Reflective Appraisal of Programs*. Ithaca, NY: Cornell University Media Services.

———. 1979. *Analyzing Impacts of Extension Programs*. Washington, DC: U.S. Department of Agriculture.

Berger, Peter L. and Thomas Luckman. 1967. *The Social Construction of Reality*. Garden City, NY: Doubleday/Anchor.

Bernstein, Ilene and Howard E. Freeman. 1975. *Academic and Entrepreneurial Research: Consequences of Diversity in Federal Evaluation Studies*. New York: Russell Sage.

Beyer, Janice M. and Harrison M. Trice. 1982. "The Utilization Process: A Conceptual Framework and Synthesis of Empirical Findings." *Administrative Science Quarterly* 27:591-622.

Bickman, Leonard. 1994. "An Optimistic View of Evaluation." *Evaluation Practice* 15(3): 255-59.

———, ed. 1990. *Advances in Program Theory* (New Directions for Program Evaluation, No. 47, Fall). San Francisco: Jossey-Bass.

———. 1985. "Improving Established Statewide Programs: A Component Theory of Evaluation." *Evaluation Review* 9(2):189-208.

Blalock, Hubert M., Jr. 1964. *Causal Inferences in Nonexperimental Research*. Chapel Hill: University of North Carolina Press.

Blanchard, Ken. 1986. *Situational Leadership* (Two volume, 12-tape audiotape set). Escondido, CA: Blanchard Training and Development, Inc.

Blumer, Herbert. 1969. *Symbolic Interactionism*. Englewood Cliffs, NJ: Prentice Hall.

Bonsignore, Michael. 1996. "How Total Quality Became Framework for Honeywell." *Minneapolis Star Tribune*, April 15, p. D3.

Boruch, R. F., A. J. McSweeny, and E. J. Soderstrom. 1978. "Randomized Field Experiments for Program Planning, Development, and Evaluation: An Illustrative Bibiliography." *Evaluation Quarterly* 2:655-95.

Boruch, Robert and David Rindskopf. 1984. "Data Analysis." Pp. 121-58 in *Evaluation Research Methods*, edited by Leonard Rutman. Beverly Hills, CA: Sage.

Boruch, Robert F. and Werner Wothke, eds. 1985. *Randomization and Field Experimentation* (New Directions for Program Evaluation, No. 28, December). San Francisco: Jossey-Bass.

Boyer, J. F. and L. I. Langbein. 1991. "Factors Influencing the Use of Health Evaluation Research in Congress." *Evaluation Review* 15:507-32.

Brandl, John. 1994. "Must Deal With the Bureaucracy—But Exactly How Is Harder to Say." *Minneapolis Star Tribune*, September 5, p. 13A.

Braskamp, L. A. and R. D. Brown, eds. 1980. *Utilization of Evaluative Information* (New Directions for Program Evaluation, vol. 5). San Francisco: Jossey-Bass.

Breul, Jonathan P. 1994. "How the Government Performance and Results Act Borrows from the Experience of OECD Countries." Paper prepared for the Fulbright Symposium on Public Sector Reform, July 22-24, Brisbane, Australia.

Brightman, Harvey and Carl Noble. 1979. "On the Ineffective Education of Decision Scientists." *Decision Sciences* 10:151-57.

Brizius, J. A. and M. D. Campbell. 1991. *Getting Results: A Guide for Government Accountability*. Washington, DC: Council of Governor's Policy Advisors.

Brock, James, Richard Schwaller, and R. L. Smith. 1985. "The Social and Local Government Impacts of the Abandonment of the Milwaukee Railroad in Montana." *Evaluation Review* 9(2):127-43.

Brookfield, Stephen D. 1994. "Tales From the Dark Side: A Phenomenography of Adult Critical Reflection." *International Journal of Lifelong Learning* 13(3):203-16.

———. 1990. *Understanding and Facilitating Adult Learning*. San Francisco: Jossey-Bass.

Broom, Michael F. and Donald C. Klein. 1995. *Power: The Infinite Game*. Amherst, MA: HRD Press.

Broskowski, A., J. Driscoll, and H. C. Schulberg. 1978. "A Management Information and Planning System for Indirect Services." Pp. 189-214 in *Evaluation of Human Service Programs*, edited by C. Clifford Attkisson et al. New York: Academic Press.

Brown, Lawrence A. 1981. *Innovation Diffusion*. London: Methuen.

Bruyn, Severyn. 1966. *The Human Perspective in Sociology: The Methodology of Participant Observation*. Englewood Cliffs, NJ: Prentice Hall.

Bryk, Anthony S., ed. 1983. *Stakeholder-Based Evaluation* (New Directions for Program Evaluation, vol. 17). San Francisco: Jossey-Bass.

Bryson, John M. 1995. *Strategic Planning for Public and Nonprofit Organizations*. San Francisco: Jossey-Bass.

Bryson, John M. and Barbara C. Crosby. 1992. *Leadership for the Common Good: Tackling Public Problems in a Shared-Power World*. San Francisco: Jossey-Bass.

Buck, Connie. 1995. "The World According to Soros." *The New Yorker*, January 23, pp. 54-78.

Bunge, Mario. 1959. *Causality*. Cambridge, MA: Harvard University Press.

Burry, James. 1984. *Synthesis of the Evaluation Use Literature*, NIE Grant Report. Los Angeles: UCLA Center for the Study of Evaluation.

Campbell, Donald T. [1971] 1991. "Methods for the Experimenting Society." *Evaluation Practice* 12(3):223-60. Reprint of 1971 presentation to the American Psychological Association.

———. 1988. *Methodology and Epistemology for Social Science: Selected Papers*, edited by E. S. Overman. Chicago: University of Chicago Press.

———. 1983. "Threats to Validity Added When Applied Social Research Is Packaged as 'Program Evaluation' in the Service of Administrative Decision Making." Presented at the Conference on Family Support Programs: The State of the Art, Sponsored by the Bush Center in Child Development and Social Policy, Yale University, New Haven, CT.

———. 1969. "Reforms as Experiments." *American Psychologist* 24:409-29.

Campbell, Donald T. and Robert F. Boruch. 1975. "Making the Case for Randomized Assignment to Treatments by Considering the Alternatives: Six Ways in Which Quasi-Experimental Evaluations in Compensatory Education Tend to Underestimate Effects." Pp. 195-296 in *Evaluation and Experiment*, edited by Carol A. Bennett and Arthur A. Lumsdaine. New York: Academic Press.

Campbell, Donald T. and Julian C. Stanley. 1963. *Experimental and Quasi-Experimental Designs for Research*. Chicago: Rand McNally.

Campbell, Jeanne L. 1994. "Issues of Cluster Evaluation Use." Presented at the 1994 meeting of the American Evaluation Association, Boston.

———. 1983. "Factors and Conditions Influencing Usefulness of Planning, Evaluation, and Reporting in Schools." Ph.D. dissertation, University of Minnesota.

Canadian Evaluation Society. 1982. *The Bottom Line: Utilization of What, by Whom?* Proceedings of the 3rd Annual Conference of the Canadian Evaluation Society. Toronto: University of Toronto.

Caracelli, Valerie and Hallie Preskill. 1996. "Evaluation Use Survey." Evaluation Use Topical Interest Group, American Evaluation Association.

Caro, Francis G., ed. 1971. *Readings in Evaluation Research*. New York: Russell Sage.

Carver, John. 1990. *Boards That Make a Difference*. San Francisco: Jossey-Bass.

Caulley, Darrel. 1993. "Evaluation: Does It Make a Difference?" *Evaluation Journal of Australia* 5(2):3-15.

CFC (Center for the Future of Children). 1995. "Long-Term Outcomes of Early Childhood Programs." In *The Future of Children* 5(3). Los Altos, CA: The David and Lucille Packard Foundation.

Chelimsky, Eleanor. 1997. "The Coming Transformations in Evaluation." In *Evaluation for the 21st Century*, edited by Eleanor Chelimsky and Will Shadish. Thousand Oaks, CA: Sage.

———. 1995a. "The Political Environment of Evaluation and What It Means for the Development of the Field." Presented as the American Evaluation Association Presidential Address, November, Vancouver. Published in *Evaluation Practice* 16(3):215-25.

———. 1995b. "Comments on the AEA Guiding Principles." Pp. 53-54 in *Guiding Principles for Evaluators* (New Directions for Program Evaluation, No. 66), edited by W. R. Shadish, D. L. Newman, M. A. Scheirer, and C. Wye. San Francisco: Jossey-Bass.

———. 1992. "Expanding Evaluation Capabilities in the General Accounting Office." Pp. 91-96 in *Evaluation in the Federal Government: Changes, Trends, and Opportunities* (New Directions for Program Evaluation, No. 55), edited by C. G. Wye and R. C. Sonnichsen. San Francisco: Jossey-Bass.

———. 1987a. "The Politics of Program Evaluation." Pp. 5-22 in *Evaluation Practice in Review* (New Directions for Program Evaluation, No. 34), edited by D. S. Cordray, H. S. Bloom, and R. J. Light. San Francisco: Jossey-Bass.

———. 1987b. "What We Have Learned About the Politics of Program Evaluation." *Educational Evaluation and Policy Analysis* 9:199-213.

———. 1983. "Improving the Cost Effectiveness of Evaluation." Pp. 149-70 in *The Costs of Evaluation*, edited by Marvin C. Alkin and Lewis C. Solmon. Beverly Hills, CA: Sage.

Chen, Huey-Tsyh. 1990. *Theory-Driven Evaluations*. Newbury Park, CA: Sage.

———, ed. 1989. "Special Issue: The Theory-Driven Perspective." *Evaluation and Program Planning* 12(4).

Chen, Huey-Tsyh and Peter Rossi. 1989. "Issues in the Theory-Driven Perspective." *Evaluation and Program Planning* 12(4): 299-306.

———. 1987. "The Theory-Driven Approach to Validity." *Evaluation and Program Planning* 10(1):95-103.

Cicarelli, Victor. 1971. "The Impact of Head Start: Executive Summary." Pp. 397-401 in *Readings in Evaluation Research*, edited by Francis G. Caro. New York: Russell Sage.

Cochran-Smith, Marilyn and Susan Lytle. 1990. "Research on Teaching and Teacher Research: The Issues That Divide." *Educational Researcher* 19(2):2-11.

Coffey, Amanda and Paul Atkinson. 1996. *Making Sense of Qualitative Data*. Thousand Oaks, CA: Sage.

Cohen, David K. 1970. "Politics and Research: Evaluation of Social Action Programs in Education." In *Educational Evaluation*, American Educational Research Association, *Review of Educational Research* (April):213-38.

Cohen, David K. and Michael S. Garet. 1975. "Reforming Educational Policy With Applied Social Research." *Harvard Educational Review* 45(February):17-41.

Cohen, David K. and Janet A. Weiss. 1977. "Social Science and Social Policy: Schools and Race." Pp. 67-84 in *Using Social Research in Public Policy Making*, edited by Carol H. Weiss. Lexington, MA: D. C. Heath.

Cole, M. B. 1984. "User-Focused Evaluation of Training Programme Effectiveness in a South African Industrial Company." Presented at the National Productivity Institute Conference, University of Witwatersrand, Johannesburg.

Combs, Arthur. 1972. *Educational Accountability: Beyond Behavioral Objectives*. Washington, DC: Association for Supervision and Curriculum Development.

Comptroller General of Canada. 1989. "Working Standards for the Evaluation of Programs in Federal Departments and Agencies." Ottawa, ON: Program Evaluation Branch, Supply & Services Canada.

Connell, J. P., A. C. Kubisch, L. B. Schorr, and C. H. Weiss (Eds.). 1995. *New Approaches to Evaluating Community Initiatives: Concepts, Methods, and Contexts*. Washington, DC: The Aspen Institute.

Connor, Ross F. 1988. "Structuring Knowledge Production Activities to Facilitate Knowledge Utilization: Thoughts on Important Utilization Issues." *Studies in Educational Evaluation* 14:273-83.

Conrad, Kendon J., ed. 1994. *Critically Evaluating the Role of Experiments* (New Directions for Program Evaluation, No. 63). San Francisco: Jossey-Bass.

Conte, Christopher. 1996. "Workfare on Trial." *Governing*, April, pp. 19-23.

Cook, T. D. and Donald T. Campbell. 1979. *Quasi-experimentation: Design and Analysis Issues for Field Settings*. Chicago: Rand McNally.

Cook, Thomas D. 1995. "Evaluation Lessons Learned." Plenary keynote address at the International Evaluation Conference, "Evaluation '95," November 4, Vancouver, B.C.

Cooley, William W. and William E. Bickel. 1985. *Decision-Oriented Educational Research*. Boston: Kluwer-Nijhoff.

Cordray, David S. 1993. "Strengthening Causal Interpretations of Nonexperimental Data: The Role of Meta-analysis." Pp. 59-97 in *Program Evaluation: A Pluralistic Enterprise* (New Directions for Program Evaluation, No. 60), edited by Lee Sechrest. San Francisco: Jossey-Bass.

Corwin, Ronald G. 1973. *Reform and Organizational Survival*. New York: Wiley Interscience.

Council on Foundations. 1993. *Evaluation for Foundations: Concepts, Cases, Guidelines, and Resources*. San Francisco: Jossey-Bass.

Cousins, J. Bradley, John J. Donohue, and Gordon Bloom. 1996. "Understanding Collaborative Evaluation: Results From a Survey of North American Evaluators." Unpublished paper submitted for publication, University of Ottawa. Inquiries: bcousins@educ1.edu.uottawa.ca.

———. 1995. "Collaborative Evaluation: Survey of Practice in North America." Unpublished paper presented at the International Evaluation Conference, Vancouver. Monograph inquiries: bcousins@educ1.edu.uottawa.ca.

Cousins, J. Bradley and Lorna M. Earl, eds. 1995. *Participatory Evaluation in Educa-*

tion: Studies in Evaluation Use and Organizational Learning. London: Falmer.

Cousins, J. Bradley and Lorna M. Earl. 1992. "The Case for Participatory Evaluation." *Educational Evaluation and Policy Analysis* 14:397-418.

Cousins, J. Bradley and K. A. Leithwood. 1986. "Current Empirical Research on Evaluation Utilization." *Review of Educational Research* 56(3):331-64.

Cranford, John. 1995. "A Guide to Award-Winning Technology." *Governing*, January, pp. 61-70.

Cronbach, Lee J. 1982. *Designing Evaluations of Educational and Social Programs*. San Francisco: Jossey-Bass.

———. 1975. "Beyond the Two Disciplines of Scientific Psychology." *American Psychologist* 30:116-17.

Cronbach, Lee J. and Associates. 1980. *Toward Reform of Program Evaluation*. San Francisco: Jossey-Bass.

Cronbach, Lee J. and P. Suppes, eds. 1969. *Research for Tomorrow's Schools: Disciplined Inquiry of Education*. New York: Macmillan.

Crozier, Michel. 1964. *The Bureaucratic Phenomenon*. Chicago: University of Chicago Press.

Cyert, Richard and James G. March. 1963. *A Behavioral Theory of the Firm*. Englewood Cliffs, NJ: Prentice Hall.

Dahl, Robert. 1957. "The Concept of Power." *Behavioral Science* 2(July):201-15.

Dalkey, N. C. 1969. *The Delphi Method: An Experimental Study of Group Opinion*. Santa Monica, CA: Rand.

Daniels, Stacey. 1996. "Process or Outcomes? Different Approaches for Different Stages." *Foundation*, March/April, pp. 46-48.

D'Aprix, Roger D. 1996. *Communicating for Change*. San Francisco: Jossey-Bass.

Datta, Lois-ellin. 1994. "Paradigm Wars: A Basis for Peaceful Coexistence and Beyond." Pp. 53-70 in *The Qualitative-Quantitative Debate: New Perspectives* (New Directions for Program Evaluation, No. 61), edited by C. S. Reichardt and S. F. Rallis. San Francisco: Jossey-Bass.

Davidson, Fred. 1996. *Principles of Statistical Data Handling*. Thousand Oaks, CA: Sage.

Davis, Howard R. and Susan E. Salasin. 1975. "The Utilization of Evaluation." Pp. 621-66 in *Handbook of Evaluation Research*, vol. 1, edited by Elmer L. Struening and Marcia Guttentag. Beverly Hills, CA: Sage.

Dawson, Gary. 1995. "Agency Evaluation Reports Disregarded by Legislators Who Had Requested Them." *Saint Paul Pioneer Press*, August 7, p. 4B.

Dawson, Judith A. and J. J. D'Amico. 1985. "Involving Program Staff in Evaluation Studies: A Strategy for Increasing Use and Enriching the Data Base." *Evaluation Review* 9(2):173-88.

Deitchman, Seymour. 1976. *The Best-Laid Schemes: A Tale of Social Research and Bureaucracy*. Cambridge: MIT Press.

Denzin, Norman K. and Yvonna S. Lincoln. 1994. *Handbook of Qualitative Research*. Thousand Oaks, CA: Sage.

Dery, D. 1981. *Computers in Welfare: The MIS-Match*. Beverly Hills, CA: Sage.

Deutscher, Irwin. 1970. "Words and Deeds: Social Science and Social Policy." Pp. 27-51 in *Qualitative Methodology*, edited by William J. Filstead. Chicago: Markham.

Dewey, John. 1956a. *The Child and the Curriculum*. Chicago: University of Chicago Press.

———. 1956b. *The School and Society*. Chicago: University of Chicago Press.

de Wilde, John C. 1967. *Experiences With Agricultural Development in Tropical Africa*. Baltimore, MD: Johns Hopkins University Press.

Dial, Micah. 1994. "The Misuse of Evaluation in Educational Programs." Pp. 61-68 in *Preventing the Misuse of Evaluation* (New Directions for Program Evaluation, No. 64), edited by C. J. Stevens and Micah Dial. San Francisco: Jossey-Bass.

Dickey, Barbara. 1981. "Utilization of Evaluation of Small-Scale Educational Projects." *Educational Evaluation and Policy Analysis* 2(6):65-77.

Dickey, Barbara and Eber Hampton. 1981. "Effective Problem-Solving for Evaluation Utilization." *Knowledge: Creation, Diffusion, Utilization* 2(3):361-74.

Donmoyer, Robert. 1996. "Educational Research in an Era of Paradigm Proliferation: What's a Journal Editor to Do?" *Educational Researcher* 25(2):19-25.

Drucker, Peter F. 1996. *The Leader of the Future*. San Francisco: Jossey-Bass.

Duffy, Barbara Poitras. 1994. "Use and Abuse of Internal Evaluation." Pp. 25-32 in *Preventing the Misuse of Evaluation* (New Directions for Program Evaluation, No. 64), edited by C. J. Stevens and Micah Dial. San Francisco: Jossey-Bass.

Dugan, Margret. 1996. "Participatory and Empowerment Evaluation: Lessons Learned in Training and Technical Assistance." Pp. 277-303 in *Empowerment Evaluation: Knowledge and Tools for Self-Assessment and Accountability*, edited by D. M. Fetterman, A. J. Kaftarian, and A. Wandersman. Newbury Park, CA: Sage.

Dunagin, Ralph. 1977. *Dunagin's People*. Sentinel Star, Field Newspaper Syndicate (August 30).

Dyer, Henry S. 1973. "Recycling the Problems in Testing." Assessment in a Pluralistic Society: Proceedings of the 1972 Invitational Conference on Testing Problems, Educational Testing Service, Princeton, NJ.

Edison, Thomas. 1983. *The Diary and Observations*. New York: Philosophical Library.

Edwards, Ward and Marcia Guttentag. 1975. "Experiments and Evaluation: A Reexamination." Pp. 409-63 in *Evaluation and Experiment: Some Critical Issues in Assessing Social Programs*, edited by Carl Bennet and Arthur Lumsdaine. New York: Academic Press.

Edwards, Ward, Marcia Guttentag, and Kurt Snapper. 1975. "A Decision-Theoretic Approach to Evaluation Research." Pp. 139-82 in *Handbook of Evaluation Research*, vol. 1, edited by Elmer L. Struening and Marcia Guttentag. Beverly Hills, CA: Sage.

Eisner, Elliot. 1991. *The Enlightened Eye: Qualitative Inquiry and the Enhancement of Educational Practice*. New York: Macmillan.

Elpers, J. R. and R. L. Chapman. 1978. "Basis of the Information System Design and Implementation Process." Pp. 173-88 in *Evaluation of Human Service Programs*, edited by C. Clifford Attkisson, W. A. Hargreaves, M. J. Horowitz, and J. E. Sorenson. New York: Academic Press.

Emery, F. W. and E. L. Trist. 1965. "The Causal Texture of Organizational Environment." *Human Relations* 18(February): 21-31.

Etheredge, Lloyd S. 1980. "Government Learning: An Overview." In *Handbook of Political Behavior*, edited by S. Long. New York: Plenum.

Etzioni, Amitai. 1968. *The Active Society: A Theory of Societal and Political Processes*. New York: Free Press.

Evaluation Research Society. 1980. *Standards for Evaluation*. Washington, DC: Evaluation Research Society.

Evans, Gerry and Roger Blunden. 1984. "A Collaborative Approach to Evaluation." *Journal of Practical Approaches to Developmental Handicaps* 8(1):14-18.

Evans, John W. 1971. "Head Start: Comments on Criticisms." Pp. 401-407 in *Readings in Evaluation Research*, edited by Francis G. Caro. New York: Russell Sage.

Feiman, Sharon. 1977. "Evaluation Teacher Centers." *Social Review* 8(May):395-411.

Fetterman, D. M., A. J. Kaftarian, and A. Wandersman, eds. 1996. *Empowerment Evalu-*

ation: Knowledge and Tools for Self-Assessment and Accountability. Newbury Park, CA: Sage.

Fetterman, David M. 1995. "In Response to Dr. Dan Stufflebeam." *Evaluation Practice* 16(2):179-99.

———. 1994a. "Empowerment Evaluation," American Evaluation Association Presidential Address. *Evaluation Practice*, 15(1): 1-15.

———. 1994b. "Steps of Empowerment Evaluation: From California to Cape Town." *Evaluation and Program Planning* 17(3): 305-13.

———. 1993. "Empowerment Evaluation: Theme for the 1993 Evaluation Meeting." *Evaluation Practice* 14(1): 115-17.

———. 1984. "Ethnography in Educational Research: The Dynamics of Diffusion." Pp. 21-35 in *Ethnography in Educational Evaluation*, edited by D. M. Fetterman. Beverly Hills, CA: Sage.

———. 1980. "Ethnographic Approaches in Educational Evaluation: An Illustration." *Journal of Thought* 15(3):31-48.

Fink, Arlene, ed. 1995. *The Survey Kit*. Thousand Oaks, CA: Sage.

Firestone, W. A. and R. E. Herriott. 1984. "Multisite Qualitative Policy Research: Some Design and Implementation Issues." Pp. 63-88 in *Ethnography in Educational Evaluation*, edited by D. M. Fetterman. Beverly Hills, CA: Sage.

Fishman, Daniel B. 1992. "Postmodernism Comes to Program Evaluation." *Evaluation and Program Planning* 15(2):263-70.

Fletcher, Joseph. 1966. *Situation Ethics: The New Morality*. London: Westminister John Knox.

Folz, David H. 1996. *Survey Research for Public Administration*. Thousand Oaks, CA: Sage.

Fossum, L. B. 1989. *Understanding Organizational Change*. Los Altos, CA: Crisp.

Fournier, Deborah M., ed. 1995. *Reasoning in Evaluation: Inferential Links and Leaps* (New Directions for Program Evaluation, vol. 68). San Francisco: Jossey-Bass.

Freeman, Howard E. 1977. "The Present Status of Evaluation Research." Pp. 17-51 in *Evaluation Studies Review Annual*, vol. 2, edited by Marcia Guttentag. Beverly Hills, CA: Sage.

Funnell, Sue. 1993. "Reporting the Performance of the Public Sector." *Evaluation Journal of Australia* 5(2):16-37.

Gardiner, Peter C. and Ward Edwards. 1975. Measurement for Social Decision Making." Pp. 1-38 in *Human Judgment and Decision Processes*, edited by Martin F. Kaplan and Steven Schwartz. New York: Academic Press.

General Accounting Office (GAO). 1996. *Scientific Research: Continued Vigilance Needed to Protect Human Subjects*, GAO/HEHS-96-72. Washington, DC: GAO.

———. 1995. *Program Evaluation: Improving the Flow of Information to the Congress*, GAO/PEMD-95-1. Washington, DC: GAO.

———. 1992a. *Program Evaluation Issues*, GAO/OCG-93-6TR. Washington, DC: GAO.

———. 1992b. *Adolescent Drug Use Prevention: Common Features of Promising Community Programs*, GAO/PEMD-92-2. Washington, DC: GAO.

———. 1992c. *The Evaluation Synthesis*, GAO/PEMD-10.1.2. Washington, DC: GAO.

———. 1992d. *Quantitative Data Analysis*, GAO/PEMD-10.1.11. Washington, DC: GAO.

———. 1991. *Designing Evaluations*, GAO/PEMD-10.1.4. Washington, DC: GAO.

———. 1990a. *Case Study Evaluation*, Transfer Paper 10.1.9. Washington, DC: GAO.

———. 1990b. *Prospective Evaluation Methods: The Prospective Evaluation Synthesis*,

Transfer Paper 10.1.10. Washington, DC: GAO.

———. 1988. *Program Evaluation Issues*, GAO/OCG-89-8TR. Washington, DC: GAO.

———. 1987. *Federal Evaluation: Fewer Units, Reduced Resources*, GAO/PEMD-87-9. Washington, DC: GAO.

———. 1981. *Federal Evaluations*. Washington, DC: Government Printing Office.

Gephart, William J. 1981. "Watercolor Painting." Pp. 247-72 in *Metaphors for Evaluation*, edited by Nick L. Smith. Beverly Hills, CA: Sage.

Glaser, Edward M., Harold H. Abelson, and Kathalee N. Garrison. 1983. *Putting Knowledge to Use*. San Francisco: Jossey-Bass.

Goodman, Ellen. 1995. "Patients, Doctors, Hospitals Must End Silence on Journey to Death." Syndicated column distributed by Washington Post Writers Group, appearing in the *Saint Paul Pioneer Press*, December 3, p.17A.

Gordimer, Nadine. 1994. *None to Accompany Me*. New York: Penguin.

Governor's Commission on Crime Prevention and Control (GCCPC). 1976. *Residential Community Corrections Programs in Minnesota: An Evaluation Report*. Saint Paul: State of Minnesota.

Grant, Donald L., ed. 1978. *Monitoring Ongoing Programs* (New Directions for Program Evaluation, vol. 3). San Francisco: Jossey-Bass.

Greene, Jennifer C. 1990. "Technical Quality Versus User Responsiveness in Evaluation Practice." *Evaluation and Program Planning* 13(3):267-74.

———. 1988a. "Communication of Results and Utilization in Participatory Program Evaluation." *Evaluation and Program Planning* 11:341-51.

———. 1988b. "Stakeholder Participation and Utilization in Program Evaluation." *Evaluation Review* 12:91-116.

Guba, Egon G. 1981. "Investigative Reporting." Pp. 67-86 in *Metaphors for Evaluation*, edited by Nick L. Smith. Beverly Hills, CA: Sage.

———. 1978. "Toward a Methodology of Naturalistic Inquiry in Educational Evaluation." Monograph Series 8, UCLA Center for the Study of Evaluation.

———. 1977. "Overcoming Resistance to Evaluation." Presented at the Second Annual Conference on Evaluation, University of North Dakota.

Guba, Egon and Yvonna Lincoln. 1994. "Competing Paradigms in Qualitative Research." Pp. 105-17 in *Handbook of Qualitative Research*, edited by N. K. Denzin and Y. S. Lincoln. Thousand Oaks, CA: Sage.

———. 1989. *Fourth Generation Evaluation*. Newbury Park, CA: Sage.

———. 1981. *Effective Evaluation: Improving the Usefulness of Evaluation Results Through Responsive and Naturalistic Approaches*. San Francisco: Jossey-Bass.

Guttentag, Marcia and Elmer L. Struening. 1975a. *Handbook of Evaluation Research*, Vols. 1 and 2. Beverly Hills, CA: Sage.

———. 1975b. "The Handbook: Its Purpose and Organization." Pp. 3-10 in *Handbook of Evaluation Research*, vol. 2, edited by Marcia Guttentag and Elmer L. Struening. Beverly Hills, CA: Sage.

Guttmann, David and Marvin B. Sussman, eds., 1995. "Exemplary Social Intervention Programs for Members and Their Families." Special issue of *Marriage and Family Review* 21(1, 2). New York: Haworth Press.

Hage, Jerald and Michael Aiken. 1970. *Social Change in Complex Organizations*. New York: Random House.

Hall, Holly. 1992. "Assessing the Work of a Whole Foundation." *The Chronicle of Philanthropy*, January 14, 9-12.

Hampden-Turner, C. 1990. *Creating Corporate Culture*. Reading, MA: Addison-Wesley.

Handy, C. B. 1993. *Understanding Organizations*. New York: Oxford University Press.

Harper's Statistical Index. 1985. *Harper's Magazine*, April, p. 11. Source: Government Accounting Office/General Services Administration.

Havelock, Ronald G. 1980. "Forward." Pp. 11-14 in *Using Research in Organizations*, edited by Jack Rothman. Beverly Hills, CA: Sage.

———. 1973. *The Change Agent's Guide to Innovation in Education*. Englewood Cliffs, NJ: Prentice Hall.

Hedrick, Terry E. 1994. "The Quantitative-Qualitative Debate: Possibilities for Integration." Pp. 45-52 in *The Qualitative-Quantitative Debate: New Perspectives* (New Directions for Program Evaluation, No. 61), edited by C. S. Reichardt and S. F. Rallis. San Francisco: Jossey-Bass.

Heilbroner, Robert. 1996. "Dismal Days for the Dismal Science." *Forbes*, April 22, pp. 65-66.

Heilman, John G. 1980. "Paradigmatic Choices in Evaluation Methodology." *Evaluation Review* 4(5):693-712.

Helmer, Olaf. 1966. *Social Technology*. New York: Basic Books.

Hendricks, M., M. F. Mangano, and W. C. Moran, eds. 1990. *Inspectors General: A New Force in Evaluation* (New Directions for Program Evaluation, No. 48). San Francisco: Jossey-Bass.

Hendricks, Michael. 1994. "Making a Splash: Reporting Evaluation Results Effectively." Pp. 549-75 in *Handbook of Practical Program Evaluation*, edited by J. S. Wholey, H. P. Hatry, and K. E. Newcomer. San Francisco: Jossey-Bass.

———. 1984. "Preparing and Using Briefing Charts." *Evaluation News* 5(3):19-20.

———. 1982. "Oral Policy Briefings." Pp. 249-58 in *Communication Strategies in Evaluation*, edited by Nick L. Smith. Beverly Hills, CA: Sage.

Hendricks, Michael, and Elisabeth A. Handley. 1990. "Improving the Recommendations From Evaluation Studies." *Evaluation and Program Planning* 13:109-17.

Hersey, Paul. 1985. *Situational Leader*. Charlotte, North Carolina: Center for Leadership.

Hevey, Denise. 1984. "An Exercise in Utilization-Focused Evaluation: The Under-Fives Coordinators." Preschool Evaluation Project, Bristol University. Unpublished manuscript.

HFRP (Harvard Family Research Project). 1996a. *Noteworthy Results-Based Accountability Publications: An Annotated Bibliography*. Cambridge, MA: Harvard Family Research Project Publications.

———. 1996b. *State Results-Based Accountability Efforts*. Cambridge, MA: Harvard Family Research Project Publications.

Hinton, Barb. 1988. "Audit Tales: Kansas Intrigue." *Legislative Program Evaluation Society (LPES) Newsletter*, Spring, p. 3.

Hoffman, Yoel. 1975. *The Sound of One Hand*. New York: Basic Books.

Holzner, Burkart and John H. Marx. 1979. *Knowledge Application: The Knowledge System in Society*. Boston: Allyn & Bacon.

Hoogerwerf, Andries. 1985. "The Anatomy of Collective Failure in the Netherlands." Pp. 47-60 in *Culture and Evaluation*, edited by M. Q. Patton. San Francisco: Jossey-Bass.

Horsch, Karen. 1996. "Results-Based Accountability Systems: Opportunities and Challenges." *The Evaluation Exchange* 2(1):2-3.

House, Ernest R. 1995. "Principled Evaluation: A Critique of the AEA Guiding Principles." Pp. 27-34 in *Guiding Principles for Evaluators* (New Directions for Program Evaluation, No. 66), edited by W. R. Shadish, D. L. Newman, M. A. Scheirer, and C. Wye. San Francisco: Jossey-Bass.

———. 1994. "Integrating the Qualitative and Quantitative." Pp. 13-22 in *The Qualitative-Quantitative Debate: New Perspectives* (New Directions for Program Evaluation,

No. 61), edited by C. S. Reichardt and S. F. Rallis. San Francisco: Jossey-Bass.

———. 1993. *Professional Evaluation: Social Impact and Political Consequences*. Newbury Park, CA: Sage.

———. 1991. "Realism in Research." *Educational Researcher* 20(6):2-9.

———. 1990a. "Trends in Evaluation." *Educational Researcher*, 19(3):24-28.

———. 1990b. "Methodology and Justice." Pp. 23-36 in *Evaluation and Social Justice: Issues in Public Education* (New Directions for Program Evaluation, No. 45), edited by K. A. Sirotnik. San Francisco: Jossey-Bass.

———. 1986. "In-House Reflection: Internal Evaluation." *Evaluation Practice* 7(1):63-64.

———. 1980. *Evaluating With Validity*. Beverly Hills, CA: Sage.

———. 1977. "The Logic of Evaluative Argument." In *CSE Monograph Lines in Evaluation*, vol. 7. Los Angeles: UCLA Center for the Study of Education.

———. 1972. "The Conscience of Educational Evaluation." *Teachers College Record* 73(3): 405-14.

Howe, K. 1988. "Against the Quantitative-Qualitative Incompatibility Thesis." *Educational Researcher* 17(8):10-16.

Huberman, Michael. 1995. "Research Utilization: The State of the Art." *Knowledge and Policy* 7(4):13-33.

Huberty, Carl J. 1988. "Another Perspective on the Role of an Internal Evaluator." *Evaluation Practice* 9(4):25-32.

Hudson, Joe. 1977. "Problems of Measurement in Criminal Justice." Pp. 73-100 *Evaluation Research Methods*, edited by Leonard Rutman. Beverly Hills, CA: Sage.

Hudson, Joe, John Mayne, and R. Thomlison, eds. 1992. *Action-Oriented Evaluation in Organizations: Canadian Practices*. Toronto: Wall and Emerson.

Hurty, Kathleen. 1976. "Report by the Women's Caucus." *Proceedings: Educational Evaluation and Public Policy, A Conference*. San Francisco: Far West Regional Laboratory for Educational Research and Development.

ICMA. 1995. *Applying Performance Measurement: A Multimedia Training Program*, CD-ROM. Junction, MD: International City/County Management Association (in conjunction with the Urban Institute, Public Technology, Inc., and American Society for Public Administration).

Independent Sector. 1993. *A Vision of Evaluation*, edited by Sandra Trice Gray. Washington, DC: Independent Sector.

IQREC. 1997. "Democratizing Inquiry Through Qualitative Research." Presented at the International Qualitative Research in Education Conference, University of Georgia, Athens.

Jacobs, Francine H. 1988. "The Five-Tiered Approach to Evaluation." Pp. 37-68 in *Evaluating Family Programs*, edited by H. B. Weiss and F. Jacobs. Hawthorne, NY: Aldine.

Janowitz, Morris. 1979. "Where Is the Cutting Edge of Sociology?" *Midwest Sociological Quarterly* 20:591-93.

Johnson, R. B. 1995. "Estimating an Evaluation Utilization Model Using Conjoint Measurement and Analysis." *Evaluation Review* 19(3):313-38.

Joint Committee on Standards for Educational Evaluation. 1994. *The Program Evaluation Standards*. Thousand Oaks, CA: Sage.

———. 1981. *Standards for Evaluations of Educational Programs, Projects, and Materials*. New York: McGraw-Hill.

Kanter, Rosabeth Moss. 1983. *The Change Masters*. New York: Simon & Schuster.

Kanter, Rosabeth Moss, B. A. Stein, and J. D. Jick. 1992. *The Challenge of Organizational Change*. New York: Free Press.

Kearns, Kevin P. 1996. *Managing for Accountability*. San Francisco: Jossey-Bass.

Kellogg Foundation. n.d. (circa 1995). *W. K. Kellogg Foundation Cluster Evaluation Model of Evolving Practices*. Battle Creek, MI: Kellogg Foundation.

Kennedy, M. M. 1983. "The Role of the In-House Evaluator." *Evaluation Review* 7(4):519-41.

Kennedy School of Government. 1995. "Innovations in America Government Awards Winners." *Governing*, November, pp. 27-42.

Kidder, Louise H. and Michelle Fine. 1987. "Qualitative and Quantitative Methods: When Stories Converge." Pp. 57-76 in *Multiple Methods in Program Evaluation* (New Directions for Program Evaluation, No. 35), edited by M. M. Mark and L. Shotland. San Francisco: Jossey-Bass.

King, Jean A. 1995. "Involving Practitioners in Evaluation Studies: How Viable Is Collaborative Evaluation in Schools." Pp. 86-102 in *Participatory Evaluation in Education: Studies in Evaluation Use and Organizational Learning*, edited by J. Bradley Cousins and Lorna Earl. London: Falmer.

———. 1988. "Research on Evaluation Use and Its Implications for the Improvement of Evaluation Research and Practice." *Studies in Educational Evaluation* 14:285-99.

———. 1985. "Existing Research on Evaluation Use and Its Implications for the Improvement of Evaluation Research and Practice." Presented at invited conference on evaluation use, UCLA Center for the Study of Evaluation.

———. 1982. "Studying the Local Use of Evaluation: A Discussion of Theoretical Issues and an Empirical Study." *Studies in Educational Evaluation* 8:175-83.

King, Jean A. and M. Peg Lonnquist. 1994a. "A Review of Writing on Action Research: 1944-Present." Unpublished paper, Center for Applied Research and Educational Improvement, University of Minnesota, Minneapolis.

———. 1994b. "The Future of Collaborative Action Research: Promises, Problems, and Prospects." Unpublished paper, College of Education, University of Minnesota, Minneapolis, based on a presentation at the Annual Meeting of the American Educational Research Association, Atlanta, 1993.

King, Jean A., Lynn Lyons Morris, and Carol T. Fitz-Gibbon. 1987. *How to Assess Program Implementation*. Newbury Park, CA: Sage.

King, Jean A. and Ellen Pechman. 1984. "Pinning a Wave to Shore: Conceptualizing School Evaluation Use. *Educational Evaluation and Policy Analysis* 6(3):241-51.

———. 1982. *Improving Evaluation Use in Local Schools*. Washington, DC: National Institute of Education.

Knapp, Kay. 1995. "Institutionalizing Performance Measurement and Evaluation in Government: Lessons Learned." Presented at the International Evaluation Conference, November 3, Vancouver. Internal publication of Performance Measurement and Evaluation, A-2303 Hennepin County Government Center, Minneapolis, Minnesota, 55487-0233.

Knapp, Michael S. 1996. "Methodological Issues in Evaluating Integrated Human Services Initiatives." Pp. 21-34 in *Evaluating Initiatives to Integrate Human Services* (New Directions for Evaluation, No. 69), edited by J. M. Marquart and E. L. Konrad.

Kneller, George F. 1972. "Goal-Free Evaluation." *Evaluation Comment: The Journal of Educational Evaluation* (Center for the Study of Evaluation, UCLA) 3(4):13-15.

Knowles, Malcolm S. 1989. *The Making of an Adult Educator: An Autobiographical Journey*. San Francisco: Jossey-Bass.

Knowles, Malcolm S. and Associates. 1985. *Andragogy in Action: Applying Modern Principles of Adult Learning*. San Francisco: Jossey-Bass.

Knox, Alan B. 1987. *Helping Adults Learn*. San Francisco: Jossey-Bass.

Kochen, Manfred. 1975. "Applications of Fuzzy Sets in Psychology." Pp. 395-407 in *Fuzzy Sets and Their Applications to Cognitive and Decision Processes*, edited by Lofti A. Zadeh, King-Sun Fu, Kokichi Tanaka, and Masamichi Shimura. New York: Academic Press.

Kottler, Jeffrey A. 1996. *Beyond Blame: Resolving Conflicts*. San Francisco: Jossey-Bass.

Kourilsky, Marilyn. 1974. "An Adversary Model for Educational Evaluation." *Evaluation Comment* 4:2.

Kouzes, James M. and Barry Z. Posner. 1995. *The Leadership Challenge*. San Francisco: Jossey-Bass.

Kuhn, Thomas. 1970. *The Structure of Scientific Revolutions*. Chicago: University of Chicago Press.

Kushner, Tony. 1994. *Angels in America. Part Two: Perestroika*. New York: Theatre Communications Group.

Laundergan, J. Clark. 1983. *Easy Does It*. Center City, MN: Hazelden Foundation.

Law, Nancy. 1996. "VP News." *Reality-Test*, The Division H Newsletter of the American Educational Research Association, January, p. 1.

Lawler, E. E., III, A. M. Mohrman, Jr., S. A. Mohrman, G. E. Ledford, Jr., T. G. Cummings, and associates. 1985. *Doing Research That Is Useful for Theory and Practice*. San Francisco: Jossey-Bass.

Layzer, Jean I. 1996. "Building Theories of Change in Family Support Programs." *The Evaluation Exchange* 2(1):10-11.

Lazarsfeld, Paul F. and Jeffrey G. Reitz. 1975. *An Introduction to Applied Sociology*. New York: Elsevier.

Leeuw F., R. Rist, and R. Sonnichsen, eds. (1993). *Comparative Perspectives on Evaluation and Organizational Learning*. New Brunswick, NJ: Transaction.

Le Guin, Ursula K. 1969. *The Left Hand of Darkness*. New York: Ace Books.

Leonard, Jennifer. 1996. "Process or Outcomes? Turn Outcome 'Sticks' Into Carrots." *Foundation*, March/April, pp. 46-48.

Lester, James P. and Leah J. Wilds. 1990. "The Utilization of Public Policy Analysis: A Conceptual Framework." *Evaluation and Program Planning* 13(3):313-19.

Levin, B. 1993. "Collaborative Research in and With Organizations." *Qualitative Studies in Education* 6(4):331-40.

Levine, Harold G., R. Gallimore, T. S. Weisner, and J. L. Turner. 1980. "Teaching Participant-Observation Research Methods: A Skills-Building Approach." *Anthropology and Education Quarterly* 9(1):38-54.

Leviton, L. A. and E. F. X. Hughes. 1981. "Research on Utilization of Evaluations: A Review and Synthesis." *Evaluation Review* 5(4):525-48.

Lewy, Arieh and Marvin Alkin. 1983. *The Impact of a Major National Evaluation Study: Israel's Van Leer Report*. Los Angeles: UCLA Center for the Study of Evaluation.

Lincoln, Yvonna S. 1991. "The Arts and Sciences of Program Evaluation." *Evaluation Practice* 12(1):1-7.

Lincoln, Yvonna S. and Egon G. Guba. 1985. *Naturalistic Inquiry*. Beverly Hills, CA: Sage.

Lindblom, Charles E. 1965. *The Intelligence of Democracy*. New York: Free Press.

———. 1959. "The Science of Muddling Through Public Administration." *Public Administration Review* 19:79-99.

Lipsey, Mark W. 1990. *Design Sensitivity: Statistical Power for Experimental Research*. Newbury Park, CA: Sage.

———. 1988. "Practice and Malpractice in Evaluation Research." *Evaluation Practice* 9(4):5-24.

Lipsey, Mark W. and John A. Pollard. 1989. "Driving Toward Theory in Program Evaluation: More Models to Choose From." In

"Special Issue: The Theory-Driven Perspective," edited by Huey-Tsyh Chen, *Evaluation and Program Planning* 12(4):317-28.

Lofland, John. 1971. *Analyzing Social Settings*. Belmont, CA: Wadsworth.

Love, Arnold J. 1991. *Internal Evaluation: Building Organizations From Within*. Newbury Park, CA: Sage.

———, ed. 1983. *Developing Effective Internal Evaluation* (New Directions for Program Evaluation, No. 20). San Francisco: Jossey-Bass.

Lucas, H. C. 1975. *Why Information Systems Fail*. New York: Columbia University Press.

Lynn, Lawrence E., Jr. 1980a. "Crafting Policy Analysis for Decision Makers." Interview conducted by Michael Kirst in *Educational Evaluation and Policy Analysis* 2:85-90.

———. 1980b. *Designing Public Policies: A Casework on the Role of Policy Analysis*. Santa Monica, CA: Goodyear.

Lynn, Lawrence E., Jr. and Susan Salasin. 1974. "Human Services: Should We, Can We Make Them Available to Everyone?" *Evaluation* (Spring Special Issue):4-5.

Lyon, Eleanor. 1989. "In-House Research: A Consideration of Roles and Advantages." *Evaluation and Program Planning* 12(3): 241-48.

MacKenzie, R. A. 1972. *The Time Trap*. New York: AMACOM.

Mann, Floyd C. and F. W. Neff. 1961. *Managing Major Change in Organizations*. Ann Arbor, MI: Foundation for Research on Human Behavior.

Mark, Melvin M. and Thomas D. Cook. 1984. "Design of Randomized Experiments and Quasi-Experiments." Pp. 65-120 in *Evaluation Research Methods*, edited by Leonard Rutman. Beverly Hills, CA: Sage.

Mark, Melvin M. and Lance Shotland, eds. 1987. *Multiple Methods in Program Evaluation* (New Directions for Program Evaluation, No. 35). San Francisco: Jossey-Bass.

Marquart, Jules M. and Ellen L. Konrad, eds. 1996. *Evaluating Initiatives to Integrate Human Services* (New Directions for Program Evaluation No. 69).

Massarik, F., ed. 1990. *Advances in Organization Development*. Norwood, NJ: Ablex.

Maxwell, Joseph A. 1996. *Qualitative Research Design*. Thousand Oaks, CA: Sage.

Maxwell, J. A., P. G. Bashook, and L. J. Sandlow. 1985. "Combining Ethnographic and Experimental Methods in Educational Research: A Case Study." In *Beyond the Status Quo: Theory, Politics, and Practice in Ethnographic Evaluation*, edited by D. M. Fetterman and M. A. Pitman. Washington, DC: Cato Institute.

Mayer, Steven E. 1996. "Building Community Capacity With Evaluation Activities That Empower." Pp. 332-75 in *Empowerment Evaluation: Knowledge and Tools for Self-Assessment and Accountability*, edited by D. M. Fetterman, A. J. Kaftarian, and A. Wandersman. Newbury Park, CA: Sage.

———. 1994. *Building Community Capacity: The Potential of Community Foundations*. Minneapolis, MN: Rainbow Research, Inc.

———. 1993. "Common Barriers to Effectiveness in the Independent Sector." Pp. 7-11 in *A Vision of Evaluation*. Washington, DC: Independent Sector.

———. 1976. *Organizational Readiness to Accept Program Evaluation Questionnaire*. Minneapolis, MN: Program Evaluation Resource Center.

———. 1975. "Are You Ready to Accept Program Evaluation" and "Assess Your Program Readiness for Program Evaluation." *Program Evaluation Resource Center Newsletter* 6(1):1-5 and 6(3):4-5. Published by Program Evaluation Resource Center, Minneapolis, MN.

———. n.d. *The Assets Model of Community Development*. Minneapolis, MN: Rainbow Research.

McIntosh, Winsome. 1996. "Process or Outcomes? Keep the Context Long-Term." *Foundation*, March/April, pp. 46-48.

McIntyre, Ken. 1976. "Evaluating Educational Programs." *Review* (University Council for Educational Administration) 18(1): 39.

McLaughlin, John A., Larry J. Weber, Robert W. Covert, and Robert B. Ingle, eds. 1988. *Evaluation Utilization* (New Directions for Program Evaluation, No. 39). San Francisco: Jossey-Bass.

McLaughlin, Milbrey. 1976. "Implementation as Mutual Adaptation." Pp. 167-80 in *Social Program Implementation*, edited by Walter Williams and Richard F. Elmore. New York: Academic Press.

McLean, A. J. 1982. *Organizational Development in Transition: An Evolving Profession*. New York: John Wiley.

McTavish, Donald, E. Brent, J. Cleary, and K. R. Knudsen. 1975. *The Systematic Assessment and Prediction of Research Methodology*, Vol. 1, *Advisory Report*. Final Report on Grant OEO 005-P-20-2-74, Minnesota Continuing Program for the Assessment and Improvement of Research. Minneapolis: University of Minnesota.

MDHS. 1996. *Focus on Client Outcomes: A Guidebook for Results-Oriented Human Services*. St. Paul, MN: Community Services Division, Minnesota Department of Human Services.

MECFE. 1992. *Changing Times, Changing Families*. Parent outcome evaluation of the Minnesota Early Childhood Parent Education Program. St. Paul, MN: Minnesota Department of Education.

Mendelow, Aubrey L. 1987. "Stakeholder Analysis for Strategic Planning and Implementation." Pp. 176-91 in *Strategic Planning and Management Handbook*, edited by W. R. King and D. I. Cleland. New York: Van Nostrand Reinhold.

Meyers, William R. 1981. *The Evaluation Enterprise*. San Francisco: Jossey-Bass.

Miles, Matthew B. and A. Michael Huberman. 1994. *Qualitative Data Analysis: An Expanded Sourcebook*, 2nd ed. Thousand Oaks, CA: Sage.

Miller, D. E. 1981. *The Book of Jargon*. New York: Macmillan.

Millett, Ricardo A. 1996. "Empowerment Evaluation and the W. K. Kellogg Foundation." Pp. 65-76 in *Empowerment Evaluation: Knowledge and Tools for Self-Assessment and Accountability*, edited by D. M. Fetterman, A. J. Kaftarian, and A. Wandersman. Newbury Park, CA: Sage.

Mills, C. Wright. 1961. *The Sociological Imagination*. New York: Grove.

———. 1959. *The Sociological Imagination*. New York: Oxford University Press.

Minnich, Elizabeth K. 1990. *Transforming Knowledge*. Philadelphia: Temple University Press.

Moe, Barbara L. 1993. "The Human Side of Evaluation: Using the Results." Pp. 19-31 in *A Vision of Evaluation*. Washington, DC: Independent Sector.

Morgan, Gareth. 1989. *Creative Organizational Theory*. Newbury Park, CA: Sage.

———. 1986. *Images of Organization*. Newbury Park, CA: Sage.

Morris, Lynn Lyons and Carol Taylor Fitz-Gibbon. 1978. *How to Deal With Goals and Objectives*. Beverly Hills, CA: Sage.

Morrison, Ann M. 1995. *The New Leaders: Leadership Diversity in America*. San Francisco: Jossey-Bass.

Moss, Pamela. 1996. "Enlarging the Dialogue in Educational Measurement: Voices From the Interpretive Research Traditions." *Educational Researcher* 25(1):20-28.

Mowbray, Carol T. 1994. "The Gradual Extinction of Evaluation Within a Government Agency." Pp. 33-48 in *Preventing the Misuse of Evaluation* (New Directions for Program Evaluation, No. 64), edited by C. J. Stevens and Micah Dial. San Francisco: Jossey-Bass.

Mueller, Marsha. 1996. *Immediate Outcomes of Lower-Income Participants in Minnesota's Universal Access Early Childhood Family Education*. St. Paul, MN: Minnesota Department of Children, Families & Learning.

Murphy, Jerome T. 1976. "Title V of ESEA: The Impact of Discretionary Funds on State Education Bureaucracies." Pp. 77-100 in *Social Program Implementation*, edited by Walter Williams and Richard Elmore. New York: Academic Press.

Nagao, Masafumi. 1995. "Evaluating Global Issues in a Community Setting." Keynote address, *Evaluation '95*, International Evaluation Conference, November 3, Vancouver.

Nagel, Ernest. 1961. *The Structure of Science*. New York: Harcourt Brace Jovanovich.

National Academy of Sciences. 1968. *The Behavioral Sciences and the Federal Government*. Washington, DC: Government Printing Office.

Newcomer, Kathryn E. and Joseph S. Wholey. 1989. "Conclusion: Evaluation Strategies for Building High-Performance Programs." Pp. 195-208 in *Improving Government Performance: Evaluation Strategies for Strengthening Public Agencies and Programs*, edited by J. S. Wholey and K. E. Newcomer. San Francisco: Jossey-Bass.

Newman, Dianna and Robert Brown. 1996. *Applied Ethics for Program Evaluation*. Newbury Park, CA: Sage.

New York Times. 1996. "Educators Show How Not to Write English." Editorial distributed by New York Times News Service and published in the *Minneapolis Star Tribune*, March 24, p. A24.

Northwest Regional Educational Laboratory (NWREL). 1977. *3-on-2 Evaluation Report, 1976-1977*, vols. 1-3. Portland, OR: NWREL.

Nowakowski, Jeri, ed. 1987. *The Client Perspective on Evaluation* (New Directions for Program Evaluation, vol. 36). San Francisco: Jossey-Bass.

Nunnally, Jim C., Jr. 1970. *Introduction to Psychological Measurement*. New York: McGraw-Hill.

Odiorne, George S. 1984. *Strategic Management of Human Resources*. San Francisco: Jossey-Bass.

Office of Program Analysis, General Accounting Office. 1976. *Federal Program Evaluations: A Directory for the Congress*. Washington, DC: Government Printing Office.

Osborne, David and Ted Gaebler. 1992. *Reinventing Government: How the Entrepreneurial Spirit Is Transforming the Public Sector From Schoolhouse to Statehouse, City Hall to the Pentagon*. Reading, MA: Addison-Wesley.

O'Toole, James O. 1995. *Leading Change*. San Francisco: Jossey-Bass.

Owen, John M. 1993. *Program Evaluation: Forms and Approaches*. New South Wales, Australia: Allen & Unwin.

Owens, Thomas. 1973. "Education Evaluation by Adversary Proceeding." In *School Evaluation: The Politics and Process*, edited by Ernest R. House. Berkeley, CA: McCutchan.

PACT. 1986. *Participatory Evaluation: A User's Guide*. New York: Private Agencies Collaborating Together.

Palumbo, Dennis J., ed. 1994. *The Politics of Program Evaluation*. Newbury Park, CA: Sage.

Palumbo, D. J., S. Maynard-Moody, and P. Wright. 1984. "Measuring Degrees of Successful Implementation." *Evaluation Review* 8(1):45-74.

Palumbo, D. J., M. Musheno, and S. Maynard-Moody. 1985. *An Evaluation of the Implementation of Community Corrections in Oregon, Colorado and Connecticut*, Final Report prepared for Grant 82-15-CUK015. Washington, DC: National Institute of Justice.

Parker, Glenn M. 1996. *Team Players and Teamwork*. San Francisco: Jossey-Bass.

Parlett, Malcolm and David Hamilton. 1976. "Evaluation as Illumination: A New Approach to the Study of Innovatory Programs." Pp. 140-57 in *Evaluation Studies Review Annual*, vol. 1, edited by Gene V. Glass. Beverly Hills, CA: Sage.

———. "Evaluation as Illumination: A New Approach to the Study of Innovative Programs." Occasional Paper 9, University of Edinburgh Center for Research in the Educational Sciences.

Parsons, Talcott. 1960. *Structure and Process in Modern Society*. New York: Free Press.

Patton, Michael Quinn. 1996. *A World Larger Than Formative and Summative* (New Directions in Program Evaluation). San Francisco: Jossey-Bass.

———. 1994a. "Developmental Evaluation." *Evaluation Practice* 15(3):311-20.

———. 1994b. "The Program Evaluation Standards Reviewed." *Evaluation Practice* 15(2):193-99.

———. 1990. *Qualitative Evaluation and Research Methods*. Newbury Park, CA: Sage.

———. 1989. "A Context and Boundaries for a Theory-Driven Approach to Validity." *Evaluation and Program Planning* 12(4): 375-78.

———. 1988. "Integrating Evaluation Into a Program for Increased Utility and Cost-Effectiveness." Pp. 85-95 in *Evaluation Utilization* (New Directions in Program Evaluation, No. 39), edited by Robert Covert et al. San Francisco: Jossey-Bass.

———. 1986. *Utilization-Focused Evaluation* 2nd ed. Beverly Hills, CA: Sage.

———, ed. 1985. *Culture and Evaluation*. San Francisco: Jossey-Bass.

———. 1984. "An Alternative Evaluation Approach for the Problem-Solving Training Program: A Utilization-Focused Evaluation Process." *Evaluation and Program Planning* 7:189-92.

———. 1983. "Similarities of Extension and Evaluation." *Journal of Extension* 21(September-October):14-21.

———. 1982a. *Practical Evaluation*. Beverly Hills, CA: Sage.

———. 1982b. "Managing Management Information Systems." Pp. 227-39 in *Practical Evaluation*, edited by M. Q. Patton. Beverly Hills, CA: Sage.

———. 1981. *Creative Evaluation*. Beverly Hills, CA: Sage.

———. 1980a. *Qualitative Evaluation Methods*. Beverly Hills, CA: Sage.

———. 1980b. *The Processes and Outcomes of Chemical Dependency*. Center City, MN: Hazelden Foundation.

———. 1978. *Utilization-Focused Evaluation*. Beverly Hills, CA: Sage.

———. 1975a. *Alternative Evaluation Research Paradigm*. Grand Forks: University of North Dakota.

———. 1975b. "Understanding the Gobbledy Gook: A People's Guide to Standardized Test Results and Statistics." In *Testing and Evaluation: New Views*. Washington, DC: Association for Childhood Education International.

———. 1973. *Structure and Diffusion of Open Education*, Report on the Trainers of Teacher Trainer Program, New School of Behavioral Studies in Education. Grand Forks: University of North Dakota.

Patton, Michael Q. with M. Bringewatt, J. Campbell, T. Dewar, and M. Mueller. 1993. *The McKnight Foundation Aid to Families in Poverty Initiative: A Synthesis of Themes, Patterns, and Lessons Learned*. Minneapolis, MN: The McKnight Foundation.

Patton, Michael Q., Patricia S. Grimes, Kathryn M. Guthrie, Nancy J. Brennan, Barbara D. French, and Dale A. Blyth. 1977. "In Search of Impact: An Analysis of the Utilization of Federal Health Evaluation Research." Pp. 141-64 in *Using Social Research in Pub-*

lic Policy Making, edited by Carol H. Weiss. Lexington, MA: D. C. Heath.

Patton, Michael Q., Kathy Guthrie, Steven Gray, Carl Hearle, Rich Wiseman, and Neala Yount. 1977. *Environments That Make a Difference: An Evaluation of Ramsey County Corrections Foster Group Homes*. Minneapolis: Minnesota Center for Social Research, University of Minnesota.

Pederson, Clara A., ed. 1977. *Informal Education: Evaluation and Record Keeping*. Grand Forks: University of North Dakota.

Perlman, Ellen. 1996. "Sirens That Repel." *Governing*, April, pp. 37-42.

Perrone, Vito. 1977. *The Abuses of Standardized Testing*. Bloomington, IN: Phi Delta Kappa Educational Foundation.

Perrone, Vito, Michael Q. Patton, and Barbara French. 1976. *Does Accountability Count Without Teacher Support?* Minneapolis: Minnesota Center for Social Research, University of Minnesota.

Perrow, Charles. 1970. *Organizational Analysis: A Sociological View*. Belmont, CA: Wadsworth.

———. 1968. "Organizational Goals." Pp. 305-11 in *International Encyclopedia of Social Sciences*. New York: Macmillan.

Peters, Thomas and Robert Waterman. 1982. *In Search of Excellence*. New York: Harper & Row.

Petrie, Hugh G. 1972. "Theories Are Tested by Observing the Facts: Or Are They?" Pp. 47-73 in *Philosophical Redirection of Educational Research: The Seventy-First Yearbook of the National Society for the Study of Education*, edited by Lawrence G. Thomas. Chicago: University of Chicago Press.

Phillips, D. C. 1995. "The Good, the Bad, and the Ugly: The Many Faces of Constructivism." *Educational Researcher* 24(7):5-12.

Plutarch. 1952. "Alexander." *The Lives of the Noble Grecians and Romans, Great Books of the Western World*, vol. 14. Chicago: Encyclopedia Britannica.

Policy Analysis Source Book for Social Programs. 1976. Washington, DC: Government Printing Office.

Popham, James W. 1995. "An Extinction-Retardation Strategy for Educational Evaluators." *Evaluation Practice* 16(3):267-74.

———. 1972. "Results Rather Than Rhetoric." *Evaluation Comment: The Journal of Educational Evaluation* (Center for the Study of Evaluation, UCLA) 3(4):12-13.

Popham, James W. and Dale Carlson. 1977. "Deep Dark Deficits of the Adversary Evaluation Model." *Educational Researcher*, June, pp. 3-6.

Posavac, Emil J. 1995. "Statistical Process Control in the Practice of Program Evaluation." *Evaluation Practice* 16(3):121-39.

———. 1994. "Misusing Program Evaluation by Asking the Wrong Questions." Pp. 69-78 in *Preventing the Misuse of Evaluation* (New Directions for Program Evaluation, No. 64), edited by C. J. Stevens and Micah Dial. San Francisco: Jossey-Bass.

Powell, Arthur B., Dawud A. Jeffries, and Aleshia E. Selby. 1989. "Participatory Research: Empowering Students and Teachers and Humanizing Mathematics." *Humanistic Mathematics Network Newsletter* 4:29-38.

Pressman, Jeffrey L. and Aaron Wildavsky. 1984. *Implementation*. Berkeley: University of California Press.

Prideaux, David. 1995. "Beyond Facilitation: Action Research as Self-Research and Self-Evaluation." *Evaluation Journal of Australia* 7(1):3-13.

Pritchett, Price. 1996. *Resistance: Moving Beyond the Barriers to Change*. Dallas, TX: Pritchett and Associates.

Provus, Malcolm. 1971. *Discrepancy Evaluation for Educational Program Improvement and Assessment*. Berkeley, CA: McCutchan.

Rafter, David O. 1984. "Three Approaches to Evaluation Research." *Knowledge: Creation, Diffusion, Utilization* 6(2):165-85.

Reichardt, Charles S. and Thomas D. Cook. 1979. "Beyond Qualitative Versus Quantitative Methods." In *Qualitative and Quantitative Methods*, edited by T. Cook and C. S. Reichardt. Beverly Hills, CA: Sage.

Reichardt, Charles S. and Sharon F. Rallis, eds. 1994a. *The Qualitative-Quantitative Debate: New Perspectives* (New Directions for Program Evaluation, No. 61). San Francisco: Jossey-Bass.

———. 1994b. "The Relationship Between the Qualitative and Quantitative Research Traditions." Pp. 5-12 in *The Qualitative-Quantitative Debate: New Perspectives* (New Directions for Program Evaluation, No. 61), edited by C. S. Reichardt and S. F. Rallis. San Francisco: Jossey-Bass.

———. 1994c. "Qualitative and Quantitative Inquiries Are Not Incompatible: A Call for a New Partnership." Pp. 85-91 in *The Qualitative-Quantitative Debate: New Perspectives* (New Directions for Program Evaluation, No. 61), edited by C. S. Reichardt and S. F. Rallis. San Francisco: Jossey-Bass.

Reicken, Henry W. and Robert F. Boruch. 1974. *Social Experimentation: A Method for Planning and Evaluating Social Intervention*. New York: Academic Press.

Resnick, Michael. 1984. "Teen Sex: How Girls Decide." *Update-Research Briefs* (University of Minnesota) 11(5):15.

Richter, M. J. 1995. "Managing Government's Documents." *Governing*, April, pp. 59-66.

Rippey, R. M. 1973. "The Nature of Transactional Evaluation." Pp. 1-16 in *Studies in Transactional Evaluation*, edited by R. M. Rippey. Berkeley, CA: McCutchan.

Rist, Raymond. 1977. "On the Relations Among Educational Research Paradigms: From Disdain to Detente." *Anthropology and Education* 8:42-49.

Rivlin, Alice M. 1971. *Systematic Thinking for Social Action*. Washington, DC: Brookings Institution.

Rizo, Felipe M. 1991. "The Controversy About Quantification in Social Research." *Educational Researcher* 20(9):9-12.

Rog, Debra J. 1985. "A Methodological Assessment of Evaluability Assessment." Ph.D. dissertation, Vanderbilt University.

Rogers, Everett. 1962. *Diffusion of Innovation*. New York: Free Press.

Rogers, Everett M. and Floyd F. Shoemaker. 1971. *Communication of Innovation*. New York: Free Press.

Rogers, Everett M. and Lynne Svenning. 1969. *Managing Change*. San Mateo, CA: Operation PEP.

Rosenthal, Elsa J. 1976. "Delphi Technique." Pp. 121-22 in *Encyclopedia of Educational Evaluation*, edited by S. Anderson et al. San Francisco: Jossey-Bass.

Rossi, Peter H. 1994. "The War Between the Quals and the Quants: Is a Lasting Peace Possible?" Pp. 23-36 in *The Qualitative-Quantitative Debate: New Perspectives* (New Directions for Program Evaluation, No. 61), edited by C. S. Reichardt and S. F. Rallis. San Francisco: Jossey-Bass.

———. 1972. "Testing for Success and Failure in Social Action." Pp. 11-65 in *Evaluating Social Programs*, edited by Peter H. Rossi and Walter Williams. New York: Seminar Press.

Rossi, Peter H. and H. E. Freeman. 1993. (1985. 1982.) *Evaluation: A Systematic Approach*. Beverly Hills, CA: Sage.

Rossi, Peter H., Howard E. Freeman, and Sonia R. Wright. 1979. *Evaluation: A Systematic Approach*. Beverly Hills, CA: Sage.

Rossi, Peter H. and Walter Williams, eds. 1972. *Evaluating Social Programs: Theory, Practice, and Politics*. New York: Seminar Press.

Rutman, Leonard. 1977. "Barriers to the Utilization of Evaluation Research." Presented at the 27th Annual Meeting of the Society for the Study of Social Problems, Chicago.

Rutman, Leonard and John Mayne. 1985. "Institutionalization of Program Evaluation in Canada: The Federal Level." Pp. 61-68 in *Culture and Evaluation*, edited by M. Q. Patton. San Francisco: Jossey-Bass.

Sanders, James. 1994. "Methodological Issues in Cluster Evaluation." Presented at the 1994 meeting of the American Evaluation Association, Boston.

Sartorius, Rolf H. 1996a. "Third Generation Logical Framework." *European Journal of Agricultural Education and Extension* March. Unpublished manuscript.

———. 1996b. "The Third Generation Logical Framework: More Effective Project and Program Management." Working paper, Social IMPACT, Reston, VA. (e-mail: socimpct@erols.com)

———. 1991. "The Logical Framework Approach to Project Design and Management." *Evaluation Practice* 12(2):139-47.

Saxe, Leonard and Daniel Koretz, eds. 1982. *Making Evaluation Research Useful to Congress*. San Francisco: Jossey-Bass.

Schalock, Robert L. 1995. *Outcome-Based Evaluation*. New York: Plenum.

Schein, Edgar H. 1985. *Organizational Culture and Leadership*. San Francisco: Jossey-Bass.

Schein, L. 1989. *A Manager's Guide to Corporate Culture*. New York: Conference Board.

Scheirer, Mary Ann. 1987. "Program Theory and Implementation Theory: Implications for Evaluators." Pp. 59-76 in *Using Program Theory in Evaluation* (New Directions for Program Evaluation, vol. 33), edited by Leonard Bickman. San Francisco: Jossey-Bass.

Schön, Donald A. 1987. *Educating the Reflective Practitioner*. San Francisco: Jossey-Bass.

———. 1983. *The Reflective Practitioner*. New York: Basic Books.

Schorr, Lisbeth. 1993. "Shifting to Outcome-Based Accountability: A Minimalist Approach for Immediate Use." Working paper of the Improved Outcomes for Children Project, Washington, DC.

———. 1988. *Within Our Reach: Breaking the Cycle of Disadvantage*. New York: Doubleday.

Schutz, Alfred. 1967. *The Phenomenology of the Social World*. Evanston, IL: Washington University Press.

Schwandt, Thomas A. 1989a. "The Politics of Verifying Trustworthiness in Evaluation Auditing." *Evaluation Practice* 10(4):33-40.

———. 1989b. "Recapturing Moral Discourse in Evaluation." *Educational Researcher* 19(8):11-16.

Schwandt, T. A. and E. S. Halpern. 1988. *Linking Auditing and Metaevaluation*. Newbury Park, CA: Sage.

Scriven, Michael. 1996. "Formative and Summative." (draft title) *Evaluation Practice*.

———. 1995. "The Logic of Evaluation and Evaluation Practice." Pp. 49-70 in *Reasoning in Evaluation: Inferential Links and Leaps* (New Directions for Program Evaluation, No. 68), edited by D. M. Fournier. San Francisco: Jossey-Bass.

———. 1994. "The Final Synthesis." *Evaluation Practice* 15(3):367-82.

———. 1993. *Hard-Won Lessons in Program Evaluation* (New Directions for Program Evaluation, No. 58). San Francisco: Jossey-Bass.

———. 1991a. "Beyond Formative and Summative Evaluation." Pp. 18-64 in *Evaluation and Education: At Quarter Century*, 90th Yearbook of the National Society for the Study of Education, edited by M. W. McLaughlin and D. C. Phillips. Chicago: University of Chicago Press.

———. 1991b. *Evaluation Thesaurus*, 4th ed. Newbury Park, CA: Sage.

———. 1983. "Evaluation Ideologies." Pp. 229-60 in G. F. Madaus, M. Scriven, and D. L. Stufflebeam, eds., *Evaluation Models:*

Viewpoints on Educational and Human Services Evaluation. Boston: Kluwer-Nijhoff.

———. 1980. *The Logic of Evaluation*. Iverness, CA: Edgepress.

———. 1972a. "Objectivity and Subjectivity in Educational Research." Pp. 94-142 in *Philosophical Redirection of Educational Research: The Seventy-First Yearbook of the National Society for the Study of Education*, edited by Lawrence G. Thomas. Chicago: University of Chicago Press.

———. 1972b. "Pros and Cons About Goal-Free Evaluation." *Evaluation Comment: The Journal of Educational Evaluation* (Center for the Study of Evaluation, UCLA) 3(4):1-7.

———. 1967. "The Methodology of Evaluation." Pp. 39-83 in *Perspectives of Curriculum Evaluation*, edited by Ralph W. Tyler et al., AERA Monograph Series on Curriculum Evaluation, 1. Chicago: Rand McNally.

Scriven, Michael and Michael Patton. 1976. "A Perspective on Evaluation." Videotape interview. Minneapolis, MN: Program Evaluation Resource Center.

Sechrest, Lee. 1992. "Roots: Back to Our First Generations." *Evaluation Practice* 13(1): 1-7.

Sechrest, Lee B. and Anne G. Scott, eds. 1993. *Understanding Causes and Generalizing About Them* (New Directions for Program Evaluation, No. 57). San Francisco: Jossey-Bass.

Senge, Peter M. 1990. *The Fifth Disciple: The Art and Practice of the Learning Organization*. New York: Doubleday.

Shadish, William R., Jr. 1987. "Program Micro- and Macrotheories: A Guide for Social Change." Pp. 93-110 in *Using Program Theory in Evaluation* (New Directions for Program Evaluation, vol. 33), edited by Leonard Bickman. San Francisco: Jossey-Bass.

Shadish, William R., Jr., Thomas D. Cook, and Laura C. Leviton. 1991. *Foundations of Program Evaluation: Theories of Practice*. Newbury Park, CA: Sage.

Shadish, W. R., Jr. and R. Epstein. 1987. "Patterns of Program Evaluation Practice Among Members of the Evaluation Research Society and Evaluation Network." *Evaluation Review* 11:555-90.

Shadish, William R., Jr., Dianna L. Newman, Mary Ann Scheirer, and Christopher Wye. 1995. *Guiding Principles for Evaluators* (New Directions for Program Evaluation, No. 66). San Francisco: Jossey-Bass.

Shah, I. 1964. *The Sufis*. Garden City, NY: Doubleday.

Shapiro, Edna. 1973. "Educational Evaluation: Rethinking the Criteria of Competence." *School Review*, November, pp. 523-49.

Sharp, Colin A. 1994. "What Is Appropriate Evaluation? Ethics and Standards in Evaluation." *Evaluation News and Comment*, The Magazine of the Australasian Evaluation Society, May, pp. 34-41.

Sharp, Colin A. and Ann Lindsay. 1992. "An Interim History of Program Evaluation in Australia and New Zealand and the Australasian Evaluation Society." Presented at the International Evaluation Conference of the Australasian Evaluation Society, July, Melbourne, Australia.

Sharpe, L. J. 1977. "The Social Scientist and Policymaking: Some Cautionary Thoughts and Transatlantic Reflections." Pp. 37-54 in *Using Social Research for Public Policy Making*, edited by Carol H. Weiss. Lexington, MA: D. C. Heath.

Siegel, Karolynn and Peter Tuckel. 1985. "The Utilization of Evaluation Research: A Case Analysis." *Evaluation Review* 9(3):307-28.

Sirotnik, Kenneth A., eds. 1990. *Evaluation and Social Justice: Issues in Public Education* (New Directions for Program Evaluation, No. 45). San Francisco: Jossey-Bass.

Smelser, Neil. 1959. *Social Change in the Industrial Revolution*. Chicago: University of Chicago Press.

Smith, Doris Shackelford. 1992. "Academic and Staff Attitudes Towards Program Evaluation in Nonformal Educational Systems." Ph.D. dissertation, University of California, Berkeley.

Smith, John K. 1988. "The Evaluator/ Researcher as Person vs. the Person as Evaluator/Researcher." *Educational Researcher* 17(2):18-23.

Smith, M. F. 1989. *Evaluability Assessment.* Boston: Kluwer Academic Publishers.

———. 1988. "Evaluation Utilization Revisited." Pp. 7-19 in *Evaluation Utilization* (New Directions for Program Evaluation, vol. 39), edited by J. A. McLaughlin, Larry J. Weber, Robert W. Covert, and Robert B. Ingle. San Francisco: Jossey-Bass.

Smith, Mary Lee. 1994. "Qualitative Plus/ Versus Quantitative." Pp. 37-44 in *The Qualitative-Quantitative Debate: New Perspectives* (New Directions for Program Evaluation, No. 61, Spring), edited by C. S. Reichardt and S. F. Rallis. San Francisco: Jossey-Bass.

Smith, Nick L., ed. 1992. *Varieties of Investigative Evaluation* (New Directions for Program Evaluation, No. 56). San Francisco: Jossey-Bass.

———, ed. 1981. *Metaphors for Evaluation: Sources of New Methods.* Beverly Hills, CA: Sage.

———. 1980. "Studying Evaluation Assumptions." *Evaluation Network Newsletter,* Winter, pp. 39-40.

Social Science Research Council, National Academy of Sciences. 1969. *The Behavioral and Social Sciences: Outlook and Need.* Englewood Cliffs, NJ: Prentice Hall.

Sonnichsen, Richard C. 1994. "Evaluators as Change Agents." Pp. 534-48 in *Handbook of Practical Prgram Evaluation,* edited by J. S. Wholey, H. P. Hatry, and K. E. Newcomer. San Francisco: Jossey-Bass.

———. 1993. "Can Governments Learn?" In *Comparative Perspectives on Evaluation and Organizational Learning,* edited by F. Leeuw, R. Rist, and R. Sonnichsen. New Brunswick, NJ: Transaction.

———. 1989. "Producing Evaluations That Make an Impact." Pp. 49-66 in *Improving Government Performance: Evaluation Strategies for Strengthening Public Agencies and Programs,* edited by J. S. Wholey and K. E. Newcomer. San Francisco: Jossey-Bass.

———. 1988. "Advocacy Evaluation: A Model for Internal Evaluation Offices." *Evaluation and Program Planning* 11(2):141-48.

———. 1987. "An Internal Evaluator Responds to Ernest House's Views on Internal Evaluation." *Evaluation Practice* 8(4): 34-36.

Special Commission on the Social Sciences, National Science Foundation. 1968. *Knowledge Into Action: Improving the Nation's Use of the Social Sciences.* Washington, DC: Government Printing Office.

"Speed." 1995. *The New Yorker,* March 27, p. 40.

Stake, Robert E. 1996. "Beyond Responsive Evaluation: Developments in This Decade." Minnesota Evaluation Studies Institute presentation, College of Education and Human Development, University of Minnesota, June 25.

———. 1995. *The Art of Case Research.* Newbury Park, CA: Sage.

———. 1981. "Case Study Methodology: An Epistemological Advocacy." Pp. 31-40 in *Case Study Methodology in Educational Evaluation,* edited by W. W. Welch. Minneapolis: Minnesota Research and Evaluation Center.

———. 1978. "Should Educational Evaluation Be More Objective or More Subjective?" Presented at the annual meeting of the American Educational Research Association, Toronto.

———. 1975. *Evaluating the Arts in Education: A Responsive Approach.* Columbus, OH: Charles E. Merrill.

Stalford, Charles B. 1983. "School Board Use of Evaluation Information." Presented at the joint meeting of the Evaluation Network and the Evaluation Research Society, Chicago.

Statewide Study of Education. 1967. *Educational Development for North Dakota, 1967-1975*. Grand Forks: University of North Dakota.

Stecher, Brian M. and W. Alan Davis. 1987. *How to Focus an Evaluation*. Newbury Park, CA: Sage.

Stevens, Carla J. and Micah Dial, eds. 1994. *Preventing the Misuse of Evaluation* (New Directions for Program Evaluation, No. 64). San Francisco: Jossey-Bass.

Stockdill, S. H., R. M. Duhon-Sells, R. A. Olson, and M. Q. Patton. 1992. "Voices in the Design and Evaluation of a Multicultural Education Program: A Developmental Approach." *New Directions in Program Evaluation*, Spring, 53:17-34.

Stone, Clarence N. 1985. "Efficiency Versus Social Learning: A Reconsideration of the Implementation Process." *Policy Studies Review* 4(3):484-96.

Strike, Kenneth. 1972. "Explaining and Understanding the Impact of Science on Our Concept of Man." Pp. 26-46 in *Philosophical Redirection of Educational Research: The Seventy-First Yearbook of the National Society for the Study of Education*, edited by Lawrence G. Thomas. Chicago: University of Chicago Press.

Studer, Sharon L. 1978. "A Validity Study of a Measure of 'Readiness to Accept Program Evaluation.' " Ph.D. dissertation, University of Minnesota.

Stufflebeam, Daniel. 1994. "Empowerment Evaluation, Objectivist Evaluation, and Evaluation Standards: Where the Future of Evaluation Should Not Go and Where It Needs to Go." *Evaluation Practice* 15(3): 321-38.

———. 1980. "An Interview With Daniel L. Stufflebeam." *Educational Evaluation and Policy Analysis* 2(4):90-92.

———. 1972. "Should or Can Evaluation Be Goal-Free?" *Evaluation Comment: The Journal of Educational Evaluation* (Center for the Study of Evaluation, UCLA) 3(4): 7-9.

Stufflebeam, Daniel L., W. J. Foley, W. J. Gephart, L. R. Hammond, H. O. Merriman, and M. M. Provus. 1971. *Educational Evaluation and Decision-Making in Education*. Itasca, IL: Peacock.

Stufflebeam, Daniel L. and Egon Guba. 1970. "Strategies for the Institutionalization of the CIPP Evaluation Model." Presented at the 11th Annual PDK Symposium on Education Research, Columbus, Ohio.

Suchman, Edward A. 1972. "Action for What? A Critique of Evaluative Research." Pp. 42-84 in *Evaluating Action Programs*, edited by Carol H. Weiss. Boston: Allyn & Bacon.

———. 1967. *Evaluative Research: Principles and Practice in Public Service and Social Action Programs*. New York: Russell Sage.

Taylor, Donald W. 1965. "Decision Making and Problem Solving." Pp. 48-86 in *Handbook of Organizations*, edited by James G. March. Chicago: Rand McNally.

Terry, Robert W. 1993. *Authentic Leadership*. San Francisco: Jossey-Bass.

Thompson, James D. 1967. *Organizations in Action*. New York: McGraw-Hill.

Thompson, Mark. 1975. *Evaluation for Decision in Social Programmes*. Lexington, MA: D. C. Heath.

Thoreau, Henry D. 1838. *Journal*, March 14.

Trend, M. G. 1978. "On Reconciliation of Qualitative and Quantitative Analysis." *Human Organization* 37:345-54.

Tripodi, Tony, Phillip Felin, and Irwin Epstein. 1971. *Social Program Evaluation Guidelines for Health, Education, and Welfare Administration*. Itasca, IL: Peacock.

Trochim, William M. K., ed. 1986. *Advances in Quasi-Experimental Design and Analysis* (New Directions for Program Evaluation, No. 31). San Francisco: Jossey-Bass.

Tucker, Eugene. 1977. "The Follow Through Planned Variation Experiment: What Is the Pay-Off?" Presented at the annual meeting of the American Educational Research Association, April. New York City, NY.

Turner, Terilyn C. and Stacey H. Stockdill, eds. 1987. *The Technology for Literacy Project Evaluation*. The Saint Paul Foundation: St. Paul, Minnesota.

Turpin, Robin. 1989. "Winner of the President's Prize on the Problem of Evaluation Politics." *Evaluation Practice* 10(10):54-57.

Uphoff, Norman. 1991. "A Field Methodology for Participatory Self-Evaluation." Special issue, Evaluation of Social Development Projects, in *Community Development Journal* 26(4):271-85.

U.S. Department of Health and Human Services. 1983. *Compendium of HHS Evaluation Studies*. Washington, DC: HHS Evaluation Documentation Center.

U.S. House of Representatives, Committee on Government Operations, Research and Technical Programs Subcommittee. 1967. *The Use of Social Research in Federal Domestic Programs*. Washington, DC: Government Printing Office.

Vroom, Phyllis I., Marie Columbo, and Neva Nahan. 1994. "Confronting Ideology and Self-Interest: Avoiding Misuse of Evaluation." Pp. 61-68 in *Preventing the Misuse of Evaluation* (New Directions for Program Evaluation, No. 64), edited by C. J. Stevens and Micah Dial. San Francisco: Jossey-Bass.

Wadsworth, Yoland. 1995. " 'Building In' Research and Evaluation to Human Services." Unpublished report to the Winston Churchill Memorial Trust of Australia, Melbourne.

———. 1993a. "What Is Participatory Action Research?" Melbourne, Australia: Action Research Issues Association, Inc.

———. 1993b. "How Can Professionals Help Groups Do Their Own Participatory Action Research?" Melbourne, Australia: Action Research Issues Association, Inc.

———. 1984. *Do It Yourself Social Research*. Melbourne, Australia: Victorian Council of Social Service and Melbourne Family Care Organisation in association with Allen and Unwin.

Walters, Jonathon. 1996. "Auditor Power!" *Governing*, April, pp. 25-29.

Ward, David, Gene Kassebaum, and Daniel Wilner. 1971. *Prison Treatment and Parole Survival: An Empirical Assessment*. New York: John Wiley.

Wargo, Michael J. 1995. "The Impact of Federal Government Reinvention on Federal Evaluation Activity." *Evaluation Practice* 16(3):227-37.

———. 1989. "Characteristics of Successful Program Evaluations." Pp. 71-82 in *Improving Government Performance: Evaluation Strategies for Strengthening Public Agencies and Programs*, edited by J. S. Wholey and K. E. Newcomer. San Francisco: Jossey-Bass.

Watkins, Karen E. and Victoria J. Marsick. 1993. *Sculpting the Learning Organization*. San Francisco: Jossey-Bass.

Weber, Max. 1947. *The Theory of Social and Economic Organizations*. New York: Oxford University Press.

Weidman, Donald R., Pamela Horst, Grace Taher, and Joseph S. Wholey. 1973. *Design of an Evaluation System for NIMH*, Contract Report 962-7. Washington, DC: Urban Institute.

Weiss, Carol H. 1993. "Where Politics and Evaluation Research Meet." *Evaluation Practice* 14(1):93-106. (Original work published 1973)

———. [1988] 1990. "Evaluation for Decisions: Is Anybody There? Does Anybody Care?" Pp. 171-84 in *Debates on Evaluation*, edited by Marvin Alkin. Newbury Park, CA: Sage. Reprinted American Evaluation Association keynote address originally published in *Evaluation Practice* 9(1):5-19.

———. 1980. "Knowledge Creep and Decision Accretion." *Knowledge: Creation, Diffusion, Utilization* 1(3):381-404.

———. 1977. "Introduction." Pp. 1-22 in *Using Social Research in Public Policy Making*, edited by Carol H. Weiss. Lexington, MA: D. C. Heath.

———, ed. 1972a. *Evaluating Action Programs*. Boston: Allyn & Bacon.

———. 1972b. *Evaluation Research: Methods of Assessing Program Effectiveness*. Englewood Cliffs, NJ: Prentice Hall.

———. 1972c. "Evaluating Educational and Social Action Programs: A 'Treeful of Owls.' " Pp. 3-27 in *Evaluating Action Programs*, edited by Carol H. Weiss. Boston: Allyn & Bacon.

———. 1972d. "Utilization of Evaluation: Toward Comparative Study." Pp. 318-26 in *Evaluating Action Programs*, edited by Carol H. Weiss. Boston: Allyn & Bacon.

Weiss, Carol H. and Michael Bucuvalas. 1980. "Truth Tests and Utility Tests: Decision Makers' Frame of Reference for Social Science Research." *American Sociological Review* 45(April):302-13.

Weiss, Heather B. and Jennifer C. Greene. 1992. "An Empowerment Partnership for Family Support and Education Programs and Evaluations." *Family Science Review* 5(1,2):145-63.

Weiss, Heather B. and F. Jacobs, eds. 1988. *Evaluating Family Programs*. Hawthorne, NY: Aldine.

Westinghouse Learning Corporation. 1969. *The Impact of Head Start: An Evaluation of the Effects of Head Start on Children's Cognitive and Affective Development*. Bladensburg, MD: Westinghouse Learning Corporation.

Whitmore, E. 1990. "Focusing on the process of evaluation: It's the "How" that counts." Presented at the American Evaluation Association annual meeting, Washington, DC.

———. 1988. "Empowerment and Evaluation: A Case Example." Presented at the American Evaluation Association annual meeting, New Orleans.

Whitmore, E. and P. Kerans. 1988. "Participation, Empowerment, and Welfare." *Canadian Review of Social Policy* 22:51-60.

Wholey, Joseph S. 1994. "Assessing the Feasibility and Likely Usefulness of Evaluation." Pp. 15-39 in *Handbook of Practical Program Evaluation*, edited by Joseph S. Wholey, Harry P. Hatry, and Kathryn E. Newcomer. San Francisco: Jossey-Bass.

Wholey, Joseph S., Harry P. Hatry, and Kathryn E. Newcomer, eds. 1994. *Handbook of Practical Program Evaluation*. San Francisco: Jossey-Bass.

Wholey, Joseph S., John W. Scanlon, Hugh G. Duffy, James S. Fukumotu, and Leona M. Vogt. 1970. *Federal Evaluation Policy: Analyzing the Effects of Public Programs*. Washington, DC: Urban Institute.

Whyte, William F., ed. 1991. *Participatory Action Research*. Newbury Park, CA: Sage.

Wildavsky, A. 1985. "The Self-Evaluating Organization." Pp. 246-65 in *Program Evaluation: Patterns and Directions*, edited by E. Chelimsky. Washington, DC: American Society for Public Administration.

Wildman, Paul. 1995. *Action Research Case Studies Newsletter* 3(1).

Willems, E. P. and H. L. Raush. 1969. *Naturalistic Viewpoint in Psychological Research*. New York: Holt, Rinehart and Winston.

Williams, David D., ed. 1986. *Naturalistic Evaluation* (New Directions for Program Evaluation, No. 30). San Francisco: Jossey-Bass.

Williams, H. S., A. Y. Webb, and W. J. Phillips. 1991. *Outcome Funding: A New Approach to Targeted Grantmaking*. Rensselaerville, NY: The Rensselaerville Institute.

Williams, Jay. 1976. *Everyone Knows What a Dragon Looks Like*. New York: Four Winds Press.

Williams, Walter. 1976. "Implementation Analysis and Assessment." Pp. 267-92 in *Social Program Implementation*, edited by W. Williams and R. F. Elmore. New York: Academic Press.

Williams, Walter and Richard F. Elmore. 1976. *Social Program Implementation*. New York: Academic Press.

Williams, Walter and John W. Evans. 1969. "The Politics of Evaluation: The Case of Head Start." *Annals of the American Academy of Political and Social Science* 385(September):118-32.

Winberg, A. 1991. "Maximizing the Contribution of Internal Evaluation Units." *Evaluation and Program Planning* 14:167-72.

Wolf, Robert L. 1975. "Trial by Jury: A New Evaluation Method." *Phi Delta Kappan* (November).

Wolf, Robert L. and Barbara Tymitz. 1976. "Whatever Happened to the Giant Wombat. An Investigation of the Impact of the Ice Age Mammals and Emergence of Man Exhibit." Mimeograph, National Museum of Natural History, Smithsonian Institutes.

Worley, D. R. 1960. "Amount and Generality of Information-Seeking Behavior in Sequential Decision Making as Dependent on Level of Incentive." Pp. 1-11 in *Experiments on Decision Making*, Technical Report 6, edited by D. W. Taylor. New Haven, CT: Yale University, Department of Industrial Administration and Psychology.

Worthen, Blaine R. 1994. "Conceptual Challenges Confronting Cluster Evaluation." Presented at the 1994 meeting of the American Evaluation Association, Boston.

Worthen, Blaine R. and James R. Sanders, eds. 1973. *Educational Evaluation: Theory and Practice*. Worthington, OH: Charles A. Jones.

Wortman, Paul M. 1995. "An Exemplary Evaluation of a Program That Worked: The High/Scope Perry Preschool Project. *Evaluation Practice* 16(3):257-65.

Wray, L. D. and J. A. Hauer. 1996. "Best Practices Reviews for Local Government." *Public Management*, January, pp. 7-11.

Wright, William and Thomas Sachse. 1977. "Survey of Hawaii Evaluation Users." Presented at the annual meeting of the American Educational Research Association. New York City, NY.

Wye, Christopher G. and Richard C. Sonnichsen, eds. 1992. *Evaluation in the Federal Government: Changes, Trends, and Opportunities* (New Directions for Program Evaluation, No. 55). San Francisco: Jossey-Bass.

Yates, Brian T. 1996. *Analyzing Costs, Procedures, Processes, and Outcome in Human Services*. Thousand Oaks, CA: Sage.

Yin, Robert K. 1994. "Evaluation: A Singular Craft." Pp. 71-84 in *The Qualitative-Quantitative Debate: New Perspectives* (New Directions for Program Evaluation, No. 61), edited by C. S. Reichardt and S. F. Rallis. San Francisco: Jossey-Bass.

Zadeh, Lofti A., King-Sun Fu, Kokichi Tanaka, and Masamichi Shimura, eds. 1975. *Fuzzy Sets and Their Applications to Cognitive and Decision Processes*. New York: Academic Press.

Index

About the Author

Michael Quinn Patton lives in St. Paul, Minnesota, where he founded and directs an organizational development consulting business: Utilization-Focused Information and Training. He is also a professor with the Union Institute Graduate School—a national, nontraditional, and nonresidential university offering doctoral degrees in interdisciplinary and applied fields. In addition to *Utilization-Focused Evaluation,* he has authored four other Sage books: *Qualitative Evaluation and Research Methods* (1990); *How to Use Qualitative Methods in Evaluation* (1987); *Creative Evaluation* (1987); and *Practical Evaluation* (1982). He also edited Volume 25 of *New Directions for Evaluation* on *Culture and Evaluation.*

Dr. Patton has served as President of the American Evaluation Association and received the Alva and Gunner Myrdal Award from the Evaluation Research Society for "outstanding contributions to evaluation use and practice." He was on the faculty of the University of Minnesota for 18 years, including 5 years as Director of the Minnesota Center for Social Research. He received the University's Morse-Amoco Award for outstanding teaching and was winner of the 1985 Storytelling Competition at the University. His doctorate is in Organizational Development and Sociology from the University of Wisconsin.

In his consulting practice, he brings an evaluation perspective to work in organizational development, strategic planning, policy analysis, futuring, board development, management consulting, and systems analysis. As an interdisciplinary evaluation generalist, his evaluations have included projects in education, health, criminal justice, agriculture, energy conservation, community development, corporate planning, human services, poverty programs, leadership development, wilderness experiences, housing, staff training, mental health, and foundation giving. He has worked on local, county, state, national, and international projects. His heavy schedule of speaking engagements before professional groups helps him stay up-to-date on the issues people are struggling with in attempting to conduct useful evaluations.

Evaluating wilderness education programs in the Southwest introduced him to the wonders of the Grand Canyon, where he backpacks at least once a year. The influence of these experiences can be found in this book by those, he says, "who know the Canyon."